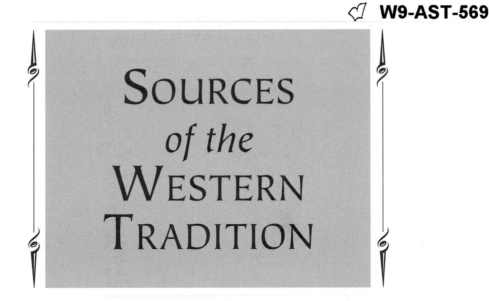

# SOURCES
### *of the*
# WESTERN
# TRADITION

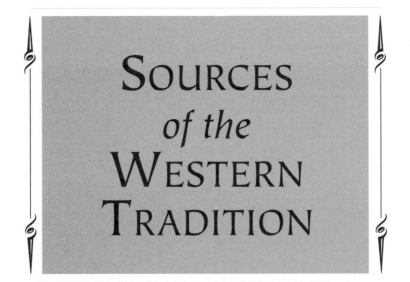

# SOURCES of the WESTERN TRADITION

## FOURTH EDITION

### VOLUME I: FROM ANCIENT TIMES TO THE ENLIGHTENMENT

## Marvin Perry
*Baruch College, City University of New York*

## Joseph R. Peden
*Baruch College, City University of New York*

## Theodore H. Von Laue
*Clark University*

*George W. Bock, Editorial Associate*

HOUGHTON MIFFLIN COMPANY    BOSTON    NEW YORK

Sponsoring Editor: Andrea Shaw
Assistant Editor: Lisa Rothrauff
Senior Project Editor: Helen Bronk
Senior Production/Design Coordinator: Jennifer Waddell
Manufacturing Manager: Florence Cadran
Marketing Manager: Sandra McGuire

Credits

Cover Image: Image Bank Boston/Patti McConville

Cover Design: Leonard Massiglia/LMA

List of Sources

**Chapter 1**
*Section 1* P. 4: From *The Epic of Gilgamesh,* translated by N.K. Sandars. Copyright © 1964. Reproduced by permission of Penguin Books Ltd. UK. *Section 2* P. 7: From James B. Pritchard (ed.), *The Ancient Near East: A New Anthology of Texts and Pictures,* Vol. 2, pp. 151–154. Published by arrangement with Princeton University Press. Copyright © 1975 by Princeton University Press. *Section 3* P. 10: From *Babylonian and Assyrian Laws, Contracts, and Letters,* ed. C.M.W. Johns (New York: Charles Scribner's Sons, 1904), pp. 44–67 passim.

Credits are continued on p. 438

Printed in the U.S.A.
ISBN: 0-395-89201-5
Library of Congress Catalog Card Number: 98-71766
  3456789-CRS-02 01 00 99

# Contents

**CHAPTER 4  *The Roman Republic  101***

**CHAPTER 5  *The Roman Empire  129***

## CHAPTER 13    *The Enlightenment* 401

# Preface

Teachers of the Western Civilization survey have long recognized the pedagogical value of primary sources, which are the raw materials of history. The fourth edition of *Sources of the Western Tradition* contains a wide assortment of documents—over 300 and virtually all primary sources—that have been carefully selected and edited to fit the needs of the survey and to supplement standard texts.

We have based our choice of documents for the two volumes on several criteria. In order to introduce students to those ideas and values that characterize the Western tradition, *Sources of the Western Tradition* emphasizes primarily the works of the great thinkers. While focusing on the great ideas that have shaped the Western heritage, however, the reader also provides a balanced treatment of political, economic, and social history. We have tried to select documents that capture the characteristic outlook of an age and that provide a sense of the movement and development of Western history. The readings are of sufficient length to convey their essential meaning, and we have carefully extracted those passages that focus on the documents' main ideas.

An important feature of the reader is the grouping of several documents that illuminate a single theme; such a constellation of related readings reinforces understanding of important themes and invites comparison, analysis, and interpretation. In Volume I, Chapter 6, for example, Section 6, "The Christian World-View," contains three readings: *The City of God,* by Saint Augustine, "The Christian Way of Life," by Saint Benedict, and "Church and State," by Gelasius. In Volume II, Chapter 8, "Politics and Society, 1845–1914," Section 2, "The Lower Classes" contains four readings: "The Pains of Poverty," by Jeanne Bouvier, "The Yearning for Social Justice," by Nikolaus Osterroth, *In Darkest England,* by William Booth, and "Working

Conditions for Women in Russian Factories," by M. I. Pokzovskaya.

An overriding concern of the editors in preparing this compilation was to make the documents accessible—to enable students to comprehend and to interpret historical documents on their own. We have provided several pedagogical features to facilitate this aim. Introductions of three types explain the historical setting, the authors' intent, and the meaning and significance of the readings. First, introductions to each of the twenty-three chapters provide comprehensive overviews to periods. Second, introductions to each numbered section or grouping treat the historical background for the reading(s) that follow(s). Third, each reading has a brief headnote that provides specific details about that reading.

Within some readings, interlinear notes, clearly set off from the text of the document, serve as transitions and suggest the main themes of the passages that follow. Used primarily in longer extracts of the great thinkers, these interlinear notes help to guide students through the readings.

To aid students' comprehension, brief, bracketed editorial definitions or notes that explain unfamiliar or foreign terms are inserted into the running text. When terms or concepts in the documents require fuller explanations, these appear at the bottom of pages as editors' footnotes. Where helpful, we have retained the notes of authors, translators, or editors from whose works the documents were acquired. (The latter have asterisks, daggers, etcetera, to distinguish them from our numbered explanatory notes.) The review questions that appear at the ends of sections enable students to check their understanding of the documents; sometimes the questions ask for comparisons with other readings, linking or contrasting key concepts.

For ancient sources, we have generally selected recent translations that are both faithful to the text and readable. For some seventeenth- and eighteenth-century English documents, the archaic spelling has been retained, when this does not preclude comprehension, in order to show students how the English language has evolved over time.

For the fourth edition, we have reworked most chapters, dropping some documents and adding new ones. All new documents have been carefully edited: extraneous passages deleted, notes inserted to explain historical events, names identified, and technical terms defined. Wherever possible, we have extended the constellation format that groups related documents into one section.

The fourth edition of Volume I contains more than thirty new sources. For example, in Chapter 1, a new section from Mesopotamian wisdom literature illustrates the pessimistic attitude that characterized the Mesopotamian outlook. A second section, "Love, Passion, and Misogyny," deals with male-female relationships in ancient Egypt. Added to Chapter 2 is a piece from Amos illustrating the prophet's concern for social justice and an excerpt from the Book of Job that raises the timeless question: Why do good people suffer? Added to Chapter 3 are passages from Herodotus, *The Histories* and from Aristotle, *Nicomachean Ethics*. Seneca's astute advice on rearing children is incorporated into Chapter 5. Inserted in Chapter 7 is material on Byzantine and Islamic civilizations, including excerpts from the *Koran*. Also in that chapter, a passage on Saint Boniface is added to the constellation "Converting the Germanic Peoples to Christianity." The most significant change in Chapter 8 is the addition of several troubadour poems. A new constellation, "The Spread of the Renaissance," which contains several passages from Shakespeare's plays, is added to Chapter 9. Chapter 11 contains two additional constellations: "The Witch Craze" and "The Court of Louis IV." In addition, accounts from two seventeenth-century slave traders are added to the section on slavery. William Harvey's report of his discovery of the circulation of blood is inserted in Chapter 12. A new constellation, "Epistemology and Education," containing passages from Locke, Helvétius, and Rousseau, is included in Chapter 13. Two other new selections in this chapter are John Howard's account of England's prisons and Condorcet's condemnation of slavery.

Volume II contains about thirty-five new selections and an added chapter (Chapter 9) on European imperialism. The constellation, "Expansion of Human Rights," inserted into Chapter 4, shows how reformers extended the ideals of revolution to women, Jews, and Blacks. In Chapter 8, the new constellation, "The Irish Potato Famine," deals with a topic that has received considerable attention in recent years. The selections in the new Chapter 9 are grouped in four constellations: "The Spirit of British Imperialism," "Seeking a Place in the Sun," "European Rule in Africa," and "British Rule in India." In Chapter 11, examples of the powerful war poetry of Siegfried Sassoon and Wilfred Owen are included. Also added to this chapter is a German woman's description of the hostility faced by newly employed female workers. Excerpts from *True Stories,* a recent work by Lev Razgon, a survivor of Stalin's camps, are included in Chapter 12. Chapter 13 contains two new selections on the battle of Stalingrad, one written by a Russian and the other by a German. Inserted in the concluding Chapter 14 is a constellation on the Cold War, which includes passages from Winston Churchill, George F. Kennan, and Nikita Khrushchev. The last section, "Toward the Twenty-First Century," contains selections by Samuel P. Huntington and Michael T. Klare assessing the direction of global tensions.

To accompany the fourth edition is a revised *Instructor's Resource Manual with Test Items* by Professor Diane Moczar of Northern Virginia Community College. In addition to an introduction with suggestions on how to use *Sources of the Western Tradition* in class, there are chapter overviews, summaries of the sections, and, for each chapter, several questions for discussion or essay assignments and ten to twenty multiple-choice questions.

We wish to thank the following instructors for their critical reading of the manuscript and for their many valuable suggestions.

Carolyn Conley, University of Alabama
at Birmingham
Duane Everhart, College of DuPage
Holger Herwig, University of Calgary
David Hendon, Baylor University
Robert Herzstein, University of South
Carolina
Michael Honhart, University of Rhode
Island
Michael Intinoli, Burlington County
College
James Kieswetter, Eastern Washington
University
Gaylen Lewis, Bakersfield College
Benjamin Martin, Louisiana State
University
Ralph Mathiesen, University of South
Carolina
Brian Nance, Coastal Carolina
University

We are also grateful to the staff of Houghton Mifflin Company who lent their talents to the project. We would like to thank Jeffrey Greene, sponsoring editor, Andrea Shaw, sponsoring editor, and Lisa Rothrauff, assistant editor, for guiding the new edition from its inception and Helen Bronk, senior project editor, for her careful attention to detail. Although Freda Alexander, Frances Gay, and Jean Woy did not work on this edition, their excellent editorial efforts in the previous editions are still very much evident in this one. We are particularly grateful to Holly Webber for her superb copyediting skills.

I wish to thank Angela Von Laue who helped to research several chapters in Volume II and read the proof for that volume. I am especially grateful to my friend, George W. Bock, who worked closely with me in every phase of the reader's development, and to my wife Phyllis Perry, for her encouragement. On a sad note, as the book goes to print, I think again of Joseph Peden, a conscientious colleague since the book's inception, who died in 1996.

M.P.

CHAPTER 1

# The Near East

STROLL IN THE GARDEN, Eighteenth Dynasty, c. 1350 B.C. This relief portrays members of the Egyptian royal family. *(Limestone, 24 cm high. Ägyptisches Museum und Papyrussammlung, Staatliche Museum zu Berlin. [Farabb. s.S. 91])*

The world's first civilizations arose some five thousand years ago in the river valleys of Mesopotamia (later Iraq) and Egypt. In these Near Eastern lands people built cities, organized states with definite boundaries, invented writing, engaged in large-scale trade, practiced specialization of labor, and erected huge monuments: all activities that historians associate with civilization. Scholars emphasize the fact that civilizations emerged in the river valleys—the Tigris and Euphrates in Mesopotamia and the Nile in Egypt. When they overflowed their banks, these rivers deposited fertile soil, which could provide a food surplus required to sustain life in cities. The early inhabitants of these valleys drained swamps and built irrigation works, enabling them to harness the rivers for human advantage. In the process they also strengthened the bonds of cooperation, a necessary ingredient of civilization.

Religion and myth were the central forces in these early civilizations. They pervaded all phases of life, providing people with satisfying explanations for the operations of nature and the mystery of death and justifying traditional rules of morality. Natural objects—the sun, the river, the mountain—were seen either as gods or as the abodes of gods. The political life of the Near East was theocratic: that is, people regarded their rulers as either divine or as representatives of the gods and believed that law originated with the gods. Near Eastern art and literature were dominated by religious themes.

The Sumerians, founders of urban life in Mesopotamia, developed twelve city-states in the region of the lower Euphrates near the Persian Gulf. Each city-state included a city and the farmland around it; each had its own government and was independent of the other city-states. In time the Sumerians were conquered, and their cities were incorporated into kingdoms and empires. However, as Akkadians, Elamites, Babylonians, and other peoples of the region adopted and built upon Sumerian religion, art, and literary forms, the Sumerian achievement became the basis of a coherent Mesopotamian civilization that lasted some three thousand years.

Early in its history Egypt became a centralized state under the rule of a pharaoh, who was viewed as both a man and a god. The pharaoh's authority was all-embracing, and all Egyptians were subservient to him. Early in their history, the Egyptians developed cultural patterns that were to endure for three thousand years; the ancient Egyptians looked to the past, seeking to maintain the ways of their ancestors.

Although the cultural patterns of both civilizations were similar—in both religion and theocratic kingship played a dominant role—there were significant differences between the two. Whereas in Egypt the pharaoh was considered divine, rulers in Mesopotamia were regarded as exceptional human beings whom the gods had selected to act as their agents. Second, the natural environment of the Egyptians fostered a sense of security and an optimistic outlook toward life. Natural barriers—deserts, the Mediterranean Sea, and cataracts in the Nile—protected Egypt from invasion, and the overflowing of the Nile was regular and predictable, ensuring a good harvest. In contrast, Mesopotamia, without natural barriers, suffered from frequent invasions, and the Tigris and Euphrates rivers were unpredictable. Sometimes there was insufficient overflow, and the land was afflicted with drought; at other times, rampaging floods devastated the fields. These conditions promoted a pessimistic outlook, which pervaded Mesopotamian civilization.

After 1500 B.C., the Near East entered a period of empire building. In the late sixth century B.C., the Persians, the greatest of the empire builders, conquered all the lands from the Nile River to the Indus River in India. Persia united Egypt, Mesopotamia, and other Near Eastern lands into a world-state and brought together the region's various cultural traditions. In the first half of the fifth century B.C., the Persians tried to add the city-states of Greece to their empire; the ensuing conflict was of critical importance for the history of Western civilization.

Egyptians, Mesopotamians, and other Near Eastern peoples developed a rich urban culture and made important contributions to later civilizations. They established bureaucracies, demonstrated creativity in art and literature, fashioned effective systems of mathematics, and advanced the knowledge of architecture, metallurgy, and engineering. The wheel, the plow, the phonetic alphabet, and the calendar derive from the Near East. Both the Hebrews and the Greeks, the principal sources of Western civilization, had contact with these older civilizations and adopted many of their cultural forms. But, as we shall see, even more important for the shaping of Western civilization was how the Hebrews and the Greeks broke with the essential style of Near Eastern society and conceived new outlooks, new points of departure for the human mind.

# 1  Mesopotamian Protest Against Death

The *Epic of Gilgamesh,* the greatest work of Mesopotamian literature, was written about 2000 B.C. It utilized legends about Gilgamesh, probably a historical figure who ruled the city of Uruk about 2600 B.C. The story deals with a profound theme—the human protest against death. In the end, Gilgamesh learns to accept reality: there is no escape from death. While the *Epic of Gilgamesh* is an expression of the pessimism that pervaded Mesopotamian life, it also reveals the Mesopotamians' struggle to come to terms with reality.

# EPIC OF GILGAMESH[1]

The *Epic of Gilgamesh* involves the gods in human activities. Because King Gilgamesh, son of a human father and the goddess Ninsun, drives his subjects too hard, they appeal to the gods for help. The gods decide that a man of Gilgamesh's immense vigor and strength requires a rival with similar attributes with whom he can contend. The creation goddess, Aruru, is instructed to create a man worthy of Gilgamesh. From clay she fashions Enkidu in the image of Anu, the god of the heavens and father of all the gods. Enkidu is a powerful man who roams with the animals and destroys traps set by hunters, one of whom appeals to King Gilgamesh. The two of them, accompanied by a harlot, find Enkidu at a watering place frequented by animals. The harlot removes her clothes and seduces Enkidu, who spends a week with her, oblivious to everything else. After this encounter, the bond between Enkidu and the animals is broken. He now enters civilization and is befriended by Gilgamesh, with whom he slays the terrible monster Humbaba.

Returning to Uruk after the encounter with Humbaba, Gilgamesh washes away the grime of battle and dons his royal clothes; thus arrayed he attracts the goddess of love, Ishtar, patroness of Uruk, who proposes marriage, but because of Ishtar's previous marriages and infidelities, Gilgamesh refuses. Ishtar falls into a bitter rage and appeals to her father, the god Anu, to unleash the fearful Bull of Heaven on Gilgamesh. However, Gilgamesh and Enkidu together slay the beast. To avenge the deaths of Humbaba and the Bull of Heaven, the gods decide that Enkidu shall die. In the following passage, Enkidu dreams of his impending death and the House of Darkness, from which no one returns.

When the daylight came Enkidu got up and cried to Gilgamesh, "O my brother, such a dream I had last night. Anu, Enlil, Ea and heavenly Shamash took counsel together, and Anu said to Enlil, 'Because they have killed the Bull of Heaven, and because they have killed Humbaba who guarded the Cedar Mountain one of the two must die.'. . ."

So Enkidu lay stretched out before Gilgamesh: his tears ran down in streams and he said to Gilgamesh, "O my brother, so dear as you are to me, brother, yet they will take me from you." Again he said, "I must sit down on the threshold of the dead and never again will I see my dear brother with my eyes."

. . . In bitterness of spirit he poured out his heart to his friend. "It was I who cut down the cedar, I who levelled the forest, I who slew Humbaba and now see what has become of me. Listen, my friend, this is the dream I dreamed last night. The heavens roared, and earth rumbled back an answer; between them stood I before an awful being, the sombre-faced man-bird; he had directed on me his purpose. His was a vampire face, his foot was a lion's foot, his hand was an eagle's talon. He fell on me and his claws were in my hair, he held me fast and I smothered; then he transformed me so that my arms became wings covered with feathers. He turned his stare towards me, and he led me away to the palace of Irkalla, the

---

[1]Throughout the text, titles original to the source appear in italics. Titles added by the editors are not italicized.

Queen of Darkness, to the house from which none who enters ever returns, down the road from which there is no coming back.

"There is the house whose people sit in darkness; dust is their food and clay their meat. They are clothed like birds with wings for covering, they see no light, they sit in darkness. I entered the house of dust and I saw the kings of the earth, their crowns put away for ever; rulers and princes, all those who once wore kingly crowns and ruled the world in the days of old. They who had stood in the place of the gods like Anu and Enlil, stood now like servants to fetch baked meats in the house of dust, to carry cooked meat and cold water from the water-skin. In the house of dust which I entered were high priests and acolytes, priests of the incantation and of ecstasy; there were servers of the temple, and there was Etana, that king of Kish whom the eagle carried to heaven in the days of old. I saw also Samuqan, god of cattle, and there was Ereshkigal the Queen of the Underworld; and Belit-Sheri squatted in front of her, she who is recorder of the gods and keeps the book of death. She held a tablet from which she read. She raised her head, she saw me and spoke: 'Who has brought this one here?' Then I awoke like a man drained of blood who wanders alone in a waste of rushes; like one whom the bailiff has seized and his heart pounds with terror."

Gilgamesh had peeled off his clothes, he listened to his words and wept quick tears, Gilgamesh listened and his tears flowed. . . .

This day on which Enkidu dreamed came to an end and he lay stricken with sickness. One whole day he lay on his bed and his suffering increased. He said to Gilgamesh, the friend on whose account he had left the wilderness, "Once I ran for you, for the water of life, and I now have nothing." A second day he lay on his bed and Gilgamesh watched over him but the sickness increased. A third day he lay on his bed, he called out to Gilgamesh, rousing him up. Now he was weak and his eyes were blind with weeping. Ten days he lay and his suffer-

ing increased, eleven and twelve days he lay on his bed of pain. Then he called to Gilgamesh, "My friend, the great goddess cursed me and I must die in shame. I shall not die like a man fallen in battle; I feared to fall, but happy is the man who falls in the battle, for I must die in shame." And Gilgamesh wept over Enkidu. With the first light of dawn he raised his voice and said to the counsellors of Uruk:

"Hear me, great ones of Uruk,
I weep for Enkidu, my friend,
Bitterly moaning like a woman mourning
I weep for my brother.
O Enkidu, my brother,
You were the axe at my side,
My hand's strength, the sword in my belt,
The shield before me,
A glorious robe, my fairest ornament;
An evil Fate has robbed me.

                    .    .    .

All the people of Eridu
Weep for you Enkidu.

                    .    .    .

What is this sleep which holds you now?
You are lost in the dark and cannot hear me."

He touched his heart but it did not beat, nor did he lift his eyes again. When Gilgamesh touched his heart it did not beat. So Gilgamesh laid a veil, as one veils the bride, over his friend. He began to rage like a lion, like a lioness robbed of her whelps. This way and that he paced round the bed, he tore out his hair and strewed it around. He dragged off his splendid robes and flung them down as though they were abominations.

In the first light of dawn Gilgamesh cried out, "I made you rest on a royal bed, you reclined on a couch at my left hand, the princes of the earth kissed your feet. I will cause all the people of Uruk to weep over you and raise the dirge of the dead. The joyful people will stoop with sorrow; and when you have gone to the earth I will let my hair grow long for your sake, I will wander through the wilderness in the skin of a lion." The next day also, in the first light, Gilgamesh lamented; seven days and seven nights he wept for Enkidu, until the worm fastened on him. Only then he gave him up to the earth, for the Anunnaki, the judges [of the dead],[2] had seized him. . . .

---

In his despair, Gilgamesh is confronted with the reality of his own death. Yearning for eternal life, he seeks Utnapishtim, legendary king of the city of Shurrupak, a man to whom the gods had granted everlasting life.

---

Bitterly Gilgamesh wept for his friend Enkidu; he wandered over the wilderness as a hunter, he roamed over the plains; in his bitterness he cried, "How can I rest, how can I be at peace? Despair is in my heart. What my brother is now, that shall I be when I am dead. Because I am afraid of death I will go as best I can to find Utnapishtim whom they call the Faraway, for he has entered the assembly of the gods." So Gilgamesh travelled over the wilderness, he wandered over the grasslands, a long journey, in search of Utnapishtim, whom the gods took after the deluge; and they set him to live in the land of Dilmun, in the garden of the sun; and to him alone of men they gave everlasting life. . . .

---

In the garden of the gods, Gilgamesh speaks with Siduri, the divine winemaker, who tells him that his search for eternal life is hopeless.

---

". . . My friend who was very dear to me and who endured dangers beside me, Enkidu my brother, whom I loved, the end of mortality has overtaken him. I wept for him seven days and nights till the worm fastened on him. Because of my brother I am afraid of death, because of

my brother I stray through the wilderness and cannot rest. But now, young woman, maker of wine, since I have seen your face do not let me see the face of death which I dread so much."

She answered, "Gilgamesh, where are you hurrying to? You will never find that life for which you are looking. When the gods created man they allotted to him death, but life they retained in their own keeping. As for you, Gilgamesh, fill your belly with good things; day and night, night and day, dance and be merry, feast and rejoice. Let your clothes be fresh, bathe yourself in water, cherish the little child that holds your hand, and make your wife happy in your embrace; for this too is the lot of man."

But Gilgamesh said to Siduri, the young woman, "How can I be silent, how can I rest, when Enkidu whom I love is dust, and I too shall die and be laid in the earth. You live by the sea-shore and look into the heart of it; young woman, tell me now, which is the way to Utnapishtim, the son of Ubara-Tutu? What directions are there for the passage; give me, oh, give me directions, I will cross the Ocean if it is possible; if it is not I will wander still farther in the wilderness.". . .

---

Siduri instructs Gilgamesh how to reach Utnapishtim. Ferried across the "waters of death" by a boatman, Gilgamesh meets Utnapishtim. But he, too, cannot give Gilgamesh the eternal life for which he yearns.

---

. . . "Oh father Utnapishtim, you who have entered the assembly of the gods, I wish to question you concerning the living and the dead, how shall I find the life for which I am searching?"

Utnapishtim said, "There is no permanence. Do we build a house to stand for ever, do we seal a contract to hold for all time? Do brothers divide an inheritance to keep for ever, does the flood-time of rivers endure? It is only the nymph of the dragon-fly who sheds her larva and sees the sun in his glory. From the days of

---

[2]Throughout the text, words in brackets have been added as glosses by the editors. Brackets around glosses from the original sources have been changed to parentheses to distinguish them.

old there is no permanence. The sleeping and the dead, how alike they are, they are like a painted death. What is there between the master and the servant when both have fulfilled their doom? When the Anunnaki, the judges, come together, and Mammetun the mother of destinies, together they decree the fates of men.

Life and death they allot but the day of death they do not disclose."

---

The tale concludes with one of several Near Eastern flood stories that preceded the account of Noah in Genesis.

---

## REVIEW QUESTIONS

1. Describe the condition of the dead as envisioned in Enkidu's dream.
2. Describe the stages of Gilgamesh's reaction to Enkidu's death. Do these seem plausible psychologically? Explain.
3. What philosophic consolation did the goddess Siduri and Utnapishtim offer Gilgamesh?
4. Historians often comment on the pessimism or sense of the tragic that is reflected in Mesopotamian literature. To what extent is this true in the story of Gilgamesh?

---

## 2  A Pessimistic View of Life

Uncertainty and danger filled life in Mesopotamia. Sometimes, the unpredictable waters of the rivers broke through dikes, flooding fields, ruining crops, and damaging cities. At other times, an insufficient overflow deprived the land of water, causing crops to fail. Great windstorms left the countryside covered with a layer of sand, and heavy thunderstorms turned fields into a sea of mud that made travel impossible. Unlike Egypt, which was protected by vast deserts, Mesopotamia had no natural barriers to invasion. Feeling themselves surrounded by unfathomable and often hostile forces, Mesopotamians lived in an atmosphere of anxiety, which permeated their civilization.

Contributing to this sense of insecurity was the belief that the gods behaved capriciously, malevolently, and vindictively. What do the gods demand of me? Is it ever possible to please them? To these questions Mesopotamians had no reassuring answers, for the gods' behavior was a mystery to mere human beings.

# MESOPOTAMIAN WISDOM LITERATURE

The following selection reveals the pessimism that pervaded Mesopotamian life. The sufferer tries to do everything that he believes the gods want of him but cannot escape misfortune.

I survived to the next year; the appointed time passed.
I turn around, but it is bad, very bad;

My ill luck increases and I cannot find what is right.
I called to my god, but he did not show his face,

I prayed to my goddess, but she did not raise her head.

Even the diviner with his divination could not make a prediction,

And the interpreter of dreams with his libation could not elucidate my case.

I sought the favor of the . . . spirit, but he would not enlighten me;

The exorcist with his ritual could not appease the divine wrath against me.

What strange conditions everywhere!

When I look behind (me), there is persecution, trouble.

Like one who has not made libations to his god,

Nor invoked his goddess when he ate,

Does not make prostrations nor recognize (the necessity of) bowing down,

In whose mouth supplication and prayer are lacking,

Who has even neglected holy days, and ignored festivals,

Who was negligent and did not observe the gods' rites,

Did not teach his people reverence and worship,

But has eaten his food without invoking his god,

And abandoned his goddess by not bringing a flour offering,

Like one who has gone crazy and forgotten his lord,

Has frivolously sworn a solemn oath by his god, (like such a one) do I appear.

For myself, I gave attention to supplication and prayer:

My prayer was discretion, sacrifice my rule.

The day for worshipping the god was a joy to my heart;

The day of the goddess's procession was profit and gain to me.

The king's blessing—that was my joy,

And the accompanying music became a delight for me.

I had my land keep the god's rites,

And brought my people to value the goddess's name.

I made the praise for the king like a god's,

And taught the people respect for the palace.

I wish I knew that these things would be pleasing to one's god!

What is good for oneself may be offense to one's god,

What in one's own heart seems despicable may be proper to one's god.

Who can know the will of the gods in heaven?

Who can understand the plans of the underworld gods?

Where have humans learned the way of a god?

He who was alive yesterday is dead today.

One moment he is worried, the next he is boisterous.

One moment he is singing a joyful song,

A moment later he wails like a professional mourner.

Their condition changes (as quickly as) opening and shutting (the *eyes*).

When starving they become like corpses,

When full they oppose their god.

In good times they speak of scaling heaven,

When they are troubled they talk of going down to hell.

I am *perplexed* at these things; I have not been able to understand their significance.

As for me, exhausted, a windstorm is driving me on!

Debilitating Disease is let loose upon me:

An Evil Wind has blown (from the) horizon,

Headache has sprung up from the surface of the underworld. . . .

(They all joined in) and came on me together.

(They *struck*) my head, they enveloped my skull;

(My) face is gloomy, my eyes flow.

They have wrenched my neck muscles and made (my) neck limp.

They struck (my chest,) beat my breast.

They affected my flesh and made me shake,

(In) my epigastrium [abdomen] they kindled a fire.

They churned up my bowels, . . . (they) . . . my . . .

Causing the discharge of phlegm, they tired out my (lungs).

They tired out my limbs and made my *fat* quake.

My upright stance they knocked down like a
  wall,
My robust figure they laid down like a rush [a
  grasslike plant] . . . .

My eyes stare straight ahead, but cannot see,
My ears are open, but cannot hear.
Feebleness has overcome my whole body,
An attack of illness has fallen upon my flesh.
Stiffness has taken over my arms,
Weakness has come upon my knees,
My feet forget their motion.
(A stroke) has got me; I choke like someone
  prostrate.
Death has (*approached*) and has covered my face.
If someone is concerned about me, I am not
  even able to answer the one who inquires.
(My . . .) weep, but I cannot control myself.
A snare is laid on my mouth,
And a bolt keeps my lips barred. . . .

My malady is indeed protracted.
Through not eating, my looks have become
  strange,

My flesh is flaccid, and my blood has ebbed
  away.
My bones look separated, and are covered
  (only) with my skin.
My flesh is inflamed, and the . . . -disease has
  afflicted me.
I have taken to a bed of *bondage*; going out is a
  pain;
My house has become my prison. . . .

I spent the night in my dung like an ox,
And wallowed in my excrement like a
  sheep.
My symptoms are beyond the exorcist,
And my omens have confused the diviner.
The exorcist could not diagnose the nature of
  my sickness,
Nor could the diviner set a time limit on my
  illness.
My god has not come to the rescue nor taken
  me by the hand;
My goddess has not shown pity on me nor
  gone by my side.

## REVIEW QUESTIONS

1. How had the writer tried to please the gods?
2. How does he account for his misfortune?

---

# 3 Mesopotamian Concepts of Justice

A significant source of information about the life of the ancient peoples of Mesopotamia is a code of laws issued about 1750 B.C. by the Babylonian king Hammurabi (1792–1750 B.C.). Discovered by archaeologists in 1901, the code was inscribed on a stone that shows the king accepting the laws from the sun god, Shamash, who was also the Babylonian god of justice.

These laws offer striking insights into the moral values, class structure, gender relationships, and roles of kingship and religion in Babylonian society. The 282 laws cover a range of public and private matters: marriage and family relations, negligence, fraud, commercial contracts, duties of public officials, property and inheritance, crimes and punishments, and techniques of legal procedure. The prologue to the code reveals the Mesopotamian concept of the priest-king—a ruler chosen by a god to administer his will on earth. In it, Hammurabi asserted that he had a divine duty to uphold justice in the land, to punish the wicked, and to further the welfare of the people.

# CODE OF HAMMURABI

Two distinct approaches to choice of punishment for crime are found in Hammurabi's code with its numerous laws. In some instances, the guilty party is required to pay a monetary compensation to the victim, a tradition traceable to the earliest known Sumerian laws. Another approach, also found in the later Hebrew codes of law, is the principle of exact retaliation: "an eye for an eye, a tooth for a tooth."

Another feature of Hammurabi's code is that the penalties vary according to the social status of the victim. Three classes are represented: free men and women (called *patricians* in the reading here); commoners (or *plebeians*), not wholly free, but dependents of the state or perhaps serfs on landed estates; and slaves. The patricians are protected by the law of retaliation. People of the lower classes receive only monetary compensation if they are victims of a crime.

196. If a man has knocked out the eye of a patrician, his eye shall be knocked out.

197. If he has broken the limb of a patrician, his limb shall be broken.

198. If he has knocked out the eye of a plebeian or has broken the limb of a plebeian, he shall pay one mina[1] of silver.

199. If he has knocked out the eye of a patrician's servant, or broken the limb of a patrician's servant, he shall pay half his value.

200. If a patrician has knocked out the tooth of a man that is his equal, his tooth shall be knocked out.

201. If he has knocked out the tooth of a plebeian, he shall pay one-third of a mina of silver. . . .

209. If a man has struck a free woman with child, and has caused her to miscarry, he shall pay ten shekels[2] for her miscarriage.

210. If that woman die, his daughter shall be killed.

211. If it be the daughter of a plebeian, that has miscarried through his blows, he shall pay five shekels of silver.

212. If that woman die, he shall pay half a mina of silver.

213. If he has struck a man's maid and caused her to miscarry, he shall pay two shekels of silver.

214. If that woman die, he shall pay one-third of a mina of silver.

---

Many laws relating to business transactions show the importance of trade in Mesopotamian society and the willingness of the government to intervene in order to regulate the practices of the marketplace.

---

218. If a surgeon has operated with the bronze lancet on a patrician for a serious injury, and has caused his death, or has removed a cataract for a patrician, with the bronze lancet, and has made him lose his eye, his hands shall be cut off.

219. If the surgeon has treated a serious injury of a plebeian's slave, with the bronze lancet, and has caused his death, he shall render slave for slave.

220. If he has removed a cataract with the bronze lancet, and made the slave lose his eye, he shall pay half his value.

221. If a surgeon has cured the limb of a patrician, or has doctored a diseased bowel, the

---

[1]The mina was a weight of silver used to express monetary value. (Throughout the text, the editors' notes carry numbers, whereas notes from the original sources are indicated by asterisks, daggers, etcetera. An exception is made for editorial notes pertaining to Scriptures, which have symbols rather than numbers.)

[2]The shekel, also a weight of monetary value, was worth far less than the mina.

patient shall pay five shekels of silver to the surgeon.

222. If he be a plebeian, he shall pay three shekels of silver.

223. If he be a man's slave, the owner of the slave shall give two shekels of silver to the doctor. . . .

228. If a builder has built a house for a man, and finished it, he shall pay him a fee of two shekels of silver, for each *SAR*³ built on.

229. If a builder has built a house for a man, and has not made his work sound, and the house he built has fallen, and caused the death of its owner, that builder shall be put to death.

230. If it is the owner's son that is killed, the builder's son shall be put to death.

231. If it is the slave of the owner that is killed, the builder shall give slave for slave to the owner of the house.

232. If he has caused the loss of goods, he shall render back whatever he has destroyed. Moreover, because he did not make sound the house he built, and it fell, at his own cost he shall rebuild the house that fell. . . .

271. If a man has hired oxen, a wagon, and its driver, he shall pay one hundred and sixty *KA*⁴ of corn daily. . . .

275. If a man has hired a boat, its hire is three *ŠE*⁵ of silver daily.

---

The outcome of some procedures depended upon the will of the gods: for example, an accused woman could place her fate in the hands of a god by plunging into a river, canal, or reservoir; if she did not drown, she was declared innocent. In other cases, legal culpability could be removed by invoking a god to bear witness to the truth of one's testimony. The law was particularly harsh on perjurers and those who made grave charges that they could not prove in court.

---

³*SAR* was a measure of land.
⁴*KA* stood for a bulk measure.
⁵*ŠE* was another monetary weight of silver.

1. If a man has accused another of laying a *nêrtu* (death spell?) upon him, but has not proved it, he shall be put to death.

2. If a man has accused another of laying a *kišpu* (spell) upon him, but has not proved it, the accused shall go to the sacred river, he shall plunge into the sacred river, and if the sacred river shall conquer him, he that accused him shall take possession of his house. If the sacred river shall show his innocence and he is saved, his accuser shall be put to death. He that plunged into the sacred river shall appropriate the house of him that accused him.

3. If a man has borne false witness in a trial, or has not established the statement that he has made, if that case be a capital trial, that man shall be put to death.

4. If he has borne false witness in a civil law case, he shall pay the damages in that suit. . . .

9. If a man has lost property and some of it be detected in the possession of another, and the holder has said, "A man sold it to me, I bought it in the presence of witnesses"; and if the claimant has said, "I can bring witnesses who know it to be property lost by me"; then the alleged buyer on his part shall produce the man who sold it to him and the witnesses before whom he bought it; the claimant shall on his part produce the witnesses who know it to be his lost property. The judge shall examine their pleas. The witnesses to the sale and the witnesses who identify the lost property shall state on oath what they know. Such a seller is the thief and shall be put to death. The owner of the lost property shall recover his lost property. The buyer shall recoup himself from the seller's estate.

---

The laws concerned with family relationships placed great power in the hands of husbands and fathers, yet the code tried to protect women and children from neglect and mistreatment. Divorce initiated by either husband or wife was permitted under specific circumstances.

141. If a man's wife, living in her husband's house, has persisted in going out, has acted the fool, has wasted her house, has belittled her husband, he shall prosecute her. If her husband has said, "I divorce her," she shall go her way; he shall give her nothing as her price of divorce. If her husband has said, "I will not divorce her," he may take another woman to wife; the wife shall live as a slave in her husband's house.

142. If a woman has hated her husband and has said, "You shall not possess me," her past shall be inquired into, as to what she lacks. If she has been discreet, and has no vice, and her husband has gone out, and has greatly belittled her, that woman has no blame, she shall take her marriage-portion and go off to her father's house.

143. If she has not been discreet, has gone out, ruined her house, belittled her husband, she shall be drowned. . . .

148. If a man has married a wife and a disease has seized her, if he is determined to marry a second wife, he shall marry her. He shall not divorce the wife whom the disease has seized. In the home they made together she shall dwell, and he shall maintain her as long as she lives. . . .

168. If a man has determined to disinherit his son and has declared before the judge, "I cut off my son," the judge shall inquire into the son's past, and, if the son has not committed a grave misdemeanor such as should cut him off from sonship, the father shall (not) disinherit his son.

169. If he has committed a grave crime against his father, which cuts him off from son-ship, for the first offence he shall pardon him. If he has committed a grave crime a second time, the father shall cut off his son from sonship. . . .

195. If a son has struck his father, his hands shall be cut off.

---

One of the most unusual features of the law dealt with the failure of the government officials of a city or a district to prevent banditry. The code held the governor responsible for the breach of the peace and required him to compensate the bandit's victim. Government officials found guilty of extortion, bribery, or use of public employees for private purposes were severely punished.

---

23. If the highwayman has not been caught, the man that has been robbed shall state on oath what he has lost and the city or district governor in whose territory or district the robbery took place shall restore to him what he has lost.

24. If a life (has been lost), the city or district governor shall pay one mina of silver to the deceased's relatives. . . .

34. If either a governor, or a prefect, has appropriated the property of a levymaster,[6] has hired him out, has robbed him by high-handedness at a trial, has taken the salary which the king gave to him, that governor, or prefect, shall be put to death. . . .

---

[6]A levymaster was a military official.

## REVIEW QUESTIONS

1. What does Hammurabi's code reveal about the social structure of Babylonian society?
2. Explain the role of religion in the administration of law in Babylonia.
3. How did Hammurabi seek to regulate business practices among the Babylonian people?
4. What do the laws indicate about the status of women in Babylonian society?
5. How did Hammurabi try to control corrupt practices among the government officials of Babylonia?

## 4  Divine Kingship in Egypt

Theocratic monarchy, in which the ruler was considered either a god or a representative of the gods, was the basic political institution of ancient Near Eastern civilization. Kings were believed to rule in accordance with divine commands, and law was viewed as god-given. Theocracy as a form of government that subordinates the individual to the gods and their earthly representatives is compatible with mythical thought that sees nature and human destiny controlled by divine beings.

The theocratic mind of the Near East did not conceive the idea of political freedom. Mesopotamians and Egyptians were not free citizens but subjects who obeyed unquestioningly the edicts of their god-kings or priest-kings. Nor did Near Easterners arrive at a rational way of analyzing the nature and purpose of government and the merits or demerits of political institutions. To them the power of their gods and rulers was absolute and not an issue for discussion or reflection.

Divine kingship was the basic political institution of ancient Egyptian civilization. The Egyptians believed their king or pharaoh to be both a god and a man, the earthly embodiment of the god Horus. He was regarded as a benevolent protector who controlled the flood waters of the Nile, kept the irrigation system in working order, maintained justice in the land, and expressed the will of the gods by his words. It was expected that when the pharaoh died and joined his fellow gods, he would still help his living subjects. The Egyptians rejoiced in the rule of their all-powerful god-king.

# HYMNS TO THE PHARAOHS

The first reading is a hymn to the new god-king Rameses IV (c. 1166 B.C.). The second reading is a hymn to a deceased pharaoh, perhaps Unnos (c. 2600 B.C.).

### TO RAMESES IV

What a happy day! Heaven and earth rejoice, (for) thou art the great lord of Egypt.

They that had fled have come again to their towns, and they that were hidden have again come forth.

They that hungered are satisfied and happy, and they that thirsted are drunken.

They that were naked are clad in fine linen, and they that were dirty have white garments.

They that were in prison are set free, and he that was in bonds is full of joy.

They that were at strife in this land are reconciled. High Niles [beneficial floods] have come from their sources, that they may refresh the hearts of others.

Widows, their houses stand open, and they suffer travellers to enter.

Maidens rejoice and repeat their songs of gladness (?). They are arrayed in ornaments and say (?): "———— he createth generation on generation. Thou ruler, thou wilt endure for ever."

The ships rejoice on the deep ————.
They come to land with wind or oars,

They are satisfied . . . when it is said:
"King Hekmaatrē-Beloved-of-Amūn[1] again
   weareth the crown.
The son of [the sun-god] Rē, Ramesses, hath
   received the office of his father."
All lands say unto him:
"Beautiful is Horus on the throne of Amūn
   who sendeth him forth,
(Amūn) the protector of the Prince, who
   bringeth every land."

## TO A DECEASED PHARAOH

The King has not died the death: he has become one who rises (like the morning sun)
from the horizon. He rests from life (like the
setting sun) in the West, but he dawns anew in
the East. O King, you have not departed dead:
you have departed living! Have you said that
he would die?—nay, he dies not: this king lives

_____
[1]Hekmaatrē was another name of this pharaoh.

for ever. He has escaped his day of death. O
lofty one among the imperishable stars!—you
shall not ever perish. Loose the embalming
bandages!—they are not bandages (at all): they
are the tresses of the goddess Nephthys (as she
leans down over you). Men fall, and their name
ceases to be: therefore God takes hold of this
king by his arm, and leads him to the sky, that
he may not die upon earth amongst men. This
king flies away from you, you mortals. He is
not of the earth, he is of the sky. He flies as
a cloud to the sky, he who was like a bird at
the masthead. He goes up to heaven like the
hawks, and his feathers are like those of the
wild geese; he rushes at heaven like a crane,
he kisses heaven like the falcon, he leaps to
heaven like the locust. He ascends to the sky!
He ascends to the sky on the wind, on the
wind! The stairs of the sky are let down for
him that he may ascend thereon to heaven. O
gods, put your arms under the king: raise him,
lift him to the sky. To the sky! To the sky! To
the great throne amongst the gods!

# GUIDELINES FOR THE RULER

**Generally, pharaohs were mindful of their responsibilities. To prepare his son
to rule, a pharaoh or his vizier (a high executive officer) might compile a list of
instructions, like the ones that follow. These instructions were most likely
composed by a vizier of King Issi (c. 2400 B.C.).**

If thou art a leader and givest command to the
multitude, strive after every excellence, until
there be no fault in thy nature. Truth is good
and its worth is lasting, and it hath not been
disturbed since the day of its creator,* whereas
he that transgresseth its ordinances is punished. It lieth as a (right) path in front of
him that knoweth nothing. Wrong-doing (?)
hath never yet brought its venture to port. Evil
indeed winneth wealth, but the strength of
truth is that it endureth, and the (upright)

_____
*Rē [the sun god], who brought truth into the world.

man saith: "It is the property of my father.". . .†

_____
The following excerpts came from the in-
structions of Amenemhet I (1991–1962
B.C.), who prepared them for his son.
_____

I gave to the poor and nourished the orphan,
I caused him that was nothing to reach the
goal, even as him that was of account. . . .

_____
†That my father brought me up in the ways of truth is the
best thing that he has bequeathed me.

None hungered in my years, none thirsted in them. Men dwelt in (peace) through that which I wrought; . . . all that I commanded was as it should be. . . .

---

These instructions were prepared for King Merikare (c. 2050 B.C.) by his father.

---

Be not evil, it is good to be kindly. Cause thy monument‡ to endure through the love of

---

‡The remembrance of thee.

thee. . . . Then men thank God on thine account, men praise thy goodness and pray for thine health. . . . But keep thine eyes open, one that is trusting will become one that is afflicted. . . .

Do right so long as thou abidest on the earth. Calm the weeper, oppress no widow, expel no man from the possessions of his father. . . . Take heed lest thou punish wrongfully.

Exalt not the son of one of high degree more than him that is of lowly birth, but take to thyself a man because of his actions.

## REVIEW QUESTIONS

1. What were the duties expected of an Egyptian king?
2. Discuss the role of religion in sustaining the authority of rulers over their subjects.

---

# 5  Religious Inspiration of Akhenaten

Pharaoh Amenhotep IV (1369–1353 B.C.) was a religious mystic who conceived of divinity in a manner approaching monotheism. He suppressed the worship of the many gods of Egypt and insisted that only Aton—the sun god—and himself, the king and son of Aton, be worshiped by the Egyptians. Aton was viewed as the creator of the world, a god of love, peace, and justice. To promote the exclusive worship of Aton and himself, Amenhotep changed his name to Akhenaten ("It is well with Aton"), and near modern Tell El-Amarna he built a new capital city, Akhataten, which became the center of the new religious cult. The new religion perished quickly after Akhenaten's death. There is no evidence that this step toward a monotheistic conception of the divine had any later influence on the Hebrews.

The masses of Egypt were not influenced by Akhenaten's religious inspiration, and he was resisted by the priests, who clung to traditional beliefs. His immediate successors abandoned the new capital and had the monuments to Aton destroyed.

## HYMN TO ATON

Akhenaten's religious outlook inspired remarkable works of art and literature. In the following hymn, Akhenaten glorifies Aton in words that are reminiscent of Psalm 104.

Thou appearest beautifully on the horizon of
  heaven,
Thou living Aton, the beginning of life!
When thou art risen on the eastern horizon,
Thou hast filled every land with thy beauty.
Thou art gracious, great, glistening, and high
  over every land;
Thy rays encompass the lands to the limit of
  all that thou hast made. . . .
At daybreak, when thou arisest on the horizon,
When thou shinest as the Aton by day,
Thou drivest away the darkness and givest thy
  rays.
The Two Lands[1] are in festivity *every day,*
Awake and standing upon (their) feet,
For thou hast raised them up.
Washing their bodies, taking (their) clothing,
Their arms are (raised) in praise at thy appear-
  ance.
All the world, they do their work.

All beasts are content with their pasturage;
Trees and plants are flourishing.
The birds which fly from their nests,
Their wings are (stretched out) in praise to thy
  *ka.*[2]
All beasts spring upon (their) feet.
Whatever flies and alights,
They live when thou hast risen (for) them.
The ships are sailing north and south as well,
For every way is open at thy appearance.
The fish in the river dart before thy face;
Thy rays are in the midst of the great green sea.

Creator of seed in women,
Thou who makest fluid into man,
Who maintainest the son in the womb of his
  mother,
Who soothest him with that which stills his
  weeping,
Thou nurse (even) in the womb,
Who givest breath to sustain all that he had
  made!
When he descends from the womb to *breathe*

On the day when he is born,
Thou openest his mouth completely,
Thou suppliest his necessities.
When the chick in the egg speaks within the
  shell,
Thou givest him breath within it to maintain
  him.
When thou hast made him his fulfillment
  within the egg, to break it,
He comes forth from the egg to speak at his
  completed (time);
He walks upon his legs when he comes forth
  from it.

How manifold it is, what thou hast made!
They are hidden from the face (of man).
O sole god, like whom there is no other!
Thou didst create the world according to thy
  desire,
Whilst thou wert alone:
All men, cattle, and wild beasts,
Whatever is on earth, going upon (its) feet,
And what is on high, flying with its wings.

The countries of Syria and Nubia,[3] the *land* of
  Egypt,
Thou settest every man in his place,
Thou suppliest their necessities:
Everyone has his food, and his time of life is
  reckoned.
Their tongues are separate in speech,
And their natures as well;
Their skins are distinguished,
As thou distinguishest the foreign peoples.
Thou makest a Nile in the underworld,[4]
Thou bringest it forth as thou desirest
To maintain the people (of Egypt)
According as thou madest them for thyself,
The lord of all of them, wearying (himself)
  with them,
The lord of every land, rising for them,
The Aton of the day, great of majesty.

---

[1]The Two Lands were the two political divisions of Egypt, Upper and Lower Egypt. They were usually governed by the same king.
[2]The *ka* was a protective and guiding spirit, which each person was thought to have.

[3]Syria was an ancient country, larger than modern Syria, north of modern Israel and Jordan; Nubia was a kingdom located south of the first cataract of the Nile. It is now in Sudan.
[4]The Egyptians believed that the source of their Nile was in a huge body of water, which they called Nun, under the earth.

1. Why was the sun a likely choice for a god conceived as one and universal?
2. What were some of the gifts of Aton to humanity?
3. What does the poem reveal about Akhenaten's view of the world and its peoples?

## 6  Love, Passion, and Misogyny in Ancient Egypt

As in most ancient societies, Egyptian women were concerned principally with marriage, children, and household. But in comparison to other societies, Egyptian women suffered fewer disabilities. They had legal rights, could enter the priesthood, a truly prestigious position, and like men, were thought to have access to the other world after death.

Both men and women came under love's power, and the Egyptians wrote numerous poems that expressed both the joy and pain of love.

# LOVE POETRY

In the first selection, a young man admires his loved one's beauty. In this instance, the word "sister"[1] is probably not to be taken literally; it is intended as an expression of endearment.

The *One,* the sister without peer,
The handsomest of all!
She looks like the rising morning star
At the start of a happy year.
Shining bright, fair of skin,
Lovely the look of her eyes,
Sweet the speech of her lips,
She has not a word too much.
Upright neck, shining breast,
Hair true lapis lazuli;
Arms surpassing gold,
Fingers like lotus buds.
Heavy thighs, narrow waist,
Her legs parade her beauty;
With graceful step she treads the ground,

Captures my heart by her movements.
She causes all men's necks
To turn about to see her;
Joy has he whom she embraces,
He is like the first of men!

Without his love the young man suffers.

*Seven* days since I saw my sister,
And sickness invaded me;
I am heavy in all my limbs,
My body has forsaken me.
When the physicians come to me,
My heart rejects their remedies;
The magicians are quite helpless,
My sickness is not discerned.
To tell me "She is here" would revive me!
Her name would make me rise;
Her messenger's coming and going,

---

[1]Since Egyptians were interested in maintaining pure bloodlines, incestuous relationships, including brother and sister, were not uncommon. Therefore, the word "sister" when used by a lover, may be taken figuratively or literally, depending on the circumstances.

That would revive my heart!
My sister is better than all prescriptions,
She does more for me than all medicines;
Her coming to me is my amulet,
The sight of her makes me well!
When she opens her eyes my body is young,
Her speaking makes me strong;
Embracing her expels my malady—
*Seven* days since she went from me!

---

Egyptian women also experience love and vent their feelings.

---

My heart *flutters* hastily,
When I think of my love of you;

It lets me not act sensibly,
It leaps (from) its place.
It lets me not put on a dress,
Nor wrap my scarf around me;
I put no paint upon my eyes,
I'm even not anointed.

"Don't wait, go there," says it to me,
As often as I think of him;
My heart, don't act so stupidly,
Why do you play the fool?
Sit still, the brother comes to you,
And many eyes as well!
Let not the people say of me:
"A woman fallen through love!"
Be steady when you think of him,
My heart, do not *flutter*!

---

# THE INSTRUCTION OF ANKHSHESHONQ

Some Egyptian men held unflattering views of women. In his advice to his son, the priest Ankhsheshonq, who lived sometime between 300 B.C. and 50 B.C., expresses such misogynist views.

Do not take to yourself a woman whose husband is alive, lest he become your enemy. . . .

Let your wife see your wealth; do not trust her with it. . . .

Do not open your heart to your wife or to your servant.

Open it to your mother; she is a woman of discretion. . . .

Instructing a woman is like having a sack of sand whose side is split open.

Her savings are stolen goods.

What she does with her husband today she does with another man tomorrow. . . .

Do not rejoice in your wife's beauty; her heart is set on her lover. . . .

A woman lets herself be loved according to the character of her husband. . . .

He who violates a married woman on the bed will have his wife violated on the ground. . . .

He who makes love to a woman of the street will have his purse cut open on its side. . . .

He who makes love to a married woman is killed on her doorstep. . . .

Do not marry an impious woman, lest she give your children an impious upbringing.

If a woman is at peace with her husband they will never fare badly.

If a woman whispers about her husband [they will never] fare well.

If a woman does not desire the property of her husband she has another man [in her] heart. . . .

If a wife is of nobler birth than her husband he should give way to her.

*REVIEW QUESTIONS*

1. On the basis of these poems, what similarities do you discern between our standards of beauty and an ancient Egyptian's?
2. Which piece of the priest's advice would a misogynist today consider the most wise?

---

## 7  Empire Builders

After 1500 B.C. Near Eastern history was marked by empire building, which led to the intermingling of peoples and cultural traditions and to the extension of civilization well beyond the river valleys. Two of the leading empire builders were the Assyrians and the Persians.

# THE ASSYRIAN EMPIRE INSCRIPTION OF TIGLATHPILESER I

The Assyrians, a Semitic people from the region of what is now northern Iraq, went through several stages of empire building. At its height in the seventh century B.C., the Assyrian Empire stretched from Egypt to Persia (modern Iran). The king, representative of the god Ashur, governed absolutely, and nobles, appointed by the crown, kept order in the provinces. Traveling inspectors checked on the performance of these officials. A network of roads and an effective messenger service enabled Assyrian rulers to keep informed about potential unrest and to crush rebellions. Conquered peoples were permitted a substantial amount of independence so long as they paid tribute to their Assyrian overlords, but uprisings were ruthlessly suppressed.

In the following reading, Tiglathpileser I (1115–1077 B.C.) described his conquests and the subjugation of rebellious subjects.

Tiglath-pileser, the powerful king, king of hosts, who has no rival, king of the four quarters (of the world), king of all rulers, lord of lords, king of kings; the lofty prince . . . who rules over the nations, . . . the legitimate shepherd whose name is exalted above all rulers; the lofty judge, whose weapons Ashur[1] has sharpened, and whose name, as ruler over the four quarters (of the world), he has proclaimed forever; the conqueror of distant lands, which form the boundaries on north and south; the brilliant day, whose splendour overthrows the world's regions; the terrible, destroying flame, which like the rush of the storm sweeps over the enemy's country; who . . . has no adversary, and overthrows the foes of Ashur.

Ashur and the great gods who have enlarged my kingdom, who have given me strength and power as my portion, commanded me to extend the territory of their (the gods') country, putting into my hand their powerful weapons, the cyclone of battle. I subjugated lands and

---

[1]Ashur was the patron god of the Assyrians. He is identified with the earlier Babylonian god Marduk.

mountains, cities and their rulers, enemies of Ashur, and conquered their territories. With sixty kings I fought, spreading terror (among them), and achieved a glorious victory over them. A rival in combat, or an adversary in battle, I did not have. To Assyria I added more land, to its people I added more people, enlarging the boundaries of my land and conquering all (neighbouring?) territories.

In the beginning of my government, five kings . . . with an army of twenty thousand men . . .—and whose power no king had ever broken and overcome in battle—trusting to their strength rushed down and conquered the land of Qummuh (Commagene).[2] With the help of Ashur, my lord, I gathered my war chariots and assembled my warriors; I made no delay, but traversed Kashiari,[3] an almost im-passable region. I waged battle in Qummuh with these five kings and their twenty thousand soldiers and accomplished their defeat. Like the Thunderer (the storm god Adad) I crushed the corpses of their warriors in the battle that caused their overthrow. I made their blood to flow over all the ravines and high places of mountains. I cut off their heads and piled them up at the walls of their cities like heaps of grain. I carried off their booty, their goods, and their property beyond reckoning. Six thousand, the rest of their troops, who had fled before my weapons and had thrown themselves at my feet, I took away as prisoners and added to the people of my country.

At that time I marched also against the people of Qummuh, who had become unsubmissive, withholding the tax and tribute due to Ashur, my lord. I conquered Qummuh to its whole extent, and carried off their booty, their goods, and their property; I burned their cities with fire, destroyed, and devastated.

---

[2]Commagene was a region along the upper Euphrates River in northern Syria.
[3]Kashiari was a mountainous area in Mesopotamia.

---

# THE PERSIAN EMPIRE INSCRIPTIONS OF CYRUS AND DARIUS I

Under Cyrus the Great and his son and successor, Cambyses, the Persians conquered all lands between the Nile in Egypt and the Indus River in India. This conquest took twenty-five years, from 550 to 525 B.C. The Near Eastern conception of absolute monarchy justified by religion reached its culminating expression in the person of the Persian king, who ruled this vast empire with divine approval. The Persian kings developed an effective system of administration—based in part on an Assyrian model—which gave stability and a degree of unity to their extensive territories.

In the following inscription, Cyrus the Great describes his accomplishments.

I am Cyrus, king of the world, great king, legitimate king, king of Babylon, king of Sumer and Akkad, king of the four rims (of the earth), son of Cambyses, great king, king of Anshan, grandson of Cyrus, great king, king of Anshan, descendant of Teispes, great king, king of Anshan, of a family (which) always (exercised) kingship; whose rule Bel and Nebo love, whom they want as king to please their hearts.

When I entered Babylon as a friend and (when) I established the seat of the government in the palace of the ruler under jubilation and rejoicing, Marduk, the great lord, (induced) the magnanimous inhabitants of Babylon (to love me), and I was daily endeavouring to worship him. My numerous troops walked around in Babylon in peace, I did not allow anybody to terrorize (any place) of the (country of Sumer) and Akkad. I strove for peace in Babylon and in all his (other) sacred cities. As to the inhabitants of Babylon, (I abolished) the corvée[1] (lit.: yoke) which was against their (social) standing. I brought relief to their dilapidated housing, putting (thus) an end to their (main) complaints. Marduk, the great lord, was well pleased with my deeds and sent friendly blessings to myself, Cyrus, the king who worships him, to Cambyses, my son, the offspring of (my) loins, as well as to all my troops, and we all (praised) his great (godhead) joyously, standing before him in peace.

All the kings of the entire world from the Upper to the Lower Sea, those who are seated in throne rooms, (those who) live in other (types of buildings as well as) all the kings of the West land living in tents,* brought their heavy tributes and kissed my feet in Babylon. (As to the region) from . . . as far as Ashur and Susa, Agade, Eshnunna, the towns Zamban, Me-Turnu, Der as well as the region of the Gutians, I returned to (these) sacred cities on the other side of the Tigris, the sanctuaries of which have been ruins for a long time, the images which (used) to live therein and established for them permanent sanctuaries. I (also) gathered all their (former) inhabitants and returned (to them) their habitations. Furthermore, I resettled upon the command of Marduk, the great lord, all the gods of Sumer and Akkad whom Nabonidus has brought into Babylon to the anger of the lord of the gods, unharmed, in their (former) chapels, the places which make them happy.

May all the gods whom I have resettled in their sacred cities ask daily Bel and Nebo for a long life for me and may they recommend me (to him); to Marduk, my lord, they may say this: "Cyrus, the king who worships you, and Cambyses, his son, . . ." . . . all of them I settled in a peaceful place . . . ducks and doves, . . . I endeavoured to fortify/repair their dwelling places. . . . (six lines destroyed)

---

[1]The corvée was labor that local authorities required of ordinary citizens, often on public works such as the maintenance of roads.
*This phrase refers either to the way of life of a nomadic or a primitive society in contradistinction to that of an urban.

Besides providing impressive political and administrative unity, the Persian Empire fused and perpetuated the various cultural traditions of the Near East. This cultural fusion is reflected in the following inscription, which describes the construction of the palace at Susa by King Darius I (522–486 B.C.).

---

A great god is Ahuramazda, who created this earth,
who created yonder firmament, who created man,
who created welfare for man, who
made Darius king, one king of many,
one lord of many.—I am Darius,
great king, king of kings, king of countries, king
of this earth, son of Ilystaspes, the Achaemenian.—Says Darius the king: Ahuramazda
the greatest of gods, he created me; he
made me king; he to me this kingdom
granted, the great (kingdom), with good horses, with
good men. By the grace of Ahuramazda my father
Hystaspes and Arsames my grandfather
then both were living when Ahuramazda
made me king of this earth. Ahuramazda
created for me the horse on the whole earth, and
man; he made me king. Ahuramazda
granted me aid, Ahuramazda I reverenced,
Ahuramazda the greatest of gods—what he told me
to do, all that by my hand was done,
all that Ahuramazda did.—By the grace of Ahuramazda this palace I made which at Susa
was made. From afar to here its ornamentation was brought.
The earth was dug until I came to rock-bottom.
When the excavation was made, then rubble was filled in, one
part 40 feet in depth, the other 20 feet in depth.
On this rubble the palace was constructed.—
And that the earth was dug down, and that rubble

was filled in and that brick was moulded, the Babylonian folk, it did (that). The timber cedar,
this—a mountain named Lebanon—from
there was
brought; the Assyrian folk, it brought it to
Babylon; from Babylon the Karkians and
Ionians
brought it to Susa. The oak from Gandara
was brought and from Carmania. The gold
from
Sardis and from Bactria was brought, which
was wrought here. The stone—lapis lazuli and
ser-
pentine—which was wrought here, this from
Sogdiana
was brought. The stone hematite, this from
Choras-
mia was brought, which was wrought here.
The silver and
the copper from Egypt were brought. The ornamentation
with which the wall was adorned, that from
Ionia

was brought. The ivory, which was brought
here, from
Ethiopia and from India and from Arachosia
was brought. The stone pillars which here
were wrought—a place named Abirāduš in
Uja—
from there were brought; the stone-masons who
there worked, those were Ionians and
Sardians.—The artisans who the structure wrought, those were Medes and Egyptians;
those who worked on the fine stones, those
were Sardians and Egyptians. The men who
worked on the brick (work), those were Babylonians
and Ionians; those who (worked) at the wall,
those were
Medes and Egyptians.—Says Darius the king:
by the grace
of Ahuramazda (this) fine well-laid well-
walled (palace)
I made. Me may Ahuramazda protect, and
what by me was
done, and what my father (has done), and my
country.

## REVIEW QUESTIONS

1. What role do the inscriptions suggest the gods played in establishing and
   extending the rule of the Assyrian and Persian kings?
2. What appear to have been the character and purposes of warfare in the Assyrian
   and Persian empires?
3. In what ways did the great royal palace at Susa symbolize both the culture and
   extent of the Persian Empire?

---

# 8   The Myth-making Outlook
## of the Ancient Near East

The civilizations of the ancient Near East were based on a way of thinking that
is fundamentally different from the modern scientific outlook. The peoples of
Mesopotamia and Egypt interpreted nature and human experience through
myths, which narrated the deeds of gods who in some distant past had brought
forth the world and human beings. These myths made the universe and life intelligible for Near Eastern people.

The difference between scientific thinking and mythical thinking is profound. The scientific mind views physical nature as an *it*—inanimate, impersonal, and governed by universal law. The myth-making (mythopoeic) mind sees nature as personified—alive, with individual wills, gods, and demons who manipulate things according to their desires. The scientific mind holds that natural objects obey universal rules; hence the location of planets, the speed of objects, and the onset of a hurricane can be predicted. The myth-making mind has no awareness of repetitive laws inherent in nature; rather it attributes all occurrences to the actions of gods, whose behavior is often unpredictable. The scientific mind appeals to reason—it analyzes nature logically and systematically and searches for general principles that govern the phenomena. The myth-making mind explains nature and human experience by narrating stories about the gods and their deeds. Myth is an expression of the poetic imagination; it proclaims a truth that is emotionally satisfying, not one produced by intellectual analysis and synthesis. It gives order to human experiences and justifies traditional rules of morality. Mythical explanations of nature and human experience, appealing essentially to the imagination, enrich perception and feeling; they make life seem less overwhelming and death less frightening.

# PERSONIFICATION OF NATURAL OBJECTS

The mythopoeic mind accounts for causation by personifying inanimate substances. To explain through personification is to seek the *who* behind events, to attribute these events to the will of a god (or to an object suffused with divine presence). Thus if a river did not rise, it was because it refused to do so; either the river or the gods were angry at the people.

The following excerpts from Mesopotamian literature are examples of personification. While we regard table salt as an ordinary mineral, to the Mesopotamians it was alive, a fellow being. In one passage, a person appeals to salt to end his bewitchment. In the second, an afflicted person who believes himself bewitched calls on fire to destroy his enemies.

## O SALT

O Salt, created in a clean place,
For food of gods did *Enlil* [father of the
    Sumerian gods] destine thee.
Without thee no meal is set out in *Ekur*,
Without thee god, king, lord, and prince do
    not smell incense.
I am so-and-so, the son of so-and-so,
Held captive by enchantment,
Held in fever by bewitchment.

O Salt, break my enchantment! Loose my spell!
Take from me the bewitchment!—And as My
    Creator
I shall extol thee.

## SCORCHING FIRE

Scorching Fire, warlike son of Heaven,
Thou, the fiercest of thy brethren,
Who like Moon and Sun decidest lawsuits—
Judge thou my case, hand down the verdict.

Burn the man and woman who bewitched me;
Burn, O Fire, the man and woman who bewitched me;
Scorch, O Fire, the man and woman who bewitched me;

Burn them, O Fire;
Scorch them, O Fire;
Take hold of them, O Fire;
Consume them, O Fire;
Destroy them, O Fire.

---

# *ENUMA ELISH*
# THE BABYLONIAN GENESIS

The Mesopotamian creation epic *Enuma elish* is another example of mythical thinking. Marduk, the chief god of Babylon, slays Tiamat, a primal mother identified with the salt sea, and then proceeds to construct the cosmos from her carcass.

"Stand thou up, that I and thou meet in single combat!"
When Tiamat heard this,
She was like one possessed; she took leave of her senses.
In fury Tiamat cried out aloud.
To the roots her legs shook both together.
She recites a charm, keeps casting her spell,
While the gods of battle sharpen their weapons.
Then joined issue Tiamat and Marduk, wisest of gods.
They strove in single combat, locked in battle.
The lord spread out his net to enfold her,
The Evil Wind, which followed behind, he let loose in her face.
When Tiamat opened her mouth to consume him,
He drove in the Evil Wind that she close not her lips.
As the fierce winds charged her belly,
Her body was distended and her mouth was wide open.
He released the arrow, it tore her belly,
It cut through her insides, splitting the heart.
Having thus subdued her, he extinguished her life.
He cast down her carcass to stand upon it.
After he had slain Tiamat, the leader,
Her band was shattered, her troupe broken up;

And the gods, her helpers who marched at her side,
Trembling with terror, turned their backs about,
In order to save and preserve their lives.
Tightly encircled, they could not escape.
He made them captives and he smashed their weapons.
Thrown into the net, they found themselves ensnared;
Placed in cells, they were filled with wailing;
Bearing his wrath, they were held imprisoned. . . .
When he had vanquished and subdued his adversaries, . . .
[Marduk] turned back to Tiamat whom he had bound.
The lord trod on the legs of Tiamat,
With his unsparing mace he crushed her skull.
When the arteries of her blood he had severed,
The North Wind bore (it) to places undisclosed.
On seeing this, his fathers were joyful and jubilant,
They brought gifts of homage, they to him.
Then the lord paused to view her dead body,
That he might divide the monster and do artful works.
He split her like a shellfish into two parts:
Half of her he set up and ceiled it as sky,

Pulled down the bar and posted guards.
He bade them to allow not her waters to
    escape.
He crossed the heavens and surveyed the
    regions. . . .

[There] He constructed stations for the great
    gods,
Fixing their astral likenesses as constella-
    tions.
He determined the year by designating the
    zones:
He set up three constellations for each of the
    twelve months. . . .

In her [Tiamat's] belly he established the
    zenith.

The Moon he caused to shine, the night (to
    him) entrusting.
He appointed him a creature of the night to
    signify the days. . . .
When Marduk hears the words of the gods,
His heart prompts (him) to fashion artful works.
Opening his mouth, he addresses [the god] Ea
To impart the plan he had conceived in his
    heart:
"Blood I will mass and cause bones to be.
I will establish a savage, 'man' shall be his
    name.
Verily, savage-man I will create.
He shall be charged with the service of the
    gods
    That they might be at ease!"

---

# LAMENT FOR UR
# THE GODS AND HUMAN DESTINY

**Mesopotamians and Egyptians believed that their destinies were determined by the gods. Drought, hurricanes, sickness, law, and foreign invasion were all attributed to divine intervention. In the "Lament for Ur," the assembly of the gods decides to punish the Sumerian city-state of Ur.**

Enlil called the storm.
    The people mourn.
Winds of abundance he took from the land.
    The people mourn.
Good winds he took away from Sumer.
    The people mourn.
Deputed [assigned] evil winds.
    The people mourn.
Entrusted them to Kingaluda, tender of
    storms.
He called the storm that annihilates the land.
    The people mourn.
He called disastrous winds.
    The people mourn.
Enlil—choosing Gibil (fire god) as his
    helper—
called the (great) hurricane of heaven.
    The people mourn.

The (blinding) hurricane howling across the
    skies—
    the people mourn—
the storm that annihilates the land roaring
    over the earth—
    the people mourn—
the tempest unsubduable like breaks through
    levees,
beats down upon, devours the city's ships,
(all these) he gathered at the base of heaven.
    The people mourn.

(Great) fires he lit that heralded the storm.
    The people mourn.
And lit on either flank of furious winds
    the searing heat of desert.
Like flaming heat of noon this fire
    scorched. . . .

The storm ordered by Enlil in hate,
   the storm which wears away the country,
covered Ur like a cloth,
   veiled it like a linen sheet. . . .

On that day did the storm leave the city;
   that city was a ruin.
O father Nanna (the moon god), that town
     was left a ruin.
   The people mourn.
On that day did the storm leave the country.
   The people mourn.
Its people ('s corpses), not potsherds,
   littered the approaches.

The walls were gaping;
the high gates, the roads,
   were piled with dead.
In the wide streets,
   where feasting crowds (once) gathered,
jumbled they lay.

In all the streets and roadways bodies lay.
In open fields that used to fill with dancers,
the people lay in heaps.

The country's blood now filled its holes.
   like metal in a mold;
bodies dissolved—like butter left in the sun.

## REVIEW QUESTIONS

1. What is myth? How does mythical thinking differ from scientific thinking?
2. It has been said that humans are myth-making animals and that all human societies sustain themselves by creating myths. Discuss.
3. On what occasions might the ancient Mesopotamians have turned to the gods for help?
4. How did the Mesopotamians explain certain natural disasters?

## CHAPTER 2

# The Hebrews

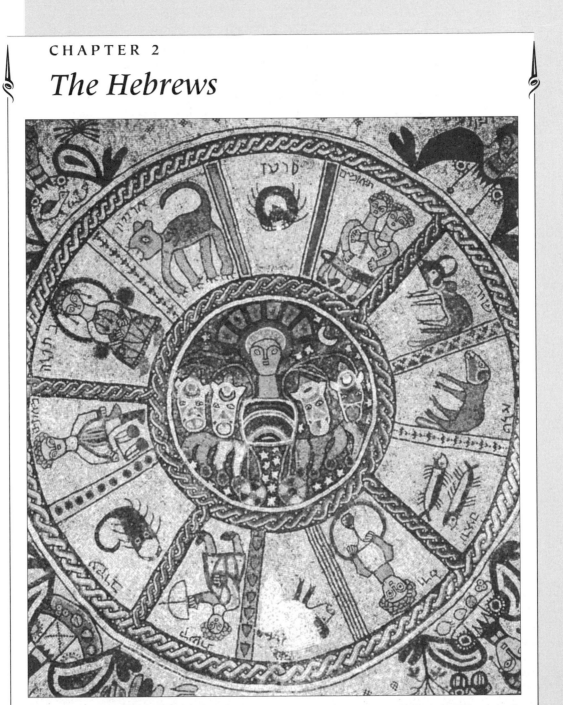

TEMPLE FLOOR MOSAIC. Images in Hebrew art are extremely rare because of the injunction in the Second Commandment against graven images. This floor mosaic from Beth Alpha synagogue in Israel is a zodiacal calendar. (©*Zev Radovan, Jerusalem*)

Two ancient peoples, the Hebrews (Jews) and the Greeks, are the principal founders of Western civilization. From the Hebrews derives the concept of *ethical monotheism*—the belief in one God who demands righteous behavior from his human creations—which is an essential element of the Western tradition.

The Hebrews originated in Mesopotamia and migrated to Canaan (Palestine). Some Hebrews who journeyed to Egypt to become farmers and herdsmen were forced to labor for the Egyptian state. In the thirteenth century B.C., Moses, who believed that he was doing God's bidding, led the Hebrews from Egypt—the biblical Exodus. While wandering in the Sinai Desert, the Hebrews were uplifted and united by a belief in Yahweh, the One God. In the eleventh century B.C., some two hundred years after they had begun the conquest of Canaan, the Hebrews were unified under the leadership of Saul, their first king. Under Solomon (d. 922 B.C.) the kingdom of Israel reached the height of its power and splendor.

The Hebrews borrowed elements from the older civilizations of the Near East. Thus there are parallels between Babylonian literature and biblical accounts of the Creation, the Flood, and the Tower of Babel. Nevertheless, Israelite religion marks a profound break with the outlook of the surrounding civilizations of the Near East.

There are two fundamental characteristics of ancient Near Eastern religion. First, the Near Eastern mind saw gods everywhere in nature; the moon and stars, rivers and mountains, thunder and wind storms were either gods or the dwelling places of gods. The Near Eastern mind invented myths—stories about the gods' birth, deeds, death, and resurrection. Second, Near Eastern gods were not fully sovereign. They were not eternal but were born or created; their very existence and power depended on some prior realm. They grew old, became ill, required food, and even died—all limitations on their power. The gods were subject to magic and destiny—forces that preceded them in time and surpassed them in power—and if the gods did wrong, destiny, or fate, punished them.

Hebrew religious thought evolved through the history and experience of the Jewish people. Over the centuries the Hebrew view of God came to differ markedly from Near Eastern ideas about the gods and the world. For the Hebrews, God was not only one, he was also *transcendent*—above nature. This means that natural objects were not divine, holy, or alive, but were merely God's creations. In contrast to the Near Eastern gods, Yahweh was fully sovereign, absolutely free; there were no limitations whatsoever on his power. He was eternal and the source of all in the universe; he did not answer to fate but himself determined the consequences of wrongdoing; he was not subject to any primordial power or to anything outside or above him.

The Hebrew conception of God led to a revolutionary view of the human being. The Hebrews believed that God had given the individual moral autonomy—the capacity to choose between good and evil.

Therefore, men and women had to measure their actions by God's laws and were responsible for their own behavior. Such an outlook led people to become aware of themselves—their moral potential and personal worth. From the Hebrews came a fundamental value of the Western tradition—the inviolable worth and dignity of the individual.

## 1  Hebrew Cosmogony and Anthropology

The Hebrew scriptures, which form the Old Testament of the Christian Bible, are a collection of thirty-nine books written over several centuries by several authors. It is a record of more than a thousand years of ancient Jewish history and religious development. Among the topics treated in Genesis, the first book of the Bible, are God's creation of the universe and human beings, the original human condition in the Garden of Eden, and the origin of evil with Adam and Eve's disobedience of God and their resultant expulsion from Eden.

## GENESIS

The first three chapters from the book of Genesis follow. The first chapter presents the *cosmogony* and *anthropology* of the Jews. Hebrew cosmogony—that is, their view of the generation of the universe and all that is in it—exemplifies God's majesty and power. Although Genesis is similar to other Near Eastern creation myths, it also sharply breaks with the essential outlook of the time. In Genesis, nature is no longer inhabited by mythical gods, and inanimate objects are not suffused with life. The Hebrews did not worship the moon and stars and mountains and rivers, but they regarded nature as the orderly creation of one supreme and eternal being.

How the Hebrews conceived of the creation of men and women and their position in the universe—the anthropology of the Jews—is dealt with in verses 26–31. The Hebrews' conception of the individual created in God's image and subordinate to nothing except God is as revolutionary as their idea of God, for this conception confers great power and dignity upon human beings.

1 In the beginning God created the heavens and the earth. ²The earth was without form and void, and darkness was upon the face of the deep; and the Spirit of God was moving over the face of the waters.

3 And God said, "Let there be light"; and there was light. ⁴And God saw that the light was good; and God separated the light from the darkness. ⁵God called the light Day, and the darkness he called Night. And there was evening and there was morning, one day.

6 And God said, "Let there be a firmament in the midst of the waters, and let it separate the waters from the waters." ⁷And God made the firmament and separated the waters which were under the firmament from the waters

which were above the firmament. And it was so. [8]And God called the firmament Heaven. And there was evening and there was morning, a second day.

9 And God said, "Let the waters under the heavens be gathered together into one place, and let the dry land appear." And it was so. [10]God called the dry land Earth, and the waters that were gathered together he called Seas. And God saw that it was good. [11]And God said, "Let the earth put forth vegetation, plants yielding seed, and fruit trees bearing fruit in which is their seed, each according to its kind, upon the earth." And it was so. [12]The earth brought forth vegetation, plants yielding seed according to their own kinds, and trees bearing fruit in which is their seed, each according to its kind. And God saw that it was good. [13]And there was evening and there was morning, a third day.

14 And God said, "Let there be lights in the firmament of the heavens to separate the day from the night; and let them be for signs and for seasons and for days and years, [15]and let them be lights in the firmament of the heavens to give light upon the earth." And it was so. [16]And God made the two great lights, the greater light to rule the day, and the lesser light to rule the night; he made the stars also. [17]And God set them in the firmament of the heavens to give light upon the earth, [18]to rule over the day and over the night, and to separate the light from the darkness. And God saw that it was good. [19]And there was evening and there was morning, a fourth day.

20 And God said, "Let the waters bring forth swarms of living creatures, and let birds fly above the earth across the firmament of the heavens." [21]So God created the great sea monsters and every living creature that moves, with which the waters swarm, according to their kinds, and every winged bird according to its kind. And God saw that it was good. [22]And God blessed them, saying, "Be fruitful and multiply and fill the waters in the seas, and let birds multiply on the earth." [23]And there was evening and there was morning, a fifth day.

24 And God said, "Let the earth bring forth living creatures according to their kinds: cattle and creeping things and beasts of the earth according to their kinds." And it was so. [25]And God made the beasts of the earth according to their kinds and the cattle according to their kinds, and everything that creeps upon the ground according to its kind. And God saw that it was good.

26 Then God said, "Let us make man in our image, after our likeness; and let them have dominion over the fish of the sea, and over the birds of the air, and over the cattle, and over all the earth, and over every creeping thing that creeps upon the earth." [27]So God created man in his own image, in the image of God he created him; male and female he created them. [28]And God blessed them, and God said to them, "Be fruitful and multiply, and fill the earth and subdue it; and have dominion over the fish of the sea and over the birds of the air and over every living thing that moves upon the earth." [29]And God said, "Behold, I have given you every plant yielding seed which is upon the face of all the earth, and every tree with seed in its fruit; you shall have them for food. [30]And to every beast of the earth, and to every bird of the air, and to everything that creeps on the earth, everything that has the breath of life, I have given every green plant for food." And it was so. [31]And God saw everything that he had made, and behold, it was very good. And there was evening and there was morning, a sixth day.

---

The second chapter of Genesis contains a retrospective view of the creation of the universe; a second account of man's creation from "the dust of the ground," a description of the Garden of Eden, into which man was placed, with the injunction that he may eat freely of every tree in the garden, except the tree of the knowledge of good and evil, and an account of God's creation of woman from the rib of man as a companion for him. In Genesis, Eden was an idyllic garden, a paradise, in which the first human beings lived. It has been compared to the mythic land of the blessed, Dilmun, described in the Babylonian epic *Gilgamesh*. In Eden, human beings were free of death, illness, pain, and a consciousness of evil, or sin.

---

2 Thus the heavens and the earth were finished, and all the host of them. 2And on the seventh day God finished his work which he had done, and he rested on the seventh day from all his work which he had done. 3So God blessed the seventh day and hallowed it, because on it God rested from all his work which he had done in creation.

4 These are the generations of the heavens and the earth when they were created.

In the day that the LORD God made the earth and the heavens, 5when no plant of the field was yet in the earth and no herb of the field had yet sprung up—for the LORD God had not caused it to rain upon the earth, and there was no man to till the ground; 6but a mist went up from the earth and watered the whole face of the ground—7then the LORD God formed man of dust from the ground, and breathed into his nostrils the breath of life; and man became a living being. 8And the LORD God planted a garden in Eden, in the east; and there he put the man whom he had formed. 9And out of the ground the LORD God made to grow every tree that is pleasant to the sight and good for food, the tree of life also in the midst of the garden, and the tree of the knowledge of good and evil. . . .

15 The LORD God took the man and put him in the garden of Eden to till it and keep it. 16And the LORD God commanded the man, saying, "You may freely eat of every tree of the garden; 17but of the tree of the knowledge of good and evil you shall not eat, for in the day that you eat of it you shall die."

18 Then the LORD God said, "It is not good that the man should be alone; I will make him a helper fit for him." 19So out of the ground the LORD God formed every beast of the field and every bird of the air, and brought them to the man to see what he would call them; and whatever the man called every living creature, that was its name. 20The man gave names to all cattle, and to the birds of the air, and to every beast of the field; but for the man there was not found a helper fit for him. 21So the LORD God caused a deep sleep to fall upon the man, and while he slept took one of his ribs and closed up its place with flesh; 22and the rib which the LORD God had taken from the man he made into a woman and brought her to the man. 23Then the man said,

"This at last is bone of my bones
    and flesh of my flesh;
she shall be called Woman,
    because she was taken out of Man."

24Therefore a man leaves his father and his mother and cleaves to his wife, and they become one flesh. 25And the man and his wife were both naked, and were not ashamed.

---

The third chapter of Genesis deals with the origin of evil. When Adam and Eve disobeyed God by eating from the tree of knowledge, they were driven from the Garden of Eden. For the Hebrews the expulsion from paradise marks the beginning of human history, suffering, and death. This passage provides one of the fundamental explanations of evil in the Western tradition, the Judaic conception, later to be refashioned by Saint Paul into the Christian notion of original sin. The language of the biblical narrative is naive and framed in mythic imagery, but the ideas present are timeless.

---

3 Now the serpent was more subtle than any other wild creature that the LORD God had made. He said to the woman, "Did God say, 'You shall not eat of any tree of the garden'?" 2And the woman said to the serpent, "We may eat of the fruit of the trees of the garden; 3but God said, 'You shall not eat of the fruit of the tree which is in the midst of the garden, neither shall you touch it, lest you die.'" 4But the serpent said to the woman, "You will not die. 5For God knows that when you eat of it your eyes will be opened, and you will be like God, knowing good and evil." 6So when the woman saw that the tree was good for food, and that it was a delight to the eyes, and that the tree was to be desired to make one wise, she took of its

fruit and ate; and she also gave some to her husband, and he ate. ⁷Then the eyes of both were opened, and they knew that they were naked; and they sewed fig leaves together and made themselves aprons.

8 And they heard the sound of the LORD God walking in the garden in the cool of the day, and the man and his wife hid themselves from the presence of the LORD God among the trees of the garden. ⁹But the LORD God called to the man, and said to him, "Where are you?" ¹⁰And he said, "I heard the sound of thee in the garden, and I was afraid, because I was naked; and I hid myself." ¹¹He said, "Who told you that you were naked? Have you eaten of the tree of which I commanded you not to eat?" ¹²The man said, "The woman whom thou gavest to be with me, she gave me fruit of the tree, and I ate." ¹³Then the LORD God said to the woman, "What is this that you have done?" The woman said, "The serpent beguiled me, and I ate."
14 The LORD God said to the serpent,
"Because you have done this,
    cursed are you above all cattle,
    and above all wild animals;
upon your belly you shall go,
    and dust you shall eat
    all the days of your life.
¹⁵I will put enmity between you and the
        woman,
    and between your seed and her seed;
he shall bruise your head,
    and you shall bruise his heel."
¹⁶To the woman he said,
"I will greatly multiply your pain in
        childbearing;

in pain you shall bring forth children,
yet your desire shall be for your husband,
    and he shall rule over you."
17 And to Adam he said,
"Because you have listened to the voice of
        your wife,
    and have eaten of the tree
of which I commanded you,
    'You shall not eat of it,'
cursed is the ground because of you;
    in toil you shall eat of it all the days of
        your life;
¹⁸thorns and thistles it shall bring forth to you;
    and you shall eat the plants of the field.
¹⁹In the sweat of your face
    you shall eat bread
till you return to the ground,
    for out of it you were taken;
you are dust,
    and to dust you shall return."

20 The man called his wife's name Eve, because she was the mother of all living. ²¹And the LORD God made for Adam and for his wife garments of skins, and clothed them.

22 Then the LORD God said, "Behold, the man has become like one of us, knowing good and evil; and now, lest he put forth his hand and take also of the tree of life, and eat, and live for ever"—²³therefore the LORD God sent him forth from the garden of Eden, to till the ground from which he was taken. ²⁴He drove out the man; and at the east of the garden of Eden he placed the cherubim [winged angels], and a flaming sword which turned every way, to guard the way to the tree of life.

## REVIEW QUESTIONS

1. Compare and contrast the Hebrew view of the creation of the world and the human race in the book of Genesis with that of the Mesopotamians in the *Enuma elish* (see page 24).
2. What does the story of Adam and Eve reveal about Hebrew conceptions of good and evil?
3. What do you learn about Hebrew conceptions of male and female relationships from the stories in the book of Genesis?
4. What relationship does the book of Genesis suggest between humans and other creations of God such as the earth, plants, and animals?

## 2  The Covenant and the Ten Commandments

Central to Hebrew religious thought was the covenant that the Hebrews believed had been made between God and themselves. The Hebrews believed that God had chosen them to be the first recipients of his law. They did not hold that this honor was bestowed on them because they were better than other nations or that they had done something special to earn it. Rather they viewed the covenant as an awesome responsibility; God had chosen them to set an example of righteous behavior to the other nations.

# *EXODUS*
# THE COVENANT

As described in Exodus, the Israelite leader Moses received the covenant on Mount Sinai at the time of the Hebrews' flight from Egypt and wanderings in the wilderness of the Sinai Desert.

3 And Moses went up to God, and the LORD called to him out of the mountain, saying, "Thus you shall say to the house of Jacob, and tell the people of Israel: ⁴You have seen what I did to the Egyptians, and how I bore you on eagles' wings and brought you to myself. ⁵Now therefore, if you will obey my voice and keep my covenant, you shall be my own possession among all peoples; for all the earth is mine, ⁶and you shall be to me a kingdom of priests and a holy nation. These are the words which you shall speak to the children of Israel."

7 So Moses came and called the elders of the people, and set before them all these words which the LORD had commanded him. ⁸And all the people answered together and said, "All that the LORD has spoken we will do." And Moses reported the words of the people to the LORD. ⁹And the LORD said to Moses, "Lo, I am coming to you in a thick cloud, that the people may hear when I speak with you, and may also believe you for ever." (Exodus 19)

# *EXODUS*
# THE TEN COMMANDMENTS

Together with the covenant, Moses received the Ten Commandments, which specified God's moral laws. Chapter 20 sets forth the Ten Commandments.

17 Then Moses brought the people out of the camp to meet God; and they took their stand at the foot of the mountain. ¹⁸And Mount Sinai was wrapped in smoke, because the LORD descended upon it in fire; and the smoke of it went up like the smoke of a kiln, and the whole mountain quaked greatly. ¹⁹And as the sound of the trumpet grew louder and louder, Moses spoke, and God answered him in thunder. ²⁰And the LORD came down upon Mount Sinai, to the top of the mountain; and the LORD called Moses to the top of the mountain, and Moses went up. (Exodus 19)

**20** And God spoke all these words, saying,

2 "I am the LORD your God, who brought you out of the land of Egypt, out of the house of bondage.

3 "You shall have no other gods before me.

4 "You shall not make yourself a graven image, or any likeness of anything that is in heaven above, or that is in the earth beneath, or that is in the water under the earth; ⁵you shall not bow down to them or serve them; for I the LORD your God am a jealous God, visiting the iniquity of the fathers upon the children to the third and the fourth generation of those who hate me, ⁶but showing steadfast love to thousands of those who love me and keep my commandments.

7 "You shall not take the name of the LORD your God in vain; for the LORD will not hold him guiltless who takes his name in vain.

8 "Remember the sabbath day, to keep it holy. ⁹Six days you shall labor, and do all your work; ¹⁰but the seventh day is a sabbath to the LORD your God; in it you shall not do any work, you, or your son, or your daughter, your manservant, or your maidservant, or your cattle, or the sojourner who is within your gates; ¹¹for in six days the LORD made heaven and earth, the sea, and all that is in them, and rested the seventh day; therefore the LORD blessed the sabbath day and hallowed it.

12 "Honor your father and your mother, that your days may be long in the land which the LORD your God gives you.

13 "You shall not kill.

14 "You shall not commit adultery.

15 "You shall not steal.

16 "You shall not bear false witness against your neighbor.

17 "You shall not covet your neighbor's house; you shall not covet your neighbor's wife, or his manservant, or his maidservant, or his ox, or his ass, or anything that is your neighbor's."

18 Now when all the people perceived the thunderings and the lightnings and the sound of the trumpet and the mountain smoking, the people were afraid and trembled; and they stood afar off, ¹⁹and said to Moses, "You speak to us, and we will hear; but let not God speak to us, lest we die." ²⁰And Moses said to the people, "Do not fear; for God has come to prove you, and that the fear of him may be before your eyes, that you may not sin."

21 And the people stood afar off, while Moses drew near to the thick cloud where God was.

## REVIEW QUESTIONS

1. What were the terms of the covenant between God and the Hebrews?
2. The belief that some laws were divine in origin was shared by many Near Eastern peoples including the Hebrews. How has this belief shaped subsequent Western civilization?

---

## 3  Humaneness of Hebrew Law

The new awareness of the individual that was produced by the Hebrew concept of God found expression in Hebrew law, which was recorded in the Torah, the first five books of the Scriptures. For the Hebrews, the source of law was, of course, God, and because God is good, his law must be concerned with human welfare. Israelite law incorporated the legal codes and oral traditions of the older civilizations of the Near East. In contrast to the other law codes of the

Near East, however, Hebrew laws were more concerned with people than with property; they expressed a humane attitude toward slaves and rejected the idea (so clearly demonstrated in the Code of Hammurabi) of one law for nobles and another for commoners.

## *LEVITICUS*
# NEIGHBOR AND COMMUNITY

To the Hebrews, laws governing economic, social, and political relationships gave practical expression to God's universal standards of morality. Leviticus, the third book in the Scriptures, contains laws governing actions dealing with neighbors and the community.

9 "When you reap the harvest of your land, you shall not reap your field to its very border, neither shall you gather the gleanings after your harvest. 10And you shall not strip your vineyard bare, neither shall you gather the fallen grapes of your vineyard; you shall leave them for the poor and for the sojourner: I am the LORD your God.

11 "You shall not steal, nor deal falsely, nor lie to one another. 12And you shall not swear by my name falsely, and so profane the name of your God: I am the LORD.

13 "You shall not oppress your neighbor or rob him. The wages of a hired servant shall not remain with you all night until the morning. 14You shall not curse the deaf or put a stumbling block before the blind, but you shall fear your God: I am the LORD.

15 "You shall do no injustice in judgment; you shall not be partial to the poor or defer to the great, but in righteousness shall you judge your neighbor. 16You shall not go up and down as a slanderer among your people, and you shall not stand forth against the life of your neighbor: I am the LORD.

17 "You shall not hate your brother in your heart, but you shall reason with your neighbor, lest you bear sin because of him. 18You shall not take vengeance or bear any grudge against the sons of your own people, but you shall love your neighbor as yourself: I am the LORD. . . .

33 "When a stranger sojourns with you in your land, you shall not do him wrong. 34The stranger who sojourns with you shall be to you as the native among you, and you shall love him as yourself. . . ." (Leviticus 19)

---

## *DEUTERONOMY*
# JUDGES, WITNESSES, AND JUSTICE

The book of Deuteronomy was composed in the seventh century B.C., some six centuries after the exodus from Egypt. Written as though it were a last speech of Moses advising the people how to govern themselves as they entered the land of Canaan, Deuteronomy reflects the new problems faced by the Hebrews who had already established a kingdom and lived in a settled urban society. In presenting their reform program, the authors of Deuteronomy linked their message to the authority of Moses. The central theme of these verses is the attainment of justice.

18 "You shall appoint judges and officers in all your towns which the LORD your God gives you, according to your tribes; and they shall judge the people with righteous judgment. 19You shall not pervert justice; you shall not show partiality; and you shall not take a bribe, for a bribe blinds the eyes of the wise and subverts the cause of the righteous. 20Justice, and only justice, you shall follow, that you may live and inherit the land which the LORD your God gives you." (Deuteronomy 16)

———

15 "A single witness shall not prevail against a man for any crime or for any wrong in connection with any offence that he has committed; only on the evidence of two witnesses, or of three witnesses, shall a charge be sustained. 16If a malicious witness rises against any man to accuse him of wrongdoing, 17then both parties to the dispute shall appear before the LORD, before the priests and the judges who are in office in those days; 18the judges shall inquire diligently, and if the witness is a false witness and has accused his brother falsely, 19then you shall do to him as he had meant to do to his brother; so you shall purge the evil from the midst of you." (Deuteronomy 19)

———

15 "You shall not give up to his master a slave who has escaped from his master to you; 16he shall dwell with you, in your midst, in the place which he shall choose within one of your towns, where it pleases him best; you shall not oppress him." (Deuteronomy 23)

———

14 "You shall not oppress a hired servant who is poor and needy, whether he is one of your brethren or one of the sojourners who are in your land within your towns; 15you shall give him his hire on the day he earns it, before the sun goes down (for he is poor, and sets his heart upon it); lest he cry against you to the LORD, and it be sin in you.

16 "The fathers shall not be put to death for the children, nor shall the children be put to death for the fathers; every man shall be put to death for his own sin.

17 "You shall not pervert the justice due to the sojourner or to the fatherless, or take a widow's garment in pledge; 18but you shall remember that you were a slave in Egypt and the LORD your God redeemed you from there; therefore I command you to do this.

19 "When you reap your harvest in your field, and have forgotten a sheaf in the field, you shall not go back to get it; it shall be for the sojourner, the fatherless, and the widow; that the LORD your God may bless you in all the work of your hands. 20When you beat your olive trees, you shall not go over the boughs again; it shall be for the sojourner, the fatherless, and the widow. 21When you gather the grapes of your vineyard, you shall not glean it afterward; it shall be for the sojourner, the fatherless, and the widow. 22You shall remember that you were a slave in the land of Egypt; therefore I command you to do this." (Deuteronomy 24)

## REVIEW QUESTIONS

1. Show how an awareness of social justice pervaded Hebrew law.
2. How did the legal procedures of Hebrew law try to ensure fair treatment of all ranks of society?

# 4 The Age of Classical Prophecy

Ancient Jewish history was marked by the rise of prophets—spiritually inspired persons who believed that God had chosen them to remind the Jews of their duties to God and his law. These prophets carried God's message to the leaders and the people and warned of divine punishments for disobedience to God's commandments.

The prophetic movement—the age of classical prophecy—which emerged in the eighth century B.C., creatively expanded Hebrew religious thought. Prophets denounced exploitation of the poor, the greed of the wealthy, and the oppressive behavior of the powerful as a betrayal of Yahweh, a violation of his moral laws. They insisted that the core of Hebrew faith was not ritual but morality. Their concern for the poor and their attack on injustice received reemphasis in the Christian faith and thus became incorporated into the Western ideal of social justice.

# AMOS AND ISAIAH SOCIAL JUSTICE

By the eighth century a significant disparity existed between the wealthy and the poor. Small farmers in debt to moneylenders faced the loss of their land or even bondage. Amos, a mid-eighth-century prophet, felt a tremendous compulsion to speak out in the name of God against these injustices.

21"I hate, I despise your feasts,
  and I take no delight in your solemn
    assemblies.
22Even though you offer me your burnt
    offerings and cereal offerings,
  I will not accept them,
and the peace offerings of your fatted beasts
  I will not look upon.
23Take away from me the noise of your songs;
  to the melody of your harps I will not
    listen.
24But let justice roll down like waters,
  and righteousness like an everflowing
    stream. (Amos 5)

The prophets' insistence that rituals were not the essence of the law and their passion for righteousness are voiced in the Scriptures by Isaiah of Jerusalem, who lived in the mid-eighth century B.C. Scholars agree that Isaiah of Jerusalem did not write all sixty-six chapters that make up the Book of Isaiah. Some material appears to have been written by his disciples and interpreters, and Chapters 40 to 55, composed two centuries later, are attributed to a person given the name Second Isaiah. The following verses come from Isaiah of Jerusalem.

11"What to me is the multitude of your
    sacrifices?
  says the LORD;
I have had enough of burnt offerings of rams
  and the fat of fed beasts;
I do not delight in the blood of bulls, or of
  lambs, or of he-goats. . . .

<sup>13</sup>Bring no more vain offerings;
   incense is an abomination to me.
New moon and sabbath and the calling of
     assemblies—
   I cannot endure iniquity and solemn
     assembly.
<sup>14</sup>Your new moons and your appointed feasts
   my soul hates;
they have become a burden to me,
   I am weary of bearing them.
<sup>15</sup>When you spread forth your hands,
   I will hide my eyes from you;
even though you make many prayers,
   I will not listen;
   your hands are full of blood.
<sup>16</sup>Wash yourselves; make yourselves clean;
   remove the evil of your doings
   from before my eyes;
cease to do evil,
<sup>17</sup>   learn to do good;

seek justice,
   correct oppression;
defend the fatherless,
   plead for the widow.
   (Isaiah 1)

---

Isaiah denounced the rich and the powerful for exploiting the poor.

---

<sup>13</sup>The LORD has taken his place to contend,
   he stands to judge his people.
<sup>14</sup>The LORD enters into judgment
   with the elders and princes of his people:
"It is you who have devoured the vineyard,
   the spoil of the poor is in your houses.
<sup>15</sup>What do you mean by crushing my people,
   by grinding the face of the poor?"
     says the Lord GOD of hosts.
     (Isaiah 3)

# *ISAIAH*
# PEACE AND HUMANITY

Isaiah of Jerusalem envisioned the unity of all people under God. This universalism drew out the full implications of Hebrew monotheism. In Isaiah's vision all peoples would live together in peace and harmony. Some of these lines are inscribed on the building that houses the United Nations in New York City.

<sup>2</sup>It shall come to pass in the latter days
   that the mountain of the house of the LORD
shall be established as the highest of the
     mountains,
   and shall be raised above the hills;
and all the nations shall flow to it,
<sup>3</sup>   and many peoples shall come, and say:
"Come, let us go up to the mountain of the
     LORD,
   to the house of the God of Jacob;
that he may teach us his ways

and that we may walk in his paths."
For out of Zion shall go forth the law,
   and the word of the LORD from Jerusalem.
<sup>4</sup>He shall judge between the nations,
   and shall decide for many peoples;
and they shall beat their swords into
     plowshares,
   and their spears into pruning hooks;
nation shall not lift up sword against nation,
   neither shall they learn war any more.
     (Isaiah 2)

REVIEW QUESTIONS

1. For the Hebrew prophets, ethical conduct was preferable to ritual acts as a way to worship God. Discuss.
2. How have the teachings of the Hebrew prophets influenced modern Western concepts of human dignity and social justice?

---

## 5   The Problem of Undeserved Suffering

Written sometime between the seventh and the fourth centuries B.C., the Book of Job is one of the best examples of Hebrew wisdom literature. It is concerned with profound questions. Why do the righteous often suffer and the wicked prosper? And why does God permit such injustice? The Book of Job does not provide conclusive answers to these questions, but it does impel us to ponder them and to think about our relationship to God.

## *BOOK OF JOB*

In the prologue, the first two chapters of the book, God tells Satan[1] that there is none like his servant Job, "a whole-hearted and an upright man that feareth God and shunneth evil." Satan replies that Job is loyal only because God has protected him from misfortune. Put an end to his good fortune, says Satan, and Job "will blaspheme Thee to Thy face." Accepting the challenge, God permits Satan to destroy Job's children, take away his possessions, and afflict him with painful boils all over his body. Still Job does not curse God.

So far Job has accepted his fate uncomplainingly. But then in the company of three friends, Eliphaz, Bildad, and Zophar, he laments his misfortune and protests that God has treated him unjustly. Why is this happening, he asks, since he has not knowingly sinned? And why does a merciful God continue to make him suffer?

3 After this Job opened his mouth and cursed the day of his birth.
[2]And Job said:
[3]"Let the day perish wherein I was born,
   and the night which said,
   'A man-child is conceived.'

[4]Let that day be darkness! . . .
[11]"Why did I not die at birth,
   come forth from the womb and expire? . . .
   (Job 3)

---

[11]"Therefore I will not restrain my mouth;
   I will speak in the anguish of my spirit;
   I will complain in the bitterness of my soul.
[12]Am I the sea, or a sea monster,
   that thou settest a guard over me?

---

[1]At this stage in Jewish thought, Satan is simply a member of God's court; he is not the enemy of God and the leader of the forces of evil as he is later depicted, particularly at the time of Jesus and in early Christian writings.

13When I say, 'My bed will comfort me,
  my couch will ease my complaint,'
14then thou dost scare me with dreams
  and terrify me with visions,
15so that I would choose strangling
  and death rather than my bones.
16I loathe my life; I would not live for ever.
  Let me alone, for my days are a breath.
17What is man, that thou dost make so much
    of him,
  and that thou dost set thy mind upon him,
18dost visit him every morning,
  and test him every moment?
19How long wilt thou not look away from me,
  nor let me alone till I swallow my spittle?
20If I sin, what do I do to thee, thou watcher
    of men?
  Why hast thou made me thy mark [target]?
  Why have I become a burden to thee?
21Why dost thou not pardon my transgression
  and take away my iniquity?
For now I shall lie in the earth;
  thou wilt seek me, but I shall not be." . . .
    (Job 7)

---

Job's friends take the orthodox position that
"God will not cast away an innocent man,
/Neither will he uphold the evil-doers. . . ."
But Job replies that God is destroying an in-
nocent man.

---

22It is all one; therefore I say,
  he destroys both the blameless and the
    wicked.
23When disaster brings sudden death,
  he mocks at the calamity¹ of the innocent.
24The earth is given into the hand of the
    wicked;
  he covers the faces of its judges—
  if it is not he, who then is it? . . . (Job 9)

---

11God gives me up to the ungodly,
  and casts me into the hands of the wicked.

12I was at ease, and he broke me asunder;
  he seized me by the neck and dashed me
    to pieces;
he set me up as his target,
13  his archers surround me.
He slashes open my kidneys, and does not
    spare;
  he pours out my gall on the ground.
14He breaks me with breach upon breach;
  he runs upon me like a warrior. . . .
16My face is red with weeping,
  and on my eyelids is deep darkness;
17although there is no violence in my hands,
  and my prayer is pure. . . . (Job 16)

---

6know then that God has put me in the
    wrong,
  and closed his net about me.
7Behold, I cry out, 'Violence!' but I am not
    answered;
  I call aloud, but there is no justice.
8He has walled up my way, so that I cannot
    pass,
  and he has set darkness upon my paths.
9He has stripped from me my glory,
  and taken the crown from my head.
10He breaks me down on every side, and I am
    gone,
  and my hope has he pulled up like a tree.
11He has kindled his wrath against me,
  and counts me as his adversary. (Job 19)

---

Job protests that the wicked often go unpunished, while he who aspired to righteousness is made to suffer.

---

7Why do the wicked live,
  reach old age, and grow mighty in power?
8Their children are established in their
    presence,
  and their offspring before their eyes.
9Their houses are safe from fear,
  and no rod of God is upon them.

¹⁰Their bull breeds without fail;
  their cow calves, and does not cast her calf.
¹¹They send forth their little ones like a flock,
  and their children dance.
¹²They sing to the tambourine and the lyre,
  and rejoice to the sound of the pipe.
¹³They spend their days in prosperity,
  and in peace they go down to Sheol.
¹⁴They say to God, 'Depart from us!
  We do not desire the knowledge of thy
    ways.
¹⁵What is the Almighty, that we should serve
    him?
  And what profit do we get if we pray to
    him?' (Job 21)

---

¹²because I delivered the poor who cried,
  and the fatherless who had none to help
    him.
¹³The blessing of him who was about to perish
    came upon me,
  and I caused the widow's heart to sing for
    joy.
¹⁴I put on righteousness, and it clothed me;
  my justice was like a robe and a turban.
¹⁵I was eyes to the blind,
  and feet to the lame.
¹⁶I was a father to the poor,
  and I searched out the cause of him whom I
    did not know.
¹⁷I broke the fangs of the unrighteous,
  and made him drop his prey from his teeth.
    (Job 29)

---

¹⁶"And now my soul is poured out within me;
  days of affliction have taken hold of me.
¹⁷The night racks my bones,
  and the pain that gnaws me takes no rest.
¹⁸With violence it seizes my garment;
  it binds me about like the collar of my
    tunic.
¹⁹God has cast me into the mire,
  and I have become like dust and ashes.
²⁰I cry to thee and thou dost not answer me;
  I stand, and thou dost not heed me.

²¹Thou hast turned cruel to me;
  with the might of thy hand thou dost
    persecute me.
²²Thou liftest me up on the wind, thou makest
    me ride on it,
  and thou tossest me about in the roar of the
    storm.
²³Yea, I know that thou wilt bring me to
    death,
  and to the house appointed for all living.
    (Job 30)

---

Elihu, a young man, joins the symposium.
He is angry with Job for his self-righteous-
ness, for trying to justify himself rather than
God, and with Job's friends, for having
found no answer to Job's dilemma. But in
proclaiming God's justice, Elihu essentially
repeats the friends' arguments.

---

¹⁰"Therefore, hear me, you men of under-
    standing,
  far be it from God that he should do
    wickedness,
  and from the Almighty that he should do
    wrong.
¹¹For according to the work of a man he will
    requite him,
  and according to his ways he will make it
    befall him.
¹²Of a truth, God will not do wickedly,
  and the Almighty will not pervert justice.
¹³Who gave him charge over the earth
  and who laid on him the whole world?
¹⁴If he should take back his spirit to himself,
  and gather to himself his breath,
¹⁵all flesh would perish together,
  and man would return to dust.
¹⁶"If you have understanding, hear this;
  listen to what I say. . . .
³¹"For has any one said to God,
  'I have borne chastisement; I will not offend
    any more;
³²teach me what I do not see:
  if I have done iniquity, I will do it no more'?

<sup>33</sup>Will he then make requital to suit you, be-
      cause you reject it?
For you must choose, and not I; therefore
      declare what you know.
<sup>34</sup>Men of understanding will say to me,
   and the wise man who hears me will say:
<sup>35</sup>'Job speaks without knowledge,
   his words are without insight.'
<sup>36</sup>Would that Job were tried to the end,
   because he answers like wicked men.
<sup>37</sup>For he adds rebellion to his sin;
   he claps his hands among us,
   and multiplies his words against God."
         (Job 34)

———

<sup>5</sup>"Behold, God is mighty, and does not despise
      any;
   he is mighty in strength of understanding.
<sup>6</sup>He does not keep the wicked alive,
   but gives the afflicted their right.
<sup>7</sup>He does not withdraw his eyes from the
      righteous,
   but with kings upon the throne
   he sets them for ever, and they are exalted.
<sup>8</sup>And if they are bound in fetters
   and caught in the cords of affliction,

<sup>9</sup>then he declares to them their work
   and their transgressions, that they are
      behaving arrogantly.
<sup>10</sup>He opens their ears to instruction,
   and commands that they return from
      iniquity.
<sup>11</sup>If they hearken and serve him,
   they complete their days in prosperity,
   and their years in pleasantness.
<sup>12</sup>But if they do not hearken, they perish by
      the sword,
   and die without knowledge. (Job 36)

---

Then God, "out of the whirlwind," replies
to Job. But in God's response, we do not
find a clear answer to the problem of undeserved suffering. Instead, God, in a series of
rhetorical questions, reminds Job that he
alone is the creator and sustainer of the universe and that it is the obligation of Job, a
mere mortal, to honor his creator and not
find fault with him. Awed by God's majesty
and power, a humbled Job declares, "I ab-
hor my words and repent." In an epilogue,
God responds by restoring Job's good fortune.

---

## REVIEW QUESTIONS

1.  Do you see ways in which Job could have strengthened his case?
2.  Do you have an answer to Job's dilemma? Explain.

# CHAPTER 3
# *The Greeks*

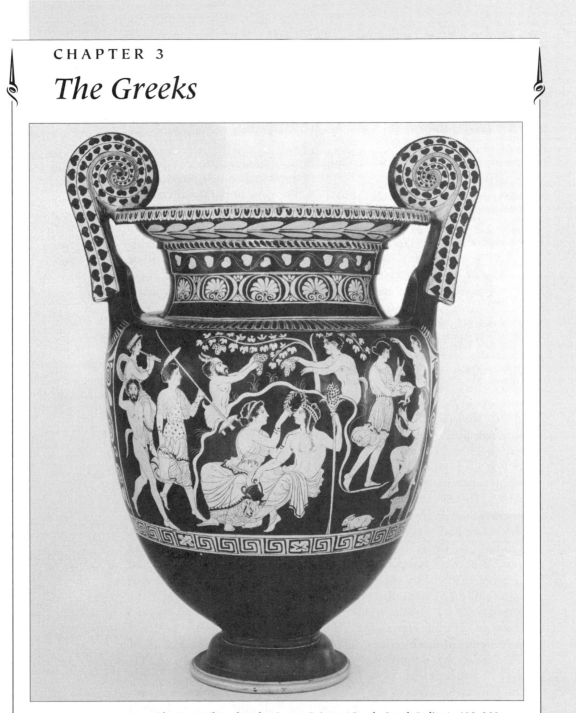

LUCANIAN, VOLUTE KRATER (side A), attributed to the Creusa Painter (Greek, South Italian), 400–380 B.C. Dionysos, the god of wine and ecstasy, is shown with his wife Ariadne. Also depicted are Pan, the god of shepherds, and three satyrs. *(The Toledo Museum of Art; Purchased with funds from the Libbey Endowment, Gift of Edward Durmmond Libbey. [1981.110])*

Hebrew ethical monotheism, which gave value to the individual, is one source of Western civilization. Another source derives from the ancient Greeks, who originated scientific and philosophic thought, created democracy, and developed a humanistic outlook. From about 750 B.C. to 338 B.C. the Greek world consisted of small, independent, and self-governing city-states. Within this political-social context, the Greeks made their outstanding contributions to civilization.

In contrast to the Egyptians and Mesopotamians, the Greeks developed rational-scientific, rather than mythical, interpretations of nature and the human community. In trying to understand nature, Greek philosophers proposed physical explanations: that is, they gradually omitted the gods from their accounts of how nature came to be the way it is. Greek intellectuals also analyzed government, law, and ethics in logical and systematic ways. It was the great achievement of Greek thinkers to rise above magic, miracles, mystery, and custom and to assert that reason was the avenue to knowledge. The emergence of rational attitudes did not, of course, end traditional religion, particularly for the peasants, who remained devoted to their ancient cults, gods, and shrines. But what distinguishes the Greeks is that alongside an older religious-mythical tradition arose a philosophic-scientific view of the natural world and human culture.

The Greeks, who defined human beings by their capacity to use reason, also defined the principle of political liberty. Egyptians and Mesopotamians were subject to the authority of god-kings and priest-kings; the common people did not participate in political life, and there was no awareness of individual liberty. In contrast, many Greek city-states, particularly Athens, developed democratic institutions and attitudes. In the middle of the fifth century B.C., when Athenian democracy was at its height, adult male citizens were eligible to hold public office and were equal before the law; in the assembly, which met some forty times a year, they debated and voted on the key issues of state. Whereas Mesopotamians and Egyptians believed that law had been given to them by the gods, the Greeks came to understand that law was a human creation, a product of human reason. The Athenians abhorred rule by absolute rulers and held that people can govern themselves. While expressing admiration for the Greek political achievement, modern critics also point out several limitations of Greek democracy, notably slavery and the inability of women to participate in political life.

The Greeks originated the Western humanist tradition. They valued the human personality and sought the full cultivation of human talent. In the Greek view, a man of worth pursued excellence, that is, he sought to mold himself in accordance with the highest standards and ideals. Greek art, for example, made the human form the focal point of attention and exalted the nobility, dignity, self-assurance, and beauty of the human being.

Greek culture has a distinctive style that enables us to see it as an organic whole. To the English classicist H. D. F. Kitto, the common thread that runs through Greek philosophy, literature, and art is "a sense of the wholeness of things"—the conviction that the universe contains an inherent order, that law governs both nature and human affairs, and that this law can be comprehended by human reason.

Although the Greek city-states shared a common culture, they frequently warred with each other. Particularly ruinous was the Peloponnesian War (431–404 B.C.) between Athens and Sparta and their allies. The drawn-out conflict, marked by massacres and civil wars within city-states, shattered the Greek world spiritually. Increasingly, a narrow individualism and worsening factional disputes weakened the bonds of community within the various city-states. Moreover, learning little from the Peloponnesian War, the Greeks continued their internecine conflicts. Finally, by 338 B.C. the weakened city-states were conquered by Philip II of Macedonia, a kingdom to the north of Greece. Although the Greek cities continued to exist, they had lost their political independence; Greek civilization was entering a new phase.

Philip's famous son, Alexander thew Great, a romantic adventurer and brilliant commander, inherited the Macedonian kingdom and conquered the vast Persian Empire. After Alexander died in 323 B.C. at the age of thirty-two, his generals could not hold together the empire, which extended from Egypt to the frontiers of India. By 275 B.C. it was broken into three parts, each named for a dynasty: the Ptolemies in Egypt, the Seleucids in Asia, and the Antigonids in Macedonia and Greece. The rulers of these kingdoms were Macedonians, and their generals and high officials were Greek; the style of government, not in the democratic tradition of the Greek city-states, was modeled after the absolute rule by priest-kings and god-kings typical of the Near East.

Alexander's conquest of the Near East marks a second stage in the evolution of Greek civilization (Hellenism). The first stage, the *Hellenic Age,* began about 800 B.C. with the earliest city-states and lasted until Alexander's death; at that time Greek civilization entered the *Hellenistic Age,* which lasted until 30 B.C., when Egypt, the last Hellenistic kingdom, lost its independence to Rome.

The Hellenistic Age inherited many cultural achievements of the earlier Hellenic Age, but crucial differences exist between the two eras. The self-sufficient and independent *polis* (city-state), the center of life in the Hellenic Age, was diminished in power and importance by larger political units, kingdoms headed by absolute monarchs. Although Greek cities continued to exercise considerable control over domestic affairs, they had lost to powerful monarchs their freedom of action in foreign affairs.

A second characteristic of the Hellenistic Age was cosmopolitanism, an intermingling of peoples and cultural traditions. In the Hellenic Age, the Greeks had drawn a sharp distinction between Greek and non-Greek. In the wake of Alexander's conquests, however, thousands of Greek soldiers, merchants, and administrators settled in Near Eastern lands, bringing with them Greek language, customs, and culture. Many upper-class citizens of Near Eastern cities, regardless of their ethnic backgrounds, came under the influence of Greek civilization. At the same time, Mesopotamian, Egyptian, and Persian ways, particularly religious practices and beliefs, spread westward into regions under the sway of Greek civilization.

# 1   Homer: The Educator of Greece

The poet Homer, who probably lived during the eighth century B.C., helped shape the Greek outlook. His great epics, *The Iliad* and *The Odyssey,* contain the embryo of the Greek humanist tradition: the concern with man and his achievements. "To strive always for excellence and to surpass all others"—in these words lies the essence of the Homeric hero's outlook. In the warrior-aristocratic world of Homer, excellence is primarily interpreted as bravery and skill in battle. The Homeric hero is driven to demonstrate his prowess, to assert himself, to win honor, and to earn a reputation.

*The Iliad* deals in poetic form with the Trojan War, which probably was waged in the thirteenth century B.C., between the Mycenaean Greeks and the Trojans of Asia Minor. At the outset Homer states his theme: the wrath of Achilles that brought so much suffering to the Greeks. Agamemnon, their king, has deprived the great warrior Achilles of his rightful prize, the captive girl Briseis. Achilles will not submit to this grave insult to his honor and refuses to join the Greeks in combat against the Trojans. In this way he intends to make Agamemnon pay for his arrogance, for without the Greeks' greatest warrior, Agamemnon will have no easy victories. With Achilles on the sidelines, the Greeks suffer severe losses.

Destiny is at work: the "wicked arrogance" of Agamemnon and the "ruinous wrath" of Achilles have caused suffering and death among the Greek forces. For Homer, human existence has a pattern—a universal plan governs human affairs. People, even the gods, operate within a certain unalterable framework; their deeds are subject to the demands of destiny or necessity. Later Greek thinkers would express this idea of a universal order in philosophic and scientific terms.

# Homer
## *THE ILIAD*

The following passages from *The Iliad* illustrate the Homeric ideal of excellence. In the first, Hector of Troy, son of King Priam, prepares for battle. Hector's wife Andromache pleads with him to stay within the city walls, but Hector, in the tradition of the Homeric hero, feels compelled to engage in combat to show his worth and gain honor.

Hector looked at his son and smiled, but said nothing. Andromache, bursting into tears, went up to him and put her hand in his. "Hector," she said, "you are possessed. This bravery of yours will be your end. You do not think of your little boy or your unhappy wife, whom you will make a widow soon. Some day the Achaeans {Greeks} are bound to kill you in a massed attack. And when I lose you I might as well be dead. There will be no comfort left, when you have met your doom—nothing but grief. I have no father, no mother, now. My father fell to the great Achilles when he sacked our lovely town, Cilician Thebe[1] of the High Gates. . . . I had seven brothers too at home. In one day all of them went down to Hades' House.[2] The great Achilles of the swift feet killed them all. . . .

"So you, Hector, are father and mother and brother to me, as well as my beloved husband. Have pity on me now; stay here on the tower; and do not make your boy an orphan and your wife a widow. . . ."

"All that, my dear," said the great Hector of the glittering helmet, "is surely my concern. But if I hid myself like a coward and refused to fight, I could never face the Trojans and the Trojan ladies in their trailing gowns. Besides, it would go against the grain, for I have trained myself always, like a good soldier, to take my place in the front line and win glory for my father and myself. . . ."

As he finished, glorious Hector held out his arms to take his boy. But the child shrank back with a cry to the bosom of his girdled nurse, alarmed by his father's appearance. He was frightened by the bronze of the helmet and the horsehair plume that he saw nodding grimly down at him. His father and his lady mother had to laugh. But noble Hector quickly took his helmet off and put the dazzling thing on the ground. Then he kissed his son, dandled him in his arms, and prayed to Zeus [the chief god] and the other gods: "Zeus, and you other gods, grant that this boy of mine may be, like me, pre-eminent in Troy; as strong and brave as I; a mighty king of Ilium [Troy]. May people say, when he comes back from battle, 'Here is a better man than his father.' Let him bring home the bloodstained armour of the enemy he has killed, and make his mother happy."

Hector handed the boy to his wife, who took him to her fragrant breast. She was smiling through her tears, and when her husband saw this he was moved. He stroked her with his hand and said: "My dear, I beg you not to be too much distressed. No one is going to send me down to Hades before my proper time. But Fate is a thing that no man born of woman, coward or hero, can escape. Go home now, and attend to your own work, the loom and the spindle, and see that the maidservants get on with theirs. War is men's business; and this war is the business of every man in Ilium, myself above all."

---

[1]In the *Iliad* the Cilices lived in southern Asia Minor.
[2]Hades refers both to the god of the underworld and to the underworld itself.

Many brave Greek warriors die in battle, including Achilles' best friend Patroclus, slain by the Trojan Hector. Achilles now sets aside his quarrel with Agamemnon (who has appealed to Achilles) and joins the battle. King Priam urges his son not to fight the mighty Achilles, but Hector, despite his fears, faces Achilles and meets his death. In this passage, the grief-stricken Priam goes to Achilles and requests Hector's body. Achilles responds with compassion. This scene shows that although Homer sees the essence of life as the pursuit of glory, he is also sensitive to life's brevity and to the suffering that pervades human existence.

. . . Big though Priam was, he came in unobserved, went up to Achilles, grasped his knees and kissed his hands, the terrible, man-killing hands that had slaughtered many of his sons. Achilles was astounded when he saw King Priam, and so were all his men. . . .

But Priam was already praying to Achilles. "Most worshipful Achilles," he said, "think of your own father, who is the same age as I, and so has nothing but miserable old age ahead of him. No doubt his neighbours are oppressing him and there is nobody to save him from their depredations. Yet he at least has one consolation. While he knows that you are still alive, he can look forward day by day to seeing his beloved son come back from Troy; whereas my fortunes are completely broken. I had the best sons in the whole of this broad realm, and now not one, not one I say, is left. There were fifty when the Achaean expedition came. Nineteen of them were borne by one mother and the rest by other ladies in my palace. Most of them have fallen in action, and Hector, the only one I still could count on, the bulwark of Troy and the Trojans, has now been killed by you, fighting for his native land. It is to get him back from you that I have come to the Achaean ships, bringing this princely ransom with me. Achilles, fear the gods, and be merciful to me, remembering your own father, though I am even more entitled to compassion, since I have brought myself to do a thing that no one else on earth has done—I have raised to my lips the hand of the man who killed my son."

Priam had set Achilles thinking of his own father and brought him to the verge of tears. Taking the old man's hand, he gently put him from him; and overcome by their memories they both broke down. Priam, crouching at Achilles' feet, wept bitterly for man-slaying Hector, and Achilles wept for his father, and then again for Patroclus. The house was filled with the sounds of their lamentation. But presently, when he had had enough of tears and recovered his composure, the excellent Achilles leapt from his chair, and in compassion for the old man's grey head and grey beard, took him by the arm and raised him. Then he spoke to him from his heart: "You are indeed a man of sorrows and have suffered much. How could you dare to come by yourself to the Achaean ships into the presence of a man who has killed so many of your gallant sons? You have a heart of iron. But pray be seated now, here on this chair, and let us leave our sorrows, bitter though they are, locked up in our own hearts, for weeping is cold comfort and does little good. We men are wretched things, and the gods, who have no cares themselves, have woven sorrow into the very pattern of our lives."

## REVIEW QUESTIONS

1.  What glimpses do we get from Homer's *Iliad* of the respective roles of men and women in Greek society?
2.  Homer's epic poems were studied and even memorized by Greek schoolchildren. What values would the poems have taught these youngsters to emulate?
3.  What lessons about the human condition did Achilles draw from the tragic events of the Trojan War?

## 2 Early Greek Philosophy: The Emancipation of Thought from Myth

In the sixth century B.C., Greeks living in the city of Miletus in Ionia, the coast of Asia Minor, conceived a nonmythical way of viewing nature, a feat that marks the origins of philosophic and scientific thought. Traditionally, natural occurrences like earthquakes and lightning had been attributed to the gods. But early Greek thinkers, called cosmologists because they were interested in the nature and structure of the universe, were the first to see nature as a system governed by laws that the intellect could ascertain. The cosmologists sought physical rather than supernatural explanations for natural events. This new approach made possible a self-conscious and systematic investigation of nature and a critical appraisal of proposed theories; in contrast, the mythical view that the gods regulate nature did not invite discussion and questioning.

# Aristotle
# THALES OF MILETUS

Thales of Miletus (c. 624–c. 548 B.C.) is considered the founder of Ionian philosophy. He wanted to know how nature came to be the way it is, and he did not turn to traditional legends for an answer. Thales said that water was the basic element of nature and that through a natural process—similar to the formation of ice or steam—water gave rise to everything else in the universe. Thales revolutionized thought because in searching for a first cause in nature he omitted the gods. What we know about Thales' view of nature comes essentially from Aristotle (see page 89). A brief reference to Thales from Aristotle's *Metaphysics* follows.

Most of the philosophers thought that principles in the form of matter were the only principles of all things: for the original source of all existing things, that from which a thing first comes-into-being and into which it is finally destroyed, the substance persisting but changing in its qualities, this they declare is the element and first principle of existing things . . . for there must be some natural substance, either one or more than one, from which the other things come-into-being, while it is preserved. Over the number, however, and the form of this kind of principle they do not all agree; but Thales, the founder of this type of philosophy, says that it is water (and therefore declared that the earth is on water), perhaps taking this supposition from seeing the nurture of all things to be moist, and the warm itself coming-to-be from this and living by this (that from which they come-to-be being the principle of all things)—taking the supposition both from this and from the seeds of all things having a moist nature, water being the natural principle of moist things.

# ANAXIMANDER

Anaximander (c. 611–547 B.C.), another Ionian, also held that a single element was the wellspring of nature, but he rejected any specific substance such as water, holding instead that something indefinite, which he called the Boundless or the Infinite, was the source of all things. Anaximander attempted to explain how natural objects and living things had derived from this primary mass. What is remarkable about Anaximander's cosmogony was the omission of the gods or any supernatural agency in the origin of life and the formation of the world. All that we know about Anaximander comes from brief passages in the writings of several ancient scholars.

Of those who say that it is one, moving, and infinite, Anaximander, son of Praxiades, a Milesian, the successor and pupil of Thales, said that the principle and element of existing things was the *apeiron* (indefinite, *or* infinite), being the first to introduce this name of the material principle. He says that it is neither water nor any other of the so-called elements, but some other *apeiron* nature, from which come into being all the heavens and the worlds in them.

————

For he (Anaximander) thought that things were born not from one substance, as Thales thought from water, but each from its own particular principles. These principles of individual things he believed to be infinite, and to give birth to innumerable worlds and whatsoever arises in them; and those worlds, he thought, are now dissolved, now born again, according to the age to which each is able to survive.

————

He says that that which is productive from the eternal of hot and cold was separated off at the coming-to-be of this world, and that a kind of sphere of flame from this was formed round the air surrounding the earth, like bark round a tree. When this was broken off and shut off in certain circles, the sun and the moon and the stars were formed. . . .

————

The heavenly bodies come into being as a circle of fire separated off from the fire in the world, and enclosed by air. There are breathing-holes, certain pipe-like passages, at which the heavenly bodies show themselves; accordingly eclipses occur when the breathing-holes are blocked up. The moon is seen now waxing, now waning according to the blocking or opening of the channels. The circle of the sun is 27 times the size of (the earth, that of) the moon (18 times); the sun is highest, and the circles of the fixed stars are lowest. . . .

————

Winds occur when the finest vapours of the air are separated off and when they are set in motion by congregation; rain occurs from the exhalation that issues upwards from the things beneath the sun, and lightning whenever wind breaks out and cleaves the clouds. . . .

————

(On thunder, lightning, thunderbolts, whirlwinds and typhoons.) Anaximander says that all these things occur as a result of wind: for whenever it is shut up in a thick cloud and then bursts out forcibly, through its fineness and lightness, then the bursting makes the noise, while the rift against the blackness of the cloud makes the flash. . . .

————

Anaximander said that the first living creatures were born in moisture, enclosed in thorny barks; and that as their age increased they came forth on to the drier part and, when the bark had broken off, they lived a different kind of life for a short time.

———

Further he says that in the beginning man was born from creatures of a different kind; because other creatures are soon self-supporting, but man alone needs prolonged nursing. For this reason he would not have survived if this had been his original form.

———

Anaximander of Miletus conceived that there arose from heated water and earth either fish or creatures very like fish; in these man grew, in the form of embryos retained within until puberty; then at last the fish-like creatures burst and men and women who were already able to nourish themselves stepped forth.

Living creatures came into being from moisture evaporated by the sun. Man was originally similar to another creature—that is, to a fish.

———

[H]e declares . . . that originally men came into being inside fishes, and that having been nurtured there—like sharks—and having become adequate to look after themselves, they then came forth and took to the land.

# Aristotle
# PYTHAGORAS

**Pythagoras (c. 580–507 B.C.) was born on the island of Samos, a major Greek cultural and commercial center in the eastern Aegean Sea; as a young man, he migrated to southern Italy, where the Greeks had established colonies. A deep religiosity pervaded the thought of Pythagoras and his followers, who sought to purify the soul and to achieve salvation. Believing that the soul undergoes a reincarnation in animals, Pythagoreans would not eat meat. The Pythagoreans' great contribution to scientific thought was their conviction that nature contains an inherent mathematical order. Thus, continuity exists between the Pythagoreans and Isaac Newton and Albert Einstein, who expressed the laws underlying the cosmos in mathematical terms more than two thousand years later. Aristotle's description of the Pythagoreans follows.**

. . . the Pythagoreans, as they are called, devoted themselves to mathematics; they were the first to advance this study, and having been brought up in it they thought its principles were the principles of all things. Since of these principles numbers are by nature the first, and in numbers they seemed to see many resemblances to the things that exist and come into being—more than in fire and earth and water (such and such a modification of numbers being justice, another being soul and reason, another being opportunity—and similarly almost all other things being numerically expressible); since, again, they saw that the attributes and the ratios of the musical scales were expressible in numbers; since, then, all other things seemed in their whole nature to be modelled after numbers, and numbers seemed to be the first things in the whole of nature, they supposed the elements of numbers to be the elements of all things, and the whole heaven to be a musical scale and a number. And all the properties of numbers and scales which they could show to agree with the attributes and parts and the whole arrangement of the heavens, they collected and fitted into their scheme.

## REVIEW QUESTIONS

1. Why is Thales considered the first philosopher in the Western world?
2. Compare the Babylonian and Hebrew accounts of the origin of the world and human beings with that of Anaximander. How do they differ in purpose and literary genre?
3. What is the significance of Pythagoras' view that nature contains an inherent mathematical order?
4. Early Greek philosophy marks a break with mythical thinking and the emergence of rational scientific thinking. Discuss this statement.

---

## 3  The Expansion of Reason

The new method of inquiry initiated by the Ionian natural philosophers found expression in other areas of Greek culture. Thus, in the Greek medical school headed by Hippocrates (c. 460–377 B.C.) on the island of Cos, doctors consciously attacked magical practices and beliefs, seeing them as hindrances to understanding causes and cures of disease. The historian Thucydides (c. 460–400 B.C.) sought logical explanations for human events, and the Sophists applied reason to traditional religion, law, and morality.

## Hippocrates
## *THE SACRED DISEASE:*
## THE SEPARATION OF MEDICINE
## FROM MYTH

In the following excerpt from "The Sacred Disease," a Hippocratic doctor rejects the belief that epilepsy is a sacred disease. Instead he maintains that epilepsy, like all other diseases, has a natural explanation and denounces as "charlatans and quacks" those who claim that gods cause the disease.

I. I am about to discuss the disease called "sacred." It is not, in my opinion, any more divine or more sacred than other diseases, but has a natural cause, and its supposed divine origin is due to men's inexperience, and to their wonder at its peculiar character. Now while men continue to believe in its divine origin because they are at a loss to understand it, they really disprove its divinity by the facile method of healing which they adopt, consisting as it does of purifications and incantations. But if it is to be considered divine just because it is wonder-ful, there will be not one sacred disease but many, for I will show that other diseases are no less wonderful and portentous, and yet nobody considers them sacred. For instance, quotidian fevers, tertians and quartans seem to me to be no less sacred and god-sent than this disease,* but nobody wonders at them. . . .

---

*Because of the regularity of the attacks of fever, which occur every day (quotidians), every other day (tertians), or with intermission of two whole days (quartans).

II. My own view is that those who first attributed a sacred character to this malady were like the magicians, purifiers, charlatans and quacks of our own day, men who claim great piety and superior knowledge. Being at a loss, and having no treatment which would help, they concealed and sheltered themselves behind superstition, and called this illness sacred, in order that their utter ignorance might not be manifest. They added a plausible story, and established a method of treatment that secured their own position. They used purifications and incantations; they forbade the use of baths, and of many foods that are unsuitable for sick folk. . . .

But if to eat or apply these things engenders and increases the disease, while to refrain works a cure, then neither is godhead to blame nor are the purifications beneficial; it is the foods that cure or hurt, and the power of godhead disappears.

III. Accordingly I hold that those who attempt in this manner to cure these diseases cannot consider them either sacred or divine; for when they are removed by such purifications and by such treatment as this, there is nothing to prevent the production of attacks in men by devices that are similar. If so, something human is to blame, and not godhead. He who by purifications and magic can take away such an affliction can also by similar means bring it on, so that by this argument the action of godhead is disproved. By these sayings and devices they claim superior knowledge, and deceive men by prescribing for them purifications and cleansings, most of their talk turning on the intervention of gods and spirits.

---

# Thucydides
# METHOD OF HISTORICAL INQUIRY

Thucydides' history was another expression of the movement from myth to reason that pervaded every aspect of Greek culture. Mesopotamians and Egyptians kept annals purporting to narrate the deeds of gods and their human agents. The Greeks carefully investigated events—the first people to examine the past with a critical eye. Thucydides examined men's actions and their motives, explicitly rejected divine explanations for human occurrences, searched for natural causes, and based his conclusions on evidence. In this approach, he was influenced by the empiricism of the Hippocratic physicians. For Thucydides, a work of history, as distinguished from poetry, was a creation of the rational mind and not an expression of the poetic imagination. Thus, in Thucydides' *History of the Peloponnesian War* there was no place for legend, for myth, for the fabulous—all hindrances to historical truth. In the following passage, Thucydides describes his method of inquiry.

I began my history at the very outbreak of the war, in the belief that it was going to be a great war and more worth writing about than any of those which had taken place in the past. My belief was based on the fact that the two sides were at the very height of their power and preparedness, and I saw, too, that the rest of the Hellenic [Greek] world was committed to one side or the other; even those who were not immediately engaged were deliberating on the courses which they were to take later. This was the greatest disturbance in the history of the Hellenes, affecting also a large part of the non-Hellenic world, and indeed, I might almost say, the whole of mankind. For though I have found it impossible, because of its remoteness in time, to acquire a really precise knowledge of the distant past or even of the history preceding our own period, yet, after looking back into it as far as I can, all the evidence leads me to conclude that these periods were not great periods either in warfare or in anything else. . . .

In investigating past history, and in forming the conclusions which I have formed, it must be admitted that one cannot rely on every detail which has come down to us by way of tradition. People are inclined to accept all stories of ancient times in an uncritical way—even when these stories concern their own native countries. . . .

. . . Most people, in fact, will not take trouble in finding out the truth, but are much more inclined to accept the first story they hear.

However, I do not think that one will be far wrong in accepting the conclusions I have reached from the evidence which I have put forward. It is better evidence than that of the poets, who exaggerate the importance of their themes, or of the prose chroniclers, who are less interested in telling the truth than in catching the attention of their public, whose authorities cannot be checked, and whose subject-matter, owing to the passage of time, is mostly lost in the unreliable streams of mythology. We may claim instead to have used only the plainest evidence and to have reached conclusions which are reasonably accurate, considering that we have been dealing with ancient history. As for this present war, even though people are apt to think that the war in which they are fighting is the greatest of all wars and, when it is over, to relapse again into their admiration of the past, nevertheless, if one looks at the facts themselves, one will see that this was the greatest war of all.

In this history I have made use of set speeches some of which were delivered just before and others during the war. I have found it difficult to remember the precise words used in the speeches which I listened to myself and my various informants have experienced the same difficulty; so my method has been, while keeping as closely as possible to the general sense of the words that were actually used, to make the speakers say what, in my opinion, was called for by each situation.

And with regard to my factual reporting of the events of the war I have made it a principle not to write down the first story that came my way, and not even to be guided by my own general impressions; either I was present myself at the events which I have described or else I heard of them from eye-witnesses whose reports I have checked with as much thoroughness as possible. Not that even so the truth was easy to discover: different eye-witnesses give different accounts of the same events, speaking out of partiality for one side or the other or else from imperfect memories. And it may well be that my history will seem less easy to read because of the absence in it of a romantic element. It will be enough for me, however, if these words of mine are judged useful by those who want to understand clearly the events which happened in the past and which (human nature being what it is) will, at some time or other and in much the same ways, be repeated in the future. My work is not a piece of writing designed to meet the taste of an immediate public, but was done to last for ever.

# Critias
# RELIGION AS A HUMAN INVENTION

**After the Greek philosophers of Asia Minor began to employ natural, rather than supernatural, explanations for nature, Greek thinkers on the mainland applied reason to human affairs. Exemplifying this trend were the Sophists, who wandered from city to city teaching rhetoric, grammar, poetry, mathematics,**

music, and gymnastics. The Sophists sought to develop their students' minds, and they created a secular curriculum—for these reasons they enriched the humanist tradition of the West.

The Sophist Critias (c. 480–403 B.C.) was a poet, philosopher, orator, and historian; also he was originally an eager follower of Socrates. Later, Critias became the most bloodthirsty of the so-called Thirty Tyrants, oligarchs who seized control of Athens in 404 B.C. and massacred their democratic opponents. The following passage, a surviving fragment of a play by Critias, demonstrates the Sophists' use of critical thought.

There was a time when the life of men was unordered, bestial and the slave of force, when there was no reward for the virtuous and no punishment for the wicked. Then, I think, men devised retributory laws, in order that Justice might be dictator and have arrogance as its slave, and if anyone sinned, he was punished. Then, when the laws forbade them to commit open crimes of violence, and they began to do them in secret, a wise and clever man invented fear (of the gods) for mortals, that there might be some means of frightening the wicked, even if they do anything or say or think it in secret. Hence he introduced the Divine (religion), saying that there is a God flourishing with immortal life, hearing and seeing with his mind, and thinking of everything and caring about these things, and having divine nature, who will hear everything said among mortals, and will be able to see all that is done. And even if you plan anything evil in secret, you will not escape the gods in this; for they have surpassing intelligence. In saying these words, he introduced the pleasantest of teachings, covering up the truth with a false theory; and he said that the gods dwelt there where he could most frighten men by saying it, whence he knew that fears exist for mortals and rewards for the hard life: in the upper periphery, where they saw lightnings and heard the dread rumblings of thunder, and the starry-faced body of heaven, the beautiful embroidery of Time the skilled craftsman, whence come forth the bright mass of the sun, and the wet shower upon the earth. With such fears did he surround mankind, through which he well established the deity with his argument, and in a fitting place, and quenched lawlessness among men. . . . Thus, I think, for the first time did someone persuade mortals to believe in a race of deities.

## REVIEW QUESTIONS

1. Hippocrates distinguishes between magic and medicine. Discuss this statement.
2. What were some of the methods that Thucydides promised to use to make his history more accurate and credible?
3. What was revolutionary about Critias' approach to religion?

# 4 Humanism

The Greeks conceived the humanist outlook, one of the pillars of Western civilization. They urged human beings to develop their physical, intellectual, and moral capacities to the fullest, to shape themselves according to the highest standards, and to make their lives as harmonious as a flawless work of art. Such an aspiration required intelligence and self-mastery.

# Pindar
# THE PURSUIT OF EXCELLENCE

The poet Pindar (c. 518–438 B.C.) expressed the Greek view of excellence in his praise for a victorious athlete. Life is essentially tragic—triumphs are short-lived, misfortunes are many, and ultimately death overtakes everyone; still, human beings must demonstrate their worth by striving for excellence.

He who wins of a sudden, some noble prize
In the rich years of youth
Is raised high with hope; his manhood takes
    wings;
He has in his heart what is better than
    wealth
But brief is the season of man's delight.

Soon it falls to the ground;
Some dire decision uproots it.
—Thing of a day! such is man: a shadow in a
    dream.
Yet when god-given splendour visits him
A bright radiance plays over him, and how
    sweet is life!

---

# Sophocles
# *ANTIGONE*   "Man the Skilled, the Brilliant"

In a famous passage from his play *Antigone,* Sophocles (c. 496–406 B.C.) lauded human talents.

Numberless wonders
terrible wonders walk the world but none the
    match for man—
that great wonder crossing the heaving gray
    sea,
    driven on by the blasts of winter
on through breakers crashing left and right,
    holds his steady course
and the oldest of the gods he wears away—
the Earth, the immortal, the inexhaustible—
as his plows go back and forth, year in, year out
    with the breed of stallions turning up the
    furrows.

And the blithe, lightheaded race of birds he
    snares,
. . . the tribes of savage beasts, the life that
    swarms the depths—
    with one fling of his nets
woven and coiled tight, he takes them all,
    man the skilled, the brilliant!
He conquers all, taming with his techniques

the prey that roams the cliffs and wild lairs,
training the stallion, clamping the yoke across
    his shaggy neck, and the tireless mountain
    bull.

And speech and thought, quick as the
    wind
and the mood and mind for law that rules the
    city—
    all these he has taught himself
and shelter from the arrows of the frost
when there's rough lodging under the cold
    clear sky
and the shafts of lashing rain—
    ready, resourceful man!
    Never without resources
never an impasse as he marches on the
    future—
only Death, from Death alone he will find no
    rescue
but from desperate plagues he has plotted his
    escapes.

Man the master, ingenious past all measure
past all dreams, the skills within his grasp—
   he forges on, now to destruction
now again to greatness. When he weaves in
the laws of the land, and the justice of the
   gods
that binds his oaths together

he and his city rise high—
   but the city casts out
that man who weds himself to inhumanity
thanks to reckless daring. Never share my
   hearth
never think my thoughts, whoever does such
   things.

## REVIEW QUESTIONS

1. What human virtues did the Greek poets extoll?
2. In what sense does Pindar consider life to be tragic?

---

## 5  The Persian Wars

In 499 B.C., the Ionian Greeks in Asia Minor revolted against their Persian rulers; Athens sent twenty ships to aid the Ionians. To punish the Athenians, Darius I, king of Persia, sent a force to the peninsula of Attica, where Athens is located. In 490 B.C. on the plains of Marathon, an Athenian army of about 10,000 men defeated the Persians. Ten years later, Xerxes, Darius' son and heir, organized a huge invasion force aimed at making Greece a Persian province. Realizing that their independence and freedom were at stake, many Greek cities put aside their quarrels and united against the common enemy. In 480 B.C. on the Bay of Salamis near Athens, the Athenian navy defeated the Persian armada, and the next year the Spartan army crushed the Persians at Plataea.

## Herodotus
## *THE HISTORIES*

Herodotus (c. 484–c. 424 B.C.), often called "the father of history," wrote about the most important events of his lifetime, the Persian Wars. Although the gods were present in Herodotus' narrative, they played a far less important role than they had in Greek mythology or in Near Eastern annals. Herodotus visited Persian lands and found much to praise there. Nevertheless, he was struck by the contrast between Greek freedom and Persian absolutism, between the free Greek citizen and the Persian subject who knew only obedience to the king's commands.

   A second theme prevalent in *The Histories* is punishment for *hubris,* or arrogance. Xerxes, in seeking to rule both Asia and Greece, was seen as exhibiting such arrogance. In the following excerpt, Herodotus discusses Xerxes' ambition.

In this book, the result of my inquiries into history, I hope to do two things: to preserve the memory of the past by putting on record the astonishing achievements both of our own and of the Asiatic peoples; secondly, and more particularly, to show how the two races came into conflict. . . .

.    .    .

Xerxes began his reign by building up an army for a campaign in Egypt. The invasion of Greece was at first by no means an object of his thoughts; but Mardonius—the son of Gobryas and Darius' sister and thus cousin to the king—who was present in court and had more influence with Xerxes than anyone else in the country, used constantly to talk to him on the subject. "Master," he would say, "the Athenians have done us great injury, and it is only right that they should be punished for their crimes. By all means finish the task you already have in hand; but when you have tamed the arrogance of Egypt, then lead an army against Athens. Do that, and your name will be held in honour all over the world, and people will think twice in future before they invade your country." And to the argument for revenge he would add that Europe was a very beautiful place; it produced every kind of garden tree; the land there was everything that land should be—it was, in short, too good for anyone in the world except the Persian king. Mardonius' motive for urging the campaign was love of mischief and adventure and the hope of becoming governor of Greece himself; and after much persistence he persuaded Xerxes to make the attempt. . . .

After the conquest of Egypt, when he was on the point of taking in hand the expedition against Athens, Xerxes called a conference of the leading men in the country, to find out their attitude towards the war and explain to them his own wishes. When they met, he addressed them as follows: "Do not suppose, gentlemen, that I am departing from precedent in the course of action I intend to undertake. We Persians have a way of living, which I have inherited from my predecessors and propose to follow. . . . Of our past history you need no reminder; for you know well enough the famous deeds of Cyrus,[1] Cambyses,[2] and my father Darius, and their additions to our empire. Now I myself, ever since my accession, have been thinking how not to fall short of the kings who have sat upon this throne before me, and how to add as much power as they did to the Persian empire. And now at last I have found a way to win for Persia not glory only but a country as large and as rich as our own—indeed richer than our own—and at the same time to get satisfaction and revenge. That, then, is the object of this meeting—that I may disclose to you what it is that I intend to do. I will bridge the Hellespont[3] and march an army through Europe into Greece, and punish the Athenians for the outrage they committed upon my father and upon us. As you saw, Darius himself was making his preparations for war against these men; but death prevented him from carrying out his purpose. I therefore on his behalf, and for the benefit of all my subjects, will not rest until I have taken Athens and burnt it to the ground, in revenge for the injury which the Athenians without provocation once did to me and my father. These men, you remember, came to Sardis with Aristagoras[4] the Milesian—a mere slave of ours—and burnt the temples, and the trees that grew about them; and you know all too well how they served our troops under Datis and Artaphernes,[5] when they landed upon Greek soil. For these reasons I have now prepared to make war upon them, and, when I consider the matter, I find several advantages in the venture; if we crush the Athenians and their neighbours in the Peloponnese,[6] we shall so extend the empire of Persia

---

[1]Cyrus, the founder of the Persian Empire, ruled from 559 to 529 B.C.

[2]Cambyses was king of Persia from 529 to 521 B.C. When he conquered Egypt, it temporarily became a Persian province.

[3]The Hellespont is the narrow strait connecting the Aegean Sea with the Sea of Marmora. At one point it is less than a mile wide.

[4]Aristagoras, the ruler of Miletus, encouraged the other cities of Ionia to revolt against the Persians.

[5]Datis and Artaphernes were the commanders of the Persian forces defeated by the Athenians at Marathon.

[6]The Peloponnese (Peloponnesus) is the largest peninsula of southern Greece.

that its boundaries will be God's own sky. With your help I shall pass through Europe from end to end and make it all one country, so that the sun will not look down upon any land beyond the boundaries of what is ours. For if what I am told is true, there is not a city or nation in the world which will be able to withstand us, once Athens and Sparta are out of the way. Thus the guilty and the innocent alike shall bear the yoke of servitude. . . ."

The first to speak after the king was Mardonius. "Of all Persians who have ever lived," he began, "and of all who are yet to be born, you, my lord, are the greatest. Every word you have spoken is true and excellent, and you will not allow the wretched Ionians in Europe to make fools of us. It would indeed be an odd thing if we who have defeated and enslaved the Sacae, Indians, Ethiopians, Assyrians,[7] and many other great nations for no fault of their own, but merely to extend the  boundaries of our empire, should fail now to punish the Greeks who have been guilty of injuring us without provocation. . . . "Well then, my lord, who is likely to resist you when you march against them with the millions of Asia at your back, and the whole Persian fleet? Believe me, it is not in the Greek character to take so desperate a risk. But should I be wrong—should the courage born of ignorance and folly drive them to do battle with us, then they will learn that we are the best soldiers in the world. Nevertheless, let us take this business seriously and spare no

pains; success is never automatic in this world—nothing is achieved without trying."

Xerxes' proposals were made to sound plausible enough by these words of Mardonius, and when he stopped speaking there was a silence. For a while nobody dared to put forward the opposite view, until Artabanus, taking courage from the fact of his relationship to the king—he was a son of Hystaspes and therefore Xerxes' uncle—rose to speak. . . . "It is my duty to tell you what you have to fear from them: you have said you mean to bridge the Hellespont and march through Europe to Greece. Now suppose—and it is not impossible—that you were to suffer a reverse by sea or land, or even both. These Greeks are said to be great fighters—and indeed one might well guess as much from the fact that the Athenians alone destroyed the great army we sent to attack them under Datis and Artaphernes. Or, if you will, suppose they were to succeed upon one element only—suppose they fell upon our fleet and defeated it, and then sailed to the Hellespont and destroyed the bridge: then, my lord, you would indeed be in peril. . . .

"I urge you, therefore, to abandon this plan; take my advice and do not run any such terrible risk when there is no necessity to do so. . . .

"You know, my lord, that amongst living creatures it is the great ones that God smites with his thunder, out of envy of their pride. The little ones do not vex him. It is always the great buildings and the tall trees which are struck by lightning. It is God's way to bring the lofty low. Often a great army is destroyed by a little one, when God in his envy puts fear into the men's hearts, or sends a thunderstorm, and they are cut to pieces in a way they do not deserve. For God tolerates pride in none but Himself."

---

[7]The Sacae lived in Bactria, above the Iranian Plateau; the Indians just west of the Indus River. Ethiopia of that time means a land along the west side of the Red Sea. The Assyrians were a people inhabiting land between the Tigris and Euphrates rivers.

## REVIEW QUESTIONS

1. What were the motives of the Persians in planning Xerxes' invasion of Greece? What do these motives suggest about the nature of the Persian imperial system?
2. What factors were considered by the Persians in choosing a strategy for the war?
3. Herodotus was not a witness to the debate between Mardonius and Artabanus. What does this indicate about his methodology?
4. What dangers did Artabanus foresee in the proposed invasion of Greece?

## 6  Greek Drama

Western drama is an art form that originated in Greece. It had its beginnings in the religious ceremonies of the Greeks and initially served a ritual function linking the Greeks with their gods. In the hands of the great Greek dramatists, drama gradually became less concerned with the activities of the gods, emphasizing instead human personality and universal human themes.

# Sophocles
# *ANTIGONE*

In *Antigone,* the dramatist Sophocles expresses the Greeks' high esteem for humanity and its potential. He also deals with a theme that recurs in Western thought over the centuries: the conflict between individual morality and the requirements of the state, between personal conscience and the state's laws. Creon, king of Thebes, forbids the burial of Polyneikes, Antigone's brother, because he rebelled against the state. The body, decrees Creon, shall remain unburied, food for dogs and vultures, despite the fact that Antigone is his niece and betrothed to his son. Antigone believes that a higher law compels her to bury her brother, even though this means certain death for her and for her sister Ismene, if the latter helps Antigone.

SCENE II

CREON                    *Wheeling on Antigone.*
You,
with your eyes fixed on the ground—speak up.
Do you deny you did this, yes or no?

ANTIGONE
I did it. I don't deny a thing.

CREON
                              *To the Sentry.*
You, get out, wherever you please—
you're clear of a very heavy charge.
                    *He leaves; Creon turns back to*
                                    *Antigone.*
You, tell me briefly, no long speeches—
were you aware a decree had forbidden this?

ANTIGONE
Well aware. How could I avoid it? It was public.

CREON
And still you had the gall to break this law?

ANTIGONE
Of course I did. It wasn't Zeus, not in the least,
who made this proclamation—not to me.
Nor did that Justice, dwelling with the gods
beneath the earth, ordain such laws for men.
Nor did I think your edict had such force
that you, a mere mortal, could override the gods,
the great unwritten, unshakable traditions.
They are alive, not just today or yesterday:
they live forever, from the first of time,
and no one knows when they first saw the light.

These laws—I was not about to break them,
not out of fear of some man's wounded pride,
and face the retribution of the gods.
Die I must, I've known it all my life—
how could I keep from knowing?—even without
your death-sentence ringing in my ears.
And if I am to die before my time

I consider that a gain. Who on earth,
alive in the midst of so much grief as I,
could fail to find his death a rich reward?
So for me, at least, to meet this doom of yours
is precious little pain. But if I had allowed
my own mother's son to rot, an unburied
    corpse—
that would have been an agony! This is nothing.
And if my present actions strike you as foolish,
let's just say I've been accused of folly
by a fool.

LEADER[1]
Like father like daughter,
passionate, wild . . .
she hasn't learned to bend before adversity.

CREON
No? Believe me, the stiffest stubborn wills
fall the hardest; the toughest iron,
tempered strong in the white-hot fire,
you'll see it crack and shatter first of all.
And I've known spirited horses you can
    break
with a light bit—proud, rebellious horses.
There's no room for pride, not in a slave,
not with the lord and master standing by.

This girl was an old hand at insolence
when she overrode the edicts we made public.
But once she'd done it—the insolence,
twice over—to glory in it, laughing,
mocking us to our face with what she'd done.
I'm not the man, not now: she is the man
if this victory goes to her and she goes free.

Never! Sister's child or closer in blood
than all my family clustered at my altar
worshiping Guardian Zeus—she'll never
    escape,
she and her blood sister [Ismene], the most
    barbaric death.
Yes, I accuse her sister of an equal part
in scheming this, this burial.
                                    *To his attendants.*
Bring her here!

I just saw her inside, hysterical, gone to
    pieces.
It never fails: the mind convicts itself
in advance, when scoundrels are up to no
    good,
plotting in the dark. Oh but I hate it more
when a traitor, caught red-handed,
tries to glorify his crimes.

ANTIGONE
Creon, what more do you want
than my arrest and execution?

CREON
Nothing. Then I have it all.

ANTIGONE
Then why delay? Your moralizing repels me,
every word you say—pray god it always will.
So naturally all I say repels you too.
Enough.
Give me glory! What greater glory could I
    win
than to give my own brother decent burial?
These citizens here would all agree.
                                    *To the Chorus.*
they'd praise me too
if their lips weren't locked in fear.
                                    *Pointing to Creon.*
Lucky tyrants—the perquisites of power!
Ruthless power to do and say whatever pleases
*them.*

CREON
You alone, of all the people in Thebes,
see things that way.

ANTIGONE
They see it just that way
but defer to you and keep their tongues in
    leash.

CREON
And you, aren't you ashamed to differ so from
    them?
So disloyal!

ANTIGONE
Not ashamed for a moment,
not to honor my brother, my own flesh and
    blood.

---

[1]This character, sometimes called the *choragos,* was a single
commentator on the action of the play.

CREON
Wasn't Eteocles a brother too—cut down, facing him?

ANTIGONE
Brother, yes, by the same mother, the same
father.

CREON
Then how can you render his enemy such
honors,
such impieties in his eyes?

ANTIGONE
He'll never testify to that,
Eteocles dead and buried.

CREON
He will—
if you honor the traitor just as much as him.

ANTIGONE
But it was his brother, not some slave that
died—

CREON
Ravaging our country!—
but Eteocles died fighting in our behalf.

ANTIGONE
No matter—Death longs for the same rites for
all.

CREON
Never the same for the patriot and the traitor.

ANTIGONE
Who, Creon, who on earth can say the ones
below
don't find this pure and uncorrupt?

CREON
Never. Once an enemy, never a friend,
not even after death.

ANTIGONE
I was born to join in love, not hate—
that is my nature.

CREON
Go down below and love,
if love you must—love the dead! While I'm
alive,

no woman is going to lord it over me.
            *Enter Ismene from the palace, under guard.*

CHORUS
Look,
Ismene's coming, weeping a sister's tears,
loving sister, under a cloud . . .
her face is flushed, her cheeks streaming.
Sorrow puts her lovely radiance in the dark.

CREON
You—
in my own house, you viper, slinking
undetected,
sucking my life-blood! I never knew
I was breeding twin disasters, the two of you
rising up against my throne. Come, tell me,
will you confess your part in the crime or
not?
Answer me. Swear to me.

ISMENE
I did it, yes—
if only she consents—I share the guilt,
the consequences too.

ANTIGONE
No,
Justice will never suffer that—not you,
you were unwilling. I never brought you in.

ISMENE
But now you face such dangers . . . I'm not
ashamed
to sail through trouble with you,
make your troubles mine.

ANTIGONE
Who did the work?
Let the dead and the god of death bear
witness!
I've no love for a friend who loves in words
alone.

ISMENE
Oh no, my sister, don't reject me, please,
let me die beside you, consecrating
the dead together.

ANTIGONE
Never share my dying,

don't lay claim to what you never touched.
My death will be enough.

ISMENE
What do I care for life, cut off from you?

ANTIGONE
Ask Creon. Your concern is all for him.

ISMENE
Why abuse me so? It doesn't help you now.

ANTIGONE
You're right—
if I mock you, I get no pleasure from it,
only pain.

ISMENE
Tell me, dear one,
what can I do to help you, even now?

ANTIGONE
Save yourself. I don't grudge you your
    survival.

ISMENE
Oh no, no, denied my portion in your death?

ANTIGONE
You chose to live, I chose to die.

ISMENE
Not, at least,
without every kind of caution I could voice.

ANTIGONE
Your wisdom appealed to one world—mine,
    another.

ISMENE
But look, we're both guilty, both condemned
    to death.

ANTIGONE
Courage! Live your life. I gave myself to death,
long ago, so I might serve the dead.

---

Haimon, grief-stricken at the condemnation
of his fiancée Antigone, approaches his father Creon, and tries to resolve the crisis.
Creon is suspicious about Haemon's loyalty.

---

SCENE III

CREON
We'll soon know, better than seers could tell
    us.
                              *Turning to Haemon.*
Son, you've heard the final verdict on your
    bride?
Are you coming now, raving against your
    father?
Or do you love me, no matter what I do?

HAEMON
Father, I'm your *son* . . . you in your wisdom
set my bearings for me—I obey you.
No marriage could ever mean more to me than
    you,
whatever good direction you may offer.

CREON
Fine, Haemon.
That's how you ought to feel within your
    heart,
subordinate to your father's will in every way.
That's what a man prays for: to produce good
    sons—
households full of them, dutiful and attentive,
so they can pay his enemy back with interest
and match the respect their father shows his
    friend.
But the man who rears a brood of useless
    children,
what has he brought into the world, I ask you?
Nothing but trouble for himself, and mockery
from his enemies laughing in his face.
Oh Haemon,
never lose your sense of judgment over a
    woman.
The warmth, the rush of pleasure, it all goes
    cold
in your arms, I warn you . . . a worthless
    woman
in your house, a misery in your bed.
What wound cuts deeper than a loved one
turned against you? Spit her out,
like a mortal enemy—let the girl go.
Let her find a husband down among the dead.

Imagine it: I caught her in naked rebellion,

the traitor, the only one in the whole city.
I'm not about to prove myself a liar,
not to my people, no, I'm going to kill her!
That's right—so let her cry for mercy, sing her
    hymns
to Zeus who defends all bonds of kindred
    blood.
Why, if I bring up my own kin to be rebels,
think what I'd suffer from the world at large.
Show me the man who rules his household
    well:
I'll show you someone fit to rule the state.
That good man, my son,
I have every confidence he and he alone
can give commands and take them too.
        Staunch
in the storm of spears he'll stand his ground,
a loyal, unflinching comrade at your side.

But whoever steps out of line, violates the laws
or presumes to hand out orders to his
    superiors,
he'll win no praise from me. But that man
the city places in authority, his orders
must be obeyed, large and small,
right and wrong.
Anarchy—
show me a greater crime in all the earth!
She, she destroys cities, rips up houses,
breaks the ranks of spearmen into headlong
    rout.
But the ones who last it out, the great mass of
    them
owe their lives to discipline. Therefore
we must defend the men who live by law,
never let some women triumph over us.
Better to fall from power, if fall we must,
at the hands of a man—never be rated
inferior to a woman, never.

LEADER
To us,
unless old age has robbed us of our wits,
you seem to say what you have to say with
    sense.

HAEMON
Father, only the gods endow a man with
    reason,

the finest of all their gifts, a treasure.
Far be it from me—I haven't the skill,
and certainly no desire, to tell you when,
if ever, you make a slip in speech . . . though
someone else might have a good suggestion.

Of course it's not for you,
in the normal run of things, to watch
whatever men say or do, or find to criticize.
The man in the street, you know, dreads your
    glance,
he'd never say anything displeasing to your
    face.
But it's for me to catch the murmurs in the
    dark,
the way the city mourns for this young girl.
"No woman," they say, "ever deserved death
    less,
and such a brutal death for such a glorious
    action.
She, with her own dear brother lying in his
    blood—
she couldn't bear to leave him dead, unburied,
food for the wild dogs or wheeling vultures.
Death? She deserves a glowing crown of gold!"
So they say, and the rumor spreads in secret,
darkly . . .
I rejoice in your success, father—
nothing more precious to me in the world.
What medal of honor brighter to his children
than a father's glowing glory? Or a child's
to his proud father? Now don't, please,
be quite so single-minded, self-involved,
or assume the world is wrong and you are
    right.
Whoever thinks that he alone possesses
    intelligence,
the gift of eloquence, he and no one else,
and character, too . . . such men, I tell you,
spread them open—you will find them empty.

No,
it's no disgrace for a man, even a wise man,
to learn many things and not to be too rigid.
You've seen trees by a raging winter torrent,
how many sway with the flood and salvage
    every twig,
but not the stubborn—they're ripped out,
    roots and all.

Bend or break. The same when a man is
   sailing:
haul your sheets too taut, never give an inch,
you'll capsize, go the rest of the voyage
keel up and the rowing-benches under.

Oh give way. Relax your anger—change!
I'm young, I know, but let me offer this:
it would be best by far, I admit,
if a man were born infallible, right by nature.
If not—and things don't often go that way,
it's best to learn from those with good advice.

LEADER
You'd do well, my lord, if he's speaking to the
   point,
to learn from him,

                    *Turning to Haemon.*

and you, my boy, from him.
You both are talking sense.

CREON
So,
men our age, we're to be lectured, are we?—
schooled by a boy his age?

HAEMON
Only in what is right. But if I seem young,
look less to my years and more to what I do.

CREON
Do? Is admiring rebels an achievement?

HAEMON
I'd never suggest that you admire treason.

CREON
Oh?—
isn't that just the sickness that's attacked her?

HAEMON
The whole city of Thebes denies it, to a man.

CREON
And is Thebes about to tell me how to rule?

HAEMON
Now, you see? Who's talking like a child?

CREON
Am I to rule this land for others—or myself?

HAEMON
It's no city at all, owned by one man alone.

CREON
What? The city *is* the king's—that's the law!

HAEMON
What a splendid king you'd make of a desert
   island—
you and you alone.

## REVIEW QUESTIONS

1. What was Antigone's justification for disobeying the command of the king?
   Provide examples of historical figures who have employed a similar justification
   for their actions.
2. Why did Creon react so violently to Antigone's action?
3. What does the text of the drama tell us about the rival political views prevalent in
   democratic Athens in the days of Sophocles?

## 7   Athenian Greatness

The fifty years following the Persian Wars marked Athens' golden age. The central
figure in Athenian political life for much of this period was Pericles (c. 495–429
B.C.), a gifted statesman and military commander. In the opening stage of the Peloponnesian War between Athens and Sparta (431–404 B.C.), Pericles delivered an
oration in honor of the Athenian war dead. In this speech, as reconstructed by the
historian Thucydides, Pericles brilliantly described Athenian greatness.

# Thucydides
# THE FUNERAL ORATION OF PERICLES

Pericles contrasted Sparta's narrow conception of excellence with the Athenian ideal of the self-sufficiency of the human spirit. The Spartans subordinated all personal goals and interests to the demands of the Spartan state. As such, Sparta—a totally militarized society—was as close as the ancient Greeks came to a modern totalitarian society. The Athenians, said Pericles, did not require grinding military discipline in order to fight bravely for their city. Their cultivation of the mind and love of beauty did not make them less courageous.

To be sure, Pericles' "Funeral Oration," intended to bolster the morale of a people locked in a brutal war, idealized Athenian society. Athenians did not always behave in accordance with Pericles' high principles. Nevertheless, as both Pericles and Thucydides knew, Athenian democracy was an extraordinary achievement.

"Let me say that our system of government does not copy the institutions of our neighbours. It is more the case of our being a model to others, than of our imitating anyone else. Our constitution is called a democracy because power is in the hands not of a minority but of the whole people. When it is a question of settling private disputes, everyone is equal before the law; when it is a question of putting one person before another in positions of public responsibility, what counts is not membership of a particular class, but the actual ability which the man possesses. No one, so long as he has it in him to be of service to the state, is kept in political obscurity because of poverty. And, just as our political life is free and open, so is our day-to-day life in our relations with each other. We do not get into a state with our next-door neighbour if he enjoys himself in his own way, nor do we give him the kind of black looks which, though they do no real harm, still do hurt people's feelings. We are free and tolerant in our private lives; but in public affairs we keep to the law. This is because it commands our deep respect.

"We give our obedience to those whom we put in positions of authority, and we obey the laws themselves, especially those which are for the protection of the oppressed, and those unwritten laws which it is an acknowledged shame to break.

"And here is another point. When our work is over, we are in a position to enjoy all kinds of recreation for our spirits. There are various kinds of contests [in poetry, drama, music, and athletics] and sacrifices regularly throughout the year; in our own homes we find a beauty and a good taste which delight us every day and which drive away our cares. Then the greatness of our city brings it about that all the good things from all over the world flow in to us, so that to us it seems just as natural to enjoy foreign goods as our own local products.

"Then there is a great difference between us and our opponents, in our attitude towards military security. Here are some examples: Our city is open to the world, and we have no periodical deportations in order to prevent people observing or finding out secrets which might be of military advantage to the enemy. This is because we rely, not on secret weapons, but on our own real courage and loyalty. There is a difference, too, in our educational systems. The Spartans, from their earliest boyhood, are submitted to the most laborious training in courage; we pass our lives without all these restrictions, and yet are just as ready to face the same dangers as they are. Here is a proof of this: When the Spartans invade our land, they do not come by themselves, but bring all their allies with them; whereas we, when we launch an attack abroad, do the job by ourselves, and, though fighting on foreign soil, do not often fail to defeat opponents who are fighting for their own hearths and homes. As a matter of fact none of our enemies has ever yet been confronted with our total strength, because we have to divide our attention between our navy and the many missions on which our troops are sent on land. Yet, if our enemies engage a detachment of our forces and defeat it, they give themselves credit for having thrown back our entire army; or, if they lose, they claim that they were beaten by us in full strength. There are certain advantages, I think, in our way of meeting danger voluntarily, with an easy mind, instead of with a laborious training, with natural rather than with state-induced courage. We do not have to spend our time practising to meet sufferings which are still in the future; and when they are actually upon us we show ourselves just as brave as these others who are always in strict training. This is one point in which, I think, our city deserves to be admired. There are also others:

"Our love of what is beautiful does not lead to extravagance; our love of the things of the mind does not make us soft. We regard wealth as something to be properly used, rather than as something to boast about. As for poverty, no one need be ashamed to admit it: the real shame is in not taking practical measures to escape from it. Here each individual is interested not only in his own affairs but in the affairs of the state as well: even those who are mostly occupied with their own business are extremely well-informed on general politics—this is a peculiarity of ours: we do not say that a man who takes no interest in politics is a man who minds his own business; we say that he has no business here at all. We Athenians, in our own persons, take our decisions on policy or submit them to proper discussions: for we do not think that there is an incompatibility between words and deeds; the worst thing is to rush into action before the consequences have been properly debated. And this is another point where

we differ from other people. We are capable at the same time of taking risks and of estimating them beforehand. Others are brave out of ignorance; and, when they stop to think, they begin to fear. But the man who can most truly be accounted brave is he who best knows the meaning of what is sweet in life and of what is terrible, and then goes out undeterred to meet what is to come.

"Again, in questions of general good feeling there is a great contrast between us and most other people. We make friends by doing good to others, not by receiving good from them. This makes our friendship all the more reliable, since we want to keep alive the gratitude of those who are in our debt by showing continued goodwill to them: whereas the feelings of one who owes us something lack the same enthusiasm, since he knows that, when he repays our kindness, it will be more like paying back a debt than giving something spontaneously. We are unique in this. When we do kindness to others, we do not do them out of any calculations of profit or loss: we do them without afterthought, relying on our free liberality. Taking everything together then, I declare that our city is an education to Greece, and I declare that in my opinion each single one of our citizens, in all the manifold aspects of life, is able to show himself the rightful lord and owner of his own person, and do this, moreover, with exceptional grace and exceptional versatility. And to show that this is no empty boasting for the present occasion, but real tangible fact, you have only to consider the power which our city possesses and which has been won by those very qualities which I have mentioned. Athens, alone of the states we know, comes to her testing time in a greatness that surpasses what was imagined of her. In her case, and in her case alone, no invading enemy is ashamed at being defeated, and no subject can complain of being governed by people unfit for their responsibilities. Mighty indeed are the marks and monuments of our empire which we have left. Future ages will wonder at us, as the present age wonders at us now."

*REVIEW QUESTIONS*

1. According to Pericles, what are the chief characteristics of a democratic society?
2. What were the attitudes of the Athenians to such things as wealth, learning, and public affairs?
3. How did the Athenians differ from the Spartans in their views on education and military training?

---

## 8  The Status of Women in Classical Greek Society

Women occupied a subordinate position in Greek society. A woman's chief functions were to bear male heirs for her husband and to manage his household. In Athens, respectable women were secluded in their homes; they did not go into the marketplace or eat at the same table as their husbands and guests. Nor did women have political rights; they could not vote or hold office. In order to exercise her property rights, a woman was represented by a male guardian—usually a father, husband, brother, or son.

Parents usually arranged the marriage of their daughters. A father who discovered that his daughter had been unchaste could sell her into slavery. Adultery was a crime. A husband was compelled by law to divorce his adulterous wife and could have her lover executed.

# Xenophon
## *OECONOMICUS*

A philosopher's notion of a woman's place in society appears in the following passage from *Oeconomicus* (Estate Management) by Xenophon (c. 428–354 B.C.). An Athenian soldier, historian, and friend of the philosopher Socrates (see page 79), Xenophon uses a conversation between Socrates and his friend Ischomachus as a way to discuss a wife's role in the Greek household.

"Ah, Ischomachus," said I, "that is just what I want to hear from you. Did you yourself train your wife to be of the right sort, or did she know her household duties when you received her from her parents?"

"Why, what knowledge could she have had, Socrates, when I took her for my wife? She was not yet fifteen years old when she came to me, and up to that time she had lived in leading-strings [cords by which children were supported when beginning to walk], seeing, hearing and saying as little as possible. . . .

"Well, Socrates, as soon as I found her docile and sufficiently domesticated to carry on conversation, I questioned her to this effect.

"'Tell me, dear, have you realised for what reason I took you and your parents gave you to me? For it is obvious to you, I am sure, that we should have had no difficulty in finding someone else to share our beds. But I for myself and your parents for you considered who was the best partner of home and children that we could get. My choice fell on you, and your parents, it appears, chose me as the best they could find. Now if God grants us children, we will then think out how we shall best train them. For one of the blessings in which we shall share is the acquisition of the very best of allies and the very best of support in old age; but at present we share in this our home. For I am paying into the common stock all that I have, and you have put in all that you brought with you. And we are not to reckon up which of us has actually contributed the greater amount, but we should know of a surety that the one who proves the better partner makes the more valuable contribution.'

"My wife's answer was as follows, Socrates: 'How can I possibly help you? What power have I? Nay, all depends on you. My duty, as my mother told me, is to be discreet.'

" 'And since both the indoor and the outdoor tasks demand labour and attention, God from the first adapted the woman's nature, I think, to the indoor and man's to the outdoor tasks and cares.

" 'For he made the man's body and mind more capable of enduring cold and heat, and journeys and campaigns; and therefore imposed on him the outdoor tasks. To the woman, since he has made her body less capable of such endurance, I take it that God has assigned the indoor tasks. And knowing that he had created in the woman and had imposed on her the nourishment of the infants, he meted out to her a larger portion of affection for new-born babes than to the man. And since he imposed on the woman the protection of the stores also, knowing that for protection a fear-ful disposition is no disadvantage, God meted out a larger share of fear to the woman than to the man; and knowing that he who deals with the outdoor tasks will have to be their defender against any wrong-doer, he meted out to him again a larger share of courage. But because both must give and take, he granted to both impartially memory and attention; and so you could not distinguish whether the male or the female sex has the larger share of these. And God also gave to both impartially the power to practise due self-control, and gave authority to whichever is the better—whether it be the man or the woman—to win a larger portion of the good that comes from it. And just because both have not the same aptitudes, they have the more need of each other, and each member of the pair is the more useful to the other, the one being competent where the other is deficient.

" 'Now since we know, dear, what duties have been assigned to each of us by God, we must endeavour, each of us, to do the duties allotted to us as well as possible. The law, moreover, approves of them, for it joins together man and woman. And as God has made them partners in their children, so the law appoints them partners in the home. And besides, the law declares those tasks to be honourable for each of them wherein God has made the one to excel the other. Thus, to the woman it is more honourable to stay indoors than to abide in the fields, but to the man it is unseemly rather to stay indoors than to attend to the work outside.' "

---

# Aristophanes
# *LYSISTRATA*

**Aristophanes** (c. 448–c. 380 B.C.), greatest Athenian comic playwright, wrote *Lysistrata* in 412 B.C. to convey his revulsion for the Peloponnesian War that was destroying Greece. In the play, the women of Athens, led by Lysistrata, resolve to refrain from sexual relations with their husbands until the men make peace. When the women seize the Acropolis—the rocky hill in the center of

Athens—the men resort to force but are doused with water. At this point a commissioner, accompanied by four constables, enters and complains about the disturbance; Koryphaios, one of the doused men, vents his anger. The ensuing dialogue between the commissioner and Lysistrata reflects some attitudes of Greek men and women toward each other.

COMMISSIONER ... That's what women are good for: a complete disaster.

MAN 1 Save your breath for actual crimes, Commissioner. Look what's happened to us. Insolence, insults, insufferable effrontery, and apart from that, they've soaked us. It looks as though we pissed in our tunics.

COMMISSIONER By Poseidon, that liquid deity, you got what you deserved. It's all our own fault. We taught them all they know. We are the forgers of fornication. We sowed in them sexual license and now we reap rebellion ... *(shrugs)* What do you expect? This is what happens. ... *(indicates doors of Acropolis)* Take my own case.

I'm the Commissioner for Public Safety. I've got men to pay. I need the money and look what happens. The women have shut me out of the public treasury. *(taking command)* All right, men. On your feet. Take up that log over there. Form a line. Get a move on. You can get drunk later. I'll give you a hand. *(They ram the gates without success. After three tries, as they are stepping back, Lysistrata opens the door. Calonike and Myrrhine accompany her.)*

LYSISTRATA Put that thing down! I'm coming out of my own free will. What we want here is not bolts and bars and locks, but common sense.

COMMISSIONER Sense? Common sense? You ... you ... you ... Where's a policeman? Arrest her! Tie her hands behind her back.

LYSISTRATA *(who is carrying wool on a spindle or a knitting needle)* By Artemis, goddess of the hunt, if he touches me, you'll be dropping one man from your payroll. *(Lysistrata jabs him)*

COMMISSIONER What's this? Retreat? Get back in there. Grab her, the two of you.

MYRRHINE *(holding a large chamber pot)* By Artemis, goddess of the dew, if you lay a hand on her, I'll kick the shit out of you.

COMMISSIONER Shit? Disgusting. Arrest her for using obscene language.

CALONIKE *(carrying a lamp)* By Artemis, goddess of light, if you lay a finger on her, you'll need a doctor.

COMMISSIONER Apprehend that woman. Get her, NOW!

BOEOTIAN *(from the roof, with a broom)* By Artemis, goddess of witchcraft, if you go near her, I'll break your head open.

COMMISSIONER Good God, what a mess. Athens' finest disgraced! Defeated by a gaggle of girls. Close ranks, men! On your marks, get set, CHARGE!

LYSISTRATA *(holds her hands up and they stop)* Hold it! We've got four battalions of fully equipped infantry women back there.

COMMISSIONER Go inside and disarm them.

LYSISTRATA *(gives a loud whistle and women crowd the bottlenecks and the doorway with brooms, pots and pans, etc.)* Attack! Destroy them, you sifters of flour and beaters of eggs, you pressers of garlic, you dough girls, you bar maids, you market militia. Scratch them and tear them, bite and kick. Fall back, don't strip the enemy—the day is ours. *(the policemen are overpowered)*

COMMISSIONER *(in tears)* Another glorious military victory for Athens!

LYSISTRATA What did you think we were? There's not an ounce of servility in us. A woman scorned is something to be reckoned with. You underestimated the capacity of free-born women.

COMMISSIONER Capacity? I sure as hell did. You'd cause a drought in the saloons if they let you in.

MAN I Your honor, there's no use talking to animals. I know you're a civil servant, but don't overdo it.

MAN II Didn't we tell you? They gave us a public bath, fully dressed, without any soap.

WOMAN I What did you expect, sonny? You made the first move—we made the second. Try it again and you'll get another black eye. *(flute)* We are really sweet little stay-at-homes by nature, all sweetness and light, good little virgins, perfect dolls *(they all rock to and fro coyly)*. But if you stick your finger in a hornet's nest, you're going to get stung.

MEN ALL *(and drums—they beat their feet rhythmically on the ground)*
Oh Zeus, Oh Zeus.
Of all the beasts that thou has wrought,
What monster's worse than woman?
Who shall encompass with his thought
Their endless crimes? Let me tell you . . . no
  man!

They've seized the heights, the rock, the
  shrine.
But to what end I know not.
There must be *reasons* for the crime *(to audience)*
*Do you know why? (pause)* I thought not.

MAN I Scrutinize those women. Assess their rebuttals.

MAN II 'Twould be culpable negligence not to probe this affair to the bottom.

COMMISSIONER *(as if before a jury)* My first question is this, gentlemen of the . . . What possible motive could you have had in seizing the Treasury?

LYSISTRATA We wanted to keep the money. *No money, no war.*

COMMISSIONER You think that money is the cause of the war?

LYSISTRATA Money is the cause of all our problems. . . . They'll not get another penny.

COMMISSIONER Then what do you propose to do?

LYSISTRATA Control the Treasury.

COMMISSIONER Control the Treasury?

LYSISTRATA Control the Treasury. National economics and home economics—they're one and the same.

COMMISSIONER No, they're not.

LYSISTRATA Why do you say so?

COMMISSIONER The national economy is for the war effort.

LYSISTRATA Who needs the war effort?

COMMISSIONER How can we protect the city?

LYSISTRATA Leave that to us.

ALL MEN You?

ALL WOMEN Us.

COMMISSIONER God save us.

LYSISTRATA Leave that to us.

COMMISSIONER Subversive nonsense!

LYSISTRATA Why get so upset? There's no stopping us now.

COMMISSIONER It's a downright crime.

LYSISTRATA We *must* save you.

COMMISSIONER *(pouting)* What if I don't want to be saved?

LYSISTRATA All the more reason to.

COMMISSIONER Might I ask where you got these ideas of war and peace?

LYSISTRATA If you'll allow me, I'll tell you.

COMMISSIONER Out with it then, or I'll . . .

LYSISTRATA Relax and put your hands down.

COMMISSIONER I can't help myself. You make me so damned angry.

CALONIKE Watch it.

COMMISSIONER Watch it yourself, you old wind bag.

LYSISTRATA Because of our natural self-restraint, we women have tolerated you men ever since this war began. We tolerated you and kept our thoughts to ourselves. (You never let us utter a peep, anyway.) But that does not mean that we were happy with you. We knew you all too well. Very often, in the evening, at suppertime, we would listen to you talk of some enormously important decision you had made. Deep down inside all we felt was pain, but we would force a smile and ask, "How was the assembly today, dear? Did you get to talk about peace?" And my husband would answer, "None of your business. Shut up!" And I would shut up.

CALONIKE I wouldn't have.

COMMISSIONER I'd have shut your mouth for you.

LYSISTRATA But then we would find out that you had passed a more disgusting resolution, and I would ask you, "Darling, how did you manage to do something so absolutely stupid?" And my husband would glare at me and threaten to slap my face if I did not attend to the distaff side of things. And then he'd always quote Homer: "The men must see to the fighting."

COMMISSIONER Well done. Well done.

LYSISTRATA What do you mean? Not to let us advise against your idiocy was bad enough, but then again we'd actually hear you out in public saying things like, "Who can we draft? There's not a man left in the country." Someone else would say, "Quite right, not a man left. Pity." And so we women got together and decided to save Greece. There was no time to lose. Therefore, you keep quiet for a change and listen to us. For we have valuable advice to give this country. If you'll listen, we'll put you back on your feet again.

COMMISSIONER You'll do what? I'm not going to put up with this. I'm not going . . .

LYSISTRATA SILENCE!

COMMISSIONER I categorically decline to be silent for a woman. Women wear hats.

LYSISTRATA If that's what is bothering you, try one on and shut up! (puts one on him)

CALONIKE Here's a spindle.

MYRRHINE And a basket of wool.

CALONIKE Go on home. There's a sweetheart. Put on your girdle, wind your wool, and mind the beans don't boil over.

LYSISTRATA "THE WOMEN MUST SEE TO THE FIGHTING."

COMMISSIONER Beside the point, beside the point. Things are in a tangle. How can you set them straight?

LYSISTRATA Simple.

COMMISSIONER Explain.

LYSISTRATA Do you know anything about weaving? Say the wool gets tangled. We lift it up, like this, and work out the knots by winding it this way and that, up and down, on the spindles. That's how we'll unravel the war. We'll send our envoys this way and that, up and down, all over Greece.

COMMISSIONER Wool? Spindles? Are you out of your mind? War is a serious business.

LYSISTRATA If you had any sense, you'd learn a lesson from women's work.

COMMISSIONER Prove it.

LYSISTRATA The first thing we have to do is give the wool a good wash, get the dirt out of the fleece. We beat out the musk and pick out the hickies. Do the same for the city. Lambast the loafers and discard the dodgers. Then our spoiled wool—that's like your job-hunting sycophants—sack the spongers, decapitate the dabblers. But toss together into the wool basket the good [resident] aliens, the allies, the strangers, and begin spinning them into a ball. The colonies are loose threads; pick up the ends and gather them in. Wind them all into one, make a great bobbin of yarn, and weave, without bias or seam, a garment of government fit for the people.

COMMISSIONER It's all very well this weaving and bobbing—when you have absolutely no earthly idea what a war means.

LYSISTRATA You disgusting excuse for a man! The pain of giving birth was only our first pain. You took our boys and sent *them to their deaths in Sicily.*

COMMISSIONER Quiet! I beg you, let that memory lie still.

LYSISTRATA And now, when youth and beauty are still with us and our blood is hot,

you take our husbands away, and we sleep alone. That's bad enough for us married women. But I pity the virgins growing old, alone in their beds.

COMMISSIONER Well, men grow old too, you know.

LYSISTRATA But it's not the same. A soldier's discharged, bald as a coot he may be, and . . . zap! he marries a nymphette. But a woman only has one summer, and when that has slipped by, she can spend her days and her years consulting oracles and fortune tellers, but they'll never send her a husband.

———

MEN ALL There's something rotten in the state of Athens.
An ominous aroma of constitutional rot.
My nose can smell a radical dissenter,
An anarchist, tyrannous, feminist plot.

The Spartans are behind it.
They must have masterminded
This anarchist, tyrannous, feminist plot.

## REVIEW QUESTIONS

1. What were the duties of a good wife and a good husband according to Xenophon?
2. What were the grievances of Greek women as listed by Aristophanes?
3. What attitudes of ancient Greek males toward females are reflected in our own modern Western society?

# 9  The Peloponnesian War

After the defeat of the Persian invaders in 479 B.C., the Athenians organized a mutual defense pact, called the Delian League, among the smaller Greek states. With the largest population and greatest wealth and naval forces, Athens became the dominant power within the league. In the course of time, Athens converted the alliance from an organization of equal sovereign states to an empire under Athenian control. This outcome aroused suspicion among the other Greek states in the Peloponnese, particularly Sparta, that an imperialistic Athens was a threat to their own independence and freedom. That fear precipitated the Peloponnesian War (431–404 B.C.), which devastated the Greek world during the late fifth century B.C.

Elected general during the war, Thucydides was banished from Athens for failing to rescue Amphipolis, a town under attack by Sparta. During his twenty-year exile, Thucydides gathered information about the war, which he correctly viewed as an event of world-historical importance. He was also right to regard his account as a unique documentary achievement that would serve as a model for future historians.

Above all, Thucydides studied politics, the lifeblood of Athenian society. For him, history was essentially the study of political behavior. Consistent with the Greek character, Thucydides sought underlying patterns and general truths pertaining to statesmanship and political power. His chronicle contains rich insights into human nature, the techniques of demagogues, the ruinous consequences of mob behavior, and the spiritual deterioration of men under the stress of war.

# Thucydides
# THE MELIAN DIALOGUE AND THE REVOLUTION AT CORCYRA

The Athenians, who saw no conflict between imperialism and democracy, considered it natural for strong states to dominate weaker ones. This view coincided with the position of those Sophists (see page 54) who argued that might makes right. The classic expression of this view is found in Thucydides' history.

During the war, Athens decided to invade the island of Melos, which resisted this unprovoked act of aggression. Thucydides reconstructed a dialogue based on a meeting between Athenian envoys and Melian officials, who tried unsuccessfully to persuade the Athenians not to launch an unjust war. Subsequently, Athens attacked. After capturing the town, the Athenians slaughtered the men, enslaved the women and children, and colonized the territory. Following is the famous Melian Dialogue.

## THE MELIAN DIALOGUE

MELIANS No one can object to each of us putting forward our own views in a calm atmosphere. That is perfectly reasonable. What is scarcely consistent with such a proposal is the present threat, indeed the certainty, of your making war on us. We see that you have come prepared to judge the argument yourselves, and that the likely end of it all will be either war, if we prove that we are in the right, and so refuse to surrender, or else slavery.

ATHENIANS If you are going to spend the time in enumerating your suspicions about the future, or if you have met here for any other reason except to look the facts in the face and on the basis of these facts to consider how you can save your city from destruction, there is no point in our going on with this discussion. If, however, you will do as we suggest, then we will speak on.

MELIANS It is natural and understandable that people who are placed as we are should have recourse to all kinds of arguments and different points of view. However, you are right in saying that we are met together here to discuss the safety of our country and, if you will have it so, the discussion shall proceed on the lines that you have laid down.

ATHENIANS  Then we on our side will use no fine phrases saying, for example, that we have a right to our empire because we defeated the Persians, or that we have come against you now because of the injuries you have done us—a great mass of words that nobody would believe. And we ask you on your side not to imagine that you will influence us by saying that you, though a colony of Sparta, have not joined Sparta in the war, or that you have never done us any harm. Instead we recommend that you should try to get what it is possible for you to get, taking into consideration what we both really do think; since you know as well as we do that when these matters are discussed by practical people, the standard of justice depends on the equality of power to compel and that in fact the strong do what they have the power to do and the weak accept what they have to accept.

MELIANS  Then in our view (since you force us to leave justice out of account and to confine ourselves to self-interest)—in our view it is at any rate useful that you should not destroy a principle that is to the general good of all men—namely, that in the case of all who fall into danger there should be such a thing as fair play and just dealing, and that such people should be allowed to use and to profit by arguments that fall short of a mathematical accuracy. And this is a principle which affects you as much as anybody, since your own fall would be visited by the most terrible vengeance and would be an example to the world.

ATHENIANS  . . . What we shall do now is to show you that it is for the good of our own empire that we are here and that it is for the preservation of your city that we shall say what we are going to say. We do not want any trouble in bringing you into our empire, and we want you to be spared for the good both of yourselves and of ourselves.

MELIANS  And how could it be just as good for us to be the slaves as for you to be the masters?

ATHENIANS  You, by giving in, would save yourselves from disaster; we, by not destroying you, would be able to profit from you.

MELIANS  So you would not agree to our being neutral, friends instead of enemies, but allies of neither side?

ATHENIANS  No, because it is not so much your hostility that injures us; it is rather the case that, if we were on friendly terms with you, our subjects would regard that as a sign of weakness in us, whereas your hatred is evidence of our power. . . . [Our subjects think] that those who still preserve their independence do so because they are strong, and that if we fail to attack them it is because we are afraid. So that by conquering you we shall increase not only the size but the security of our empire. We rule the sea and you are islanders, and weaker islanders too than the others; it is therefore particularly important that you should not escape. . . .

MELIANS  Then surely, if such hazards are taken by you to keep your empire . . . we who are still free would show ourselves great cowards and weaklings if we failed to face everything that comes rather than submit to slavery.

ATHENIANS  No, not if you are sensible. This is no fair fight, with honour on one side and shame on the other. It is rather a question of saving your lives and not resisting those who are far too strong for you.

MELIANS  Yet we know that in war fortune sometimes makes the odds more level than could be expected from the difference in numbers of the two sides. And if we surrender, then all our hope is lost at once, whereas, so long as we remain in action, there is still a hope that we may yet stand upright.

ATHENIANS  Hope, that comforter in danger! If one already has solid advantages to fall back upon, one can indulge in hope. . . . [D]o not be like those people who, as so commonly happens, miss the chance of saving themselves in a human and practical way, and, when every clear and distinct hope has left them in their adversity, turn to what is blind and vague, to prophecies and oracles and such things which by encouraging hope lead men to ruin.

MELIANS It is difficult, and you may be sure that we know it, for us to oppose your power. . . . Nevertheless we trust that the gods will give us fortune as good as yours, because we are standing for what is right against what is wrong; and as for what we lack in power, we trust that it will be made up for by our alliance with the Spartans, who are bound, if for no other reason, then for honour's sake, and because we are their kinsmen, to come to our help. Our confidence, therefore, is not so entirely irrational as you think.

ATHENIANS . . . Our opinion of the gods and our knowledge of men lead us to conclude that it is a general and necessary law of nature to rule wherever one can. . . . [W]ith regard to your views about Sparta and your confidence that she, out of a sense of honour, will come to your aid, we must say that we congratulate you on your simplicity but do not envy you your folly. . . .

. . . You, if you take the right view . . . will see that there is nothing disgraceful in giving way to the greatest city in Hellas when she is offering you such reasonable terms—alliance on a tribute-paying basis and liberty to enjoy your own property. And, when you are allowed to choose between war and safety, you will not be so insensitively arrogant as to make the wrong choice. This is the safe rule—to stand up to one's equals, to behave with deference towards one's superiors, and to treat one's inferiors with moderation. Think it over again, then, when we have withdrawn from the meeting, and let this be a point that constantly recurs to your minds—that you are discussing the fate of your country, that you have only one country, and that its future for good or ill depends on this one single decision which you are going to make.

The Athenians then withdrew from the discussion. The Melians, left to themselves, reached a conclusion which was much the same as they had indicated in their previous replies. Their answer was as follows:

MELIANS Our decision, Athenians, is just the same as it was at first. We are not prepared to give up in a short moment the liberty which our city has enjoyed from its foundation for 700 years. We put our trust in the fortune that the gods will send and which has saved us up to now, and in the help of men—that is, of the Spartans; and so we shall try to save ourselves. But we invite you to allow us to be friends of yours and enemies to neither side, to make a treaty which shall be agreeable to both you and us, and so to leave our country.

---

During the war, revolutions broke out in several city-states as democrats, those who believed in decision making by citizen participation, and oligarchs, those who wanted the rule of a select few, competed for power. In these conflicts, traditional standards of morality were set aside and dangerous passions were unleashed. Thucydides' account of the revolution at Corcyra shows how the stresses of war precipitated a moral collapse and a deterioration in the quality of political life.

---

. . . The Corcyraeans continued to massacre those of their own citizens whom they considered to be their enemies. Their victims were accused of conspiring to overthrow the democracy, but in fact men were often killed on grounds of personal hatred or else by their debtors because of the money that they owed. There was death in every shape and form. And, as usually happens in such situations, people went to every extreme and beyond it. There were fathers who killed their sons; men were dragged from the temples or butchered on the very altars; some were actually walled up in the temple of Dionysus [a god of drunken revelry] and died there.

So savage was the progress of this revolution, and it seemed all the more so because it was one of the first which had broken out. Later, of course, practically the whole of the Hellenic world was convulsed, with rival parties in every state—democratic leaders trying to bring in the Athenians, and oligarchs trying to bring in the Spartans. In peacetime there would have been no excuse and no desire for calling them in, but in time of war, when each party could always count upon an alliance which would do harm to its opponents and at the same time strengthen its own position, it became a natural thing for anyone who wanted a change of government to call in help from outside. In the various cities these revolutions were the cause of many calamities—as happens and always will happen while human nature is what it is, though there may be different degrees of savagery, and, as different circumstances arise, the general rules will admit of some variety. In times of peace and prosperity cities and individuals alike follow higher standards, because they are not forced into a situation where they have to do what they do not want to do. But war is a stern teacher; in depriving them of the power of easily satisfying their daily wants, it brings most people's minds down to the level of their actual circumstances.

So revolutions broke out in city after city, and in places where the revolutions occurred late the knowledge of what had happened previously in other places caused still new extravagances of revolutionary zeal, expressed by an elaboration in the methods of seizing power and by unheard-of atrocities in revenge. To fit in with the change of events, words, too, had to change their usual meanings. What used to be described as a thoughtless act of aggression was now regarded as the courage one would expect to find in a party member; to think of the future and wait was merely another way of saying one was a coward; any idea of moderation

was just an attempt to disguise one's unmanly character; ability to understand a question from all sides meant that one was totally unfitted for action. Fanatical enthusiasm was the mark of a real man, and to plot against an enemy behind his back was perfectly legitimate self-defence. Anyone who held violent opinions could always be trusted, and anyone who objected to them became a suspect. To plot successfully was a sign of intelligence, but it was still cleverer to see that a plot was hatching. If one attempted to provide against having to do either, one was disrupting the unity of the party and acting out of fear of the opposition. In short, it was equally praiseworthy to get one's blow in first against someone who was going to do wrong, and to denounce someone who had no intention of doing any wrong at all. Family relations were a weaker tie than party membership, since party members were more ready to go to any extreme for any reason whatever. These parties were not formed to enjoy the benefits of the established laws, but to acquire power by overthrowing the existing regime and the members of these parties felt confidence in each other not because of any fellowship in a religious communion, but because they were partners in crime. If an opponent made a reasonable speech, the party in power, so far from giving it a generous reception, took every precaution to see that it had no practical effect. . . .

Love of power, operating through greed and through personal ambition, was the cause of all these evils. To this must be added the violent fanaticism which came into play once the struggle had broken out. Leaders of parties in the cities had programmes which appeared admirable—on one side political equality for the masses, on the other the safe and sound government of the aristocracy—but in professing to serve the public interest they were seeking to win the prizes for themselves. In their struggles for ascendancy nothing was barred; terrible indeed were the actions to which they committed themselves, and in taking revenge they went farther still. Here they were deterred neither by the claims of justice nor by the interests of the state; their one standard was the pleasure of their own party at that particular moment, and so, either by means of condemning their enemies on an illegal vote or by violently usurping power over them, they were always ready to satisfy the hatreds of the hour. Thus neither side had any use for conscientious motives; more interest was shown in those who could produce attractive arguments to justify some disgraceful action. As for the citizens who held moderate views, they were destroyed by both the extreme parties, either for not taking part in the struggle or in envy at the possibility that they might survive.

As the result of these revolutions, there was a general deterioration of character throughout the Greek world. The simple way of looking at things, which is so much the mark of a noble nature, was regarded as a ridiculous quality and soon ceased to exist. Society had become divided into two ideologically hostile camps, and each side viewed the other with suspicion. As for ending this state of affairs, no guarantee could be given that would be trusted, no oath sworn that people would fear to break; everyone had come to the conclusion that it was hopeless to expect a permanent settlement and so, instead of being able to feel confident in others, they devoted their energies to providing against being injured themselves. As a rule those who were least remarkable for intelligence showed the greater powers of survival. Such people recognized their own deficiencies and the superior intelligence of their opponents; fearing that they might lose a debate or find themselves outmanoeuvred in intrigue by their quick-witted enemies, they boldly launched straight into action; while their opponents, over-confident in the belief that they would see what was happening in advance, and not thinking it necessary to seize by force what they could secure by policy, were the more easily destroyed because they were off their guard.

Certainly it was in Corcyra that there occurred the first examples of the breakdown of law and order. There was the revenge taken in their hour of triumph by those who had in the past been arrogantly oppressed instead of wisely governed; there were the wicked resolutions taken by those who, particularly under the pressure of misfortune, wished to escape from their usual poverty and coveted the property of their neighbours; there were the savage and pitiless actions into which men were carried not so much for the sake of gain as because they were swept away into an internecine struggle by their ungovernable passions. Then, with the ordinary conventions of civilized life thrown into confusion, human nature, always ready to offend even where laws exist, showed itself proudly in its true colours, as something incapable of controlling passion, insubordinate to the idea of justice, the enemy to anything superior to itself; for, if it had not been for the pernicious power of envy, men would not so have exalted vengeance above innocence and profit above justice. Indeed, it is true that in these acts of revenge on others men take it upon themselves to begin the process of repealing those general laws of humanity which are there to give a hope of salvation to all who are in distress, instead of leaving those laws in existence, remembering that there may come a time when they, too, will be in danger and will need their protection.

## REVIEW QUESTIONS

1. In what way did the debate between the Athenians and Melians reflect the new rationalist spirit in Greek society?
2. Evaluate the performance of the Melian negotiators.
3. What types of political behavior did Thucydides hold in contempt?

## 10 Socrates: The Rational Individual

Socrates (469–399 B.C.) marked a decisive turning point in Greek philosophy and in the history of Western thought. The Socratic conception of the rational individual became an essential component of the tradition of classical humanism. Socrates agreed with the Sophists that the study of physical nature was less important than the study of man. But whereas the Sophists concentrated on teaching specific skills—how to excel in debates, for example—Socrates was concerned with comprehending and improving human character. Although ethical concerns lay at the center of Socrates' thought, he never provided a list of ethical commands; in Socratic philosophy, there is nothing comparable to the Ten Commandments. What he did provide was a method—the dialectic or dialogue—of arriving at knowledge, including moral values.

For Socrates, the dialogue (the asking and answering of questions between two or more individuals) was the sole avenue to moral insights and self-knowledge. The interchange implied that a human mind was not a passive vessel into which a teacher poured knowledge. Participants in a dialogue were obliged to play an active role and to think critically about human values. The use of the dialogue implied further that relations between people should involve rational discussion through which people learn from each other and improve themselves.

When Socrates was seventy, he was accused by his enemies of corrupting the youth of Athens and of not believing in the city's gods but in other, new divinities, and he went on trial for his life.

# Plato
# *THE APOLOGY*

Knowledge of Socrates' trial comes principally from *The Apology* written by Plato (see page 83), Socrates' most illustrious student. (The original meaning of *apology* was a defense or explanation.) In the first passage from *The Apology,* presented below, Socrates tells the court that the Delphic Oracle, the prophetess of Apollo at Delphi, had said that there was no one wiser than Socrates. Not considering himself wise, Socrates resolved to discover what the oracle meant, by conversing with people reputed to be wise.

I went to a man who seemed wise: thinking that there, if anywhere, I should prove the answer wrong, and be able to say to the oracle, "You said that I am the wisest of men; but this man is wiser than I am." So I examined him—I need not tell you his name, he was a public man, but this was the result, Athenians. When I conversed with him, I came to see that, though many persons, and chiefly he himself, thought that he was wise, yet he was not wise. And then I tried to show him that he was not wise, though he fancied that he was; and by that I gained his hatred, and the hatred of many of the bystanders. So when I went away, I thought to myself, "I am wiser than this man: neither of us probably knows anything that is really good, but he thinks that he has knowledge, when he has it not, while I, seeing that I have no knowledge, do not think that I have." In this point, at least, I seem to be a little wiser than he is; I do not think that I know what I do not know. Next I went to another man, who seemed to be still wiser, with just the same result. And there again I gained his hatred. . . . After the public men I went to the poets, tragic, dithyrambic [frenzied], and others, thinking there to find myself manifestly more ignorant than they. So I took up the poems on which I thought that they had spent most pains, and asked them what they meant wishing also for instruction. I am ashamed to tell you the truth, my friends, but I must say it. In short, almost any of the bystanders would have spoken better about the works of these poets than the poets themselves. So I soon found that it is not by wisdom that the poets create their works, but by a certain natural power, and by inspiration, like soothsayers and prophets: for though such persons say many fine things, they know nothing of what they say. And the poets seemed to me to be in a like case. And at the same time I perceived that, because of their poetry, they thought that they were the wisest of men in other matters too, which they were not. So I went away again, thinking that I had the same advantage over them as over the public men.

Finally I went to the artisans: for I was conscious, in a word, that I had no knowledge at all, and I was sure that I should find that they knew many fine things. And in that I was not mistaken. They knew what I did not know, and so far they were wiser than I. But, Athenians, it seemed to me that the skilled craftsmen made the same mistake as the poets. Each of them claimed to have great wisdom in the highest matters because he was skilful in his own art; and this fault of theirs threw their real wisdom into the shade. So I asked myself on behalf of the oracle whether I would choose to remain as I was, neither wise in their wisdom

nor ignorant in their ignorance, or to have both, as they had them. And I made answer to myself and to the oracle that it were better for me to remain as I was.

This search, Athenians, has gained me much hatred of a very fierce and bitter kind, which has caused many false accusations against me; and I am called by the name of wise. For the bystanders always think that I am wise myself in any matter wherein I convict another man of ignorance. But in truth, my friends, perhaps it is God who is wise: and by this oracle he may have meant that man's wisdom is worth little or nothing. He did not mean, I think, that Socrates is wise: he only took me as an example, and made use of my name, as though he would say to men: "He among you is wisest, who, like Socrates, is convinced that for wisdom he is verily worthless." And therefore I still go about searching and testing every man whom I think wise, whether he be a citizen or a stranger, according to the word of the God [Apollo]; and whenever I find that he is not wise, I point that out to him in the service of the God. And I am so busy in this pursuit that I have never had leisure to take any part worth mentioning in public matters, or to look after my private affairs. I am in very great poverty by my service to the God.

And besides this, the young men who follow me about, who are the sons of wealthy persons and with much leisure, by nature delight in hearing men cross-questioned: and they often imitate me among themselves: then they try their hand at cross-questioning other people. And, I imagine, they find a great abundance of men who think that they know a great deal, when in truth they know little or nothing. And then the persons who are cross-questioned are angry with me instead of with themselves: and say that Socrates is an abominable fellow who corrupts the young. And when they are asked, Why, what does he do? what does he teach? they have nothing to say; but, not to seem at a loss, they repeat the stock charges against all philosophers, and say that he investigates things in the air and under the earth, and that he teaches people to disbelieve in the gods, and "to make the worst appear the better reason." For I fancy they would not like to confess the truth, that they are shown up as mere ignorant pretenders to knowledge. And so they have filled your ears with their fierce slanders for a long time, for they are zealous and fierce, and numerous: they are well-disciplined too, and plausible in speech. . . .

---

Had Socrates been willing to compromise and to stop teaching his philosophy, it is likely that he would not have received the death penalty. However, for Socrates the pursuit of truth was the highest human activity; it involved the person's whole being. It transformed the individual, enabling him to live in accordance with moral values that had been arrived at through thought and that could be defended rationally.

---

. . . But I know well that it is evil and base to do wrong and to disobey my better, whether he be man or god. And I will never choose what I know to be evil, and fear and fly from what may possibly be a good. And so, even if you acquit me now, and do not listen to Anytus' [his prosecutor's] argument that I ought never to have been brought to trial, if I was to be acquitted; and that as it is, you are bound to put me to death, because if I were to escape, all your children would forthwith be utterly corrupted by practising what Socrates teaches: if you were therefore to say to me, "Socrates, this time we will not listen to Anytus: we will let you go: but on this condition, that you cease from carrying on this search, and from philosophy: if you are found doing that again, you shall die:" I say, if you offered to let me go on these terms, I should reply:—"Athenians, I hold you in the highest regard and love; but I will obey the God rather than you: and as long as I have breath and power I will not cease from philosophy, and from exhorting you and setting forth the truth to any of you whom I meet, saying as I am wont, 'My excellent friend, you are a citizen of Athens, a city very

great and very famous for wisdom and power of mind: are you not ashamed of caring so much for the making of money, and for reputation and honour? Will you not spend thought or care on wisdom and truth and the perfecting of your soul?' " And if he dispute my words, and say that he does care for these things, I shall not forthwith release him and go away: I shall question him and cross-examine him: and if I think that he has not virtue, though he says that he has, I shall reproach him for setting the least value on the most important things; and the greater value on the more worthless. This shall I do to every one whom I meet, old or young, citizen or stranger; but especially to the citizens, for they are more nearly akin to me. For know well, the God commands me so to do. And I think that nothing better has ever happened to you in your city than my service to the God. For I spend my whole life in going about persuading you all, both young and old, to give your first and chiefest care to the perfection of your souls: and not till you have done that to care for your bodies or your wealth. I tell you, that virtue does not come from wealth, but that wealth and every other good, whether public or private, which men have, come from virtue. If then I corrupt the youth by this teaching, the mischief is great; but if any man says that I teach anything else, he speaks falsely. And therefore, Athenians, I say, either listen to Anytus, or do not listen to him: either acquit me, or do not acquit me: but be sure that I shall not alter my life; no, not if I have to die for it many times.

Do not interrupt me, Athenians. Remember the request which I made to you, and listen to my words. I think that it will do you good to hear them. I have something more to say to you, at which perhaps you will cry out: but do not do that. Be sure that if you kill me, a man such as I say I am, you will harm yourselves more than you will harm me. Meletus [another prosecutor] and Anytus can do me no harm; that is impossible, for I do not think that God will allow a good man to be harmed by a bad one. They may indeed kill me, or drive me into exile, or deprive me of my civil rights; and perhaps Meletus and others think these things great evils. But I do not think so: I think that to do as he is doing, and to try to kill a man unjustly, is a much greater evil. And now, Athenians, I am not going to argue for my own sake at all, as you might think, but for yours, that you may not sin against the God and reject his gift to you, by condemning me. If you put me to death, you will hardly find another man to fill my place. The God has sent me to attack the city, if I may use a ludicrous simile, just as if it were a great and noble horse, which was rather sluggish from its size and needed a gadfly to rouse it: and I think that I am the gadfly that the God has set upon the city: for I never cease settling on you as it were at every point, and rousing, and exhorting, and reproaching each man of you all day long. You will hardly find any one else, my friends, to fill my place: and, if you take my advice, you will spare my life. You are indignant, as drowsy persons are when they are awakened, and, of course, if you are persuaded by Anytus, you could easily kill me with a single blow, and then sleep on undisturbed for the rest of your lives. . . .

Perhaps someone will say, "Why cannot you withdraw from Athens, Socrates, and hold your peace?" It is the most difficult thing in the world to make you understand why I cannot do that. If I say that I cannot hold my peace because that would be to disobey the God, you will think that I am not in earnest and will not believe me. And if I tell you that no greater good can happen to a man than to discuss human excellence every day and the other matters about which you have heard me arguing and examining myself and others, and that an unexamined life is not worth living, then you will believe me still less. But that is so, my friends, though it is not easy to persuade you. . . .

---

Socrates is convicted and sentenced to death.

---

. . . Perhaps, my friends, you think that I have been convicted because I was wanting in the arguments by which I could have persuaded you to acquit me, if I had thought it right to do or to say anything to escape punishment. It is not so. I have been convicted because I was wanting, not in arguments, but in impudence and shamelessness—because I would not plead before you as you would have liked to hear me plead, or appeal to you with weeping and wailing, or say and do many other things which I maintain are unworthy of me, but which you have been accustomed to from other men. But when I was defending myself, I thought that I ought not to do anything unworthy of a free man because of the danger which I ran, and I have not changed my mind now. I would very much rather defend myself as I did, and die, than as you would have had me do, and live. . . .

And now I wish to prophesy to you, Athenians, who have condemned me. For I am going to die, and that is the time when men have most prophetic power. And I prophesy to you who have sentenced me to death that a far more severe punishment than you have inflicted on me will surely overtake you as soon as I am dead. You have done this thing, thinking that you will be relieved from having to give an account of your lives. But I say that the result will be very different. There will be more men who will call you to account, whom I have held back, though you did not recognize it. And they will be harsher toward you than I have been, for they will be younger, and you will be more indignant with them. For if you think that you will restrain men from reproaching you for not living as you should, by putting them to death, you are very much mistaken. That way of escape is neither possible nor honorable. It is much more honorable and much easier not to suppress others, but to make yourselves as good as you can. This is my parting prophecy to you who have condemned me.

## REVIEW QUESTIONS

1. What is the nature of Socrates' wisdom?
2. Was Socrates a subversive force in Athenian society? Explain your answer.
3. According to Socrates, what is the true vocation of a philosopher? What price may the philosopher pay for his effort?
4. Compare the vocation of Socrates as a philosopher to that of the Hebrew prophets.
5. Why did some Athenians believe that Socrates corrupted the young?
6. What did Socrates say would be his reaction if he were offered an acquittal on the condition that he give up teaching his philosophy? What were his reasons?

---

## 11  Plato: The Philosopher-King

Plato (c. 429–347 B.C.), an Athenian aristocrat and disciple of Socrates, based his philosophy on Socrates' teachings. Plato was greatly affected by the deterioration of Athenian politics during and immediately after the Peloponnesian War. The rise of demagogues, the violent conflicts between oligarchs and democrats, and the execution of Socrates convinced Plato that Athenian democracy was a failure. His hostility toward democracy also stemmed from his upper-class background and temperament.

Socratic philosophy held promise of reforming the individual through the critical use of reason. Plato felt that the individual could not undergo a moral transformation while living in a wicked and corrupt society. If the individual were to achieve virtue, the state must be reformed.

# Plato
# *THE REPUBLIC*

In *The Republic,* Plato proposed organizing government in harmony with the needs of human nature. Those people who are driven by a desire for food, possessions, and sexual gratification, Plato said, should be farmers, tradesmen, or artisans. Those who are naturally courageous and assertive should be soldiers. And the few who have the capacity for wisdom—the philosophers—should be entrusted with political power.

In the ideal state, Plato asserted, the many would be ruled by the few who have a natural endowment for leadership. These philosopher-kings, the finest product of the state's carefully designed educational program, would wield absolute power: the people would lose their right to participate in political affairs, and the state would manufacture propaganda and strictly control education in order to keep the masses obedient. In exchange, the citizens would gain leaders distinguished by their rationality, wisdom, and virtue. In the form of a dialogue between Socrates and a man called Glaucon, Plato in the following reading presented his views on the character of the philosopher.

[SOCRATES] Unless either philosophers become kings in their countries or those who are now called kings and rulers come to be sufficiently inspired with a genuine desire for wisdom; unless that is to say, political power and philosophy meet together . . . there can be no rest from troubles, my dear Glaucon, for states, nor yet, as I believe, for all mankind. . . . There is no other way of happiness either for the state or for the individual. . . .

Now . . . we must, I think, define . . . whom we mean by these lovers of wisdom who, we have dared to assert, ought to be our rulers. Once we have a clear view of their character, we shall be able to defend our position by pointing to some who are naturally fitted to combine philosophic study with political leadership, while the rest of the world should accept their guidance and let philosophy alone.

[GLAUCON] Yes, this is the moment for a definition. . . .

[S] . . . One trait of the philosophic nature we may take as already granted: a constant passion for any knowledge that will reveal to them something of that reality which endures for ever and is not always passing into and out of existence. And, we may add, their desire is to know the whole of that reality; they will not willingly renounce any part of it as relatively small and insignificant, as we said before when we compared them to the lover and to the man who covets honour.

[G] True.

[S] Is there not another trait which the nature we are seeking cannot fail to possess—truthfulness, a love of truth and a hatred for falsehood that will not tolerate untruth in any form?

[G] Yes, it is natural to expect that.

[S] It is not merely natural, but entirely necessary that an instinctive passion for any object should extend to all that is closely akin to it; and there is nothing more closely akin to wisdom than truth. So the same nature cannot love wisdom and falsehood; the genuine lover of knowledge cannot fail, from his youth up, to strive after the whole of truth.

[G] I perfectly agree.

[S] Now we surely know that when a man's desires set strongly in one direction, in every other channel they flow more feebly, like a stream diverted into another bed. So when the current has set towards knowledge and all that goes with it, desire will abandon those pleasures of which the body is the instrument and be concerned only with the pleasure which the soul enjoys independently—if, that is to say, the love of wisdom is more than a mere pretence. Accordingly, such a one will be temperate and no lover of money; for he will be the last person to care about the things for the sake of which money is eagerly sought and lavishly spent.

[G] That is true.

[S] Again, in seeking to distinguish the philosophic nature, you must not overlook the least touch of meanness. Nothing could be more contrary than pettiness to a mind constantly bent on grasping the whole of things, both divine and human.

[G] Quite true.

[S] And do you suppose that one who is so high-minded and whose thought can contemplate all time and all existence will count this life of man a matter of much concern?

[G] No, he could not.

[S] So for such a man death will have no terrors.

[G] None.

[S] A mean and cowardly nature, then, can have no part in the genuine pursuit of wisdom.

[G] I think not.

[S] And if a man is temperate and free from the love of money, meanness, pretentiousness, and cowardice, he will not be hard to deal with or dishonest. So, as another indication of the philosophic temper, you will observe whether, from youth up, he is fair-minded, gentle, and sociable.

[G] Certainly.

[S] Also you will not fail to notice whether he is quick or slow to learn. No one can be expected to take a reasonable delight in a task in which much painful effort makes little headway. And if he cannot retain what he learns, his forgetfulness will leave no room in his head for knowledge; and so, having all his toil for nothing, he can only end by hating himself as well as his fruitless occupation. We must not, then, count a forgetful mind as competent to pursue wisdom; we must require a good memory.

{G} By all means.

{S} Further, there is in some natures a crudity and awkwardness that can only tend to a lack of measure and proportion; and there is a close affinity between proportion and truth. Hence, besides our other requirements, we shall look for a mind endowed with measure and grace, which will be instinctively drawn to see every reality in its true light.

{G} Yes.

{S} Well then, now that we have enumerated the qualities of a mind destined to take its full part in the apprehension of reality, have you any doubt about their being indispensable and all necessarily going together?

{G} None whatever.

{S} Then have you any fault to find with a pursuit which none can worthily follow who is not by nature quick to learn and to remember, magnanimous and gracious, the friend and kinsman of truth, justice, courage, temperance?

Plato said that genuine philosophers are "those whose passion it is to see the truth." For Plato, unlike the Sophists, standards of beauty, justice, and goodness exist that are universally valid—that apply to all peoples at all times. Plato held that these standards are in a higher world, the realm of Forms or Ideas. This world of Forms is known only through the mind, not the senses. For example, a sculptor observes many bodies but they all possess flaws; in his mind's eye he perceives the world of Ideas and tries to reproduce with his art the perfect human form. Plato says that the ordinary person, basing opinion on everyday experience, has an imperfect understanding of beauty, goodness, and justice, whereas the philosopher, through reason, reaches beyond sense perception to the realm of Forms and discovers truth. Such people are the natural

rulers of the state; only they are capable of a correct understanding of justice; only they have the wisdom to reform the state in the best interests of all its citizens.

The distinction between a higher world of truth and a lower world of imperfection, deception, and illusion is illustrated in Plato's famous Allegory of the Cave. Plato, through the dialogue of Socrates and Glaucon, compares those persons without a knowledge of the Forms to prisoners in a dark cave.

---

{S} Next, said I, here is a parable to illustrate the degrees in which our nature may be enlightened or unenlightened. Imagine the condition of men living in a sort of cavernous chamber underground, with an entrance open to the light and a long passage all down the cave. Here they have been from childhood, chained by the leg and also by the neck, so that they cannot move and can see only what is in front of them, because the chains will not let them turn their heads. At some distance higher up is the light of a fire burning behind them; and between the prisoners and the fire is a track with a parapet built along it, like the screen at a puppet-show, which hides the performers while they show their puppets over the top.

{G} I see, said he.

{S} Now behind this parapet imagine persons carrying along various artificial objects, including figures of men and animals in wood or stone or other materials, which project above the parapet. Naturally, some of these persons will be talking, others silent.

{G} It is a strange picture, he said, and a strange sort of prisoners.

{S} Like ourselves, I replied; for in the first place prisoners so confined would have seen nothing of themselves or of one another, except the shadows thrown by the fire-light on the wall of the Cave facing them, would they?

{G} Not if all their lives they had been prevented from moving their heads.

{S} And they would have seen as little of the objects carried past.

{G} Of course.

[S] Now, if they could talk to one another, would they not suppose that their words referred only to those passing shadows which they saw?

[G] Necessarily.

[S] And suppose their prison had an echo from the wall facing them? When one of the people crossing behind them spoke, they could only suppose that the sound came from the shadow passing before their eyes.

[G] No doubt.

[S] In every way, then, such prisoners would recognize as reality nothing but the shadows of those artificial objects.

[G] Inevitably. . . .

---

To the prisoners chained in the cave, the shadows of the artificial objects constitute reality. When a freed prisoner ascends from the cave to the sunlight, he sees a totally different world. Returning to the cave, he tries to tell the prisoners that the shadows are only poor imitations of reality, but they laugh at him, for their opinions have been shaped by the only world they know. The meaning of the parable is clear: the philosophers who ascend to the higher world of Forms possess true knowledge; everyone else possesses mere opinions, deceptive beliefs, and illusions. The philosophers have a duty to guide the ignorant.

---

[S] Now consider what would happen if their release from the chains and the healing of their unwisdom should come about in this way. Suppose one of them were set free and forced suddenly to stand up, turn his head, and walk with eyes lifted to the light; all these movements would be painful, and he would be too dazzled to make out the objects whose shadows he had been used to see. What do you think he would say, if someone told him that what he had formerly seen was meaningless illusion, but now, being somewhat nearer to reality and turned towards more real objects, he was getting a truer view? Suppose further that he were shown the various objects being car-

ried by and were made to say, in reply to questions, what each of them was. Would he not be perplexed and believe the objects now shown him to be not so real as what he formerly saw?

[G] Yes, not nearly so real.

[S] And if he were forced to look at the fire-light itself, would not his eyes ache, so that he would try to escape and turn back to the things which he could see distinctly, convinced that they really were clearer than these other objects now being shown to him?

[G] Yes.

[S] And suppose someone were to drag him away forcibly up the steep and rugged ascent and not let him go until he had hauled him out into the sunlight, would he not suffer pain and vexation at such treatment, and, when he had come out into the light, find his eyes so full of its radiance that he could not see a single one of the things that he was now told were real?

[G] Certainly he would not see them all at once.

[S] He would need, then, to grow accustomed before he could see things in that upper world. At first it would be easiest to make out shadows, and then the images of men and things reflected in water, and later on the things themselves. After that, it would be easier to watch the heavenly bodies and the sky itself by night, looking at the light of the moon and stars rather than the Sun and the Sun's light in the day-time.

[G] Yes, surely.

[S] Last of all, he would be able to look at the Sun and contemplate its nature, not as it appears when reflected in water or any alien medium, but as it is in itself in its own domain.

[G] No doubt.

[S] And now he would begin to draw the conclusion that it is the Sun that produces the seasons and the course of the year and controls everything in the visible world, and moreover is in a way the cause of all that he and his companions used to see.

[G] Clearly he would come at last to that conclusion.

[S] Then if he called to mind his fellow prisoners and what passed for wisdom in his former dwelling place, he would surely think himself happy in the change and be sorry for them. They may have had a practice of honouring and commending one another, with prizes for the man who had the keenest eye for the passing shadows and the best memory for the order in which they followed or accompanied one another, so that he could make a good guess as to which was going to come next. Would our released prisoner be likely to covet those prizes or to envy the men exalted to honour and power in the Cave? Would he not feel like Homer's Achilles, that he would far sooner "be on earth as a hired servant in the house of a landless man" or endure anything rather than go back to his old beliefs and live in the old way?

[G] Yes, he would prefer any fate to such a life.

[S] Now imagine what would happen if he went down again to take his former seat in the Cave. Coming suddenly out of the sunlight, his eyes would be filled with darkness. He might be required once more to deliver his opinion on those shadows, in competition with the prisoners who had never been released, while his eyesight was still dim and unsteady; and it might take some time to become used to the darkness. They would laugh at him and say that he had gone up only to come back with his sight ruined; it was worth no one's while even to attempt the ascent. If they could lay hands on the man who was trying to set them free and lead them up, they would kill him.

[G] Yes, they would.

[S] Every feature in this parable, my dear Glaucon, is meant to fit our earlier analysis. The prison dwelling corresponds to the region revealed to us through the sense of sight, and the firelight within it to the power of the Sun. The ascent to see the things in the upper world you may take as standing for the upward journey of the soul into the region of the intelligible; then you will be in possession of what I surmise, since that is what you wish to be told.

Heaven knows whether it is true; but this, at any rate, is how it appears to me. In the world of knowledge, the last thing to be perceived and only with great difficulty is the essential Form of Goodness. Once it is perceived, the conclusion must follow that, for all things, this is the cause of whatever is right and good; in the visible world it gives birth to light and to the lord of light, while it is itself sovereign in the intelligible world and the parent of intelligence and truth. Without having had a vision of this Form no one can act with wisdom, either in his own life or in matters of state. . . .

---

For Plato, the perfect state, like the well-formed soul, is one governed by reason. By contrast, in the imperfect state, as in the imperfect soul, greed, selfishness, desire, and disorder predominate. Democracy is flawed, said Plato, because most people lack the ability to deal intelligently with matters of state. In the end, said Plato, the democratic state degenerates into anarchy, and the way is prepared for a tyrant. Plato viewed the tyrant as the most despicable of persons. A slave to his own passions, said Plato, the tyrant is like a lunatic who "dreams that he can lord it over all mankind and heaven besides." The character of the philosopher is the very opposite of the sick soul of the tyrant. In the following passage, Plato discusses what he regards as democracy's weaknesses.

---

[S] And when the poor win, the result is a democracy. They kill some of the opposite party, banish others, and grant the rest an equal share in civil rights and government, officials being usually appointed by lot.

[G] Yes, that is how a democracy comes to be established, whether by force of arms or because the other party is terrorized into giving way.

[S] Now what is the character of this new régime? Obviously the way they govern themselves will throw light on the democratic type of man.

[G] No doubt.

[S] First of all, they are free. Liberty and free speech are rife everywhere; anyone is allowed to do what he likes.

[G] Yes, so we are told.

[S] That being so, every man will arrange his own manner of life to suit his pleasure. The result will be a greater variety of individuals than under any other constitution. So it may be the finest of all, with its variegated pattern of all sorts of characters. Many people may think it the best, just as women and children might admire a mixture of colours of every shade in the pattern of a dress. At any rate if we are in search of a constitution, here is a good place to look for one. A democracy is so free that it contains a sample of every kind; and perhaps anyone who intends to found a state, as we have been doing, ought first to visit this emporium of constitutions and choose the model he likes best.

[G] He will find plenty to choose from.

[S] Here, too, you are not obliged to be in authority, however competent you may be, or to submit to authority, if you do not like it; you need not fight when your fellow citizens are at war, nor remain at peace when they do, unless you want peace; and though you may have no legal right to hold office or sit on juries, you will do so all the same if the fancy takes you. . . .

. . . When he [the democrat] is told that some pleasures should be sought and valued as arising from desires of a higher order, others chastised and enslaved because the desires are base, he will shut the gates of the citadel against the messengers of truth, shaking his head and declaring that one appetite is as good as another and all must have their equal rights. So he spends his days indulging the pleasure of the moment, now intoxicated with wine and music, and then taking to a spare diet and drinking nothing but water; one day in hard training, the next doing nothing at all, the third apparently immersed in study. Every now and then he takes a part in politics, leaping to his feet to say or do whatever comes into his

head. . . . His life is subject to no order or restraint, and he has no wish to change an existence which he calls pleasant, free, and happy.

That well describes the life of one whose motto is liberty and equality. . . .

In a democratic country you will be told that liberty is its noblest possession, which makes it the only fit place for a free spirit to live in.

[G] True; that is often said.

[S] Well then, as I was saying, perhaps the insatiable desire for this good to the neglect of everything else may transform a democracy and lead to a demand for despotism. A democratic state may fall under the influence of unprincipled leaders, ready to minister to its thirst for liberty with too deep draughts of this heady wine; and then, if its rulers are not complaisant enough to give it unstinted freedom, they will be arraigned as accursed oligarchs and punished. Law-abiding citizens will be insulted as nonentities who hug their chains; and all praise and honour will be bestowed, both publicly and in private, on rulers who behave like subjects and subjects who behave like rulers. In such a state the spirit of liberty is bound to go to all lengths. . . .

. . . The parent falls into the habit of behaving like the child, and the child like the parent: the father is afraid of his sons, and they show no fear or respect for their parents, in order to assert their freedom. . . . To descend to smaller matters, the schoolmaster timidly flatters his pupils, and the pupils make light of their masters as well as of their attendants. Generally speaking, the young copy their elders, argue with them, and will not do as they are told; while the old, anxious not to be thought disagreeable tyrants, imitate the young and condescend to enter into their jokes and amusements. . . .

Putting all these items together, you can see the result: the citizens become so sensitive that they resent the slightest application of control as intolerable tyranny, and in their resolve to have no master they end by disregarding even the law, written or unwritten.

[G] Yes, I know that only too well.

[S] Such then, I should say, is the seed, so full of fair promise, from which springs despotism.

## REVIEW QUESTIONS

1. According to Plato, what were the character traits a philosopher should possess? What traits should he avoid?
2. In terms of the Allegory of the Cave, what is real and what is illusion?
3. Why did Plato believe that philosophers would make the best rulers?
4. In Plato's view, what were the principal arguments against democracy? What is your assessment of his critique?

---

## 12 Aristotle: Science, Politics, and Ethics

Aristotle (384–322 B.C.) was born at Stagira, a Greek city-state on the Macedonian coast. About 367 B.C., he came to Athens to study with Plato, and he remained a member of Plato's Academy for twenty years. In 342 B.C., Philip II, king of Macedonia, invited Aristotle to tutor his son Alexander, who was then fourteen years old. When Alexander succeeded Philip and set out to conquer the Persian Empire, Aristotle left Macedonia for Athens, where he opened a school of philosophy called the Lyceum, named for a nearby temple to Apollo Lyceus. Aristotle synthesized the thought of earlier philosophers, including his teacher Plato, and was the leading authority of his day in virtually every field of knowledge.

## Aristotle
## *HISTORY OF ANIMALS, POLITICS, AND NICOMACHEAN ETHICS*

Scientific thinking encompasses both rationalism and empiricism. Rationalism—pursuit of truth through thought alone, independent of experience with the natural world—was advocated by Plato. This approach points in the direction of theoretical mathematics. Like Plato, Aristotle valued reason, but unlike his teacher he also had great respect for the concrete details of nature obtained through sense experience. In *History of Animals,* Aristotle demonstrated his empirical approach: observing nature and collecting, classifying, and analyzing data. Aristotle's empiricism is the foundation of such sciences as geology, botany, and biology. The first excerpt, a careful observation of the development of a chick embryo, illustrates Aristotle's empiricism.

When he turned to the study of politics, Aristotle also followed an empirical methodology. He undertook a series of historical studies of the constitutions of

158 Greek states. The most significant and complete study that has survived describes the constitution of Athens. On the basis of these extensive surveys, Aristotle proceeded to write *Politics,* his masterwork of political philosophy, excerpted in the second reading.

Like Socrates and Plato, Aristotle based his ethics on reason. People could achieve moral well-being, said Aristotle, when they avoided extremes of behavior and rationally chose the way of moderation. In his *Nicomachean Ethics,* dedicated to his son Nicomachus, Aristotle described the "proud man." This passage, excerpted in the third reading, sketches characteristics that make up the Greek ideal of excellence.

## HISTORY OF ANIMALS

. . . With the common hen after three days and three nights there is the first indication of the embryo; with larger birds the interval being longer, with smaller birds shorter. Meanwhile the yolk comes into being, rising towards the sharp end, where the primal element of the egg is situated, and where the egg gets hatched; and the heart appears, like a speck of blood, in the white of the egg. This point beats and moves as though endowed with life, . . . and a membrane carrying bloody fibres now envelops the yolk. . . . A little afterwards the body is differentiated, at first very small and white. The head is clearly distinguished, and in it the eyes, swollen out to a great extent. This condition of the eyes lasts on for a good while, as it is only by degrees that they diminish in size and collapse. At the outset the under portion of the body appears insignificant in comparison with the upper portion. . . . The life-element of the chick is in the white of the egg, and the nutriment comes through the navel-string out of the yolk.

When the egg is now ten days old the chick and all its parts are distinctly visible. The head is still larger than the rest of its body, and the eyes larger than the head, but still devoid of vision. The eyes, if removed about this time, are found to be larger than beans, and black; if the cuticle be peeled off them there is a white and cold liquid inside, quite glittering in the sunlight, but there is no hard substance whatsoever. Such is the condition of the head and eyes. At this time also the larger internal organs are visible. . . .

About the twentieth day, if you open the egg and touch the chick, it moves inside and chirps; and it is already coming to be covered with down, when, after the twentieth day is past, the chick begins to break the shell. The head is situated over the right leg close to the flank, and the wing is placed over the head. . . .

---

In the following selection from *Politics,* Aristotle begins by defining the nature of a state and its purpose.

---

## POLITICS

It is clear therefore that the state cannot be defined merely as a community dwelling in the same place and preventing its members from wrong-doing and promoting the exchange of goods and services. Certainly all these must be present if there is to be a state, but even the presence of every one of them does not *ipso facto* [by that fact] make a state. The state is intended to enable all, in their households and their kinships, to live *well,* meaning by that a full and satisfying life. . . .

. . . [W]e must lay it down that the political association which we call a state exists not simply for the purpose of living together but for the sake of noble actions. Those who do noble deeds are therefore contributing to the quality of the political association, and those who contribute most are entitled to a larger share [of political power] than those who, though they may be equal or even superior in free birth and family, are inferior in noble deeds and so in the essential goodness that belongs to the *polis.* Similarly, they are entitled to a larger share than those who are superior in riches but inferior in goodness.

---

He then addresses the problem of where the sovereign power of the state ought to reside.

---

. . . "Where ought the sovereign power of the state to reside?" With the people? With the propertied classes? With the good? With one man, the best of all the good? With one man, the tyrant? There are objections to all these. Thus suppose we say the people is the supreme authority, then if they use their numerical superiority to make a distribution of the property of the rich, is not that unjust? It has been done by a valid decision of the sovereign power, yet what can we call it save the very height of injustice? Again, if the majority, having laid their hands on everything, distribute the possessions of the few, they are obviously destroying the state. But that cannot be goodness which destroys its possessor and justice cannot be destructive of the state. So it is clear that this process, though it may be the law, cannot be just. Or, if that is just, the actions taken by a tyrant must be just; his superior power enables him to use force, just as the masses force their will on the rich. Thirdly, if it is just for the few and wealthy to rule, and if they too rob and plunder and help themselves to the goods of the many, is that just? If it is, then it is just in the former case also. The answer clearly is that all these three are bad and unjust. The fourth alternative, that the good should rule and have the supreme authority, is also not free from objection; it means that all the rest must be without official standing, debarred from holding office under the constitution. The fifth alternative, that one man, the best, should rule, is no better; by making the number of rulers fewer we leave still larger numbers without official standing. It might be

objected too that it is a bad thing for any human being, subject to all possible disorders and affections of the human mind, to be the sovereign authority, which ought to be reserved for the law itself. But that will not make any difference to the cases we have been discussing; the law itself may have a bias towards oligarchy or democracy, so that exactly the same results will ensue. . . .

. . . [A]t the moment it would seem that the most defensible, perhaps even the truest, answer to the question would be to say that the majority ought to be sovereign, rather than the best, where the best are few. For it is possible that the many, no one of whom taken singly is a good man, may yet taken all together be better than the few, not individually but collectively, in the same way that a feast to which all contribute is better than one given at one man's expense. For where there are many people, each has some share of goodness and intelligence, and when these are brought together, they become as it were one multiple man with many pairs of feet and hands and many minds. So too in regard to character and powers of perception. That is why the general public is a better judge of works of music and poetry; some judge some parts, some others, but their joint pronouncement is a verdict upon the whole. And it is this assembling in one what was before separate that gives the good man his superiority over any individual man from the masses.

---

Aristotle seeks to determine what is the best constitution. His conclusion reflects the premise developed in his Ethics that moderation, or the middle way, is the path to virtue in all things. So, Aristotle says that in forming a constitution for the state, power should reside in the hands of the middle class rather than the aristocracy or the poor.

---

If we were right when in our *Ethics* we stated that Virtue is a Mean and that the happy life is life free and unhindered and according to virtue, then the best life must be the middle way, [or the mean] . . . between two extremes which it is open to those at either end to attain. And the same principle must be applicable to the goodness or badness of cities and states. For the constitution of a city is really the way it lives.

In all states there are three sections of the community—the very well-off, the very badly-off, and those in between. Seeing therefore that it is agreed that moderation and a middle position are best, it is clear that in the matter of possessions to own a middling amount is best of all. This condition is most obedient to reason, and following reason is just what is difficult both for the exceedingly rich, handsome, strong, and well-born, and for the opposite, the extremely poor, the weak, and the downtrodden. The former commit deeds of violence on a large scale, the latter are delinquent and wicked in petty ways. The misdeeds of the one class are due to *hubris* [overweening pride, arrogance], the misdeeds of the other to rascality. Add the fact that it is among the members of the middle section that you find least reluctance to hold office as well as least eagerness to do so; and both these are detrimental to states. There are other drawbacks about the two extremes. Those who have a super-abundance of all that makes for success, strength, riches, friends, and so forth, neither wish to hold office nor understand the work; and this is ingrained in them from childhood on; even at school they are so full of their superiority that they have never learned to do what they are told. Those on the other hand who are greatly deficient in these qualities are too subservient. So they cannot command and can only obey in a servile régime, while the others cannot obey in any régime and can command only in a master-slave relationship. The result is a state not of free men but of slaves and masters, the one full of envy, the other of contempt. Nothing could be farther removed from friendship or from the whole idea of a shared partnership in a state. Sharing is a token of friendship; one does not share even a journey with people one

does not like. The state aims to consist as far as possible of those who are like and equal, a condition found chiefly among the middle section. And so the best government is certain to be found in this kind of city, whose composition is, we maintain, a natural one. The middle class is also the steadiest element, the least eager for change. They neither covet, like the poor, the possessions of others, nor do others covet theirs, as the poor covet those of the rich. So they live less risky lives, not scheming and not being schemed against. Phocylides's [sixth-century B.C. poet] wish was therefore justified when he wrote "Those in the middle have many advantages; that is where I wish to be in society."

It is clear then both that the political partnership which operates through the middle class is best, and also that those cities have every chance of being well-governed in which the middle class is large, stronger if possible than the other two together, or at any rate stronger than one of them. For the addition of its weight to either side will turn the balance and prevent the extravagances of the opposition. For this reason it is a happy state of affairs when those who take part in the life of the state have a moderate but adequate amount of property; for where one set of people possesses a great deal and the other nothing, the result is either extreme democracy or unmixed oligarchy or a tyranny due to the excesses of the other two. Tyranny often emerges from an over-enthusiastic democracy or from an oligarchy, but much more rarely from middle-class constitutions or from those very near to them.

The superiority of the middle type of constitution is clear also from the fact that it alone is free from fighting among factions. Where the middle element is large, there least of all arise faction and counter-faction among citizens. And for the same reason the larger states are free from danger of splitting; they are strong in the middle. In small states it is easy for the whole body of citizens to become divided into two, leaving no middle at all, and they are nearly all either rich or poor. Democracies too are safer than oligarchies in this respect and longer lasting thanks to their middle class, which is always more numerous and more politically important in democracies than in oligarchies. For when the unpropertied class without the support of a middle class gets on top by weight of numbers, things go badly and they soon come to grief.

---

The following selection from *Ethics* shows how Aristotle's ethical theory rests on the principles of moderation and balance. Aristotle notes that some people become "angry at the wrong things, more than is right, and longer, and cannot be appeased until they inflict vengeance or punishment." On the other extreme, foolish and slavish people endure every insult without defending themselves. Between these extremes is the proud man, "who is angry at the right thing and with the right people, and, further, as he ought, when he ought, and as long as he ought." Even-tempered and moderate in all things, such a man "tends to be unperturbed and not to be led by passion."

---

## ETHICS

... In the first place, then, as has been said, the proud man is concerned with honours; yet he will also bear himself with moderation towards wealth and power and all good or evil fortune, whatever may befall him, and will be neither over-joyed by good fortune nor over-pained by evil. For not even towards honour does he bear himself as if it were a very great thing. . . .

He does not run into trifling dangers, nor is he fond of danger, because he honours few things; but he will face great dangers, and when he is in danger he is unsparing of his life, knowing that there are conditions on which life is not worth having. And he is the sort of man to confer benefits, but he is ashamed of receiving them; for the one is the mark of a supe-

rior, the other of an inferior. And he is apt to confer greater benefits in return; for thus the original benefactor besides being paid will incur a debt to him, and will be the gainer by the transaction. They seem also to remember any service they have done, but not those they have received (for he who receives a service is inferior to him who has done it, but the proud man wishes to be superior), and to hear of the former with pleasure, of the latter with displeasure. . . . It is a mark of the proud man also to ask for nothing or scarcely anything, but to give help readily, and to be dignified towards people who enjoy high position and good fortune, but unassuming towards those of the middle class; for it is a difficult and lofty thing to be superior to the former, but easy to be so to the latter, and a lofty bearing over the former is no mark of ill-breeding, but among humble people it is as vulgar as a display of strength against the weak. Again, it is characteristic of the proud man not to aim at the things commonly held in honour, or the things in which others excel; to be sluggish and to hold back except where great honour or a great work is at stake, and to be a man of few deeds, but of great and notable ones. He must also be open in his hate and in his love (for to conceal one's feelings, i.e. to care less for truth than for what people will think, is a coward's part), and must speak and act openly; for he is free of speech because he is contemptuous, and he is given to telling the truth, except when he speaks in irony to the vulgar. He must be unable to make his life revolve round another, unless it be a friend; for this is slavish, and for this reason all flatterers are servile and people lacking in self-respect are flatterers. Nor is he given to admiration; for nothing to him is great. Nor is he mindful of wrongs; for it is not the part of a proud man to have a long memory, especially for wrongs, but rather to overlook them. Nor is he a gossip; for he will speak neither about himself nor about another, since he cares not to be praised nor for others to be blamed; nor again is he given to praise; and for the same reason he is not an evil-speaker, even about his enemies, except from haughtiness. With regard to necessary or small matters he is least of all men given to lamentation or the asking of favours; for it is the part of one who takes such matters seriously to behave so with respect to them. He is one who will possess beautiful and profitless things rather than profitable and useful ones; for this is more proper to a character that suffices to itself.

Further, a slow step is thought proper to the proud man, a deep voice, and a level utterance; for the man who takes few things seriously is not likely to be hurried, nor the man who thinks nothing great to be excited, while a shrill voice and a rapid gait are the results of hurry and excitement.

Such, then, is the proud man; the man who falls short of him is unduly humble, and the man who goes beyond him is vain.

## REVIEW QUESTIONS

1. What evidence in Aristotle's description of chick embryo development illustrates his use of empirical methods of scientific inquiry?
2. According to Aristotle, what are the characteristic features of a true political community?
3. Why did Aristotle believe that state power was best left in the hands of the middle classes? Why did he fear government by the poor, the tyrant, the few, the good, or the rich?
4. According to Aristotle, how did the "proud man," a man of excellence, relate to others? To worldly success and riches?
5. What kind of moral values did the proud man cultivate?
6. What kind of personal demeanor should a proud man assume?
7. Aristotle urged both self-sufficiency and moderation as guiding principles in human life. In what specific ways would the proud man demonstrate these virtues?

# 13 Hellenistic Philosophy: Epicureanism

Hellenistic philosophy marks a second stage in the evolution of Greek thought. In the Hellenic Age, philosophers dealt primarily with the individual's relationship to the city-state. In the Hellenistic Age, philosophers were concerned with defining the individual's relationship to a wider, often competitive and hostile community that consisted of a plurality of peoples and a variety of cultures. In particular, the later philosophers sought to help people become ethically self-sufficient so that they could attain peace of mind in such an environment. Among the most significant schools of philosophy that emerged during the Hellenistic Age were Stoicism (see pages 124 and 140) and Epicureanism.

Epicureanism was named for its founder, Epicurus (341–270 B.C.), who established a school at Athens in 307 or 306 B.C. To achieve peace of mind, taught Epicurus, one should refrain from worrying about death or pleasing the gods, avoid intense involvements in public affairs, cultivate friendships, and pursue pleasure prudently.

# Epicurus
# THE PRUDENT PURSUIT OF PLEASURE

The following excerpts from Epicurus' works reveal his prescription for achieving emotional well-being. The passages have been grouped according to particular subjects.

## THE GODS

. . . We must grasp this point, that the principal disturbance in the minds of men arises because they think that these celestial bodies are blessed and immortal, and yet have wills and actions and motives inconsistent with these attributes; and because they are always expecting or imagining some everlasting misery [inflicted on them by the gods], such as is depicted in legends, or even fear the loss of feeling in death . . . and, again, because they are brought to this pass not by reasoned opinion, but rather by some irrational presentiment . . . and, by learning the true causes of celestial phenomena and all other occurrences that come to pass from time to time, we shall free ourselves from all which produces the utmost fear in other men.

––––––––

It is vain to ask of the gods what a man is capable of supplying for himself.

## DEATH

. . . So death, the most terrifying of ills, is nothing to us, since so long as we exist, death is not with us; but when death comes, then we do not exist. It does not then concern either the living or the dead, since for the former it is not, and the latter are no more.

But the many at one moment shun death as the greatest of evils, at another yearn for it as a respite from the evils in life. But the wise man neither seeks to escape life nor fears the cessation of life, for neither does life offend him nor does the absence of life seem to be any evil. And just as with food he does not seek simply the larger share and nothing else, but rather the most pleasant, so he seeks to enjoy not the longest period of time, but the most pleasant.

## REASON AND PHILOSOPHY

Let no one when young delay to study philosophy, nor when he is old grow weary of his study. For no one can come too early or too late to secure the health of his soul. And the man who says that the age for philosophy has either not yet come or has gone by is like the man who says that the age for happiness is not yet come to him, or has passed away. Wherefore both when young and old a man must study philosophy, that as he grows old he may be young in blessings through the grateful recollection of what has been and that in youth he may be old as well, since he will know no fear of what is to come. We must then meditate on the things that make our happiness, seeing that when that is with us we have all, but when it is absent we do all to win it.

––––––––

A man cannot dispel his fear about the most important matters if he does not know what is the nature of the universe but suspects the truth of some mythical story. So that without natural science it is not possible to attain our pleasures unalloyed.

––––––––

We must not pretend to study philosophy, but study it in reality: for it is not the appearance of health that we need, but real health.

## LIVING WELL

When, therefore, we maintain that pleasure is the end, we do not mean the pleasures of profligates and those that consist in sensuality, as is supposed by some who are either ignorant or disagree with us or do not understand, but freedom from pain in the body and from trouble in the mind. For it is not continuous drinkings and revellings, nor the satisfaction of lusts, nor the enjoyment of fish and other luxuries of the wealthy table, which produce a pleasant life, but sober reasoning, searching out the motives for all choice and avoidance, and banishing mere opinions, to which are due the greatest disturbance of the spirit.

Of all this the beginning and the greatest good is prudence. Wherefore prudence is a more precious thing even than philosophy; for from prudence are sprung all the other virtues, and it teaches us that it is not possible to live pleasantly without living prudently and honourably and justly. . . .

Of all the things which wisdom acquires to produce the blessedness of the complete life, far the greatest is the possession of friendship.

———

We must release ourselves from the prison of affairs and politics.

———

A free life cannot acquire many possessions, because this is not easy to do without servility to mobs or monarchs. . . .

———

The noble soul occupies itself with wisdom and friendship. . . .

———

The first measure of security is to watch over one's youth and to guard against what makes havoc of all by means of pestering desires.

## REVIEW QUESTIONS

1. What did Epicurus believe were the chief causes of emotional distress among human beings?
2. What advice did he offer for achieving inner peace and happiness?
3. Why did Epicurean teaching represent a radical attack on traditional Greek institutions and values?

# 14 Greek Culture and the Jews in the Hellenistic Age

During the Hellenistic Age, Greek civilization spread to the Near East in the wake of Alexander's conquests, and Mesopotamian, Egyptian, Persian, and Jewish traditions—particularly religious beliefs—moved westwards. Thousands of Greeks settled in newly established cities throughout the ancient Near East, carrying with them Greek urban institutions and culture, laws, cults, educational methods, artistic and architectural styles, customs and dress. The new Hellenistic cities were dominated by a Greek upper class, which recruited native non-Greeks to its ranks to the degree that they became *Hellenized,* that is, adopted the Greek language and lifestyle. Through intermarriage, education in Greek schools, and the prospect of political and economic advantage, many

non-Greeks came to participate in and contribute to a common Greek civilization that spread from the western Mediterranean to the Indus River.

# FIRST BOOK OF MACCABEES
# JEWISH RESISTANCE TO
# FORCED HELLENIZATION

Like other Near Eastern people, the Jews—both in Judea and the Diaspora (Jews
who lived outside Palestine)—came under the influence of Hellenism. As Greek
settlements sprang up in Judea, Jews had increasing contact with Greek soldiers,
artisans, and merchants. Some Jewish scholars came to admire the rich Greek
philosophical tradition. The Hebrew Scriptures were translated into Greek for use
by Greek-speaking Jews, Greek words entered the Hebrew language, and newly
constructed synagogues employed Hellenistic architectural styles. Radical Hell-
enizers, mainly prosperous aristocrats, adopted Greek games, dress, entertainment, and eating habits; these efforts to assimilate pagan ways were resisted by
simple folk and the devout who clung tenaciously to Mosaic law.

The clash of cultures came to a head when the Seleucid king Antiochus IV
(174–163 B.C.) decided to impose Hellenization upon the Jews of Judea. (His
predecessor, Antiochus III, had seized Palestine from Ptolemaic Egypt.) In 167
B.C. he desecrated the Temple in Jerusalem by erecting an altar to Zeus in the
Temple court and offering pigs, unclean animals in Jewish law, as a sacrifice.
He forbade ritual circumcision, the sign of the covenant between Jews and
their god, Yahweh. In the following selection from the first book of the Maccabees, an anonymous Jewish historian writing shortly after 134 B.C. describes
the causes of great rebellion against forced Hellenization. The text reveals that
some Jews were already so Hellenized that they supported the policies of the
Seleucid king.

The outrage of loyalist Jews against forced Hellenization was epitomized by
Mattathias whose battle cry was "Let everybody who is zealous for the Law and
stands by the covenant come out after me." Led by one of Mattathias' sons,
Judah the Maccabeus (the "hammerer"), the Jews successfully fought the Syrians, venting their anger also against the Hellenized Jews who sided with Antiochus. In 140 B.C., the Jews, under Judah's brother Simon, regained their
independence.

## 1 MAC 1:41–64: THE PERSECUTION

[41]Then the king wrote to his whole kingdom
that all should be one people, [42]and that each
should give up his customs. [43]All the Gentiles
accepted the command of the king. Many even
from Israel gladly adopted his religion; they
sacrificed to idols and profaned the sabbath.

[44]And the king sent letters by messengers to
Jerusalem and the cities of Judah; he directed
them to follow customs strange to the land,
[45]to forbid burnt offerings and sacrifices and
drink offerings in the sanctuary, to profane
sabbaths and feasts, [46]to defile the sanctuary
and the priests, [47]to build altars and sacred
precincts and shrines for idols, to sacrifice

swine and unclean animals, [48]and to leave their sons uncircumcised. They were to make themselves abominable by everything unclean and profane, [49]so that they should forget the [Mosaic] law and change all the ordinances. [50]"And whoever does not obey the command of the king shall die."

[51]In such words he wrote to his whole kingdom. And he appointed inspectors over all the people and commanded the cities of Judah to offer sacrifice, city by city. [52]Many of the people, every one who forsook the law, joined them, and they did evil in the land; [53]they drove Israel into hiding in every place of refuge they had.

[54]Now on the fifteenth day of Chislev [in 167 B.C.] they erected a desolating sacrilege upon the altar of burnt offering. They also built altars in the surrounding cities of Judah, [55]and burned incense at the doors of the houses and in the streets. [56]The books of the law which they found they tore to pieces and burned with fire. [57]Where the book of the covenant was found in the possession of any one, or if any one adhered to the law, the decree of the king condemned him to death. [58]They kept using violence against Israel, against those found month after month in the cities. [59]And on the twenty-fifth day of the month they offered sacrifice on the altar which was upon the altar of burnt offering. [60]According to the decree, they put to death the women who had their children circumcised, [61]and their families and those who circumcised them; and they hung the infants from their mothers' necks.

[62]But many in Israel stood firm and were resolved in their hearts not to eat unclean food. [63]They chose to die rather than to be defiled by food or to profane the holy covenant; and they did die. [64]And very great wrath came upon Israel.

---

# Philo of Alexandria
# APPRECIATION OF GREEK CULTURE AND SYNTHESIS OF REASON AND REVELATION

Living in the cosmopolitan world of Alexandria dominated by Greek thought and culture, Alexandrian Jews felt compelled to demonstrate that their faith was not incompatible with reason, that there was no insurmountable gulf separating Mosaic religion from Greek philosophy. The leading figure in this effort to explain and justify the Hebrew Scriptures in terms of Greek philosophy—to prove that Mosaic law, revealed by God, was compatible with truth discovered by natural reason—was Philo of Alexandria (c. 20 B.C.–50 A.D.). Scion of a wealthy, aristocratic Jewish family, Philo was intimately familiar with the Greek cultural tradition and greatly admired Plato. He believed that Plato's view of God, as presented in the *Timaeus,* was compatible with Hebrew Scripture. In that work Plato had posited an eternal God who had existed prior to his creation of the world and continued to exist as an incorporeal and transcendent being.

On several points Philo disagreed with Greek philosophy. For example, holding that only God was eternal, he could not accept the Platonic view of the eternity of Ideas or Forms. Nor could he accept the position of Greek philosophy that the laws of nature were inexorable, for this precluded divine miracles. In these and other instances, Philo skillfully used the tools of Greek logic to harmonize differing viewpoints. His blending of Platonism with Scripture would be continued by Christian thinkers who admired Philo's achievement.

In the following selections, Philo expresses his admiration for Greek culture.

There was a time when I had leisure for philosophy and for the contemplation of the universe and its contents, when I made its spirit my own in all its beauty and loveliness and true blessedness, when my constant companions were divine themes and verities, wherein I rejoiced with a joy that never cloyed or sated. I had no base or abject thoughts nor grovelled in search of reputation or of wealth or bodily comforts, but seemed always to be borne aloft into the heights with a soul possessed by some God-sent inspiration, a fellow-traveller with the sun and moon and the whole heaven and universe. Ah then I gazed down from the upper air, and straining the mind's eye beheld, as from some commanding peak, the multitudinous world-wide spectacles of earthly things, and blessed my lot in that I had escaped by main force from the plagues of mortal life. But, as it proved, my steps were dogged by the deadliest of mischiefs, the hater of the good, envy, which suddenly set upon me and ceased not to pull me down with violence till it had plunged me in the ocean of civil cares, in which I am swept away, unable even to raise my head above the water. Yet amid my groans I hold my own, for, planted in my soul from my earliest days I keep the yearning for culture which ever has pity and compassion for me, lifts me up and relieves my pain. To this I owe it that sometimes I raise my head and with the soul's eyes—dimly indeed because the mist of extraneous affairs has clouded their clear vision—I yet make shift to look around me in my desire to inhale a breath of life pure and unmixed with evil. And if unexpectedly I obtain a spell of fine weather and a calm from civil turmoils, I get me wings and ride the waves and almost tread the lower air, wafted by the breezes of knowledge which often urges me to come to spend my days with her, a truant as it were from merciless masters in the shape not only of men but of affairs, which pour in upon me like a torrent from different sides. Yet it is well for me to give thanks to God even for this, that though submerged I am not sucked down into the depths, but can also open the soul's eyes, which in my despair of comforting hope I thought had now lost their sight, and am irradiated by the light of wisdom, and am not given over to lifelong darkness. So behold me daring, not only to read the sacred messages of Moses, but also in my love of knowledge to peer into each of them and unfold and reveal what is not known to the multitude.

———

. . . For instance when first I was incited by the goads of philosophy to desire her I consorted in early youth with one of her handmaids, Grammar, and all that I begat by her, writing, reading and study of the writings of the poets, I dedicated to her mistress. And again I kept company with another, namely Geometry, and was charmed with her beauty, for she shewed symmetry and proportion in every part. Yet I took none of her children for my private use, but brought them as a gift to the lawful wife. Again my ardour moved me to keep company with a third; rich in rhythm, harmony and melody was she, and her name was Music, and from her I begat diatonics, chromatics and enharmonics, conjunct and disjunct melodies, conforming with the consonance of the fourth, fifth or octave intervals. And again of none of these did I make a secret hoard, wishing to see the lawful wife a lady of wealth with a host of servants ministering to her.

Philo sought to demonstrate the truth of Judaism to a non-Jewish culture. In the selections below, he employs the categories of Greek philosophy to provide proof for God's existence and his creation of the universe.

---

Doubtless hard to unriddle and hard to apprehend is the Father and Ruler of all, but that is no reason why we should shrink from searching for Him. But in such searching two principal questions arise which demand the consideration of the genuine philosopher. One is whether the Deity exists, a question necessitated by those who practise atheism, the worst form of wickedness, the other is what the Deity is in essence. Now to answer the first question does not need much labour, but the second is not only difficult but perhaps impossible to solve. Still, both must be examined. We see then that any piece of work always involves the knowledge of a workman. Who can look upon statues or painting without thinking at once of a sculptor or painter? Who can see clothes or ships or houses without getting the idea of a weaver and a shipwright and a housebuilder? And when one enters a well-ordered city in which the arrangements for civil life are very admirably managed, what else will he suppose but that this city is directed by good rulers? So then he who comes to the truly Great City, this world, and beholds hills and plains teeming with animals and plants, the rivers, spring-fed or winter torrents, streaming along, the seas with their expanses, the air with its happily tempered phases, the yearly seasons passing into each other, and then the sun and moon ruling the day and night, and the other heavenly bodies fixed or planetary and the whole firmament revolving in rhythmic order, must he not naturally or rather necessarily gain the conception of the Maker and Father and Ruler also? For none of the works of human art is self-made, and the highest art and knowledge is shewn in this universe, so that surely it has been wrought by one of excellent knowledge and absolute perfection. In this way we have gained the conception of the existence of God.

## REVIEW QUESTIONS

1. What is meant by the concept *Hellenization?*
2. Did all Jews react similarly to the process of Hellenization?
3. How did the directives of Antiochus IV violate Jewish beliefs?
4. What Hellenistic elements can be seen in the writings of Philo of Alexandria?

# CHAPTER 4
# *The Roman Republic*

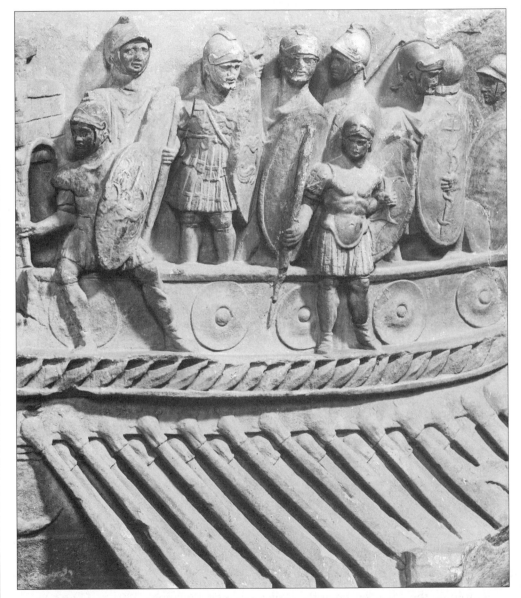

A ROMAN WARSHIP WITH LEGIONNAIRES, on a relief from the Temple of Fortuna Primigenia, first century B.C. Roman soldiers fought on sea as well as on land, conquering nations throughout the Mediterranean area during the eras of the Republic and the Empire. *(Alinari/Art Resource, N.Y.)*

The city-state was the foundation of Greek society in the Hellenic Age; in the Hellenistic Age, Greek cities became subordinate to larger political units, ruled by autocratic monarchs. Hellenistic philosophers conceived of a still broader political arrangement: a world-state in which people of different nationalities were bound together by the ties of common citizenship and law that applied to all. It was Rome's great achievement to construct such a world-state.

Roman history falls into two broad periods—the Republic and the Empire. The Roman Republic began in 509 B.C. with the overthrow of the Etruscan monarchy and lasted until 27 B.C., when Octavian (Augustus) became in effect the first Roman emperor, ending almost five hundred years of republican self-government. For the next five hundred years, Rome would be governed by emperors.

In 264 B.C., when the Roman Republic had established dominion over the Italian peninsula, there were four other great powers in the Mediterranean world. Carthage controlled North Africa, Corsica, Sardinia, and parts of Spain and Sicily. The other powers—Macedonia, Egypt, and Syria—were the three Hellenistic kingdoms carved out of the empire of Alexander the Great. By 146 B.C., Rome had emerged victorious over the other powers, and by 30 B.C. they were all Roman provinces.

The Roman Republic, which had conquered a vast empire, was not destroyed by foreign armies but by internal weaknesses. In the century after 133 B.C., the senate, which had governed Rome well during its march to empire, degenerated into a self-seeking oligarchy; it failed to resolve critical domestic problems and fought to preserve its own power and prestige. When Rome had been threatened by foreign enemies, all classes united in a spirit of patriotism. This social harmony broke down when the threat from outside diminished, and the Republic was torn by internal dissension and civil war.

## 1  Rome's March to World Empire

The Hellenistic Age was characterized by a movement away from the parochial outlook of the city-state to a cosmopolitan world-view. Rome's expansion from a city-state to a world empire that embraced many different nationalities exemplified the universalism of the Hellenistic Age. Polybius (c. 204–c. 122 B.C.), the greatest historian of the era, sought to explain Rome's accomplishment. His world history is a concrete illustration of this cosmopolitanism.

In the tradition of Thucydides, Polybius, also Greek, believed that the duty of the historian was to teach moral lessons, to enlighten and not to entertain.

Like Thucydides, too, he analyzed events with clinical objectivity and looked for laws that might govern the course of history. He wrote: "For as a living creature is rendered wholly useless if deprived of its eyes, so if you take truth from History what is left is but an idle unprofitable tale." But whereas Thucydides wrote about the Peloponnesian War that convulsed the Greek city-states, Polybius took the entire Mediterranean world as his subject. The historian, said Polybius, was required to do more than describe this or that episode; he must assemble the parts in order to obtain a clearer picture of the whole.

# Polybius
# THE ROMAN ARMY

The discipline and dedication of the citizen-soldiers helps explain Rome's success in conquering a world empire. In the following account, Polybius tells how the commanders enforced obedience and fostered heroism.

A court-martial composed of the tribunes immediately sits to try him [a soldier], and if he is found guilty, he is punished by beating (*fustuarium*). This is carried out as follows. The tribune takes a cudgel and lightly touches the condemned man with it, whereupon all the soldiers fall upon him with clubs and stones, and usually kill him in the camp itself. But even those who contrive to escape are no better off. How indeed could they be? They are not allowed to return to their homes, and none of their family would dare to receive such a man into the house. Those who have once fallen into this misfortune are completely and finally ruined. The *optio* [lieutenant] and the *decurio* [sergeant] of the squadron are liable to the same punishment if they fail to pass on the proper orders at the proper moment to the patrols and the *decurio* of the next squadron. The consequence of the extreme severity of this penalty and of the absolute impossibility of avoiding it is that the night watches of the Roman army are faultlessly kept.

The ordinary soldiers are answerable to the tribunes [elected military administrators] and the tribunes to the consuls [commanders]. A tribune, and in the case of the allies a prefect [commander of a large unit], has power to inflict fines, distrain on [confiscate] goods, and

to order a flogging. The punishment of beating to death is also inflicted upon those who steal from the camp, those who give false evidence, those who in full manhood commit homosexual offences, and finally upon anyone who has been punished three times for the same offence. The above are the offences which are punished as crimes. The following actions are regarded as unmanly and dishonourable in a soldier: to make a false report to the tribune of your courage in the field in order to earn distinction; to leave the post to which you have been assigned in a covering force because of fear; and similarly to throw away out of fear any of your weapons on the field of battle. For this reason the men who have been posted to a covering force are often doomed to certain death. This is because they will remain at their posts even when they are overwhelmingly outnumbered on account of their dread of the punishment that awaits them. Again, those who have lost a shield or a sword or any other weapon on the battlefield often hurl themselves upon the enemy hoping that they will either recover the weapon they have lost, or else escape by death from the inevitable disgrace and the humiliations they would suffer at home.

If it ever happens that a large body of men break and run in this way and whole maniples [units of 120 to 300 men] desert their posts under extreme pressure, the officers reject the idea of beating to death or executing all who are guilty, but the solution they adopt is as effective as it is terrifying. The tribune calls the legion [large military unit] on parade and brings to the front those who are guilty of having left the ranks. He then reprimands them sharply, and finally chooses by lot some five or eight or twenty of the offenders, the number being calculated so that it represents about a tenth[1] of those who have shown themselves guilty of cowardice. Those on whom the lot has fallen are mercilessly clubbed to death in the manner I have already described. The rest are put on rations of barley instead of wheat, and are ordered to quarter themselves outside the camp in a place which has no defences. The danger and the fear of drawing the fatal lot threatens every man equally, and since there is no certainty on whom it may fall, and the public disgrace of receiving rations of barley is shared by all alike, the Romans have adopted the best possible practice both to inspire terror and to repair the harm done by any weakening of their warlike spirit.

The Romans also have an excellent method of encouraging young soldiers to face danger. Whenever any have especially distinguished themselves in a battle, the general assembles the troops and calls forward those he considers to have shown exceptional courage. He praises them first for their gallantry in action and for anything in their previous conduct which is particularly worthy of mention, and then he distributes gifts such as the following: to a man who has wounded one of the enemy, a spear; to one who has killed and stripped an enemy, a cup

if he is in the infantry, or horse-trappings if in the cavalry—originally the gift was simply a lance. These presentations are not made to men who have wounded or stripped an enemy in the course of a pitched battle, or at the storming of a city, but to those who during a skirmish or some similar situation in which there is no necessity to engage in single combat, have voluntarily and deliberately exposed themselves to danger.

At the storming of a city the first man to scale the wall is awarded a crown of gold. In the same way those who have shielded and saved one of their fellow-citizens or of the allies are honoured with gifts from the consul, and the men whose lives they have preserved present them of their own free will with a crown; if not, they are compelled to do so by the tribunes who judge the case. Moreover, a man who has been saved in this way reveres his rescuer as a father for the rest of his life and must treat him as if he were a parent. And so by means of such incentives even those who stay at home feel the impulse to emulate such achievements in the field no less than those who are present and see and hear what takes place. For the men who receive these trophies not only enjoy great prestige in the army and soon afterwards in their homes, but they are also singled out for precedence in religious processions when they return. On these occasions nobody is allowed to wear decorations save those who have been honoured for their bravery by the consuls, and it is the custom to hang up the trophies they have won in the most conspicuous places in their houses, and to regard them as proofs and visible symbols of their valour. So when we consider this people's almost obsessive concern with military rewards and punishments, and the immense importance which they attach to both, it is not surprising that they emerge with brilliant success from every war in which they engage.

[1]This custom is the origin of the word *decimate,* from the Latin *decem,* ten.

## REVIEW QUESTIONS

1. How did the Romans ensure good discipline among their soldiers?
2. What factors mentioned by Polybius help explain Rome's emergence as a great power?

## 2  The Punic Wars

In 264 B.C., Rome, which had just completed its conquest of Italy, went to war with Carthage, the dominant power in the western Mediterranean. A threat to the north Sicilian city of Messana (now Messina) was the immediate cause of the war. Rome feared that Carthage might use Messana as a springboard from which to attack the cities of southern Italy, which were allied to Rome, or to interfere with their trade. The First Punic War (264–241 B.C.) was a grueling conflict; drawing manpower from its loyal allies, Rome finally prevailed. Carthage surrendered Sicily to Rome, and three years later Rome seized the large islands of Corsica and Sardinia, west of Italy, from a weakened Carthage.

# Livy
# THE SECOND PUNIC WAR: THE THREAT FROM HANNIBAL

Carthaginian expansion in Spain led to the Second Punic War (218–201 B.C.). The Carthaginian army was led by Hannibal (247–183 B.C.), whose military genius impressed and frightened Rome. Hannibal brought the battle to Rome by leading his seasoned army, including war elephants, across the Alps into Italy.

Hannibal demonstrated his superb generalship at the battle of Cannae in 216 B.C., where the Carthaginians destroyed a Roman army of sixty thousand. Hannibal removed some of his soldiers in the center and commanded the thin line to retreat as the Romans charged. Believing that the enemy was on the run, the Romans continued their headlong thrust into the Carthaginian center. Then, according to plan, Carthaginian troops stationed on the wings attacked the Roman flanks and the cavalry closed in on the Roman rear, completely encircling the Roman troops. News of the disaster, one of the worst in the Republic's history, brought anguish to Romans, who feared that Hannibal would march on the capital itself. Adding to Rome's distress was the desertion of some of its Italian allies to Hannibal. In the following passage, the Roman historian Livy (59 B.C.–A.D. 17) describes the mood in Rome after Cannae.

. . . Never, without an enemy actually within the gates, had there been such terror and confusion in the city [Rome]. To write of it is beyond my strength, so I shall not attempt to describe what any words of mine would only make less than the truth. In the previous year a consul and his army had been lost at Trasimene [location of an overwhelming defeat for Rome], and now there was news not merely of another similar blow, but of a multiple calamity—two consular armies annihilated, both consuls[1] dead, Rome left without a

---

[1]The consuls served dual offices as elected magistrates of Rome in peacetime and commanders-in-chief of the Roman army.

force in the field, without a commander, without a single soldier, Apulia and Samnium [two provinces in southern Italy] in Hannibal's hands, and now nearly the whole of Italy overrun. No other nation in the world could have suffered so tremendous a series of disasters, and not been overwhelmed. It was unparalleled in history: the naval defeat off the Aegates islands,* a defeat which forced the Carthaginians to abandon Sicily and Sardinia and suffer themselves to pay taxes and tribute to Rome; the final defeat in Africa to which Hannibal himself afterwards succumbed—neither the one nor the other was in any way comparable to what Rome had now to face, except in the fact that they were not borne with so high a courage.

The praetors[2] Philus and Pomponius summoned the Senate[3] to meet . . . to consider the defence of the City, as nobody doubted that Hannibal, now that the armies were destroyed, would attack Rome—the final operation to crown his victory. It was not easy to work out a plan: their troubles, already great enough, were made worse by the lack of firm news; the streets were loud with the wailing and weeping of women, and nothing yet being clearly known, living and dead alike were being mourned in nearly every house in the city. In these circumstances, Quintus Fabius Maximus[4] put forward some proposals: riders, he suggested, lightly equipped, should be sent out along the Appian and Latin Ways[5] to

question any survivors they might meet roaming the countryside, and report any tidings they could get from them of what had happened to the consuls and the armies. If the gods, in pity for the empire, had suffered any of the Roman name to survive, they should inquire where they were, where Hannibal went after the battle, what his plans were, what he was doing, and what he was likely to do next. The task of collecting this information should be entrusted to vigorous and active men. There was also a task, Fabius suggested, for the Senate itself to perform, as there was a lack of public officers: this was, to get rid of the general confusion in the city and restore some sort of order. Women must be forbidden to appear out of doors, and compelled to stay in their homes; family mourning should be checked, and silence imposed everywhere; anyone with news to report should be taken to the praetors, and all individuals should await in their homes the news which personally concerned them. Furthermore, guards should be posted at the gates to prevent anyone from leaving the city, and every man and woman should be made to believe that there was no hope of safety except within the walls of Rome. Once, he ended, the present noise and disorder were under control, then would be the proper time to recall the Senate and debate measures for defence.

The proposals of Fabius won unanimous support. The city magistrates cleared the crowds out of the forum and the senators went off to restore some sort of order in the streets. . . .

How much more serious was the defeat at Cannae than those which had preceded it can be seen by the behaviour of Rome's allies: before that fatal day their loyalty had remained unshaken; now it began to waver, for the simple reason that they despaired of the survival of Roman power. The following peoples went over to the Carthaginian cause: the Atellani, Calatini, Hirpini, some of the Apulians, all the Samnites except the Pentri, the Bruttii, the

---

*The end of the First Punic war in 241 B.C.

[2]Praetors were magistrates who governed the city of Rome when the consuls were absent.

[3]The senate, originally drawn from the patrician caste, was the true ruler of Rome. It advised the magistrates on all matters of public policy.

[4]Fabius (Quintus Fabius Maximum Verrucosus, nicknamed "the Delayer," d. 203 B.C.) was elected consul several times, but his tactics in trying to avoid pitched battles displeased the Romans. However, Fabius' successors were totally defeated at Cannae, and Fabius, elected consul for the fifth time, recaptured Tarentum in 209.

[5]The Appian Way, parts of which exist today, was the main highway from Rome southward to Campania. The Latin Way (Via Latina), a parallel route, passed through hill towns before rejoining the Appian Way.

Lucanians, the Uzentini, and nearly all the Greek settlements on the coast, namely Tarentum, Metapontum, Croton, and Locri, and all the Gauls on the Italian side of the Alps.

But neither the defeats they had suffered nor the subsequent defection of all these allied peoples moved the Romans ever to breathe a word about peace.

---

# Appian of Alexandria
# THE THIRD PUNIC WAR:
# THE DESTRUCTION OF CARTHAGE

Despite his brilliant victory at Cannae, Hannibal lacked the manpower to deal Rome a knockout blow, and the Romans, respecting Hannibal's generalship, refused to engage his army in another major encounter. Finally, when Rome invaded North Africa and threatened Carthage, Hannibal quit Italy to defend his homeland and was defeated at the battle of Zama in 202 B.C.

Although Carthage, now a second-rate power, no longer posed a threat, Rome started the Third Punic War in 149 B.C. Driven by old hatreds and the traumatic memory of Hannibal's near conquest of Italy, Rome resolved to destroy Carthage. After Carthage fell in 146 B.C., Rome sold the survivors into slavery, obliterated the city, and turned the land into a province, which was named Africa. The savage and irrational behavior of Rome toward a helpless Carthage showed an early deterioration in senatorial leadership. In the following passage, Appian of Alexandria (A.D. 95–c. 165) describes the destruction of Carthage by the Romans under Scipio Aemilianus (185–129 B.C.).

Now Scipio hastened to the attack of Byrsa, the strongest part of the city [of Carthage], where the greater part of the inhabitants had taken refuge. There were three streets ascending from the forum to this fortress, along which, on either side, were houses built closely together and six stories high, from which the Romans were assailed with missiles. They were compelled, therefore, to possess themselves of the first ones and use those as a means of expelling the occupants of the next. When they had mastered the first, they threw timbers from one to another over the narrow passageways, and crossed as on bridges. While war was raging in this way on the roofs, another fight was going on among those who met each other in the streets below. All places were filled with groans, shrieks, shouts, and every kind of agony. Some were stabbed, others were hurled alive from the roofs to the pavement, some of them alighting on the heads of spears or other pointed weapons, or swords. No one dared to set fire to the houses on account of those who were still on the roofs, until Scipio reached Byrsa. Then he set fire to the three streets all together, and gave orders to keep the passageways clear of burning material so that the army might move back and forth freely.

Then came new scenes of horror. As the fire spread and carried everything down, the soldiers did not wait to destroy the buildings little by little, but all in a heap. So the crashing grew louder, and many corpses fell with the stones into the midst. Others were seen still living, especially old men, women, and young children who had hidden in the inmost nooks of the houses, some of them wounded, some more or less burned, and uttering piteous cries. Still others, thrust out and falling from such a height with the stones, timbers, and fire, were torn asunder in all shapes of horror, crushed and mangled. Nor was this the end of their miseries, for the street cleaners, who were removing the rubbish with axes, mattocks, and forks, and making the roads passable, tossed with these instruments the dead and the living together into holes in the ground, dragging them along like sticks and stones and turning them over with their iron tools. Trenches were filled with men. Some who were thrown in head foremost, with their legs sticking out of the ground, writhed a long time. Others fell with their feet downward and their heads above ground. Horses ran over them, crushing their faces and skulls, not purposely on the part of the riders, but in their headlong haste. Nor did the street cleaners do these things on purpose; but the tug of war, the glory of approaching victory, the rush of the soldiery, the orders of the officers, the blast of the trumpets, tribunes and centurions[1] marching their cohorts hither and thither—all together made everybody frantic and heedless of the spectacles under their eyes.

Six days and nights were consumed in this kind of fighting, the soldiers being changed so that they might not be worn out with toil, slaughter, want of sleep, and these horrid sights. . . .

---

[1]Centurions were noncommissioned officers, each commanding a hundred men; attached to each legion were six military tribunes, who had been voted in by the citizens of Rome in the general elections.

Scipio, beholding this city, which had flourished 700 years from its foundation and had ruled over so many lands, islands, and seas, rich with arms and fleets, elephants and money, equal to the mightiest monarchies but far surpassing them in bravery and high spirit (since without ships or arms, and in the face of famine, it had sustained continuous war for three years), now come to its end in total destruction—Scipio, beholding this spectacle, is said to have shed tears and publicly lamented the fortune of the enemy. After meditating by himself a long time and reflecting on the rise and fall of cities, nations, and empires, as well as of individuals, upon the fate of Troy, that once proud city, upon that of the Assyrians, the Medes, and the Persians, greatest of all, and later the splendid Macedonian empire, either voluntarily or otherwise the words of the poet escaped his lips:—

"The day shall come in which our
    sacred Troy
And Priam,[2] and the people over
    whom
Spear-bearing Priam rules, shall
    perish all."
        (*Iliad,* vi, 448, 449;
        Bryant's translation.)

Being asked by Polybius in familiar conversation (for Polybius had been his tutor) what he meant by using these words, he said that he did not hesitate frankly to name his own country, for whose fate he feared when he considered the mutability of human affairs. And Polybius wrote this down just as he heard it.

---

[2]Priam, in Homer's epic poem *The Iliad,* was the king of Troy at the time of the Trojan War.

## REVIEW QUESTIONS

1. Ancient historians believed their task was to shape the character of youth through edifying accounts of the experiences of past generations. What lessons did Livy intend to teach in his account of the Punic Wars?
2. What do you think prompted Scipio Aemilianus to quote the lines from Homer's *Iliad?*

## 3  Exploitation of the Provinces

The Greeks expressed their genius in philosophy and the arts, the Romans in government and law. Rome generally allowed its subjects a large measure of self-government, respected local religions and customs, and reduced the constant warfare that had plagued the Mediterranean world. But there was also a negative side to Roman rule. The conquest of a great number of lands and peoples gave the Roman ruling class innumerable opportunities to enhance their wealth by exploiting the empire's subjects. Senators appointed to govern provinces frequently amassed large fortunes through bribery, extortion, the confiscation of properties, and the enslavement and sale of the captured populace.

Efforts by provincial victims to seek justice by prosecuting the malefactors before the extortion court in Rome were often thwarted by collusion between the senators accused and the senators who served as judges and jurors. One such case was the trial of Gaius Verres, ex-governor of Sicily, who was prosecuted for his crimes by the great orator Marcus Tullius Cicero (106–43 B.C.).

# Cicero
# ORATION AGAINST VERRES

Cicero, acting on behalf of the Sicilians, portrays Verres' crimes while the defendant was governor of Sicily. He links them to the greater problem of the disastrous decline in the moral reputation and authority of the whole senatorial order. After Cicero's devastating revelations, Verres, recognizing the futility of a defense, fled into exile.

. . . Nothing, [Verres] declares, is too sacred to be corrupted by money; nothing too strong to resist its attack. If the secrecy with which his projects are put into effect were comparable to the criminality which inspires their design, he might, to some extent or at some stage, have kept them from my notice. But so far, conveniently enough, his unbelievable unscrupulousness has been matched by a peculiar degree of folly. He has grabbed his wealth without any attempt at concealment; and he has let everyone see the schemes and intrigues by which he hopes to corrupt his judges. . . .

But the most conspicuous and numerous instances and demonstrations of his criminal-ity come from his governorship in Sicily. For three long years he so thoroughly despoiled and pillaged the province that its restoration to its previous state is out of the question. A succession of honest governors, over a period of many years, could scarcely achieve even a partial rehabilitation. While Verres was governor the Sicilians enjoyed the benefit neither of their own laws, nor of the Roman Senate's decrees, nor even of the rights to which everyone in the world is entitled. All the property that anyone in Sicily still has for his own today is merely what happened to escape the attention of this avaricious lecher, or survived his glutted appetites.

In Sicily, during those three years, not a single lawsuit was decided without his connivance. Inheritances from a father or grandfather, however authentic, were cancelled—if Verres said the word. Under a new and immoral ruling, the properties of farmers were robbed of countless sums. Allies of unassailable loyalty were treated as enemies; Roman citizens were tortured and put to death like slaves. Criminals of the deepest dye would bribe their way to acquittal, while men of impeccable honesty were prosecuted in their absence, and convicted and banished unheard. Powerfully fortified harbours, great and well-protected cities, were left open for pirates and robbers to attack. Sicilian soldiers and sailors, allies and friends of ours, were starved to death. Splendid, beautifully equipped fleets were squandered and thrown away. It was an appalling disgrace for our country.

Then again, ancient monuments given by wealthy monarchs to adorn the cities of Sicily, or presented or restored to them by victorious Roman generals, were ravaged and stripped bare, one and all, by this same governor. Nor was it only statues and public monuments that he treated in this manner. Among the most sacred and revered Sicilian sanctuaries, there was not a single one which he failed to plunder; not one single god, if only Verres detected a good work of art or a valuable antique, did he leave in the possession of the Sicilians.

When I turn to his adulteries and similar outrages, considerations of decency deter me from giving details of these loathsome manifestations of his lusts. Besides, I do not want, by describing them, to worsen the calamities of the people who have not been permitted to save their children and their wives from Verres' sexual passions. It is, however, incontestable that he himself did not take the slightest precaution to prevent these abominations from becoming universally known. On the contrary, I believe that every man alive who has heard the name of Verres would be able to recount the atrocities which he has committed. . . .

---

Since the Senate took control of the extortion court ten years earlier, says Cicero, worsening corruption has sullied the reputation of the entire senatorial order. Such behavior has grave political consequences.

---

For I am going to disclose to you, with full corroborating evidence, the whole story of all the abominable crimes which have been perpetrated in the courts during these ten years since they were first transferred to the Senate. Gentlemen, here are the facts which I am going to reveal to the people of Rome. While the Order of Knights[1] controlled the courts, for nearly fifty years not one single knight who was a judge incurred the slightest suspicion of allowing his verdict to be influenced by a bribe. Yet after the courts had been transferred to the Senate—after you had escaped, every one of you, from the Roman people's control—Quintus Calidius,[2] on being found guilty, was able to remark that no ex-praetor could honourably be convicted for less than three million sesterces![3]

Again, then the Senator Publius Septimius Scaevola[4] was condemned by an extortion court presided over by Quintus Hortensius[5]—then praetor—his fine had to be expressly adjusted because, while a member of a court, he had accepted a bribe. The successful prosecutions of other Senators . . . for stealing public funds,

---

[1]The Order of Knights (the Equestrian Order) originated as cavalry members in the Roman army, but during the years of the late Republic, they constituted a special legal caste and were selected on the basis of their assessed wealth.
[2]Quintus Calidius, a senator who had been governor of Spain, had been condemned for extortion in 77 B.C.
[3]Sesterces were Roman coins. Originally of silver, they were later made of bronze. One sestertius was worth a quarter of a silver denarius, the basic coin of the Roman monetary system.
[4]Publius Septimius Scaevola had been a senator; he was punished in 72 B.C. for extortion.
[5]Quintus Hortensius (114–50 B.C.), a famous Roman orator, often worked with Cicero on legal cases.

and . . . for high treason, likewise clearly established that they had been bribed while serving as judges. . . .

You can imagine, then, how I shall feel if I discover that the same kind of criminal irregularity has occurred in the present case! In this connexion I must record a fact which many witnesses can corroborate. When Gaius Verres was in Sicily, a number of people heard him saying this sort of thing on various occasions: "I have a powerful friend! Whatever I steal from the province, I am sure he will protect me. My intention is not just to make money for myself: I have mapped out the three years of my Sicilian governorship like this. I shall consider myself to be doing nicely if I can earmark one year's profits for my own use, the second year's for my protectors and counsel, and the whole of the third year's—the richest and most lucrative—for the judges who try me!"

This reminds me of a remark I made . . . recently, when the judges for this case were being challenged . . . that, one of these days, communities from the provinces would send deputations to the people of Rome requesting that the extortion law and its court should be abolished. For if no such court existed, they suppose that each governor would only take away with him enough for himself and his children. At present, on the other hand, with the courts as they are, a governor takes enough for himself, and his protectors, and his counsel, and the president of the court, and the judges! In other words there is no end to it. A greedy man's lust for gain they could satisfy, but they cannot afford a guilty man's acquittal. How peculiarly glorious our courts have become, how scintillating is our Order's prestige, when Rome's allies pray that the courts which our ancestors created for their benefit should be struck out of existence!

Besides, would Verres ever have been so optimistic unless he, too, had absorbed this same deplorable opinion concerning yourselves? His evident agreement with this view ought—if possible—to make you hate him even more than other Romans do: seeing that in greed, criminality, and perjury he regards you as his equals.

In God's name, gentlemen, I pray you to devote all your care and all your foresight to facing this situation. It is evident to me, and I give you solemn warning, that heaven itself has vouchsafed you this opportunity of rescuing our entire Order from its present unpopularity, disgrace, ill-fame, and scandal. People believe that strictness and good faith are not to be found in our courts—indeed, that the courts themselves no longer have any reality. So we Senators are scorned and despised by the people of Rome: long have we laboured under this painful burden of disrepute.

## REVIEW QUESTIONS

1. What was the character of political ethics in the late Republic according to Cicero?
2. Why was Cicero so outraged by Verres' conduct and fearful of its consequences?

# 4 Roman Slavery

Slavery was practiced in ancient times, in many lands and among most peoples. Although conditions might vary in detail from place to place, essentially a slave was considered legally to be a piece of property, not a person with normal citizen's rights. Age, sex, skills, ethnic origin, demeanor, appearance, and personal character determined a slave's value in the marketplace. The status of slave was usually hereditary, but a person might be enslaved for debt or as a penalty for crime. Pirates would kidnap and sell their captives as slaves. But the most common source of slaves was defeated people captured during wars. They were assigned to all kinds of work, and their labors were vital in sustaining the luxury and leisure of the Roman upper classes. Even families of modest fortunes could usually afford a slave to do domestic chores, to help farm, or to assist in the family's business or craft.

# Diodorus Siculus
# SLAVES: TORMENT AND REVOLT

The Roman war machine created hundreds of thousands of slaves during the last centuries of the Republic and the early centuries of the imperial age. Under the Republic, the Romans were notably harsh toward slaves; until the full influence of Greek Stoic philosophy penetrated the governing class, little was done to protect them from the absolute power of their Roman masters. Diodorus Siculus (of Sicily) (c. 80–c. 29 B.C.), a Greek historian, describes the condition of Roman slaves toiling in silver and gold mines in Iberia (present-day Spain) and then tells of an uprising of slaves that lasted from 135 to 132 B.C.

## THE ORDEAL OF SLAVES IN THE MINES

. . . After the Romans had made themselves masters of Iberia, a multitude of Italians have swarmed to the mines and taken great wealth away with them, such was their greed. For they purchase a multitude of slaves whom they turn over to the overseers of the working of the mines; and these men, opening shafts in a number of places and digging deep into the ground, seek out the seams of earth which are rich in silver and gold; and not only do they go into the ground a great distance, but they also push their diggings many stades [measure equalling about 607 feet] in depth and run galleries off at every angle, turning this way and that, in this manner bringing up from the depths the ore which gives them the profit they are seeking. . . .

But to continue with the mines, the slaves who are engaged in the working of them produce for their masters revenues in sums defy-ing belief, but they themselves wear out their bodies both by day and by night in the diggings under the earth, dying in large numbers because of the exceptional hardships they endure. For no respite or pause is granted them in their labours, but compelled beneath blows of the overseers to endure the severity of their plight, they throw away their lives in this wretched manner, although certain of them who can endure it, by virtue of their bodily strength and their persevering souls, suffer such hardships over a long period; indeed death in their eyes is more to be desired than life, because of the magnitude of the hardships they must bear.

## A SLAVE REVOLT IN SICILY

There was never a sedition of slaves so great as that which occurred in Sicily, whereby many cities met with grave calamities, innumerable men and women, together with their children, experienced the greatest misfortunes, and all the island was in danger of falling into the power of fugitive slaves. . . .

. . . The Servile [slave] War broke out for the following reason. The Sicilians, having shot up in prosperity and acquired great wealth, began to purchase a vast number of slaves, to whose bodies, as they were brought in droves from the slave markets, they at once applied marks and brands. The young men they used as cowherds, the others in such ways as they happened to be useful. But they treated them with a heavy hand in their service, and granted them the most meagre care, the bare minimum for food and clothing. . . .

The slaves, distressed by their hardships, and frequently outraged and beaten beyond all reason, could not endure their treatment. Getting together as opportunity offered, they discussed the possibility of revolt, until at last they put their plans into action. . . . The beginning of the whole revolt took place as follows.

There was a certain Damophilus of Enna [a city in central Sicily], a man of great wealth but insolent of manner; he had abused his slaves to excess, and his wife Megallis vied even with her husband in punishing the slaves and in her general inhumanity towards them. The slaves, reduced by this degrading treatment to the level of brutes, conspired to revolt and to murder their masters. Going to Eunus [a Syrian slave believed to be a seer and magician] they asked him whether their resolve had the favour of the gods. He, resorting to his usual mummery, promised them the favour of the gods, and soon persuaded them to act at once. Immediately, therefore, they brought together four hundred of their fellow slaves and, having armed themselves in such ways as opportunity permitted, they fell upon the city of Enna, with Eunus at their head and working his miracle of the flames of fire for their benefit. When they found their way into the houses they shed much blood, sparing not even suckling babes. Rather they tore them from the breast and dashed them to the ground, while as

for the women—and under their husbands' very eyes—but words cannot tell the extent of their outrages and acts of lewdness! By now a great multitude of slaves from the city had joined them, who, after first demonstrating against their own masters their utter ruthlessness, then turned to the slaughter of others. When Eunus and his men learned that Damophilus and his wife were in the garden that lay near the city, they sent some of their band and dragged them off, both the man and his wife, fettered and with hands bound behind their backs, subjecting them to many outrages along the way. Only in the case of the couple's daughter were the slaves seen to show consideration throughout, and this was because of her kindly nature, in that to the extent of her power she was always compassionate and ready to succour the slaves. Thereby it was demonstrated that the others were treated as they were, not because of some "natural savagery of slaves," but rather in revenge for wrongs previously received. The men appointed to the task, having dragged Damophilus and Megallis into the city, as we said, brought them to the theatre, where the crowd of rebels had assembled. But when Damophilus attempted to devise a plea to get them off safe and was winning over many of the crowd with his words, Hermeias and Zeuxis, men bitterly disposed towards him, denounced him as a cheat, and without waiting for a formal trial by the assembly the one ran him through the chest with a sword, the other chopped off his head with an axe. Thereupon Eunus was chosen king, not for his manly courage or his ability as a military leader, but solely for his marvels and his setting of the revolt in motion. . . .

Established as the rebels' supreme commander, he called an assembly and put to death all the citizenry of Enna except for those who were skilled in the manufacture of arms: these he put in chains and assigned to this task. He gave Megallis to the maidservants to deal with as they might wish; they subjected her to torture and threw her over a precipice. He himself murdered his own masters, Antigenes and Pytho. Having set a diadem upon his head, and arrayed himself in full royal style, he proclaimed his wife queen (she was a fellow Syrian and of the same city), and appointed to the royal council such men as seemed to be gifted with superior intelligence. . . .

. . . In three days Eunus had armed, as best he could, more than six thousand men, besides others in his train who had only axes and hatchets, or slings, or sickles, or fire-hardened stakes, or even kitchen spits; and he went about ravaging the countryside. Then, since he kept recruiting untold numbers of slaves, he ventured even to do battle with Roman generals, and on joining combat repeatedly overcame them with his superior numbers, for he now had more than ten thousand soldiers.

Soon after, engaging in battle with a general arrived from Rome, Lucius Hypsaeus [the Roman governor], who had eight thousand Sicilian troops, the rebels were victorious, since they now numbered twenty thousand. Before long their band reached a total of two hundred thousand,[1] and in numerous battles with the Romans they acquitted themselves well, and failed but seldom. As word of this was bruited about, a revolt of one hundred and fifty slaves, banded together, flared up in Rome, of more than a thousand in Attica, and of yet others in Delos [an island off the southeastern Greek coast] and many other places. But

[1]The ancients often exaggerated numbers; the slaves probably raised an army of some 70,000.

thanks to the speed with which forces were brought up and to the severity of their punitive measures, the magistrates of these communities at once disposed of the rebels and brought to their senses any who were wavering on the verge of revolt. In Sicily, however, the trouble grew. Cities were captured with all their inhabitants, and many armies were cut to pieces by the rebels, until Rupilius, the Roman commander, recovered Tauromenium [Taormina] for the Romans by placing it under strict siege and confining the rebels under conditions of unspeakable duress and famine: conditions such that, beginning by eating the children, they progressed to the women, and did not altogether abstain even from eating one another. . . .

Finally, after Sarapion, a Syrian, had betrayed the citadel, the general laid hands on all the runaway slaves in the city, whom, after torture, he threw over a cliff. From there he advanced to Enna, which he put under siege in much the same manner, bringing the rebels into extreme straits and frustrating their hopes. . . . Rupilius captured this city also by betrayal, since its strength was impregnable to force of arms. Eunus, taking with him his bodyguards, a thousand strong, fled in unmanly fashion. . . .

. . . He met such an end as befitted his knavery, and died at Morgantina [in central Sicily]. Thereupon Rupilius, traversing the whole of Sicily with a few picked troops, sooner than had been expected rid it of every nest of robbers.

## REVIEW QUESTIONS

1. What was the character of slavery under the early Romans?
2. According to these selections, what was the impact of slavery on the moral character of both masters and slaves?

## 5  Women in Republican Society

The status of women in late republican Roman society was considerably better than that of Greek women during the classical age. Like the Greek, Roman law had originally placed each female under the jurisdiction of a male, the *paterfamilias* (literally, "family father"), but Roman women obtained some freedom from male control during the times of the late Republic and the early Empire. Although women never achieved full civil equality and they could not formally participate in the political institutions of Rome, they did eventually exercise much practical control over their own property and indirectly exercised political influence through their husbands, sons, and fathers.

# Livy
# CATO PROTESTS AGAINST THE DEMANDS OF ROMAN WOMEN

A remarkable example of the political power and public participation of women in Roman society was recorded by the Roman historian Livy (Titus Livius, 59 B.C.–A.D. 17). The incident centered on a demand in 195 B.C. by Roman women that the senate repeal a law passed in 215 B.C. during the Second Punic War. In the following reading from his *History of Rome,* Livy presents the demands of the women and then reports the speech of Consul Marcus Porcius Cato the Elder (234–149 B.C.), a strong defender of traditional Roman morals and manners.

Amid the anxieties of great wars, either scarce finished or soon to come, an incident occurred, trivial to relate, but which, by reason of the passions it aroused, developed into a violent contention. Marcus Fundanius and Lucius Valerius, tribunes of the people, proposed to the assembly the abrogation of the Oppian law. The tribune Gaius Oppius had carried this law in the heat of the Punic War, in the consulship of Quintus Fabius and Tiberius Sempronius,* that no woman should possess more than half an ounce of gold or wear a parti-coloured garment or ride in a carriage in the City or in a town within a mile thereof, except on the occasion of a religious festival. The tribunes Mar-

cus and Publius Iunius Brutus were supporting the Oppian law, and averred that they would not permit its repeal; many distinguished men came forward to speak for and against it; the Capitoline[1] was filled with crowds of supporters and opponents of the bill. The matrons could not be kept at home by advice or modesty or their husbands' orders, but blocked all the streets and approaches to the Forum,[2] begging the men as they came down to the Forum that, in the prosperous condition of the state,

---

*215 B.C.

[1]"Capitoline," the name of a prominent citadel in Rome, refers here to a public space on that hill where popular assemblies were frequently held to hear political debates or to conduct elections.
[2]The Forum was the main square in ancient Rome. It lay at the foot of the Capitoline Hill.

when the private fortunes of all men were daily increasing, they should allow the women too to have their former distinctions restored. The crowd of women grew larger day by day; for they were now coming in from the towns and rural districts. Soon they dared even to approach and appeal to the consuls, the praetors, and the other officials, but one consul, at least, they found adamant, Marcus Porcius Cato, who spoke thus in favour of the law whose repeal was being urged.

"If each of us, citizens, had determined to assert his rights and dignity as a husband with respect to his own spouse, we should have less trouble with the sex as a whole; as it is, our liberty, destroyed at home by female violence, even here in the Forum is crushed and trodden underfoot, and because we have not kept them individually under control, we dread them collectively. . . . But from no class is there not the greatest danger if you permit them meetings and gatherings and secret consultations. . . .

". . . For myself, I could not conceal my blushes a while ago, when I had to make my way to the Forum through a crowd of women. Had not respect for the dignity and modesty of some individuals among them rather than of the sex as a whole kept me silent, lest they should seem to have been rebuked by a consul, I should have said, 'What sort of practice is this, of running out into the streets and blocking the roads and speaking to other women's husbands? Could you not have made the same requests, each of your own husband, at home? Or are you more attractive outside and to other women's husbands than to your own? And yet, not even at home, if modesty would keep matrons within the limits of their proper rights, did it become you to concern yourselves with the question of what laws should be adopted in this place or repealed.' Our ancestors permitted no woman to conduct even personal business without a guardian to intervene in her behalf; they wished them to be under the control of fathers, brothers, husbands; we (Heaven help us!) allow them now even to interfere in public affairs, yes, and to visit the

Forum and our informal and formal sessions. What else are they doing now on the streets and at the corners except urging the bill of the tribunes and voting for the repeal of the law? Give loose rein to their uncontrollable nature and to this untamed creature and expect that they will themselves set bounds to their licence; unless you act, this is the least of the things enjoined upon women by custom or law and to which they submit with a feeling of injustice. It is complete liberty or, rather, if we wish to speak the truth, complete licence that they desire.

"If they win in this, what will they not attempt? Review all the laws with which your forefathers restrained their licence and made them subject to their husbands; even with all these bonds you can scarcely control them. What of this? If you suffer them to seize these bonds one by one and wrench themselves free and finally to be placed on a parity with their husbands, do you think that you will be able to endure them? The moment they begin to be your equals, they will be your superiors. . . .

". . . No law is entirely convenient for everyone; this alone is asked, whether it is good for the majority and on the whole. . . . I should like to know what it is which has caused the panic-stricken matrons to rush out into the streets and barely refrain from entering the Forum and a public meeting. . . .

". . . What pretext, respectable even to mention, is now given for this insurrection of the women? 'That we may glitter with gold and purple,' says one, 'that we may ride in carriages on holidays and ordinary days, that we may be borne through the city as if in triumph over the conquered and vanquished law and over the votes which we have captured and wrested from you; that there may be no limits to our spending and our luxury.'

"You have often heard me complaining of the extravagance of the women and often of the men, both private citizens and magistrates even, and lamenting that the state is suffering from those two opposing evils, avarice and luxury, which have been the destruction of every great empire. The better and the happier becomes the fortune of our commonwealth day by day and the greater the empire grows—and already we have crossed into Greece and Asia, places filled with all the allurements of vice, and we are handling the treasures of kings—the more I fear that these things will capture us rather than we them. . . .

". . . Do you wish, citizens, to start a race like this among your wives, so that the rich shall want to own what no other woman can have and the poor, lest they be despised for their poverty, shall spend beyond their means? Once let these women begin to be ashamed of what they should not be ashamed, and they will not be ashamed of what they ought. She who can buy from her own purse will buy; she who cannot will beg her husband. Poor wretch that husband, both he who yields and he who yields not, since what he will not himself give he will see given by another man. . . ."

. . . When these speeches against and for the bill had been delivered, the next day an even greater crowd of women appeared in public, and all of them in a body beset the doors of those tribunes, who were vetoing their colleagues' proposal, and they did not desist until the threat of veto was withdrawn by the tribunes. After that there was no question that all the tribes would vote to repeal the law. The law was repealed twenty years after it was passed.

# Quintus Lucretius Vespillo
# A FUNERAL EULOGY FOR A ROMAN WIFE

Documenting intimate relationships between Roman men and women is difficult because ordinary people were unlikely to write about such things. Although personal records are scant or now lost, glimpses have survived in the writings of historians and poets or as inscriptions on tombstones.

In the late Republic, it became more common for distinguished men to pronounce funeral eulogies for distinguished female as well as male members of their families. One such eulogy was composed by the ex-Consul Quintus Lucretius Vespillo for his wife Turia, who died about 8 B.C. Though marriages among persons of the higher social ranks were usually undertaken for political and economic considerations, clearly this couple had gone beyond such a formal alliance to achieve a most touching love.

Before the day fixed for our marriage, you were suddenly left an orphan, by the murder of your parents in the solitude of the country. . . .

Through your efforts chiefly, their death did not remain unavenged. . . .

In our day, marriages of such long duration, not dissolved by divorce, but terminated by death alone, are indeed rare. For our union was prolonged in unclouded happiness for forty-one years. Would that it had been my lot to put an end to this our good fortune and that I as the older—which was more just—had yielded to fate.

Why recall your inestimable qualities, your modesty, deference, affability, your amiable disposition, your faithful attendance to the household duties, your enlightened religion, your unassuming elegance, the modest simplicity and refinement of your manners? Need I speak of your attachment to your kindred, your affection for your family—when you respected my mother as you did your own parents and cared for her tomb as you did for that of your own mother and father,—you who share countless other virtues with Roman ladies most jealous of their fair name? These qualities which I claim for you are your own, equalled or excelled by but few; for the experience of men teaches us how rare they are.

With common prudence we have preserved all the patrimony which you received from your parents. Intrusting it all to me, you were not troubled with the care of increasing it; thus did we share the task of administering it, that I undertook to protect your fortune, and you to guard mine. . . .

You gave proof of your generosity not only towards several of your kin, but especially in your filial devotion. . . . You brought up in your own home, in the enjoyment of mutual benefits, some young girls of your kinship. And that these might attain to a station in life worthy of our family, you provided them with dowries. . . .

I owe you no less a debt than Cæsar Augustus [27 B.C.–A.D. 14, emperor of Rome] himself, for this my return from exile to my native land. For unless you had prepared the way for my safety, even Cæsar's promises of assistance had been of no avail. So I owe no less a debt to your loyal devotion than to the clemency of Cæsar.

Why shall I now conjure up the memory of our domestic counsels and plans stored away in the hidden recesses of the heart?—That, aroused by the sudden arrival of messages from you to a realization of the present and imminent perils, I was saved by your counsel? That you suffered me not to be recklessly carried away by a foolish rashness, or that, when bent on more temperate plans, you provided for me a safe retreat, having as sharers in your plans for my safety, when an exile,—fraught with danger as they were for you all,—your sister and her husband. . . .

---

Vespillo then relates what happened to his wife when she begged his enemy M. Lepidus to honor her husband's writ of pardon from Octavian Caesar.

---

. . . Then prostrating yourself at his feet, he not only did not raise you up,—but, dragged along and abused as though a common slave, your body all covered with bruises, yet with unflinching steadfastness of purpose, you recalled to him Cæsar's edict (of pardon) and the letter of felicitation on my return, that accompanied it. Braving his taunts and suffering the most brutal treatment, you denounced these cruelties publicly so that he (Lepidus) was branded as the author of all my perils and misfortunes. And his punishment was not long delayed.

Could such courage remain without effect? Your unexampled patience furnished the occasion for Cæsar's clemency, and, by guarding my life, he branded the infamous and savage cruelty (of the tyrant Lepidus). . . .

When all the world was again at peace and the Republic reestablished, peaceful and happy days followed. We longed for children, which an envious fate denied us. Had Fortune smiled on us in this, what had been lacking to complete our happiness? But an adverse destiny put an end to our hopes. . . . Disconsolate to see me without children . . . you wished to put an end to my chagrin by proposing to me a divorce, offering to yield the place to another spouse more fertile, with the only intention of searching for and providing for me a spouse worthy of our mutual affection, whose children you assured me you would have treated as your own. . . .

I will admit that I was so irritated and shocked by such a proposition that I had difficulty in restraining my anger and remaining master of myself. You spoke of divorce before the decree of fate [death] had forced us to separate, and I could not comprehend how you could conceive of any reason why you, still living, should not be my wife, you who during my exile had always remained most faithful and loyal. . . .

Would that our time of life had permitted our union to have endured until I, the older, had passed away—which was more just—and that you might perform for me the last sad rites and that I might have departed, leaving you behind, with a daughter to replace me at your side.

By fate's decree your course was run before mine. You left me the grief, the heart-ache, the longing for you, the sad fate to live alone. . . .

The conclusion of this discourse will be that you have deserved all, and that I remain with the chagrin of not being able to give you all. Your wishes have always been my supreme law; and whatever it will be permitted me to accord them still, in this I shall not fail.

May the gods, the Manes [spirits of dead ancestors, considered godlike], assure and protect your repose!

## REVIEW QUESTIONS

1. What did Cato's remarks reveal about the attitudes held toward women by the more old-fashioned Roman males?
2. What virtues did a Roman husband expect in his wife? What did he consider her duties to be?

---

## 6 Tiberius Gracchus and the Crisis in Agriculture

The wars of expansion had a disastrous effect on Roman agriculture. Hannibal's ravaging of Italian farmlands and the obligatory military service that kept peasants away from their fields for long periods left many small farms in near ruins. The importation of thousands of prisoners of war to work as slaves on large plantations also squeezed small farmers out of business. Sinking ever deeper into debt and poverty, many lost their lands and went to Rome, where lack of jobs condemned them to permanent poverty. The once sturdy and independent Roman farmer, who had done all that his country had asked of him, became part of a vast urban underclass—poor, embittered, and alienated.

# Plutarch
# TIBERIUS GRACCHUS

Tiberius Gracchus (163–133 B.C.), a scion of one of Rome's most honored families, was distressed by this injustice. Moreover, he realized that small landowners were the backbone of the Roman army. Elected tribune (an office created in 493 B.C. to protect plebeian rights), Tiberius Gracchus in 133 B.C. proposed land reforms that the senatorial nobility regarded as a potential menace to their property. They also viewed Tiberius Gracchus as a threat to their political authority. The Roman nobility feared that this popular reformer was building a following among the commoners in order to undermine senatorial rule and that his real ambition was to subvert republican institutions and to become a tyrant, a one-man ruler. This fear was strengthened when Tiberius, in violation of constitutional custom, announced that he would seek reelection as tribune. Senatorial extremists killed Tiberius Gracchus and some three hundred of his followers. The Republic had entered an age of political violence that would eventually destroy it. (Tiberius' younger brother, Gaius, became tribune in 123 B.C. and suffered a fate similar to his brother's.) The following account of Tiberius Gracchus is by Plutarch, the second-century Greek biographer.

Of the territory which the Romans won in war from their neighbours, a part they sold, and a part they made common land, and assigned it for occupation to the poor and indigent among the citizens, on payment of a small rent into the public treasury. And when the rich began to offer larger rents and drove out the poor, a law was enacted forbidding the holding by one person of more than five hundred acres of land. For a short time this enactment gave a check to the rapacity of the rich, and was of assistance to the poor, who remained in their places on the land which they had rented and occupied the allotment which each had held from the outset. But later on the neighbouring rich men, by means of fictitious personages, transferred these rentals to themselves, and finally held most of the land openly in their own names. Then the poor, who had been ejected from their land, no longer showed themselves eager for military service, and neglected the bringing up of children, so that soon all Italy was conscious of a dearth of freemen, and was filled with gangs of foreign slaves, by whose aid the rich cultivated their estates, from which they had driven away the free citizens. An attempt was therefore made to rectify this evil, and by Caius Laelius[1] the comrade of Scipio; but the men of influence opposed his measures, and he, fearing the disturbance which might ensue, desisted, and received the surname of *Wise* or *Prudent* [for the Latin word "sapiens" would seem to have either meaning]. Tiberius, however, on being elected tribune

of the people, took the matter directly in hand. . . .

He did not, however, draw up his law by himself, but took counsel with the citizens who were foremost in virtue and reputation. . . .

. . . And it is thought that a law dealing with injustice and rapacity so great was never drawn up in milder and gentler terms. For men who ought to have been punished for their disobedience and to have surrendered with payment of a fine the land which they were illegally enjoying, these men it merely ordered to abandon their injust acquisitions upon being paid their value, and to admit into ownership of them such citizens as needed assistance. But although the rectification of the wrong was so considerate, the people were satisfied to let bygones be bygones if they could be secure from such wrong in the future; the men of wealth and substance, however, were led by their greed to hate the law, and by their wrath and contentiousness to hate the law-giver, and tried to dissuade the people by alleging that Tiberius was introducing a re-distribution of land for the confusion of the body politic, and was stirring up a general revolution.

But they accomplished nothing; for Tiberius, striving to support a measure which was honourable and just with an eloquence that would have adorned even a meaner cause, was formidable and invincible, whenever, with the people crowding around the rostra [speaker's platforms], he took his stand there and pleaded for the poor. "The wild beasts that roam over Italy," he would say, "have every one of them a cave or lair to lurk in; but the men who fight and die for Italy enjoy the common air and light, indeed, but nothing else; houseless and

[1]Caius Laelius Sapiens, a leading military hero in the Third Punic War and a close friend of Scipio Aemilianus, the conqueror of Carthage, attempted unsuccessfully to resettle the poor on public land.

homeless they wander about with their wives and children. And it is with lying lips that their imperators[2] exhort the soldiers in their battles to defend sepulchres and shrines from the enemy; for not a man of them has an hereditary altar, not one of all these many Romans an ancestral tomb, but they fight and die to support others in wealth and luxury, and though they are styled masters of the world, they have not a single clod of earth that is their own."

Such words as these, the product of a lofty spirit and genuine feeling, and falling upon the ears of a people profoundly moved and fully aroused to the speaker's support, no adversary of Tiberius could successfully withstand.

_____

[2]First, a commander, general, or captain in the army, later *imperator* meant "emperor."

## REVIEW QUESTIONS

1. What factors created a socioeconomic class struggle in the late Roman Republic?
2. According to Plutarch, what was the reaction of the senatorial order to the reforms proposed by Tiberius Gracchus?

## 7   The Decline of the Republic

In 133 B.C. the Romans effectively controlled all the lands that touched the Mediterranean Sea. The old enemies of Rome, Carthage and Macedonia, had become Roman provinces; the Hellenistic kingdoms of Syria and Egypt were clients of Rome without effective power to challenge Roman hegemony. The Mediterranean Sea had become a "Roman lake."

Yet, at the very moment of its imperial supremacy, the internal order and institutions of the Roman Republic began to break down. The senatorial leaders, who had served Rome responsibly in its march to empire, no longer governed effectively. The ruling class engaged in shameless corruption in administering the provinces, resorted to bribery and force to maintain control over public offices, and failed to solve the deeply rooted problems that afflicted the state. In the century following the assassination of Tiberius Gracchus in 133 B.C., the Republic was torn by conspiracies to seize the state, civil wars, assassinations, mob violence, and confiscations of property by political opponents.

## Sallust
## *THE CONSPIRACY OF CATILINE*

In the dark days of the Republic after the assassination of Julius Caesar in 44 B.C., the Roman politician and historian Sallust (Gaius Sallustius Crispus, 86–35 B.C.) reflected on the causes of the Republic's collapse. In his account of a failed coup d'état that occurred in 63 B.C., Sallust contrasted the virtues of the early Republic with the moral decline that set in after the destruction of Carthage.

Having failed to be elected consul in 63 B.C., Catiline, a Roman noble, organized a conspiracy to seize the state. The coup d'état was thwarted by the vigorous action of the consul Cicero, who arrested the known conspirators and had them executed. Catiline, who led an army against the forces loyal to the government, was defeated and killed.

## MORAL DETERIORATION

In peace and war [in the early Republic], as I have said, virtue was held in high esteem. The closest unity prevailed, and avarice was a thing almost unknown. Justice and righteousness were upheld not so much by law as by natural instinct. They quarrelled and fought with their country's foes; between themselves the citizens contended only for honour. In making offerings to the gods they spared no expense; at home they lived frugally and never betrayed a friend. By combining boldness in war with fair dealing when peace was restored, they protected themselves and the state. There are convincing proofs of this. In time of war, soldiers were often punished for attacking against orders or for being slow to obey a signal of recall from battle, whereas few ever ventured to desert their standards or to give ground when hard pressed. In peace, they governed by conferring benefits on their subjects, not by intimidation; and when wronged they would rather pardon than seek vengeance.

Thus by hard work and just dealing the power of the state increased. Mighty kings were vanquished, savage tribes and huge nations were brought to their knees; and when Carthage, Rome's rival in her quest for empire, had been annihilated [in 146 B.C.], every land and sea lay open to her. It was then that fortune turned unkind and confounded all her enterprises. To the men who had so easily endured toil and peril, anxiety and adversity, the leisure and riches which are generally regarded as so desirable proved a burden and a curse. Growing love of money, and the lust for power which followed it, engendered every kind of evil. Avarice destroyed honour, integrity, and every other virtue, and instead taught men to be proud and cruel, to neglect religion, and to hold nothing too sacred to sell. Ambition

tempted many to be false, to have one thought hidden in their hearts, another ready on their tongues, to become a man's friend or enemy not because they judged him worthy or unworthy but because they thought it would pay them, and to put on the semblance of virtues that they had not. At first these vices grew slowly and sometimes met with punishment; later on, when the disease had spread like a plague, Rome changed: her government, once so just and admirable, became harsh and unendurable.

---

Reflecting on the last stages of the Republic's decline, Sallust believed that men had learned a most dangerous lesson: that they could gain power and wealth through violence and corruption rather than through virtue and self-restraint.

---

Never in its history—it seems to me—had the empire of Rome been in such a miserable plight. From east to west all the world had been vanquished by her armies and obeyed her will; at home there was profound peace and abundance of wealth, which mortal men esteem the chiefest of blessings. Yet there were Roman citizens obstinately determined to destroy both themselves and their country. In spite of two senatorial decrees, not one man among all the conspirators was induced by the promise of reward to betray their plans, and not one deserted from Catiline's camp. A deadly moral contagion had infected all their minds. And this madness was not confined to those actually implicated in the plot. The whole of the lower orders, impatient for a new régime, looked with favour on Catiline's enterprise.* In this they only did what might have

---

*This surely cannot have been true. Sallust must be exaggerating the popular support for the conspiracy.

been expected of them. In every country paupers envy respectable citizens and make heroes of unprincipled characters, hating the established order of things and hankering after innovation; discontented with their own lot, they are bent on general upheaval. Turmoil and rebellion bring them carefree profit, since poverty has nothing to lose.

The city populace were especially eager to fling themselves into a revolutionary adventure. There were several reasons for this. To begin with, those who had made themselves conspicuous anywhere by vice and shameless audacity, those who had wasted their substance by disgraceful excesses, and those whom scandalous or criminal conduct had exiled from their homes— all these had poured into Rome till it was like a sewer. Many, remembering Sulla's victory,[1] and seeing men who had served under him as common soldiers now risen to be senators, or so rich that they lived as luxuriously as kings, began to hope that they too, if they took up arms, might find victory a source of profit. Young men from the country, whose labour on the farms had barely kept them from starvation, had been attracted by the private and public doles available at Rome, and preferred an idle city life to such thankless toil. These, like all the rest, stood to gain by public calamities. It is no wonder, therefore, that these paupers, devoid of moral scruple and incited by ambitious hopes, should have held their country as cheap as they held themselves. Those also to whom Sulla's victory had brought disaster by the proscription of their parents, the confiscation of their property, and the curtailment of their civil rights, looked forward with no less sanguine expectations to what might result from the coming struggle. Moreover, all the factions opposed to the Senate would rather see the state embroiled than accept their own exclusion from political power.

Such was the evil condition by which, after an interval of some years, Rome was once more afflicted. After the restoration of the power of the tribunes in the consulship of Pompey and Crassus,†[2] this very important office was obtained by certain men whose youth intensified their natural aggressiveness. These tribunes began to rouse the mob by inveighing against the Senate, and then inflamed popular passion still further by handing out bribes and promises, whereby they won renown and influence for themselves. They were strenuously opposed by most of the nobility, who posed as defenders of the Senate but were really concerned to maintain their own privileged position. The whole truth—to put it in a word—is that although all disturbers of the peace in this period put forward specious pretexts, claiming either to be protecting the rights of the people or to be strengthening the authority of the Senate, this was mere pretence: in reality, every one of them was fighting for his personal aggrandizement. Lacking all self-restraint, they [stopped] at nothing to gain their ends, and both sides made ruthless use of any successes they won.

---

[1]Lucius Cornelius Sulla (c. 138–78 B.C.) was a successful politician and general, whose rivalry with another politician and general, Gaius Marius (c. 155–86 B.C.), led to civil war. After seizing Rome and massacring his opponents, Sulla made himself dictator and increased the power of the aristocratic senate, suppressing the office of tribune of the people. The latter had been used by Tiberius and Gaius Gracchus, among others (see page 119), to better the condition of the poorer classes.

---

†In 70 B.C.
[2]Pompey (Gnaeus Pompeius, 106–48 B.C.) and Crassus (Marcus Licinius Crassus, c. 115–53 B.C.) held the office of consul in 55 B.C. In 59 B.C., together with Julius Caesar, they had formed a political alliance called a triumvirate (meaning "group of three men"), which dominated Roman government for the next decade.

## REVIEW QUESTIONS

1. To what virtues did Sallust attribute the greatness of Rome?
2. What vices did Sallust believe could ruin a great state? Does his analysis have any contemporary significance?

## 8   Cicero: Statesman and Philosopher

Marcus Tullius Cicero (106–43 B.C.), a leading Roman statesman, was also a distinguished orator, an unsurpassed Latin stylist, and a student of Greek philosophy. His letters, more than eight hundred of which have survived, provide modern historians with valuable insights into late republican politics. His orations before the Senate and law courts have been models of eloquence and rhetorical technique for students of Latin and later European languages. (See his oration against Verres, page 109.)

# Cicero
# ADVOCATE OF STOICISM

Cicero adopted the Stoic belief that natural law governs the universe and applies to all and that all belong to a common humanity. The gift of reason, which is common to all people, enables us to comprehend this natural law and to order our lives in accordance with its principles, which are unchangeable and eternal. Natural law as understood by right reason commands people to do what is right and deters them from doing what is wrong. Thus there is a unity of knowledge and virtue. For Cicero, the laws of the state should accord with the natural law underlying the universe. Adherence to such rationally formulated laws creates a moral bond among citizens and the peoples of all nations and states. In the following passage from his philosophic treatise, *The Laws,* Cicero explored the implications of the Stoic concept of natural law.

. . . Now let us investigate the origins of Justice.

Well then, the most learned men have determined to begin with Law, and it would seem that they are right, if, according to their definition, Law is the highest reason, implanted in Nature, which commands what ought to be done and forbids the opposite. This reason, when firmly fixed and fully developed in the human mind, is Law. And so they believe that Law is intelligence whose natural function it is to command right conduct and forbid wrongdoing. They think that this quality has derived its name in Greek from the idea of granting to every man his own, and in our language I believe it has been named from the idea of choosing. For as they have

attributed the idea of fairness to the word law, so we have given it that of selection, though both ideas properly belong to Law. Now if this is correct, as I think it to be in general, then the origin of Justice is to be found in Law, for Law is a natural force; it is the mind and reason of the intelligent man, the standard by which Justice and Injustice are measured. But since our whole discussion has to do with the reasoning of the populace, it will sometimes be necessary to speak in the popular manner, and give the name of law to that which in written form decrees whatever it wishes, either by command or prohibition. For such is the crowd's definition of law. But in determining what Justice is, let us begin with that supreme Law which had its origin ages before any written law existed or any State had been established.

. . . I shall seek the root of Justice in Nature, under whose guidance our whole discussion must be conducted.

. . . [T]hat animal which we call man, endowed with foresight and quick intelligence, complex, keen, possessing memory, full of reason and prudence, has been given a certain distinguished status by the supreme God who created him; for he is the only one among so many different kinds and varieties of living beings who has a share in reason and thought, while all the rest are deprived of it. But what is more divine, I will not say in man only, but in all heaven and earth, than reason? And reason, when it is full grown and perfected, is rightly called wisdom. Therefore, since there is nothing better than reason, and since it exists both in man and God, the first common possession of man and God is reason. But those who have reason in common must also have right reason in common. And since right reason is Law, we must believe that men have Law also in common with the gods. Further, those who share Law must also share Justice; and those who share these are to be regarded as members of the same commonwealth. If indeed they obey the same authorities and powers, this is true in a far greater degree; but as a matter of fact they do obey this celestial system, the divine mind, and the God of transcendent power. Hence we must now conceive of this whole universe as one commonwealth of which both gods and men are members.

Moreover, virtue exists in man and God alike, but in no other creature besides; virtue, however, is nothing else than Nature perfected and developed to its highest point; therefore there is a likeness between man and God. As this is true, what relationship could be closer or clearer than this one? For this reason, Nature has lavishly yielded such a wealth of things adapted to man's convenience and use that what she produces seems intended as a gift to us, and not brought forth by chance; and this is true, not only of what the fertile earth bountifully bestows in the form of grain and fruit, but also of the animals; for it is clear that some of them have been created to be man's slaves, some to supply him with their products, and others to serve as his food. Moreover innumerable arts have been discovered through the teachings of Nature; for it is by a skilful imitation of her that reason has acquired the necessities of life. . . .

. . . [O]ut of all the material of the philosophers' discussions, surely there comes nothing more valuable than the full realization that we are born for Justice, and that right is based, not upon men's opinions, but upon Nature. This fact will immediately be plain if you once get a clear conception of man's fellowship and union with his fellow-men. For no single thing is so like another, so exactly its counterpart, as all of us are to one another. Nay, if bad habits and false beliefs did not twist the weaker minds and turn them in whatever direction they are inclined, no one would be so like his own self as all men would be like all others. And so, however we may define man, a single definition will apply to all. This is a sufficient proof that there is no difference in kind between man and man; for if there were, one definition could not be applicable to all men; and indeed reason, which alone raises us above the level of the beasts and enables us to draw inferences, to prove and disprove, to discuss and solve problems, and to come to conclusions, is certainly common to us all, and, though varying in what it learns, at least in the capacity to learn it is invariable. For the same things are invariably perceived by the senses, and those things which stimulate the senses, stimulate them in the same way in all men; and those rudimentary beginnings of intelligence to which I have referred, which are imprinted on our minds, are imprinted on all minds alike; and speech, the mind's interpreter, though differing in the choice of words, agrees in the sentiments expressed. In fact, there is no human being of any race who, if he finds a guide, cannot attain to virtue.

## REVIEW QUESTIONS

1. What is Cicero's view on the nature of law and what conclusions does he derive from it?
2. According to Cicero, what is virtue and how do men attain it?
3. Why does Cicero conclude that the sense of justice is common to all humans? What implication does he draw from this conclusion?

## 9   The Meaning of Caesar's Assassination

In 49 B.C., Julius Caesar (100–44 B.C.), a talented and ambitious commander marched on Rome. After defeating the Senate's forces, he was appointed dictator for ten years. A creative statesman, Caesar introduced reforms to resolve the grievances of Romans and provincials. Some senators feared that Caesar aimed to establish a typical Hellenistic monarchy over Rome with himself as absolute king. The very word *king* was abhorrent to patriotic Romans, who gloried in their status as free citizens of a five-centuries-old republic. Finally, on the Ides (the fifteenth) of March, 44 B.C., Julius Caesar was slain by some sixty senators, who acted, they said, to restore the liberty of the Roman people. Their leaders were Marcus Junius Brutus (82–42 B.C.) and Gaius Cassius (d. 42 B.C.), both of whom Caesar had previously pardoned.

## Cicero
# JUSTIFYING THE ASSASSINATION

In the following reading from *On Duties,* Cicero, who was not one of the assassins, justifies the killing of Caesar.

Our tyrant deserved his death for having made an exception of the one thing that was the blackest crime of all. Why do we gather instances of petty crime—legacies criminally obtained and fraudulent buying and selling? Behold, here you have a man who was ambitious to be king of the Roman People and master of the whole world; and he achieved it! The man who maintains that such an ambition is morally right is a madman; for he justifies the destruction of law and liberty and thinks their hideous and detestable suppression glorious.

But if anyone agrees that it is not morally right to be king in a state that once was free and that ought to be free now, and yet imagines that it is advantageous for him who can reach that position, with what remonstrance or rather with what appeal should I try to tear him away from so strange a delusion? For, oh ye immortal gods! can the most horrible and hideous of all murders—that of fatherland—bring advantage to anybody, even though he who has committed such a crime receives from his enslaved fellow-citizens the title of "Father of his Country"?

# Dio Cassius
# IN DEFENSE OF CAESAR
# AND MONARCHY

The reputation of Julius Caesar changed over the centuries. Some 250 years after Caesar's assassination, the Roman historian and politician Dio Cassius (c. A.D. 150–235), writing in Greek, acknowledged that Caesar was not blameless in bringing about the tragedy that led to his death and renewal of civil war between Caesar's friends and enemies. Yet, examining events since Caesar's time, he argued that monarchy is superior to republicanism and condemned the assassination.

. . . [A] baleful frenzy . . . fell upon certain men through jealousy of [Caesar's] advancement and hatred of his preferment to themselves caused his death unlawfully, while it added a new name to the annals of infamy; it scattered [Caesar's] decrees to the winds and brought upon the Romans seditions and civil wars once more after a state of harmony. His slayers, to be sure, declared that they had shown themselves at once destroyers of Caesar and liberators of the people: but in reality they impiously plotted against him, and they threw the city into disorder when at last it possessed a stable government. Democracy, indeed, has a fair-appearing name and conveys the impression of bringing equal rights to all through equal laws, but its results are seen not to agree at all with its title. Monarchy, on the contrary, has an unpleasant sound, but is a most practical form of government to live under. For it is easier to find a single excellent man than many of them, and if even this seems to some a difficult feat, it is quite inevitable that the other alternative should be acknowledged to be impossible; for it does not belong to the majority of men to acquire virtue. And again, even though a base man should obtain supreme power, yet he is preferable to the masses of like character, as the history of the Greeks and barbarians and of the Romans themselves proves. For successes have always been greater and more frequent in the case both of cities and of individuals under kings than under popular rule, and disasters do [not] happen [so frequently] under monarchies as under mob-rule. Indeed, if ever there has been a prosperous democracy, it has in any case been at its best for only a brief period, so long, that is, as the people had neither the numbers nor the strength sufficient to cause insolence to spring up among them as the result of good fortune or jealousy as the result of ambition. But for a city, not only so large in itself, but also ruling the finest and the greatest part of the known world, holding sway over men of many and diverse natures, possessing many men of great wealth, occupied with every imaginable pursuit, enjoying every imaginable fortune, both individually and collectively, —for such a city, I say, to practise moderation under a democracy is impossible, and still more is it impossible for the people, unless moderation prevails, to be harmonious. Therefore, if Marcus Brutus and Gaius Cassius had only reflected upon these things, they would never have killed the city's head and protector nor have made themselves the cause of countless ills both to themselves and to all the rest of mankind then living.

It happened as follows, and his death was due to the cause now to be given. He had aroused dislike that was not altogether unjustified, except in so far as it was the senators themselves who had by their novel and excessive honours encouraged him and puffed him up, only to find fault with him on this very account and to spread slanderous reports how glad he was to accept them and how he behaved more haughtily as a result of them. It is true that Caesar did now and then err by accepting some of the honours voted him and believing that he really deserved them; yet those were most blameworthy who, after beginning to honour him as he deserved, led him on and brought blame upon him for the measures they had passed. He neither dared, of course, to thrust them all aside, for fear of being thought contemptuous, nor, again, could he be safe in accepting them; for excessive honour and praise render even the most modest men conceited, especially if they seem to be bestowed with sincerity.

## REVIEW QUESTIONS

1. Why did Cicero consider Caesar guilty of "the blackest crime of all"?
2. What were Dio Cassius' criticisms of the Roman republicans and of democracy as a form of government?

# CHAPTER 5
# *The Roman Empire*

MARCUS AURELIUS, Roman emperor (161–180). In this relief, Marcus rides through the Roman Forum, having been accorded a triumph after defending the empire against barbarian incursions. *(Alinari/Art Resource, N.Y.)*

In the chaotic years following Julius Caesar's assassination in 44 B.C., Octavian (Augustus) emerged victorious over his rivals, becoming the unchallenged ruler of Rome. Although eager for personal power, Augustus was by no means a self-seeking tyrant; he was a creative statesman who prevented the renewal of civil war that had plagued the Republic and introduced needed reforms in Italy and the provinces. His long reign, from 27 B.C. to A.D. 14, marks the beginning of the *Pax Romana,* the Roman Peace, which endured until A.D. 180.

The period of the Pax Romana was one of the finest in the ancient world. Revolts against Roman rule were few, and Roman legions ably defended the Empire's borders. The Mediterranean world had never enjoyed so many years of peace, effective government, and economic well-being. Stretching from Britain to the Arabian Desert and from the Danube River to the sands of the Sahara, the Roman Empire united some seventy million people. In many ways the Roman Empire was the fulfillment of the universalism and cosmopolitanism of the Hellenistic Age. The same law bound together Italians, Spaniards, North Africans, Greeks, Syrians, and other peoples. Although dissatisfaction was sometimes violently expressed and separatist tendencies persisted, notably in Judea and Gaul, people from diverse backgrounds viewed themselves as Romans even though they had never set foot in the capital city.

In the seventy years following Augustus' reign, political life was sometimes marred by conspiracies and assassinations, particularly after an emperor's death left the throne vacant. Marcus Cocceius Nerva, who reigned from A.D. 96 to 98, introduced a practice that led to orderly succession and gave Rome four exceptionally competent emperors. He adopted as his son and designated as his heir Trajan (Marcus Ulpius Traianus), a man of proven ability. From the accession of Nerva to the death of Marcus Aurelius Antoninus in A.D. 180, the Roman Empire was ruled by the "Five Good Emperors." Marcus Aurelius abandoned the use of adoption and allowed his son Commodus (Marcus Aurelius Commodus Antoninus, A.D. 180–192) to succeed to the throne. An extravagant despot, Commodus was murdered in A.D. 192.

During the third century the Roman Empire suffered hard times, and the ordered civilization of the Pax Romana was destroyed. The Empire was plunged into anarchy as generals vied for the throne. Taking advantage of the weakened border defenses, the barbarians (Germanic tribesmen) crossed the Danube frontier and pillaged Roman cities. Both civil war and barbarian attacks greatly disrupted the Roman economy, which even during good times suffered from basic weaknesses.

Two later emperors—Diocletian (G. Aurelius Valerius Diocletianus, A.D. 285–305) and Constantine (Flavius Valerius Constantinus,

A.D. 306–337)—tried to keep the Empire from dissolution by tightening control over the citizenry. Although heavy taxes, requisitioning of goods, and forced labor provided some stability, these measures also turned many citizens against the oppressive state. At the end of the fourth and the opening of the fifth century, several barbarian tribes poured into the Empire in great numbers. In succeeding decades Germanic tribes overran Roman provinces and set up kingdoms on lands that had been Roman. The Roman Empire in the west fell; the eastern provinces, however, survived as the Byzantine Empire.

The history of the Roman Empire influenced Western civilization in many ways. From Latin, the language of Rome, came the Romance languages: French, Italian, Spanish, Portuguese, and Romanian. Roman law became the basis of the legal codes of most modern European states. Rome preserved Greek culture, the foundation of Western learning and aesthetics, and spread it to other lands. And Christianity, the religion of the West, was born in the Roman Empire.

# 1 The Imperial Office

The greatest achievement of Caesar Augustus (Octavian), grandnephew and adopted son of Julius Caesar, was undoubtedly the step-by-step building of a new constitutional structure for the Roman Empire. This political system, called by modern historians the Principate, has been described as a monarchy disguised as an oligarchical republic. The Roman antimonarchial tradition, nurtured for five centuries under the Republican regime, had contributed directly to Julius Caesar's assassination. Augustus was wise enough, as he created a stable central executive office for the Empire, to camouflage the monarchial reality of his regime by maintaining the outer forms of the old Republic's constitution.

Augustus' chief innovation was creating the office of *Princeps* (First Citizen), which combined a number of Republican offices and powers and placed them at the disposal of one man. Desiring to maintain the appearance of traditional republican government, he refused to be called king. The Senate gave him the semi-religious and revered name Augustus (venerable). In effect, however, he was the first Roman emperor. He cultivated the support of the traditional constituents of the Roman state—the senatorial nobility, knights, and public contractors, residents of the capital, soldiers and veterans, and the wealthy and politically useful provincial subjects of Rome. At the time of his death in A.D. 14, Augustus successfully passed on his imperial office to his chosen heir, his adopted son Tiberius.

# Augustus
## *THE ACHIEVEMENTS OF THE DIVINE AUGUSTUS*

In *Res gestae divi Augusti (The Achievements of the Divine Augustus),* a document composed shortly before his death and left to be published with his will, Augustus gave an account of those achievements for which he wanted to be remembered. A careful reading reveals the image Augustus chose to promote to justify his emperorship. It also describes the many responsibilities of holders of that office.

I drove into exile the murderers of my father [Julius Caesar], avenging their crime through tribunals established by law; and afterwards, when they made war on the republic, I twice defeated them in battle.

I undertook many civil and foreign wars by land and sea throughout the world, and as victor I spared the lives of all citizens who asked for mercy. When foreign peoples could safely be pardoned I preferred to preserve rather than to exterminate them. The Roman citizens who took the soldier's oath of obedience to me numbered about 500,000. I settled rather more than 300,000 of these in colonies or sent them back to their home towns after their period of service; to all these I assigned lands or gave money as rewards for their military service. . . .

The dictatorship was offered to me by both senate and people in my absence and when I was at Rome in the consulship of Marcus Marcellus and Lucius Arruntius, but I refused it. I did not decline in the great dearth of corn to undertake the charge of the corn-supply, which I so administered that within a few days I delivered the whole city from apprehension and immediate danger at my own cost and by my own efforts. . . . The senate and people of Rome agreed that I should be appointed supervisor of laws and morals without a colleague and with supreme power, but I would not accept any office inconsistent with the custom of our ancestors. The measures that the senate then desired me to take I carried out in virtue of my tribunician power. . . .

To each member of the Roman plebs [common populace] I paid under my father's will 300 sesterces,[1] and in my own name I gave them 400 each from the booty of war in my fifth consulship, and once again in my tenth consulship I paid out 400 sesterces as a largesse to each man from my own patrimony, and in my eleventh consulship I bought grain with my own money and distributed twelve rations apiece, and in the twelfth year of my tribunician power I gave every man 400 sesterces for the third time. These largesses of mine never reached fewer than 250,000 persons. . . .

. . . I paid monetary rewards to soldiers whom I settled in their home towns after completion of their service, and on this account I expended about 400,000,000 sesterces.

Four times I assisted the treasury with my own money, so that I transferred to the administrators of the treasury 150,000,000 sesterces. . . .

I restored the Capitol[2] and the theatre of Pompey, both works at great expense without inscribing my own name on either. I restored

---

[1]Sesterces, during the reign of Augustus, were small coins of bronze, each worth one hundredth of a gold *aureus,* or a quarter of a silver denarius, the basic coin of the Roman monetary system. Brunt (editor of source) notes that a Roman legionary soldier of this period earned 900 sesterces a year, out of which the cost of uniform, food, and arms was deducted. A Roman whose assessed wealth came to at least 400,000 sesterces qualified to enter the order of knights; to be a senator required one million sesterces.
[2]Here "Capitol" refers to the temple of Jupiter, patron of Rome, on the Capitoline Hill.

the channels of the aqueducts, which in several places were falling into disrepair through age, and I brought water from a new spring into the aqueduct called Marcia, doubling the supply. I completed the Forum Julium[3] and the basilica between the temples of Castor and Saturn,[4] works begun and almost finished by my father. . . .

I gave three gladiatorial games in my own name and five in that of my sons or grandsons; at these games some 10,000 men took part in combat. Twice in my own name and a third time in that of my grandson I presented to the people displays by athletes summoned from all parts. I produced shows in my own name four times and in place of other magistrates twenty-three times. . . . I gave beast-hunts of African beasts in my own name or in that of my sons and grandsons in the circus or forum or amphitheatre on twenty-six occasions, on which about 3,500 beasts were destroyed.

I made the sea peaceful and freed it of pirates. In that war I captured about 30,000 slaves who had escaped from their masters and taken up arms against the republic, and I handed them over to their masters for punishment.

I extended the territory of all those provinces of the Roman people on whose borders lay peoples not subject to our government. I brought peace to the Gallic and Spanish provinces as well as to Germany, throughout the area bordering on the [Atlantic] Ocean from Cadiz [in Spain] to the mouth of the Elbe [in northwestern Germany]. I secured the pacification of the Alps. . . . The Pannonian peoples [in western Hungary] . . . were conquered through the agency of Tiberius Nero[5] who was then my stepson and legate; I brought them into the empire of the Roman people, and extended the frontier of Illyricum[6] to the banks of the Danube. . . .

In my sixth and seventh consulships, after I had extinguished civil wars, and at a time when with universal consent I was in complete control of affairs, I transferred the republic from my power to the dominion of the senate and people of Rome. For this service of mine I was named Augustus by decree of the senate, and the door-posts of my house were publicly wreathed with bay leaves and a civic crown was fixed over my door and a golden shield was set in the Curia Julia,[7] which, as attested by the inscription thereon, was given me by the senate and people of Rome on account of my courage, clemency, justice and piety. After this time I excelled all in influence, although I possessed no more official power than others who were my colleagues in the several magistracies.

In my thirteenth consulship the senate, the equestrian order and the whole people of Rome gave me the title of Father of my Country. . . .

[3]The Forum (Square) Julium was surrounded by a covered portico. Begun by Julius Caesar, it was finished by Augustus.
[4]Saturn was a Roman agricultural god associated with the Greek god Cronus. Castor, brother of Pollux and Helen of Troy, was the son of Jupiter by a mortal. The twins Castor and Pollux were deified in Rome for having helped the Romans in a battle.

[5]Tiberius Nero, Augustus' adopted son and designated heir, reigned as emperor from A.D. 14 to 37.
[6]Illyricum was a Roman province on the Adriatic Sea in the former Yugoslavia.
[7]The Curia Julia, also begun by Julius Caesar and completed by Augustus, was a courthouse.

# Tacitus
# THE IMPOSITION OF ONE-MAN RULE

Not all Romans accepted Augustus' own evaluation of his achievements. In this reading, the Roman historian Cornelius Tacitus (c. A.D. 55–c. 117) described how Augustus seduced the Roman people into accepting monarchial rule.

[Augustus] seduced the army with bonuses, and his cheap food policy was successful bait for civilians. Indeed, he attracted everybody's goodwill by the enjoyable gift of peace. Then he gradually pushed ahead and absorbed the functions of the senate, the officials, and even the law. Opposition did not exist. War or judicial murder had disposed of all men of spirit. Upper-class survivors found that slavish obedience was the way to succeed, both politically and financially. They had profited from the revolution, and so now they liked the security of the existing arrangement better than the dangerous uncertainties of the old régime. Besides, the new order was popular in the provinces. There, government by Senate and People was looked upon sceptically as a matter of sparring dignitaries and extortionate officials. The legal system had provided no remedy against these, since it was wholly incapacitated by violence, favouritism, and—most of all—bribery.

To safeguard his domination Augustus made his sister's son Marcellus a priest and an aedile[1]—in spite of his extreme youth—and singled out Marcus Agrippa,[2] a commoner but a first-rate soldier who had helped to win his victories, by the award of two consecutive consulships; after the death of Marcellus, Agrippa was chosen by Augustus as his son-in-law. Next the emperor had his stepsons Tiberius and Nero Drusus[3] hailed publicly as victorious generals. . . .

At this time there was no longer any fighting—except a war against the Germans. . . . In the capital the situation was calm. The titles of officials remained the same. Actium[4] had been won before the younger men were born. Even most of the older generation had come into a world of civil wars. Practically no one had ever seen truly Republican government. The country had been transformed, and there was nothing left of the fine old Roman character. Political equality was a thing of the past; all eyes watched for imperial commands.

[1]An aedile was a minor municipal magistrate, responsible for petty criminal cases, and for the supervision of markets and public games—gladiator combats and chariot races.

[2]Marcus Agrippa (c. 63–12 B.C.), Augustus' son-in-law, was his closest associate and virtually co-emperor; he predeceased Augustus.
[3]Nero Drusus (38–9 B.C.), one of Augustus' stepsons, was the father of Emperor Claudius (ruled A.D. 41–54).
[4]The Battle of Actium, fought in the sea off west-central Greece, pitted forces of Antony and Cleopatra against those of Octavian (Augustus). Octavian's victory gave him sole control of the Roman Empire.

## REVIEW QUESTIONS

1. Describe the functions of a Roman emperor as suggested by the career of Caesar Augustus.
2. What constituencies did Caesar Augustus have to serve?
3. How did Augustus disguise the monarchial character of his regime?

## 2  Imperial Culture

The reign of Augustus marks the golden age of Latin literature. This outpouring of literary works stemmed in part from the patronage of authors by Augustus and other prominent Romans. Roman poets and dramatists used Greek models, just as Roman philosophers, mathematicians, scientists, doctors, and geographers did. Not surprisingly, writers of the Augustan Age often expressed strong patriotic sentiments and were extravagant in their praise of Augustus.

# Virgil
## *THE AENEID*

The poet Virgil (Publius Vergilius Maro, 70–19 B.C.) admired Augustus, who was his patron, for ending the civil wars and bringing order to the Roman world. Augustus urged Virgil to compose a grand opus that would glorify Rome's imperial achievement—the emperor knew that he would find an honored place in such a work. It took Virgil ten years to produce the *Aeneid,* which was not fully completed when he died. Augustus disobeyed Virgil's deathbed request that the manuscript be destroyed, and the patriotic poem became Rome's national epic.

The *Aeneid* was greatly influenced by Homer's *Iliad* and *Odyssey* (see Chapter 3). In *The Iliad,* Homer dealt with the conflict between the early Greeks and the Trojans. Roman legend held that a Trojan remnant led by Prince Aeneas, son of Venus (the goddess of love) and a mortal father, Anchises, escaped the sacking of Troy. (Caesar Augustus claimed descent from the goddess Venus through Aeneas.) In book six, Aeneas, escorted by the Sybil, prophetess and priestess of Apollo, descends to the underworld in order to reach his father. There his father's soul describes the illustrious future that will be Rome's.

. . . Turn your two eyes
This way and see this people, your own Romans.
Here is Caesar, and all the line of Iulus
   [founder of the Julian family],
All who shall one day pass under the dome
Of the great sky: this is the man, this one,
Of whom so often you have heard the promise,
Caesar Augustus, son of the deified [Julius
   Caesar],
Who shall bring once again an Age of Gold
To Latium,[1] to the land where Saturn [Roman
   god] reigned
In early times. He will extend his power

Beyond the Garamants[2] and Indians,
Over far territories north and south
   . . .
Others will cast more tenderly in bronze
Their breathing figures, I can well believe,
And bring more lifelike portraits out of
   marble;
Argue more eloquently, use the pointer
To trace the paths of heaven accurately
And accurately foretell the rising stars.
Roman, remember by your strength to rule
Earth's peoples—for your arts are to be these:
To pacify, to impose the rule of law,
To spare the conquered, battle down the
   proud.

[1]Latium was the ancient country in which stood the towns of Lavinium and Alba Longa; Rome was established in that region and became its most significant city.

[2]The Garamants (Garamantes) were a warlike nomadic people living in the northwestern Sahara.

# Quintilian
## *THE EDUCATION OF THE ORATOR*

Quintilian (Marcus Fabius Quintilianus, c. A.D. 35–c. 90), the leading Roman rhetorician of his day, was born in Spain and educated in Rome. After many years of teaching the children of the Roman elite, Quintilian wrote a systematic treatise on education, *The Education of the Orator,* which provided shrewd insights into the learning process and emphasized the making of well-rounded, cultured orators and good citizens as important goals for the instructor. Excerpts from this work are given below.

My aim, then, is the education of the perfect orator. The first essential for such an one is that he should be a good man, and consequently we demand of him not merely the possession of exceptional gifts of speech, but of all the excellences of character as well. For I will not admit that the principles of upright and honourable living should, as some have held, be regarded as the peculiar concern of philosophy. The man who can really play his part as a citizen and is capable of meeting the demands both of public and private business, the man who can guide a state by his counsels, give it a firm basis by his legislation and purge its vices by his decisions as a judge, is assuredly no other than the orator of our quest. . . .

I prefer that a boy should begin with Greek, because Latin, being in general use, will be picked up by him whether we will or no; while the fact that Latin learning is derived from Greek is a further reason for his being first instructed in the latter. . . . The study of Latin ought therefore to follow at no great distance and in a short time proceed side by side with Greek. The result will be that, as soon as we begin to give equal attention to both languages, neither will prove a hindrance to the other.

Some hold that boys should not be taught to read till they are seven years old, that being the earliest age at which they can derive profit from instruction and endure the strain of learning. . . . Those however who hold that a child's mind should not be allowed to lie fallow for a moment are wiser. Why, again, since children are capable of moral training, should they not be capable of literary education? I am well aware that during the whole period of which I am speaking we can expect scarcely the same amount of progress that one year will effect afterwards. . . .

I am not however so blind to differences of age as to think that the very young should be forced on prematurely or given real work to do. Above all things we must take care that the child, who is not yet old enough to love his studies, does not come to hate them and dread the bitterness which he has once tasted, even when the years of infancy are left behind. His studies must be made an amusement: he must be questioned and praised and taught to rejoice when he has done well; sometimes, too, when he refuses instruction, it should be given to some other to excite his envy, at times also he must be engaged in competition and should be allowed to believe himself successful more often than not, while he should be encouraged to do his best by such rewards as may appeal to his tender years. . . .

. . . It is the master's duty as well, if he is engaged on the task of training unformed minds and prefers practical utility to a more ambitious programme, not to burden his pupils at once with tasks to which their strength is unequal, but to curb his energies and refrain from talking over the heads of his audience. Vessels with narrow mouths will not receive liquids if too much be poured into them at a time, but are easily filled if the liquid is admitted in a gentle stream or, it may be, drop by drop; similarly you must consider how much a child's mind is capable of receiving: the things which are beyond their grasp will not enter their minds, which have not opened out sufficiently to take them in. . . .

Still, all our pupils will require some relaxation, not merely because there is nothing in this world that can stand continued strain . . . but because study depends on the good will of the student, a quality that cannot be secured by compulsion. Consequently if restored and refreshed by a holiday they will bring greater energy to their learning and approach their work with greater spirit of a kind that will not submit to be driven. I approve of play in the young; it is a sign of a lively disposition; nor will you ever lead me to believe that a boy who is gloomy and in a continual state of depression is ever likely to show alertness of mind in his work, lacking as he does the impulse most natural to boys of his age. Such relaxation must not however be unlimited: otherwise the refusal to give a holiday will make boys hate their work, while excessive indulgence will accustom them to idleness. There are moreover certain games which have an education value for boys. . . . Games too reveal character in the most natural way, at least that is so if the teacher will bear in mind that there is no child so young as to be unable to learn to distinguish between right and wrong, and that the character is best moulded, when it is still guiltless of deceit and most susceptible to instruction: for once a bad habit has become engrained, it is easier to break than bend. There must be no delay, then, in warning a boy that his actions must be unselfish, honest, self-controlled, and we must never forget the words of Virgil, "So strong is custom formed in early years."

I disapprove of flogging, although it is the regular custom and meets with the acquiescence of Chrysippus,[1] because . . . it is a disgraceful form of punishment and fit only for slaves, and is in any case an insult, as you will realise if you imagine its infliction at a later age. . . . And though you may compel a child with blows, what are you to do with him when he is a young man no longer amenable to such threats and confronted with tasks of far greater difficulty? Moreover when children are beaten, pain or fear frequently have results of which it is not pleasant to speak and which are likely subsequently to be a source of shame, a shame which unnerves and depresses the mind and leads the child to shun and loathe the light. . . . I will content myself with saying that children are helpless and easily victimised, and that

therefore no one should be given unlimited power over them. I will now proceed to describe the subjects in which the boy must be trained, if he is to become an orator, and to indicate the age at which each should be commenced.

As soon as the boy has learned to read and write without difficulty, it is the turn for the teacher of literature. My words apply equally to Greek and Latin masters, though I prefer that a start should be made with a Greek: in either case the method is the same. This profession may be most briefly considered under two heads, the art of speaking correctly and the interpretation of the poets; but there is more beneath the surface than meets the eye. For the art of writing is combined with that of speaking, and correct reading precedes interpretation, while in each of these cases criticism has its work to perform. . . . Nor is it sufficient to have read the poets only; every kind of writer must be carefully studied, not merely for the subject matter, but for the vocabulary; for words often acquire authority from their use by a particular author. Nor can such training be regarded as complete if it stop short of music, for the teacher of literature has to speak of metre and rhythm: nor again if he be ignorant of astronomy, can he understand the poets; for they, to mention no further points, frequently give their indications of time by reference to the rising and setting of the stars. Ignorance of philosophy is an equal drawback, since there are numerous passages in almost every poem based on the most intricate questions of natural philosophy. . . . No small powers of eloquence also are required to enable the teacher to speak appropriately and fluently on the various points which have just been mentioned. For this reason those who criticise the art of teaching literature as trivial and lacking in substance put themselves out of court. Unless the foundations of oratory are well and truly laid by the teaching of literature, the superstructure will collapse. The study of literature is a necessity for boys and the delight of old age, the sweet companion of our privacy and the sole branch of study which has more solid substance than display.

---

[1]Chrysippus (280–207 B.C.) was considered second only to Zeno among the Stoic philosophers.

# Juvenal
## *THE SATIRES*

Juvenal (Decimus Junius Juvenalis, c. A.D. 60–c. 131), Rome's greatest satirical poet, found much fault with the Rome of his day. The streets were crowded, noisy, and unsafe; bullies itched to fight; criminals stole and murdered; the poor suffered even more than other Romans. The following excerpt from *The Satires* is Juvenal's account of the underside of life in Rome.

. . . A man's word
Is believed just to the extent of the
    wealth in his coffers stored.
Though he swear on all the altars from
    here to Samothrace,[1]
A poor man isn't believed. . . .

Anyway, a poor man's the butt of jokes if
    his cloak has a rip
Or is dirty, if his toga is slightly soiled, if
    a strip
Of leather is split in his shoes and gapes,
    if coarse thread shows
New stitches patching not one but many
    holes. Of the woes
Of unhappy poverty, none is more
    difficult to bear
Than that it heaps men with ridicule.
    Says an usher, "How dare
You sit there? Get out of the rows
    reserved for knights to share. . . ."

. . . What poor man ever inherits
A fortune or gets appointed as clerk to a
    magistrate?
Long ago the penniless Romans ought to
    have staged a great
Mass walkout. It's no easy job for a man
    to advance
When his talents are balked by his
    impoverished circumstance,

But in Rome it's harder than
    elsewhere. . . .
Here most of the sick die off because
    they get no sleep
(But the sickness is brought on by the
    undigested heap
Of sour food in their burning stomachs),
    for what rented flat
Allows you to sleep? Only rich men in
    this city have that.
There lies the root of the illness—carts
    rumbling in narrow streets
And cursing drivers stalled in a traffic
    jam—it defeats
All hope of rest. . . .

. . . Though we hurry, we merely crawl;
We're blocked by a surging mass ahead,
    a pushing wall
Of people behind. A man jabs me,
    elbowing through, one socks
A chair pole against me, one cracks my
    skull with a beam, one knocks
A wine cask against my ear. My legs are
    caked with splashing
Mud, from all sides the weight of
    enormous feet comes smashing
On mine, and a soldier stamps his
    hobnails through to my sole. . . .

. . . a piece of a pot
Falls down on my head, how often a
    broken vessel is shot
From the upper windows, with what a
    force it strikes and dints
The cobblestones! . . .

---

[1]Samothrace, an island in the northern Aegean Sea, is best known today as the place where the famous statue of the Winged Victory (Nike) was found.

The besotted bully, denied his chance in
 the shabby bars
Of killing somebody, suffers torments,
 itching to fight.
Like Achilles[2] bemoaning his friend, he
 tosses about all night,
Now flat on his face, now on his back—
 there's no way at all
He can rest, for some men can't sleep till
 after a bloody brawl.
But however rash and hot with youth
 and flushed with wine,
He avoids the noble whose crimson cloak
 and long double line
Of guards with brass lamps and torches
 show they're too much to handle.
But for me, whom the moon escorts, or
 the feeble light of a candle
Whose wick I husband and trim—he
 has no respect for me.
Now hear how the pitiful fight begins—
 if a fight it be,

When he delivers the punches and I am
 beaten to pulp.
He blocks my way and tells me to stop. I
 stop, with a gulp—
What else can you do when a madman
 stronger than you attacks? . . .

This is the poor man's freedom: having
 been soundly mauled
And cut to pieces by fists, he begs and
 prays, half dead,
To be allowed to go home with a few
 teeth still in his head.

But these aren't your only terrors. For
 you can never restrain
The criminal element. Lock up your
 house, put bolt and chain
On your shop, but when all's quiet,
 someone will rob you or he'll
Be a cutthroat perhaps and do you in
 quickly with cold steel. . . .

---

[2]Achilles, the Greeks' most formidable warrior in
Homer's *Iliad*, was torn by grief when his best friend Patroclus was killed by the Trojans.

---

Juvenal gives us an unflattering picture of
women and marriage.

---

You once had your wits about you,
 Postumus; but now you think
Of taking a wife? What Fury, what
 serpents, are driving you mad?

Can you let a termagant [shrewish woman]
 boss you when rope is so easily had
And so many windows open on dizzy
 leaps and the height
Of the Aemilian bridge so handy?
 If none of these modes of flight
Is to your taste, don't you think it
 might be better to take
Some boy as bedmate, who'd never
 quarrel all night, or make
You promise gifts as you twine, or
 complain if you resist
His pleas and sleep, instead of panting,
 and leave him unkissed? . . .

And who is so deeply in love he never
 shrinks at all
From the very woman he praises to the
 skies—what's more,
Hates her at least sixteen hours out
 of the twenty-four? . . .

If you don't intend to love the woman
 you embrace
And marry in legal form, there seems
 no reason for you
To marry, no reason why you should
 waste the supper and new
Wedding cakes that must be given to
 well-stuffed guests who leave
When the party's over, or waste the
 gift of the bridal eve,
The rich tray gleaming with coins
 engraved with victories
In Dacia and Germany. If you simply
 must appease
Yourself with a wife and are devoted
 to one, incline

Your head, submit your neck to the
      marriage yoke. You'll find
No woman who spares the man who loves
      her. Though she glow
With passion, she loves to torment
      and plunder her lover. So,
The more he's good and desirable as
      a husband, the less
Beneficial by far will be his wife.
      You'll never address
A gift if she says no, never sell
      things if she objects,
Never buy anything unless she consents.
      And she will select
Your friends for you and turn your now
      aged friend from the door. . . .

You'll have to despair of knowing
      any peace at home
If your mother-in-law's alive. She
      teaches your wife to delight

In stripping you of wealth. . . .

There's hardly a case in court that
      a woman's fuss didn't start.

The bed where a wife lies never is free
      of complaints and a host
Of quarrels back and forth. There'll
      be little sleep in that bed.
There she assails her husband, worse
      than a tigress is said
To be at the loss of her cubs. Aware
      of her own secret deeds,
She pretends to grieve, denounces
      the boys he's known, and weeps
At some feigned mistress, always with
      floods of tears at hand
Ever ready at their station, waiting
      for her command
On how they should flow. You think,
      poor worm, it's love they show. . . .

## REVIEW QUESTIONS

1. What role do poets play in shaping the ideals and values of a culture?
2. According to Virgil, what was Rome's destiny and the basis of its greatness?
3. What kind of human being did Quintilian hope to create with his curriculum and ideas on education?
4. What argument did Quintilian make against flogging students?
5. According to Juvenal, what were some of the hazards of urban life in ancient Rome?
6. Why did Juvenal expect all men to be unhappy in marriage?

# 3  Roman Stoicism

Stoicism, the leading school of thought in the Hellenistic world, appealed to Roman thinkers. Founded by Zeno of Citium (335–267 B.C.), who established an academy in Athens, Stoicism taught that universal principles, or natural law, underlay the universe. Natural laws applied to all people and were grasped through reason, which was common to all human beings. Stoicism gave expression to the universalism of the Hellenistic Age; it held that all people—Greek and barbarian, free and slave, rich and poor—were essentially equal, for they all had the capacity to reason and were all governed by the same universal laws. Living according to the law of reason that pervades the cosmos provides the individual with the inner fortitude to deal with life's misfortunes, said the

Stoics; it is the path to virtue. In the tradition of Socrates, the Stoics regarded people as morally self-sufficient, capable of regulating their own lives. The Romans valued the Stoic emphasis on self-discipline and the molding of character according to worthy standards. The Stoic doctrine of natural law that applied to all peoples harmonized with the requirements of Rome's multinational Empire.

# Seneca
# *THE MORAL EPISTLES*

Lucius Annaeus Seneca (4 B.C.–A.D. 65) was born at Corduba (Cordova), Spain, into a highly educated family: his father, for example, was a distinguished rhetorician, politician, and historian. Sent to school in Rome, Seneca studied rhetoric and philosophy, particularly Stoicism. From A.D. 54 to 62, he was a key advisor to the emperor Nero (A.D. 54–68). Later the notoriously unstable emperor accused Seneca of participating in a conspiracy against him and compelled him to commit suicide.

In traditional Stoic fashion, Seneca held that individuals belong to two commonwealths, the city where they are born and the kingdom of humanity, which is worldwide. In serving this superior commonwealth, individuals become aware of their moral potential. The virtuous tone of Seneca's writings (they had a great appeal to Christians) contrasted with the realities of his life, for Seneca used his political influence for self-enrichment and condoned murder to enhance his political power. Despite this discrepancy between Seneca's words and deeds, he was one of the few Romans to denounce the gladiatorial events as barbaric, and he urged humane treatment of slaves.

The sentiments expressed in the first two moral essays, written in the form of epistles (letters) to his friend Lucilius, a prominent Roman civil servant, reveal Seneca's Stoic humanitarianism. In the third selection, dealing with the rearing of the young, Seneca blends common sense with wisdom.

## ON GLADIATORS

But nothing is more harmful to a good disposition than to while the time away at some public show. I return from such entertainments more greedy, more dissipated, nay, even more cruel and inhuman. By chance I fell in with a public show at midday, expecting some sport, buffoonery [clownish amusement], or other relaxation, now that the spectators had seen their fill of human gore. All the bloody deeds of the morning were mere mercy: for now, all trifling apart, they commit downright murder. The combatants have nothing with which to shield the body; they are exposed to every stroke of their antagonist; and every stroke is a wound. And this some prefer to their fighting well armored! There is no helmet or shield to repel the blow; no defense, no art—for these are but so many balks and delays of death. In the morning men are exposed to lions and bears; at noon gladiators who fight to the death are ordered out against one another, and the conqueror is detained for another slaughter. Death alone puts an end to this business. "Kill, burn, scourge," is all they cry. "Why is he so afraid of the sword's point? Why is he so timorous to kill? Why does he not die more manfully?" They are urged on with floggings if they refuse to fight and are obliged to give and take wounds with an open breast. They are called upon to cut one another's throats.

## ON SLAVERY

It by no means displeases me, Lucilius, to hear from those who confer with you, that you live on friendly terms with your slaves. This attests to your good sense and education. Are they slaves? No, they are men; they are comrades; they are humble friends. Nay, rather fellow-servants, if you reflect on the equal power of Fortune over both you and them. I therefore laugh at those who think it scandalous for a gentleman to permit, at times, his servant to sit down with him at supper. Why should he not? It is only proud custom that has ordained that a master dine surrounded by at least a dozen slaves and stuff himself, while the poor servants are not allowed to open their lips, even to speak. The slightest murmur is restrained by a rod; nor are mere accidents excused, such as a cough, a sneeze, or a hiccup. Silence interrupted by a word is sure to be punished severely. Thus the slaves must stand, perhaps the whole night, without taking a bit of food or drink or speaking a word. Whence it often happens that such as are not allowed to speak before their masters will speak disrespectfully of them behind their backs. In contrast, those slaves who have been allowed not only to speak before their masters, but sometimes with them, whose mouths were not sewed up, have been ready to incur the most imminent danger, even to the sacrificing of their lives, for their master's safety. Slaves are not naturally our enemies, but we make them such.

I pass by the more cruel and inhuman actions, wherein we treat slaves not as men but as beasts of burden. . . .

Were you to consider, that he whom you call your slave, is sprung from the same origin, enjoys the same climate, breathes the same air, and is subject to the same condition of life and death as yourself, you will think it possible to see him as a free-born person, as he is free to see you as a slave. After the fall of Marius,[1] how many people born of the most splendid parentage and not unjustly expecting a senatorial office for their exploits in war, did fortune cut down? She made one a shepherd, another a caretaker of a country cottage. Can you now despise the man whose fortune is such, into which, while you despise it, you may fall?

I will not discuss at length the treatment of slaves towards whom we behave cruelly and arrogantly. But this is the essence of what I would prescribe: treat your inferiors as you would have a superior treat you. As often as you think of the power that you have over a slave, reflect on the power that your master has over you. But you say, "I have no master." Be it so. The world goes well with you at present; it may not do so always. You may one day be a slave yourself. Do you know at what time Hecuba[2] became a slave, or Croesus,[3] or the mother of Darius,[4] or Plato, or Diogenes?[5] Live therefore courteously with your slave; talk with him, dine with him.

## ON REARING CHILDREN

It will be of the utmost profit, I say, to give children sound training from the very beginning; guidance, however, is difficult, because we ought to take pains neither to develop in them anger nor to blunt their native spirit. The mat-

---

[1]Gaius Marius (c. 155–86 B.C.) was a famous Roman general.
[2]In the *Iliad*, Hecuba, the wife of Priam, king of Troy, was enslaved by the Greeks after their conquest of Troy.
[3]Croesus, king of Lydia in Asia Minor from 560 to 546 B.C., was famous for his wealth, but died in slavery after losing his kingdom in battle.
[4]Darius III of Persia (336–330 B.C.) was defeated by Alexander the Great, who also captured Darius' mother, wives, and children.
[5]Diogenes (c. 412–323 B.C.), a famous Greek philosopher of the Cynic school, was captured by pirates and put up for sale in Crete. He is reported to have said, "Sell me to that man; he needs a master." He was bought by a wealthy Greek, who restored his freedom.

ter requires careful watching; for both qualities—that which should be encouraged and that which should be checked—are fed by like things, and like things easily deceive even a close observer. By freedom the spirit grows, by servitude it is crushed; if it is commended and is led to expect good things of itself, it mounts up, but these same measures breed insolence and temper; therefore we must guide the child between the two extremes, using now the curb, now the spur. He should be subjected to nothing that is humiliating, nothing that is servile; it should never be necessary for him to beg submissively, nor should begging ever prove profitable—rather let his own desert and his past conduct and good promise of it in the future be rewarded. In struggles with his playmates we should not permit him either to be beaten or to get angry; we should take pains to see that he is friendly toward those with whom it is his practice to engage in order that in the struggle he may form the habit of wishing not to hurt his opponent but merely to win. Whenever he gets the upper hand and does something praiseworthy, we should allow him to be encouraged but not elated, for joy leads to exultation, exultation to over-conceit and a too high opinion of oneself. We shall grant him some relaxation, though we shall not let him lapse into sloth and ease, and we shall keep him far from all taint of pampering; for there is nothing that makes the child hot-tempered so much as a soft and coddling bringing up. Therefore the more an only

child is indulged, and the more liberty a ward is allowed, the more will his disposition be spoiled. He will not withstand rebuffs who has never been denied anything, whose tears have always been wiped away by an anxious mother, who has been allowed to have his own way with his tutor [the slave who was the child's special guardian]. . . . Childhood, therefore, should be kept far from all contact with flattery; let a child hear the truth, sometimes even let him fear, let him be respectful always, let him rise before his elders. Let him gain no request by anger; when he is quiet let him be offered what was refused when he wept. Let him, moreover, have the sight but not the use of his parents' wealth. When he has done wrong, let him be reproved. It will work to the advantage of children to give them teachers and tutors of a quiet disposition. Every young thing attaches itself to what is nearest and grows to be like it; the character of their nurses and tutors is presently reproduced in that of the young men. There was a boy who had been brought up in the house of Plato, and when he had returned to his parents and saw his father in a blustering rage, his comment was: "I never saw this sort of thing at Plato's." I doubt not that he was quicker to copy his father than he was to copy Plato! Above all, let his food be simple, his clothing inexpensive, and his style of living like that of his companions. The boy will never be angry at some one being counted equal to himself, whom you have from the first treated as the equal of many.

# Marcus Aurelius
## *MEDITATIONS*

**Emperor Marcus Aurelius Antoninus (A.D. 161–180) was the last of the great Roman Stoics and the last of the so-called Five Good Emperors. His death brought an end to the Pax Romana. A gentle and peace-loving man, Marcus Aurelius was not spared violence and personal misfortune during his reign. Troops returning from Syria brought back a plague, which spread throughout the Empire. Marcus hurried to the east to quell an uprising by the commander of the forces in Asia, who declared himself emperor. Although the mutiny**

quickly died out, Marcus Aurelius' wife perished on the journey. Four of his five sons died young, and his fifth son, Commodus, who succeeded to the throne, was a tyrant.

For the last fourteen years of his life, Marcus Aurelius had to deal with tribesmen from north of the Danube who broke through the defenses and plundered what is now the Balkan peninsula. Marcus took personal command of the hard-pressed legions on the frontier. During this period he wrote the *Meditations,* twelve books containing his reflections on duty, human dignity, the self-sufficiency of reason, and other themes traditionally discussed by Stoic thinkers. Written in Greek, this deeply personal expression of Stoic philosophy has been called "the highest ethical product of the ancient mind." Excerpts from the *Meditations* follow.

## BOOK TWO

Begin each day by telling yourself: Today I shall be meeting with interference, ingratitude, insolence, disloyalty, ill-will, and selfishness—all of them due to the offenders' ignorance of what is good or evil. But for my part I have long perceived the nature of good and its nobility, the nature of evil and its meanness, and also the nature of the [evildoer] himself, who is my brother (not in the physical sense, but as a fellow-creature similarly endowed with reason and a share of the divine); therefore none of those things can injure me, for nobody can implicate me in what is degrading. Neither can I be angry with my brother or fall foul of him; for he and I were born to work together, like a man's two hands, feet, or eyelids, or like the upper and lower rows of his teeth. To obstruct each other is against Nature's law—and what is irritation or aversion but a form of obstruction?

A little flesh, a little breath, and a Reason to rule all—that is myself. . . . As one already on the threshold of death, think nothing of the first—of its viscid [thick] blood, its bones, its web of nerves and veins and arteries. The breath, too; what is that? A whiff of wind; and not even the same wind, but every moment puffed out and drawn in anew. But the third, the Reason, the master—on this you must concentrate. Now that your hairs are grey, let it play the part of a slave no more, twitching puppetwise at every pull of self-interest; and

cease to fume at destiny by ever grumbling at today or lamenting over tomorrow. . . .

Hour by hour resolve firmly, like a Roman and a man, to do what comes to hand with correct and natural dignity, and with humanity, independence, and justice. Allow your mind freedom from all other considerations. This you can do, if you will approach each action as though it were your last, dismissing the wayward thought, the emotional recoil from the commands of reason, the desire to create an impression, the admiration of self, the discontent with your lot. See how little a man needs to master, for his days to flow on in quietness and piety: he has but to observe these few counsels, and the gods will ask nothing more.

## BOOK THREE

If mortal life can offer you anything better than justice and truth, self-control and courage—that is, peace of mind in the evident conformity of your actions to the laws of reason, and peace of mind under the visitations of a destiny you cannot control—if, I say, you can discern any higher ideal, why, turn to it with your whole soul, and rejoice in the prize you have found. . . .

Never value the advantages derived from anything involving breach of faith, loss of self-respect, hatred, suspicion, or execration of others, insincerity, or the desire for something which has to be veiled and curtained. One whose chief regard is for his own mind, and for the divinity within him and the service of its goodness, will strike no poses, utter no complaints, and crave neither for solitude nor yet for a crowd. . . . No other care has he in life but to keep his mind from straying into paths incompatible with those of an intelligent and social being. . . .

## BOOK FOUR

Men seek for seclusion in the wilderness, by the seashore, or in the mountains—a dream you have cherished only too fondly yourself. But such fancies are wholly unworthy of a philosopher, since at any moment you choose you can retire within yourself. Nowhere can man find a quieter or more untroubled retreat than in his own soul; above all, he who possesses resources in himself, which he need only contemplate to secure immediate ease of mind—the ease that is but another word for a well-ordered spirit. Avail yourself often, then, of this retirement, and so continually renew yourself. Make your rules of life brief, yet so as to embrace the fundamentals; recurrence to them will then suffice to remove all vexation, and send you back without fretting to the duties to which you must return. . . .

If the power of thought is universal among mankind, so likewise is the possession of reason, making us rational creatures. It follows, therefore, that this reason speaks no less universally to us all with its "thou shalt" or "thou shalt not." So then there is a world-law; which in turn means that we are all fellow-citizens and share a common citizenship, and that the world is a single city. Is there any other common citizenship that can be claimed by all humanity? And it is from this world-polity that mind, reason, and law themselves derive. If not, whence else? As the earthy portion of me has its origin from earth, the watery from a different element, my breath from one source and my hot and fiery parts from another of their own elsewhere (for nothing comes from nothing, or can return to nothing), so too there must be an origin for the mind. . . .

## BOOK FIVE

At day's first light have in readiness, against disinclination to leave your bed, the thought that "I am rising for the work of man." Must I grumble at setting out to do what I was born for, and for the sake of which I have been brought into the world? Is this the purpose of my creation, to lie here under the blankets and keep myself warm? "Ah, but it is a great deal more pleasant!" Was it for pleasure, then, that you were born, and not for work, not for effort? Look at the plants, the sparrows, ants, spiders, bees, all busy at their own tasks, each doing his part towards a coherent world-order; and will you refuse man's share of the work, instead of being prompt to carry out Nature's bidding? "Yes, but one must have some repose as well." Granted; but repose has its limits set by nature, in the same way as food and drink have; and you overstep these limits, you go beyond the point of sufficiency; while on the other hand, when action is in question, you stop short of what you could well achieve.

## *REVIEW QUESTIONS*

1. What virtues did Stoics believe should guide human actions?
2. What Stoic philosophic principle influenced Seneca's view of the proper relationship between slaves and masters?
3. Which of Seneca's guidelines for rearing children do you like the best? Which do you like the least? Explain.
4. According to Marcus Aurelius, what was the purpose of human life?
5. How did a Stoic seek to achieve tranquility of mind and spirit?

## 4  Roman Law

One of the most significant legacies of Rome to Western civilization is the system of law developed by the Romans over many centuries. Roman law evolved into three distinct types: the civil law *(ius civile),* which was peculiar to the Roman state and applicable only to its citizens; the law of nature *(ius naturale),* an unchanging, everlasting, universal law that was binding on all persons by reason of their common humanity; the law of nations *(ius gentium),* an international law governing the relationship between Romans and other peoples. The law of nations was fashioned by Roman jurists as Rome came into contact with and conquered other cultures; it incorporated elements from Roman civil law and the legal traditions of the other peoples, particularly the Greeks. Roman jurists held that the law of nations accorded with natural law: that is, it rested upon principles of reason that were common to all humans.

Roman law eventually became the basis for the legal systems of all modern European states except England and Ireland. As Europeans established colonial empires in Asia, Africa, and the Americas, they carried with them the principles inherited from Roman law.

# Justinian
# *CORPUS IURIS CIVILIS*

The principles of Roman law are drawn from many sources, from the statutes of emperors, edicts of magistrates, and commentaries of learned jurists, such as Ulpian (Domitius Ulpianus, d. A.D. 228), Gaius (c. A.D. 130–180), and Julius Paulus (second–third century A.D.). These past laws and judicial commentaries were culled and selectively incorporated in the *Corpus Iuris Civilis,* the imperial code drawn up by order of Emperor Justinian (A.D. 527–565) and promulgated in A.D. 534. It has been said that next to the Bible, no book has had a deeper impact on Western civilization than Justinian's code. It became the official body of laws of the eastern Roman (or Byzantine) Empire through the Middle Ages and was gradually reintroduced into western Europe in the twelfth century. Roman law continued in the postmedieval world and formed the basis of common law in all Western lands except England and its dependencies, where its influence was less marked. Some principles of Roman law are readily recognizable in today's legal systems, as the following excerpts indicate.

• The Divine Trajan stated in a Rescript addressed to Julius Frontonus that anyone who is absent should not be convicted of crime. Likewise, no one should be convicted on suspicion; for the Divine Trajan stated in a Rescript to Assiduus Severus: "It is better to permit the crime of a guilty person to go unpunished than to condemn one who is innocent."

• No one suffers a penalty for merely thinking.

- Proof is incumbent upon the party who affirms a fact, not upon him who denies it.

- In inflicting penalties, the age and inexperience of the guilty party must always be taken into account.

- Nothing is so opposed to consent, which is the basis of *bona fide* contracts, as force and fear; and to approve anything of this kind is contrary to good morals.

- The crime or the punishment of a father can place no stigma upon his son; for each one is subjected to fate in accordance with his conduct, and no one is appointed the successor of the crime of another.

- Women are excluded from all civil or public employments; therefore they cannot be judges, or perform the duties of magistrates, or bring suits in court, or become sureties for others, or act as attorneys.

- A minor, also, must abstain from all civil employments.

- Every person should support his own offspring, and anyone who thinks that he can abandon his child shall be subjected to the penalty prescribed by law. We do not give any right to masters or to patrons to recover children who have been abandoned, when children exposed by them, as it were, to death, have been rescued through motives of pity, for no one can say that a child whom he has left to perish belongs to him.

- The authority and observance of long-established custom should not be treated with contempt, but it should not prevail to the extent of overcoming either reason or law.

---

Not all principles of Roman law have been incorporated into the legal codes of modern societies. One example is the use of torture to test the testimony of witnesses, particularly those of low social status. In those lands where Roman law remained in effect, torture was legal until the eighteenth century, when it was purged from European judicial systems.

---

- Torture is employed in the detection of crime, but a beginning should not be made with its application; and, therefore, in the first place, evidence should be resorted to, and if the party is liable to suspicion, he shall be compelled by torture to reveal his accomplices and crimes.

- Where several culprits are implicated in the same offence, they should be examined in such a way as to begin with the one who appears to be more timid than the others, and of tender age.

- Torture is not applied in pecuniary matters, unless when an investigation is made with reference to property belonging to an estate; other things, however, are established by oath, or by the evidence of witnesses.

- Torture should not be inflicted upon a minor under fourteen years of age, as the Divine Pius stated in a Rescript addressed to Caecilius Jubentinus.

- All persons, however, without exception, shall be tortured in a case of high treason which has reference to princes, if their testimony is necessary, and circumstances demand it.

- Torture should not be applied to the extent that the accuser demands, but as reason and moderation may dictate.

- In questions where freedom is involved it is not necessary to seek for the truth by the torture of those whose status is in dispute.

- It was declared by the Imperial Constitutions that while confidence should not always be reposed in torture, it ought not to be rejected as absolutely unworthy of it, as the evidence obtained is weak and dangerous, and inimical to the truth; for most persons, either through their power of endurance, or through the severity of the torment, so despise suffering that the truth can in no way be extorted from them. Others are so little able to suffer that they prefer to lie rather than to endure the question, and hence it happens that they make confessions of different kinds, and they not only implicate themselves, but others as well.

• The Edict of the Divine Augustus, which he published during the Consulate of Vivius Avitus and Lucius Apronianus, is as follows: "I do not think that torture should be inflicted in every instance, and upon every person; but when capital and atrocious crimes cannot be detected and proved except by means of the torture of slaves, I hold that it is most effective for ascertaining the truth, and should be employed."

## REVIEW QUESTIONS

1. What is the *ius naturale* and what are its implications when applied to particular legal cases?
2. What is the *ius gentium* and what were its origins?
3. What provisions of Justinian's code are reflected in present-day legal systems in Europe and America?
4. Why are both torture and slavery in the modern world seen as incompatible with the basic premises of natural law?

---

## 5   Provincial Administration

During the Pax Romana, Roman officials governed territories that extended from Britain, Spain, and present-day Morocco in the west to Mesopotamia and Armenia in the east; from the Rhine and Danube rivers in western and central Europe to the Sahara in northern Africa. The Empire reached its greatest geographic extent under Emperor Trajan (A.D. 98–117), who conquered Dacia (heartland of modern Romania). The basic unit of political administration, the city, met most of the daily political and social needs of the population. Above the level of the city governments were the Roman provincial authorities, led by governors usually appointed by and responsible directly to the emperor. The senate's role in governing the provinces gradually declined, and the burdens of ruling the vast territory fell largely on the emperor. This enormous task proved daunting for all but the most energetic and conscientious emperors.

# CORRESPONDENCE BETWEEN PLINY THE YOUNGER AND EMPEROR TRAJAN

A series of letters exchanged between Emperor Trajan and Gaius Plinius Caecilius (Pliny the Younger, c. A.D. 61–c. 112), governor of the Roman province of Bithynia, located in the northwestern corner of Asia Minor, reveal the many problems Roman provincial officials faced. Given the highly personal character of the imperial office, provincial officials like Pliny, even when urged not to do so, tended to refer most problems directly to the emperor for policy guidance.

## XXXIII

*Pliny to the Emperor Trajan*

While I was visiting another part of the province, a widespread fire broke out in Nicomedia[1] which destroyed many private houses and also two public buildings (the Elder Citizens' Club and the Temple of Isis)[2] although a road runs between them. It was fanned by the strong breeze in the early stages, but it would not have spread so far but for the apathy of the populace; for it is generally agreed that people stood watching the disaster without bestirring themselves to do anything to stop it. Apart from this, there is not a single fire engine anywhere in the town, not a bucket nor any apparatus for fighting a fire. These will now be provided on my instructions.

Will you, Sir, consider whether you think a company of firemen might be formed, limited to 150 members? I will see that no one shall be admitted who is not genuinely a fireman, and that the privileges granted shall not be abused: it will not be difficult to keep such small numbers under observation.

## XXXIV

*Trajan to Pliny*

You may very well have had the idea that it should be possible to form a company of firemen at Nicomedia on the model of those existing elsewhere, but we must remember that it is societies like these which have been responsible for the political disturbances in your province, particularly in its towns. If people assemble for a common purpose, whatever name we give them and for whatever reason, they soon turn into a political club. It is a better policy then to provide the equipment necessary for dealing with fires, and to instruct

property owners to make use of it, calling on the help of the crowds which collect if they find it necessary.

## XXXIX

*Pliny to the Emperor Trajan*

The theatre at Nicaea,[3] Sir, is more than half built but is still unfinished, and has already cost more than ten million sesterces,[4] or so I am told—I have not yet examined the relevant accounts. I am afraid it may be money wasted. The building is sinking and showing immense cracks, either because the soil is damp and soft or the stone used was poor and friable [crumbly]. We shall certainly have to consider whether it is to be finished or abandoned, or even demolished, as the foundations and substructure intended to hold up the building may have cost a lot but look none too solid to me. There are many additions to the theatre promised by private individuals, such as a colonnade on either side and a gallery above the auditorium,[5] but all these are now held up by the stoppage of work on the main building which must be finished first.

The citizens of Nicaea have also begun to rebuild their gymnasium[6] (which was destroyed by fire before my arrival) on a much larger and more extensive scale than before. They have already spent a large sum, which may be to little

---

[1]Nicomedia was the capital city of the province of Bithynia.

[2]Isis, the chief Egyptian goddess and consort of Osiris, was widely worshipped throughout the Roman Empire.

[3]Nicaea was another city in Bithynia. The Roman theater was an open-air structure, consisting of the flat stage used by the performers, the orchestra (close to the stage, a place where senators and nobles sat), and the auditorium, a sloped stand or rows of stone benches on which the rest of the audience sat. Dramas and declamations of poetry were given in the theaters.

[4]One sestertius (plural, sesterces) equals one quarter of a silver denarius.

[5]The word *auditorium* was also used in the modern sense, a lecture room or courtroom; the word means "listening place."

[6]As now, a gymnasium was a place where Greek and Roman wrestlers competed, and other small-scale athletic feats were performed. It was also a hall where citizens heard lectures or debates and socialized.

purpose, for the buildings are badly planned and too scattered. Moreover, an architect—admittedly a rival of the one who drew up the designs—has given the opinion that the walls cannot support the superstructure in spite of being twenty-two feet thick, as the rubble core has no facing of brick.

The people of Claudiopolis[7] are also building, or rather excavating, an enormous public bath in a hollow at the foot of a mountain. The money for this is coming either from the admission fees already paid by the new members of the town council elected by your gracious favour, or from what they will pay at my demand. So I am afraid there is misapplication of public funds at Nicaea. . . .

. . . I am therefore compelled to ask you to send out an architect to inspect both theatre and bath and decide whether it will be more practicable, in view of what has already been spent, to keep to the original plans and finish both buildings as best we can, or to make any necessary alterations and changes of site so that we do not throw away more money in an attempt to make some use of the original outlay.

# XL
## *Trajan to Pliny*

The future of the unfinished theatre at Nicaea can best be settled by you on the spot. It will be sufficient for me if you let me know your decision. But, once the main building is finished, you will have to see that private individuals carry out their promises of adding to the theatre.

These poor Greeks all love a gymnasium; so it may be that they were too ambitious in their plans at Nicaea. They will have to be content with one which suits their real needs.

As for the bath at Claudiopolis, which you say has been started in an unsuitable site,

you must decide yourself what advice to give. You cannot lack architects: every province has skilled men trained for this work. It is a mistake to think they can be sent out more quickly from Rome when they usually come to us from Greece.

# XXXI
## *Pliny to the Emperor Trajan*

You may stoop when necessary, Sir, to give ear to my problems, without prejudice to your eminent position, seeing that I have your authority to refer to you when in doubt.

In several cities, notably Nicomedia and Nicaea, there are people who were sentenced to service in the mines or the arena, or to other similar punishments, but are now performing the duties of public slaves and receiving an annual salary for their work. Since this was told me I have long been debating what to do. I felt it was too hard on the men to send them back to work out their sentences after a lapse of many years, when most of them are old by now, and by all accounts are quietly leading honest lives, but I did not think it quite right to retain criminals in public service; and though I realized there was nothing to be gained by supporting these men at public expense if they did no work, they might be a potential danger if they were left to starve. I was therefore obliged to leave the whole question in suspense until I could consult you.

You may perhaps want to know how they came to be released from the sentences passed on them. I asked this question myself, but received no satisfactory answer to give you, and although the records of their sentences were produced, there were no documents to prove their release. But people have stated on their behalf that they had been released by order of the previous governors or their deputies, and this is confirmed by the unlikelihood that any unauthorized person would take this responsibility.

---

[7]Claudiopolis was another city in the Roman province of Bithynia.

## XXXII
### Trajan to Pliny

Let us not forget that the chief reason for sending you to your province was the evident need for many reforms. Nothing in fact stands more in need of correction than the situation described in your letter, where criminals under sentence have not only been released without authority but are actually restored to the status of honest officials. Those among them who were sentenced within the last ten years and were released by no proper authority must therefore be sent back to work out their sentences. But if the men are elderly and have sentences dating back farther than ten years, they can be employed in work not far removed from penal labour, cleaning public baths and sewers, or repairing streets and highways, the usual employment for men of this type.

## XXVI
### Pliny to the Emperor Trajan

As a result of your generosity to me, Sir, Rosianus Geminus became one of my closest friends; for when I was consul he was my quaestor [financial officer]. I always found him devoted to my interests, and ever since then he has treated me with the greatest deference and increased the warmth of our public relations by many personal services. I therefore pray you to give your personal attention to my request for his advancement; if you place any confidence in my advice you will bestow on him your favour. He will not fail to earn further promotion in whatever post you place him. I am sparing in my praises because I trust that his sincerity, integrity and application are well known to you already from the high offices he has held in Rome beneath your own eyes, as well as from his service in the army under your command.

I still feel that I have not given adequate expression to the warmth of my affection, and so once more I pray you, Sir, most urgently, to permit me to rejoice as soon as possible in the due promotion of my quaestor—that is to say, in my own advancement in his person.

## LXV
### Pliny to the Emperor Trajan

A very considerable question, Sir, in which the whole province is interested, has been lately started, concerning the state and maintenance of what are called *foundlings.* I have examined the rulings of former Princes upon this head, but not finding any thing in them either particular or general relating to the Bithynians, I thought it necessary to apply to you for your directions. For in a point which requires the special interposition of your authority, I could not content myself with following precedents.

An edict of the Emperor Augustus (as pretended) was read to me, concerning Asia*; also a letter from Vespasian to the Lacedaemonians, and another from Titus to the same, with one likewise from him to the Achaeans. Also a letter from Domitian to the Proconsuls Avidius Nigrinus and Armenius Brocchus, and another to the Lacedaemonians: but I have not transmitted them to you, as well because they were ill-copied (and some of them, too, of doubtful authority) as because I imagine the true copies are preserved in your Record Office.

## LXVI
### Trajan to Pliny

The question concerning free-born persons who have been exposed [abandoned] as infants and reared in slavery by those who took them up, has been frequently discussed; but I do not find in the archives of the Princes my predecessors, any general regulation upon this head, extending to all the provinces. There are, indeed, letters of Domitian to Avidius Nigrinus and

*i.e. the Roman province so called.

Armenius Brocchus, which perhaps ought to be observed; but Bithynia is not comprehended in the provinces therein mentioned. I am of opinion therefore, that those who desire emancipation upon this ground should not be debarred from publicly asserting their freedom, nor be obliged to purchase it by repaying the cost of their maintenance.

## REVIEW QUESTION

1. What kinds of political and administrative problems in the Roman empire are suggested by the letters of Trajan and Pliny?

---

## 6  The Roman Peace

The two-hundred-year period from Augustus' assumption of sole power in 27 B.C. to the death of Emperor Marcus Aurelius in A.D. 180 marks the Pax Romana, the Roman Peace. Roman poets and officials extolled the Roman achievement—the creation of a well-run world-state that brought order and stability to the different nations of the Mediterranean world.

## Aelius Aristides
## *THE ROMAN ORATION*
## THE BLESSINGS OF THE PAX ROMANA

In the following reading, Aelius Aristides, a second-century Greek intellectual, glowingly praises the Pax Romana in an oration that was probably delivered in Rome. In the tradition of Roman orators, Aelius used hyperbole and exaggeration. Nevertheless, the oration does capture the universalism and cosmopolitanism that characterized the Roman Empire.

"If one considers the vast extent of your empire he must be amazed that so small a fraction of it rules the world, but when he beholds the city and its spaciousness it is not astonishing that all the habitable world is ruled by such a capital. . . . Your possessions equal the sun's course. . . . You do not rule within fixed boundaries, nor can anyone dictate the limits of your sway. . . . Whatever any people produces can be found here, at all times and in abundance. . . . Egypt, Sicily, and the civilized part of Africa are your farms; ships are continually coming and going. . . .

"Vast as it is, your empire is more remarkable for its thoroughness than its scope: there are no dissident or rebellious enclaves. . . . The whole world prays in unison that your empire may endure forever.

"Governors sent out to cities and peoples each rule their charges, but in their relations to each other they are equally subjects. The principal difference between governors and their charges is this—they demonstrate the proper way to be a subject. So great is their reverence for the great Ruler [the emperor], who administers all things. Him they believe to know their business better than they themselves do, and hence they respect and heed him more than one would a master overseeing a task and giving orders. No one is so self-assured that he can remain unmoved upon hearing the emperor's name; he rises in prayer and adoration and utters a twofold prayer—to the gods for the Ruler, and to the Ruler for himself. And if the governors are in the least doubt concerning the justice of claims or suits of the governed, public or private, they send to the Ruler for instructions at once and await his reply, as a chorus awaits its trainer's directions. Hence the Ruler need not exhaust himself by traveling to various parts to settle matters in person. It is easy for him to abide in his place and manage the world through letters; these arrive almost as soon as written, as if borne on wings.

"But the most marvelous and admirable achievement of all, and the one deserving our fullest gratitude, is this. . . . You alone of the imperial powers of history rule over men who are free. You have not assigned this or that region to this nabob or that mogul; no people has been turned over as a domestic and bound holding—to a man not himself free. But just as citizens in an individual city might designate magistrates, so you, whose city is the whole world, appoint governors to protect and provide for the governed, as if they were elective, not to lord it over their charges. As a result, so far from disputing the office as if it were their own, governors make way for their successors readily when their term is up, and may not even await their coming. Appeals to a higher jurisdiction are as easy as appeals from parish to county. . . .

"But the most notable and praiseworthy feature of all, a thing unparalleled, is your magnanimous conception of citizenship. All of your subjects (and this implies the whole world) you have divided into two parts: the better endowed and more virile, wherever they may be, you have granted citizenship and even kinship; the rest you govern as obedient subjects. Neither the seas nor expanse of land bars citizenship; Asia and Europe are not differentiated. Careers are open to talent. . . . Rich and poor find contentment and profit in your system; there is no other way of life. Your polity is a single and all-embracing harmony. . . .

"You have not put walls around your city, as if you were hiding it or avoiding your subjects; to do so you considered ignoble and inconsistent with your principles, as if a master should show fear of his slaves. You did not overlook walls, however, but placed them round the empire, not the city. The splendid and distant walls you erected are worthy of you; to men within their circuit they are visible, but it requires a journey of months and years from the city to see them. Beyond the outermost ring of the civilized world you drew a second circle, larger in radius and easier to defend, like the outer fortifications of a city. Here you built walls and established cities in diverse parts. The cities you filled with colonists; you introduced arts and crafts and established an orderly culture. . . . Your military organization makes all others childish. Your soldiers and officers you train to prevail not only over the enemy but over themselves. The soldier lives under discipline daily, and none ever deserts the post assigned him.

"You alone are, so to speak, natural rulers. Your predecessors were masters and slaves in turn; as rulers they were counterfeits, and reversed their positions like players in a ball game. . . . You have measured out the world, bridged rivers, cut roads through mountains, filled the wastes with posting stations, introduced orderly and refined modes of life. . . .

"Be all gods and their offspring invoked to grant that this empire and this city flourish forever and never cease until stones float upon the sea and trees forbear to sprout in the springtide. May the great Ruler and his sons be preserved to administer all things well."

## Tacitus
# THE OTHER SIDE OF THE PAX ROMANA

Not all peoples in the Roman Empire welcomed Roman rule. Some nations, particularly Jews, Gauls, Britons, and Egyptians, saw themselves as victims of brutal domination and rose in revolt against their Roman governors. Our knowledge of their motives and grievances is usually secondhand, being found in the records of their enemies—the Romans and their collaborators.

Cornelius Tacitus, Roman historian and orator (see also page 133), wrote a biography of his father-in-law, Agricola, a general who completed the conquest of northern Britain. In this work, Tacitus describes the character and motives of Roman imperialism from a Briton's viewpoint. The speech that follows is uttered by Calgacus, a leader of the northern, or Caledonian, tribes during the Roman campaign in the years A.D. 77–83. The ideas expressed, however, are those that Tacitus, a well-informed Roman of high social rank, believed the victims of Roman military conquest held about their situation.

"Whenever I consider why we are fighting and how we have reached this crisis, I have a strong sense that this day of your splendid rally may mean the dawn of liberty for the whole of Britain. You have mustered to a man, and to a man you are free. There are no lands behind us, and even the sea is menaced by the Roman fleet. The clash of battle—the hero's glory—has become the safest refuge for the coward. Battles against Rome have been lost and won before—but never without hope; we were always there in reserve. We, the choice flower of Britain, were treasured in her most secret places. Out of sight of subject shores, we kept even our eyes free from the defilement of tyranny. We, the last men on earth, the last of the free, have been shielded till to-day by the very remoteness and the seclusion for which we are famed. We have enjoyed the impressiveness of the unknown. But to-day the boundary of Britain is exposed; beyond us lies no nation, nothing but waves and rocks and the Romans, more deadly still than they, for you find in them an arrogance which no reasonable submission can elude. Brigands of the world, they have exhausted the land by their indiscriminate plunder, and now they ransack the sea.

The wealth of an enemy excites their [greed], his poverty their lust of power. East and West have failed to glut their maw [stomach]. They are unique in being as violently tempted to attack the poor as the wealthy. Robbery, butchery, rapine, the liars call Empire; they create a desolation and call it peace.

"We instinctively love our children and our kinsmen above all else. These are torn from us by conscription to slave in other lands. Our wives and sisters, even if they are not raped by Roman enemies, are seduced by them in the guise of guests and friends. Our goods and fortunes are ground down to pay tribute, our land and its harvest to supply corn, our bodies and hands to build roads through woods and swamps—all under blows and insults. Slaves, born into slavery, once sold, get their keep from their masters. But as for Britain, never a day passes but she pays and feeds her enslavers. In a private household it is the latest arrival who is always the butt of his fellow-slaves; so, in this establishment, where all the world have long been slaves, it is we, the cheap new acquisitions, who are picked out for extirpation. You see, we have no fertile lands, no mines, no harbours, which we might be spared to work.

Courage and martial spirit we have, but the master does not relish them in the subject. Even our remoteness and seclusion, while they protect, expose us to suspicion. Abandon, then, all hope of mercy and at last take courage, whether it is life or honour that you hold most dear. . . . Let us, then, uncorrupted, unconquered as we are, ready to fight for freedom but never to repent failure, prove at the first clash of arms what heroes Caledonia[1] has been holding in reserve. . . . Or can you seriously think that those Gauls or Germans[2]—and, to our bitter shame, many Britons too!—

are bound to Rome by genuine loyalty or love? They may be lending their life-blood to foreign tyrants, but they were enemies of Rome much longer than they have been her slaves. Apprehension and terror are weak bonds of affection; once break them, and, where fear ends, hatred will begin. All that can goad men to victory is on our side. . . . In the ranks of our very enemies we shall find hands to help us. . . . They [the Romans] have nothing in reserve that need alarm us—only forts without garrisons, colonies of grey-beards, towns sick and distracted between rebel subjects and tyrant masters. Here before us is their general, here his army; behind are the tribute, the mines and all the other whips to scourge slaves. Whether you are to endure these for ever or take summary vengeance, this field must decide. On, then, into action and, as you go, think of those that went before you and of those that shall come after."

---

[1]Caledonia was the name given by the Romans to the section of Scotland north of what is now the Firth of Forth.
[2]The Gauls consisted of several groups of tribes in modern Belgium, the Netherlands, France, and Switzerland. The Germans (Germani) who had been conquered by Rome lived north of the Gauls, just south of the Rhine; the rest of the Germani occupied a large territory north and east of the Rhine.

# Josephus
# RESISTANCE TO ROMAN RULE IN JUDEA

The Jews of Judea were a particularly thorny problem for Rome. Tolerant of the diverse religions of the empire and aware of the Jews' commitment to strict monotheism, the Romans did not interfere with Jewish beliefs and exempted Jews from emperor worship. However, at times the Romans offended Jewish sensibilities; Emperor Caligula (A.D. 37–41), for example, ordered a golden statue of himself to be placed in Jerusalem's holy temple. Refusing to accept loss of political independence and subjection to hated idolaters, Jewish militants launched a full-scale war of liberation in A.D. 66. After a terrible struggle, the Jews finally were crushed by superior Roman might.

Emperor Vespasian (Titus Flavius Sabinus Vespasianus), who reigned A.D. 69–79, and his son Titus (A.D. 79–81), who was commander of the victorious Roman forces and heir-apparent to the throne—staged a triumphal procession in Rome. Behind their chariot, Jewish captives were paraded in chains, and Roman soldiers carried Jewish sacred objects taken from the temple. To commemorate the event, the Romans erected the Arch of Titus, which still stands.

The Jewish revolt was described by Flavius Josephus (originally Joseph ben Mathias, c. A.D. 37–c. 100), a Jewish commander who surrendered to Rome and became an active collaborator. In the following reading, Josephus gives his report of a speech by Herod Agrippa II, the Jewish king of Chalcis, to the north of Palestine. According to Josephus, Herod Agrippa felt that a revolt against the overwhelming power of Rome was doomed. Jewish militants did not heed pleas for caution.

"... I grant that the ministers of Rome are unbearably harsh; does it follow that all the Romans are persecuting you, including Caesar? Yet it is on them that you are going to make war! It is not by their wish that an unscrupulous governor comes from Rome, nor can western eyes see the goings-on in the east; it is not easy in Rome even to get up-to-date news of what happens here. It would be absurd because of the trifling misdemeanours of one man to go to war with a whole nation, and such a nation—a nation that does not even know what it is all about! Our grievances can be quickly put right; the same procurator [Roman governor] will not be here for ever, and his successors are almost sure to be more reasonable. But once set on foot, war cannot easily be either broken off or fought to a conclusion without disaster. . . .

"Where are the men, where are the weapons you count on? Where is the fleet that is to sweep the Roman seas? Where are the funds to pay for your expeditions? Do you think you are going to war with Egyptians and Arabs? Look at the far-flung empire of Rome and contrast your own impotence. Why, our forces have been worsted even by our neighbours again and again, while their arms have triumphed over the whole world! And even the world is not big enough to satisfy them; Euphrates is not far enough to the east, or Danube to the north, or Libya and the desert beyond to the south, or Cadiz to the west; but beyond the Ocean they have sought a new world, carrying their arms as far as Britain, that land of mystery. Why not face facts? Are you richer than the Gauls, stronger than the Germans, cleverer than the Greeks, more numerous than all the nations of the world? What gives you confidence to defy the power of Rome?

"It is terrible to be enslaved, it will be said. How much worse for Greeks, who surpass every nation under the sun in nobility and fill such a wide domain, and yet bow before the fasces[1] of a Roman governor, as do the Macedonians, who have a better right than you to demand their liberty! And what of the five hundred cities of Asia [a large province in Asia Minor]? Do they not without a garrison bow before one governor and the consular fasces? Need I mention the Heniochi, the Colchians, and the Tauric race,[2] the peoples near the Bosporus,[3] the Black Sea, and the Sea of Azov?[4] At one time they recognized not even a native ruler, and now they submit to 3,000 legionaries, while forty warships keep the peace on the sea where before none but pirates sailed. How justly Bithynia, Cappadocia, Pamphylia, Lycia, and Cilicia[5] might demand liberty! Yet without armed pressure they pay their dues.

"Then there are the Thracians [in modern Bulgaria], spread over a country five days' march in width and seven in length, more rugged and much more defensible than yours, a country whose icy blasts are enough to halt an invader. Yet 2,000 Roman guards suffice to maintain order. Their neighbours the Illyrians, whose land extends from Dalmatia [contempo-

---

[1]Fasces, a bundle of birch rods with an ax tied into the center and protruding above them, were carried in the presence of a Roman consul as a symbol of his magisterial powers of punishment over the people.
[2]The Heniochi, Colchians, and Taurians (Tauri) were tribes that lived along the northeastern borders of the Black Sea, the Sea of Azov, and in the Crimea.
[3]The Bosporus, in this context, was the Crimean peninsula and land to the east of it. Today, the term is used for a narrow passage of water between the part of Turkey in Asia Minor and the part in Europe.
[4]Called in Roman times the Palus Maeotis, the Sea of Azov is a body of water bordered by Ukraine and opening through a narrow strait into the Black Sea.
[5]Bithynia, Cappadocia, Pamphylia, Lycia, and Cilicia, former independent kingdoms conquered by the Romans, made up almost all of Asia Minor.

rary Croatia] to the Danube frontier, need only two legions to keep them quiet; in fact Illyrians unite with Romans to halt Dacian [tribes from the area of Romania] raids. The Dalmatians again, who have so often tried to shake off the yoke and have always been driven by defeat to rally their forces and revolt again, now live peaceably under one Roman legion!

"But if any people might reasonably be tempted to rebel by its peculiar advantages, that people is the Gauls, provided as they are with such marvellous natural defences, on the east the Alps, on the north the Rhine, on the south the Pyrenees, on the west the [Atlantic] Ocean. Yet in spite of these immense obstacles, in spite of the huge total of 305 nations [tribes], in spite of the prosperity that wells up from their soil and enables them to flood the whole world with their goods, they submit to being the milch cow of Rome and receiving from her hands what they themselves have produced! And this they tolerate, not from effeminacy or racial inferiority—they fought for eighty years to save their liberty—but because they are overawed by the might of Rome and still more by her destiny, which wins her more victories than do her arms. So Gaul is kept in order by 1,200 soldiers—hardly more men than she has cities!

"Then Spain—in the fight for independence the gold from her soil could not save her, nor could the vast stretch of land and sea that separates her from Rome, nor the tribes of Lusitania [modern Portugal] and Cantabria [north coastal Spain] with their passion for fighting, nor the neighbouring Ocean that terrifies even the natives with its tides. Crossing the cloud-capped Pyrenees and advancing their arms beyond the Pillars of Hercules[6] the Romans enslaved Spain too. Yet to guard this remote and almost invincible nation requires but one legion![7]

"Which of you has not heard of the Germans,[8] with their inexhaustible manpower? You have, I am sure, seen their magnificent physique on many occasions, for on every side Roman masters have German slaves; yet this people occupies an immense area, their physique is surpassed by their pride, from the bottom of their hearts they despise death, and when enraged they are more dangerous than the fiercest of wild beasts. Yet the Rhine is the limit of their aggression and the Romans with eight legions have tamed them, enslaving the prisoners and driving the entire nation to seek refuge in flight.

"Consider the defences of the Britons, you who feel so sure of the defences of Jerusalem. They are surrounded by the Ocean and inhabit an island as big as this continent; yet the Romans crossed the sea and enslaved them, and four legions keep that huge island quiet. But why should I say more about that, when even the Parthians [of western Iran], the most warlike race of all, rulers of so many nations and protected by such vast forces, send hostages to Rome, and on Italian soil may be seen, humbly submitting for the sake of peace, the aristocrats of the east.

"Almost every nation under the sun bows down before the might of Rome. . . .

"Possibly some of you suppose that you are making war in accordance with agreed rules, and that when the Romans have won they will be kind to you, and will not think of making you an example to other nations by burning down your Holy City [Jerusalem] and destroying your entire race. I tell you, not even if you survive will you find a place of refuge, since every people recognizes the lordship of Rome or fears that it will have to do so. Again, the danger threatens not only ourselves here but also those who live in other cities; for there is not a region in the world without its Jewish colony. All these, if you go to war, will be massacred by your opponents, and through the folly of a few men every city will run with Jewish blood. . . ."

---

[6]The peaks on either side of the Strait of Gibraltar, which connects the Mediterranean Sea and the Atlantic Ocean, were called the Pillars of Hercules.

[7]The Roman legion was a military unit, subdivided into smaller groups as in a modern army brigade, and comprised about six thousand men.

[8]For the Germans, see note 2 on page 155.

REVIEW QUESTIONS

1. What did the friends of Rome find so admirable in its imperial system?
2. What were the faults of the Roman imperial system as seen by its subjects?
3. What faults in the Romans' administration of their subject peoples were readily admitted by Herod Agrippa in his speech to the Jews, as reported by Josephus?
4. Why did Agrippa feel that a revolt against Rome was doomed to fail?

---

## 7   Third-Century Crisis

An extravagant tyrant, Marcus Aurelius' son Commodus (Lucius Aelius Aurelius, A.D. 180–192) was an unworthy successor, and his reign marks the close of the Pax Romana. For the next hundred years the Empire was burdened by economic, political, and military crises. For much of the third century, barbarian tribesmen broke through the northern frontier defenses and plundered the Balkans, Greece, Asia Minor, northern Italy, Gaul, and Spain; the Persians invaded the Empire from the east. The legions, consisting predominantly of the least Romanized provincials, used their weapons to place their own commanders on the throne. During the ensuing civil wars, the soldiers looted the towns as if they were an invading army. Rome was drifting into anarchy.

The devastations by barbarians and the soldiers wrecked the economy, which was further damaged by crushing taxes and requisitions of goods and by inflation caused by debased coinage. Everywhere, people were fleeing from plundering barbarians or soldiers, from warring armies, and from government officials who extorted taxes and goods and services from an already overburdened population.

## Dio Cassius
# CARACALLA'S EXTORTIONS

The reign (A.D. 211–217) of Caracalla provides an early example of the crushing demands imposed by the state on its citizenry. The following account comes from the *Roman History* of Dio Cassius.

[Caracalla] was fond of spending money upon the soldiers, great numbers of whom he kept in attendance upon him, alleging one excuse after another and one war after another; but he made it his business to strip, despoil, and grind down all the rest of mankind, and the senators by no means least. In the first place, there were the gold crowns that he was repeatedly demanding, on the constant pretext that he had conquered some enemy or other; and I am not referring, either, to the actual manufacture of the crowns—for what does that amount to?—but to the vast amount of money constantly being given under that name by the cities for the customary "crowning," as it is called, of the emperors. Then there were the provisions that we were required to furnish in great quantities on all occasions, and this without receiving any remuneration and sometimes actually at additional cost to ourselves—all of which supplies he either bestowed upon the soldiers or else peddled out; and there were the gifts which he demanded from the wealthy citizens and from the various communities; and the taxes, both the new ones which he promulgated and the ten per cent. tax that he instituted in place of the five per cent. tax applying to the emancipation of slaves, to bequests, and to all legacies. . . . But apart from all these burdens, we were also compelled to build at our own expense all sorts of houses for him whenever he set out from Rome, and costly lodgings in the middle of even the very shortest journeys; yet he not only never lived in them, but in some cases was not destined even to see them. Moreover, we constructed amphitheatres and race-courses wherever he spent the winter or expected to spend it, all without receiving any contribution from him; and they were all promptly demolished, the sole reason for their being built in the first place being, apparently, that we might become impoverished.

The emperor himself kept spending the money upon the soldiers, as we have said, and upon wild beasts and horses; for he was for ever killing vast numbers of animals, both wild and domesticated, forcing us to furnish most of them, though he did buy a few. One day he slew a hundred boars at one time with his own hands. . . . In everything he was very hot-headed and very fickle, and he furthermore possessed the craftiness of his mother and the Syrians, to which race she belonged. He would appoint some freedman or other wealthy person to be director of the games in order that the man might spend money in this way also; and he would salute the spectators with his whip from the arena below and beg for gold pieces like a performer of the lowest class. . . . To such an extent was the entire world, so far as it owned his sway, devastated throughout his whole reign, that on one occasion the Romans at a horse-race shouted in unison this, among other things: "We shall do the living to death,* that we may bury the dead." Indeed, he often used to say: "Nobody in the world should have money but me; and I want it to bestow upon the soldiers." Once when Julia [Domna, his mother] chided him for spending vast sums upon them and said, "There is no longer any source of revenue, either just or unjust, left to us," he replied, exhibiting his sword, "Be of good cheer, mother: for as long as we have this, we shall not run short of money."

Moreover to those who flattered him he distributed both money and goods.

---

*Or . . . "We are stripping the living."

---

# PETITION TO EMPEROR PHILIP

**A petition presented about A.D. 245 to Emperor Philip (M. Julius Philippus, 244–249) reveals the desperation of the peasants.**

We who flee as suppliants to the refuge of your divinity are the entire population of your most sacred estate. We are suffering extortion and illegal exactions beyond all reason at the hands of those who ought to preserve the public welfare. . . . Military commanders, soldiers, and powerful and influential men in the city and your officials . . . swoop down upon us, take us away from our work, requisition our plow oxen, and illegally exact what is not due them. As a result we are suffering extraordinary injustice by this extortion. We wrote about all this to your majesty, Augustus,[1] when you held the prefecture of the Prae-

---

[1] The title Augustus was originally given by the senate to Octavian, the first emperor. It later became the title of all his successors. (See page 131.)

torian Guard[2] . . . and how your divinity was moved the rescript [emperor's official answer] quoted herewith makes clear: "We have transmitted the content of your petition to the governor, who will see to it that there is no further cause for complaint." But inasmuch as this rescript has brought us no aid, it has resulted that we are still suffering throughout the countryside illegal exactions of what is not owing, as certain parties assault us and trample upon us unjustly, and we are still suffering extraordinary extortion at the hands of the officials, and our resources have been exhausted and the estates deserted.

---

[2]The Praetorian Guard, commanded by a prefect (*praefectus*), was the official troop of imperial bodyguards.

---

# Herodian
# EXTORTIONS OF MAXIMINUS

Raised to imperial office by his own rebellious troops, Maximinus (A.D. 235–238) was desperate for money to pay the soldiers and to run the state. He therefore robbed the urban middle class. This account of Maximinus comes from Herodian of Antioch (c. A.D. 165–c. 255), a Syrian Greek who served in the imperial bureaucracy. He wrote a history of the Roman Empire that covered the time from the death of Marcus Aurelius (A.D. 180) to the accession of Gordian III (A.D. 238).

. . . Other battles took place in which Maximinus won praise for his personal participation, for fighting with his own hands, and for being in every conflict the best man on the field. . . . He threatened (and was determined) to defeat and subjugate the German nations as far as the ocean.

This is the kind of military man the emperor was, and his actions would have added to his reputation if he had not been much too ruthless and severe toward his associates and subjects. What profit was there in killing barbarians when greater slaughter occurred in Rome and the provinces? Or in carrying off booty captured from the enemy when he robbed his fellow countrymen of all their property? . . . Anyone who was merely summoned into court by an informer was immediately judged guilty, and left with all his property confiscated. It was thus possible every day to see men who yesterday had been rich, today reduced to paupers, so great was the avarice of the tyrant, who pretended to be insuring a continuous supply of money for the soldiers. The emperor's ears were always open to slanderous charges, and he spared neither age nor position. He arrested on slight and trivial charges many men who had governed provinces and commanded armies, who had won the honor of a consulship, or had gained fame by military victories. . . . After insulting and torturing these prisoners, he condemned them to exile or death.

As long as his actions affected only individuals and the calamities suffered were wholly private, the people of the cities and provinces were not particularly concerned with what the emperor was doing. Unpleasant things which happen to those who seem to be fortunate or wealthy are not only a matter of indifference to the mob, but they often bring pleasure to mean and malicious men, who envy the powerful and the prosperous. After Maximinus had impoverished most of the distinguished men and confiscated their estates, which he considered small and insignificant and not sufficient for his purposes, he turned to the public treasuries; all the funds which had been collected for the citizens' welfare or for gifts, all the funds being held in reserve for shows or festivals, he transferred to his own personal fortune. The offerings which belonged to the temples, the statues of the gods, the tokens of honor of the heroes, the decorations on public buildings, the adornments of the city, in short, any material suitable for making coins, he handed over to the mints. But what especially irked the people and aroused public indignation was the fact that, although no fighting was going on and no enemy was under arms anywhere, Rome appeared to be a city under siege. Some citizens, with angry shaking of fists, set guards around the temples, preferring to die before the altars than to stand by and see their country ravaged. From that time on, particularly in the cities and the provinces, the hearts of the people were filled with rage. The soldiers too were disgusted with his activities, for their relatives and fellow citizens complained that Maximinus was acting solely for the benefit of the military.

For these reasons, and justifiably, the people were aroused to hatred and thoughts of revolt.

## REVIEW QUESTIONS

1. How did the Roman emperors abuse their power?
2. What evidence do these documents provide of the citizens' growing hate for the Roman state?

## 8 The Demise of Rome

The conquest of the western provinces of the Roman Empire by various Germanic tribes in the fifth century A.D. was made easier by the apathy and frequent collaboration of Roman citizens themselves. Many Romans had grown to hate the bureaucratic oppressors who crushed them with constant demands for excessive and unfair taxes, forced labor on government projects, extortion, and all the evils of a police state. In some areas of Gaul and Spain, peasants had revolted and successfully defended their homes and farms against the Roman authorities. When such barbarians as the Visigoths, Vandals, and Ostrogoths entered the region, many Romans welcomed them as liberators and cooperated with them in establishing their new kingdoms.

## Salvian
## POLITICAL AND SOCIAL INJUSTICE

The conditions that made such dramatic conquests possible are well delineated in a book called *The Governance of God,* by Salvian (Salvianus) of Marseilles (c. A.D. 400–470). A Christian priest, Salvian was an eyewitness to the end of Roman rule in Gaul. He describes the political and moral causes of the collapse of the Roman state in the west in the following reading.

What towns, as well as what municipalities and villages are there in which there are not as many tyrants as *curiales*.[1] Perhaps they glory in this name of tyrant because it seems to be considered powerful and honored. For, almost all robbers rejoice and boast, if they are said to be more fierce than they really are. What place is there, as I have said, where the bowels of widows and orphans are not devoured by the leading men of the cities, and with them those of almost all holy men? . . . Not one of them [widows and orphans], therefore, is safe. In a manner, except for the very powerful, neither is anyone safe from the devastation of general brigandage, unless they are like the robbers themselves. To this state of affairs, indeed, to this crime has the world come that, unless one is bad, he cannot be safe. . . .

All the while, the poor are despoiled, the widows groan, the orphans are tread underfoot, so much so that many of them, and they are not of obscure birth and have received a liberal education, flee to the enemy lest they die from the pain of public persecution. They seek among the barbarians the dignity of the Roman because they cannot bear barbarous indignity among the Romans. Although these Romans differ in religion and language from the barbarians to whom they flee, and differ from them in respect to filthiness of body and clothing, nevertheless, as I have said, they prefer to bear among the barbarians a worship unlike their own rather than rampant injustice among the Romans.

---

Salvian tells how Roman citizens are deserting Rome to live under the rule of the Goths and other barbarian invaders. Moreover, in many parts of Spain and Gaul (France), peasants called *Bagaudae* have rebelled and established zones free from Roman authority.

---

[1]The *curiales* were members of the municipal councils. In the late years of the Roman Empire, they were forced to act as tax collectors for the central government and to pay from their own pockets whatever sums they could not collect from the overtaxed inhabitants.

Thus, far and wide, they migrate either to the Goths[2] or to the Bagaudae, or to other barbarians everywhere in power; yet they do not repent having migrated. They prefer to live as freemen under an outward form of captivity than as captives under an appearance of liberty. Therefore, the name of Roman citizens, at one time not only greatly valued but dearly bought, is now repudiated and fled from, and it is almost considered not only base but even deserving of abhorrence.

And what can be a greater testimony of Roman wickedness than that many men, upright and noble and to whom the position of being a Roman citizen should be considered as of the highest splendor and dignity, have been driven by the cruelty of Roman wickedness to such a state of mind that they do not wish to be Romans? . . .

I am now about to speak of the Bagaudae who were despoiled, oppressed and murdered by evil and cruel judges. After they had lost the right of Roman citizenship, they also lost the honor of bearing the Roman name. We blame their misfortunes on themselves. We ascribe to them a name which signifies their downfall. We give to them a name of which we ourselves are the cause. We call them rebels. We call those outlaws whom we compelled to be criminal.

For, by what other ways did they become Bagaudae, except by our wickedness, except by the wicked ways of judges, except by the proscription and pillage of those who have turned the assessments of public taxes into the benefit of their own gain and have made the tax levies their own booty? Like wild beasts, they did not rule but devoured their subjects, and feasted not only on the spoils of men, as most robbers are wont to do, but even on their torn flesh and, as I may say, on their blood.

---

[2]The Goths were Germanic tribes that invaded Rome. The Visigoths invaded Italy in the early fifth century and seized Rome for a few days. This was the first time in eight centuries that a foreign enemy had entered the capital. Later the Visigoths occupied large areas of Spain and Gaul. In the late fifth century, the Ostrogoths invaded and conquered Italy, establishing a kingdom there.

Thus it happened that men, strangled and killed by the robberies of judges, began to live as barbarians because they were not permitted to be Romans. They became satisfied to be what they were not, because they were not permitted to be what they were. They were compelled to defend their lives at least, because they saw that they had already completely lost their liberty. . . .

But what else can these wretched people wish for, they who suffer the incessant and even continuous destruction of public tax levies. To them there is always imminent a heavy and relentless proscription. They desert their homes, lest they be tortured in their very homes. They seek exile, lest they suffer torture. The enemy is more lenient to them than the tax collectors. This is proved by this very fact, that they flee to the enemy in order to avoid the full force of the heavy tax levy. This very tax levying, although hard and inhuman, would nevertheless be less heavy and harsh if all would bear it equally and in common. Taxation is made more shameful and burdensome because all do not bear the burden of all. They extort tribute from the poor man for the taxes of the rich, and the weaker carry the load for the stronger. There is no other reason that they cannot bear all the taxation except that the burden imposed on the wretched is greater than their resources. . . .

Therefore, in the districts taken over by the barbarians, there is one desire among all the Romans, that they should never again find it necessary to pass under Roman jurisdiction. In those regions, it is the one and general prayer of the Roman people that they be allowed to carry on the life they lead with the barbarians. And we wonder why the Goths are not conquered by our portion of the population, when the Romans prefer to live among them rather than with us. Our brothers, therefore, are not only altogether unwilling to flee to us from them, but they even cast us aside in order to flee to them.

---

# Jerome
# THE FATE OF ROME

Saint Jerome (Hieronymus, c. A.D. 340–420) was one of the major theologians and scriptural scholars of the late Roman period. He left Rome itself to join a monastery in Bethlehem in Judea, where he studied Hebrew and began work on a monumental new translation of the Hebrew and Christian Scriptures into Latin. This new edition, called the Vulgate (written in the Latin of the common people), became the standard text of the Bible in the Western church for more than a thousand years. In the following letter to Agenuchia, a highborn lady of Gaul, Saint Jerome bemoans the fate of Rome, once so proud and powerful. The letter, dated A.D. 409, was written at a critical moment: the Visigoths had accepted a huge ransom to end their siege of Rome.

Nations innumerable and most savage have invaded all Gaul. The whole region between the Alps and the Pyrenees, the ocean and the Rhine, has been devastated by the Quadi, the Vandals, the Sarmati, the Alani, the Gepidae, the hostile Heruli, the Saxons, the Burgundians, the Alemanni, and the Pannonians [barbarian tribes]. O wretched Empire! Mayence [Mainz], formerly so noble a city, has been taken and ruined, and in the church many thousands of men have been massacred. Worms has been destroyed after a long siege. Rheims, that powerful city, Amiens, Arras, Speyer, Strasburg,*—all have seen their citizens led away captive into Germany. Aquitaine and the provinces of Lyons and Narbonne, all save a few towns, have been depopulated; and these the sword threatens without, while hunger ravages within. I cannot speak without tears of Toulouse, which the merits of the holy Bishop Exuperius have prevailed so far to save from destruction. Spain, even, is in daily terror lest it perish, remembering the invasion of the Cimbri;[1] and whatsoever the other provinces have suffered once, they continue to suffer in their fear.

I will keep silence concerning the rest, lest I seem to despair of the mercy of God. For a long time, from the Black Sea to the Julian Alps,[2] those things which are ours have not been ours; and for thirty years, since the Danube boundary was broken, war has been waged in the very midst of the Roman Empire. Our tears are dried by old age. Except a few old men, all were born in captivity and siege, and do not desire the liberty they never knew. . . .

---

When the Visigoths led by Alaric sacked Rome in 410, Jerome lamented in another passage.

---

Who could believe that Rome, built upon the conquest of the whole world, would fall to the ground? that the mother herself would become the tomb of her peoples?

---

*The names of modern cities here used are not in all cases exact equivalents for the names of the regions mentioned by Jerome.
[1]The Cimbri, originally from what is now Denmark, spread southward to invade Spain, Gaul, and Italy in the late part of the second century B.C. They were defeated by the Roman general Marius (c. 157–86 B.C.).

[2]The mountains called the Julian Alps are in the former Yugoslavia.

# Pope Gregory I
# THE END OF ROMAN GLORY

In the late sixth century, the Lombards, the last Germanic tribe to invade those lands that had once been Roman, swept down the Tiber valley and in 593 were at the gates of Rome. At that time, Pope Gregory I, the Great (590–604), descendant of a prominent and wealthy Roman senatorial family, reflected on Rome, once the mistress of the world.

We see on all sides sorrows; we hear on all sides groans. Cities are destroyed, fortifications razed to the ground, fields devastated, the land reduced to solitude. No husbandman is left in the field, few inhabitants remain in the cities, and yet these scanty remnants of the human race are still each day smitten without ceasing. . . . Some men are led away captive, others are mutilated, others slain before our eyes.

What is there, then, my brethren to please us in this world?

What Rome herself, once deemed the Mistress of the World, has now become, we see—wasted away with afflictions, grievous and many, with the loss of citizens, the assaults of enemies, the frequent fall of ruined buildings. . . . For where is the Senate? Where is the People [the State]? The bones are dissolved, the flesh is consumed, all the pomp of the dignities of this world is gone. . . .

Yet even we who remain few as we are, still are daily smitten with the sword, still are daily crushed by innumerable afflictions. . . . For the Senate is no more, and the People has perished, yet sorrow and sighing are multiplied daily among the few that are left. Rome is, as it were, already empty and burning. . . . But where are they who once rejoiced in her glory? Where is their pomp? Where their pride? Where their constant and immediate joy? . . .

. . . The Sons of men of the world, when they wished for worldly advancement came together from all parts of the earth to this city. But now behold! she is desolate. Behold! she is wasted away. No one hastens to her for worldly advancement.

## REVIEW QUESTIONS

1. What conditions in late Roman society undermined the social and political bonds between the rulers and the ruled?
2. What were the consequences of the Germanic invasions as depicted by Saint Jerome and Pope Gregory I?

## CHAPTER 6

# Early Christianity

THE ASCENSION OF JESUS INTO HEAVEN, miniature painting c. A.D. 586. From a gospel book transcribed by the monk Rabbula at Saint John's Abbey in Zagba, Mesopotamia. *(Biblioteca Laurenziana, Florence, Italy. Scala/Art Resource, N.Y.)*

Christianity, the core religion of Western civilization, emerged during the first century of the Roman Empire. The first Christians were followers of Jesus Christ, a Jew, who, in the tradition of the Hebrew prophets, called for a moral reformation of the individual. Jesus' life, teachings, crucifixion, and the belief that he had risen from the dead convinced his followers that Jesus had shown humanity the way to salvation. Dedicated disciples spread this message throughout the Mediterranean world.

Surviving persecution and gaining in numbers, Christians influenced all classes from slave to aristocrat, and Christianity had become the state religion of Rome by the end of the fourth century. The reasons for the spread and triumph of Christianity are diverse. The poor and oppressed of the Roman world were drawn to Jesus' message of love and compassion, his concern for humanity; the promise of eternal life had an immense attraction to people who were burdened with misfortune and fearful of death. Jesus' call for a moral transformation of the individual addressed itself to the inner conscience of men and women of all social classes.

The Judeo-Christian and Greco-Roman (classical humanist) traditions constitute the foundations of Western civilization. Nevertheless, they represent two contrasting views of the world. For classical humanists, the ultimate aim of life was the achievement of excellence in this world, the maximum cultivation of human talent; Christians subordinated this world to a higher reality. For Christians, the principal purpose of life was the attainment of salvation—entrance into a heavenly kingdom after death.

In the Greco-Roman tradition, reason was autonomous: that is, the intellect depended on its own powers and neither required nor accepted guidance from a supernatural authority. For example, Socrates held that ethical standards were arrived at through rational thought alone; they were not divine commandments revealed to human beings by a heavenly lawmaker. Conservative Christian churchmen, believing that Greek intellectualism posed a threat to Christian teachings, wanted nothing to do with Greek philosophy. But other Christians, recognizing the value of Greek philosophy, sought to integrate Greek learning into the Christian framework. Greek philosophy, they said, could help Christians clarify, organize, and explain their teachings. Those who advocated studying and utilizing Greek philosophy prevailed; thus Christianity preserved rational thought, the priceless achievement of the Greek mind. In the process, however, philosophy lost its autonomy, for early Christian thinkers insisted that to reason properly one must first believe in God and his revelation, with the Bible as the ultimate authority. Without these prior conditions, the Christians argued, reason would lead to error. Thus, for early Christian thinkers, unlike their Greek predecessors, reason was not autonomous: it was subject to divine authority as interpreted by the church.

In the late Roman Empire, when Roman institutions were breaking down and classical values were being discarded, Christianity was a dynamic movement. Surviving the barbarian invasions, the Christian church gave form and direction to the European culture that emerged in the Middle Ages.

## 1   The Teachings of Jesus

During the reign (A.D. 14–37) of the Emperor Tiberius, the Roman governor in Judea, Pontius Pilate, executed on charges of sedition an obscure Jewish religious teacher, Jesus of Nazareth. While performing healings and exorcisms, Jesus expounded a message of hope and salvation for sinners who repented. To the Jews who were attracted to Jesus' person and teachings, Jesus appeared to be a new prophet or even the long-awaited Messiah, the divinely promised leader who would restore Israel to freedom and usher in a new age.

Jesus made enemies among those powerful Jewish leaders who believed that the popular preacher was undermining their authority and weakening respect for their teachings on the requirements of Jewish law. The Romans viewed Jesus as a political agitator who might lead the Jews in a revolt against Roman rule. Some Jewish leaders denounced Jesus to the Roman authorities, who executed him.

After the death of Jesus, his loyal followers, who believed in his resurrection, continued to preach his teachings, forming small congregations of those faithful to his mission and words. They soon spread out as missionaries to Jewish and Gentile communities throughout the Roman Empire. These followers of Jesus, the Messiah, or in Greek, *Christos* (the Anointed One), were the founders of the Christian church.

Like Socrates, Jesus himself never wrote a book; all we know of his life and teachings are the recollections of his disciples, passed down orally until put in written form some thirty to seventy years after his death. These primary sources include the gospels ("good news") attributed to the Saints Mark, Matthew, Luke, and John; the letters of Saint Paul and others; the Acts of the Apostles, a historical account of their missionary work; and the book of Revelation, a prophetic portrayal of the coming messianic kingdom of Jesus and God's destruction of the powers of evil. These works, written several decades after Jesus' death and collected together definitively in the fourth century, comprise the New Testament, the Christian sacred scriptures. They reflect the ways in which the early Christians remembered Jesus' teachings and the meaning of his life and ministry.

## THE GOSPEL ACCORDING TO SAINT MARK

In this reading from Saint Mark's gospel, Jesus stated in a few words the core of his ethical teaching.

28 And one of the scribes* came up and heard them disputing with one another, and seeing that he answered them well, asked him, "Which commandment is the first of all?" ²⁹Jesus answered, "The first is, 'Hear, O Israel: The Lord our God, the Lord is one;†³⁰and you shall love the Lord your God with all your heart, and with all your soul, and with all your mind, and with all your strength.' ³¹The second is this, 'You shall love your neighbor as yourself.' There is no other commandment greater than these." ³²And the scribe said to him, "You are right, Teacher; you have truly said that he is one, and there is no other but he; ³³and to love him with all the heart, and with all the understanding, and with all the strength, and to love one's neighbor as oneself, is much more than all whole burnt offerings and sacrifices." ³⁴And when Jesus saw that he answered wisely, he said to him, "You are not far from the kingdom of God." And after that no one dared to ask him any question. (Mark 12)

*Scribes were not only copyists of the scrolls that contained Jewish law, but they were also students of that law. Editors' footnotes for Bible readings in this chapter are not numbered, to eliminate confusion with verse numbers.—Eds.

†"Hear, O Israel" occurs in the Book of Deuteronomy in the Hebrew Scriptures as the "first law," that of monotheism (one God). Here, as a Jew, Jesus was reminding his followers of this fact.—Eds.

# THE GOSPEL ACCORDING TO SAINT MATTHEW

In the gospel of Saint Matthew, Jesus outlined to his disciples the attitudes pleasing to God; this is the famous Sermon on the Mount.

5 Seeing the crowds, he went up on the mountain, and when he sat down his disciples came to him. ²And he opened his mouth and taught them, saying:

3 "Blessed are the poor in spirit, for theirs is the kingdom of heaven.

4 "Blessed are those who mourn, for they shall be comforted.

5 "Blessed are the meek, for they shall inherit the earth.

6 "Blessed are those who hunger and thirst for righteousness, for they shall be satisfied.

7 "Blessed are the merciful, for they shall obtain mercy.

8 "Blessed are the pure in heart, for they shall see God.

9 "Blessed are the peacemakers, for they shall be called sons of God.

10 "Blessed are those who are persecuted for righteousness' sake, for theirs is the kingdom of heaven.

11 "Blessed are you when men revile you and persecute you and utter all kinds of evil against you falsely on my account. ¹²Rejoice and be glad, for your reward is great in heaven, for so men persecuted the prophets who were before you. . . ." (Matthew 5)

A characteristic feature of Jesus' teaching— one that angered the Jewish leaders— was a demand that his followers go beyond the letter of the Jewish law. In the tradition of the Hebrew prophets, Jesus stressed the ethical demands that underlie this law and urged a moral transformation of human character, based on a love of God and neighbor. In the next reading from Saint Matthew, Jesus reinterpreted the Hebrew commandments on killing, adultery, divorce, vengeance, the definition of a neighbor, and almsgiving.

17 "Think not that I have come to abolish the law and the prophets; I have come not to abolish them but to fulfil them. ¹⁸For truly, I say to you, till heaven and earth pass away, not an iota, not a dot, will pass from the law until

all is accomplished. ¹⁹Whoever then relaxes one of the least of these commandments and teaches men so, shall be called least in the kingdom of heaven; but he who does them and teaches them shall be called great in the kingdom of heaven. ²⁰For I tell you, unless your righteousness exceeds that of the scribes and Pharisees,* you will never enter the kingdom of heaven.

21 "You have heard that it was said to the men of old, 'You shall not kill; and whoever kills shall be liable to judgment.' ²²But I say to you that every one who is angry with his brother shall be liable to judgment; whoever insults his brother shall be liable to the council, and whoever says, 'You fool!' shall be liable to the hell of fire. ²³So if you are offering your gift at the altar, and there remember that your brother has something against you, ²⁴leave your gift there before the altar and go; first be reconciled to your brother, and then come and offer your gift. ²⁵Make friends quickly with your accuser, while you are going with him to court, lest your accuser hand you over to the judge, and the judge to the guard, and you be put in prison; ²⁶truly, I say to you, you will never get out till you have paid the last penny.

27 "You have heard that it was said, 'You shall not commit adultery.' ²⁸But I say to you that every one who looks at a woman lustfully has already committed adultery with her in his heart. ²⁹If your right eye causes you to sin, pluck it out and throw it away; it is better that you lose one of your members than that your whole body be thrown into hell. ³⁰And if your right hand causes you to sin, cut it off and throw it away; it is better that you lose one of your members than that your whole body go into hell.

31 "It was also said, 'Whoever divorces his wife, let him give her a certificate of divorce.'

³²But I say to you that every one who divorces his wife, except on the ground of unchastity, makes her an adulteress; and whoever marries a divorced woman commits adultery.

33 "Again you have heard that it was said to the men of old, 'You shall not swear falsely, but shall perform to the Lord what you have sworn.' ³⁴But I say to you, Do not swear at all, either by heaven, for it is the throne of God, ³⁵or by the earth, for it is his footstool, or by Jerusalem, for it is the city of the great King. ³⁶And do not swear by your head, for you cannot make one hair white or black. ³⁷Let what you say be simply 'Yes' or 'No'; anything more than this comes from evil.

38 "You have heard that it was said, 'An eye for an eye and a tooth for a tooth.' ³⁹But I say to you, Do not resist one who is evil. But if any one strikes you on the right cheek, turn to him the other also; ⁴⁰and if any one would sue you and take your coat, let him have your cloak as well; ⁴¹and if any one forces you to go one mile, go with him two miles. ⁴²Give to him who begs from you, and do not refuse him who would borrow from you.

43 "You have heard that it was said, 'You shall love your neighbor and hate your enemy.' ⁴⁴But I say to you, Love your enemies and pray for those who persecute you, ⁴⁵so that you may be sons of your Father who is in heaven; for he makes his sun rise on the evil and on the good, and sends rain on the just and on the unjust. ⁴⁶For if you love those who love you, what reward have you? Do not even the tax collectors do the same? ⁴⁷And if you salute only your brethren, what more are you doing than others? Do not even the Gentiles†do the same? ⁴⁸You, therefore, must be perfect, as your heavenly Father is perfect.

6 "Beware of practicing your piety before men in order to be seen by them; for then you will have no reward from your Father who is in heaven.

---

*The Pharisees were a sect within Judaism; they adopted a flexible attitude toward Mosaic Law, allowing for various interpretations and granting authority to oral tradition as well as to written Scripture. Unlike the aristocratic Sadducees, the Pharisees were concerned with social injustice and had the support of the common people—Eds.

†Gentiles meant non-Jews; many religions were represented in the cosmopolitan Roman Empire of that period.—Eds.

²"Thus, when you give alms, sound no trumpet before you, as the hypocrites do in the

synagogues‡ and in the streets, that they may be praised by men. Truly, I say to you, they have their reward. ³But when you give alms, do not let your left hand know what your right hand is doing, ⁴so that your alms may be in secret; and your Father who sees in secret will reward you. . . ." (Matthew 5–6)

---

‡Synagogues, originally a name given to substitutes outside Judea for the Temple in Jerusalem, coexisted with the Temple; they were places for public prayer and study of the Hebrew Scriptures.—Eds.

## REVIEW QUESTIONS

1. What did Jesus believe to be the basic tenets of his teachings?
2. How did Jesus react to identifying true religion with a written law?

---

## 2  Saint Paul's View of Jesus, His Mission, and His Teaching

After the execution of Jesus by the Roman authorities in Judea around A.D. 30, his disciples, believing that he had risen from the dead, sought a clearer understanding of his life and teachings. They became convinced that Jesus' mission, calling people to repent their sins and receive God's forgiveness and to conduct their lives according to a high code of ethics, must be carried on. They proceeded to spread the "good news" to their fellow Jews and eventually to other peoples throughout the Roman world.

The disciples of Jesus were soon joined in this great mission by a man known to us as Saint Paul, the first great theologian of the new Christian church. Saint Paul started life as a pious Jew named Saul. He was born in Tarsus, a Greek city in Asia Minor. A Roman citizen as well as a Pharisee, Paul studied the Hebrew Scriptures in Judea and joined in the early persecution of Jesus' followers. But, through a visionary experience, Paul was converted to the belief that Jesus was the Messiah. He traveled widely throughout Syria, Asia Minor, and Greece, converting both Jews and non-Jews. He kept in touch with the new Christian communities by visits and letters. Several of the latter are included in the New Testament. He died around A.D. 65.

## THE LETTER OF PAUL TO THE EPHESIANS

In the following letter addressed to the Christian community in Ephesus, a major Greek city in western Asia Minor, Paul explains the meaning of Jesus as the Messiah, and tells how that meaning should be reflected in a Christian's daily life. The Letter to the Ephesians has been attributed to Paul, but now many scholars, on the basis of linguistic analysis, believe that the author was not Paul himself, but a close adherent of Pauline theology.

17 Now this I affirm and testify in the Lord, that you must no longer live as the Gentiles do, in the futility of their minds; [18]they are darkened in their understanding, alienated from the life of God because of the ignorance that is in them, due to their hardness of heart; [19]they have become callous and have given themselves up to licentiousness, greedy to practice every kind of uncleanness. [20]You did not so learn Christ!—[21]assuming that you have heard about him and were taught in him, as the truth is in Jesus. [22]Put off your old nature which belongs to your former manner of life and is corrupt through deceitful lusts, [23]and be renewed in the spirit of your minds, [24]and put on the new nature, created after the likeness of God in true righteousness and holiness.

[25]Therefore, putting away falsehood, let every one speak the truth with his neighbor, for we are members one of another. [26]Be angry but do not sin; do not let the sun go down on your anger, [27]and give no opportunity to the devil. [28]Let the thief no longer steal, but rather let him labor, doing honest work with his hands, so that he may be able to give to those in need. [29]Let no evil talk come out of your mouths, but only such as is good for edifying, as fits the occasion, that it may impart grace to those who hear. [30]And do not grieve the Holy Spirit of God, in whom you were sealed for the day of redemption. [31]Let all bitterness and wrath and anger and clamor and slander be put away from you, with all malice, [32]and be kind to one another, tenderhearted, forgiving one another, as God in Christ forgave you. (Ephesians 4)

---

# THE FIRST LETTER OF PAUL TO THE CORINTHIANS

**In a letter to the Christians of Corinth, the great commercial center of Roman Greece, Paul defined love and declared it to be the essential foundation of a Christian life. In the second excerpt, Paul discusses the resurrection, the central doctrine of Christianity.**

**13** If I speak in the tongues of men and of angels, but have not love, I am a noisy gong or a clanging cymbal. [2]And if I have prophetic powers, and understand all mysteries and all knowledge, and if I have all faith, so as to remove mountains, but have not love, I am nothing. [3]If I give away all I have, and if I deliver my body to be burned, but have not love, I gain nothing.

[4]Love is patient and kind; love is not jealous or boastful; [5]it is not arrogant or rude. Love does not insist on its own way; it is not irritable or resentful; [6]it does not rejoice at wrong, but rejoices in the right. [7]Love bears all things, believes all things, hopes all things, endures all things.

[8]Love never ends; as for prophecy, it will pass away; as for tongues, they will cease; as for knowledge, it will pass away. [9]For our knowledge is imperfect and our prophecy is imperfect; [10]but when the perfect comes, the imperfect will pass away. [11]When I was a child, I spoke like a child, I thought like a child, I reasoned like a child; when I became a man, I gave up childish ways. [12]For now we see in a mirror* dimly, but then face to face. Now I know in part; then I shall understand fully,

---

*The mirror of the ancients was made of a highly polished metal; it would not reflect, however, as clearly as a modern one.—Eds.

even as I have been fully understood. [13]So faith, hope, love abide, these three; but the greatest of these is love. (1 Corinthians 12–13)

———

15 Now I would remind you, brethren, in what terms I preached to you the gospel, which you received, in which you stand, [2]by which you are saved, if you hold it fast— unless you believed in vain.

3 For I delivered to you as of first importance what I also received, that Christ died for our sins in accordance with the scriptures, [4]that he was buried, that he was raised on the third day in accordance with the scriptures, [5]and that he appeared to Cephas, then to the twelve. [6]Then he appeared to more than five hundred brethren at one time, most of whom are still alive, though some have fallen asleep. [7]Then he appeared to James, then to all the apostles. [8]Last of all, as to one untimely born, he appeared also to me. [9]For I am the least of the apostles, unfit to be called an apostle, because I persecuted the church of God. [10]But by the grace of God I am what I am, and his grace toward me was not in vain. On the contrary, I worked harder than any of them, though it was not I, but the grace of God which is with me. [11]Whether then it was I or they, so we preach and so you believed.

12 Now if Christ is preached as raised from the dead, how can some of you say that there is no resurrection of the dead? [13]But if there is no resurrection of the dead, then Christ has not been raised; [14]if Christ has not been raised, then our preaching is in vain and your faith is in vain. [15]We are even found to be misrepresenting God, because we testified of God that he raised Christ, whom he did not raise if it is true that the dead are not raised. [16]For if the dead are not raised, then Christ has not been raised. [17]If Christ has not been raised, your faith is futile and you are still in your sins. [18]Then those also who have fallen asleep in Christ have perished. [19]If in this life we who are in Christ have only hope, we are of all men most to be pitied.

20 But in fact Christ has been raised from the dead, the first fruits of those who have fallen asleep. [21]For as by a man came death, by a man has come also the resurrection of the dead. [22]For as in Adam all die, so also in Christ shall all be made alive. [23]But each in his own order: Christ the first fruits, then at his coming those who belong to Christ. [24]Then comes the end, when he delivers the kingdom to God the Father after destroying every rule and every authority and power. [25]For he must reign until he has put all his enemies under his feet. [26]The last enemy to be destroyed is death.

## REVIEW QUESTIONS

1. How did Saint Paul expand the meaning of Jesus' teachings on love?
2. Do you agree with Paul that love is more essential than knowledge?
3. Why for Paul is belief in the resurrection essential for a Christian?

———

## 3  Christianity and Society

**Although the principal concern of Jesus' followers was the attainment of salvation, Christians still had to deal with the world and its ways. In the process of doing so, they developed attitudes and customs that have had an enduring influence on Western culture.**

# Athenagoras
# SEXUALITY AND FAMILY LIFE

Christians, Paul taught, expected each other to uphold high standards of personal chastity, avoiding all occasions of sexual impurity by thought or deed. Even within marriage, sexual intercourse was linked to procreation, not pleasure. Many even condemned a second marriage, challenging widows and widowers to remain chaste. Abortion was condemned, as was divorce. Athenagoras, a contemporary of Emperor Marcus Aurelius, was an Athenian philosopher who became a Christian. Writing in the late second century, Athenagoras described what he saw as Christian attitudes toward sex and family morals.

. . . But we are so far from practising promiscuous intercourse, that it is not lawful among us to indulge even a lustful look. "For," saith He, "he that looketh on a woman to lust after her, hath committed adultery already in his heart." [Matthew 5:28] Those, then, who are forbidden to look at anything more than that for which God formed the eyes, which were intended to be a light to us, and to whom a wanton look is adultery, the eyes being made for other purposes, and who are to be called to account for their very thoughts, how can any one doubt that such persons practise self-control? For our account lies not with human laws, which a bad man can evade, . . . but we have a law which makes the measure of rectitude to consist in dealing with our neighbour as ourselves. On this account, too, according to age, we recognise some as sons and daughters, others we regard as brothers and sisters, and to the more advanced in life we give the honour due to fathers and mothers. On behalf of those, then, to whom we apply the names of brothers and sisters, and other designations of relationship, we exercise the greatest care that their bodies should remain undefiled and uncorrupted; for the Logos[1] again says to us, "If any one kiss a second time because it has given him pleasure, (he sins);" adding, "Therefore the kiss, or rather the salutation, should be given

with the greatest care, since, if there be mixed with it the least defilement of thought, it excludes us from eternal life." (Probably from an Apocryphal gospel not included by the church in the New Testament)

## CHAPTER XXXIII
### *Chastity of the Christians with Respect to Marriage*

Therefore, having the hope of eternal life, we despise the things of this life, even to the pleasures of the soul, each of us reckoning her his wife whom he has married according to the laws laid down by us, and that only for the purpose of having children. For as the husbandman throwing the seed into the ground awaits the harvest, not sowing more upon it, so to us the procreation of children is the measure of our indulgence in appetite. Nay, you would find many among us, both men and women, growing old unmarried, in the hope of living in closer communion with God. But if the remaining in virginity and in the state of an eunuch brings nearer to God, while the indulgence of carnal thought and desire leads away from Him, in those cases in which we shun the thoughts, much more do we reject the deeds. For we bestow our attention, not on the study of words, but on the exhibition and teaching of actions,—that a person should either remain as he was born, or be content with one marriage; for a second marriage is only a specious adul-

---

[1]*Logos,* Greek for *word,* is used in the New Testament in the Gospel of John to designate both God and Jesus, as a divinity. The Stoics used *logos* to mean Divine Reason.

tery. "For whosoever puts away his wife," says He, "and marries another, commits adultery;" [Matthew 19:9] not permitting a man to send her away whose virginity he has brought to an end, nor to marry again. For he who deprives himself of his first wife, even though she be dead, is a cloaked adulterer, resisting the hand of God—because in the beginning God made one man and one woman—and dissolving the strictest union of flesh with flesh, formed for the intercourse of the race. . . .

---

Early Christians, who were repelled by all forms of violence, were particularly incensed by the malicious accusation that they engaged in cannibalism. Athenagoras responds to this charge.

---

## CHAPTER XXXV
*The Christians Condemn and Detest All Cruelty*

What man of sound mind, therefore, will affirm, while such is our character, that we are murderers? For we cannot eat human flesh till we have killed some one. The former charge, therefore, being false, if any one should ask them in regard to the second, whether they have seen what they assert, not one of them would be so barefaced as to say that he had. And yet we have slaves, some more and some fewer, by whom we could not help being seen; but even of these, not one has been found to invent even such things against us. For when they know that we cannot endure even to see a man put to death, though justly, who of them can accuse us of murder or cannibalism? Who does not reckon among the things of greatest interest the contests of gladiators and wild beasts, especially those which are given by you? But we, deeming that to see a man put to death is much the same as killing him, have abjured such spectacles. How, then, when we do not even look on, lest we should contract guilt and pollution, can we put people to death? And when we say that those women who use drugs to bring on abortion commit murder, and will have to give an account to God for the abortion, on what principle should we commit murder?

## REVIEW QUESTIONS

1. How did Christian moral values differ from those of their non-Christian neighbors?
2. Do the moral teachings of Athenagoras find echo in modern society?

---

# 4 The Persecutions

Under Roman law, all cults had to be approved by the authorities, and religious associations were licensed by the state. At first, the Christians were assumed to be members of a Jewish sect, and as Judaism was a legal religion, the authorities did not intervene in the work of the Christian missionaries except as they were involved in disputes within the Jewish community. By the reign of Emperor Nero (A.D. 54–68), Roman officials had become aware that the new Christian churches were composed of many Gentiles as well as Jews, and could no longer reasonably be considered a legitimate part of the privileged Jewish religious community. The first major persecution broke out in the city of Rome when Nero, to put down a rumor that he had set afire a large section of the city, decided to focus blame for the disaster on the small Christian community. When the unpopular Christians were arrested, they pleaded guilty not to arson, but to the crime of being Christians: that is, to belonging to an illegal sect or association. The penalty for such unlicensed association was death. Those who denied they were Christians and agreed to offer sacrifice to the gods of Rome were released.

# PERSECUTIONS AT LYONS AND VIENNE

During the second century, Christians were at times victims of mob actions, usually stimulated by some disaster like an outbreak of disease, an earthquake, a drought, or other communal catastrophe attributed to the anger of the gods. Christians' pacifism and their refusal to participate in the worship of the state deities, in processions and festivals, and in theatrical performances and gladiatorial games made them increasingly unpopular.

The next reading is a letter sent in A.D. 177 by the Christians of the cities of Lyons and Vienne in Gaul (France) to fellow Christians in Asia and Phrygia (both in modern Turkey). The letter describes a group of Christians arrested and reviled by enraged mobs.

First, indeed, they [the Christians] endured nobly the sufferings heaped upon them by the general populace, clamors, blows, being dragged along, robberies, stonings, imprisonments, and all that an enraged mob loves to inflict on opponents and enemies. Then they were taken to the forum by . . . the ordained authorities of the city and were examined in the presence of the whole multitude. Having confessed, they were imprisoned until the arrival of the governor. When they were afterwards brought before him and he treated us with all manner of cruelty. . . .

. . . [Some refused to renounce their faith in Christ, but others] appeared unprepared and untrained and still weak, unable to endure the strain of a great contest. Of these about ten became apostates [renounced their religion], who caused us great pain and excessive sorrow, and weakened the zeal of the others who had not yet been seized, and who, although suffering all kinds of evil, were constantly with the martyrs and did not abandon them. . . . And some of our servants who were heathens were seized because the governor had ordered that we should all be examined in public.

These by the wiles of Satan, fearing the tortures which they saw the saints suffering and urged by the soldiers to do this, accused us falsely of Thyestean banquets[1] and Oedipodean incests[2] and of deeds which it is not lawful for us to speak of, or think of, and which we do not believe men ever committed. When these accusations were reported all raged like wild beasts against us. . . . Then finally the holy martyrs endured sufferings beyond all description and Satan strove earnestly that some blasphemies might be uttered by them also.

But the whole rage of the people, governor and soldiers was aroused exceedingly against Sanctus, deacon from Vienne, and against Maturus, a recent convert but a noble combatant, and against Attalus, a native of Pergamum [a city in Asia Minor], who had always been a pillar and a foundation in that place, and against Blandina [a slave] through whom

---

[1]Thyestes, in Greek myth, was forced to eat his own sons at a banquet; the reference is to cannibalism.
[2]Oedipus, the protagonist of several Greek dramas, unwittingly committed incest with his mother.

Christ showed that what appears mean, deformed and contemptible to men is of great glory with God through love for Him, shown in power and not boasting in appearance. For while we all, together with her mistress on earth, who was herself also one of the combatants among the martyrs, feared lest in the strife she should be unable to make her confession on account of her bodily weakness, Blandina was filled with such power that she was delivered and raised above those who took turns in torturing her in every manner from dawn till evening; and they confessed that they were defeated and had nothing more which they could do to her. They marvelled at her endurance, for her whole body was mangled and broken; and they testified that one form of torture was sufficient to destroy life, to say nothing of so many and so great tortures. But the blessed one, like a noble athlete, renewed her strength . . ., and her comfort, refreshment and relief from suffering was in saying, "I am a Christian" and "Nothing vile is done by us."

. . . Maturus, Sanctus, Blandina and Attalus were therefore led to the wild beasts in the amphitheatre, and in order to give to the heathen public a spectacle of cruelty, a day was especially appointed for our people to fight with the wild beasts. Accordingly Maturus and Sanctus again passed through the whole torture in the amphitheatre, not as if they had suffered nothing at all before, but rather as if having overcome the adversary already in many kinds of contests they were now striving for the crown itself. They endured again the running the gauntlet customary in that place and the attacks from the wild beasts and everything that the raging multitude, who cried out from one place or another, desired, and at last the iron chair in which their bodies were roasted and tormented them with the fumes. Not even with this did the tortures cease, but they raged still more, desiring to overcome their patience, and they did not hear a word from Sanctus except the confession [that he was a Christian] which he had made from the beginning. These accordingly after their life

had continued for a very long time through the great conflict, died at last, after having furnished a spectacle to the world throughout that day instead of all the varieties of gladiatorial combats.

But Blandina suspended on a stake was exposed as food for the wild beasts which should fall upon her. Because she seemed to be suspended in the manner of a cross and because of her earnest prayers, she encouraged the contestants greatly. They looking upon her in her conflict, beheld with their eyes, through their sister, Him who had suffered for them in order to persuade those who trust in Him that everyone who suffers for the glory of Christ has eternal fellowship with the living God. And as none of the beasts touched her at that time, she was taken down from the stake and led away again to the prison, to be preserved for another contest. . . .

---

The Roman authorities frequently set free anyone who denied his Christian faith and was willing to worship a Roman god, usually the divine emperor.

---

. . . For Caesar had written that these [Christians] should be put to death, but if any should deny they should be dismissed. At the beginning of the festival held there, which is attended by throngs of people from all nations, the governor had the blessed ones brought to the judgment-seat to be a show and spectacle for the multitude. Therefore he examined them again, and as many as seemed to be Roman citizens he had beheaded, the others he sent to the wild beasts.

Christ was glorified greatly in those who had previously denied him, for contrary to the expectation of the heathen, they confessed. For these were examined separately as about to be set free, and when they confessed, they were added to the number of the martyrs. But those who never had a particle of faith . . . or any thought of the fear of God . . . blasphemed the way through their apostasy. . . .

... The bodies of the martyrs after having been exposed and exhibited in every manner for six days, were afterwards burned and reduced to ashes by the lawless men and thrown in the river Rhone which flows close by, so that no remnants of them might still be seen on the earth. And they did this as if they were able to overcome God and prevent their coming to life again, in order, as some said, "that they may have no hope of a resurrection, trusting in which they bring to us a certain foreign and strange religion, and despise awful punishments and are ready with joy to suffer death. Now let us see whether they will rise again, and if their God is able to aid them and rescue them from our hands."

## REVIEW QUESTIONS

1. What do the stories of the martyrs tell us about the character of Roman society?
2. Tertullian claimed that "the blood of the martyrs was the seed of the faith." How did the persecutions foster Christianity?

---

## 5   Christianity and Greco-Roman Learning

Should the cultural inheritance of the Greco-Roman world be retained or discarded? This was a formidable problem for early Christian thinkers. Those who urged abandoning Greco-Roman learning argued that such knowledge would corrupt the morality of the young and would lead Christians to doubt Scripture. On the other hand, several Christian intellectuals, particularly those educated in the Greco-Roman classics, defended the study of pagan works. Their view ultimately prevailed.

Christians preserved the intellectual tradition of Greece. However, philosophy underwent a crucial change: philosophic thought among Christians had to be directed in accordance with the requirements of their faith. The intellect was not fully autonomous; it could not question or challenge Christian teachings but had to accept the church's dictums regarding God's existence, the creation of the universe, the mission of Jesus, and the purpose of life and death.

## Tertullian
# WHAT HAS JERUSALEM TO DO WITH ATHENS?

A native of Carthage, Tertullian (Quintus Septimus Florens Tertullianus, c. A.D. 160–c. 240) became a Christian about A.D. 190 and thereafter was a defender of Christian morals against both pagans and less rigorous Christians. He emphasized the sacredness of life and the Christian abhorrence of violence. His *Prescriptions Against Heretics* reveals hostility toward Greco-Roman learning, an attitude shared by some other early Christian thinkers.

. . . Worldly wisdom culminates in philosophy with its rash interpretation of God's nature and purpose. It is philosophy that supplies the heresies[1] with their equipment. . . . The idea of a mortal soul was picked up from the Epicureans,[2] and the denial of the restitution of the flesh was taken from the common tradition of the philosophical schools. . . . Heretics and philosophers [ponder] the same themes and are caught up in the same discussions. What is the origin of evil and why? The origin of man, and how? . . . A plague on Aristotle, who taught them dialectic [logical argumentation], the art which destroys as much as it builds, which changes its opinions like a coat, forces its conjectures, is stubborn in argument, works hard at being contentious and is a burden even to itself. For it reconsiders every point to make sure it never finishes a discussion.

From philosophy come those fables and . . . fruitless questionings, those "words that creep like as doth a canker." To hold us back from such things, the Apostle [Paul] testifies expressly in his letter to the Colossians [Colos-

sians 2:8] that we should beware of philosophy. "Take heed lest any man [beguile] you through philosophy or vain deceit, after the tradition of men," against the providence of the Holy Ghost. He had been at Athens where he had come to grips with the human wisdom which attacks and perverts truth, being itself divided up into its own swarm of heresies by the variety of its mutually antagonistic sects. What has Jerusalem to do with Athens, the Church with [Plato's] Academy, the Christian with the heretic? Our principles come from the Porch of Solomon,[3] who had himself taught that the Lord is to be sought in simplicity of heart. I have no use for a Stoic or a Platonic or a dialectic Christianity. After Jesus Christ we have no need of speculation, after the Gospel no need of research. When we come to believe, we have no desire to believe anything else; for we begin by believing that there is nothing else which we have to believe.

---

[1] A heresy is any belief that differs from official or standard doctrine.

[2] Chapter 3, page 94.

[3] The Stoic philosophers took their name from the Greek word *stoa,* porch, the place where Zeno, their founder, used to teach. *Porch of Solomon* is used to designate the teachings of King Solomon, who built the great Temple in Jerusalem. Tertullian makes it clear he follows Solomon's wisdom.

---

# Clement of Alexandria
# IN DEFENSE OF GREEK LEARNING

In the following passage, Clement of Alexandria (c. A.D. 150–c. 220) expresses his admiration for Greek learning. A Greek Christian theologian, Clement combined Christianity with Platonism.

The Greeks should not be condemned by those who have merely glanced at their writings, for comprehension of these works requires careful investigation. Philosophy is not the originator of false practices and base deeds as some have calumniated it; nor does it beguile us and lead us away from faith.

Rather philosophy is a clear image of truth, a divine gift to the Greeks. Before the advent of the Lord, philosophy helped the Greeks to attain righteousness, and it is now conducive to piety; it supplies a preparatory teaching for those who will later embrace the faith. God is the cause of all good things:

some given primarily in the form of the Old and the New Testament; others are the consequence of philosophy. Perchance too philosophy was given to the Greeks primarily till the Lord should call the Greeks to serve him. Thus philosophy acted as a schoolmaster to the Greeks, preparing them for Christ, as the laws of the Jews prepared them for Christ.

The way of truth is one. But into it, as into a perennial river, streams flow from all sides. We assert that philosophy, which is characterized by investigation into the form and nature of things, is the truth of which the Lord Himself said, "I am the truth." Thus Greek preparatory culture, including philosophy itself, is shown to have come down from God to men.

Some do not wish to touch either philosophy or logic or to learn natural science. They demand bare faith alone, as if they wished, without bestowing any care on the vine, straightway to gather clusters from the first. I call him truly learned who brings everything to bear on the truth; so that from geometry, music, grammar, and philosophy itself, he culls what is useful and guards the faith against assault. And he who brings everything to bear on a right life, learning from Greeks and non-Greeks, this man is an experienced searcher after truth. And how necessary it is for him who desires to be partaker of the power of God to treat of intellectual subjects by philosophising.

According to some, Greek philosophy apprehended the truth accidentally, dimly, partially. Others will have it that Greek philosophy was instituted by the devil. Several hold that certain powers descending from heaven inspired the whole of philosophy. But if Greek philosophy does not comprehend the whole of truth and does not encompass God's commandments, yet it prepares the way for God's teachings; training in some way or other, molding character, and fitting him who believes in Providence for the reception of truth.

## REVIEW QUESTIONS

1. Why did Tertullian oppose the study of pagan literature on the part of Christians?
2. Why did Clement of Alexandria favor the study of pagan learning?
3. What might have been the consequences if the Christian church had followed the advice of Tertullian rather than Clement?

## 6  Monastic Life

In the late third century A.D., inspired by Jesus' example of self-denial and seeking to escape from the distractions of worldly concerns, some zealous Christians withdrew to the deserts of Roman Egypt in search of peace and isolation. They turned their minds wholly to prayer, contemplation, and ascetic practices. These hermits were the earliest Christian monks. In time, some hermits banded together to form monastic communities, living under written rules that established a form of monastic government and way of life.

The hermit or monk "took up the Cross"—that is, emulated the way of Christ through a life of prayer, introspective self-examination, hard work, and ascetic practices like fasting, sexual abstinence, physical deprivation, and poverty. The hermitage and the monastery were schools for sanctity; thus the hermits and monks have been the spiritual models for many male and female Christians from late Roman times down to the present age.

# Saint Benedict of Nursia
# THE BENEDICTINE RULE

The monastic way of life soon spread from Egypt to Palestine and Syria and eventually throughout the Christian Roman Empire. In Italy, Benedict of Nursia (c. 480–547), scion of a wealthy Roman family, founded twelve monasteries, the best known being at Monte Cassino in the mountains of southern Italy. Benedict wrote a set of rules for the governance of his monks; the Benedictine Rule became the model for many monasteries throughout Latin Christendom. In the following extract, Benedict summarizes the purpose and principles of monastic life.

. . . Therefore we are constrained to found a school for the service of the Lord. In its organization we hope we shall ordain nothing severe, nothing burdensome; but if there should result anything a little irksome by the demands of justice for the correction of vices and the persevering of charity, do not therefore, through fear, avoid the way of salvation, which cannot be entered upon save through a narrow entrance, but in which, as life progresses and the heart becomes filled with faith, one walks in the unspeakable sweetness of love; but never departing from His control, and persevering in His doctrine in the monastery until death, let us with patience share in the sufferings of Christ, that we may be worthy to be partakers in His kingdom. . . .

## WHAT THE ABBOT SHOULD BE LIKE

The abbot who is worthy to rule a monastery ought to remember by what name they are called, and to justify by their deeds the name of a superior. For he is believed to take the place of Christ in the monastery, since he is called by his name, as the apostle says: "Ye have received the spirit of adoption of sons, whereby we call, Abba, Father."

And so the abbot ought not (God forbid) to teach or decree or order anything apart from the precept of the Lord; but his rules and his teaching ought always to be leavened with the leaven of divine justice in the minds of his disciples; and let the abbot be always mindful that in the great judgment of God, both his teaching and the obedience of his disciples will be weighed in the balance. And let the abbot know that whatever the master finds lacking in the sheep will be charged to the fault of the shepherd. Only in case the pastor has shown the greatest diligence in his management of an unruly and disobedient flock, and has given his whole care to the correction of their evil doings, will that pastor be cleared at the judgment of God and be able to say with the prophet, "I have not hid thy righteousness within my heart, I have declared thy faithfulness and thy salvation, but they despising have scorned me"; then let the punishment of eternal death itself fall upon the disobedient sheep of his care.

Therefore when anyone takes on himself the name of abbot, he should govern his disciples by a twofold teaching, that is, let him show forth all the good and holy things by his deeds rather than by his words; to ready disciples he ought to set forth the commands of God in words, but to the hard of heart, and to the simple-minded he ought to illustrate the divine precepts in his deeds. And all things which he has taught his disciples to be wrong, let him demonstrate in his action that they should not be done, lest sometime God should say to him, a sinner: "Why dost thou declare my statutes or take my testimony in thy mouth? Thou hast hated instruction and cast My word behind thee"; and again: "Thou who hast seen the mote in thy brother's eyes, hast not seen the beam in thine own eye."

Let him not be a respecter of persons in the monastery. Let not one be loved more than another, unless he shall have found someone to be better than another in good deeds and in obedience; let not a freeman be preferred to one coming from servitude, unless there be some good and reasonable cause; but if according to the dictates of justice it shall have seemed best to the abbot, let him do this with anyone of any rank whatsoever; otherwise let each keep his own place, since, whether bond or free, we are all one in Christ, and under one God we bear the same burden of service, for there is no respect of persons with God; only in this regard are we distinguished with him if we are found better and more humble than others in our good deeds. Therefore let his love for all be the same, and let one discipline be put upon all according to merit. . . .

## ABOUT CALLING THE BROTHERS TO COUNCIL

Whenever anything especial is to be done in the monastery, the abbot shall convoke the whole body and himself set forth the matter at issue. And after listening to the advice of the brothers, he shall consider it by himself, and shall do what he shall have judged most useful. Now we say all should be called to the council, because the Lord often reveals to the younger brother what is best to be done.

But let the brothers give advice with all subjection of humility and not presume to defend boldly what seemed good to them, but rather rely on the judgment of the abbot, and all obey him in what he has judged to be for their welfare. But just as it is fitting that the disciples obey the master, so is it incumbent on him to dispose everything wisely and justly.

Therefore, let all follow the rule of the master in all things, and let no one depart from it rashly; let no one in the monastery follow the desire of his own heart. And let no one strive

with his abbot shamelessly either within or without the monastery; and if he shall have presumed to do so, let him be subjected to the regular discipline. And let the abbot himself do all things in the fear of God and in the observance of the rule, knowing that he must without doubt render account unto God, the most just judge, for all his judgments.

If there are any matters of minor importance to be done for the welfare of the monastery, let the abbot take the advice only of the elders, as it is written: "Do all things with counsel, and after it is done thou wilt not repent."

## CONCERNING THOSE WHO, BEING OFTEN REBUKED, DO NOT AMEND

If any brother, having frequently been rebuked for any fault, do not amend even after he has been excommunicated, a more severe rebuke shall fall upon him;—that is, the punishment of the lash shall be inflicted upon him. But if he do not even then amend; or, if perchance—which God forbid,—swelled with pride he try even to defend his works: then the abbot shall act as a wise physician. If he have applied . . . the ointments of exhortation, the medicaments [medicines] of the Divine Scriptures; if he have proceeded to the last blasting of excommunication, or to blows with rods, and if he sees that his efforts avail nothing: let him also—what is greater—call in the prayer of himself and all the brothers for him: that God who can do all things may work a cure upon an infirm brother. But if he be not healed even in this way, then at last the abbot may use the pruning knife, as the apostle says: "Remove evil from you," etc.: lest one diseased sheep contaminate the whole flock.

## WHETHER BROTHERS WHO LEAVE THE MONASTERY OUGHT AGAIN TO BE RECEIVED

A brother who goes out, or is cast out, of the monastery for his own fault, if he wish to return, shall first promise every amends for the fault on account of which he departed; and thus he shall be received into the lowest degree—so that thereby his humility may be proved. But if he again depart, up to the third time he shall be received. Knowing that after this every opportunity of return is denied to him.

## CONCERNING BOYS UNDER AGE, HOW THEY SHALL BE CORRECTED

Every age or intelligence ought to have its proper bounds. Therefore as often as boys or youths, or those who are less able to understand how great is the punishment of excommunication: as often as such persons offend, they shall either be afflicted with excessive fasts, or coerced with severe blows, that they may be healed.

## CONCERNING THE RECEPTION OF GUESTS

All guests who come shall be received as though they were Christ; for He Himself said: "I was a stranger and ye took Me in." And to all, fitting honour shall be shown; but, most of all, to servants of the faith and to pilgrims. When, therefore, a guest is announced, the prior or the brothers shall run to meet him, with every office of love. And first they shall pray together; and thus they shall be joined together in peace. Which kiss of peace shall not first be offered, unless a prayer have preceded; on account of the wiles of the devil. In the salutation itself, moreover, all humility shall be exhibited. In the case of all guests humility shall be exhibited. In the case of all guests arriving or departing: with inclined head, or with prostrating of the whole body upon the ground, Christ, who is also received in them, shall be adored.

---

The monks gathered together for prayer seven times in the course of the day. Prayers were chanted from set texts.

---

## CONCERNING THE ART OF SINGING

Whereas we believe that there is a divine presence, and that the eyes of the Lord look down everywhere upon the good and the evil: chiefly then, without any doubt, we may believe that this is the case when we are assisting at divine service. Therefore let us always be mindful of what the prophets say: "Serve the Lord in all fear"; and before the face of the Divinity and His angels; and let us so stand and again, "Sing wisely"; and "in the sight of the angels I will sing unto thee." Therefore let us consider how we ought to conduct ourselves and sing that our voice may accord with our intention.

## CONCERNING REVERENCE FOR PRAYER

If when to powerful men we wish to suggest anything, we do not presume to do it unless with reverence and humility: how much more should we supplicate with all humility, and devotion of purity, God who is the Lord of all. And let us know that we are heard, not for much speaking, but for purity of heart and compunction of tears. And, therefore, prayer ought to be brief and pure; unless perchance it be prolonged by the influence of the inspiration of the divine grace. When assembled together, then, let the prayer be altogether brief; and, the sign being given by the prior, let us rise together.

## CONCERNING THE DAILY MANUAL LABOR

Idleness is the enemy of the soul. And therefore, at fixed times, the brothers ought to be occupied in manual labour; and again, at fixed times, in sacred reading.

## CONCERNING HUMILITY

. . . If we wish to attain to the height of the greatest humility, and to that divine exaltation which is attained by the humility of this present life, we must mount by our own acts that ladder which appeared in a dream to Jacob,[1] upon which angels appeared unto him ascending and descending. For that ascent and descent can only be understood by us to be this: to ascend by humility, to descend through pride. . . .

Now the first grade of humility is this: keeping the fear of God before his eyes, let him avoid forgetfulness and ever remember all the precepts of the Lord; and continually consider in his heart that eternal life which is prepared for those who fear God, just as the mockers of God fall into hell. . . .

The fifth grade of humility is this, if one reveals to the abbot in humble confession all the vain imaginings that come into his heart, and all the evil he has done in secret. . . .

This is the eighth grade of humility; if a monk do nothing except what the common rule of the monastery or the examples of his superior urges him to do.

The ninth grade of humility is this: if a monk keep his tongue from speaking and

keeping silence speaks only in answer to questions, since the Scripture says that "sin is not escaped by much speaking," and "a talkative man is not established in the earth."

The tenth grade of humility is this, that he be not easily moved nor prompt to laughter, since it is written: "The fool raiseth his voice in laughter."

The eleventh grade of humility is this: if, when the monk speaks, he says few words and those to the point, slowly and without laughter, humbly and gravely; and be not loud of voice, as it is written: "A wise man is known by his few words."

The twelfth grade of humility is this: that a monk conduct himself with humility not only in his heart but also in his bearing, in the sight of all; that is, in the service of God, in the oratory [chapel], in the monastery, in the garden, on the road, in the field; and everywhere, sitting or walking or standing, let him always have his head bowed, and his eyes fixed on the ground. Always mindful of his sins, let him think of himself as being already tried in the great judgment, saying in his heart what that publican, spoken of in the gospel, said with his eyes fixed on the earth: "Lord, I a sinner am not worthy to lift mine eyes to the heavens;" and again with the prophet: "I am bowed down and humbled wheresoever I go." . . .

---

[1]Jacob, a patriarch of ancient Israel, had a dream about angels ascending and descending a ladder between heaven and earth; the dream is recounted in the Old Testament.

## REVIEW QUESTIONS

1. Describe the government of a Benedictine monastery.
2. How did monasticism help to shape Western cultural values?

---

## 7  The Christian World-View

Building on the life and teachings of Jesus as reported in the Gospels and apostolic letters collected in the New Testament, the early Christian thinkers formulated a comprehensive world-view. The Christian view stressed the sinful nature of human beings—their almost unlimited capacity for evildoing. The church taught that only through the gift of God's grace could individuals overcome the consequences of sin and obtain salvation. Christian leaders drew a sharp distinction between a spiritual realm (called the City of God by Saint Augustine) and the secular world (the City of Man), where Christians had to live out their earthly, material existence. Christians were urged to live in the world, but not to live by its values. Rather, they were to imitate the ways of Jesus in thought, word, and deed, as interpreted by the authorities of the church.

The task of living a Christian life in a secular world was not easy. Not the least of the problems was how Christians could relate to the political power structure of earthly societies. The task of finding a Christian basis for relations between church and state has been a continuous process since early Christian times. It has had wide repercussions in creating a distinctive Christian view of the legitimate powers of the state.

# Saint Augustine
## *THE CITY OF GOD*

Augustine (Aurelius Augustinus, A.D. 354–430), bishop of Hippo (now Souk-Ahras in modern Algeria), was one of the great theologians of the early Christian church. He formulated a view of life and of the individual that became definitive for Western Christians until it was partially superseded by the writings of Thomas Aquinas in the thirteenth century. Although Augustine admired the achievements of Socrates and Plato, he could not accept their central premise: that in the search for truth the individual relied on reason alone.

The sacking of Rome by the Visigoths in A.D. 410 shocked the entire Roman world. Pagans blamed the catastrophe on the Christians; by abandoning the old gods, said pagans, Christians had brought down the wrath of heaven on Rome. In reply to these charges, Saint Augustine wrote the *City of God,* setting forth the Christian view of the world and humanity.

The theme of the first group of passages from Augustine's *City of God* is a crucial element in the Christian outlook: that when human beings turn away from God to follow their own desires as Adam and Eve did, they fall into evil and become afflicted with many miseries, which can only be relieved through God's grace.

I have already said, in previous Books, that God had two purposes in deriving all men from one man. His first purpose was to give unity to the human race by the likeness of nature. His second purpose was to bind mankind by the bond of peace, through blood relationship, into one harmonious whole. I have said further that no member of this race would ever have died had not the first two [Adam and Eve]—one created from nothing and the second from the first—merited this death by disobedience. The sin which they committed was so great that it impaired all human nature—in this sense, that the nature has been transmitted to posterity with a propensity to sin and a necessity to die. . . .

When a man lives "according to man" and not "according to God" he is like the Devil. . . .

When man lives according to himself, that is to say, according to human ways and not according to God's will, then surely he lives according to falsehood. Man himself, of course, is not a lie, since God who is his Author and Creator could not be the Author and Creator of a lie. Rather, man has been so constituted in truth that he was meant to live not according to himself but to Him who made him—that is, he was meant to do the will of God rather than his own. It is a lie not to live as a man was created to live.

Man indeed desires happiness even when he does so live as to make happiness impossible. . . . The happiness of man can come not from himself but only from God, and that to live according to oneself is to sin, and to sin is to lose God. . . .

Moreover, our first parents [Adam and Eve] only fell openly into the sin of disobedience because, secretly, they had begun to be guilty. Actually, their bad deed could not have been done had not bad will preceded it; what is more, the root of their bad will was nothing else than pride. For, "pride is the beginning of all sin." And what is pride but an appetite for inordinate exaltation? Now, exaltation is inordinate when the soul cuts itself off from the very Source [God] to which it should keep close and somehow makes itself and becomes an end to itself. This takes place when the soul becomes inordinately pleased with itself, and such self-pleasing occurs when the soul falls away from the unchangeable Good which ought to please the soul far more than the soul can please itself. Now, this falling away is the soul's own doing, for, if the will had merely remained firm in the love of that higher immutable Good which lighted its mind into knowledge and warmed its will into love, it would not have turned away in search of satisfaction in itself and, by so doing, have lost that light and warmth. And thus Eve would not have believed that the serpent's lie was true, nor would Adam have preferred the will of his wife to the will of God. . . .

This life of ours—if a life so full of such great ills can properly be called a life—bears witness to the fact that, from its very start, the race of mortal men has been a race condemned. Think,

first, of that dreadful abyss of ignorance from which all error flows and so engulfs the sons of Adam in a darksome pool that no one can escape without the toll of toils and tears and fears. Then, take our very love for all those things that prove so vain and poisonous and breed so many heartaches, troubles, griefs, and fears; such insane joys in discord, strife, and war; such wrath and plots of enemies, deceivers, sycophants; such fraud and theft and robbery; such perfidy and pride, envy and ambition, homicide and murder, cruelty and savagery, lawlessness and lust; all the shameless passions of the impure—fornication and adultery, incest and unnatural sins, rape and countless other uncleannesses too nasty to be mentioned; the sins against religion—sacrilege and heresy, blasphemy and perjury; the iniquities against our neighbors—calumnies and cheating, lies and false witness, violence to persons and property; the injustices of the courts and the innumerable other miseries and maladies that fill the world, yet escape attention.

It is true that it is wicked men who do such things, but the source of all such sins is that radical canker [sinfulness] in the mind and will that is innate in every son of Adam. . . .

Yet, for all this blight of ignorance and folly, fallen man has not been left without some ministries of Providence, nor has God, in His anger, shut up His mercies. There are still within the reach of man himself, if only he will pay the price of toil and trouble, the twin resources of law and education. With the one, he can make war on human passion; with the other, he can keep the light of learning lit even in the darkness of our native ignorance. . . .

From this all but hell of unhappiness here on earth, nothing can save us but the grace of Jesus Christ, who is our Saviour, Lord and God. In fact, the very meaning of the name, Jesus, is Saviour, and when we say "save" we mean, especially, that He saves us from passing from the misery of this mortal life to a still more miserable condition, which is not so much a life as death. . . .

Augustine saw a conflict between the earthly city, visible, temporal, and corrupt, and the City of God, invisible, eternal, and perfect. Those Christians favored with God's grace lived in this earthly city as strangers and pilgrims passing through on their journey to their true homeland, the heavenly kingdom. The fate of the earthly city was of no ultimate concern to these Christians. For Augustine, this earthly world represented the forces of evil that would finally be destroyed at the end of time, when Christ would come again.

What we see, then, is that two societies have issued from two kinds of love. Worldly society has flowered from a selfish love which dared to despise even God, whereas the communion of saints is rooted in a love of God that is ready to trample on self. In a word, this latter relies on the Lord, whereas the other boasts that it can get along by itself. The city of man seeks the praise of men, whereas the height of glory for the other is to hear God in the witness of conscience. The one lifts up its head in its own boasting; the other says to God: "Thou art my glory, thou liftest up my head."

In the city of the world both the rulers themselves and the people they dominate are dominated by the lust for domination; whereas in the City of God all citizens serve one another in charity, whether they serve by the responsibilities of office or by the duties of obedience. The one city loves its leaders as symbols of its own strength; the other says to its God: "I love thee, O Lord, my strength." Hence, even the wise men in the city of man live according to man, and their only goal has been the goods of their bodies or of the mind or of both; though some of them have reached a knowledge of God, "they did not glorify him as God or give thanks but became vain in their reasonings, and their senseless minds have been darkened. For while professing to be wise" (that is to say, while glorying in their own wisdom, under the domination of pride),

"they have become fools, and they have changed the glory of the incorruptible God for an image made like to corruptible man and to birds and four-footed beasts and creeping things" (meaning that they either led their people, or imitated them, in adoring idols shaped like these things), "and they worshiped and served the creature rather than the Creator who is blessed forever." In the City of God, on the contrary, there is no merely human wisdom, but there is a piety which worships the true God as He should be worshiped and has as its goal that reward of all holiness whether in the society of saints on earth or in that of angels of heaven, which is "that God may be all in all." . . .

Augustine says that history reveals the intermingling of the City of God and the City of Man in time and space, and the incessant combat between the partisans of these two cities. This struggle will continue until time itself is annulled by God when Christ returns—and the saints are separated from sinners at the Last Judgment. Then the saints will join Jesus and be with him for eternity, and the sinners will be separated from God and confined to hell, also for eternity.

. . . In the eternal City of God, each and all of the citizens are personally immortal with an immortality which the holy angels never lost and which even human beings can come to share. This is to be achieved by the supreme omnipotence of the Creator, the Founder of the City. . . .

Who can measure the happiness of heaven, where no evil at all can touch us, no good will be out of reach; where life is to be one long laud extolling God, who will be all in all; where there will be no weariness to call for rest, no need to call for toil, no place for any energy but praise. . . .

. . . There will be such poise, such grace, such beauty as become a place where nothing unbecoming can be found. Wherever the spirit wills, there, in a flash, will the body be. Nor will the spirit ever will anything unbecoming either to itself or to the body.

In heaven, all glory will be true glory, since no one could ever err in praising too little or too much. True honor will never be denied where due, never be given where undeserved, and, since none but the worthy are permitted there, no one will unworthily ambition glory. Perfect peace will reign, since nothing in ourselves or in any others could disturb this peace.

---

# Saint Benedict of Nursia
# THE CHRISTIAN WAY OF LIFE

*In the following selection from his monastic book of rules, Saint Benedict of Nursia advises his monks on the attitudes and conduct necessary to live a virtuous Christian life.*

## WHAT ARE THE INSTRUMENTS OF GOOD WORKS

In the first place, to love the Lord God with the whole heart, whole soul, whole strength, then his neighbor as himself.

Then not to kill, not to commit adultery, not to steal, not to covet, not to bear false witness, to honor all men, and what anyone would not have done to him, let him not do to another. To deny himself, that he may follow Christ, to chasten the body, to renounce luxuries, to love fasting. To relieve the poor, to clothe the naked, to visit the sick, to bury the dead, to help in tribulation, to console the afflicted.

To make himself a stranger to the affairs of the world, to prefer nothing before the love of Christ, not to give way to anger, not to bear any grudge, not to harbour deceit in the heart, not to forsake charity. Not to swear, lest haply he perjure himself, to utter truth from his heart and his mouth. Not to return evil for evil, not to do injuries, but rather to bear them patiently, to love his enemies, not to curse again those who curse him, but rather to bless them, to endure persecution for righteousness' sake. Not to be proud, not given to wine, not gluttonous, not addicted to sleep, not slothful, not given to murmur, not a slanderer. To commit his hope to God; when he sees anything good in himself to attribute it to God, and not to himself, but let him always know that which is evil is his own doing, and impute it to himself. To fear the day of judgment, to dread hell, to desire eternal life with all spiritual longing, to have the expectation of death every day before his eyes. To watch over his actions at all times, to know certainly that in all places the eye of God is upon him; those evil thoughts which come into his heart to dash to pieces on Christ, and to make them known to his spiritual senior. To keep his lips from evil and wicked discourse, not to be fond of much talking, not to speak vain words or such as provoke laughter, not to love much or violent laughter. To give willing attention to the sacred readings, to pray frequently every day, to confess his past sins to God, in prayer, with tears and groanings; from thence forward to reform as to those sins.

Not to fulfill the desires of the flesh, to hate his own will, in all things to obey the commands of the abbot, even though he himself (which God forbid) should do otherwise, remembering our Lord's commands: "What they say, do; but what they do, do ye not." Not to desire to be called a saint before he is one, but first to be one that he may be truly called one;

every day to fulfill the commands of God in his deeds, to love chastity, to hate no one, not to have jealousy or envy, not to love contention, to avoid self-conceit; to reverence seniors, to love juniors, to pray for enemies in the love of Christ, to be reconciled with his adversary, before the going down of the sun, and never to despair of the mercy of God. . . .

---

# Pope Gelasius I
# CHURCH AND STATE

Emperor Constantine's conversion to Christianity in the early fourth century dramatically changed the Christian church's relationship to the Roman state. After nearly three centuries of periodic persecution, the church now enjoyed imperial patronage, and Christianity was an accepted religion. Though still not a majority of the population, the Christian community grew rapidly through the fourth century and gained new power.

Finally, about 392, Emperor Theodosius I (A.D. 379–395) outlawed the traditional pagan cults and established Christianity as the official religion of the Roman state. Though welcome, this new status created problems for the church, which was treated more and more as if it were a department of the imperial government. Interference in matters of doctrine and discipline by imperial rulers was resisted by a clergy used to internal freedom of action, who recognized no spiritual authority but Christ and the Scriptures.

In the late fifth century, Pope Gelasius I (492–496), the bishop of Rome, tried to establish clear boundaries between the legitimate sphere of authority of the state and that of the church. In the following letter to the Emperor Anastasius (491–518), written in 494, Pope Gelasius I established the church's theoretical ground rules for future church-state relations.

. . . Two there are, august emperor, by which this world is chiefly ruled, the sacred authority (*auctoritas*) of the priesthood and the royal power (*potestas*). Of these the responsibility of the priests is more weighty in so far as they will answer for the kings of men themselves at the divine judgement. You know, most clement son, that, although you take precedence over all mankind in dignity, nevertheless you piously bow the neck to those who have charge of divine affairs and seek from them the means of your salvation, and hence you realize that, in the order of religion, in matters concerning the reception and right administration of the heavenly sacraments, you ought to submit yourself rather than rule, and that in these matters you should depend on their judgment rather than seek to bend them to your will. For if the bishops themselves, recognizing that the imperial office was conferred on you by divine disposition, obey your laws so far as the sphere of public order is concerned lest they seem to obstruct your decrees in mundane matters, with what zeal, I ask you, ought you to obey those who have been charged with administering the sacred mysteries? Moreover, just as no light risk attends pontiffs[1] who keep silent in matters concerning the service of God, so too no little

---

[1]Originally designating a Roman magistrate, the Latin word *pontifex* became applied to any priest. Here it refers to bishops.

danger threatens those who show scorn—which God forbid—when they ought to obey. And if the hearts of the faithful should be submitted to all priests in general who rightly administer divine things, how much more should assent be given to the bishop of that see[2] which the Most High [God] wished to be preeminent over all priests, and which the devotion of the whole church has honored ever since. As Your Piety is certainly well aware, no one can ever raise himself by purely human means to the privilege and place of him whom the voice of Christ has set before all, whom the church has always venerated and held in devotion as its primate.[3] The things which are established by divine judgement can be assailed by human presumption; they cannot be overthrown by anyone's power.

------

[2]A see is a bishop's center of authority or community, over which he has power of decision in religious matters.

[3]The primate (originally from a Latin word for first) is the "first" bishop: that is, the bishop of Rome, who, as the successor of Saint Peter, was here recognized as the presiding bishop over the entire Christian church.

## REVIEW QUESTIONS

1. According to Saint Augustine, what was the origin of the unity of the human race? What was the origin of human sinfulness?
2. Describe Augustine's conception of the two cities—the City of God and the City of Man—and the radical implications of this teaching in shaping Christian culture.
3. Describe the teachings of Pope Gelasius on the proper relationship between church and state. What was radically new in this doctrine?

CHAPTER 7
# The Early Middle Ages

HISTOIRE DE CHARLEMAGNE (detail). This fifteenth-century tapestry shows Charlemagne wearing the heraldric insignia of France and the Holy Roman Empire. His courtiers surround him. *(Wool, 2.55 × 1.45 m. Musée des Beaux-Arts, Dijon.)*

The establishment of Germanic kingdoms in the fifth and sixth centuries on Roman lands marked the end of the ancient world and the start of the Middle Ages, a period that spanned a thousand years. During the Middle Ages the center of Western civilization shifted northward from the lands bordering the Mediterranean Sea to parts of Europe that Greco-Roman civilization had barely penetrated.

The Early Middle Ages (500–1050) marked an age of transition. The humanist culture that characterized the Greco-Roman past had disintegrated, and a new civilization was emerging in Latin Christendom, which covered western and central Europe. Medieval civilization consisted of a blending of the remnants of Greco-Roman culture with Germanic customs and Christian principles. The central element was Christianity; the Christian view of a transcendent God and the quest for salvation pervaded the medieval outlook, and the church was the dominant institution.

During the Early Middle Ages, Latin Christendom was a pioneer society struggling to overcome invasions, a breakdown of central authority, a decline in trade and town life, and a deterioration of highly refined culture. The Latin Christian church, centered in Rome and headed by the pope, progressively gave form and unity to the new civilization. Christian clergy preserved some of the learning of the ancient world, which they incorporated into the Christian outlook. Dedicated missionaries converted various Germanic, Celtic, and Slavic peoples to Latin Christianity. From Italy to the North Sea and from Ireland to Poland, an emerging Christian tradition was providing unity to people with differing cultural traditions.

The center of emerging medieval civilization was the kingdom of the Franks, located in Gaul (France) and western Germany. Migrating westward from their homeland in the valley of the Rhine River, the Germanic Franks conquered Roman Gaul in the fifth and sixth centuries. Charlemagne (768–814), the greatest of the Frankish rulers, added large areas of Germany and Italy to his kingdom. On Christmas Day in the year 800, Pope Leo III crowned Charlemagne emperor of the Romans, a sign that the memory of Imperial Rome still persisted. Without Roman law, a professional civil service, and great cities serving as centers of trade, however, Charlemagne's empire was only a pale shadow of the Roman Empire. Rather, the crowning of a German king as emperor of the Romans by the pope signified something new: the intermingling of Germanic, Christian, and Roman elements that came to characterize medieval Latin Christendom.

Charlemagne's empire rested more on the strength of the emperor's personality than it did on viable institutions. Charlemagne's heirs were unable to hold the empire together; power passed gradually into the hands of large landholders, who exercised governmental authority in their own regions. Also contributing to this decline in centralized authority were devastating raids by Muslims from Spain, North Africa, and Mediterranean islands; Northmen from Scandinavia; and Magyars from western Asia. Europe had entered an age of feudalism, in which public authority was dispersed among lords and held as if it were private inheritable property.

Feudalism rested on an economic base known as manorialism. Although family farms owned by free peasants still existed, the essential agricultural arrangement in medieval society was the village community (manor), headed by a lord or his steward and farmed by serfs, who were bound to the land. A lord controlled at least one manorial village; great lords might possess scores. Much land was held by various clerical institutions; the church's manors were similar to those run by nonclerics.

Feudalism was an improvised response to the challenge posed by ineffectual central authority, and it provided some order and law during a period of breakdown. Medieval feudal practices were not uniform but differed from region to region. In later centuries, when kings reasserted their authority and fashioned strong central governments, the power of lords declined.

Latin Christendom (western and central Europe) was only one of three new civilizations based on religion that emerged after the decline of the Roman Empire; Byzantium and Islam were the other two. During the Early Middle Ages both of these eastern civilizations were far more advanced than Latin Christendom. And yet it was Latin Christendom, not Byzantine or Islamic civilizations, that eventually produced the modern world.

# 1 Islam

The vital new religion of Islam emerged in the seventh century among the Arabs of Arabia. Its founder was Muhammad (c. 570–632), a prosperous merchant in Mecca, a trading city near the Red Sea. When Muhammad was about forty, he believed that he was visited by the angel Gabriel, who ordered him to "recite in the name of the Lord!" Transformed by this vision, Muhammad was convinced that he had been chosen to serve as a prophet.

Although most desert Arabs worshiped tribal gods, in the towns and trading centers many Arabs were familiar with Judaism and Christianity, and some had accepted the idea of one God. Rejecting the many deities of the tribal religions, Muhammad offered the Arabs a new monotheistic faith, Islam, which means "surrender to Allah" (God).

# Muhammad
## *THE KORAN*

Islamic standards of morality and rules governing daily life are set by the Koran, the book that Muslims believe contains the words of Allah as revealed to Muhammad. Muslims see their religion as the completion and perfection of Judaism and Christianity. They regard the ancient Hebrew prophets as sent from God and value their messages about compassion and the oneness of humanity. Muslims also regard Jesus as a great prophet but do not consider him divine. They see Muhammad as the last and greatest of the prophets and believe that he was entirely human, not divine. Muslims worship only Allah, the creator and ruler of heaven and earth, a single, all-powerful God who is merciful, compassionate, and just. Following are excerpts from the *Koran*:

## GOD

God: there is no god but Him, the Living, the Eternal One. Neither slumber nor sleep overtakes Him. His is what the heavens and the earth contain. Who can intercede with Him except by His permission? He knows what is before and behind men. They can grasp only that part of His knowledge which He wills. His throne is as vast as the heavens and the earth, and the preservation of both does not weary Him. He is the Exalted, the Immense One. (2:255–257)

————

*In the Name of God, the Compassionate, the Merciful*

It is the Merciful who has taught the Koran.

He created man and taught him articulate speech. The sun and the moon pursue their ordered course. The plants and the trees bow down in adoration.

He raised the heaven on high and set the balance of all things, that you might not transgress that balance. Give just weight and full measure.

He laid the earth for His creatures, with all its fruits and blossom-bearing palm, chaff-covered grain and scented herbs. Which of your Lord's blessings would you deny?

He created man from potter's clay, and the jinn from smokeless fire. Which of your Lord's blessings would you deny? (55:1–18)

————

All that is in the heavens and the earth gives glory to God. He is the Mighty, the Wise One.

It is He that has sovereignty over the heavens and the earth. He ordains life and death, and has power over all things.

He is the First and the Last, the Visible and the Unseen. He has knowledge of all things.

It was He who created the heavens and the earth in six days, and then mounted the throne. He knows all that goes into the earth and all that emerges from it, all that comes down from heaven and all that ascends to it. He is with you wherever you are. God is cognizant of all your actions.

He has sovereignty over the heavens and earth. To God shall all things return. He causes the night to pass into the day, and causes the day to pass into the night. He has knowledge of the inmost thoughts of men. (57:1–7)

## RIGHTEOUSNESS AND MERCY

Righteousness does not consist in whether you face towards the East or the West. The righteous man is he who believes in God and the Last Day, in the angels and the Book and the prophets; who, though he loves it dearly, gives away his wealth to kinsfolk, to orphans, to the destitute, to the traveller in need and to beggars, and for the redemption of captives; who attends to his prayers and renders the alms levy; who is true to his promises and steadfast in trial and adversity and in times of war. Such are the true believers; such are the God-fearing. (2:176–178)

———

Serve God and associate none with Him. Show kindness to parents and kindred, to orphans and to the destitute, to near and distant neighbours, to those that keep company with you, to the traveller in need, and to the slaves you own. God does not love arrogant and boastful men, who are themselves niggardly and enjoin others to be niggardly; who conceal the riches which God of His bounty has bestowed upon them (We have prepared a shameful punishment for the unbelievers); and who spend their wealth for the sake of ostentation, believing neither in God nor in the Last Day. He that chooses Satan for his friend, an evil friend has he. (4:36–39)

## CHRISTIANITY

And remember the angels' words to Mary. They said:* 'God has chosen you. He has made you pure and exalted you above womankind. Mary, be obedient to your Lord; bow down and worship with the worshippers.'

This is an account of a divine secret. We reveal it to you.† You were not present when they cast lots to see which of them should have charge of Mary; nor were you present when they argued about her.

The angels said to Mary: 'God bids you rejoice in a word from Him. His name is the Messiah, Jesus the son of Mary. He shall be noble in this world and in the hereafter, and shall be

one of those who are favoured. He shall preach to men in his cradle and in the prime of manhood, and shall lead a righteous life.'

'Lord,' she said, 'how can I bear a child when no man has touched me?'

He replied: 'Even thus. God creates whom He will. When He decrees a thing He need only say: "Be," and it is. He will instruct him in the Scriptures and in wisdom, in the Torah and in the Gospel, and send him forth as an apostle to the Israelites. He will say: "I bring you a sign from your Lord. From clay I will make for you the likeness of a bird. I shall breathe into it and, by God's leave, it shall become a living bird. By God's leave I shall heal the blind man and the leper, and raise the dead to life. I shall tell you what to eat and what to store up in your houses. Surely that will be a sign for you, if you are true believers. I come to confirm the Torah which preceded me and to make lawful to you some of the things you are forbidden. I bring you a sign from your Lord: therefore fear God and obey me. God is my Lord and your Lord: therefore serve Him. That is a straight path. (3:42–51)

———

People of the Book,‡ do not transgress the bounds of your religion. Speak nothing but the truth about God. The Messiah, Jesus the son of Mary, was no more than God's apostle and His Word which He cast to Mary: a spirit from Him. So believe in God and His apostles and do not say: 'Three.' Forbear, and it shall be better for you. God is but one God. God forbid that He should have a son! His is all that the heavens and the earth contain. God is the all-sufficient protector. The Messiah does not disdain to be a servant of God, nor do the angels who are nearest to Him. Those who through arrogance disdain His service shall all be brought before Him. (4:171–172)

———

*Cf. Luke i, 26–38.
†Muḥammad.

‡Christians.

## HEAVEN AND HELL

### THAT WHICH IS COMING

*In the Name of God, the Compassionate, the Merciful*

When that which is coming comes—and no soul shall then deny its coming—some shall be abased and others exalted.

When the earth shakes and quivers, and the mountains crumble away and scatter abroad into fine dust, you shall be divided into three multitudes: those on the right (blessed shall be those on the right); those on the left (damned shall be those on the left); and those to the fore (foremost shall be those). Such are they that shall be brought near to their Lord in the gardens of delight: a whole multitude from the men of old, but only a few from the latter generations.

They shall recline on jewelled couches face to face, and there shall wait on them immortal youths with bowls and ewers and a cup of purest wine (that will neither pain their heads nor take away their reason); with fruits of their own choice and flesh of fowls that they relish. And theirs shall be the dark-eyed houris [beautiful virgins], chaste as hidden pearls: a guerdon [reward] for their deeds.

There they shall hear no idle talk, no sinful speech, but only the greeting, 'Peace! Peace!'

Those on the right hand – happy shall be those on the right hand! They shall recline on couches raised on high in the shade of thornless sidrs and clusters of talh;* amidst gushing waters and abundant fruits, unforbidden, never-ending.

We created the houris and made them virgins, loving companions for those on the right

hand: a multitude from the men of old, and a multitude from the latter generations.

As for those on the left hand (wretched shall be those on the left hand!) they shall dwell amidst scorching winds and seething water: in the shade of pitch-black smoke, neither cool nor refreshing. For they have lived in comfort and persisted in the heinous sin,† saying: 'When we are once dead and turned to dust and bones, shall we be raised to life? And our forefathers, too?'

Say: 'Those of old, and those of the present age, shall be brought together on an appointed day. As for you sinners who deny the truth, you shall eat the fruit of the Zaqqūm tree and fill your bellies with it. You shall drink scalding water: yet you shall drink it as the thirsty camel drinks.'

Such shall be their fare on the Day of Reckoning. (56:1–56)

## WOMEN

Men have authority over women because God has made the one superior to the other, and because they spend their wealth to maintain them. Good women are obedient. They guard their unseen parts because God has guarded them. As for those from whom you fear disobedience, admonish them and send them to beds apart and beat them. Then if they obey you, take no further action against them. Surely God is high, supreme.

If you fear a breach between a man and his wife, appoint an arbiter from his people and another from hers. If they wish to be reconciled God will bring them together again. Surely God is all-knowing and wise. (4:34–35)

---

*Probably the banana fruit.

†Idolatry.

## REVIEW QUESTIONS

1. Compare and contrast the views of God and morality described in the Koran with those found in the Hebrew Scriptures and the New Testament.
2. What advice does the Koran give to Christians?

## 2  Preservation of Ancient Learning in the East

During the Early Middle Ages, when learning was in retreat in Latin Christendom, both Byzantine and Islamic civilizations preserved the intellectual traditions of ancient Greece. Contacts with Byzantine and Muslim learning during the High Middle Ages stimulated learning in the Latin West.

## Theophylact Simocattes
# THE VALUE OF REASON AND HISTORY

In the following selection Theophylact Simocattes, a seventh-century Byzantine historian, shows respect for the tradition of reason that was inherited from the classical world and familiarity with Homer, the wellspring of Greek literature. Like Thucydides, he values history, considering it a far better avenue to knowledge than the myths and fables created or embellished by poets.

Man is adorned not only by the endowments of nature but also by the fruits of his own efforts. For reason, which he possesses, is an admirable and divine trait by which he renders to God his adoration and homage. Through reason he enters into knowledge of himself and does not remain ignorant of the ordering of his creation. Accordingly, through reason men come together with each other and, turning away from external considerations, they direct their thoughts toward the mystery of their own nature.

Reason has given many good things to men and is an excellent helpmate of nature. The things which nature has withheld from man, reason provides in the most effective manner, embellishing those things which are seen, adding spice to those that are tasted, roughening or softening things to the touch, composing poetry and music for the ear, soothing the soul by lessening discord, and bringing sounds into concord. Is not reason also the most persuasive master of the crafts?—reason which has made a well-woven tunic from wool, which from wood has constructed carts for farmers, oars for sailors, and small wicker shields for soldiers as protection against the dangers of the battlefield.

Most important of all, reason provides the hearer with that pleasure which reflects the greatest amount of experience, the study of history, which is the instructor of the spirit. Nothing can be more seductive than history for the minds of those who desire to learn. It is sufficient to cite an example from Homer to demonstrate this: Soon after he had been thrown on the beach by violent waves of the sea, the son of Laertes, Odysseus, almost naked and with his body emaciated from the mishap of the shipwreck, was graciously received at the court of Alcinous. There he was clothed in a bright robe and given a place at the table of the king. Although only just arrived, he was granted permission to speak and an opportunity to relate his adventures. His recital pleased the Phocaeans so much that the banquet seemed to have changed into a theater. Indeed, they lent him an attention altogether remarkable, nor did they feel during his long narration any tedium, although he described the many misfortunes he had suffered. For listening brings an overwhelming desire (to hear more) and thus easily accepts a strange tale.

It is for this reason that in learning the poets are considered most estimable, for they realize that the spirits of men are fond of stories, always yearning to acquire knowledge and thirsty for strange narrations. Thus the poets create myths for men and clothe their phrases with adornments, fleshing out the fables with method, and embellishing their nonsense with meter as if with enchanted spells. This artifice has succeeded so well that poets are considered to be theologians, intimately associated with the gods. It is believed that through the poets' mouths the gods reveal their own personal affairs and also whether a felicitous or a calamitous event will happen to men in their lifetime.

This being so, one may term history the common teacher of all men: it shows which course to follow and which to avoid as profitless. The most competent generals are those who have been instructed by history, for history reveals how to draw up troops and by what means to outmaneuver the enemy through ambush. History renders these generals more prudent because they know about the misfortunes of others, and it directs them through observation of the mistakes of others. Similarly, it has shown that men become happier through good conduct, pushing men to higher peaks of virtue through gradual advances. For the old man history is his support and staff, while for the young, it is the fairest and wisest instructor, applying (the fruit of) great experience to new situations and thus anticipating somewhat the lessons of time. I now dedicate my own zeal and efforts to history, although I know that I am undertaking a greater task than I am able to fulfill effectively, since I lack elegance of expression, profundity of thought, purity of syntax, and skill in composition. If any parts of my work should prove pleasing in any way, let this be ascribed rather to the result of chance than to my own skill.

# Avicenna
# LOVE OF LEARNING

In the eighth and ninth centuries, Muslim civilization, which creatively integrated Arabic, Byzantine, Persian, and Indian cultural traditions, entered its golden age.

Muslim science, philosophy, and mathematics, based largely on the achievements of the ancient Greeks, made brilliant contributions to the sum of knowledge at a time when Latin Christendom had lost much of Greco-Roman thought and culture. The Muslims had acquired Greek learning from the older Persian and Byzantine civilizations, which had kept alive the Greek inheritance. By translating Greek works into Arabic and commenting on them, Muslim scholars performed the great historical task of preserving the philosophical and scientific heritage of ancient Greece. Along with this heritage, the original contributions of Muslim scholars and scientists were also passed on to Christian Europe.

The most eminent Muslim thinker, Ibn-Sina, known to the West as Avicenna (980–1037), was a poet, doctor, scientist, and philosopher who wrote on every field of knowledge. His philosophical works, which relied heavily on Aristotle, had an important influence on medieval Christian thinkers. In his autobiography, excerpted below, Avicenna describes his love for learning and his debt to ancient Greece.

[In] Bukhara [in present-day Uzbekistan] I was put under teachers of the Koran and of letters. By the time I was ten I had mastered the Koran and a great deal of literature, so that I was marvelled at for my aptitude.... Then there came to Bukhara a man called Abū ʿAbd Allāh al-Nātilī who claimed to be a philosopher; my father invited him to stay in our house, hoping that I would learn from him also. Before his advent I had already occupied myself with Muslim jurisprudence, attending Ismāʿīl the Ascetic; so I was an excellent enquirer, having become familiar with the methods of postulation and the techniques of rebuttal according to the usages of the canon lawyers. I now commenced reading the *Isagoge* (of Porphyry)[1] with al-Nātilī: when he mentioned to me the definition of *genus* as a term applied to a number of things of different species in answer to the question "What is it?" I set about verifying this definition in a manner such as he had never heard. He marvelled at me exceedingly, and warned my father that I should not engage in any other occupation but learning; whatever problem he stated to me, I showed a better mental conception of it than he. So I continued until I had read all the straightforward parts of Logic with him; as for the subtler points, he had no acquaintance with them.

From then onward I took to reading texts by myself; I studied the commentaries, until I had completely mastered the science of Logic. Similarly with Euclid[2] I read the first five or six figures with him, and thereafter undertook on my own account to solve the entire remainder of the book. Next I moved on to the *Almagest* (of Ptolemy)[3]; when I had finished the prolegomena [introductory essay] and reached the geometrical figures, al-Nātilī told me to go on reading and to solve the problems by myself; I should merely revise what I read with him, so that he might indicate to me what was right and what was wrong. The truth is that he did not really teach this book; I began to solve the work, and many were the complicated figures of which he had no knowledge until I presented them to him, and made him understand them. Then al-Nātilī took leave of me, setting out for Gurganj.

I now occupied myself with mastering the various texts and commentaries on natural science and metaphysics, until all the gates of knowledge were open to me. Next I desired to study medicine, and proceeded to read all the books that have been written on this subject. Medicine is not a difficult science, and naturally I excelled in it in a very short time, so that qualified physicians began to read medicine with me. I also undertook to treat the sick, and methods of treatment derived from practical experience revealed themselves to me such as baffle description. At the same time I continued between whiles to study and dispute on law, being now sixteen years of age.

The next eighteen months I devoted entirely to reading; I studied Logic once again, and all the parts of philosophy. During all this time I did not sleep one night through, nor devoted my attention to any other matter by day. I prepared a set of files; with each proof I examined, I set down the syllogistic premises and put them in order in the files, then I examined what deductions might be drawn from them. I observed methodically the conditions of the premises, and proceeded until the truth of each particular problem was confirmed for me. Whenever I found myself perplexed by a problem, or could not find the middle term in any syllogism, I would repair to the mosque and pray, adoring the All-Creator, until my puzzle was resolved and my difficulty made easy. At night I would return home, set the lamp before me, and busy myself with reading and writing; whenever sleep overcame me or I was conscious of some weakness, I turned aside to drink a glass of wine until

---

[1]Porphyry (A.D. 233–c. 305) wrote a history of philosophy and edited the lectures of Plotinus, the Neoplatonist. The *Isagoge* was Porphyry's introduction to the categories of Aristotle.

[2]Euclid, an Alexandrian mathematician who lived around 300 B.C. He creatively synthesized earlier developments in geometry.

[3]Ptolemy, a mathematician, geographer, and astronomer who worked at Alexandria in the second century A.D. His *Almagest,* a Greek-Arabic term meaning "the greatest" summed up antiquity's knowledge of astronomy and became the authoritative text during the Middle Ages.

my strength returned to me; then I went back to my reading. If ever the least slumber overtook me, I would dream of the precise problem which I was considering as I fell asleep; in that way many problems revealed themselves to me while sleeping. So I continued until I had made myself master of all the sciences; I now comprehended them to the limits of human possibility. All that I learned during that time is exactly as I know it now; I have added nothing more to my knowledge to this day.

I was now a master of Logic, natural sciences and mathematics. I therefore returned to metaphysics; I read the *Metaphysica* (of Aristotle), but did not understand its contents and was baffled by the author's intention; I read it over forty times, until I had the text by heart. Even then I did not understand it or what the author meant, and I despaired within myself, saying, "This is a book which there is no way of understanding." But one day at noon I chanced to be in the booksellers' quarter, and a broker was there with a volume in his hand which he was calling for sale. He offered it to me, but I returned it to him impatiently, believing that there was no use in this particular science. However he said to me, "Buy this book from me: it is cheap, and I will sell it to you for four dirhams. The owner is in need of the money." So I bought it, and found that it was a book by Abū Naṣr al-Fārābī *On the Objects of the Metaphysica*. I returned home and hastened to read it; and at once the objects of that book became clear to me, for I had it all by heart. I rejoiced at this,

and upon the next day distributed much in alms to the poor in gratitude to Almighty God.

Now the Sultan of Bukhara at that time was Nūḥ ibn Manṣūr, and it happened that he fell sick of a malady which baffled all the physicians. My name was famous among them because of the breadth of my reading; they therefore mentioned me in his presence, and begged him to summon me. I attended the sick-room, and collaborated with them in treating the royal patient. So I came to be enrolled in his service. One day I asked his leave to enter their library, to examine the contents and read the books on medicine; he granted my request, and I entered a mansion with many chambers, each chamber having chests of books piled one upon another. In one apartment were books on language and poetry, in another law, and so on; each apartment was set aside for books on a single science. I glanced through the catalogue of the works of the ancient Greeks, and asked for those which I required; and I saw books whose very names are as yet unknown to many—works which I had never seen before and have not seen since. I read these books, taking notes of their contents; I came to realize the place each man occupied in his particular science.

So by the time I reached my eighteenth year I had exhausted all these sciences. My memory for learning was at that period of my life better than it is now, but to-day I am more mature; apart from this my knowledge is exactly the same, nothing further having been added to my store since then.

## REVIEW QUESTIONS

1. Why did Theophylact value reason? History?
2. Provide examples of Avicenna's familiarity with Greek learning.

---

## 3   Converting the Germanic Peoples to Christianity

From its beginnings, Christianity sought to carry to all peoples its offer of salvation through faith in Jesus. After Christianity had become the religion of the Roman state, pagan cults were suppressed. When the western Roman provinces fell under the power of invading Germanic tribes, Christian Romans faced the task of converting their new rulers to their religion.

The ability of the Christian religion to penetrate and absorb alien cultures while preserving its own core beliefs was continually to be tested in the Early Middle Ages. Roman Britain had been invaded in the fifth century by various tribes from northwestern Germany, Denmark, and the Netherlands. Among these tribes were the Angles (from which the word *English* is derived), the Saxons, and the Jutes. The Romano-Britons, who were Christians, were forced to retreat westward to occupy what became the Celtic-speaking Christian principalities of Cornwall, Wales, and Cumberland. Pagan Germans ruled the rest of England.

# Bede
## *HISTORY OF THE ENGLISH CHURCH AND PEOPLE*

The English monk called the Venerable Bede (673–735), in his *History of the English Church and People,* cites a letter from Pope Gregory I (the Great) written in 601. In the letter, the pope forwarded instructions for Augustine of Canterbury, whom he had appointed leader of a mission to convert the English to Christianity. He wrote his emissary to tell Augustine to win the favor of the pagan English by accommodating the requirements of Christian beliefs to the existing non-Christian cultural practices, as the first excerpt shows.

Conducting missionary work among the Germanic peoples was almost impossible without the permission of their rulers. Since Germanic kings were responsible for fostering the goodwill of the tribal gods toward their people, any change in religion held a political as well as a religious connotation, as the second passage reveals.

When these [missionaries] had left, the holy father Gregory sent after them letters worthy of our notice, which show most clearly his unwearying interest in the salvation of our nation. The letter runs as follows:

"To our well loved son Abbot[1] Mellitus: Gregory, servant of the servants of God.

"Since the departure of yourself and your companions, we have been somewhat anxious, because we have received no news of the success of your journey. Therefore, when by God's help you reach our most reverend brother, Bishop Augustine,[2] we wish you to inform him that we have been giving careful thought to the affairs of the English, and have come to the conclusion that the temples of the idols in that country should on no account be destroyed. He is to destroy the idols, but the temples themselves are to be aspersed [sprinkled] with holy water, altars set up, and relics enclosed in

[1]The elected head of a monastic community, the abbot was supposed to rule justly and paternally following the constitution (rule) of the community.

[2]Augustine (not to be confused with Augustine of Hippo) was an Italian monk who was sent in 597 to convert the English to Christianity. He established his see (bishopric) at Canterbury and founded others at Rochester and London, successfully directing missionary activity in the southern part of what is now England.

them. For if these temples are well built, they are to be purified from devil-worship,[3] and dedicated to the service of the true God. In this way, we hope that the people, seeing that its temples are not destroyed, may abandon idolatry and resort to these places as before, and may come to know and adore the true God. And since they have a custom of sacrificing many oxen to devils, let some other solemnity be substituted in its place, such as a day of Dedication[4] or the Festivals of the holy martyrs [saints' days] whose relics are enshrined there. On such occasions they might well construct shelters of boughs for themselves around the churches that were once temples, and celebrate the solemnity with devout feasting. They are no longer to sacrifice beasts to the Devil, but they may kill them for food to the praise of God, and give thanks to the Giver of all gifts for His bounty. If the people are allowed some worldly pleasures in this way, they will more readily come to desire the joys of the spirit. For it is certainly impossible to eradicate all errors from obstinate minds at one stroke, and whoever wishes to climb to a mountain top climbs gradually step by step, and not in one leap. It was in this way that God revealed Himself to the Israelite people in Egypt, permitting the sacrifices formerly offered to the Devil to be offered thenceforward to Himself instead. So He bade them sacrifice beasts to Him, so that, once they became enlightened, they might abandon a wrong conception of sacrifice, and adopt the right. For, while they were to continue to offer beasts as before, they were to offer them to God instead of to idols, thus transforming the idea of sacrifice. Of your kindness, you are to inform our brother Augustine of this policy, so that he may consider how he may best implement it on the spot. God keep you safe, my very dear son." . . .

In this passage from Bede's history, King Edwin (585–633) of Northumbria, one of seven kingdoms of Britain, seeks his leading councillors' approval before converting to Christianity. Some motives for accepting Christianity are revealed in the royal council's discussion.

When Paulinus[5] had spoken, the king answered that he was both willing and obliged to accept the Faith which he taught, but said that he must discuss the matter with his principal advisers and friends, so that if they were in agreement, they might all be cleansed [baptized] together in Christ the Fount of Life. Paulinus agreed, and the king kept his promise. He summoned a council of the wise men, and asked each in turn his opinion of this new faith and new God being proclaimed.

Coifi, the High Priest, replied without hesitation: "Your Majesty, let us give careful consideration to this new teaching, for I frankly admit that, in my experience, the religion that we have hitherto professed seems valueless and powerless. None of your subjects has been more devoted to the service of the gods than myself, yet there are many to whom you show greater favour, who receive greater honours, and who are more successful in all their undertakings. Now, if the gods had any power, they would surely have favoured myself, who have been more zealous in their service. Therefore, if on examination these new teachings are found to be better and more effectual, let us not hesitate to accept them."

Another of the king's chief men signified his agreement with this prudent argument, and went on to say: "Your Majesty, when we compare the present life of man with that time of which we have no knowledge, it seems to me like the swift flight of a lone sparrow through the banqueting-hall where you sit in the winter

---

[3]As Christianity was monotheistic, it denied the validity of any other gods. Therefore, Christians customarily designated the pagan deities as "devils," or evil spirits.
[4]The anniversary of the dedication or consecration of a church was celebrated as a holiday.

[5]Paulinus was a Roman monk sent in 601 by Pope Gregory I to aid Augustine of Canterbury. In 627 he was consecrated bishop of York, where he baptized King Edwin of Northumbria.

months to dine with your thanes[6] and counsellors. Inside there is a comforting fire to warm the room; outside, the wintry storms of snow and rain are raging. This sparrow flies swiftly in through one door of the hall, and out through another. While he is inside, he is safe from the winter storms; but after a few moments of comfort, he vanishes from sight into the darkness whence he came. Similarly, man appears on earth for a little while, but we know nothing of what went before this life, and what follows. Therefore if this new teaching can reveal any more certain knowledge, it seems only right that we should follow it." The other elders and counsellors of the king, under God's guidance, gave the same advice.

Coifi then added that he wished to hear Paulinus' teaching about God in greater detail; and when, at the king's bidding, this had been given, the High Priest said: "I have long realized that there is nothing in what we worshipped, for the more diligently I sought after truth in our religion, the less I found. I now publicly confess that this teaching clearly reveals truths that will afford us the blessings of life, salvation, and eternal happiness. Therefore, your Majesty, I submit that the temples and altars that we have dedicated to no advantage be immediately desecrated and burned." In short, the king granted blessed Paulinus full permission to preach, renounced idolatry, and professed his acceptance of the Faith of Christ. And when he asked the High Priest who should be the first to profane the altars and shrines of the idols, together with the enclosures that sur-

rounded them, Coifi replied: "I will do this myself, for now that the true God has granted me knowledge, who more suitably than I can set a public example, and destroy the idols that I worshipped in ignorance?" So he formally renounced his empty superstitions, and asked the king to give him arms and a stallion—for hitherto it had not been lawful for the High Priest to carry arms, or to ride anything but a mare—and, thus equipped, he set out to destroy the idols. Girded with a sword and with a spear in his hand, he mounted the king's stallion and rode up to the idols. When the crowd saw him, they thought he had gone mad, but without hesitation, as soon as he reached the temple, he cast a spear into it and profaned it. Then, full of joy at his knowledge of the worship of the true God, he told his companions to set fire to the temple and its enclosures and destroy them. The site where these idols once stood is still shown, not far east of York,[7] beyond the river Derwent, and is known as Goodmanham. Here it was that the High Priest, inspired by the true God, desecrated and destroyed the altars that he had himself dedicated.

So King Edwin, with all the nobility and a large number of humbler folk, accepted the Faith and were washed in the cleansing waters of Baptism in the eleventh year of his reign, which was the year 627, and about one hundred and eighty years after the first arrival of the English in Britain.

---

[6]A thane ranked just below a nobleman.

[7]York (founded by the Romans as Eboracum) was the principal town of northern Britain during the Middle Ages. It became an archbishopric (major see) in the early eighth century, and later a major political center during the period of Viking rule.

# Saint Boniface
# SACRED MISSION TO GERMANY

**Of the many English monks and nuns who converted inhabitants of the Netherlands and Germany, none was more important than Saint Boniface (c. 680–754). In 716, Boniface, then a monk called Wynfrid, who had earned a reputation as a Latin scholar, left England for Frisia in order to restore the churches that had**

been destroyed when the Frisians revolted against Frankish rule and Christian proselytizing. Consecrated bishop in 722, he extended his missionary activity into Bavaria and Thuringia. Working closely with the papacy, he founded monasteries, including the famous Abbey of Fulda, converted pagans, and imposed Christian standards of behavior on both clergy and laypeople. In this passage, Bishop Daniel of Winchester advises Boniface not to mock the beliefs of the Germans but to win them over with logic (and salesmanship).

To the venerable and beloved prelate Boniface, Daniel, servant of the people of God.

I rejoice, beloved brother and fellow priest, that you are deserving of the highest prize of virtue. You have approached the hitherto stony and barren hearts of the pagans, trusting in the plenitude of your faith, and have labored untiringly with the plowshare of Gospel preaching, striving by your daily toil to change them into fertile fields. To you may well be applied the Gospel saying: "The voice of one crying in the wilderness," etc. Yet a part of the second prize shall be given, not unfittingly, to those who support so pious and useful a work with what help they can give and supplement the poverty of those laborers with means sufficient to carry on zealously the work of preaching which has already been begun and to raise up new sons to Christ.

And so I have with affectionate good will taken pains to suggest to Your Prudence a few things that may show you how, according to my ideas, you may most readily overcome the resistance of those uncivilized people. Do not begin by arguing with them about the origin of their gods, false as those are, but let them affirm that some of them were begotten by others through the intercourse of male with female, so that you may at least prove that gods and goddesses born after the manner of men are men and not gods and, since they did not exist before, must have had a beginning.

Then, when they have been compelled to learn that their gods had a beginning since some were begotten by others, they must be asked in the same way whether they believe that the world had a beginning or was always in existence without beginning. If it had a be-

ginning, who created it? Certainly they can find no place where begotten gods could dwell before the universe was made. I mean by "universe" not merely this visible earth and sky, but the whole vast extent of space, and this the heathen too can imagine in their thoughts. But if they argue that the world always existed without beginning, you should strive to refute this and to convince them by many documents and arguments. Ask your opponents who governed the world before the gods were born, who was the ruler? How could they bring under their dominion or subject to their law a universe that had always existed before them? And whence, or from whom or when, was the first god or goddess set up or begotten? Now, do they imagine that gods and goddesses still go on begetting others? Or, if they are no longer begetting, when or why did they cease from intercourse and births? And if they are still producing offspring, then the number of gods must already be infinite. . . .

Do they think the gods are to be worshiped for the sake of temporal and immediate good or for future eternal blessedness? If for temporal things, let them tell in what respect the heathen are better off than Christians. . . .

These and many similar things which it would take long to enumerate you ought to put before them, not offensively or so as to anger them, but calmly and with great moderation. At intervals you should compare their superstitions with our Christian doctrines, touching upon them from the flank, as it were, so that the pagans, thrown into confusion rather than angered, may be ashamed of their absurd ideas and may understand that their infamous ceremonies and fables are well known to us.

This point is also to be made: if the gods are all-powerful, beneficent, and just, they not only reward their worshipers but punish those who reject them. If, then, they do this in temporal matters, how is it that they spare us Christians who are turning almost the whole earth away from their worship and overthrowing their idols? And while these, that is, the Christians, possess lands rich in oil and wine and abounding in other resources, they have left to those, that is, the pagans, lands stiff with cold. . . .

# Einhard
# FORCIBLE CONVERSION UNDER CHARLEMAGNE

**Although most conversions were based on peaceful persuasion or a voluntary act of consent, occasionally Christianity was imposed by force. Thus, after his long wars against the pagan Saxons, Charlemagne required the Saxons to adopt Christianity and be assimilated into the Frankish kingdom. In his biography of Charlemagne, the Frankish historian Einhard (770–840) described this event.**

No war ever undertaken by the Frank nation was carried on with such persistence and bitterness, or cost so much labor, because the Saxons,[1] like almost all the tribes of Germany, were a fierce people, given to the worship of devils, and hostile to our religion, and did not consider it dishonorable to transgress and violate all law, human and divine. Then there were peculiar circumstances that tended to cause a breach of peace every day. Except in a few places, where large forests or mountain ridges intervened and made the bounds certain, the line between ourselves and the Saxons passed almost in its whole extent through an open country, so that there was no end to the murders, thefts, and arsons on both sides. In this way the Franks became so embittered that they at last resolved to make reprisals no longer, but to come to open war with the Saxons [in 772]. Accordingly war was begun against them, and was waged for thirty-three successive years with great fury; more, however, to the disadvantage of the Saxons than of the Franks. It could doubtless have been brought to an end sooner, had it not been for the faithlessness of the Saxons. It is hard to say how often they were conquered, and humbly submitting to the King, promised to do what was enjoined upon them, gave without hesitation the required hostages, and received the officers sent them from the King. They were sometimes so much weakened and reduced that they promised to renounce the worship of devils, and to adopt Christianity, but they were no less ready to violate these terms than prompt to accept them, so that it is impossible to tell which came easier to them to do; scarcely a year passed from the beginning of the war without such changes on their part. But the King did not suffer his high purpose and steadfastness—firm alike in good and evil

---

[1]The Saxons were members of a Germanic tribe living between the Rhine and Elbe rivers.

fortune—to be wearied by any fickleness on their part, or to be turned from the task that he had undertaken; on the contrary, he never allowed their faithless behavior to go unpunished, but either took the field against them in person, or sent his counts[2] with an army to wreak vengeance and exact righteous satisfaction. At last, after conquering and subduing all who had offered resistance, he took ten thousand of those that lived on the banks of the Elbe,[3] and settled them, with their wives and children, in many different bodies here and there in Gaul and Germany. The war that had lasted so many years was at length ended by their acceding to the terms offered by the King; which were renunciation of their national religious customs and the worship of devils, acceptance of the sacraments of the Christian faith and religion, and union with the Franks to form one people.

---

[2]Counts were royal officials exercising the king's authority in districts called counties.

[3]The Elbe River, in central Germany, flows northwestward into the North Sea.

## REVIEW QUESTIONS

1. How did Pope Gregory hope to ease the transition of the English from pagan to Christian beliefs and practices?
2. What considerations motivated the English kings and their councillors to convert to Christianity?
3. Give examples of the logic Bishop Daniel urged Boniface to employ in his conversion of pagans.
4. What role did politics play in the conversion of the Saxon peoples to Christianity?

---

# 4  The Transmission of Learning

Learning, which had been in retreat in the Late Roman Empire, continued its decline in the unsettled conditions following Rome's demise. The old Roman schools closed, and many scientific and literary works of the ancient world were either lost or neglected. Knowledge of the Greek language in western Europe virtually disappeared, and except for clerics, few people could read or write Latin. The few learned people generally did not engage in original thought but preserved and transmitted surviving elements of the Greco-Roman past.

One such scholar was Cassiodorus (c. 490–575), who served three Ostrogothic kings in Italy. Cassiodorus wrote theological treatises and the twelve-volume *History of the Goths,* but his principal achievement was collecting Greek and Latin manuscripts. Like other Christian scholars before and after him, Cassiodorus maintained that the study of secular literature was an aid to understanding sacred writings. He retired to a monastery where he fostered the monastic practice of copying Christian and pagan manuscripts. Without this effort of monks, many important secular and Christian writings might have perished.

# Cassiodorus
# THE MONK AS SCRIBE

In the following reading from his Introduction to *Divine and Human Readings*, Cassiodorus gave his views on the importance of the monastic scribe's vocation. Cassiodorus believed that through his pen the scribe preaches the word of God and is inspired by his text to know God more fully.

## ON SCRIBES AND THE REMEMBERING OF CORRECT SPELLING

1. I admit that among those of your tasks which require physical effort that of the scribe,[1] if he writes correctly, appeals most to me; and it appeals, perhaps not without reason, for by reading the Divine Scriptures he wholesomely instructs his own mind and by copying the precepts of the Lord he spreads them far and wide. Happy his design, praiseworthy his zeal, to preach to men with the hand alone, to unleash tongues with the fingers, to give salvation silently to mortals, and to fight against the illicit temptations of the devil with pen and ink. Every word of the Lord written by the scribe is a wound inflicted on Satan. And so, though seated in one spot, with the dissemination of his work he travels through different provinces. The product of his toil is read in holy places; people hear the means by which they may turn themselves away from base desire and serve the Lord with heart undefiled. Though absent, he labors at his task. I cannot deny that he may receive a renovation of life from these many blessings, if only he accomplishes things of this sort, not with a vain show of ambition, but with upright zeal. Man multiplies the heavenly words, and in a certain metaphorical sense, if one may so express himself, that which the virtue of the Holy Trinity utters is written by a trinity of fingers. O sight glorious to those who contemplate it carefully! With gliding pen the heavenly words are copied so that the devil's craft, by means of which he caused the head of the Lord to be struck during His passion, may be destroyed. They deserve praise too for seeming in some way to imitate the action of the Lord, who, though it was expressed figuratively, wrote His law with the use of His all-powerful finger. Much indeed is there to be said about such a distinguished art, but it is enough to mention the fact that those men are called scribes *(librarii)* who serve zealously the just scales *(libra)* of the Lord.

2. But lest in performing this great service copyists introduce faulty words with letters changed or lest an untutored corrector fail to know how to correct mistakes, let them read the works of ancient authors on orthography [spelling]. . . .

. . . I have collected as many of these works as possible with eager curiosity. . . . [If you] read [them] with unremitting zeal, they will completely free you from the fog of ignorance, so that what was previously unknown may become for the most part very well known.

3. In addition to these things we have provided workers skilled in bookbinding, in order that a handsome external form may clothe the beauty of sacred letters; in some measure, perhaps, we imitate the example in the parable of the Lord,* who amid the glory of the heavenly banquet has clothed in wedding garments

---

[1]Scribes were persons trained to copy by hand the texts of books, or to take dictation.

*Matthew 22:11.

those whom He judges worthy of being invited to the table. And for the binders, in fitting manner, unless I err, we have represented various styles of binding in a single codex,[2] that he who so desires may choose for himself the type of cover he prefers.

4. We have also prepared cleverly constructed lamps which preserve their illuminating flames and feed their own fire and without human attendance abundantly maintain a very full clearness of most copious light; and the fat oil in them does not fail, although it is burned continually with a bright flame.

5. Nor have we by any means allowed you to be unacquainted with the hour meters which have been discovered to be very useful to the human race. I have provided a sundial for you for bright days and a water clock which points out the hour continually both day and night, since on some days the bright sun is frequently absent, and rain water passes in marvellous fashion into the ground, because the fiery force of the sun, regulated from above, fails. And so the art of man has brought into harmony elements which are naturally separated; the hour meters are so reliable that you consider an act of either as having been arranged by messengers. These instruments, then, have been provided in order that the soldiers of Christ,[3] warned by most definite signs, may be summoned to the carrying out of their divine task as if by sounding trumpets.

---

[2]A codex consists of the rectangular sheets on which scribes have written, bound together on one side, like a modern book. Invented in the late first century A.D., the codex gradually replaced scrolls as the predominant way to store written texts.

---

[3]"Soldiers of Christ" is a metaphor to describe the monks in their vocation.

## REVIEW QUESTIONS

1. Why was it necessary for monks to be literate and even learned?
2. What contributions did the monasteries make in the development of medieval culture?

---

# 5   The Carolingian Renaissance

The Early Middle Ages witnessed a marked decline in learning and the arts. Patronage of both the liberal and the visual arts by the old Roman aristocracy was not widely copied by the Germanic ruling class that replaced the Romans. Support for learning and the arts shifted from secular to ecclesiastical patrons. Monasteries became the new centers for intellectual and artistic activities, and Christian themes and values almost entirely displaced the worldly values of Greco-Roman culture.

Under the patronage of Charlemagne (742–814), the great Frankish emperor, a conscious revival of classical Greek and Roman learning and the visual arts occurred. Charlemagne realized that his great empire could not be effectively governed without a cadre of literate clergy and administrators. To educate the leaders of the Frankish empire, Charlemagne sponsored a number of reforms designed to improve the educational institutions and the quality of literacy and learning in his realm. At court, he completely reformed the school conducted for the children of his family and his courtiers and recruited the best scholars in western Europe to staff it. Among these scholars was the English deacon Alcuin of York (735–804), who became his chief advisor on educational and religious affairs. They aimed at restoring classical learning to serve the needs of the new Christian culture.

# Einhard
# CHARLEMAGNE'S APPRECIATION OF LEARNING

The revival of classical learning and the visual arts under Charlemagne is called the Carolingian Renaissance, a cultural awakening that helped shape medieval civilization. One of Charlemagne's most significant decisions was ordering the making of copies of old manuscripts dating back to Roman times. Much of to-day's knowledge of Roman learning and literature comes from surviving Carolingian copies of older Latin texts that no longer exist. In the first reading, Charlemagne's biographer Einhard describes western Europe's greatest royal patron of the liberal arts since the fall of the western Roman Empire.

Charles [Charlemagne] had the gift of ready and fluent speech, and could express whatever he had to say with the utmost clearness. He was not satisfied with command of his native language merely, but gave attention to the study of foreign ones, and in particular was such a master of Latin that he could speak it as well as his native tongue; but he could understand Greek better than he could speak it. He was so eloquent, indeed, that he might have passed for a teacher of eloquence. He most zealously cultivated the liberal arts, held those who taught them in great esteem, and conferred great honors upon them. He took lessons in grammar of the deacon Peter of Pisa,[1] at that time an aged man. Another deacon, Albin of Britain, surnamed Alcuin, a man of Saxon extraction, who was the greatest scholar of the day, was his teacher in other branches of learning. The King spent much

time and labor with him studying rhetoric, dialectics, and especially astronomy; he learned to reckon, and used to investigate the motions of the heavenly bodies most curiously, with an intelligent scrutiny. He also tried to write, and used to keep tablets and blanks in bed under his pillow, that at leisure hours he might accustom his hand to form the letters; however, as he did not begin his efforts in due season, but late in life, they met with ill success.

He cherished with the greatest fervor and devotion the principles of the Christian religion, which had been instilled into him from infancy. Hence it was that he built the beautiful basilica[2] at Aix-la-Chapelle,[3] which he adorned with gold and silver and lamps, and with rails and doors of solid brass. He had the columns and marbles for this structure brought from Rome

---

[1]Peter of Pisa, a famous grammarian (in Latin, the international language of the Middle Ages), was brought from Italy to teach at the school in Charlemagne's palace. He encouraged interest in pre-Christian classical writing, which influenced the court poets of that era.

[2]A basilica is usually a rectangular-shaped church, whose main chamber is divided by columns into a central nave and side aisles. There was usually a semi-circular apse at the narrow end facing the east, which was the visual focal point and the location of the main altar.

[3]Aix-la-Chapelle, now Aachen, was Charlemagne's capital. It was located in what is now western Germany, near the Netherlands-Belgium frontier.

and Ravenna,[4] for he could not find such as were suitable elsewhere. He was a constant worshipper at this church as long as his health permitted, going morning and evening, even after nightfall, besides attending mass; and he took care that all the services there conducted should be administered with the utmost possible propriety, very often warning the sextons not to let any improper or unclean thing be brought into the building or remain in it. He provided it with a great number of sacred vessels of gold and silver and with such a quantity of clerical robes that not even the doorkeepers who fill the humblest office in the church were obliged to wear their everyday clothes when in the exercise of their duties. He was at great pains to improve the church reading and psalmody [singing], for he was well skilled in both, although he neither read in public nor sang, except in a low tone and with others.

He was very forward in succoring the poor, and in that gratuitous generosity which the Greeks call alms, so much so that he not only made a point of giving in his own country and his own kingdom, but when he discovered that there were Christians living in poverty in Syria, Egypt, and Africa, at Jerusalem, Alexandria, and Carthage, he had compassion on their wants, and used to send money over the seas to them. . . .

---

[4]Ravenna, in northeastern Italy, was the final capital of the western Roman Empire, in the fifth century; in the sixth and seventh centuries it was the capital of the Byzantine governors of Italy. Ravenna is famous for its magnificent sixth-century churches and mosaic art.

---

## Charlemagne
# AN INJUNCTION TO MONASTERIES TO CULTIVATE LETTERS

**In a letter to the Abbot Baugulf of Fulda (in Germany), Charlemagne announced his decision to use monasteries as schools for training future clergymen in grammar, writing, and rhetoric.**

Charles, by the grace of God, King of the Franks and Lombards and Patrician of the Romans, to Abbot Baugulf and to all the congregation, also to the faithful committed to you, we have directed a loving greeting by our ambassadors in the name of omnipotent God.

Be it known, therefore, to your devotion pleasing to God, that we, together with our faithful, have considered it to be useful that the bishoprics and monasteries entrusted by the favor of Christ to our control, in addition to the [rule] of monastic life and the intercourse of holy religion, . . . also ought to be zealous in [the cultivation of letters], teaching those who by the gift of God are able to learn, according to the capacity of each individual, so that just as the observance of the rule imparts order and grace to honesty of morals, so also zeal in teaching and learning may do the same for sentences, so that those who desire to please God by living rightly should not neglect to please him also by speaking correctly. For it is written: "Either from thy words thou shalt be justified or from thy words thou shalt be condemned."*

For although correct conduct may be better than knowledge, nevertheless knowledge precedes conduct. Therefore, each one ought to study what he desires to accomplish, so that . . . the mind may know more fully what ought

---

*Matthew, xii. 37.

to be done, as the tongue hastens in the praises of omnipotent God without the hindrances of errors. For since errors should be shunned by all men, . . . the more they ought to be avoided as far as possible by those who are chosen for this very purpose alone, so that they ought to be the especial servants of truth. For when in the years . . . [past], letters were often written to us from several monasteries in which it was stated that the brethren who dwelt there offered up in our behalf sacred and pious prayers, we have recognized in most of these letters both correct thoughts and uncouth expressions; because what pious devotion dictated faithfully to the mind, the tongue, uneducated on account of the neglect of study, was not able to express in the letter without error. . . . We began to fear lest perchance, as the skill in writing was less, so also the wisdom for understanding the Holy Scriptures might be much less than it rightly ought to be. And we all know well that, although errors of speech are dangerous, far more dangerous are errors of the understanding. Therefore, we exhort you not only not to neglect the study of letters, but also with most humble mind, pleasing to God, to study earnestly in order that you may be able more easily and more correctly to penetrate the mysteries of the divine Scriptures. Since, moreover, images . . . and similar figures are found in the sacred pages, no one doubts that each one in reading these will understand the spiritual sense more quickly if previously he shall have been fully instructed in the mastery of letters. Such men truly are to be chosen for this work as have both the will and the ability to learn and a desire to instruct others. And may this be done with a zeal as great as the earnestness with which we command it.

## REVIEW QUESTIONS

1. Why was Charlemagne so anxious to raise the educational standards of both the clergy and laity of his empire?
2. Why has Charlemagne been regarded as one of the greatest kings of the Early Middle Ages?

# 6 The Feudal Lord: Vassal and Warrior

In societies in which the state's role in regulating human relationships is minimal, law and order are maintained through custom and contract. This condition prevailed in the Early Middle Ages, particularly among the Germanic peoples. Laws were based on the community's assumptions about what was right and wrong, enforced by public opinion and community-approved use of force. To enforce law and to protect oneself and one's family, a person formed contractual ties with others and sought security and justice in mutual aid. A principal form of such a contract was called vassalage. By its terms, two free men of different means bound themselves to assistance and loyal support. The socially and economically superior man was called the lord; the man of inferior social status was called the vassal. The vassal pledged to be loyal and fight on behalf of his lord when called upon, in return for the lord's loyalty and protection when they were needed. The contract was lifelong and had deep emotional meaning in addition to the obvious self-interest of both parties.

Vassalage was a dynamic relationship, ever changing in content and meaning according to time, place, and circumstances. In the Carolingian Empire, vassalage was practiced by all members of the free class wealthy enough to afford weapons. Charlemagne and his successors tried to use vassalage as a means of controlling their warlike subjects and organizing them to serve more effectively for the defense of their realms. Eventually, the kings' vassals used their military skills, their own landed wealth, and political power to diminish royal power. The royal vassals then became the true center of authority within medieval society.

An important part of the lord–vassal relationship was the lord's grant of a fief to his vassal. The fief might be any object of value that reflected the vassal's social status and the lord's respect for his services. A fief could be a war horse, sword, and suit of armor, a public office, a right to collect a tax or toll or authority to hold a court of justice in a specified district. The most sought-after fief was a land grant—one or more manors from which to draw income. Fiefs were held for the duration of the bond of vassalage. If the bond was broken by death or disloyalty, the fief was forfeited to its grantor. By the late ninth century, however, fiefs had become hereditary, as had the right to be a vassal to a specific lord.

## Galbert of Bruges
# COMMENDATION AND THE OATH OF FEALTY

This reading contains an eyewitness account of the ceremony of commendation or investiture in which vassals swore an oath of fealty (loyalty) to their new lord, William Clito, the count of Flanders, in 1127, and were then invested with their fiefs. The account comes from an early twelfth-century chronicle written by a Flemish notary, Galbert of Bruges (a major medieval commercial city in Flanders, now part of Belgium).

Through the whole remaining part of the day those who had been previously enfeoffed [given fiefs] by the most pious count Charles,[1] did homage to the count, taking up now again their fiefs and offices and whatever they had before rightfully and legitimately obtained. On Thursday the seventh of April, homages were again made to the count being completed in the following order of faith and security.

First they did their homage thus: The count asked if he was willing to become completely his man, and the other replied, "I am willing;" and with clasped hands, surrounded by the hands of the count, they were bound together by a kiss. Secondly, he who had done homage gave his fealty to the representative of the count in these words, "I promise on my faith that I will in future be faithful to count William, and will observe my homage to him completely against all persons in good faith and without deceit," and thirdly, he took his oath to this upon the relics of the saints. Afterward, with a little rod which the count held in his hand, he gave investitures to all who by this agreement had given their security and homage and accompanying oath.

---

[1]Charles, count of Flanders, was murdered on March 2, 1127.

# Fulbert, Bishop of Chartres
# OBLIGATIONS OF LORDS AND VASSALS

In a letter written in 1020 to William, Duke of Aquitaine, Bishop Fulbert (c. 920–1028) of Chartres summarizes the obligations of the lord and the vassal.

To William most glorious duke of the Aquitanians,[1] bishop Fulbert [asks] the favor of his prayers.

Asked to write something concerning the form of fealty, I have noted briefly for you on the authority of the books the things which follow. He who swears fealty to his lord ought always to have these six things in memory; what is harmless, safe, honorable, useful, easy, practicable. Harmless, that is to say that he should not be injurious to his lord in his body; safe, that he should not be injurious to him in his secrets or in the defences through which he is able to be secure; honorable, that he should not be injurious to him in his justice or in other matters that pertain to his honor; useful, that he should not be injurious to him in his

possessions; easy or practicable, that that good which his lord is able to do easily, he make not difficult, nor that which is practicable he make impossible to him.

However, that the faithful vassal should avoid these injuries is proper, but not for this does he deserve his holding; for it is not sufficient to abstain from evil, unless what is good is done also. It remains, therefore, that in the same six things mentioned above he should faithfully counsel and aid his lord, if he wishes to be looked upon as worthy of his benefice and to be safe concerning the fealty which he has sworn.

The lord also ought to act toward his faithful vassal reciprocally in all these things. And if he does not do this he will be justly considered guilty of bad faith, just as the former, if he should be detected in the avoidance of or the doing of or the consenting to them, would be perfidious and perjured.

---

[1]The Aquitanians inhabited the kingdom of Aquitaine in southwestern France—later a province of France.

# Bertran de Born
# IN PRAISE OF COMBAT

Feudal lords did not engage in productive labor as did serfs, merchants, and craftsmen. Manual labor and commerce were considered degrading for men of their rank and skills. Lords were professional warriors; combat was what they relished, trained for, and eagerly sought. They used their wealth to obtain armor and weapons, and even their sports, hunting and tournaments, prepared them for battle.

The spirit of the feudal warrior is expressed in the following poem by Bertran de Born (c. 1140–c. 1215), a French nobleman from the bishopric of Perigord in southern France. He is ackowledged to have been a superior poet of his day, a good warrior, and a clever intriguer who stirred up troubles between the kings of France and England. His poetry captures the excitement and pageantry of medieval warfare.

I love the springtide of the year
When leaves and blossoms do abound,
And well it pleases me to hear
The birds that make the woods resound
With their exulting voices.
And very well it pleases me
Tents and pavilions pitched to see,
And oh, my heart rejoices

To see armed knights in panoply [full armor]
Of war on meadow and on lea [pasture].

I like to see men put to flight
By scouts throughout the countryside,
I like to see, armed for the fight,
A host of men together ride;
And my delight's unbounded

When castles strong I see assailed,
And outworks smashed, whose strength has
    failed,
And near the walls, surrounded
By moats, and by strong stakes enrailed,
The host that has the ramparts scaled.

And well I like a noble lord
When boldly the attack he leads,
For he, whene'er he wields his sword,
Inspires his men by his brave deeds,
Their hearts with courage filling.
When tide of battle's at the flood,

Each soldier then, in fighting mood,
To follow should be willing,
For no man is accounted good
Till blows he's given and withstood.

Axes and swords and spears and darts,
Shields battered in with many a blow,
We'll see when first the battle starts,
And clash of arms as foe meets foe;
The steeds of dead and dying
Wildly will rush throughout the field,
And all who wish to be revealed
As brave will e'er be trying
How best their axes they may wield,
For they would rather die than yield.

Not so much joy in sleep have I,
Eating and drinking please me less
Than hearing on all sides the cry
"At them!" and horses riderless
Among the woodlands neighing.
And well I like to hear the call
Of "Help!" and see the wounded fall,
Loudly for mercy praying,
And see the dead, both great and small,
Pierced by sharp spearheads one and all.

Barons, without delaying,
Pawn every city, castle, hall,
And never cease to fight and brawl.

## REVIEW QUESTIONS

1. In the Middle Ages, contracts were symbolized and publicly noted by the use of various ritual acts or gestures. Explain how the contract of vassalage was signified by specific rituals or actions.
2. What were some of the ethical and emotive dimensions of vassalage? Describe the mutual obligations of lords and vassals.
3. What personal qualities were expected from a medieval leader in combat? What challenge did the Germanic warrior spirit present to the leaders of the Christian Church?

---

# 7   The Burdens of Serfdom

The feudal lord's way of life was made possible by the toil of the serfs who worked on the manors. Serfs, who were not free persons, had some rights but many burdensome obligations. Unlike slaves, they could not be sold off the land or dispossessed from their landholdings. Their tenure on their farms was hereditary, but they owed heavy rent to the landlord in the form of labor and a share of their crops and livestock. There were many restrictions on their personal freedom: they needed the landlord's permission to leave the estate, to marry, or to pass on personal property to their heirs. In return, they received security; they were defended by the landlords against outside aggressors or fellow serfs.

The labor services usually took up half the work week of the serf. He was required to plow, plant, and harvest the lord's fields, repair roads, fix fences, clear ditches, and cart goods to barns and markets. Although specific obligations varied from time to time and manor to manor, they were sufficiently onerous to encourage the serfs to seek freedom; in later centuries, when the opportunity presented itself, a serf might flee to a nearby town or to newly developed lands, or might purchase certain freedoms from the manorial lord. The serfs' struggle to rid themselves of the burdens of serfdom took centuries. It was largely successful in western Europe by the fifteenth century. But in eastern Europe, serfdom was imposed on the formerly free peasantry in the sixteenth and seventeenth centuries. Remnants of serfdom in western Europe survived until the French Revolution. Serfdom was abolished in central and eastern Europe in the mid-nineteenth century.

# THE CUSTOMS OF THE MANOR OF DARNHALL

The following reading from the customs of the manor of Darnhall (variously spelled in the original manuscripts) in Cheshire, a rural county in northwestern England, details the general burdens of serfs. The manor of Darnhall belonged to an order of monks. In the year 1326, the abbot of the monastery drew up this custumal, a document reaffirming his rights over the serfs. Although this document comes from the Late Middle Ages, it does characterize essential elements of serfdom.

Here begin the customs of the bond-tenants[1] of the manor of Dernale [Darnhall].

One is that they ought to [appear in] court at the will of the lord, or of his bailiff,[2] upon being summoned only, even during the night, and they ought all to come the next day.

And whereas some of them have been accustomed to give part of their land to their sons, so that it came about that after their death their sons have by the carelessness of the bailiffs of the place been received as holding those same lands without doing to the lord anything for their seisin[3] in their father's time; those sons who hold land ought to do suit of court [to sue], or obtain the lord's grace to redeem the suit at the will of the lord, on account of the great loss which has by this means been suffered by the lord.

Also they all [must use] the mill under pain of forfeiture of their grain, if they at any time

---

[1]*Bond-tenants* was another name for serfs; they were also known as bondmen.

[2]The bailiff was an agent appointed by the landlord (that is, the lord of the manor) to manage the manor, collect rents, and levy fines for breaches of the lord's rules (custom).

[3]*Seisin* is a legal term meaning possession of property.

withdraw suit; and every year they owe pannage[4] for their pigs.

Also they ought to make redemption of their daughters, if they wish to marry out of the manor, at the will of the lord.

They will also give *leyrwithe*[5] for their daughters, if they fall into carnal sin.

Also, when any one of them dieth, the lord shall have all the pigs of the deceased, all his goats, all his mares at grass, and his horse also, if he had one for his personal use, all his bees, all his bacon-pigs, all his cloth of wool and flax, and whatsoever can be found of gold and silver. The lord also shall have all his brass pots or pot, if he have one (but who of these bond-tenants will have a brass pot for cooking his food in?), because at their death the lord ought to have all things of metal. . . .

Also the lord shall have the best ox for a "hereghett,"[6] and holy Church another. After this the rest of the animals ought to be divided thus, if the deceased has children, to wit, into three parts—one for the lord, one for the wife, one for the children; and if he leaves no children, they shall be divided into two parts—one for the lord and one for the wife of the deceased, equally. Also if they have corn, in grange [barn] or in field, then the wife of the deceased ought to choose her part, to wit, half the corn in the grange or the field, as she chooses. And if she choose her part in the field, then all the corn in the grange shall remain wholly to the lord; and if she choose her part in the grange, then all the corn in the fields shall remain wholly to the lord, together with his moiety [half] and share in the granges; always provided that, wheresoever

the wife shall choose her part, whether in grange or in field, the lord shall have his moiety and part, with her and against her; and all the other corn, in the place where the woman does not choose, shall remain to the lord; and if he has children, or a child, the division shall be made in the same way into three parts, to wit, among the lord, the wife of the deceased and his children; also if there are many children [their share shall be divided] among them.

Also it is not lawful for the bond-tenant to make a will, or bequeath anything, without licence of the lord of the manor.

And as to the sheep, let them be divided like all the other goods of the deceased which ought to be divided. But this is inserted in this place by itself, because, when the convent first came to Darnhale, the bond-tenants said that no division ought to be made of the sheep, but that all the sheep ought to remain wholly to the wife of the deceased. Which is quite false, because they always used to divide them without gainsaying it at all, until Warin le Grantuenour was bailiff of Darnhale; and while he was bailiff he was corrupted with presents, and did not exact the lord's share of all things in his time; and afterwards the bond tenants endeavoured to make this a precedent and custom, which they by no means ought to do, because they have been accustomed so to do according to the customs of this manor in the times of former lords.

Moreover, the whole land of the deceased shall be in the hands of the lord, until he who is next, that is to say, he who ought to succeed the deceased—whom, according to the custom of the neighbourhood, they call the heir—shall make such a fine with the lord as shall correspond with the value of the land and the will of the lord. . . .

. . . Also, if the lord wishes to buy corn or oats, or anything else, and they have such things to sell, it shall not be lawful to them to sell anything elsewhere, except with the lord's licence [permission], if the lord is willing to pay them a reasonable price.

---

[4]Pannage was the right to pasture swine in the lord's forest.
[5]*Leyrwithe* (also *leyrwite*) was the name given to the fine levied by the lord on a female serf found guilty of fornication.
[6]*Hereghett,* usually spelled *heriot* or *heregeld,* was any property that had been lent by a lord to a now-deceased serf, plus a fine levied on his property and paid to the lord after his death. It often consisted of the lord's choice of the serf's best livestock.

Also it is to be known that it is the custom of the manor to pay assize[7] rents equally at the four terms of the year, to wit, at Christmas, the Annunciation of the Blessed Mary [March 25], at the feasts of St. John the Baptist [June 24] and St. Michael [September 29].

Amercements [fines] of courts ought always to be levied within a fortnight after the holding of the court, or sooner, if the lord will; . . . and the lord's mercy [fine] is according to his will or the will of his bailiff, so that they can take according to the amount of the trespass and measure of the offence.

---

[7]The rent of assize was a fixed rent paid by the freeholder to the lord.

## REVIEW QUESTIONS

1. Why did the manorial lord regulate the marital and sexual practices of his serfs?
2. What restraints were placed on the property rights of the serfs at Darnhall?
3. What restrictions were placed on the serfs' rights to buy or sell their goods and services where they pleased? Why?
4. Discuss the judicial procedures of the manorial courts and their similarity to modern practices.

# CHAPTER 8
# The High and Late Middle Ages

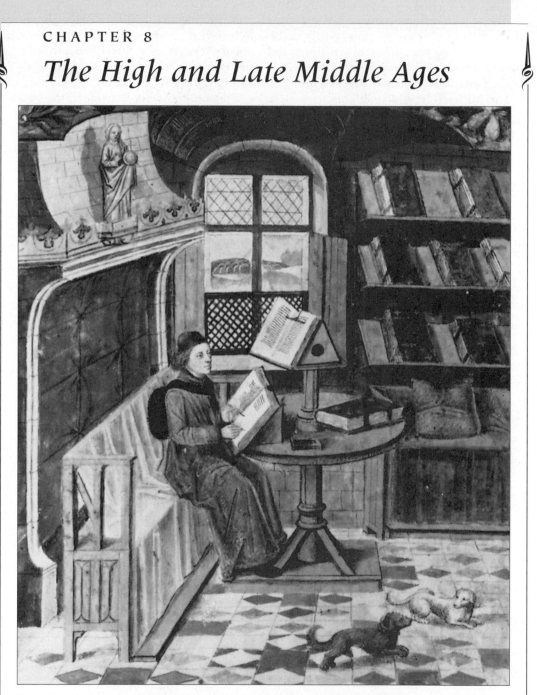

THE MEDIEVAL SCHOLAR on this page is shown surrounded by bound manuscripts. In the Middle Ages, the first universities were established. There is continuity between these medieval universities and universities today. *(Osterreichische Nationalbibliothek)*

The High Middle Ages (1050–1300) were an era of growth and vitality in Latin Christendom. Improvements in technology and cultivation of new lands led to an increase in agricultural production; the growing food supply, in turn, reduced the number of deaths from starvation and malnutrition, and better cultivation methods freed more people to engage in nonagricultural pursuits, particularly commerce.

During the Early Middle Ages, Italian towns had maintained a weak link with the Byzantine lands in the eastern Mediterranean. In the eleventh century, the Italians gained ascendancy over Muslim fleets in the Mediterranean and rapidly expanded their trade with the Byzantine Empire and North Africa. The growing population provided a market for silk, sugar, spices, dyes, and other Eastern goods. Other mercantile avenues opened up between Scandinavia and the Atlantic coast; between northern France, Flanders, and England; and along the rivers between the Baltic Sea in the north and the Black Sea and Constantinople in the southeast.

The revival of trade and the improved production of food led to the rebirth of towns in the eleventh century. During the Early Middle Ages, urban life had largely disappeared in Latin Christendom except in Italy, and even Italian towns had declined since Roman times both in population and as centers of trade and culture. During the twelfth century, towns throughout Latin Christendom became active centers of commerce and intellectual life. The rebirth of town life made possible the rise of a new social class: the middle class, consisting of merchants and artisans. These townspeople differed significantly from the clergy, the nobles, and the serfs—the other social strata in medieval society. The world of the townspeople was the marketplace rather than the church, the castle, or the manorial village. These merchants and artisans resisted efforts by lords to impose obligations upon them, as their livelihood required freedom from such constraints. The middle class became a dynamic force for change.

The High Middle Ages were also characterized by political and religious vitality. Strong kings extended their authority over more and more territory, often at the expense of feudal lords; in the process, they laid the foundation of the modern European state system. By the eleventh century the autonomy of the church—its freedom to select its own leaders and to fulfill its moral responsibilities—was threatened by kings and lords who appointed bishops and abbots to ecclesiastical offices. In effect, the churches and monasteries were at the mercy of temporal rulers, who distributed church positions as patronage, awarding them to their families, vassals, and loyal servants. These political appointees often lacked the spiritual character to maintain high standards of discipline among the priests or monks they supervised. Many clergy resented the subordination of the church to the economic and political interests of kings and lords. They held that for the church to fulfill its spiritual mission, it must be free from lay control.

The crisis within the church was dramatically addressed by a small band of clergy, mostly monks, who managed to elect to the papacy a series of committed reformers. These popes condemned clerical marriages, deeming them uncanonical, because they risked subordinating the church's interests to those of the clergymen's wives and children. Priests were required to be celibate like bishops and monks. The reformers also pressed for the systematic exclusion of the laity from participation in the governing of the church. In calling for the abolition of lay investiture, that is, the formal installation of clergy to their office by temporal lords, the papacy encountered bitter opposition. As head of the church, charged with the mission of saving souls, popes refused to accept a subordinate position to temporal rulers.

Economic, political, and religious vitality was complemented by a cultural and intellectual awakening. The twelfth and thirteenth centuries marked the high point of medieval civilization. The Christian outlook, with its otherworldly emphasis, shaped and inspired this awakening. Christian scholars rediscovered the writings of ancient Greek thinkers, which they tried to harmonize with Christian teachings. In the process, they constructed an impressive philosophical system that integrated Greek rationalism into the Christian worldview. The study of Roman law was revived, and some of its elements were incorporated into church law. A varied literature expressed both secular and religious themes, and a distinctive form of architecture, the Gothic, conveyed the overriding Christian concern with things spiritual.

During the Late Middle Ages, roughly the fourteenth and early fifteenth centuries, medieval civilization declined. In contrast to the vigor of the twelfth and thirteenth centuries, the fourteenth century was burdened by crop failures, famine, plagues, and reduced population. The church also came under attack from reformers who challenged clerical authority and questioned church teachings, from powerful kings who resisted papal interference in the political life of their kingdoms, and from political theorists who asserted that the pope had no authority to intervene in matters of state. In the city-states of Italy, a growing secularism signified a break with medieval other-worldliness and heralded the emergence of the modern outlook.

# 1 The Revival of Trade and the Growth of Towns

Several factors contributed to economic vitality in the High Middle Ages: the end of the Viking raids in northwestern Europe, greater political stability provided by kings and powerful lords, and increased agricultural productivity, which freed some people to work at other pursuits and facilitated a population increase. The prime movers in trade were the merchant adventurers, a new class of entrepreneurs. Neither bound to the soil nor obligated to lifelong military service, merchants traveled the sea lanes and land roads to distant places in search of goods that could profitably be traded in other markets.

# HOW TO SUCCEED IN BUSINESS

In the following reading from *The King's Mirror,* an anonymous thirteenth-century Norseman outlined the characteristics and skills a merchant needed and described the hazards of the job. In typical medieval fashion, he emphasized the moral dimensions of commercial transactions.

The man who is to be a trader will have to brave many perils, sometimes at sea and sometimes in heathen lands, but nearly always among alien peoples; and it must be his constant purpose to act discreetly wherever he happens to be. On the sea he must be alert and fearless.

When you are in a market town, or wherever you are, be polite and agreeable; then you will secure the friendship of all good men. Make it a habit to rise early in the morning, and go first and immediately to church. . . .

. . . When the services are over, go out to look after your business affairs. If you are unacquainted with the traffic of the town, observe carefully how those who are reputed the best and most prominent merchants conduct their business. You must also be careful to examine the wares that you buy before the purchase is finally made to make sure that they are sound and flawless. And whenever you make a purchase, call in a few trusty men

to serve as witnesses as to how the bargain was made.

You should keep occupied with your business till breakfast or, if necessity demands it, till midday; after that you should eat your meal. Keep your table well provided and set with a white cloth, clean victuals, and good drinks. Serve enjoyable meals, if you can afford it. After the meal you may either take a nap or stroll about a little while for pastime and to see what other good merchants are employed with, or whether any new wares have come to the borough which you ought to buy. On returning to your lodgings examine your wares, lest they suffer damage after coming into your hands. If they are found to be injured and you are about to dispose of them, do not conceal the flaws from the purchaser: show him what the defects are and make such a bargain as you can; then you cannot be called a deceiver. Also put a good price on your wares, though not too high, and yet very near what you see can be obtained; then you cannot be called a foister [trickster].

Finally, remember this, that whenever you have an hour to spare you should give thought to your studies, especially to the law books; for it is clear that those who gain knowledge from books have keener wits than others, since those who are the most learned have the best proofs for their knowledge. Make a study of all the laws. . . . If you are acquainted with the law, you will not be annoyed by quibbles when you have suits to bring against men of your own class, but will be able to plead according to law in every case.

But although I have most to say about laws, I regard no man perfect in knowledge unless he has thoroughly learned and mastered the customs of the place where he is sojourning. And if you wish to become perfect in knowledge, you must learn all the languages, first of all Latin and French, for these idioms are most widely used; and yet, do not neglect your native tongue or speech.

. . . Train yourself to be as active as possible, though not so as to injure your health. Strive never to be downcast, for a downcast mind is always morbid; try rather to be friendly and genial at all times, of an even temper and never moody. Be upright and teach the right to every man who wishes to learn from you; and always associate with the best men. Guard your tongue carefully; this is good counsel, for your tongue may honor you, but it may also condemn you. Though you be angry speak few words and never in passion; for unless one is careful, he may utter words in wrath that he would later give gold to have unspoken. On the whole, I know of no revenge, though many employ it, that profits a man less than to bandy heated words with another, even though he has a quarrel to settle with him. You shall know of a truth that no virtue is higher or stronger than the power to keep one's tongue from foul or profane speech, tattling, or slanderous talk in any form. If children be given to you, let them not grow up without learning a trade; for we may expect a man to keep closer to knowledge

and business when he comes of age, if he is trained in youth while under control.

And further, there are certain things which you must beware of and shun like the devil himself: these are drinking, chess, harlots, quarreling, and throwing dice for stakes. For upon such foundations the greatest calamities are built; and unless they strive to avoid these things, few only are able to live long without blame or sin.

Observe carefully how the sky is lighted, the course of the heavenly bodies, the grouping of the hours, and the points of the horizon. Learn also how to mark the movements of the ocean and to discern how its turmoil ebbs and swells; for that is knowledge which all must possess who wish to trade abroad. Learn arithmetic thoroughly, for merchants have great need of that.

If you come to a place where the king or some other chief who is in authority has his officials, seek to win their friendship; and if they demand any necessary fees on the ruler's behalf, be prompt to render all such payments, lest by holding too tightly to little things you lose the greater. . . . If you can dispose of your wares at suitable prices, do not hold them long; for it is the wont of merchants to buy constantly and to sell rapidly. . . .

. . . If you attend carefully to all these things, with God's mercy you may hope for success. This, too, you must keep constantly in mind, if you wish to be counted a wise man, that you ought never to let a day pass without learning something that will profit you. Be not like those who think it beneath their dignity to hear or learn from others such things even as might avail them much if they knew them. For a man must regard it as great an honor to learn as to teach, if he wishes to be considered thoroughly informed. . . .

. . . Always buy good clothes and eat good fare if your means permit; and never keep unruly or quarrelsome men as attendants or messmates. Keep your temper calm though not to the point of suffering abuse or bringing upon yourself the reproach of cowardice. Though necessity may force you into strife, be not in a hurry to take revenge; first make sure that your effort will succeed and strike where it ought. Never display a heated temper when you see that you are likely to fail, but be sure to maintain your honor at some later time, unless your opponent should offer a satisfactory atonement.

If your wealth takes on rapid growth, divide it and invest it in a partnership trade in fields where you do not yourself travel; but be cautious in selecting partners. Always let Almighty God, the holy Virgin Mary, and the saint whom you have most frequently called upon to intercede for you be counted among your partners. Watch with care over the property which the saints are to share with you and always bring it faithfully to the place to which it was originally promised.

# ORDINANCES OF THE GUILD MERCHANT OF SOUTHAMPTON

Along with revived trade and burgeoning towns in the High Middle Ages came the formation of businessmen's associations, called guilds. Merchant guilds encompassed all townspeople engaged in commerce. Carpenters, bakers, shoemakers, and other skilled craftsmen formed guilds that specialized in each occupation. Though women were employed in many trades, working under male guild masters, they were rarely admitted to full membership. Guilds composed exclusively of women existed in only a few places like Paris and Cologne. Guilds tried to eliminate competition by barring outsiders from doing business in the town, by limiting membership, by fixing the price of their goods, and by setting quality standards. Guilds provided for the social needs of their members, too, as the following selection of guild regulations for the seaport of Southampton, England, show. The document itself belongs to the fourteenth century, but several of the regulations had been framed earlier.

6. . . . And if a guildsman be ill and in town, one shall send to him two loaves and a gallon of wine, and one dish of cooked food; and two of the approved men of the guild shall go to visit him and look to his condition.

7. And when a guildsman dies, all those who are of the guild and in the town shall be at the service of the dead, and guildsmen shall carry the body, and bring it to the place of sepulture [burial]. And he who will not do this shall pay, on his oath, twopence to be given to the poor. And those of the ward where the dead man shall be, shall find a man to watch with the body the night that the dead person shall lie in his house. . . .

9. And when a guildsman dies, his eldest-born son or his next heir shall have the seat of his father, or of his uncle, if his father was not a guildsman, but of no one else. Nor can any husband, by reason of his wife, either have a seat in the guild or demand it by any right of his wife's ancestors. . . .

10. And no one ought nor can lawfully sell or give his seat in the guild to any man. And the son of a guildsman, other than his eldest, shall be admitted to the guild on payment of ten shillings [120 pence], and shall take the oath.

11. And if any guildsman be imprisoned in England in time of peace, the alderman, with the seneschal[1] . . . shall go at the cost of the

---

[1] An alderman was the chief of the guild, and a seneschal acted as its treasurer and vice-president.

guild to procure the release of him that is in prison.

12. And if any guildsman strike another with his fist, and be thereof attainted [found guilty], he shall lose his guildship until he has purchased it again for ten shillings, and shall take the oath like a new member. And if a guildsman strike another with a stick or a knife, or any other weapon, whatever it may be, he shall lose his guildship and his franchise,[2] and shall be held a stranger, until he be reconciled to good people of the guild, and have made satisfaction to the person whom he has injured, and be fined to the guild twenty shillings, which shall not be [forgiven or refunded]. . . .

19. And no one shall buy anything in the town of Southampton to sell it again in the same town, unless he be of the guild merchant or of the franchise. And if any one do so and be attainted (thereof), all that he has so bought shall be forfeited to the king. And no one shall be quit of custom unless he has done so as to be of the guild or of the franchise, and this from year to year.

20. And no one shall buy honey, seim [lard], salt herring, or any kind of oil, or millstones, or fresh hides, or any kind of fresh skins, except a guildsman; nor keep a tavern for wine, or sell cloth by retail, except on a market day or fair day; nor keep above five quarters of corn in his granary to sell by retail, if he is not a guildsman; and whoever shall do this, and be attainted (thereof), shall forfeit all to the king.

21. No one of the guild shall be partner or joint dealer in any of the foresaid merchandises with any person who is (not?) of the guild, by any manner of coverture [concealment], art, contrivance, collusion, or any other manner. And whosoever shall do this, and be attainted (thereof), the goods so bought shall be forfeited to the king, and the guildsman shall lose his guildship.

22. And if any guildsman fall into poverty and have not wherewith to live, and cannot work, he shall be provided for: when the guild shall be held he shall have one mark from the guild to relieve his condition. No one of the guild or franchise shall avow another's goods for his own, by which the custom of the town may be defrauded. And if any one so do, and be attainted (thereof), he shall lose the guildship and the franchise, and the merchandise so avowed shall be forfeited to the king. . . .

41. No butcher or cook shall sell to any man other than wholesome and clean provisions, and well cooked; and if any do, and he be thereof attainted, he shall be put in the pillory an hour of the day, or give two shillings to the town for the offence.

42. And that no butcher or cook throw into the street any filth or other matter whereby the town or the street become more dirty, filthy, or corrupt; and if any one do this, and be attainted, he shall pay a fine of twelve pence, as often as he shall offend in the manner aforesaid.

43. No man shall have any pigs going about in the street, or have before his door, or in the street, muck or dung beyond two nights; and if any one has, let whoever will take it away; and he who shall have acted contrary to this statute shall be grievously fined.

---

[2]A person's franchise was the privilege of citizenship in the town.

## REVIEW QUESTIONS

1. What attitudes were merchants encouraged to cultivate when dealing with customers and fellow merchants?
2. What business practices were recommended to merchants?
3. What was a guild and how did it benefit its members?
4. What kind of special privileges did guilds like the one at Southampton seek from royal rulers?

## 2 Theological Basis for Papal Power

The authority of the papacy was weakened by lords who dominated churches and monasteries by appointing bishops and abbots and by collecting the income from church taxes. These bishops and abbots, appointed for political reasons, lacked the spiritual devotion to maintain high standards of discipline among priests and monks. Church reformers were determined to end this subordination of the church to lay authority.

The practice of lay investiture led to a conflict between the papacy and the German monarchy. It began when the German king and future Holy Roman Emperor Henry IV (1056–1108) invested the new archbishop of Milan with his pastoral staff and ring, symbols of the episcopal office. Henry was immediately challenged and threatened with excommunication by Pope Gregory VII (1073–1085), a most ardent champion of reform. Gregory's action sparked a struggle between the papacy and the Holy Roman Empire that lasted for half a century. Later, after he was actually excommunicated for a second time, Henry invaded Italy, and Pope Gregory fled from Rome to the monastery of Monte Cassino and died in 1085. Civil war broke out in the imperial territories between partisans of the pope and those of the empire, and widespread death and destruction ensued. Although a compromise was effected at a synod (council of bishops) at Worms, Germany, in 1122, the ideological principles raised in the dispute were never wholly resolved.

## Pope Gregory VII
# THE SECOND LETTER TO BISHOP HERMAN OF METZ AND THE *DICTATUS PAPAE*

Like no other pope before him, Gregory VII had asserted the preeminence of the papacy over secular rulers. He declared that princes should "not seek to subdue or subject holy Church to themselves as a handmaiden; but indeed let them fittingly strive to honor her eyes, namely the priests of the Lord, by acknowledging them as masters and fathers." His exaltation of the spiritual authority of the church encouraged future popes to challenge the state whenever it threatened the supremacy of Christian moral teachings or the church's freedom to carry out its mission. The first reading is a letter written by Pope Gregory VII to a German bishop, Herman of Metz, at the height of the lay investiture struggle. The pope outlined the theological basis for the authority and powers he claimed. The exalted conception of the papacy as the central authority in the Christian church was expressed in its most extreme and detailed form in a series of propositions called the *Dictatus papae* (Rules of the Pope), which appear as numbered paragraphs in the second excerpt.

You ask us to fortify you against the madness of those who babble with accursed tongues about the authority of the Holy Apostolic See [the bishopric of Rome] not being able to excommunicate King Henry as one who despises the law of Christ, a destroyer of churches and of the empire, a promoter and partner of heresies, nor to release anyone from his oath of fidelity to him; but it has not seemed necessary to reply to this request, seeing that so many and such convincing proofs are to be found in Holy Scripture. . . .

To cite but a few out of the multitude of proofs: Who does not remember the words of our Lord and Savior Jesus Christ: "Thou art Peter and on this rock I will build my Church, and the gates of hell shall not prevail against it. And I will give thee the keys of the kingdom of heaven and whatsoever thou shalt bind on earth shall be bound in heaven and whatsoever thou shalt loose on earth shall be loosed in heaven." Are kings excepted here? Or are they not of the sheep which the Son of God committed to St. Peter? Who, I ask, thinks himself excluded from this universal grant of the power of binding and loosing to St. Peter unless, perchance, that unhappy man who, being unwilling to bear the yoke of the Lord, subjects himself to the burden of the Devil and refuses to be numbered in the flock of Christ? His wretched liberty shall profit him nothing; for if he shakes off from his proud neck the power divinely granted to Peter, so much the heavier shall it be for him in the day of judgment.

This institution of the divine will, this foundation of the rule of the Church, this privilege granted and sealed especially by a heavenly decree to St. Peter, chief of the Apostles, has been accepted and maintained with great reverence by the holy fathers, and they have given to the Holy Roman Church, as well in general councils as in their other acts and writings, the name of "universal mother." They have not only accepted her expositions of doctrine and her instructions in (our) holy religion, but they have also recognized her

judicial decisions. They have agreed as with one spirit and one voice that all major cases, all especially important affairs and the judgments of all churches ought to be referred to her as to their head and mother, that from her there shall be no appeal, that her judgments may not and cannot be reviewed or reversed by anyone.

Thus Pope Gelasius [492–496], writing to the [Byzantine] emperor Anastasius, gave him these instructions as to the right theory of the principate of the Holy and Apostolic See, based upon divine authority:

Although it is fitting that all the faithful should submit themselves to all priests who perform their sacred functions properly, how much the more should they accept the judgment of that prelate who has been appointed by the supreme divine ruler to be superior to all priests and whom the loyalty of the whole later Church has recognized as such. Your Wisdom sees plainly that no human capacity *(concilium)* whatsoever can equal that of him [Saint Peter] whom the word of Christ raised above all others and whom the reverend Church has always confessed and still devotedly holds as its Head.

---

Pope Gregory then comments on the origins of the authority of civil rulers and their motives when they seek to govern the clergy. Gregory argues that church and state are separate spheres of governing authority and that the responsibility of clergymen is greater than that of civil rulers.

---

Who does not know that kings and princes derive their origin from men ignorant of God who raised themselves above their fellows by pride, plunder, treachery, murder—in short, by every kind of crime—at the instigation of the Devil, the prince of this world, men blind with greed and intolerable in their audacity? If, then, they strive to bend the priests of God to their will, to whom may they more properly be compared than to him who is chief over all the sons of pride? For he, tempting our High Priest [Jesus], head of all priests, son of the Most High, offering him all the kingdoms of this world, said: "All these will I give thee if thou wilt fall down and worship me."

Does anyone doubt that the priests of Christ are to be considered as fathers and masters of kings and princes and of all believers? Would it not be regarded as pitiable madness if a son should try to rule his father or a pupil his master and to bind with unjust obligations the one through whom he expects to be bound or loosed, not only on earth but also in heaven? Evidently recognizing this the emperor Constantine the Great, lord over all kings and princes throughout almost the entire earth, as St. Gregory [pope, 590–604] relates in his letter to the emperor Mauritius [Maurice, Byzantine ruler, 582–602], at the holy synod of 'Nicaea'[1] took his place below all the bishops and did not venture to pass any judgment upon them but, even addressing them as gods, felt that they ought not to be subject to his judgment but that he ought to be bound by their decisions.

Pope Gelasius, urging upon the emperor Anastasius not to feel himself wronged by the truth that was called to his attention said: "There are two powers, O august Emperor, by which the world is governed, the sacred authority of the priesthood and the power of kings. Of these the priestly is by so much the greater as they will have to answer for kings themselves in the day of divine judgment;" and a little further: "Know that you are subject to their judgment, not that they are to be subjected to your will."

In reliance upon such declarations and such authorities, many prelates [popes or other powerful church officials] have excommunicated kings or emperors.

Drawn up by the papal government during the pontificate of Gregory VII, the *Dictatus papae* represents claims and ambitions that would inspire many popes and theologians throughout the Middle Ages.

## RULES OF THE POPE

1. That the Roman church was established by God alone.

2. That the Roman pontiff [bishop] alone is rightly called universal.

3. That he alone has the power to depose and reinstate bishops.

4. That his legate [emissary], even if he be of lower ecclesiastical rank, presides over bishops in council, and has the power to give sentence of deposition against them.

5. That the pope has the power to depose those who are absent (*i.e.,* without giving them a hearing).

6. That, among other things, we ought not to remain in the same house with those whom he has excommunicated.

7. That he alone has the right, according to the necessity of the occasion, to make new laws, to create new bishoprics, to make a monastery of a chapter of canons,[2] and *vice versa,* and either to divide a rich bishopric or to unite several poor ones.

8. That he alone may use the imperial insignia.

9. That all princes shall kiss the foot of the pope alone.

10. That his name alone is to be recited in the churches.

11. That the name applied to him belongs to him alone.

12. That he has the power to depose emperors.

---

[1]The council of Nicaea in Asia Minor mentioned here took place in 325; it was the first ecumenical council of the church—all bishops were invited to participate.

[2]A chapter of canons is a corporate ecclesiastical body composed of priests who administer cathedrals or monastic communities.

13. That he has the right to transfer bishops from one see to another when it becomes necessary.

14. That he has the right to ordain as a cleric anyone from any part of the church whatsoever.

15. That anyone ordained by him may rule (as bishop) over another church, but cannot serve (as priest) in it, and that such a cleric may not receive a higher rank from any other bishop.

16. That no general synod may be called without his order.

17. That no action of a synod and no book shall be regarded as canonical [official] without his authority.

18. That his decree can be annulled by no one, and that he can annul the decrees of anyone.

19. That he can be judged by no one.

20. That no one shall dare to condemn a person who has appealed to the apostolic seat.

21. That the important cases of any church whatsoever shall be referred to the Roman church (that is, to the pope).

22. That the Roman church has never erred and will never err to all eternity, according to the testimony of the holy scriptures.

23. That the Roman pontiff who has been canonically ordained is made holy by the merits of St. Peter, according to the testimony of St. Ennodius, bishop of Pavia, which is confirmed by many of the holy fathers, as is shown by the decrees of the blessed pope Symmachus [498–513].

24. That by his command or permission subjects may accuse their rulers.

25. That he can depose and reinstate bishops without the calling of a synod.

26. That no one can be regarded as catholic who does not agree with the Roman church.

27. That he has the power to absolve subjects from their oath of fidelity to wicked rulers.

## REVIEW QUESTIONS

1. What was the scriptural basis claimed by Pope Gregory VII for his authority as head of the church?
2. What were Gregory VII's views on the origin and limits of royal authority?
3. What powers did Gregory VII claim over secular princes? Over the bishops of the church?
4. In what sense did Gregory VII revolutionize earlier views on the proper relationship between church and state? (See Gelasius I, page 189.)

---

## 3   The First Crusade

In the eleventh century the Seljuk Turks, recent converts to Islam, conquered vast regions of the Near East including most of Asia Minor, the heartland of the Byzantine Empire. When the Seljuk empire crumbled, Byzantine emperor Alexius I Comnenus (1081–1118), seeing an opportunity to regain lost lands, appealed to Latin princes and the pope for assistance, an appeal answered by Urban II (1088–1099).

In 1095 at the Council of Clermont, Pope Urban II in a dramatic speech urged Frankish lords to take up the sword against the Muslims, an event that marked the beginning of the Crusades—the struggle to regain the Holy Land from Islam. A Christian army mobilized by the papacy to defend the Christian faith accorded with the papal concept of a just war. Moreover, Urban hoped that such a venture might bring the Byzantine church under papal authority. Nobles viewed Urban's appeal as a great adventure that held the promise of glory, wealth, and new lands; they were also motivated by religious reasons: recovery of Christian holy places and a church-approved way of doing penance for their sins.

The Crusades also demonstrated the growing strength and confidence of Latin Christendom, which previously had been on the defensive against Islam, and thus represented part of a wider movement of expansion on the part of Latin Christians. In the eleventh century, Italians had already driven the Muslims from Sardinia; Normans had taken Sicily from the Muslims and southern Italy from Byzantium; and Christian knights, supported by the papacy, were engaged in a long struggle to expel the Muslim Moors from Spain.

The First Crusade demonstrated Christian fanaticism as well as idealism and growing power, as contingents of crusaders robbed and massacred thousands of Jews in the Rhineland (see page 244). The First Crusade was climaxed by the storming of Jerusalem in June 1099 and the slaughter of the city's inhabitants.

## Robert the Monk
## APPEAL OF URBAN II TO THE FRANKS

Pope Urban's speech, as reported by Robert the Monk, shows how skillfully the pope appealed to the Frankish lords.

"O race of the Franks, O people who live beyond the mountains, O people loved and chosen of God, as is clear from your many deeds, distinguished over all other nations by the situation of your land, your catholic faith, and your regard for the holy church, we have a special message and exhortation for you. For we wish you to know what a grave matter has brought us to your country. The sad news has come from Jerusalem and Constantinople that the people of Persia, an accursed and foreign race [the Turks], enemies of God, 'a generation that set not their heart aright, and whose spirit was not steadfast with God' (Ps. 78:8), have invaded the lands of those Christians and devastated them with the sword, rapine, and fire. Some of the Christians they have carried away as slaves, others they have put to death. The churches they have either destroyed or turned into mosques. They desecrate and overthrow the altars. . . . They have taken from the Greek empire a tract of land so large that it takes

more than two months to walk through it. Whose duty is it to avenge this and recover that land, if not yours? For to you more than to other nations the Lord has given the military spirit, courage, agile bodies, and the bravery to strike down those who resist you. Let your minds be stirred to bravery by the deeds of your forefathers, and by the efficiency and greatness of . . . [Charlemagne], and of . . . his son [Louis the Pious], and of the other kings who have destroyed [Muslim] kingdoms, and established Christianity in their lands. You should be moved especially by the holy grave of our Lord and Saviour which is now held by unclean peoples, and by the holy places which are treated with dishonor and irreverently befouled with their uncleanness.

"O bravest of knights, descendants of unconquered ancestors, do not be weaker than they, but remember their courage. . . . Let no possessions keep you back, no solicitude for your property. Your land [France] is shut in on all sides by the sea and mountains, and is too thickly populated. There is not much wealth here, and the soil scarcely yields enough to support you. On this account you kill and devour each other, and carry on war and mutually destroy each other. Let your hatred and quarrels cease, your civil wars come to an end, and all your dissensions stop. Set out on the road to the holy sepulchre [site of Jesus' burial], take the land from that wicked people, and make it your own. That land which, as the Scripture says, is flowing with milk and honey, God gave to the children of Israel. Jerusalem is the best of all lands, more fruitful than all others, as it were a second Paradise of delights. This land our Saviour [Jesus] made illustrious by his birth, beautiful with his life, and sacred with his suffering; he redeemed it with his death and glorified it with his tomb. This royal city is now held captive by her enemies, and made pagan by those who know not God. She asks and longs to be liberated and does not cease to beg you to come to her aid. She asks aid especially from you because, as I have said, God has given more of the military spirit to you than to

other nations. Set out on this journey and you will obtain the remission of your sins and be sure of the incorruptible glory of the kingdom of heaven."

When Pope Urban had said this and much more of the same sort, all who were present were moved to cry out with one accord, "It is the will of God, it is the will of God." When the pope heard this he raised his eyes to heaven and gave thanks to God, and, commanding silence with a gesture of his hand, he said: "My dear brethren. . . . [L]et these words be your battle cry, because God caused you to speak them. Whenever you meet the enemy in battle, you shall all cry out, 'It is the will of God, it is the will of God.' . . . Whoever therefore shall determine to make this journey and shall make a vow to God and shall offer himself as a living sacrifice, holy, acceptable to God (Rom. 12:1), shall wear a cross on his brow or on his breast. And when he returns after having fulfilled his vow he shall wear the cross on his back. In this way he will obey the command of the Lord, 'Whosoever doth not bear his cross and come after me is not worthy of me'" (Luke 14:27).

## REVIEW QUESTIONS

1. Modern political propaganda frequently uses popular fears, prejudices, moral idealism, and patriotic fervor to shape public opinion. Discuss the techniques used by Pope Urban II to create public support for the Crusade.
2. What types of people did Urban II address and what were his motives?

---

# 4 Religious Dissent

Like many groups held together by common ideology, the medieval church wanted to protect its doctrines from novel, dissident, or erroneous interpretations. To ensure orthodoxy and competency, therefore, all preachers were licensed by the bishop; unlicensed preaching, especially by unschooled laymen, was forbidden. In the western church, heresy had not been a serious problem in the post-Roman period. But in the twelfth century, two heretical movements attracted significant numbers of supporters among both the clergy and laity and cut across frontiers and social classes. The first group was the Waldensians, or Poor Men of Lyons, founded about 1173 by Peter Waldo (d. 1217), a

rich merchant of Lyons, France, who gave away his wealth to the poor and began to preach in villages in southeastern France.

The second major heretical movement was that of the Cathari, more commonly called the Albigensians. The Albigensian heresy apparently entered
western Europe from the Balkans, where similar religious ideas could be traced
back to non-Christian sects of the early Roman Empire. The Albigensians were
not Christians in any orthodox sense: they rejected the Old Testament and
claimed the God of Israel to be the Evil One, who created the material world in
which souls were trapped, separating them from the Good God. Although the
Albigensians accepted the New Testament with their own emendations, they
rejected the Christian doctrine of Jesus as both God and Man; they believed that
Jesus was a disembodied spirit, and that all flesh was evil, marriage was evil,
and the begetting of children was evil. Rejecting the medieval church, they
constituted an alternative religion in the midst of Christian southern France
and Italy.

# Bernard Gui
# THE WALDENSIAN TEACHINGS

Neither a priest nor a theologian, Waldo had the Bible translated from Latin
into the common language of the people and preached the gospel message
without the consent of church authorities. Small groups of Waldo's converts
soon were found in towns and villages throughout southeastern France, northern Italy, and Switzerland. Within less than a decade, the Waldensians had
aroused the clergy's hostility and were condemned as heretics by Pope Lucius
III at a council in Verona in 1184. Gradually, influenced by other heretical
groups, the Waldensians adopted a more radical stance toward the medieval
church. In the following reading from *Manual of an Inquisitor,* a fourteenth-
century Dominican friar, Bernard Gui, describes the origin and the teachings
of the Waldensians. The Waldensian criticisms of the church would be echoed
in the writings of the great Protestant reformers of the sixteenth century.

The sect and heresy of the Waldenses or Poor of
Lyons began about the year of our Lord 1170.
Its moving spirit and founder was a certain citizen of Lyons named Waldes, or Waldens, from
whom his followers received their name. He
was a rich man who, having given up all his
property, resolved to devote himself to poverty
and to evangelical perfection, just as the apostles had done. He had procured for himself
translations of the Gospels and some other
books of the Bible in vernacular French, also
some texts from St. Augustine, St. Jerome, St.
Ambrose, and St. Gregory, arranged topically,

which he and his adherents called "sentences."
On frequently reading these over among themselves, although very seldom understanding
them aright, they were carried away by their
emotions and, although they had but little
learning, they usurped the function of the
apostles by daring to preach "in the streets and
the broad ways."

This man Waldes, or Waldens, won over to a
like presumption many people of both sexes,
made men and women his accomplices, and
sent them out to preach as his disciples. They,
men and women alike, although they were

stupid and uneducated, wandered through villages, entered homes, preached in the squares and even in churches, the men especially, and spread many errors everywhere. Moreover, when they were summoned by the archbishop of Lyons, John of the Fair Hands, and by him forbidden such audacity, they were not at all willing to obey, alleging as excuse for their madness that "we ought to obey God rather than men," Who had commanded His apostles to "preach the gospel to every creature." By virtue of a false profession of poverty and a feigned appearance of sanctity, they arrogated to themselves what had been said to the apostles. Boldly declaring that they were imitators and successors of these apostles, they cast aspersions upon prelates and clergy for abundant wealth and lives of luxury.

Thus, through presumptuously usurping the office of preaching, they became teachers of error. After they had been warned to desist, they rendered themselves disobedient and contumacious, for which they were excommunicated and driven from that city and their native land. Finally, indeed, because they remained obdurate, they were pronounced schismatics [rebels] at a certain council which was held at Rome . . . and were then condemned as heretics. And so, as they had grown in number on the earth, they scattered throughout that province and neighboring areas and into the region of Lombardy [northern Italy]. Separated and cut off from the Church, when they mingled with other heretics and imbibed their errors, they combined with their own fantasies the errors and heresies of heretics of earlier days. . . .

. . . Now, the principal heresy of the aforesaid Waldenses was and still continues to be contempt of ecclesiastical authority. Then, having been excommunicated for this and given over to Satan, they were plunged by him into countless errors, and they combined with their own fantasies the errors of heretics of an earlier day.

The foolish followers and impious teachers of this sect hold and teach that they are not subject to our lord pope, the Roman pontiff, or to other prelates of the Roman Church, for

they declare that the Roman Church persecutes and censures them unjustly and unduly. Also, they declare positively that they cannot be excommunicated by the said Roman pontiff and prelates, to none of whom ought obedience be given should he enjoin or command the members and teachers of this sect to desert and abjure it—this despite the fact that it has been condemned as heretical by the Roman Church.

Also, they hold and teach that every oath, in or out of court, without exception or qualification, has been forbidden by God as unlawful and sinful. . . .

Also, out of the same font of error, the aforesaid sect and heresy declares that any judicial process is forbidden by God and is, consequently, a sin and that it is contrary to God's command for any judge, in any case or for any reason, to sentence a man to corporal punishment involving bloodshed, or to death. They seize on the words of the Holy Gospels—"Judge not that ye be not judged"; "Thou shalt not kill"; and other similar passages—without the proper explanation essential to their interpretation. This they do without understanding the sense or accepting the signification or explanation which the Holy Roman Church wisely perceives and transmits to the faithful in accordance with the teaching of the Fathers [early Christian theologians], the doctors, and the canonical decrees.

Also, as it strays from the way and the right path, this sect does not accept or consider valid, but despises, rejects, and damns the canonical decrees, the decretals [judgments] of the supreme pontiffs, the rules concerning observance of fasts and holy days, and the precepts of the Fathers.

Also, in a more pernicious error in respect of the sacrament of penance and the keys [papal powers to legislate] of the Church, these [Waldensians] hold, and teach that, just as the apostles had it from Christ, they have from God alone and from no other the power to hear confessions from men and women who wish to confess to them, to give absolution, and to impose penance. And they do hear the confessions of such persons, they do give absolution [forgiveness] and impose penance, although they are not priests or clerics ordained by any bishop of the Roman Church but are laymen and nothing more. They do not claim to have any such power from the Roman Church, but rather disclaim it. . . .

Also, this sect and heresy ridicules the indulgences [remissions of canonical punishments due to sin] which are published and granted by prelates of the Church, asserting that they are of no value whatever.

In regard to the sacrament of the Eucharist [communion, celebration of the Last Supper] they err, saying, not publicly but in private among themselves, that if the priest who celebrates or consecrates the Mass is a sinner, the bread and wine do not change into the body and blood of Christ in the sacrament of the altar; and in their view anyone is a sinner who is not a member of their sect. Also, they say that any righteous person, even though he be a layman and not a cleric ordained by a Catholic bishop, can perform the consecration of the body and blood of Christ, provided only that he be a member of their sect. This they apply even to women, with the same proviso that they belong to their sect. Thus they teach that every holy person is a priest.

---

# Emperor Frederick II
# HERETICS: ENEMIES OF GOD
# AND HUMANITY

The new religious movements threatened to undermine the existing religious, social, and political order. Pope Gregory IX in 1231 decided to create special courts of inquisition to seek out the dissenters, or heretics. Those who repented could be sent to prison for life; those who remained unrepentant were excommunicated from the church and turned over to the secular authorities, who executed them. The property of the guilty was confiscated and divided equally among the local bishop, the inquisitors, and the local civil ruler. The ordinary procedural standards of European penal law were abandoned in the courts of inquisition. The inquiry was secret, witnesses were not identified to the accused, guilt was presumed, legal counsel was denied, and torture was applied to verify statements given under oath.

The papal inquisitors were not permitted to function everywhere. The rulers of the northern and eastern European kingdoms forbade them entry, as did England, Portugal, and Castile. In the next reading, from the first section of the Constitutions of Melfi, promulgated for the kingdom of Sicily by the Emperor Frederick II (1220–1250) in 1231, the typical attitude of medieval Christians toward heretics (or those who gave them aid or comfort) and the savage penalties imposed are graphically depicted. Ironically, in 1245, Frederick II himself was accused of heresy and deposed by Pope Innocent IV (1243–1254), leading to a war between the emperor and the papacy.

Heretics try to tear the seamless robe of our God. As slaves to the vice of a word that means division [sect], they strive to introduce division into the unity of the indivisible faith and to separate the flock from the care of Peter [the Pope], the shepherd to whom the Good Shepherd [Christ] entrusted it. Inside they are violent wolves, but they pretend the tameness of sheep until they can get inside the sheepfold of the Lord. They are the most evil angels. They are sons of depravity from the father of wickedness and the author of evil, who are resolved to deceive simple souls. They are snakes who deceive doves. They are serpents who seem to creep in secretly and, under the sweetness of honey, spew out poison. While they pretend to administer the food of life, they strike from their tails. They mix up a potion of death as a certain very deadly poison.

. . . Indeed, these miserable Patarines [Patarenes, one group of heretics], who do not possess the holy faith of the Eternal Trinity,[1] offend at the same time three persons under one cover of wickedness: God, their neighbors, and themselves. They offend God because they do not know the faith of God, and they do not know his son. They deceive their neighbors insofar as they administer the delights of heretical wickedness to them under the guise of spiritual nourishment. They rage against themselves even more cruelly insofar as, besides risking their souls, these sectaries, lavish of life and improvident with death, also expose their bodies to the enticements of cruel death which they could avoid by true knowledge and the steadfastness of true faith. What is even worse, the survivors are not frightened by the example. We cannot contain our emotions against such men so hostile to God, to themselves, and to mankind. Therefore, we draw the sword of righteous vengeance against them, and we pursue them more urgently insofar as they are known to practice the crimes of their superstition within the Roman Church herself, which is considered the head of all the other

---

[1]The central Christian doctrine that teaches that there are three divine persons in one God: Father, Son, and Holy Spirit, who are coequal, coeternal, and consubstantial.

churches, to the more evident injury of the Christian faith. . . . Because we consider this so repulsive, we have decided in the first place that the crime of heresy and these condemned sects should be numbered among the public crimes as it was promulgated in the ancient laws. . . . In order to expose the wickedness of those who, because they do not follow God, walk in darkness, even if no one reports it, we desire that the perpetrators of these crimes should be investigated diligently and should be sought after by our officials like other criminals. We order that those who become known by an inquisition [trial], even if they are touched by the evidence of a slight suspicion, should be examined by ecclesiastics and prelates. If they should be found by them to deviate from the Catholic faith in the least wise, and if, after they have been admonished by them in a pastoral way, they should be unwilling to relinquish the insidious darkness of the Devil and to recognize the God of Light, but they persist in the constancy of conceived error, we order by the promulgation of our present law that these Patarines should be condemned to suffer the death for which they strive. Committed to the judgment of the flames, they should be burned alive in the sight of the people. We do not grieve that in this we satisfy their desire, from which they obtain punishment alone and no other fruit of their error. No one should presume to intervene with us in behalf of such persons. But if anyone does, we shall turn against him the deserved stings of our indignation. . . .

. . . We order that the shelterers, believers, accomplices of Patarines, and those who support them in any way at all, who give no heed to fear for themselves so that they can protect others from punishment, should be sent into perpetual exile and all their goods confiscated.

## REVIEW QUESTIONS

1. Why were the Waldensian teachings so threatening to the clergy of the Catholic Church?
2. How did Frederick II view heretics and what methods did he determine to use to eliminate them?

## 5 Medieval Learning: Synthesis of Reason and Christian Faith

The twelfth century witnessed a revived interest in classical learning and the founding of universities. Traditional theology was broadened by the application of a new system of critical analysis, called scholasticism. Scholastic thinkers assumed that some teachings of Christianity, which they accepted as true by faith, could also be demonstrated to be true by reason. They sought to explain and clarify theological doctrines by subjecting them to logical analysis.

# Peter Abelard
# INQUIRY INTO DIVERGENT VIEWS OF CHURCH FATHERS

Dialectics, a method of logical analysis applied to the Bible and the writings of early Christian thinkers, was brilliantly taught by Peter Abelard (1079–1142) in the cathedral school at Paris. In his book *Sic et Non (Yes and No),* Abelard listed some hundred and fifty questions on which the early church authorities had taken differing positions over the centuries. He suggested that these issues could be resolved by the careful application of the dialectical method to the language of the texts.

Although he never intended to challenge the Christian faith, Abelard raised, with his critical scrutiny, fears that the dialectical approach would undermine faith and foster heresy. Saint Bernard of Clairvaux, a Cistercian monk and mystic, challenged the new methods of the Parisian professor and sought to silence him. In 1141, Abelard was forced to quit his teaching post, and he retired to a monastery, where he died the following year. Despite Bernard's apparent victory, the new scholastic rationalistic approach swept the schools of Europe. In the following reading, the critical use of rational methods in textual analysis is described by Abelard.

We must be careful not to be led astray by attributing views to the [Church] Fathers which they did not hold. This may happen if a wrong author's name is given to a book or if a text is corrupt. For many works are falsely attributed to one of the Fathers to give them authority, and some passages, even in the Bible, are corrupt through the errors of copyists. . . . We must be equally careful to make sure that an opinion quoted from a Father was not withdrawn or corrected by him in the light of later and better knowledge. . . . Again the passage in question may not give the Father's own opinion, but that of some other writer whom he is quoting. . . .

We must also make a thorough inquiry when different decisions are given on the same matter under canon [church] law. We must discover the underlying purpose of the opinion, whether it is meant to grant an indulgence or exhort to some perfection. In this way we may clear up the apparent contradiction. . . . If the opinion is a definitive judgment, we must determine whether it is of general application or directed to a particular case. . . . The when and why of the order must also be considered because what is allowed at one time is often forbidden at another, and what is often laid down as the strict letter of the law may be sometimes moderated by a dispensation. . . .

Furthermore we customarily talk of things as they appear to our bodily senses and not as they are in actual fact. So judging by what we see we say it is a starry sky or it is not, and that the sun is hot or has no heat at all, when these things though variable in appearance are ever constant. Can we be surprised, then, that some matters have been stated by the Fathers as opinions rather than the truth? Then again many controversies would be quickly settled if we could be

on our guard against a particular word used in different senses by different authors. . . .

A careful reader will employ all these ways of reconciling contradictions in the writings of the Fathers. But if the contradictions are so glaring that they cannot be reconciled, then the rival authorities must be compared and the view that has the heaviest backing be adopted. . . .

By collecting contrasting divergent opinions I hope to provoke young readers to push themselves to the limit in the search for truth, so that their wits may be sharpened by their investigation. It is by doubting that we come to investigate, and by investigating that we recognise the truth.

# Saint Thomas Aquinas
# *SUMMA THEOLOGICA*
# AND *SUMMA CONTRA GENTILES*

For most of the Middle Ages, religious thought was dominated by the influence of Saint Augustine (d. 430), the greatest of the Latin church fathers (see page 185). Augustine placed little value on the study of nature; for him, the City of Man (the world) was a sinful place from which people tried to escape in order to enter the City of God (heaven). Regarding God as the source of knowing, he held that reason by itself was an inadequate guide to knowledge: without faith in revealed truth, there could be no understanding. An alternative approach to that of Augustine was provided by Thomas Aquinas (1225–1274), a friar of the Order of Preachers (Dominicans), who taught theology at Paris and later in Italy. Both Augustine and Aquinas believed that God was the source of all truth, that human nature was corrupted by the imprint of the original sin of Adam and Eve, and that God revealed himself through the Bible and in the person of Jesus Christ. But, in contrast to Augustine, Aquinas expressed great confidence in the power of reason and favored applying it to investigate the natural world.

Aquinas held that as both faith and reason came from God, they were not in opposition to each other; properly understood, they supported each other. Because reason was no enemy of faith, it should not be feared. In addition to showing renewed respect for reason, Aquinas—influenced by Aristotelian empiricism (the acquisition of knowledge of nature through experience)—valued knowledge of the natural world. He saw the natural and supernatural worlds not as irreconcilable and hostile to each other, but as a continuous ascending hierarchy of divinely created orders of being moving progressively toward the Supreme Being. In constructing a synthesis of Christianity and Aristotelianism, Aquinas gave renewed importance to the natural world, human reason, and the creative human spirit. Nevertheless, by holding that reason was subordinate to faith, he remained a typically medieval thinker.

In the opening reading from his most ambitious work, the *Summa Theologica,* Thomas Aquinas asserts that reason by itself is insufficient to lead human beings to salvation. Also included in this grouping is a selection from another work, *Summa Contra Gentiles,* a theological defense of Christian doctrines that relies extensively on natural reason.

## SUMMA THEOLOGICA

### *Whether, Besides the Philosophical Sciences, Any Further Doctrine Is Required?*

It was necessary for man's salvation that there should be a knowledge revealed by God, besides the philosophical sciences investigated by human reason. First, because man is directed to God as to an end that surpasses the grasp of his reason. . . . But the end must first be known by men who are to direct their thoughts and actions to the end. Hence it was necessary for the salvation of man that certain truths which exceed human reason should be made known to him by divine revelation. Even as regards those truths about God which human reason can investigate, it was necessary that man be taught by a divine revelation. For the truth about God, such as reason can know it, would only be known by a few, and that after a long time, and with the admixture of many errors; whereas man's whole salvation, which is in God, depends upon the knowledge of this truth. Therefore, in order that the salvation of men might be brought about more fitly and more surely, it was necessary that they be taught divine truths by divine revelation. It was therefore necessary that, besides the philosophical sciences investigated by reason, there should be a sacred science by way of revelation.

---

In the next selection, Aquinas uses the categories of Aristotelian philosophy to demonstrate through natural reason God's existence.

---

### *Whether God Exists?*

The existence of God can be proved in five ways.

The first and more manifest way is the argument from motion. It is certain, and evident to our senses, that in the world some things are in motion. Now whatever is moved is moved by another, for nothing can be moved except it is in potentiality to that towards which it is moved; whereas a thing moves inasmuch as it is in act. For motion is nothing else than the reduction of something from potentiality to actuality. But nothing can be reduced from potentiality to actuality, except by something in a state of actuality. Thus that which is actually hot, as fire, makes wood, which is potentially hot, to be actually hot, and thereby moves and changes it. Now it is not possible that the same thing should be at once in actuality and potentiality in the same respect, but only in different respects. For what is actually hot cannot simultaneously be potentially hot; but it is simultaneously potentially cold. It is therefore impossible that in the same respect and in the same way a thing should be both mover and moved, *i.e.,* that it should move itself. Therefore, whatever is moved must be moved by another. If that by which it is moved be itself moved, then this also must needs be moved by another, and that by another again. But this cannot go on to infinity, because then there would be no first mover, and, consequently, no other mover, seeing that subsequent movers move only inasmuch as they are moved by the first mover; as the staff moves only because it is moved by the hand. Therefore it is necessary to arrive at a first mover, moved by no other; and this everyone understands to be God.

The second way is from the nature of efficient cause. In the world of sensible things we find there is an order of efficient causes. There is no case known (neither is it, indeed, possible) in which a thing is found to be the efficient cause of itself; for so it would be prior to itself, which is impossible. Now in efficient causes it is not possible to go on to infinity, because in all efficient causes following in order, the first is the cause of the intermediate cause, and the intermediate is the cause of the ultimate cause, whether the intermediate cause be several, or one only. Now to take away the cause is to take away the effect. Therefore, if there be no first cause among efficient causes, there will be no ultimate, nor any intermediate, cause. But if in efficient causes it is possible to go on to infinity, there will be no first efficient cause, neither will there be an ultimate effect, nor any intermediate efficient causes; all of which is plainly false. Therefore it is necessary to admit a first efficient cause, to which everyone gives the name of God.

The third way is taken from possibility and necessity, and runs thus. We find in nature things that are possible to be and not to be, since they are found to be generated, and to be corrupted, and consequently, it is possible for them to be and not to be. But it is impossible for these always to exist, for that which can not-be at some time is not. Therefore, if everything can not-be, then at one time there was nothing in existence. Now if this were true, even now there would be nothing in existence, because that which does not exist begins to exist only through something already existing. Therefore, if at one time nothing was in existence, it would have been impossible for anything to have begun to exist; and thus even now nothing would be in existence—which is absurd. Therefore, not all beings are merely possible, but there must exist something the existence of which is necessary. But every necessary thing either has its necessity caused by another, or not. Now it is impossible

to go on to infinity in necessary things which have their necessity caused by another, as has been already proved in regard to efficient causes. Therefore we cannot but admit the existence of some being having of itself its own necessity, and not receiving it from another, but rather causing in others their necessity. This all men speak of as God.

The fourth way is taken from the graduation to be found in things. Among beings there are some more and some less good, true, noble, and the like. But *more* and *less* are predicated of different things according as they resemble in their different ways something which is the maximum, as a thing is said to be hotter according as it more nearly resembles that which is hottest; so that there is something which is truest, something best, something noblest, and, consequently, something which is most being, for those things that are greatest in truth are greatest in being. . . . Now the maximum in any genus is the cause of all in that genus, as fire, which is the maximum of heat, is the cause of all hot things. . . . Therefore there must also be something which is to all beings the cause of their being, goodness, and every other perfection; and this we call God.

The fifth way is taken from the governance of the world. We see that things which lack knowledge, such as natural bodies, act for an end, and this is evident from their acting always, or nearly always, in the same way, so as to obtain the best result. Hence it is plain that they achieve their end, not fortuitously, but designedly. Now whatever lacks knowledge cannot move towards an end, unless it be directed by some being endowed with knowledge and intelligence; as the arrow is directed by the archer. Therefore some intelligent being exists by whom all natural things are directed to their end; and this being we call God.

---

The next reading shows Aquinas' great respect for reason. He defines a human being by the capacity to regulate actions through reason and will.

## *Does Man Choose with Necessity or Freely?*

Man does not choose of necessity. . . . For man can will and not will, act and not act . . . can will this or that, and do this or that. The reason for this is to be found in the very power of the reason. For the will can tend to whatever the reason can apprehend as good. Now the reason can apprehend as good not only this, viz., *to will* or *to act,* but also this, viz., *not to will* and *not to act.* Again, in all particular goods, the reason can consider the nature of some good, and the lack of some good, which has the nature of an evil; and in this way, it can apprehend any single one of such goods as to be chosen or to be avoided. . . . Therefore, man chooses, not of necessity, but freely.

---

In the following selection Aquinas stresses the necessity of assenting to the truths of faith even if they are beyond the grasp of reason.

---

## SUMMA CONTRA GENTILES

Another benefit that comes from the revelation to men of truths that exceed the reason is the curbing of presumption, which is the mother of error. For there are some who have such a presumptuous opinion of their own ability that they deem themselves able to measure the nature of everything; I mean to say that, in their estimation, everything is true that seems to them so, and everything is false that does not. So that the human mind, therefore, might be freed from this presumption and come to a humble inquiry after truth, it was necessary that some things should be proposed to man by God that would completely surpass his intellect.

A still further benefit may also be seen in what Aristotle says in the *Ethics.* There was a certain Simonides who exhorted people to put aside the knowledge of divine things and to apply their talents to human occupations. He said that "he who is a man should know human things, and he who is mortal, things that are mortal." Against Simonides Aristotle says that "man should draw himself towards what is immortal and divine as much as he can." And so he says in the *De animalibus* that, although what we know of the higher substances is very little, yet that little is loved and desired more than all the knowledge that we have about less noble substances. He also says in the *De caelo et mundo* that when questions about the heavenly bodies can be given even a modest and merely plausible solution, he who hears this experiences intense joy. From all these considerations it is clear that even the most imperfect knowledge about the most noble realities brings the greatest perfection to the soul. Therefore, although the human reason cannot grasp fully the truths that are above it, yet, if it somehow holds these truths at least by faith, it acquires great perfection for itself.

Therefore it is written: "For many things are shown to thee above the understanding of men" (Ecclus. 3:25). . . .

Those who place their faith in this truth, however, "for which the human reason offers no experimental evidence," do not believe foolishly, as though "following artificial fables" (II Peter 1:16). For these "secrets of divine Wisdom" (Job 11:6) the divine Wisdom itself, which knows all things to the full, has deigned to reveal to men. It reveals its own presence, as well as the truth of its teaching and inspiration, by fitting arguments; and in order to confirm those truths that exceed natural knowledge, it gives visible manifestation to works that surpass the ability of all nature. Thus, there are the wonderful cures of illnesses, there is the raising of the dead. . . . [A]nd what is more wonderful, there is the inspiration given to human minds, so that simple and untutored persons, filled with the gift of the Holy Spirit, come to possess instantaneously the highest wisdom and the readiest eloquence. When these arguments were examined [in Roman times], . . . in the midst of the tyranny of the persecutors, an innumerable throng of people, both simple and most learned, flocked to the Christian faith. In this faith there are truths preached that surpass every human intellect, the pleasures of the flesh are curbed; it is taught that the things of the world should be spurned. Now, for the minds of mortal men to assent to these things is the greatest of miracles, just as it is a manifest work of divine inspiration that, spurning visible things, men should seek only what is invisible. Now, that this has happened . . . as a result of the disposition of God, is clear from the fact that through many pronouncements of the ancient prophets God had foretold that He would do this. The books of these prophets are held in veneration among us Christians, since they give witness to our faith.

## REVIEW QUESTIONS

1. Describe the methods of literary analysis promoted by Peter Abelard in his courses on rhetoric and logic at the University of Paris.
2. Why did Abelard's new methods of textual analysis create so much controversy?
3. According to Thomas Aquinas, why does a person require more than reason?
4. Show how Aquinas used both logic and an empirical method to prove the existence of God.
5. What is the ethical and legal significance of Aquinas' argument that human beings are free to choose their course of action?

---

## 6  Medieval Universities

The twelfth century witnessed a revival of classical learning and cultural creativity. Gothic cathedrals, an enduring testament to the creativeness of the religious spirit, were erected throughout Europe. Roman authors were again read and their style imitated. Latin translations of Greek philosophical and scientific texts stimulated scholars; the reintroduction of the study of Roman law began to influence political theory and institutions. These were some of the major changes that would leave a permanent mark on subsequent Western culture.

A significant achievement of this age was the emergence of universities. Arising spontaneously among teachers of the liberal arts and students of the higher studies of law, theology, and medicine, the universities gave more formal and lasting institutional structure to the more advanced levels of schooling. The medieval universities were largely dedicated to educating young men for careers as lawyers, judges, teachers, diplomats, and administrators of both church and state. The educational foundation for such professional careers was the study of the liberal arts.

## John of Salisbury
## ON THE LIBERAL ARTS

The standard curriculum of medieval schools was based on intensive study of the seven liberal arts divided into two programs: the *trivium,* consisting of

Latin grammar, rhetoric, and dialectic (or logic), and the *quadrivium,* consisting of arithmetic, geometry, astronomy, and music. The brilliant, twelfth-century scholar and churchman John of Salisbury (c. 1115–1180) wrote the *Metalogicon,* a defense of the liberal arts curriculum, which was under attack from conservative theologians.

## WHY SOME ARTS ARE CALLED "LIBERAL"

While there are many sorts of arts, the first to proffer their services to the natural abilities of those who philosophize are the liberal arts. All of the latter are included in the courses of the Trivium and Quadrivium. The liberal arts are said to have become so efficacious among our ancestors, who studied them diligently, that they enabled them to comprehend everything they read, elevated their understanding to all things, and empowered them to cut through the knots of all problems possible of solution. Those to whom the system of the Trivium has disclosed the significance of all words, or the rules of the Quadrivium have unveiled the secrets of all nature, do not need the help of a teacher in order to understand the meaning of books and to find the solutions of questions. They (the branches of learning included in the Trivium and Quadrivium) are called "arts" because they . . . strengthen minds to apprehend the ways of wisdom. . . . They are called "liberal," either because the ancients took care to have their children instructed in them; or because their object is to effect man's liberation, so that, freed from cares, he may devote himself to wisdom. More often than not, they liberate us from cares incompatible with wisdom. They often even free us from worry about (material) necessities, so that the mind may have still greater liberty to apply itself to philosophy.

Among all the liberal arts, the first is logic, and specifically that part of logic which gives initial instruction about words. . . . [T]he word "logic" has a broad meaning, and is not restricted exclusively to the science of argumentative reasoning. (It includes) Grammar (which is "the science of speaking and writing correctly—the starting point of all liberal studies." Grammar is the cradle of all philosophy, and in a manner of speaking, the first nurse of the whole study of letters. It takes all of us as tender babes, newly born from nature's bosom. It nurses us in our infancy, and guides our every forward step in philosophy. With motherly care, it fosters and protects the philosopher from the start to the finish (of his pursuits). It is called "grammar" from the basic elements of writing and speaking. *Grama* means a letter or line. . . .

## THE IMPORTANCE OF STUDYING GRAMMAR

[It] is clear that (the function of) grammar is not narrowly confined to one subject. Rather, grammar prepares the mind to understand everything that can be taught in words. Consequently, everyone can appreciate how much all other studies depend on grammar. . . . Gaius [Julius] Caesar [100–44 B.C.] wrote books *On Analogy,* conscious that, without grammar, one cannot master philosophy (with which he was thoroughly familiar) or eloquence (in which he was most proficient). Quintilian [A.D. 35–c. 100] also praises this art to the point of declaring that we should continue the use of grammar and the love of reading "not merely during our school days, but to the very end of our life." For grammar equips us both to receive and to impart knowledge. It modulates our accent, and regulates our very voice so that it is suited to all persons and matters. Poetry should be recited in one way; prose in another.

. . . [Grammar] is . . . the key to everything written as well as the mother and arbiter of all speech. . . .

# WHAT IS A SCHOLAR?

In the next selection, the vocation of the medieval scholar and his duties are summarized in a dialogue that was used in medieval schools.

—Are you a scholar?

—Yes.

—What is a scholar?

—Somebody who earnestly and diligently applies himself to the virtues.

—Where are you a scholar?

—Here, everywhere and in every seemly place.

—How many seemly places are there?

—Four: the church, the school, at home with my parents and in the company of orderly men.

—How many unseemly places are there?

—They too are four in number: the dance-floor, the brothel, public roads and inns not frequented by orderly men. More places could be added to this list.

—Are you a scholar?

—Yes.

—What kind of scholar are you?

—As God has created me.

—How many duties does a scholar have?

—Six.

—What are they?

—To get up early, dress immediately, comb my hair, wash my hands, pray to God and go willingly to school.

—Are you a scholar?

—Yes.

—What is the substance of a scholar?

—An animated physical substance susceptible of knowledge and virtue.

—Are you a human being?

—Yes.

—What is a human being?

—A corporal, physical, rational and mortal substance created by God to attain immortal life.

—What is God?

—The best and highest conceivable being who endows everything with its existence and life.

---

# Geoffrey Chaucer
# AN OXFORD CLERIC

In his masterpiece, *The Canterbury Tales,* English poet and diplomat Geoffrey Chaucer (c. 1340–1400) describes a typical student on pilgrimage to the shrine of Saint Thomas Becket in Canterbury.

An *Oxford Cleric,* still a student though,
One who had taken logic long ago,
Was there; his horse was thinner than a rake,
And he was not too fat, I undertake,
But had a hollow look, a sober stare.
The thread upon his overcoat was bare;

He had found no preferment [employment] in
   the church
And he was too unworldly to make search
For secular employment. By his bed
He preferred having twenty books, in red
And black, of Aristotle's philosophy,
To having fine clothes, fiddle, or psaltery [a
   book of Psalms used for daily prayer].
Though a philosopher, as I have told,
He had not found the stone for making gold.[1]
Whatever money from his friends he took
He spent on learning or another book

And prayed for them most earnestly, returning
Thanks to them thus for paying for his learning.
His only care was study, and indeed
He never spoke a word more than was need,
Formal at that, respectful in the extreme,
Short, to the point, and lofty in this theme.
The thought of moral virtue filled his speech
And he would gladly learn, and gladly teach.

---

[1] The *philosopher's stone* was the name given to the mythical substance, searched for by alchemists, that would turn base metals into gold.

---

# STUDENT LETTERS

**The relationship between fathers and their sons enrolled at universities has not changed all that much since the Middle Ages, as the letters that follow demonstrate.**

## FATHERS TO SONS

### I

I have recently discovered that you live dissolutely and slothfully, preferring license to restraint and play to work and strumming a guitar while the others are at their studies, whence it happens that you have read but one volume of law while your more industrious companions have read several. Wherefore I have decided to exhort you herewith to repent utterly of your dissolute and careless ways, that you may no longer be called a waster and your shame may be turned to good repute.

### II

I have learned—not from your master, although he ought not to hide such things from me, but from a certain trustworthy source—that you do not study in your room or act in the schools as a good student should, but play and wander about, disobedient to your master and indulging in sport and in certain other dis-honorable practices which I do not now care to explain by letter.

## SONS TO FATHERS

### I

"Well-beloved father, I have not a penny, nor can I get any save through you, for all things at the University are so dear: nor can I study in my Code or my Digest, for they are all tattered. Moreover, I owe ten crowns in dues to the Provost, and can find no man to lend them to me; I send you word of greetings and of money.

The Student hath need of many things if he will profit here; his father and his kin must needs supply him freely, that he be not compelled to pawn his books, but have ready money in his purse, with gowns and furs and decent clothing, or he will be damned for a beggar; wherefore, that men may not take me for a beast, I send you word of greetings and of money.

Wines are dear, and hostels, and other good things; I owe in every street, and am hard bested to free myself from such snares. Dear father, deign to help me! I fear to be excommunicated; already have I been cited, and there is not even a dry bone in my larder. If I find not the money before this feast of Easter, the church door will be shut in my face: wherefore grant my supplication, for I send you word of greetings and of money.

### L'ENVOY

Well-beloved father, to ease my debts contracted at the tavern, at the baker's, with the doctor and the bedells [a minor college official], and to pay my subscriptions to the laundress and the barber, I send you word of greetings and of money."

### II

Sing unto the Lord a new song, praise him with stringed instruments and organs, rejoice upon the high-sounding cymbals, for your son has held a glorious disputation, which was attended by a great number of teachers and scholars. He answered all questions without a mistake, and no one could get the better of him or prevail against his arguments. Moreover he celebrated a famous banquet, at which both rich and poor were honoured as never before, and he has duly begun to give lectures which are already so popular that others' classrooms are deserted and his own are filled.

## REVIEW QUESTIONS

1. What meaning does John of Salisbury give to the word *liberal* in his discussion of liberal arts?
2. Is there any connection between modern learning and the fostering of virtuous citizens? Explain.
3. How do medieval scholars resemble their modern counterparts? How do they differ?

## 7  The Jews in the Middle Ages

Toward the end of the eleventh century, small communities of Jews were living in many of the larger towns of Christian Europe. Most of these Jews were descended from Jewish inhabitants of the Roman Empire. Under the protection of the Roman law or of individual Germanic kings, they had managed to survive amid a sometimes hostile Christian population. But religious fanaticism unleashed by the call for the First Crusade undermined Christian–Jewish relations gravely. Bands of Crusaders began systematically to attack and massacre the Jewish inhabitants of Rhineland towns. Thousands were killed—many because they refused to become converts to Christianity; their houses were looted and burned. Efforts by the bishops and civil authorities to protect their Jewish subjects were largely ineffective. Anti-Semitism became endemic in Latin Christendom.

# Albert of Aix-la-Chapelle
# MASSACRE OF THE JEWS OF MAINZ

**In the next reading, Albert, a twelfth-century priest of the city of Aix-la-Chapelle, describes the massacre of Jews (1096) at the beginning of the First Crusade.**

At the beginning of summer in the same year in which Peter [the Hermit] and Gottschalk,[1] after collecting an army, had set out, there assembled in like fashion a large and innumerable host of Christians from diverse kingdoms and lands; namely, from the realms of France, England, Flanders, and Lorraine. . . . I know not whether by a judgment of the Lord, or by some error of mind, they rose in a spirit of cruelty against the Jewish people scattered throughout these cities and slaughtered them without mercy, especially in the Kingdom of Lorraine,[2] asserting it to be the beginning of their expedition and their duty against the enemies of the Christian faith. This slaughter of Jews was done first by citizens of Cologne.[3] These suddenly fell upon a small band of Jews and severely wounded and killed many; they destroyed the houses and synagogues of the Jews and divided among themselves a very large amount of money. When the Jews saw this cruelty, about two hundred in the silence of the night began flight by boat to Neuss. The pilgrims and crusaders discovered them, and after taking away all their possessions, inflicted on them similar slaughter, leaving not even one alive.

Not long after this, they started upon their journey, as they had vowed, and arrived in a great multitude at the city of Mainz. There Count Emico, a nobleman, a very mighty man in this region, was awaiting, with a large band of Teutons [German soldiers], the arrival of the pilgrims who were coming thither from diverse lands by the King's highway.

The Jews of this city, knowing of the slaughter of their brethren, and that they themselves could not escape the hands of so many, fled in hope of safety to Bishop Rothard. They put an infinite treasure in his guard and trust, having much faith in his protection, because he was Bishop of the city. Then that excellent Bishop of the city cautiously set aside the incredible amount of money received from them. He placed the Jews in the very spacious hall of his own house, away from the sight of Count Emico and his followers, that they might remain safe and sound in a very secure and strong place.

But Emico and the rest of his band held a council and, after sunrise, attacked the Jews in the hall with arrows and lances. Breaking the bolts and doors, they killed the Jews, about seven hundred in number, who in vain resisted the force and attack of so many thousands. They killed the women, also, and with their swords pierced tender children of whatever age and sex. The Jews, seeing that their Christian enemies were attacking them and their children, and that they were sparing no

---

[1]A brilliant propagandist, Peter the Hermit raised a large army of poor and sparsely armed Frenchmen, who marched to Cologne to begin a Crusade to the Holy Land. Most of them were killed by Turkish forces after crossing into Asia Minor. Gottschalk was a German priest who gathered a band of undisciplined soldiers to join the First Crusade. His forces were killed by Hungarians defending their families and property from these Crusaders.

[2]Lorraine, a duchy in the western part of the Holy Roman Empire, is now part of France.

[3]Cologne (Köln), founded by the Romans in the first century A.D., was the largest city in the Rhine Valley, a center of commerce, industry, and learning. Its politically powerful archbishop was a prince of the Holy Roman Empire.

age, likewise fell upon one another, brother, children, wives, and sisters, and thus they perished at each other's hands. Horrible to say, mothers cut the throats of nursing children with knives and stabbed others, preferring them to perish thus by their own hands rather than to be killed by the weapons of the uncircumcised.

From this cruel slaughter of the Jews a few escaped; and a few because of fear, rather than because of love of the Christian faith, were baptized. With very great spoils taken from these people, Count Emico, Clarebold, Thomas, and all that intolerable company of men and women then continued on their way to Jerusalem.

# A DECREE BY POPE INNOCENT III

Regarding the Jews as wicked because they refused to accept Christ, the church wanted them to live in humiliation. However, the church did at times seek to protect them from violence.

The Fourth Lateran Council, which was organized by Innocent III (1198–1216), the most powerful of medieval popes, barred Jews from public office and required them to wear a distinguishing badge on their clothing, a sign of their degradation. Yet Innocent, as the following passage indicates, also cautioned against harming Jews. The passage, however, reveals some of the torments faced by Jews.

... We decree that no Christian shall use violence to compel the Jews to accept baptism. But if a Jew, of his own accord, because of a change in his faith, shall have taken refuge with Christians, after his wish has been made known, he may be made a Christian without any opposition. For anyone who has not of his own will sought Christian baptism cannot have the true Christian faith. No Christian shall do the Jews any personal injury, except in executing the judgments of a judge, or deprive them of their possessions, or change the rights and privileges which they have been accustomed to have. During the celebration of their festivals, no one shall disturb them by beating them with clubs or by throwing stones at them. No one shall compel them to render any services except those which they have been accustomed to render. And to prevent the baseness and avarice of wicked men we forbid anyone to deface or damage their cemeteries or to extort money from them by threatening to exhume the bodies of their dead. ...

# THE LIBEL OF RITUAL MURDER

Despite efforts by some popes to protect Jews, outbreaks of violence toward them persisted and bizarre myths about them emerged. Jews were seen as agents of Satan conspiring to destroy Christendom and as sorcerers employing black magic against Christians. Perhaps the most absurd (and dangerous) charge against the Jewish people was the accusation of ritual murder—that the Jews, requiring Christian blood for the Passover service, sacrificed a Christian child. Despite the vehement denials of Jews and the protests of some enlightened Christian leaders, hundreds of such libelous accusations were made, resulting in the torture, trials, murder, and expulsion of many Jews. Allegations of ritual murder and accompanying trials persisted into the twentieth century, to the consternation and anger of enlightened people who regarded the charge as so much nonsense, a lingering medieval fabrication and superstition.

In the next passage, an English chronicler reports on the death of one young Harold of Gloucester purported to be murdered by Jews in 1168.

. . . [The eight-year-old] boy Harold, who is buried in the Church of St. Peter the Apostle, at Gloucester . . ., is said to have been carried away secretly by Jews, in the opinion of many,* on Feb. 21, and by them hidden till March 16. On that night, on the sixth of the preceding feast, the Jews of all England coming together as if to circumcise a certain boy, pretend deceitfully that they are about to celebrate the feast [Passover] appointed by law in such case, and deceiving the citizens of Gloucester with that fraud, they tortured the lad placed before them with immense tortures. It is true no Christian was present, or saw or heard the deed, nor have

we found that anything was betrayed by any Jew. But a little while after when the whole convent of monks of Gloucester and almost all the citizens of that city, and innumerable persons coming to the spectacle, saw the wounds of the dead body, scars of fire, the thorns fixed on his head, and liquid wax poured into the eyes and face, and touched it with the diligent examination of their hands, those tortures were believed or guessed to have been inflicted on him in that manner. It was clear that they had made him a glorious martyr to Christ, being slain without sin, and having bound his feet with his own girdle, threw him into the river Severn. (The body is taken to St. Peter's Church, and there performs miracles.)

---

*Even the chronicler puts it doubly doubtfully.

---

# Maimonides
# JEWISH LEARNING

Medieval Jews, despite frequent persecution, carried on a rich cultural and intellectual life based on their ancestral religion. The foremost Jewish scholar of the Middle Ages was Moses ben Maimon, also called by the Greek name Maimonides (1135–1204), who was born in Córdoba, Spain, then under Muslim rule. After his family emigrated from Spain, Maimonides went to Egypt, where he became physician to the sultan. During his lifetime, Maimonides achieved fame as a philosopher, theologian, mathematician, and physician; he was recognized as the leading Jewish sage of his day, and his writings were respected by Christian and Muslim thinkers as well. Like Christian scholastics and Muslim philosophers, Maimonides tried to harmonize faith with reason, to reconcile the Hebrew Scriptures and the Talmud (Jewish biblical commentary) with Greek philosophy. In his writings on ethical themes, Maimonides demonstrated piety, wisdom, and humanity. In the following passages, he discusses education and charity.

## EDUCATION

Every man in Israel [every Jew] is obliged to study the Torah,[1] whether he be poor or rich, whether he be physically healthy or ailing, whether he be in full vigor of youth or of great age and weakened vitality; even if he be dependent upon alms for his livelihood, or going around from door to door begging his daily bread, yea, even he who has a wife and children to support is obliged to have an appointed time for the study of the Torah, both during the day and at night, for it is said: "But thou shalt meditate therein day and night" (Joshua, I.8).

Some of the great scholars in Israel were hewers of wood, some of them drawers of water, and some of them blind: nevertheless they engaged themselves in the study of the Torah by day and by night. Moreover, they are included among those who translated the tradition as it was transmitted from mouth of man to mouth of man, even from the mouth of Moses our Master [the biblical Moses].

Until what age in life is one obliged to study the Torah? Even until the day of one's demise; for it is said: "And lest they depart from thy heart all the days of thy life" (Deut. 4.9). Forsooth, as long as one will not occupy himself with study he forgets what he did study.

One is obligated to divide his time of study by three; one third for the study of Holy Writ, one third for the study of the Oral Torah [the interpretations of the Torah], and one third for thinking and reflecting so that he may understand the end of a thing from its beginning, and deduct one matter from another, and compare one matter to another. . . .

When a master gave a lesson which the disciples did not understand, he should not get angry at them and be moody, but go over it

again and repeat it even many times, until they will understand the depth of the treatise. Likewise, a disciple shall not say, I understood, and he did not understand; but he should repeat and ask even many times. If the master angers at him and becomes moody, he may say to him: "Master, it is Torah, and I need instruction, but my mind is short of understanding!"

A disciple shall not feel ashamed before his fellows who mastered the subject the first or the second time, whereas he did not grasp it until after hearing it many times, for if he will be ashamed of such a thing, he will find himself coming in and going out of the . . . [school] without any instructions at all. The sages, therefore, said: "he who is bashful cannot be instructed and he who is in an angry mood cannot instruct." . . .

Even as a man is under command to honor his father and fear him, so is he obliged to honor his master, but fear him yet more than his father; his father brought him to life upon this world but his master who taught him wisdom, brings him to life in the world to come. . . .

---

Care for the poor is ingrained in the Jewish tradition. Rabbis gave the highest value to assistance, given in secret, that helps a poor person to become self-supporting. Maimonides drew upon this rabbinical tradition in his discussion of charity.

---

## CHARITY

The law of the Torah commanded us to practise *tsedakah,*[2] support the needy and help them financially. The command in connection with this duty occurs in various expressions; e.g., "Thou shalt surely open thy hand unto him" (Deut. xv. 8), "Thou shalt uphold him; as a stranger and a settler shall he live with thee" (Lev. xxv. 35). The intention in these passages

---

[1] The Torah refers to the first five books of the Hebrew Scriptures, which the Jews believed were written by Moses. In time, *Torah* also acquired a broader meaning that encompassed the entire Hebrew Scriptures and the various commentaries.

[2] The term *tsedakah* is derived from *tsédek* (righteousness); it denotes showing kindness to others.

is identical, viz., that we should console the poor man and support him to the extent of sufficiency. . . .

There are eight degrees in alms-giving, one higher than the other: Supreme above all is to give assistance to a co-religionist who has fallen on evil times by presenting him with a gift or loan, or entering into a partnership with him, or procuring him work, thereby helping him to become self-supporting.

Inferior to this is giving charity to the poor in such a way that the giver and recipient are unknown to each other. This is, indeed, the performance of a commandment from disinterested motives; and it is exemplified by the Institution of the Chamber of the Silent which existed in the Temple,[3] where the righteous secretly deposited their alms and the respectable poor were secretly assisted.*

Next in order is the donation of money to the charitable fund of the Community, to

which no contribution should be made without the donors feeling confident that the administration is honest, prudent and capable of proper management.

Below this degree is the instance where the donor is aware to whom he is giving the alms but the recipient is unaware from whom he received them; as, e.g., the great Sages who used to go about secretly throwing money through the doors of the poor. This is quite a proper course to adopt and a great virtue where the administrators of a charitable fund are not acting fairly.

Inferior to this degree is the case where the recipient knows the identity of the donor, but not *vice versa;* as, e.g., the great Sages who used to tie sums of money in linen bundles and throw them behind their backs for poor men to pick up, so that they should not feel shame.

The next four degrees in their order are: the man who gives money to the poor before he is asked; the man who gives money to the poor after he is asked; the man who gives less than he should, but does it with good grace; and lastly, he who gives grudgingly.

---

[3]The Temple to which Maimonides refers was the Temple in Jerusalem, destroyed by the Romans in A.D. 70.
*This system of charity was adopted by Jews in several Palestinian and Babylonian cities.

## REVIEW QUESTIONS

1. What were the apparent motives of those who attacked the Jews at Cologne and elsewhere at the time of the First Crusade?
2. What harassments and abuses were Jews likely to suffer in late medieval society?
3. What was the attitude of the papacy towards Jews?
4. Discuss the role of scholarship, education, and charity in Jewish medieval culture.

---

## 8   Troubadour Love Songs

In the late twelfth century, new kinds of poetry with a distinctive set of themes began to be created at the castles and courts in France, Italy, Spain, and Germany. The poets were themselves knights or noblewomen who composed their poems to be sung or read aloud for the entertainment of fellow feudal nobles. The subject was always that of the love between man and woman.

The original inspiration for the new troubadour poetry was probably the Arab poetry of Spain and Sicily, where the theme of courtly love was developed earlier. What was revolutionary in later European poetry was its treatment of the relationship between men and women. The troubadours reversed the traditional view of men as superior and women as inferior and dependent in their relationships. They introduced what is called "courtly love," a love relationship in which the woman is the superior and dominant figure, the man inferior and dependent. The male courts the lady, paying homage to her beauty and virtue. He suffers humiliation and frustration at her will and expresses the erotic tensions that consume him.

# LOVE AS JOYOUS, PAINFUL, AND HUMOROUS

The following poems were all composed by southern French troubadours. In the first selection a poet sings the praises of his beloved.

I wandered through a garden, 'twas
   filled with flowers the rarest,
And of all these brilliant blossoms
   I culled the very fairest;
So fine its shape, so sweet its scent, its
   hues so richly blent,
That heaven, I'm sure, created it itself
   to represent.
My lady is so charming, my lady is so
   meek,
Such tenderness is in her smile, such
   beauty in her cheek;
Such kisses blossom on her lip, such
   love illumines her eye—
Oh, never was there neath the stars a
   man so blest as I!
I gaze, I thrill with joy, I weep, in song
   my feelings flow—
A song of hope, delight, desire, with
   passion all aglow—
A fervent song, a pleading song, a song
   in every line—
Of thanks and praise to her who lists no
   other songs but mine.
Oh, hear me sweet! Oh, kiss me sweet!
   Oh, clasp me tenderly!
Thy beauties many, many touch, but
   none that love like me.

---

The following two poems tell of a lover's failure to win the affections of his beloved.

---

Now that the air is fresher
and the world turned green,
I shall sing once more
of the one I love and desire,
but we are so far apart
that I cannot go and witness
how my words might please her.

And nothing can console me
but death, for evil tongues
(may God curse them)
have made us part.
And alas, I so desired her
that now I moan and cry
half mad with grief.

I sing of her, yet her beauty
is greater than I can tell,
with her fresh color, lovely eyes,
and white skin, untanned
and untainted by rouge.
She is so pure and noble
that no one can speak ill of her.

But above all, one must praise,
it seems to me, her truthfulness,
her manners and her gracious speech,

for she never would betray a friend;
and I was mad to believe
what I heard tell of her
and thus cause her to be angry.

I never intended to complain;
and even now, if she so desires,
she could bring me happiness
by granting what I seek.
I cannot go on like this much longer,
for since she's been so far away
I've scarcely slept or eaten.

Love is sweet to look upon
but bitter upon parting;
one day it makes you weep
and another skip and dance,
for now I know that the more
one enters love's service,
the more fickle it becomes.

Messenger, go with Godspeed
and bring this to my lady,
for I cannot stay here much longer
and live, or be cured elsewhere,
unless I have her next to me,
naked, to kiss and embrace
within a curtained room.

————

I said my heart was like to break,
   And that my soul was cast,
By passion's tide, just like a wreck
   Disabled by the blast.

I swore an oath that what I felt
   Was like to turn my head;
I sighed—such sighs!—and then I knelt,
   But not a word she said!

I preached of Grace in moving strain;
   I told her she was fair;
I whispered what renown she'd gain,
   By listening to my prayer.

I spoke of needle and of pole,
   And other things I'd read;
But unto all my rigmarole—
   Why not a word she said!

I prayed her then my love to test,
   To send me near or far—

I'd squelch the dragon in his den,
   I'd yoke him to my car.

I'd risk for her, as faithful knight,
   My eyes, or limbs, or head,
Being quite prepared to fool or fight—
   But not a word she said!

I argued that, if poor in cash,
   Yet I was rich in mind;
Of rivals vowed to make a hash,
   When such I chanced to find.

I knit my brows, I clenched my hand,
   I tried to wake her dread;
In quiet wise, you'll understand—
   But not a word she said!

————

Troubadours could also be playful. Sometimes they mocked women who labored too hard to preserve a youthful beauty.

————

That creature so splendid is but an
   old jade;
Of ointment and padding her beauty
   is made;
Unpainted if you had the hap to
   behold her,
You'd find her all wrinkles from
   forehead to shoulder.

What a shame for a woman who has
   lost all her grace
To waste thus her time in bedaubing
   her face!
To neglect her poor soul I am sure is
   not right of her,
For a body that's going to corruption
   in spite of her.

————

Sometimes they even mocked this obsession with romance.

————

You say the moon is all aglow,
   The nightingale a-singing—
I'd rather watch the red wine flow,
   And hear the goblets ringing.

| | |
|---|---|
| You say 'tis sweet to hear the gale | You say 'tis sweet the stars to view |
|   Creep sighing through the willows— |   Upon the waters gleaming— |
| I'd rather hear a merry tale, | I'd rather see, 'twixt me and you |
|   'Mid a group of jolly fellows! |   And the post, my supper steaming. |

### REVIEW QUESTION

1. What aspects of the "courtly love" tradition can be identified in the troubadours' love songs?

---

# 9  The Status of Women in Medieval Society

The precise status of a woman in medieval society differed immensely depending on the time, the place, and her class. The majority of women managed families and households, often taking part in farmwork or other crafts connected with the family livelihood. However, their legal rights, social standing, and power were inferior to those of adult males in their own families. During the High Middle Ages, the Christian church increasingly supported a patriarchal structure of authority in church and civil society that left women effectively under the domination of males, clerical and lay. Although the teachings of Aristotle about women tended to demean their status among intellectuals, several of the church's teachings recognized the inherent dignity of a woman. The church regarded marriage as a sacrament, considered adultery a sin, and subjected men and women to the same moral standards. Neither sex had any special advantage in attaining salvation.

Despite legal, social, and economic handicaps imposed upon them by males, some women successfully assumed positions of power and achievement. A few ruled kingdoms and principalities or headed convents and religious orders. Others organized guilds; founded nunneries; practiced various crafts; served as teachers, physicians, and midwives; and operated small businesses. Some showed talent as poets, dramatists, and artists.

## Jakob Sprenger and Heinrich Krämer ANTIFEMALE PREJUDICES

The ambivalence in the male attitude (particularly of the intellectuals) toward women arose from several sources. First, medieval and Renaissance authors, who highly esteemed the classical works of the ancient Greco-Roman civilization, were influenced by the hostility evident in the writings of that era toward women who did not accept their position as subordinate and inferior to men. Second, the Christian view of men and women as equals in the sight of God was obscured by certain scriptural texts, such as Saint Paul's "Let your women keep silence in the churches: for it is not permitted unto them to speak" (1 Corinthians 14:34); and "Wives, submit yourselves unto your own husbands, as unto the Lord" (Ephesians 5:22). This ambivalent view of women was symbolized by the Old Testament portrait of Eve as the archetypal temptress, who led Adam to sin, and the New Testament picture of the Virgin Mary, whose acceptance of her role as the mother of Jesus made salvation possible for all people. Third, the clerical insistence that celibacy was superior to marriage (because the former avoided the distractions of the flesh and family life and allowed concentration on spiritual matters) encouraged prejudice against women. In the following passages from *The Hammer of Witches* (1486), the classic textbook on sorcery and witchcraft, the German clergymen Jakob Sprenger and Heinrich Krämer give vent to anti-female prejudices that were not uncommon then.

Now the wickedness of women is spoken of in *Ecclesiasticus xxv* [Old Testament book]: There is no head above the head of a serpent: and there is no wrath above the wrath of a woman. I had rather dwell with a lion and a dragon than to keep house with a wicked woman. And among much which in that place precedes and follows about a wicked woman, he concludes: All wickedness is but little to the wickedness of a woman. Wherefore [Saint] John Chrysostom [fourth-century bishop] says on the text, It is not good to marry *(S. Matthew* xix): What else is woman but a foe to friendship, an unescapable punishment, a necessary evil, a natural temptation, a desirable calamity, a domestic danger, a delectable detriment, an evil of nature, painted with fair colours! Therefore if it be a sin to divorce her when she ought to be kept, it is indeed a necessary torture; for either we commit adultery by divorcing her, or we must endure daily strife. Cicero [Roman statesman and philosopher] in his second book of *The Rhetorics* says: The many lusts of men lead them into one sin, but the one lust of women leads them into all sins; for the root of all woman's vices is avarice. And Seneca [Roman dramatist] says in his *Tragedies:* A woman either loves or hates; there is no third grade. And the tears of a woman are a deception, for they may spring from true grief, or they may be a snare. When a woman thinks alone, she thinks evil. . . .

Others again have propounded other reasons why there are more superstitious women found

than men. And the first is, that they are more credulous; and since the chief aim of the devil is to corrupt faith, therefore he rather attacks them. See *Ecclesiasticus* xix: He that is quick to believe is light-minded, and shall be diminished. The second reason is, that women are naturally more impressionable, and more ready to receive the influence of a disembodied spirit; and that when they use this quality well they are very good, but when they use it ill they are very evil.

The third reason is that they have slippery tongues, and are unable to conceal from their fellow-women those things which by evil arts they know; and, since they are weak, they find an easy and secret manner of vindicating themselves by witchcraft. . . .

. . . [S]ince they are feebler both in mind and body, it is not surprising that they should come more under the spell of witchcraft.

For as regards intellect, or the understanding of spiritual things, they seem to be of a different nature from men; a fact which is vouched for by the logic of the authorities, backed by various examples from the Scriptures. Terence [Roman dramatist] says: Women are intellectually like children. And Lactantius [fourth-century Christian writer] (*Institutiones,* III): No woman understood philosophy except Temeste. . . .

But the natural reason is that she is more carnal than a man, as is clear from her many carnal abominations. And it should be noted that there was a defect in the formation of the first woman, since she was formed from a bent rib, that is, a rib of the breast, which is bent as it were in a contrary direction to a man. And since through this defect she is an imperfect animal, she always deceives. For Cato [Roman statesman] says: When a woman weeps she weaves snares. And again: When a woman weeps, she labours to deceive a man. And this is shown by Samson's wife [Delilah], who coaxed him to tell her the riddle he had propounded to the Philistines, and told them the answer, and so deceived him. And it is clear in the case of the first woman [Eve] that she had little faith; for when the serpent asked why they did not eat of every tree in Paradise, she answered: Of every tree, etc.—lest perchance we die. Thereby she showed that she doubted, and had little faith in the word of God. And all this is indicated by the etymology of the word; for *Femina* [woman] comes from *Fe* [to produce] and *Minus* [less], since she is ever weaker to hold and preserve the faith. And this as regards faith is of her very nature; although both by grace and nature faith never failed in the Blessed Virgin [Mary], even at the time of Christ's Passion, when it failed in all men.

Therefore a wicked woman is by her nature quicker to waver in her faith, and consequently quicker to abjure the faith, which is the root of witchcraft.

And as to her other mental quality, that is, her natural will; when she hates someone whom she formerly loved, then she seethes with anger and impatience in her whole soul, just as the tides of the sea are always heaving and boiling. Many authorities allude to this cause. *Ecclesiasticus* xxv: There is no wrath above the wrath of a woman. And Seneca (*Tragedies,* VIII): No might of the flames or of the swollen winds, no deadly weapon is so much to be feared as the lust and hatred of a woman who has been divorced from the marriage bed.

And indeed, just as through the first defect in their intelligence they are more prone to abjure the faith; so through their second defect of inordinate affections and passions they search for, brood over, and inflict various vengeances, either by witchcraft, or by some other means. Wherefore it is no wonder that so great a number of witches exist in this sex.

Women also have weak memories; and it is a natural vice in them not to be disciplined, but to follow their own impulses without any sense of what is due. . . .

To conclude. All witchcraft comes from carnal lust, which is in women insatiable. See *Proverbs* xxx [Old Testament book]: There are three things that are never satisfied, yea, a fourth thing . . . the mouth of the womb. Wherefore for the sake of fulfilling their lusts they consort even with devils. More such reasons could be brought forward, but to the understanding it is sufficiently clear that it is no matter for wonder that there are more women than men found infected with the heresy of witchcraft. And in consequence of this, it is better called the heresy of witches than of wizards, since the name is taken from the more powerful party. And blessed be the Highest Who has so far preserved the male sex from so great a crime. . . .

# Christine de Pisan
# *THE CITY OF LADIES*

In the early Renaissance, a remarkable woman took up the task of defending women from their many male detractors. Christine de Pisan (1364–1429?) was born in Venice but moved with her parents to Paris, where her father was court physician and astrologer. She married a court notary when she was fifteen, had three children, and was left a widow and penniless ten years later. She decided to use her unusually good education to become a professional writer, an unheard-of occupation for a woman at that time. She won the patronage and friendship of noble ladies at the French royal court and produced many poems and books, including a biography of King Charles V and several polemical attacks upon the poets who slandered womankind. The most famous of these is *The City of Ladies,* written in 1405. In it Christine de Pisan questioned three allegorical figures—Reason, Rectitude, and Justice—about the lies and slanders of males concerning the virtues and achievements of women. The book is really a history of famous women and their accomplishments in many fields of endeavour. In the following passages, she challenged the traditional medieval attitude toward women. In questioning Lady Reason about the alleged inferiority of women to men, de Pisan cleverly changed the subject to that of virtue, proclaiming the equality of the sexes in attaining it.

"My lady [Lady Reason], according to what I understand from you, woman is a most noble creature. But even so, Cicero [Roman statesman] says that a man should never serve any woman and that he who does so debases himself, for no man should ever serve anyone lower than him."

She replied, "The man or the woman in whom resides greater virtue is the higher; neither the loftiness nor the lowliness of a person lies in the body according to the sex, but in the perfection of conduct and virtues. And surely he is happy who serves the Virgin [Mary, the mother of Jesus], who is above all the angels."

"My lady, one of the Catos[1]—who was such a great orator—said, nevertheless, that if this world were without women, we would converse with the gods."

She replied, "You can now see the foolishness of the man who is considered wise, because, thanks to a woman, man reigns with God. And if anyone would say that man was banished because of Lady Eve, I tell you that he gained more through [the Virgin] Mary than he lost through Eve when humanity was conjoined to the Godhead,[2] which would never have taken place if Eve's misdeed [eating the

forbidden fruit] had not occurred. Thus man and woman should be glad for this sin, through which such an honor has come about. For as low as human nature fell through this creature woman, was human nature lifted higher by this same creature. And as for conversing with the gods, as this Cato has said, if there had been no woman, he spoke truer than he knew, for he was a pagan, and among those of this belief, gods were thought to reside in Hell as well as in Heaven, that is, the devils whom they called the gods of Hell—so that it is no lie that these gods would have conversed with men, if Mary had not lived."

---

In this next passage, de Pisan discusses the slander that women are not as intelligent as men.

---

". . . But please enlighten me again, whether it has ever pleased this God, who has bestowed so many favors on women, to honor the feminine sex with the privilege of the virtue of high understanding and great learning, and whether women ever have a clever enough mind for this. I wish very much to know this because men maintain that the mind of women can learn only a little."

She [Lady Reason] answered, "My daughter, since I told you before, you know quite well that the opposite of their opinion is true,

[1]Several Roman statesmen bore the name Cato. Cato the Censor (234–149 B.C.) was a vigorous critic of women.
[2]This clause refers to the Christian belief that God became a human being in the person of Jesus Christ.

and to show you this even more clearly, I will give you proof through examples. I tell you again—and don't doubt the contrary—if it were customary to send daughters to school like sons, and if they were then taught the natural sciences, they would learn as thoroughly and understand the subtleties of all the arts and sciences as well as sons. And by chance there happen to be such women, for, as I touched on before, just as women have more delicate bodies than men, weaker and less able to perform many tasks, so do they have minds that are freer and sharper whenever they apply themselves."

"My lady, what are you saying? With all due respect, could you dwell longer on this point, please. Certainly men would never admit this answer is true, unless it is explained more plainly, for they believe that one normally sees that men know more than women do."

She answered, "Do you know why women know less?"

"Not unless you tell me, my lady."

"Without the slightest doubt, it is because they are not involved in many different things, but stay at home, where it is enough for them to run the household, and there is nothing which so instructs a reasonable creature as the exercise and experience of many different things."

"My lady, since they have minds skilled in conceptualizing and learning, just like men, why don't women learn more?"

She replied, "Because, my daughter, the public does not require them to get involved in the affairs which men are commissioned to execute, just as I told you before. It is enough for women to perform the usual duties to which they are ordained. As for judging from experience, since one sees that women usually know less than men, that therefore their capacity for understanding is less, look at men who farm the flatlands or who live in the mountains. You will find that in many countries they seem completely savage because they are so simpleminded. All the same, there is no doubt that Nature provided them with the qualities of body and mind found in the wisest and most learned men. . . ."

---

Next, Christine de Pisan argues in favor of giving young women the same opportunities for learning as men.

---

Following these remarks, I, Christine, spoke, "My lady, I realize that women have accomplished many good things and that even if evil women have done evil, it seems to me, nevertheless, that the benefits accrued and still accruing because of good women—particularly the wise and literary ones and those educated in the natural sciences whom I mentioned above—outweigh the evil. Therefore, I am amazed by the opinion of some men who claim that they do not want their daughters, wives, or kinswomen to be educated because their mores would be ruined as a result."

She responded, "Here you can clearly see that not all opinions of men are based on reason and that these men are wrong. For it must not be presumed that mores necessarily grow worse from knowing the moral sciences, which teach the virtues, indeed, there is not the slightest doubt that moral education amends and ennobles them. How could anyone think or believe that whoever follows good teaching or doctrine is the worse for it? Such an opinion cannot be expressed or maintained. I do not mean that it would be good for a man or a woman to study the art of divination or those fields of learning which are forbidden—for the holy Church did not remove them from common use without good reason—but it should not be believed that women are the worse for knowing what is good. . . .

". . . To speak of more recent times, without searching for examples in ancient history, Giovanni Andrea, a solemn law professor in Bologna [Italy] not quite sixty years ago, was not of the opinion that it was bad for women to be educated. He had a fair and good daughter, named Novella, who was educated in the law to such an advanced degree that when he was occupied by some task and not at leisure to present his lectures to his students, he would send Novella, his daughter, in his place to lecture to the students from his chair. And to prevent her beauty from distracting the concentration of her audience, she had a little curtain drawn in front of her. In this manner she could on occasion supplement and lighten her father's occupation. . . ."

---

# A Merchant of Paris
# ON LOVE AND MARRIAGE

It is difficult to generalize about so intimate a relationship as marriage. It is too intensely individual, and marital love is seldom captured by words that are not either trite or highly poetic in character. But in the late fourteenth century (c. 1393), a merchant of Paris, a man of mature years and experience, tried to put in words for his fifteen-year-old child bride some practical advice as to what a good wife should be and should do for her loving husband. The young lady was of higher social status than her husband, and he clearly expected that she would marry again after his death. His instructions were for her eyes only, but the manuscript survived in at least three copies. Discovered and published in French in 1846, it offers a rare look at the marital values and expectations of a wealthy, pious, and practical businessman living in one of the largest and most cosmopolitan cities of late medieval Europe.

## WHEN TWO GOOD AND HONEST PEOPLE ARE MARRIED

I believe that when two good and honest people are married, all other affections, except their love for each other, are withdrawn, annulled, and forgotten. It seems to me that when they are together they look at each other more than they look at others, they come together and embrace each other, and they would rather talk and communicate with each other than with anyone else. When they are separated, they think of each other and say in their hearts: "This is what I will do, this is what I will say, this is what I will ask him when I see him again." All their special pleasures, greatest desires, and perfect joys are in pleasing and obeying each other. But if they don't love one another, they have no more than a routine sense of duty and respect for each other, which is not enough between many couples.

## BE VERY LOVING AND INTIMATE WITH YOUR HUSBAND

You ought to be very loving and intimate with your husband, more than with all other living creatures; moderately loving and intimate with your good and nearest kinsfolk and your husband's kinsfolk; very distant with all other men; and entirely aloof from conceited and idle young men who have more expenses than income, and who, without property or good lineage, go dancing; and also distant from courtiers of very great lords. Moreover, have nothing to do with men and women who are said to lead corrupt, amorous, or dissolute lives.

Concerning what I have said about being very loving to your husband, it is certainly true that every man ought to love and cherish his wife, and every woman should love and cherish her husband: for he is her beginning. I can prove this, for it is found in the second chapter of the first book of the Bible, called Genesis. . . .

Do not think that someone else will hide for you that which you yourself have not been able to conceal. Be secretive and discreet with everyone except your husband. For you should conceal nothing from him, but tell him everything, and he should also tell you everything. . . . You two, man and woman, ought to be as one, and at all times and in all places the one should act on the other's advice. This is how good and wise people act and ought to act. . . .

## HOW GOOD WIVES ACT TOWARD THEIR HUSBANDS, AND GOOD HUSBANDS TOWARD THEIR WIVES, WHEN THEY GO ASTRAY

Husbands ought to hide and conceal the follies of their wives and lovingly protect them from future mistakes, as did an honorable man of Venice.

In that city there was a married couple with three children. As the wife lay on her deathbed, she confessed, among other things, that one of the children was not her husband's. The confessor at length told her that he would seek advice about how to counsel her and return. This confessor went to the doctor who was looking after her and asked the nature of her illness. The doctor said that she would not be able to recover from it. Then the confessor went to her and told her that he didn't see how God would give her salvation unless she begged her husband for forgiveness for the wrong she had done him. She summoned her husband; had everyone removed from the room except her mother and her confessor, who placed her, and held her, on her knees on the bed: and before her husband, with folded hands, humbly begged pardon for having sinned in the law of his marriage and having had one of her children with another man. She would have said more, but her husband cried out: "Stop! Stop!

Stop! Don't say anything else." Then he kissed her and pardoned her, saying: "Say no more. Don't tell me or anyone else which of your children it is; for I want to love each as much as the other—so equally that you will not be blamed during your lifetime or after your death. For through your blame, I will be dishonored, and because of it, your children, and others through them—that is, our relations—will receive vile and everlasting reproach. Therefore, don't say anything. I don't want to know any more. So that no one can ever say that I do wrong by the other two, whichever it is, I will give him in my lifetime what would come to him under our laws of succession."

So, dear sister, you see that the wise man bent his heart to save his wife's reputation, which would affect his children. This shows you what wise men and women ought to do for each other to save their honor.

## CHERISH YOUR HUSBAND'S PERSON CAREFULLY

Dear sister, if you have another husband after me, be aware that you must take very good care of his person. For generally when a woman has lost her first husband and marriage, it is hard for her, depending on her social status, to find a second who is to her liking, and she remains forsaken and helpless for a long time, and even more so when she loses the second. Therefore, cherish your husband's person carefully.

I entreat you to keep his linen clean, for this is up to you. Because the care of outside affairs is men's work, a husband must look after these things, and go and come, run here and there in rain, wind, snow, and hail—sometimes wet, sometimes dry, sometimes sweating, other times shivering, badly fed, badly housed, badly shod, badly bedded—and nothing harms him because he is cheered by the anticipation of the care his wife will take of him on his return—of the pleasures, joys, and comforts she will provide, or have provided for him in her presence:

to have his shoes off before a good fire, to have his feet washed, to have clean shoes and hose, to be well fed, provided with good drink, well served, well honored, well bedded in white sheets and white nightcaps, well covered with good furs, and comforted with other joys and amusements, intimacies, affections, and secrets about which I am silent. And on the next day fresh linen and garments.

Indeed, dear sister, these favors cause a man to love and desire the return home and the sight of his good wife, and to be reserved with others. And so I advise you to comfort your second husband on all his homecomings, and persevere in this.

Also keep peace with him. Remember the country proverb that says there are three things that drive a good man from his home: a house with a bad roof, a smoking chimney, and a quarrelsome woman. Dear sister, I beg you, in order to preserve your husband's love and good will, be loving, amiable, and sweet with him. . . . By my soul! I believe doing good is the only enchantment, and one can no better bewitch a man than by giving him what pleases him.

Therefore, dear sister, I pray you to bewitch and bewitch again the husband whom you will have, preserve him from a badly covered house and a smoky chimney, and be not quarrelsome with him, but be sweet, amiable, and peaceful. Mind that in winter he has a good fire without smoke, and that he is well couched and covered between your breasts, and there bewitch him.

## REVIEW QUESTIONS

1. Evaluate the arguments Jakob Sprenger and Heinrich Krämer used to show that women were naturally deceptive and sinful. What sources did they cite as authorities on the subject?
2. Evaluate the arguments used by Christine de Pisan in her defense of women.
3. Which of the merchant's instructions to his wife do you consider most valuable in a good marriage?

## 10 Medieval Contributions to the Tradition of Liberty

In several ways the Middle Ages contributed to the development of liberty in the Western world. Townsmen organized themselves into revolutionary associations called communes to demand freedom from the domination of feudal lords. They successfully won personal liberties, the end of feudal labor services and arbitrary tax levies, and a system of municipal self-government. Another development crucial to the tradition of liberty was the resistance of lords to kings who attempted to interfere with the lords' customary rights. These actions helped to establish the tradition that kings were not above the law and could not rule arbitrarily or absolutely. There is a direct link between modern parliaments and medieval representative institutions, particularly in the case of the English Parliament.

Medieval theologians made a significant contribution to the growth of liberty. They held that a monarch's powers were limited by God's laws and by what was for the common good of Christian people. Some argued that a monarch who ignored or violated the laws and liberties of the people or the church became a tyrant and forfeited his right to be ruler. Such rulers could be, and some in fact were, deposed.

# John of Salisbury
# *POLICRATICUS*
# A DEFENSE OF TYRANNICIDE

One prelate who opposed the rule of tyrants was an Englishman, John of Salisbury (see page 240), who became bishop of Chartres, France, in 1176. He composed a statesman's handbook, *Policraticus,* explicitly defending the assassination of tyrants. Paraphrasing the Roman statesman Cicero, John held that it was right, lawful, and just to slay a tyrant.

. . . A tyrant, then, as the philosophers have described him, is one who oppresses the people by the rulership based upon force, while he who rules in accordance with the laws is a prince. Law is the gift of God, the model of equity, a standard of justice, a likeness of the divine will, the guardian of well-being, a bond of union and solidarity between peoples, a rule defining duties, a barrier against the vices and the destroyer thereof, a punishment of violence and all wrong-doing. The law is assailed by force or by fraud, and, as it were, either wrecked by the fury of the lion or undermined by the wiles of the serpent. In whatever way this comes to pass, it is plain that it is the grace of God which is being assailed and that it is God himself who in a sense is challenged to battle. The prince fights for the laws and the liberty of the people; the tyrant thinks nothing done unless he brings the laws to nought and reduces the people to slavery. Hence the prince is a kind of likeness of divinity; and the tyrant, on the contrary, a likeness of the boldness of the Adversary [the devil], even of the wickedness of Lucifer. . . . The prince, as the likeness of the Deity, is to be loved, worshipped and cherished; the tyrant, the likeness of wickedness, is generally to be even killed. The origin of tyranny is iniquity, and springing from a poisonous root, it is a tree which grows and sprouts into a baleful pestilent growth, and to which the axe must by all means be laid.

# *MAGNA CARTA*

The feudal nobles sought freedom by limiting the arbitrary powers of the kings, compelling them to issue written charters of liberties. These earliest constitutions spelled out the rights of subjects and the obligations of rulers. In 1215 King John of England (1199–1216) was compelled to recognize the liberties of his vassals, the clergy, and the towns in the Great Charter *(Magna Carta).* The king and his agents were forbidden to act arbitrarily, and the king swore to govern by due process of law. Similar written constitutions checking the powers of kings and princes were achieved in other parts of Europe.

The Magna Carta asserted the feudal rights of the subjects of a monarch who allegedly tried to rule by personal will rather than by law. Though many of its detailed clauses subsequently lost their significance, three notions embedded in the Magna Carta became rooted in English constitutional tradition: that the king cannot levy a tax without the consent of his feudal council (later Parliament); that no one may be imprisoned or otherwise damaged except through due process of law and trial by jury of his (or her) peers; and that the king himself is subject to the law and, if he violates the rights of his subjects, he may be legally disobeyed and deposed. Significant portions of the document follow.

1.  In the first place [I, John,] have granted to God and by this our present Charter have confirmed, for us and our heirs in perpetuity, that the English church shall be free, and shall have its rights undiminished and its liberties unimpaired. . . . We have also granted to all the free men of our realm for ourselves and our heirs for ever, all the liberties written below, to have and hold, them and their heirs from us and our heirs. . . .

12.  No scutage[1] or aid[2] is to be levied in our realm except by the common counsel of our realm, unless it is for the ransom of our person, the knighting of our eldest son or the first marriage of our eldest daughter; and for these only a reasonable aid is to be levied. Aids from the city of London are to be treated likewise.

13.  And the city of London is to have all its ancient liberties and free customs both by land and water. Furthermore, we will and grant that all other cities, boroughs, towns and ports shall have all their liberties and free customs.

14.  And to obtain the common counsel of the realm for the assessment of an aid (except in the three cases aforesaid) or a scutage, we will have archbishops, bishops, abbots, earls and greater barons[3] summoned individually by our letters; and we shall also have summoned generally through our sheriffs and bailiffs[4] all those who hold of us in chief [hold a fief from the king], with at least forty days' notice, and at a fixed place; and in all letters of summons we will state the reason for the summons. And when the summons has thus been made, the business shall go forward on the day arranged according to the counsel of those present, even if not all those summoned have come. . . .

20.  A free man shall not be amerced [fined] for a trivial offence, except in accordance with the degree of the offence; and for a serious offence he shall be amerced according to its gravity, saving his livelihood; and a merchant likewise, saving his merchandise; in the same way a villein [serf] shall be amerced saving his wainage;[5] if they fall into our mercy. And none of the aforesaid amercements shall be imposed except by the testimony of reputable men of the neighbourhood.

21.  Earls and barons shall not be amerced except by their peers and only in accordance with the nature of the offence. . . .

38.  Henceforth no bailiff shall put anyone on trial by his own unsupported allegation, without bringing credible witnesses to the charge.

39.  No free man shall be taken or imprisoned or disseised [dispossessed] or outlawed or

---

[1]Scutage was a tax paid by knights to the king of England, their feudal overlord, in place of performing actual military service. In the absence of danger of war, the levying of scutage was considered an abuse of the king's authority.
[2]Aid, in this sense, was any obligation, usually financial, due from a vassal to his lord. The word was later used to indicate a tax on income or property paid by his subjects to the English king.
[3]Barons were vassals holding fiefs directly from the king; earls ("counts" in other lands) were nobles who managed counties or shires.

[4]The sheriff was a royal official responsible for the carrying out of laws in a shire or county; bailiffs were his assistants.
[5]*Wainage* (or *gainage*) is a collective term meaning farming tools and implements, including such things as wagons (wains).

exiled or in any way ruined, nor will we go or send against him, except by the lawful judgement of his peers or by the law of the land.

40. To no one will we sell, to no one will we deny or delay right or justice.

41. All merchants are to be safe and secure in leaving and entering England, and in staying and travelling in England, both by land and by water, to buy and sell free from all maletotes [unjust taxes] by the ancient and rightful customs, except, in time of war, such as come from an enemy country. And if such are found in our land at the outbreak of war they shall be detained without damage to their persons or goods, until we or our chief justiciar [legal official] know how the merchants of our land are treated in the enemy country; and if ours are safe there, the others shall be safe in our land.

42. Henceforth anyone, saving his allegiance due to us, may leave our realm and return safe and secure by land and water, save for a short period in time of war on account of the general interest of the realm and excepting those imprisoned and outlawed according to the law of the land, and natives of an enemy country, and merchants, who shall be treated as aforesaid. . . .

---

# Edward I of England
# WRITS OF SUMMONS TO PARLIAMENT

The emergence of constitutional government was a major achievement of medieval civilization. The law came to be viewed as a reflection of the moral consent of the whole society rather than the arbitrary will of a despot. The rulers, in principle, governed by consent of the ruled. From the thirteenth century on, that consent was obtained through formal institutions called parliaments or assemblies. In these bodies, members of the different social classes, particularly the clergy, the nobles, small landholders, and townsmen, were present either in person or through their elected representatives. Through the latter, at least some of the populace participated in making new laws, levying taxes, and forming the general policies of the government.

A central principle in calling together assemblies or parliaments was found in Roman law and the canon law of the church: "what affects all should be approved by all" *(Quod omnes tangit ab omnibus approbetur)*. Frequently appearing in medieval documents relating to administration of both church and government, the principle is cited in the first of the following three summonses issued in 1295 by King Edward I (1272–1307), calling on his subjects to attend his parliament at Westminster Palace near London to deal with the threat of war with France. In the first summons, the king calls his ecclesiastical vassal, the archbishop, and other clergymen to a royal meeting.

The King to the venerable father in Christ, Robert, by the same grace Archbishop of Canterbury, primate [presiding bishop] of all England, greeting. As a most just law, established by the careful providence of sacred princes, exhorts and decrees that what affects all, should be approved by all, so also, very evidently should common danger be met by means provided in common. You know sufficiently well, and it is now, as we believe, known through all regions of the world, how the King of France fraudulently and craftily deprived us of our land of Gascony,[1] by withholding it unjustly from us. Now, however, not satisfied with the aforesaid fraud and injustice, having gathered together for the conquest of our kingdom a very great fleet, and a very large force of warriors, with which he has made a hostile attack on our kingdom and the inhabitants of the kingdom, he now proposes to stamp out the English language altogether from the earth if his power should be equal to the detestable task of the proposed iniquity, which God forbid. Because, therefore, darts seen beforehand do less injury, and your interest especially, as that of other fellow citizens of the same realm, is concerned in this affair, we command you, strictly enjoining you in the fidelity and love in which you are bound to us, that on the Lord's day [Sunday] next after the feast of St. Martin [November 11], in the approaching winter, you be present in person at Westminster; citing beforehand the dean [elected head] and chapter [corporate body of clergy] of your church, the archdeacons and all the clergy of your diocese, causing the same dean and archdeacons in their own persons, and the said chapter by one suitable proctor,[2] and the said clergy by two, to be present along with you, having full and sufficient power of themselves from the chapter and clergy, for considering, ordaining and providing along with us and with the rest of the prelates and principal men and other inhabitants of our kingdom how the dangers and threatened evils of this kind are to be met. Witness, the King at Wengham, the thirtieth day of September.

---

The king summons his kinsman and vassal the Earl of Cornwall to meet with the other "principal men" of the kingdom.

---

[1]Gascony was a duchy (dukedom) in the south of France; at this time it was a fief held from the king of France by the king of England, his most powerful vassal.
[2]A proctor in this sense is someone empowered to act for someone else, a proxy.

The King to his beloved and faithful kinsman, Edmund, Earl of Cornwall, greeting. Because we wish to have a conference and meeting with you and with the rest of the principal men of our kingdom, to provide remedies for the dangers which in these days threaten our whole kingdom; we command you, strictly enjoining you by the fidelity and love in which you are bound to us, that on the Lord's day next after the feast of St. Martin, in the approaching winter, you be present in person at Westminster, for considering, ordaining and doing with us, and with the prelates, and the rest of the magnates[3] and other inhabitants of our kingdom, as may be necessary to meet dangers of this kind. Witness, the King at Canterbury, on the first day of October.

---

The king summons, for the first time, representatives of the knightly class and of the non-noble citizens of the towns and cities. Their meeting in 1295 constitutes the first formal session of what will be the Parliament of England, divided into two separate bodies, the House of Lords and the House of Commons.

---

The King to the sheriff of Northamptonshire [a county in central England]. Since we purpose to have a conference and meeting, with the earls, barons, and other principal men of our kingdom to provide remedies for the dangers which in these days threaten the same kingdom; and on that account, have commanded them to be with us, on the Lord's day next after the feast of St. Martin, in the approaching winter, at Westminster, to consider, ordain, and do, as may be necessary for the avoidance of these dangers; we strictly require you to cause two knights from the aforesaid county, two citizens from each city in the same county, and two burgesses from each borough, of the more discreet and capable, to be elected

---

[3]Magnates were any feudal lords whose wealth and military power gave them exceptional political and social importance.

without delay, and to cause them to come to us, at the aforesaid time and place.

Moreover, the said knights are to have full and sufficient power, for themselves and for the commonalty of the aforesaid county, and the said citizens and burgesses for themselves and for the commonalty of the aforesaid cities and boroughs separately, then and there to do what shall be ordained by the common advice in the premises; so that the aforesaid business shall not remain unfinished in any way for defect of this power. And you shall have there the names of the knights, citizens and burgesses, and this writ.

Witness, the King at Canterbury, on the third day of October.

## REVIEW QUESTIONS

1.  How does John of Salisbury distinguish a legitimate king from a tyrant?
2.  Compare John of Salisbury's view of tyranny with Thomas Jefferson's use of the term (see page 407).
3.  In the selected passages of the Magna Carta, what specific liberties were guaranteed by the king to his subjects?
4.  Why are the summonses of Edward I important documents in English constitutional history? What do they reveal about medieval English society?
5.  What medieval political principles appear at the core of modern democratic political theory and institutions?

---

# 11  Fourteenth-Century Pestilence

Until the fourteenth century, the population of Europe had increased steadily from its low point in the centuries immediately following the fall of the Roman Empire in the West. Particularly from the eleventh century on, landlords tried to raise their income by bringing new land into cultivation. By improving farming technology, building dikes, draining marshland, and clearing forests, European peasants produced much more food, which permitted more people to survive and multiply. That advance in population tapered off by the early fourteenth century due to many crop failures and wars, which wasted the countryside and led to economic stagnation. But the greatest catastrophe began in the fall of 1347, when sailors returning to Sicily from eastern Mediterranean ports brought with them a new disease, bubonic plague. Within the next three years, from one quarter to one third of the population of Europe died from what became known, because of some of its symptoms, as the Black Death. Most who caught the plague died, though some survived. No one knew its cause or cure. We now know that the bacteria were transmitted by fleas from infected rats. The unsanitary living conditions of medieval towns and low standards of personal cleanliness helped to spread the disease. The people were so terrified by the incomprehensible pattern of the disease's progress that superstition, hysteria, and breakdown of civility were common.

# Jean de Venette
# THE BLACK DEATH

The progress of the plague as it made its way through Europe and speculation on its causes, the terrible toll of victims, and various moral responses to the crisis are described in the following reading from the chronicle of Jean de Venette, a fourteenth-century French friar who lived through the events described.

In A.D. 1348, the people of France and of almost the whole world were struck by a blow other than war. For in addition to the famine which I described in the beginning and to the wars which I described in the course of this narrative, pestilence and its attendant tribulations appeared again in various parts of the world. . . . All this year and the next, the mortality of men and women, of the young even more than of the old, in Paris and in the kingdom of France, and also, it is said, in other parts of the world, was so great that it was almost impossible to bury the dead. People lay ill little more than two or three days and died suddenly, as it were in full health. He who was well one day was dead the next and being carried to his grave. Swellings appeared suddenly in the armpit or in the groin—in many cases both—and they were infallible signs of death. This sickness or pestilence was called an epidemic by the doctors. Nothing like the great numbers who died in the years 1348 and 1349 has been heard of or seen or read of in times past. This plague and disease came from *ymaginatione* or association and contagion, for if a well man visited the sick he only rarely evaded the risk of death. Wherefore in many towns timid priests withdrew, leaving the exercise of their ministry to such of the religious as were more daring. In many places not two out of twenty remained alive. So high was the mortality at the Hôtel-Dieu [an early hospital] in Paris that for a long time, more than five hundred dead were carried daily with great devotion in carts to the cemetery of the Holy Innocents in Paris for burial. A very great

number of the saintly sisters of the Hôtel-Dieu who, not fearing to die, nursed the sick in all sweetness and humility, with no thought of honor, a number too often renewed by death, rest in peace with Christ, as we may piously believe.

This plague, it is said, began among the unbelievers [Muslims], came to Italy, and then crossing the Alps reached Avignon [site of the papacy in that period], where it attacked several cardinals and took from them their whole household. Then it spread, unforeseen, to France, through Gascony [now part of the south of France] and Spain, little by little, from town to town, from village to village, from house to house, and finally from person to person. It even crossed over to Germany, though it was not so bad there as with us. During the epidemic, God of His accustomed goodness deigned to grant this grace, that however suddenly men died, almost all awaited death joyfully. Nor was there anyone who died without confessing his sins and receiving the holy viaticum [the Eucharistic bread given to the sick or dying]. . . .

Some said that this pestilence was caused by infection of the air and waters, since there was at this time no famine nor lack of food supplies, but on the contrary great abundance. As a result of this theory of infected water and air as the source of the plague the Jews were suddenly and violently charged with infecting wells and water and corrupting the air. The whole world rose up against them cruelly on this account. In Germany and other parts of the world where Jews lived, they were massacred and slaughtered by Christians, and many thousands were burned everywhere, indiscriminately. The unshaken, if fatuous, constancy of the [Jewish] men and their wives was remarkable. For mothers hurled their children first into the fire that they might not be baptized and then leaped in after them to burn with their husbands and children. It is said that many bad Christians were found who in a like manner put poison into wells. But in truth, such poisonings, granted that they actually were perpetrated, could not have caused so great a plague nor have infected so many people. There were other causes; for example, the will of God and the corrupt humors and evil inherent in air and earth. Perhaps the poisonings, if they actually took place in some localities, reenforced these causes. The plague lasted in France for the greater part of the years 1348 and 1349 and then ceased. Many country villages and many houses in good towns remained empty and deserted. Many houses, including some splendid dwellings, very soon fell into ruins. Even in Paris several houses were thus ruined, though fewer here than elsewhere.

After the cessation of the epidemic, pestilence, or plague, the men and women who survived married each other. There was no sterility among the women, but on the contrary fertility beyond the ordinary. Pregnant women were seen on every side. . . . But woe is me! the world was not changed for the better but for the worse by this renewal of population. For men were more avaricious and grasping than before, even though they had far greater possessions. They were more covetous and disturbed each other more frequently with suits, brawls, disputes, and pleas. Nor by the mortality resulting from this terrible plague inflicted by God was peace between kings and lords established. On the contrary, the enemies of the king of France and of the Church were stronger and wickeder than before and stirred up wars on sea and on land. Greater evils than before [swarmed] everywhere in the world. And this fact was very remarkable. Although there was an abundance of all goods, yet everything was

twice as dear, whether it were utensils, victuals, or merchandise, hired helpers or peasants and serfs, except for some hereditary domains which remained abundantly stocked with everything. Charity began to cool, and iniquity with ignorance and sin to abound, for few could be found in the good towns and castles who knew how or were willing to instruct children in the rudiments of grammar.

---

Jean de Venette vividly describes one of the more bizarre reactions to the terrible plague, the sudden appearance of the Flagellants. Marching like pilgrims across the countryside, the Flagellants were a group of laymen and laywomen who sought divine pardon for their sins by preaching repentance to others and scourging themselves in a quasi-liturgical ceremony in local churches or marketplaces. The movement foreshadowed events in which moral, social, and economic discontent would increasingly manifest itself in the form of religiously justified popular uprisings against civil and clerical authorities.

---

In the year 1349, while the plague was still active and spreading from town to town, men in Germany, Flanders, Hainaut [east of Flanders], and Lorraine uprose and began a new sect on their own authority. Stripped to the waist, they gathered in large groups and bands and marched in procession through the crossroads and squares of cities and good towns. There they formed circles and beat upon their backs with weighted scourges, rejoicing as they did so in loud voices and singing hymns suitable to their rite and newly composed for it. Thus for thirty-three days they marched through many towns doing their penance and affording a great spectacle to the wondering people. They flogged their shoulders and arms with scourges tipped with iron points so zealously as to draw blood. But they did not come to Paris nor to any part of France, for they were forbidden to do so by the king of France, who did not want them. He acted on the advice of the masters of theology of the University of Paris, who said that this new sect had been formed contrary to the will of God, to the rites of Holy Mother Church, and to the salvation of all their souls. That indeed this was and is true appeared shortly. For Pope Clement VI was fully informed concerning this fatuous new rite by the masters of Paris through emissaries reverently sent to him and, on the grounds that it had been damnably formed, contrary to law, he forbade the Flagellants under threat of anathema [excommunication] to practise in the future the public penance which they had so presumptuously undertaken. His prohibition was just, for the Flagellants, supported by certain fatuous priests and monks, were enunciating doctrines and opinions which were beyond measure evil, erroneous, and fallacious. For example, they said that their blood thus drawn by the scourge and poured out was mingled with the blood of Christ. Their many errors showed how little they knew of the Catholic faith. Wherefore, as they had begun fatuously of themselves and not of God, so in a short time they were reduced to nothing. On being warned, they desisted and humbly received absolution and penance at the hands of their prelates as the pope's representatives. Many honorable women and devout matrons, it must be added, had done this penance with scourges, marching and singing through towns and churches like the men, but after a little like the others they desisted.

## REVIEW QUESTIONS

1. In the absence of any scientific knowledge about the nature and causes of the bubonic plague, how did the populace react to the mysterious spread of the disease?
2. In the chronicler's opinion, what were some of the long-term moral, social, and economic consequences of the plague?
3. Why did church authorities take steps to suppress the Flagellant movement?

---

## 12  Lower-Class Rebellions

At times the discontent of European lower classes in town and countryside erupted into rebellions against the ruling authorities. One reason for the discontent of urban laborers and artisans was their exclusion from town affairs by the wealthy merchants and bankers who controlled municipal government. Peasants wanted to end their heavy obligations to lords who exploited their labor and dominated their personal lives. Over the centuries, peasants gained greater personal liberty by purchasing the lords' rights over them, by escaping to towns, or by moving to new lands where ties to lords were less burdensome. At times, peasants resorted to violence in order to gain concessions from lords.

# Sir John Froissart
# THE PEASANT REVOLT OF 1381

In 1381, a rebellion of peasants and poor artisans in England threatened the political power of the ruling class. The rebellion, which was crushed and whose leaders were betrayed and executed, revealed the massive discontent of the lower classes and the specter of social upheaval that hovered over late medieval society. The following account of the rebellion is by Sir John Froissart (c. 1337–c. 1410), a French historian and poet who chronicled the Hundred Years' War between France and England, which wreaked havoc in the countries concerned.

While these conferences [of English nobles] were going forward there happened great commotions among the lower orders in England, by which that country was nearly ruined. In order that this disastrous rebellion may serve as an example to mankind, I will speak of all that was done from the information I had at the time. It is customary in England, as well as in several other countries, for the nobility to have great privileges over the commonality; that is to say, the lower orders are bound by law to plough the lands of the gentry, to harvest their grain, to carry it home to the barn, to thrash and winnow it; they are also bound to harvest and carry home the hay. All these services the prelates and gentlemen exact of their inferiors; and in the counties of Kent, Essex, Sussex, and Bedford, these services are more oppressive than in other parts of the kingdom. In consequence of this the evil[ly] disposed in these districts began to murmur, saying, that in the beginning of the world there were no slaves, and that no one ought to be treated as such, unless he had committed treason against his lord, as Lucifer had done against God; but they had done no such thing, for they were neither angels nor spirits, but men formed after the same likeness as these lords who treated them as beasts. This they would bear no longer; they were determined to be free, and if they laboured or did any work, they would be paid for it. A crazy priest in the county of Kent, called John Ball, who for his absurd preaching had thrice been confined in prison by the Archbishop of Canterbury, was greatly instrumental in exciting these rebellious ideas. Every Sunday after mass, as the people were coming out of church, this John Ball was accustomed to assemble a crowd around him in the marketplace and preach to them. On such occasions he would say, "My good friends, matters cannot go on well in England until all things shall be in common; when there shall be neither vassals nor lords; when the lords shall be no more masters than ourselves. How ill they behave to us! for what reason do they thus hold us in bondage? Are we not all descended from the same parents, Adam and Eve? And what can they show, or what reason can they give, why they should be more masters than ourselves? They are clothed in velvet and rich stuffs, ornamented with ermine and other furs, while we are forced to wear poor clothing. They have wines, spices, and fine bread, while we have only rye and the refuse of the straw; and when we drink, it must be water. They have handsome seats and manors, while we must brave the wind and rain in our labours in the field; and it is by our labour they have wherewith to support their pomp. We are called slaves, and if we do not perform our service we are beaten, and we have no sovereign to whom we can complain or who would be willing to hear us. Let us go to the king and remonstrate with him; he is young, and from him we may obtain a favourable answer, and if not we must ourselves seek to amend our condition." With such language as this did John Ball harangue the people of his village every Sunday after mass. The archbishop, on being informed of it, had him arrested and imprisoned for two or three months by way of punishment; but the moment he was out of prison, he returned to his former course. Many in the city of London envious of the rich and noble, having heard of John Ball's preaching, said among themselves that the country was badly governed, and that the nobility had seized upon all the gold and silver. These wicked Londoners, therefore, began to assemble in parties, and to show signs of rebellion; they also invited all those who held like opinions in the adjoining counties to come to London; telling them that they would find the town open to them and the commonalty of the same way of thinking as themselves, and that they would so press the king, that there should no longer be a slave in England.

By this means the men of Kent, Essex, Sussex, Bedford, and the adjoining counties, in number about 60,000, were brought to London, under command of Wat Tyler, Jack Straw, and John Ball. This Wat Tyler, who was chief of the three, had been a tiler of houses—a bad man and a great enemy to the nobility. . . .

With regard to the common people of London, numbers entertained these rebellious opinions, and on assembling at the bridge asked of the guards, "Why will you refuse admittance to these honest men? they are our friends, and what they are doing is for our good." So urgent were they, that it was found necessary to open the gates, when crowds rushed in and took possession of those shops which seemed best stocked with provisions; indeed, wherever they went, meat and drink were placed before them, and nothing was refused in the hope of appeasing them. Their leaders, John Ball, Jack Straw, and Wat Tyler, then marched through London, attended by more than 20,000 men, to the palace of the Savoy, which is a handsome building belonging to the Duke of Lancaster [the king's uncle], situated on the banks of the Thames on the road to Westminster: here they immediately killed the porters, pushed into the house, and set it on fire. Not content with this outrage, they went to the house of the Knight-hospitalers of Rhodes, dedicated to St. John of Mount Carmel, which they burnt together with their church and hospital.

After this they paraded the streets, and killed every Fleming [citizen of Flanders] they could find, whether in house, church, or hospital: they broke open several houses of the Lombards [Italian bankers], taking whatever money they could lay their hands upon. They murdered a rich citizen, by name Richard Lyon, to whom Wat Tyler had formerly been servant in France, but having once beaten him, the [scoundrel] had never forgotten it; and when he had carried his men to his house, he ordered his head to be cut off, placed upon a pike, and carried through the streets of London. Thus did these wicked people act, and on this Thursday they did much damage to the city of London. Towards evening they fixed their quarters in a square, called St. Catherine's, before the Tower, declaring that they would not depart until they had obtained from the king every thing they wanted—until the Chancellor [chief financial officer] of England had accounted to them, and shown how the great sums which were raised had been expended. Considering the mischief which the mob had already done, you may easily imagine how miserable, at this time, was the situation of the king and those who were with him. . . .

. . . Now observe how fortunately matters turned out, for had these scoundrels succeeded in their intentions, all the nobility of England would have been destroyed; and after such success as this the people of other nations would have rebelled also, taking example from those of Ghent and Flanders, who at the time were in actual rebellion against their lord; the Parisians indeed the same year acted in a somewhat similar manner; upwards of 20,000 of them armed themselves with leaden maces and caused a rebellion. . . .

## REVIEW QUESTIONS

1. What specific grievances motivated uprisings in England and France in the late fourteenth century?
2. What political principles were invoked by the leaders of the rebellion of 1381 to justify their demands and actions?

# 13  The Medieval World-View

The modern world is linked in many ways to the Middle Ages. European cities, the middle class, the state system, English common law, representative institutions, universities—all had their origins in the Middle Ages. Despite these elements of continuity, the characteristic outlook of medieval people is markedly different from that of people today. Whereas science and secularism shape the modern point of view, religion was the foundation of the Middle Ages. Christian beliefs as formulated by the church made life and death purposeful and intelligible.

Medieval thinkers drew a sharp distinction between a higher, spiritual world and a lower, material world. God, the creator of the universe and the source of moral values, dwelled in the higher celestial world, an abode of perfection. The universe was organized as a hierarchy with God at the summit and hell at the other extremity. Earth, composed of base matter, stood just above hell. By believing in Christ and adhering to God's commandments as taught by the church, people could overcome their sinful nature and ascend to God's world. Sinners, on the other hand, would descend to hell, a fearful place the existence of which medieval people never doubted.

Scholastic philosophy, which sought to demonstrate through reason the truth of Christian doctrines, and the Gothic cathedral, which seemed to soar from the material world to heaven, were two great expressions of the medieval mind. A third was *The Divine Comedy* of Dante Alighieri, the greatest literary figure of the Middle Ages.

# Lothario dei Segni (Pope Innocent III)
# *ON THE MISERY OF THE HUMAN CONDITION*

At the center of medieval belief was the image of a perfect God and a wretched and sinful human being. God had given Adam and Eve freedom to choose; rebellious and presumptuous, they had used their freedom to disobey God. In doing so, they made evil an intrinsic part of the human personality. But God, who had not stopped loving human beings, showed them the way out of sin. God became man and died so that human beings might be saved. Men and women were weak, egocentric, and sinful. With God's grace they could overcome their sinful nature and gain salvation; without grace they were utterly helpless. A classic expression of this pessimistic view of human nature was written in the late twelfth century by an Italian canon lawyer, Lothario dei Segni (c. 1160–1216), who was later elected pope in 1198, taking the name Innocent III. *On the Misery of the Human Condition* was enormously popular and inspired numerous rhetorical writings on the same theme as late as the seventeenth century. Scattered excerpts follow.

• For sure man was formed out of earth, conceived in guilt, born to punishment. What he does is depraved and illicit, is shameful and improper, vain and unprofitable. He will become fuel for the eternal fires, food for worms, a mass of rottenness.

I shall try to make my explanation clearer and my treatment fuller. Man was formed of dust, slime, and ashes; what is even more vile, of the filthiest seed. He was conceived from the itch of the flesh, in the heat of passion and the stench of lust, and worse yet, with the stain of sin. He was born to toil, dread, and trouble; and more wretched still, was born only to die. He commits depraved acts by which he offends God, his neighbor, and himself; shameful acts by which he defiles his name, his person, and his conscience; and vain acts by which he ignores all things important, useful, and necessary. He will become fuel for those fires which are forever hot and burn forever bright; food for the worm which forever nibbles and digests; a mass of rottenness which will forever stink and reek.

• A bird is born to fly; man is born to toil. All his days are full of toil and hardship, and at night his mind has no rest.

• How much anxiety tortures mortals! They suffer all kinds of cares, are burdened with worry, tremble and shrink with fears and terrors, are weighted down with sorrow. Their nervousness makes them depressed, and their depression makes them nervous. Rich or poor, master or slave, married or single, good and bad alike—all suffer worldly torments and are tormented by worldly vexations.

• For sudden sorrow always follows worldly joy: what begins in gaiety ends in grief. Worldly happiness is besprinkled indeed with much bitterness.

• Then, suddenly, when least expected, misfortune strikes, a calamity befalls us, disease attacks; or death, which no one can escape, carries us off.

• Men strive especially for three things: riches, pleasures, and honors. Riches lead to immorality, pleasures to shame, and honors to vanity.

• But suppose a man is lifted up high, suppose he is raised to the very peak. At once his cares grow heavy, his worries mount up, he eats less and cannot sleep. And so nature is corrupted, his spirit weakened, his sleep disturbed, his appetite lost; his strength is diminished, he loses weight. Exhausting himself, he scarcely lives half a lifetime and ends his wretched days with a more wretched death.

• Almost the whole life of mortals is full of mortal sin, so that one can scarcely find anyone who does not go astray, does not return to his own vomit and rot in his own dung. Instead they "are glad when they have done evil and rejoice in most wicked things." "Being filled with all iniquity, malice, fornication, avarice, wickedness, full of envy, murders, contention, deceit, evil, being whisperers, detractors, hateful to God, irreverent, proud, haughty, plotters of evil, disobedient to parents, foolish, dissolute, without affection, without fidelity, without mercy." This world is full of such and worse; it abounds in heretics and schismatics [Christians who reject the authority of the pope], traitors and tyrants, simonists [buyers or sellers of spiritual offices or sacred items] and hypocrites; the ambitious and the covetous, robbers and brigands, violent men, extortionists, usurers, forgers; the impious and sacreligious, the betrayers and liars, the flatterers and deceivers; gossips, tricksters, gluttons, drunkards; adulterers, incestuous men, deviates, and the dirty-minded; the lazy, the careless, the vain, the prodigal, the impetuous, the irascible, the impatient and inconstant; poisoners, fortune tellers, perjurers, cursers; men who are presumptuous and arrogant, unbelieving and desperate; and finally those ensnared in all vices together.

# Dante Alighieri
## *THE DIVINE COMEDY*

Dante Alighieri was a poet, political philosopher, soldier, and politician. Born in 1265 in Florence, Italy, he died in exile in 1321. His greatest work, *The Divine Comedy,* was composed of one hundred cantos (individual poems) and written not in Latin, the language of learning, but in the Tuscan Italian dialect of the common people. The poem is an elaborate allegory in which each character and event can be understood on two or more levels—for example, a literal description of the levels of hell and Dante's (and every Christian's) struggle to overcome a flawed human nature and to ward off worldly sin. Dante, representing all human beings, is guided through the afterworlds: hell (inferno), purgatory, and heaven (paradise). The Roman poet Virgil conducts him through hell and purgatory; Beatrice, his long-dead beloved, leads him through heaven to the point where he sees God in all his glory.

In the descent through the nine concentric circles of hell, Virgil describes the nature and significance of each region through which they pass. In each section of hell, sinners are punished in proportion to their earthly sins. Over the entrance gate to hell, Dante reads these words:

THROUGH ME YOU GO INTO THE CITY OF
    GRIEF,
THROUGH ME YOU GO INTO THE PAIN THAT
    IS ETERNAL,
THROUGH ME YOU GO AMONG PEOPLE LOST.

JUSTICE MOVED MY EXALTED CREATOR;
THE DIVINE POWER MADE ME,
THE SUPREME WISDOM, AND THE PRIMAL
    LOVE.

BEFORE ME ALL CREATED THINGS WERE
    ETERNAL,
AND ETERNAL I WILL LAST.
ABANDON EVERY HOPE, YOU WHO ENTER
    HERE.

---

Dante descends from the first circle to the second circle, where he finds the souls of those who had been guilty of sins of the flesh.

---

Now I begin to hear the sad notes of pain,
now I have come to where
loud cries beat upon my ears.

I have reached a place mute of all light
which roars like the sea in a tempest
when beaten by conflicting winds.

The infernal storm which never stops
drives the spirit in its blast;
whirling and beating, it torments them.

When they come in front of the landslide,
they utter laments, moans, and shrieks;
there they curse the Divine Power.

I learned that to such a torment
carnal sinners are condemned
who subject their reason to desire.

And, as starlings are borne by their wings
in the cold season, in a broad and dense flock,
so that blast carries the evil spirits.

Here, there, up, and down, it blows them;
no hope ever comforts them
of rest or even of less pain.

And as cranes go chanting their lays,
making a long line of themselves in the air,
so I saw coming, uttering laments,

shades borne by that strife of winds.

---

Finally the two poets reach the ninth and lowest circle, a frozen wasteland reserved for Satan and traitors.

---

". . . look ahead,"
my master [Virgil] said, "and try to discern him."

As, when a thick mist covers the land
or when night darkens our hemisphere,
a windmill, turning, appears from afar,

so now I seemed to see such a structure;
then because of the wind, I drew back
behind my guide, for there was no other
    protection.

Already—and with fear I put it into verse—
I was where the shades are covered in the ice
and show through like bits of straw in glass.

Some were lying, some standing erect,
some on their heads, others on their feet,
still others like a bow bent face to toes.

When we had gone so far ahead
that my master was pleased to show me
the creature (Lucifer)[1] that once had been so
    fair,

he stood from in front of me, and made me
    stop,
saying, "Behold, Dis![2] Here is the place
where you must arm yourself with courage."

How faint and frozen I then became,
do not ask, Reader, for I do not write it down,
since all words would be inadequate.

I did not die and did not stay alive:
think now for yourself, if you have the wit,
how I became, without life or death.

The emperor of the dolorous realm
from mid-breast protruded from the ice,
and I compare better in size

with the giants than they do with his arms.
Consider how big the whole must be,
proportioned as it is to such a part.

If he were once as handsome as he is ugly now,
and still presumed to lift his hand against his
    Maker,
all affliction must indeed come from him.

Oh, how great a marvel appeared to me
when I saw three faces on his head!
The one in front (hatred) was fiery red;

the two others which were joined to it
over the middle of each shoulder
were fused together at the top.

The right one (impotence) seemed between
    white and yellow;
the left (ignorance) was in color like those
who come from where the Nile rises.

Under each two great wings spread
of a size fitting to such a bird;
I have never seen such sails on the sea.

They had no feathers, and seemed
like those of a bat, and they flapped,
so that three blasts came from them.

Thence all Cocytus[3] was frozen.
With six eyes he wept, and over his three chins
he let tears drip and bloody foam.

In each mouth he chewed a sinner with his
    teeth
in the manner of a hemp brake,[4]
so that he kept three in pain.

---

[1]Lucifer (light-bringer) was an archangel who led a rebellion against God and was cast into hell for punishment. He was identified with Satan.
[2]Dis was another name for Pluto or Hades, the god of the dead and ruler of the underworld.

[3]The Cocytus, a river in western Greece, was alleged to lead to the underworld.
[4]A hemp brake was a tool used to break up hemp fibers so that they could be made into rope.

To the one in front the biting was nothing
compared to the scratching, for at times,
his back was stripped of skin.

"The soul up there with the greatest
    punishment,"
said my master, "is Judas Iscariot.[5] His head
is inside the mouth, and he kicks with his
    legs.

Of the other two whose heads are down,
the one hanging from the black face is
    Brutus;[6]
see how he twists and says nothing.

The other who seems so heavy set is Cassius.[7]
But night is rising again now,
and it is time to leave, for we have seen all."

---

Dante and Beatrice make the ascent to the
highest heaven, the Empyrean, which is located beyond Saturn, the last of the seven
planets, beyond the circle of stars that en-
closes the planets, and above the Primum
Mobile—the outermost sphere revolving
around the earth. Here at the summit of the
universe is a realm of pure light that radi-
ates truth, goodness, and happiness, where
God is found. Dante is permitted to look at
God, but words cannot describe "the glory
of Him who moves us all."

---

For my sight, growing pure, penetrated
ever deeper into the rays
of the Light [God] which is true in Itself.

From then on my vision was greater
than our speech which fails at such a sight,
just as memory is overcome by the excess.

As one who in a dream sees clearly,
and the feeling impressed remains afterward,
although nothing else comes back to mind,

so am I; for my vision disappears
almost wholly, and yet the sweetness
caused by it is still distilled within my heart.

Thus, in sunlight, the snow melts away;
thus the sayings of the Sibyl [a Roman
    oracle], written
on light leaves, were lost in the wind.

O Supreme Light that risest so high
above mortal concepts, give back to my mind
a little of what Thou didst appear,

and make my tongue strong,
so that it may leave to future peoples
at least a spark of Thy glory!

For, by returning to my memory
and by sounding a little in these verses
more of Thy victory will be conceived.

By the keenness of the living ray I endured
I believe I would have been dazed
if my eyes had turned away from it;

and I remember that I was bolder
because of that to sustain the view
until my sight *attained* the Infinite Worth
    [God].

O abundant grace through which I presumed
to fix my eyes on the Eternal Light
so long that I consumed my vision on it!

In its depths I saw contained, bound with love
in one volume, what is scattered
on leaves throughout the world—

substances (things) and accidents (qualities)
    and their modes
as if fused together in such a way
that what I speak of is a single light.

The universal form (principle) of this unity
I believe I saw, because more abundantly
in saying this I feel that I rejoice.

---

[5]Judas Iscariot was the disciple who betrayed Jesus to the
authorities.
[6]Brutus, a first-century Roman statesman, conspired to
murder Julius Caesar.
[7]Cassius, another Roman statesman, was a co-conspirator
with Brutus.

One moment obscures more for me than
    twenty-five centuries
have clouded since the adventure which made
    Neptune [the sea god]
wonder at the shadow of the Argo (the first
    ship).[8]

Thus my mind with rapt attention
gazed fixedly, motionless and attentive,
continually enflamed by its very gazing.

In that light we become such
that we can never consent
to turn from it for another sight,

inasmuch as the good which is the object
of the will is all in it, and outside of it
whatever is perfect there is defective.

Now my speech, even for what I remember,
will be shorter than that of an infant
who still bathes his tongue at the breast.

Not that more than a single semblance
was in the living light I gazed upon
(for it is always as it was before),

but in my vision which gained strength
as I looked the single appearance,
through a change in me, was transformed.

Within the deep and clear subsistence
of the great light three circles of three colors
and of one dimension (the Trinity) appeared to
    me,

and one (the Son) seemed reflected from the
    other (the Father)

as Iris by Iris,[9] and the third (the Holy Spirit)
seemed fire emanating equally from both.

O how poor our speech is and how feeble
for my conception! Compared to what I saw
to say its power is "little" is to say too much.

O Eternal Light (Father), abiding in Thyself
    alone,
Thou (Son) alone understanding Thyself, and
    Thou (Holy Spirit)

understood only by Thee, Thou dost love and
    smile!

The circle which appeared in Thee
as a reflected light (the Son)
when contemplated a while

seemed depicted with our image within itself
and of its own (the Circle's) color,
so that my eyes were wholly fixed on it.

Like the geometer who strives
to square the circle and cannot find
by thinking the principle he needs

I was at that new sight. I wanted to see
how the (human) image was conformed
to the (divine) circle and has a place in it,

but my own wings were not enough for
    that—
except that my mind was illuminated by a
    flash
(of Grace) through which its wish was
    realized.

For the great imagination here power failed;
but already my desire and will (in harmony)
were turning like a wheel moved evenly

by the Love which turns the sun and the other
    stars.

---

[8]The *Argo,* in Greek legends, was the ship in which the hero Jason and his companions sailed in search of the Golden Fleece. A Greek poet, Apollonius of Rhodes, wrote an epic poem, the *Argonautica,* about it in the mid-third century B.C.

[9]Iris, goddess of the rainbow, was the messenger of the gods.

JAN VAN EYCK, *The Last Judgment,* c. 1422–1441, tempera and oil on canvas, transferred to wood. *(The Metropolitan Museum of Art, Fletcher Fund, 1933)*

# Van Eyck
## *THE LAST JUDGMENT*

In *The Last Judgment* (c. 1420–1425), Hubert or Jan Van Eyck (Flemish painters and brothers, one of whom is thought to have painted this work) provided a clear visual image of the medieval world-view—a universe centered around God, whose creatures are defined by their relationship with him. Van Eyck depicted what to the medieval mind was the culminating event in history, that moment when Christ returns, judges humanity, separates the saved from the damned, consigns them either to an eternity in heaven or hell, and brings time and the world to an end.

Van Eyck also graphically revealed the medieval vision of a hierarchical space reaching upward to an apex in God and heaven and downward to Satan and the pit of hell. The painting is divided by a horizon line into two contrasting halves, the upper half representing heaven, the lower half hell. Above the horizon everything is clear, orderly, symmetrical, and calm as the saved gather around the throne of Christ, flanked by the angels and apostles. Below the horizon everything is murky, turbulent, and chaotic as human figures are seen plunging into the horrors of hell. The entire scene is charged with a violent downward hysterical motion spreading out into formlessness, as human shapes are progressively entangled with monstrous forms.

## *REVIEW QUESTIONS*

1. Compare Innocent III's view of the human condition with that of ancient Greeks such as Homer, Pindar, and Sophocles. What comfort did each offer for the tragic nature of the human condition?
2. How did Dante conceive the nature of evil and the moral ordering of specific sins?
3. Van Eyck's painting *The Last Judgment* is a visual summary of Christian doctrines. Using the specific detail seen in the painting, spell out the details of the Christian teachings. Then, taking the picture in its entirety, explain how it exemplifies the medieval view of the world.
4. Write an essay on the medieval view of the human condition and its relation to the idea of God. Cite at least three sources from your reading to illustrate your viewpoint.

CHAPTER 9

# The Renaissance

THE TRIUMPH OF GALETEA, Raphael, 1513. This fresco from the Palazzo della Farnesina in Rome exemplifies the Renaissance artist's elevation of the human form. The mythological subject is also humanistic in its evocation of the ancient Greek tradition. *(Giraudon/Art Resource, N.Y.)*

From the fifteenth through the seventeenth centuries, medieval attitudes and institutions broke down, and distinctly modern cultural, economic, and political forms emerged. For many historians, the Renaissance, which originated in the city-states of Italy, marks the starting point of the modern era. The Renaissance was characterized by a rebirth of interest in the humanist culture and outlook of ancient Greece and Rome. Although Renaissance individuals did not repudiate Christianity, they valued worldly activities and interests to a much greater degree than did the people of the Middle Ages, whose outlook was dominated by Christian otherworldliness. Renaissance individuals were fascinated by *this* world and by life's possibilities; they aspired to live a rich and creative life on earth and to fulfill themselves through artistic and literary activity.

Individualism was a hallmark of the Renaissance. The urban elite sought to demonstrate their unique talents, to assert their own individuality, and to gain recognition for their accomplishments. The most admired person during the Renaissance was the multi-talented individual, the "universal man," who distinguished himself as a writer, artist, linguist, athlete. Disdaining Christian humility, Renaissance individuals took pride in their talents and worldly accomplishments—"I can work miracles," said the great Leonardo da Vinci.

During the High Middle Ages there had been a revival of Greek and Roman learning. Yet there were two important differences between the period called the Twelfth-Century Awakening and the Renaissance. First, many more ancient works were restored to circulation during the Renaissance than during the cultural revival of the Middle Ages. Second, medieval scholastics had tried to fit the ideas of the ancients into a Christian framework; they used Greek philosophy to explain Christian teachings. Renaissance scholars, on the other hand, valued ancient works for their own sake, believing that Greek and Roman authors could teach much about the art of living.

A distinguishing feature of the Renaissance period was the humanist movement, an educational and cultural program based on the study of ancient Greek and Latin literature. By studying the humanities—history, literature, rhetoric, moral and political philosophy—humanists aimed to revive the worldly spirit of the ancient Greeks and Romans, which they believed had been lost in the Middle Ages.

Humanists were thus fascinated by the writings of the ancients. From the works of Thucydides, Plato, Cicero, Seneca, and other ancient authors, humanists sought guidelines for living life well in this world and looked for stylistic models for their own literary efforts. To the humanists, the ancients had written brilliantly, in an incomparable literary style, on friendship, citizenship, love, bravery, statesmanship, beauty, excellence, and every other topic devoted to the enrichment of human life.

Like the humanist movement, Renaissance art also marked a break with medieval culture. The art of the Middle Ages had served a religious function; its purpose was to lift the mind to God. It depicted a spiritual universe in which the supernatural was the supreme reality. The Gothic cathedral, with its flying buttresses, soared toward heaven, rising in ascending tiers; it reflected the medieval conception of a hierarchical universe with God at its apex. Painting also expressed gradations of spiritual values. Traditionally, the left side of a painting portrayed the damned, the right side the saved; dark colors expressed evil, light colors good. Spatial proportion was relative to spirituality—the less spiritually valuable a thing was, the less form it had (or the more deformed it was). Medieval art perfectly expressed the Christian view of the universe and the individual. The Renaissance shattered the dominance of religion over art, shifting attention from heaven to the natural world and to the human being; Renaissance artists often dealt with religious themes, but they placed their subjects in a naturalistic setting. Renaissance art also developed a new concept of visual space that was defined from the standpoint of the individual observer. It was a quantitative space in which the artist, employing reason and mathematics, portrayed the essential form of the object as it appeared in three dimensions to the human eye, that is, it depicted the object in perspective.

The Renaissance began in the middle of the fourteenth century in the northern Italian city-states, which had grown prosperous from the revival of trade in the Middle Ages. Italian merchants and bankers had the wealth to acquire libraries and fine works of art and to support art, literature, and scholarship. Surrounded by reminders of ancient Rome—amphitheaters, monuments, and sculpture—the well-to-do took an interest in classical culture and thought. In the late fifteenth and the sixteenth centuries, Renaissance ideas spread to Germany, France, Spain, and England through books available in great numbers due to the invention of the printing press.

# 1 The Humanists' Fascination with Antiquity

Humanists believed that a refined person must know the literature of Greece and Rome. They strove to imitate the style of the ancients, to speak and write as eloquently as the Greeks and Romans. Toward these ends, they sought to read, print, and restore to circulation every scrap of ancient literature that could still be found.

# Petrarch
# THE FATHER OF HUMANISM

During his lifetime, Francesco Petrarca, or Petrarch (1304–1374), had an astounding reputation as a poet and scholar. Often called the "father of humanism," he inspired other humanists through his love for classical learning; his criticism of medieval Latin as barbaric in contrast to the style of Cicero, Seneca, and other Romans; and his literary works based on classical models. Petrarch saw his own age as a restoration of classical brilliance after an interval of medieval darkness.

A distinctly modern element in Petrarch's thought is the subjective and individualistic character of his writing. In talking about himself and probing his own feelings, Petrarch demonstrates a self-consciousness characteristic of the modern outlook.

Like many other humanists, Petrarch remained devoted to Christianity: "When it comes to thinking or speaking of religion, that is, of the highest truth, of true happiness and eternal salvation," he declared, "I certainly am not a Ciceronian or a Platonist but a Christian." Petrarch was a forerunner of the Christian humanism best represented by Erasmus. Christian humanists combined an intense devotion to Christianity with a great love for classical literature, which they much preferred to the dull and turgid treatises written by scholastic philosophers and theologians. In the following passage, Petrarch criticizes his contemporaries for their ignorance of ancient writers and shows his commitment to classical learning.

. . . O inglorious age! that scorns antiquity, its mother, to whom it owes every noble art—that dares to declare itself not only equal but superior to the glorious past. I say nothing of the vulgar, the dregs of mankind, whose sayings and opinions may raise a laugh but hardly merit serious censure. . . .

. . . But what can be said in defense of men of education who ought not to be ignorant of antiquity and yet are plunged in this same darkness and delusion?

You see that I cannot speak of these matters without the greatest irritation and indignation. There has arisen of late a set of dialecticians [experts in logical argument], who are not only ignorant but demented. Like a black army of ants from some old rotten oak, they swarm forth from their hiding places and devastate the fields of sound learning. They condemn Plato and Aristotle, and laugh at Socrates and Pythagoras.[1] And, good God! under what silly and incompetent leaders these opinions are put forth. . . . What shall we say of men who scorn Marcus Tullius Cicero,[2] the bright sun of eloquence? Of those who scoff at Varro and Seneca,[3] and are scandalized at what

---

[1]The work of Aristotle (384–322 B.C.), a leading Greek philosopher, had an enormous influence among medieval and Renaissance scholars. A student of the philosopher Socrates, Plato (c. 427–347 B.C.) was one of the greatest philosophers of ancient Greece. His work grew to be extremely influential in the West during the Renaissance period, as new texts of his writings were discovered and translated into Latin and more Westerners could read the originals in Greek. Pythagoras (c. 582–c. 507 B.C.) was a Greek philosopher whose work influenced both Socrates and Plato.

[2]Cicero (106–43 B.C.) was a Roman statesman and rhetorician. His Latin style was especially admired and emulated during the Renaissance.

[3]Varro (116–27 B.C.) was a Roman scholar and historian. Seneca (4 B.C.–A.D. 65) was a Roman statesman, dramatist, and Stoic philosopher whose literary style was greatly admired during the Renaissance.

they choose to call the crude, unfinished style of Livy and Sallust [Roman historians]? . . .

Such are the times, my friend, upon which we have fallen; such is the period in which we live and are growing old. Such are the critics of today, as I so often have occasion to lament and complain—men who are innocent of knowledge and virtue, and yet harbour the most exalted opinion of themselves. Not content with losing the words of the ancients, they must attack their genius and their ashes. They rejoice in their ignorance, as if what they did not know were not worth knowing. They give full rein to their license and conceit, and freely introduce among us new authors and outlandish teachings.

# Leonardo Bruni
# STUDY OF GREEK LITERATURE AND A HUMANIST EDUCATIONAL PROGRAM

Leonardo Bruni (1374–1444) was a Florentine humanist who extolled both intellectual study and active involvement in public affairs, an outlook called civic humanism. In the first reading from his *History of His Own Times in Italy*, Bruni expresses the humanist's love for ancient Greek literature and language.

In a treatise, *De Studiis et Literis (On Learning and Literature)*, addressed to the noble lady Baptista di Montefeltro (1383–1450), daughter of the Count of Urbino, Bruni outlines the basic course of studies that the humanists recommended as the best preparation for a life of wisdom and virtue. In addition to the study of Christian literature, Bruni encourages a wide familiarity with the best minds and stylists of ancient Greek and Latin cultures.

## LOVE FOR GREEK LITERATURE

Then first came a knowledge of Greek, which had not been in use among us for seven hundred years. Chrysoloras the Byzantine,[1] a man of noble birth and well versed in Greek letters, brought Greek learning to us. When his country was invaded by the Turks, he came by sea, first to Venice. The report of him soon spread, and he was cordially invited and besought and promised a public stipend, to come to Florence and open his store of riches to the youth. I was then studying Civil Law,[2] but . . . I burned with love of academic studies, and had spent no little pains on dialectic and rhetoric. At the coming of Chrysoloras I was torn in mind, deeming it shameful to desert the law, and yet a crime to lose such a chance of studying Greek literature; and often with youthful impulse I would say to myself: "Thou, when it is permitted thee to gaze on Homer, Plato and Demosthenes,[3] and the other [Greek] poets, philosophers, orators, of whom such glorious things are spread abroad, and speak with them and be instructed in their admirable teaching, wilt thou desert and rob thyself? Wilt thou neglect this opportunity so divinely offered? For seven hundred years, no one in Italy has possessed Greek letters; and yet we confess that all

[1]Chrysoloras (c. 1355–1415), a Byzantine writer and teacher, introduced the study of Greek literature to the Italians, helping to open a new age of Western humanistic learning.
[2]Civil Law refers to the Roman law as codified by Emperor Justinian in the early sixth century A.D. and studied in medieval law schools.

[3]Demosthenes (384–322 B.C.) was an Athenian statesman and orator whose oratorical style was much admired by Renaissance humanists.

knowledge is derived from them. How great advantage to your knowledge, enhancement of your fame, increase of your pleasure, will come from an understanding of this tongue? There are doctors of civil law everywhere; and the chance of learning will not fail thee. But if this one and only doctor of Greek letters disappears, no one can be found to teach thee." Overcome at length by these reasons, I gave myself to Chrysoloras, with such zeal to learn, that what through the wakeful day I gathered, I followed after in the night, even when asleep.

## ON LEARNING AND LITERATURE

. . . The foundations of all true learning must be laid in the sound and thorough knowledge of Latin: which implies study marked by a broad spirit, accurate scholarship, and careful attention to details. Unless this solid basis be secured it is useless to attempt to rear an enduring edifice. Without it the great monuments of literature are unintelligible, and the art of composition impossible. To attain this essential knowledge we must never relax our careful attention to the grammar of the language, but perpetually confirm and extend our acquaintance with it until it is thoroughly our own. . . . To this end we must be supremely careful in our choice of authors, lest an inartistic and debased style infect our own writing and degrade our taste; which danger is best avoided by bringing a keen, critical sense to bear upon select works, observing the sense of each passage, the structure of the sentence, the force of every word down to the least important particle. In this way our reading reacts directly upon our style. . . .

But we must not forget that true distinction is to be gained by a wide and varied range of such studies as conduce to the profitable enjoyment of life, in which, however, we must observe due proportion in the attention and time we devote to them.

First amongst such studies I place History: a subject which must not on any account be neglected by one who aspires to true cultivation.

For it is our duty to understand the origins of our own history and its development; and the achievements of Peoples and of Kings.

For the careful study of the past enlarges our foresight in contemporary affairs and affords to citizens and to monarchs lessons of incitement or warning in the ordering of public policy. From History, also, we draw our store of examples of moral precepts.

In the monuments of ancient literature which have come down to us History holds a position of great distinction. We specially prize such [Roman] authors as Livy, Sallust and Curtius;[4] and, perhaps even above these, Julius Caesar; the style of whose Commentaries, so elegant and so limpid, entitles them to our warm admiration. . . .

The great Orators of antiquity must by all means be included. Nowhere do we find the virtues more warmly extolled, the vices so fiercely decried. From them we may learn, also, how to express consolation, encouragement, dissuasion or advice. If the principles which orators set forth are portrayed for us by philosophers, it is from the former that we learn how to employ the emotions—such as indignation, or pity—in driving home their application in individual cases. Further, from oratory we derive our store of those elegant or striking turns of expression which are used with so much effect in literary compositions. Lastly, in oratory we find that wealth of vocabulary, that clear easy-flowing style, that verve and force, which are invaluable to us both in writing and in conversation.

I come now to Poetry and the Poets. . . . For we cannot point to any great mind of the past for whom the Poets had not a powerful attraction. Aristotle, in constantly quoting Homer, Hesiod, Pindar, Euripides and other [Greek] poets, proves that he knew their works hardly less intimately than those of the philosophers. Plato, also, frequently appeals to them, and in this way covers them with his approval. If we

---

[4]Q. Curtius Rufus, a Roman historian and rhetorician of the mid-first century A.D., composed a biography of Alexander the Great.

turn to Cicero, we find him not content with quoting Ennius, Accius,[5] and others of the Latins, but rendering poems from the Greek and employing them habitually. . . . Hence my view that familiarity with the great poets of antiquity is essential to any claim to true education. For in their writings we find deep speculations upon Nature, and upon the Causes and Origins of things, which must carry weight with us both from their antiquity and from their authorship. Besides these, many important truths upon matters of daily life are suggested or illustrated. All this is expressed with such grace and dignity as demands our admiration. . . . To sum up what I have endeavoured to set forth. That high standard of education to which I referred at the outset is only to be reached by one who has seen many things and read much. Poet, Orator, Historian, and the rest, all must be studied, each must

contribute a share. Our learning thus becomes full, ready, varied and elegant, available for action or for discourse in all subjects. But to enable us to make effectual use of what we know we must add to our knowledge the power of expression. These two sides of learning, indeed, should not be separated: they afford mutual aid and distinction. Proficiency in literary form, not accompanied by broad acquaintance with facts and truths, is a barren attainment; whilst information, however vast, which lacks all grace of expression, would seem to be put under a bushel or partly thrown away. Indeed, one may fairly ask what advantage it is to possess profound and varied learning if one cannot convey it in language worthy of the subject. Where, however, this double capacity exists— breadth of learning and grace of style—we allow the highest title to distinction and to abiding fame. If we review the great names of ancient [Greek and Roman] literature, Plato, Democritus, Aristotle, Theophrastus, Varro, Cicero, Seneca, Augustine, Jerome, Lactantius, we shall find it hard to say whether we admire more their attainments or their literary power.

---

[5]Ennius (239–169 B.C.) wrote the first great Latin epic poem, which was based on the legends of Rome's founding and its early history. Accius (c. 170–c. 90 B.C.), also a Roman, authored a history of Greek and Latin literature.

## REVIEW QUESTIONS

1. What do historians mean by the term "Renaissance humanism"?
2. What made Petrarch aware that a renaissance, or rebirth, of classical learning was necessary in his time?
3. Why did Leonardo Bruni abandon his earlier course of studies to pursue the study of Greek literature?
4. What subjects made up the basic course of studies advocated by Bruni?

---

## 2  Human Dignity

In his short lifetime, Giovanni Pico della Mirandola (1463–1494) mastered Greek, Latin, Hebrew, and Arabic and aspired to synthesize the Hebrew, Greek, and Christian traditions. His most renowned work, *Oration on the Dignity of Man,* has been called the humanist manifesto.

# Pico della Mirandola
# *ORATION ON THE DIGNITY OF MAN*

In the opening section of the *Oration,* Pico declares that unlike other creatures, human beings have not been assigned a fixed place in the universe. Our destiny is not determined by anything outside us. Rather, God has bestowed upon us a unique distinction: the liberty to determine the form and value our lives shall acquire. The notion that people have the power to shape their own lives is a key element in the emergence of the modern outlook.

I have read in the records of the Arabians, reverend Fathers, that Abdala the Saracen,[1] when questioned as to what on this stage of the world, as it were, could be seen most worthy of wonder, replied: "There is nothing to be seen more wonderful than man." In agreement with this opinion is the saying of Hermes Trismegistus: "A great miracle, Asclepius, is man."[2] But when I weighed the reason for these maxims, the many grounds for the excellence of human nature reported by many men failed to satisfy me—that man is the intermediary between creatures, the intimate of the gods, the king of the lower beings, by the acuteness of his senses, by the discernment of his reason, and by the light of his intelligence the interpreter of nature, the interval between fixed eternity and fleeting time, and (as the Persians say) the bond, nay, rather, the marriage song of the world, on David's [biblical king] testimony but little lower than the angels. Admittedly great though these reasons be, they are not the principal grounds, that is, those which may rightfully claim for themselves the privilege of the highest admiration. For why should we not admire more the angels themselves and the blessed choirs of heaven? At last it seems to me I have come to understand why man is the most fortunate of creatures and consequently worthy of all admiration and what precisely is that rank which is his lot in the universal chain of Being—a rank to be envied not only by brutes but even by the stars and by minds beyond this world. It is a matter past faith and a wondrous one. Why should it not be? For it is on this very account that man is rightly called and judged a great miracle and a wonderful creature indeed. . . .

. . . God the Father, the supreme Architect, had already built this cosmic home we behold, the most sacred temple of His godhead, by the laws of His mysterious wisdom. The region above the heavens He had adorned with Intelligences, the heavenly spheres He had quickened with eternal souls, and the excrementary and filthy parts of the lower world He had filled with a multitude of animals of every kind. But, when the work was finished, the Craftsman kept wishing that there were someone to ponder the plan of so great a work, to love its beauty, and to wonder at its vastness. Therefore, when everything was done (as Moses and Timaeus[3] bear witness), He finally took thought concerning the creation of man. But there was not among His archetypes that from which He could fashion a new offspring, nor was there in His treasurehouses anything which He might bestow on His new son as an

---

[1] Abdala the Saracen possibly refers to the eighth-century A.D. writer Abd-Allah Ibn al-Muqaffa.
[2] Ancient writings dealing with magic, alchemy, astrology, and occult philosophy were erroneously attributed to an assumed Egyptian priest, Hermes Trismegistus. Asclepius was a Greek god of healing.

[3] Timaeus, a Greek Pythagorean philosopher, was a central character in Plato's famous dialogue *Timaeus.*

inheritance, nor was there in the seats of all the world a place where the latter might sit to contemplate the universe. All was now complete; all things had been assigned to the highest, the middle, and the lowest orders. But in its final creation it was not the part of the Father's power to fail as though exhausted. It was not the part of His wisdom to waver in a needful matter through poverty of counsel. It was not the part of His kindly love that he who was to praise God's divine generosity in regard to others should be compelled to condemn it in regard to himself.

At last the best of artisans [God] ordained that that creature to whom He had been able to give nothing proper to himself should have joint possession of whatever had been peculiar to each of the different kinds of being. He therefore took man as a creature of indeterminate nature and, assigning him a place in the middle of the world, addressed him thus: "Neither a fixed abode nor a form that is thine alone nor any function peculiar to thyself have we given thee, Adam, to the end that according to thy longing and according to thy judgment thou mayest have and possess what abode, what form, and what functions thou thyself shalt desire. The nature of all other beings is limited and constrained within the bounds of laws prescribed by Us. Thou, constrained by no limits, in accordance with thine own free will, in whose hand We have placed thee, shalt ordain for thyself the limits of thy nature. We have set thee at the world's center that thou mayest from thence more easily observe whatever is in the world. We have made

thee neither of heaven nor of earth, neither mortal nor immortal, so that with freedom of choice and with honor, as though the maker and molder of thyself, thou mayest fashion thyself in whatever shape thou shalt prefer. Thou shalt have the power to degenerate into the lower forms of life, which are brutish. Thou shalt have the power, out of thy soul's judgment, to be reborn into the higher forms, which are divine."

O supreme generosity of God the Father, O highest and most marvelous felicity of man! To him it is granted to have whatever he chooses, to be whatever he wills. Beasts as soon as they are born (so says Lucilius)[4] bring with them from their mother's womb all they will ever possess. Spiritual beings [angels], either from the beginning or soon thereafter, become what they are to be for ever and ever. On man when he came into life the Father conferred the seeds of all kinds and the germs of every way of life. Whatever seeds each man cultivates will grow to maturity and bear in him their own fruit. If they be vegetative, he will be like a plant. If sensitive, he will become brutish. If rational, he will grow into a heavenly being. If intellectual, he will be an angel and the son of God. And if, happy in the lot of no created thing, he withdraws into the center of his own unity, his spirit, made one with God, in the solitary darkness of God, who is set above all things, shall surpass them all.

---

[4]Lucilius, a first-century A.D. Roman poet and Stoic philosopher, was a close friend of Seneca, the philosopher-dramatist.

## REVIEW QUESTIONS

1. According to Pico della Mirandola, what quality did humans alone possess? What did its possession allow them to do?
2. Compare Pico's view of the individual with that of Saint Augustine (see page 185) and Innocent III (see page 270).

# 3  Break with Medieval Political Theory

Turning away from the religious orientation of the Middle Ages, Renaissance thinkers discussed the human condition in secular terms and opened up possibilities for thinking about moral and political problems in new ways. Thus, Niccolò Machiavelli (1469–1527), a Florentine statesman and political theorist, broke with medieval political theory. Medieval political thinkers held that the ruler derived power from God and had a religious obligation to rule in accordance with God's precepts. Machiavelli, though, ascribed no divine origin to kingship, nor did he attribute events to the mysterious will of God; and he explicitly rejected the principle that kings should adhere to Christian moral teachings. For Machiavelli, the state was a purely human creation. Successful kings or princes, he asserted, should be concerned only with preserving and strengthening the state's power and must ignore questions of good and evil, morality and immorality. Machiavelli did not assert that religion was supernatural in origin and rejected prevailing belief that Christian morality should guide political life. For him, religion's value derived from other factors: a ruler could utilize religion to unite his subjects and to foster obedience to law.

## Niccolò Machiavelli
## *THE PRINCE*

In contrast to medieval thinkers, Machiavelli did not seek to construct an ideal Christian community but to discover how politics was *really* conducted. He studied politics in the cold light of reason, as the following passage from *The Prince* illustrates.

It now remains to be seen what are the methods and rules for a prince as regards his subjects and friends. And as I know that many have written of this, I fear that my writing about it may be deemed presumptuous, differing as I do, especially in this matter, from the opinions of others. But my intention being to write something of use to those who understand, it appears to me more proper to go to the real truth of the matter than to its imagination; and many have imagined republics and principalities which have never been seen or known to exist in reality; for how we live is so far removed from how we ought to live, that he who abandons what is done for what ought to

be done, will rather learn to bring about his own ruin than his preservation.

---

Machiavelli removed ethics from political thinking. A successful ruler, he contended, is indifferent to moral and religious considerations. But will not the prince be punished on the Day of Judgment for violating Christian teachings? In startling contrast to medieval theorists, Machiavelli simply ignored the question. The action of a prince, he said, should be governed solely by necessity.

---

A man who wishes to make a profession of goodness in everything must necessarily come to grief among so many who are not good. Therefore it is necessary for a prince, who wishes to maintain himself, to learn how not to be good, and to use this knowledge and not use it, according to the necessity of the case.

Leaving on one side, then, those things which concern only an imaginary prince, and speaking of those that are real, I state that all men, and especially princes, who are placed at a greater height, are reputed for certain qualities which bring them either praise or blame. Thus one is considered liberal, another . . . miserly; . . . one a free giver, another rapacious; one cruel, another merciful; one a breaker of his word, another trustworthy; one effeminate and pusillanimous, another fierce and high-spirited; one humane, another haughty; one lascivious, another chaste; one frank, another astute; one hard, another easy; one serious, another frivolous; one religious, another an unbeliever, and so on. I know that every one will admit that it would be highly praiseworthy in a prince to possess all the above-named qualities that are reputed good, but as they cannot all be possessed or observed, human conditions not permitting of it, it is necessary that he should be prudent enough to avoid the scandal of those vices which would lose him the state, and guard himself if possible against those which will not lose it [for] him, but if not able to, he can indulge them with less scruple. And yet he must not mind incurring the scandal of those vices, without which it would be difficult to save the state, for if one considers well, it will be found that some things which seem virtues would, if followed, lead to one's ruin, and some others which appear vices result in one's greater security and wellbeing. . . .

. . . I say that every prince must desire to be considered merciful and not cruel. He must, however, take care not to misuse this mercifulness. Cesare Borgia was considered cruel, but his cruelty had brought order to the Romagna,[1] united it, and reduced it to peace and fealty. If this is considered well, it will be seen that he was really much more merciful than the Florentine people, who, to avoid the name of cruelty, allowed Pistoia[2] to be destroyed. A prince, therefore, must not mind incurring the charge of cruelty for the purpose of keeping his subjects united and faithful; for, with a very few examples, he will be more merciful than those who, from excess of tenderness, allow disorders to arise, from whence spring bloodshed and rapine; for these as a rule injure the whole community, while the executions carried out by the prince injure only individuals. . . .

---

Machiavelli's rigorous investigation of politics led him to view human nature from the standpoint of its limitations and imperfections. The astute prince, he said, recognizes that human beings are by nature selfish, cowardly, and dishonest, and regulates his political strategy accordingly.

---

From this arises the question whether it is better to be loved more than feared, or feared more than loved. The reply is, that one ought to be both feared and loved, but as it is difficult for the two to go together, it is much safer to be feared than loved, if one of the two has to be wanting. For it may be said of men in general that they are ungrateful, voluble, dissemblers, anxious to avoid danger, and covetous of gain; as long as you benefit them, they are entirely yours; they offer you their blood, their goods, their life, and their children, as I have before said, when the necessity is remote; but when it approaches, they revolt. And the prince who has relied solely on their words, without making other preparations, is ruined; for the

---

[1]Cesare Borgia (c. 1476–1507) was the bastard son of Rodrigo Borgia, then a Spanish cardinal, and later Pope Alexander VI (1492–1503). With his father's aid he attempted to carve out for himself an independent duchy in north-central Italy, with Romagna as its heart. Through cruelty, violence, and treachery, he succeeded at first in his ambition, but ultimately his principality collapsed. Romagna was eventually incorporated into the Papal State under Pope Julius II (1503–1513).

[2]Pistoia, a small Italian city in Tuscany, came under the control of Florence in the fourteenth century.

friendship which is gained by purchase and not through grandeur and nobility of spirit is bought but not secured, and at a pinch is not to be expended in your service. And men have less scruple in offending one who makes himself loved than one who makes himself feared; for love is held by a chain of obligation which, men being selfish, is broken whenever it serves their purpose; but fear is maintained by a dread of punishment which never fails.

Still, a prince should make himself feared in such a way that if he does not gain love, he at any rate avoids hatred; for fear and the absence of hatred may well go together, and will be always attained by one who abstains from interfering with the property of his citizens and subjects or with their women. And when he is obliged to take the life of any one, let him do so when there is a proper justification and manifest reason for it; but above all he must abstain from taking the property of others, for men forget more easily the death of their father than the loss of their patrimony. Then also pretexts for seizing property are never wanting, and one who begins to live by rapine will always find some reason for taking the goods of others, whereas causes for taking life are rarer and more fleeting.

But when the prince is with his army and has a large number of soldiers under his control, then it is extremely necessary that he should not mind being thought cruel; for without this reputation he could not keep an army united or disposed to any duty. Among the noteworthy actions of Hannibal[3] is numbered this, that although he had an enormous army, composed of men of all nations and fighting in foreign countries, there never arose any dissension either among them or against the prince, either in good fortune or in bad. This could not be due to anything but his inhuman cruelty, which together with his infinite other virtues, made him always venerated and terrible in the sight of his soldiers, and without it his other virtues would not have sufficed to produce that effect. Thoughtless writers admire on the one hand his actions, and on the other blame the principal cause of them. . . .

---

Again in marked contrast to the teachings of Christian (and ancient) moralists, Machiavelli said that the successful prince will use any means to achieve and sustain political power. If the end is desirable, all means are justified.

---

How laudable it is for a prince to keep good faith and live with integrity, and not with astuteness, every one knows. Still the experience of our times shows those princes to have done great things who have had little regard for good faith, and have been able by astuteness to confuse men's brains, and who have ultimately overcome those who have made loyalty their foundation.

You must know, then, that there are two methods of fighting, the one by law, the other by force: the first method is that of men, the second of beasts; but as the first method is often insufficient, one must have recourse to the second. It is therefore necessary for a prince to know well how to use both the beast and the man. . . .

A prince being thus obliged to know well how to act as a beast must imitate the fox and the lion, for the lion cannot protect himself from traps, and the fox cannot defend himself from wolves. One must therefore be a fox to recognise traps, and a lion to frighten wolves. Those that wish to be only lions do not understand this. Therefore, a prudent ruler ought not to keep faith when by so doing it would be against his interest, and when the reasons which made him bind himself no longer exist. If men were all good, this precept would not be a good one; but as they are bad, and would not observe their faith with you, so you are not bound to keep faith with them. Nor have legitimate grounds ever failed a prince who wished to show [plausible] excuse for the non-fulfilment of his promise. Of this

---

[3]Hannibal (247–182 B.C.) was a brilliant Carthaginian general whose military victories almost destroyed Roman power. He was finally defeated at the battle of Zama in 202 B.C. by the Roman general Scipio Africanus.

one could furnish an infinite number of modern examples, and show how many times peace has been broken, and how many promises rendered worthless, by the faithlessness of princes, and those that have been best able to imitate the fox have succeeded best. But it is necessary to be able to disguise this character well, and to be a great feigner and dissembler; and men are so simple and so ready to obey present necessities, that one who deceives will always find those who allow themselves to be deceived. . . .

. . . Thus it is well to seem merciful, faithful, humane, sincere, religious, and also to be so; but you must have the mind so disposed that when it is needful to be otherwise you may be able to change to the opposite qualities. And it must be understood that a prince, and especially a new prince, cannot observe all those things which are considered good in men, being often obliged, in order to maintain the state, to act against faith, against charity, against humanity, and against religion. And, therefore, he must have a mind disposed to adapt itself according to the wind, and as the variations of fortune dictate, and, as I said before, not deviate from what is good, if possible, but be able to do evil if constrained.

A prince must take great care that nothing goes out of his mouth which is not full of the above-named five qualities, and, to see and hear him, he should seem to be all mercy, faith, integrity, humanity, and religion. And nothing is more necessary than to seem to have this last quality, for men in general judge more by the eyes than by the hands, for every one can see, but very few have to feel. Everybody sees what you appear to be, few feel what you are, and those few will not dare to oppose themselves to the many, who have the majesty of the state to defend them; and in the actions of men, and especially of princes, from which there is no appeal, the end justifies the means. Let a prince therefore aim at conquering and maintaining the state, and the means will always be judged honourable and praised by every one, for the vulgar is always taken by appearances and the issue of the event; and the world consists only of the vulgar, and the few who are not vulgar are isolated when the many have a rallying point in the prince. A certain prince of the present time, whom it is well not to name, never does anything but preach peace and good faith, but he is really a great enemy to both, and either of them, had he observed them, would have lost him state or repuation on many occasions.

## REVIEW QUESTIONS

1. In what ways was Niccolò Machiavelli's advice to princes a break from the teachings of medieval political and moral philosophers?
2. How does Machiavelli's image of human nature compare with that of Pico della Mirandola, of Pope Gregory VII (see page 225), and of Innocent III (see page 270).
3. Would Machiavelli's political advice help or hurt a politician in a modern democratic society?

---

# 4  Renaissance Florence

Florence was the city of the Renaissance par excellence. Many Florentines were distinguished humanist scholars, painters, sculptors, architects, and artisans; humanists were appointed to the post of chancellor; the aristocracy funded professional humanists and artists; and many leading families produced humanist scholars. The state sponsored grand architectural projects and gave public recognition to distinguished artists and writers. Because of its reputation, leading scholars and artists from other cities sought to live in Florence.

# Francesco Guicciardini
# THE GREATNESS OF LORENZO DE MEDICI

For much of the fifteenth century, the Medici family, which had made its fortune in banking, dominated Florentine politics and patronized the arts. In the following reading from his *History of Florence,* Francesco Guicciardini (1483–1540), a Florentine historian and student of politics, described the contribution of Lorenzo de Medici (1449–1492) to Florentine cultural life.

He desired glory and excellence more than any man, but he can be criticized for having carried this desire even into unimportant matters. In versifying, in games, and in other pursuits he got very angry with anyone who equalled or imitated him. The desire was too strong in important matters too. He wanted to equal and compete with all the princes of Italy in everything. . . . On the whole, though, his ambition was praiseworthy and brought him glory and fame everywhere, even outside Italy, for it caused him to strive to make the Florence of his time stand out above all other Italian cities in all arts and skills. He had a university founded in Pisa, principally for the study of letters. When people adduced many reasons to show that it could not have as many students as Padua or Pavia, he said he would be satisfied to have more faculty members than the others. In this time, all the most excellent and most famous men in Italy taught there and received very high salaries, for he avoided neither expense nor labor to get them. In Florence, the study of the humanities flourished under messer Agnolo Poliziano, Greek under messer Demetrio [Chalcondylas] and then under [Constantine] Lascaris, philosophy and art under Marsilio Ficino, Giorgio Benigno, Count Pico della Mirandola, and other excellent men. Lorenzo showed the same favor to poetry in the vernacular, to music, architecture, painting, sculpture, and to all the arts of mind and hand, so that the city overflowed with all these exquisite things. And these arts flourished all the more because Lorenzo, a universal man, could pass judgment and distinguish among men, so that they competed with one another to please him. Furthermore, there was his infinite liberality, which provided all talented men with livelihoods and with all the instruments necessary for their work. To give an example: when he decided to establish a Greek library, he sent the very learned Lascaris all the way to Greece to look for good ancient books.

The same liberality preserved his fame and his friendship with princes in Italy and abroad; for he omitted no form of magnificence—no matter how costly—that might enable him to keep the favor of the powerful. The result was that at Lyons, Milan, Bruges, and other places where he had business interests, his magnificence and his gifts caused his expenses to multiply, whereas his profits diminished because his affairs were governed by men of little ability, such as Lionetto de'Rossi and Tommaso Portinari. Moreover, his accounts were not well rendered, for he knew little and cared less about business. On several occasions his affairs were in such disorder that he was on the verge of bankruptcy, and was forced to avail himself of his friends' money or of public funds.

# Benedetto Dei
# FLORENCE, 1472

In the following letter written to a Venetian in 1472, Benedetto Dei (*fl.* late fifteenth century), a Florentine merchant, describes the economy of his native city under the domination of Lorenzo de Medici, comparing it favorably to that of Venice and other leading Italian city-states.

Florence is more beautiful and five hundred forty years older than your Venice. We spring from triply noble blood. We are one-third Roman, one-third Frankish, and one-third Fiesolan.[1] . . . We have round about us thirty thousand estates, owned by noblemen and merchants, citizens and craftsmen, yielding us yearly bread and meat, wine and oil, vegetables and cheese, hay and wood, to the value of nine hundred thousand ducats in cash, as you Venetians, Genoese, Chians, and Rhodians who come to buy them know well enough. We have two trades greater than any four of yours in Venice put together—the trades of wool and silk. Witness the Roman court and that of the King of Naples, the Marches and Sicily, Constantinople and Pera, Broussa and Adrianople, Salonika and Gallipoli, Chios and Rhodes [cities and areas in Italy and the eastern Mediterranean], where, to your envy and disgust, in all of those places there are Florentine consuls and merchants, churches and houses, banks and offices, and whither go more Florentine wares of all kinds, especially silken stuffs and gold and silver brocades, than from Venice, Genoa, and Lucca put together. Ask your merchants who visit Marseilles, Avignon, and the whole of Provence, Bruges, Antwerp, London, and other cities where there are great banks and royal warehouses, fine dwellings, and stately churches; ask those who should know, as they go to fairs every year, whether they have seen the [Florentine] banks of the Medici, the Pazzi, the Capponi, the Buondelmonti, the Corsini, the Falconieri, the Portinari and the Ghini,* and a hundred of others which I will not name, be-

cause to do so I should need at least a ream of paper. You say we are bankrupt since Cosimo's [de Medici, 1389–1464] death. If we have had losses, it is owing to your dishonesty and the wickedness of your Levantine merchants, who have made us lose thousands of florins [gold coins]; it is the fault of those with well-known names who have filled Constantinople and Pera with failures, whereof our great houses could tell many a tale. But though Cosimo is dead and buried, he did not take his gold florins and the rest of his money and bonds with him into the other world, nor his banks and storehouses, nor his woolen and silken cloths, nor his plate and jewelry; but he left them all to his worthy sons and grandsons, who take pains to keep them and to add to them, to the everlasting vexation of the Venetians and other envious foes whose tongues are more malicious and slanderous than if they were Sienese. . . . Our beautiful Florence contains within the city in this present year two hundred seventy shops belonging to the wool merchants' guild, from whence their wares are sent to Rome and the Marches, Naples and Sicily, Constantinople and Pera, Adrianople, Broussa and the whole of Turkey. It contains also eighty-three rich and splendid warehouses of the silk merchants' guild, and furnishes gold and silver stuffs, velvet, brocade, damask, taffeta, and satin to Rome, Naples, Catalonia, and the whole of Spain, especially Seville, and to Turkey and Barbary. The principal fairs to which these wares go are those of Genoa, the Marches, Ferrara, Mantua, and the whole of Italy; Lyons, Avignon, Montpellier, Antwerp, and London. The number of banks amounts to thirty-three; the shops of the cabinetmakers, whose business is carving and inlaid work, to eighty-four; and the workshops of the stonecutters and marble workers in

---

[1]Fiesole is an ancient Etruscan hill town three miles northeast of Florence.
*The bank of the Medici and their partners at Milan.

the city and its immediate neighborhood, to fifty-four. There are forty-four goldsmiths' and jewelers' shops, thirty gold-beaters, silver wire-drawers, and a wax-figure maker.†... Go through all the cities of the world, nowhere will you ever be able to find artists in wax equal to those we now have in Florence, and to whom the figures in the Nunziata‡ can bear witness. An-

other flourishing industry is the making of light and elegant gold and silver wreaths and garlands, which are worn by young maidens of high degree, and which have given their names to the artist family of Ghirlandaio. Sixty-six is the number of the apothecaries' and grocer shops; seventy that of the butchers, besides eight large shops in which are sold fowls of all kinds, as well as game and also the native wine called Trebbiano, from San Giovanni in the upper Arno Valley; it would awaken the dead in its praise.

†This was at that time a profitable industry, as such images were used in all churches.

‡SS [Sanctissima] Annuziata [Church of the Most Holy Annunciation].

## REVIEW QUESTIONS

1. Lorenzo de Medici is presented to us by Francesco Guicciardini as a model of the Renaissance prince. What values and character traits did he display? What weaknesses?
2. What factors contributed to the wealth and power of Renaissance Florence?

## 5  Renaissance Art

Renaissance artists were inspired by the art of classical antiquity, which was representational and aspired to show nature as it appeared to the eye. In stressing the importance of depicting the object truly as it is viewed, the Renaissance artist, like his classical predecessors, also emphasized the immeasurable importance of the viewer. Renaissance art gave a renewed and original expression to classical humanism, which celebrated the dignity, worth, and creative capacity of the individual and the beauty of the human form.

## Leon Battista Alberti
## *ON PAINTING*

In his work *Della pittura (On Painting)* Leon Battista Alberti (1404–1472), the first modern art theoretician, formulated the mathematical theory of artistic perspective, which became commonly used by the artists of the time. His purpose was to enable artists to depict objects as if they were seen through a glass window, creating the illusion of depth, of three dimensions on a two-dimensional surface. This illusion involved establishing a precise mathematical relationship between the object and the observer. By defining visual space and the relationship between the object and the observer in mathematical terms, Renaissance art and artistic theory helped pave the way for the development of the modern scientific approach to nature, which later found expression in the astronomy of Copernicus and the physics of Galileo (see Chapter 12).

In all this discussion, I beg you to consider me not as a mathematician but as a painter writing of these things. Mathematicians measure with their minds alone the forms of things separated from all matter. Since we wish the object to be seen, we will use a more sensate wisdom. . . .

The painter is concerned solely with representing what can be seen. . . .

---

Alberti uses a triangle or pyramid to show how light rays coming from the object converge in the viewer's eyes.

---

Vision makes a triangle. The base of [this triangle] is the quantity seen and the sides are those rays which are extended from the quantity to the eye. It is, therefore, very certain that no quantity can be seen without the triangle. The angles in this visual triangle are first, the two points of the quantity, the third, that which is opposite the base and located within the eye. . . .

Here is a rule: as the angle within the eye becomes more acute, so the quantity seen appears smaller. From this it is clear why a very distant quantity seems to be no larger than a point . . . as more rays are used in seeing, so the thing seen appears greater; and the fewer the rays, the smaller. . . .

Up to this point we have talked of planes and rays; we have said how a pyramid is made in vision; we have proved the importance of distance and position of the centric ray together with the reception of light. Now, since in a single glance not only one plane but several are seen, we will investigate in what way many conjoined [planes] are seen. Each plane contains in itself its pyramid of colours and lights. Since bodies are covered with planes, all the planes of a body seen at one glance will make a pyramid packed with as many smaller pyramids as there are planes.

[Every painter] should know that they circumscribe the plane with their lines. When they fill the circumscribed places with colours,

they should only seek to present the forms of things seen on this plane as if it were of transparent glass. Thus the visual pyramid could pass through it, placed at a definite distance with definite lights and a definite position of centre in space and in a definite place in respect to the observer. Each painter, endowed with his natural instinct, demonstrates this when, in painting this plane, he places himself at a distance as if searching the point and angle of the pyramid from which point he understands the thing painted is best seen. . . .

---

Alberti describes his use of the human figure as a basis for a precise ratio between objects in the painting.

---

. . . Here alone, leaving aside other things, I will tell what I do when I paint.

First of all about where I draw. I inscribe a quadrangle of right angles, as large as I wish, which is considered to be an open window through which I see what I want to paint. Here I determine as it pleases me the size of the men in my picture. I divide the length of this man in three parts. These parts to me are proportional to that measurement called a *braccio* [two feet], for, in measuring the average man it is seen that he is about three *braccia*. With these *braccia* I divide the base line of the rectangle into as many parts as it will receive. To me this base line of the quadrangle is proportional to the nearest transverse [crossing line] and equidistant quantity seen on the pavement. Then, within this quadrangle, where it seems best to me, I make a point which occupies that place where the central ray strikes. For this it is called the centric point. This point is properly placed when it is no higher from the base line of the quadrangle than the height of the man that I have to paint there. Thus both the beholder and the painted things he sees will appear to be on the same plane. . . .

Know that a painted thing can never appear truthful where there is not a definite distance for seeing it.

# Leonardo da Vinci
# ART AND SCIENCE

The works of Leonardo da Vinci (1452–1519)—his drawings, paintings, sculpture, innumerable inventions, and copious writings—exemplify the Renaissance spirit. They announced a new way of looking at nature and the individual. Leonardo examined objects in all their diversity and represented them realistically. For Leonardo, visual art was a means of arriving at nature's truths. Truth was attained when the artist brought both human reason and human creative capacity to bear on the direct experiences of the senses. Leonardo visually delineated the natural world with unprecedented scientific precision and simultaneously asserted his spiritual and intellectual freedom to do so. Through his art, Leonardo helped lay the foundations for modern science.

In his notebooks, Leonardo sketched an infinite variety of objects—inorganic, organic, human—and recorded fragmentary thoughts about them. Everywhere, he demonstrated a concern for the concrete specificity of things, which he depicted in minute detail. In the following excerpts, Leonardo affirms the rigorous and direct observation of nature as a source of truth.

How painting surpasses all human works by reason of the subtle possibilities which it contains:

The eye, which is called the window of the soul, is the chief means whereby the understanding may most fully and abundantly appreciate the infinite works of nature; and the ear is the second, inasmuch as it acquires its importance from the fact that it hears the things which the eye has seen. If you historians, or poets, or mathematicians had never seen things with your eyes you would be ill able to describe them in your writings. And if you, O poet, represent a story by depicting it with your pen, the painter with his brush will so render it as to be more easily satisfying and less tedious to understand. . . .

## OF THE ORDER TO BE OBSERVED IN STUDY

I say that one ought first to learn about the limbs and how they are worked, and after having completed this knowledge one ought to study their actions in the different conditions in which men are placed, and thirdly to devise figure compositions, the study for these being taken from natural actions made on occasion as opportunities offered; and one should be on the watch in the streets and squares and fields and there make sketches with rapid strokes to represent features, that is for a head one may make an *o,* and for an arm a straight or curved line, and so in like manner for the legs and trunk, afterwards when back at home working up these notes in a completed form.

My opponent says that in order to gain experience and to learn how to work readily, it is better that the first period of study should be spent in copying various compositions made by different masters either on sheets of paper or on walls, since from these one acquires rapidity in execution and a good method. But to this it may be replied that the ensuing method would be good if it was founded upon works that were excellent in composition and by diligent masters; and

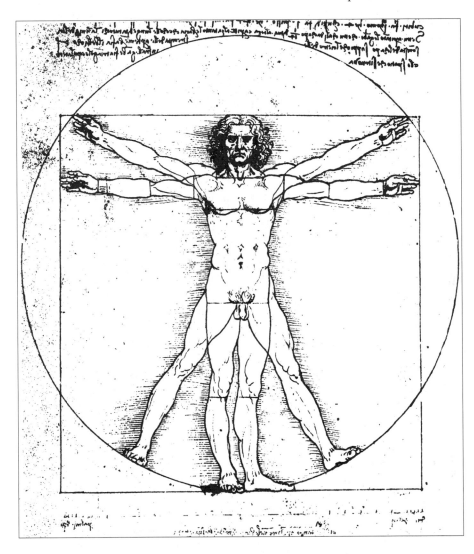

LEONARDO DA VINCI, *The Proportions of Man,* from his notebooks. See below where Leonardo discusses the proportions that this drawing illustrates. *(Stock Montage)*

since such masters are so rare that few are to be found, it is safer to go direct to the works of nature than to those which have been imitated from her originals with great deterioration and thereby to acquire a bad method, for he who has access to the fountain does not go to the water-pot. . . .

Equally important to Leonardo was the innate ability of the rational mind to use mathematics and to give order, form, and clarity to the individual's experiences of the world. Here he explains the use of mathematical perspective in art.

## THE LIFE OF THE PAINTER IN THE COUNTRY

The painter requires such knowledge of mathematics as belongs to painting, and severance from companions who are not in sympathy with his studies, and his brain should have the power of adapting itself to the tenor of the objects which present themselves before it, and he should be freed from all other cares.

And if while considering and examining one subject a second should intervene, as happens when an object occupies the mind, he ought to decide which of these subjects presents greater difficulties in investigation, and follow that until it becomes entirely clear, and afterwards pursue the investigation of the other. And above all he should keep his mind as clear as the surface of a mirror, which becomes changed to as many different colours as are those of the objects within it, and his companions should resemble him in a taste for these studies, and if he fail to find any such he should accustom himself to be alone in his investigations, for in the end he will find no more profitable companionship. . . .

## OF THE REQUISITES OF PAINTING

The first requisite of painting is that the bodies which it represents should appear in relief, and that the scenes which surround them with effects of distance should seem to enter into the plane in which the picture is produced by means of the three parts of perspective, namely the diminution in the distinctness of the form of bodies, the diminution in their size, and the diminution in their colour. Of these three divisions of perspective, the first has its origin in the eye, the two others are derived from the atmosphere that is interposed between the eye and the objects which the eye beholds. . . .

## WALL OF GLASS

Perspective is nothing else than the seeing of an object behind a sheet of glass, smooth and quite transparent, on the surface of which all the things may be marked that are behind this glass; these things approach the point of the eye in pyramids, and these pyramids are cut by the said glass.

## OF THE DIMINUTION OF OBJECTS AT VARIOUS DISTANCES

A second object as far removed from the first as the first is from the eye will appear half the size of the first, although they are of the same size.

A small object near at hand and a large one at a distance, when seen between equal angles will appear the same size. . . .

Perspective is a rational demonstration whereby experience confirms how all things transmit their images to the eye by pyramidal lines. By pyramidal lines I mean those which start from the extremities of the surface of bodies, and by gradually converging from a distance arrive at the same point; the said point being . . . in this particular case located in the eye, which is the universal judge of all objects. . . .

---

Leonardo was always engaged in a quest for the essential living form of a thing, the relationship of its parts to the whole, the numerical ratios subsisting among the parts, and the laws operative in the ratios. He found such ratios and laws everywhere in both animate and inanimate objects. In the following excerpt he tries to define the ratio of parts to the whole of the male human body. His written observations are accompanied by a marvelous sketch of the body, conceived and framed with realism and mathematical proportion.

---

If you set your legs so far apart as to take a fourteenth part from your height, and you open and raise your arms until you touch the line of the crown of the head with your middle fingers, you must know that the centre of the circle formed by the extremities of the outstretched limbs will be the navel, and the space between the legs will form an equilateral triangle.

The span of a man's outstretched arms is equal to his height.

From the beginning of the hair to the end of the bottom of the chin is the tenth part of a man's height; from the bottom of the chin to the crown of the head is the eighth of the man's height; from the top of the breast to the crown of the head is the sixth of the man; from the top of the breast to where the hair commences is the seventh part of the whole man; from the nipples to the crown of the head is a fourth part of the man. The maximum width of the shoulders is in itself the fourth part of a man; from the elbow to the tip of the middle finger is the fifth part; from this elbow to the end of the shoulder is the eighth part. The complete hand will be the tenth part. The penis begins at the centre of the man. The foot is the seventh part of the man. From the sole of the foot to just below the knee is the fourth part of the man. From below the knee to where the penis begins is the fourth part of the man.

The parts that find themselves between the chin and the nose and between the places where the hair and the eyebrows start each of itself compares with that of the ear, and is a third of the face.

## REVIEW QUESTION

1. How did mathematics, an empirical approach, and nature influence the painters and architects of the Renaissance? Why was this a significant development?

---

## 6 The Spread of the Renaissance

In the late fifteenth and the sixteenth centuries, the Renaissance spread to Germany, France, England, and Spain. Exemplifying the Renaissance spirit in France was François Rabelais (c. 1495–c. 1553), a Benedictine monk (until he resigned from the order), a physician, and a humanist scholar. *Gargantua and Pantagruel,* Rabelais's satirical epic, attacked clerical education and monastic orders and expressed an appreciation for secular learning and a confidence in human nature. Like other Renaissance humanists, Rabelais criticized medieval philosophy for its overriding concern with obscure, confused, and irrelevant questions and censured a narrow-minded clergy who deprived people of life's joys. Expressing his aversion to medieval asceticism, he attacked monasticism as life-denying and extolled worldly pleasure as a legitimate need and aim of human nature.

# François Rabelais
# CELEBRATION OF THE WORLDLY LIFE

The following reading from *Gargantua and Pantagruel* contains a description of life at an imagined monastery, the abbey of Thélème, whose rules differed markedly from those of traditional medieval monasteries. Here Rabelais expressed the Renaissance celebration of the worldly life.

## THE RULES ACCORDING TO WHICH THE THÉLÈMITES LIVED

All their life was regulated not by laws, statutes, or rules, but according to their free will and pleasure. They rose from bed when they pleased, and drank, ate, worked, and slept when the fancy seized them. Nobody woke them; nobody compelled them either to eat or to drink, or to do anything else whatever. So it was that Gargantua has established it. In their rules there was only one clause:

### DO WHAT YOU WILL

because people who are free, well-born, well-bred, and easy in honest company have a natural spur and instinct which drives them to virtuous deeds and deflects them from vice; and this they called honour. When these same men are depressed and enslaved by vile constraint and subjection, they use this noble quality which once impelled them freely towards virtue, to throw off and break this yoke of slavery. For we always strive after things forbidden and covet what is denied us.

Making use of this liberty, they most laudably rivalled one another in all of them doing what they saw pleased one. If some man or woman said, "Let us drink," they all drank; if he or she said, "Let us play," they all played; if it was "Let us go and amuse ourselves in the fields," everyone went there. If it were for hawking or hunting, the ladies, mounted on fine mares, with their grand palfreys following, each carried on their daintily gloved wrists a sparrow-hawk, a lanneret, or a merlin, the men carrying the other birds.[1]

So nobly were they instructed that there was not a man or woman among them who could not read, write, sing, play musical instruments, speak five or six languages, and compose in them both verse and prose. Never were seen such worthy knights, so valiant, so nimble both on foot and horse; knights more vigorous, more agile, handier with all weapons than they were. Never were seen ladies so good-looking, so dainty, less tiresome, more skilled with the fingers and the needle, and in every free and honest womanly pursuit than they were. . . .

---

Gargantua writes to his son Pantagruel, studying in Paris; in the letter, he describes a truly liberal education, one befitting a Renaissance humanist.

---

Now every method of teaching has been restored, and the study of languages has been revived: of Greek, without which it is disgraceful for a man to call himself a scholar, and of Hebrew, [other ancient Semitic languages], and Latin. The elegant and accurate art of printing, which is now in use, was invented in my time, by divine inspiration; as, by contrast, artillery was inspired by diabolical suggestion. The whole world is full of learned men, of very erudite tutors, and of most extensive libraries, and it is my opinion that neither in the time of Plato, of Cicero, nor of Papinian[2] were there such facilities for study as one finds today. No one, in future, will risk appearing in public or in any company, who is not well polished in Minerva's [Roman goddess of wisdom] workshop. I find robbers, hangmen, freebooters, and grooms nowadays more learned than the doctors and preachers were in my time.

Why, the very women and girls aspire to the glory and reach out for the celestial manna[3] of sound learning. So much so that at my present age I have been compelled to learn Greek,

---

[1]*Palfreys* and *lanneret,* archaic terms, refer respectively to a saddle horse usually ridden by women and to a small male falcon native to the Mediterranean area. A merlin is a small black and white European falcon, now also called a pigeon hawk.

[2]Papinian was a Roman jurist of the late second to early third century A.D. whose legal opinions were considered authoritative in late Roman law.
[3]*Manna* refers to a food miraculously provided by God for the Hebrews during their exodus out of Egypt during Moses' time (Exodus 16:14–36).

which I had not despised like Cato,[4] but which I had not the leisure to learn in my youth. Indeed I find great delight in reading the *Morals* of Plutarch, Plato's magnificent *Dialogues,* the *Monuments* of Pausanias, and the *Antiquities* of Athenaeus,[5] while I wait for the hour when it will please God, my Creator, to call me and bid me leave this earth.

Therefore, my son, I beg you to devote your youth to the firm pursuit of your studies and to the attainment of virtue. You are in Paris. There you will find many praiseworthy examples to follow. You have Epistemon for your tutor, and he can give you living instruction by word of mouth. It is my earnest wish that you shall become a perfect master of languages. First of Greek, as Quintilian [Roman educational theorist] advises; secondly, of Latin; and then of Hebrew, on account of the Holy Scriptures; also of Chaldean and Arabic, for the same reason; and I would have you model your Greek style on Plato's and your Latin on that of Cicero. Keep your memory well stocked with every tale from history, and here you will find help in the Cosmographes[6] of the historians. Of the liberal arts, geometry, arithmetic, and music, I gave you some smattering when you were still small, at the age of five or six. Go on and learn the rest, also the rules of astronomy.

But leave divinatory astrology and Lully's[7] art alone, I beg of you, for they are frauds and vanities. Of Civil Law I would have you learn the best texts by heart, and relate them to the art of philosophy. And as for the knowledge of Nature's works, I should like you to give careful attention to that too; so that there may be no sea, river, or spring of which you do not know the fish. All the birds of the air, all the trees, shrubs, and bushes of the forest, all the herbs of the field, all the metals deep in the bowels of the earth, the precious stones of the whole East and the South—let none of them be unknown to you.

Then scrupulously peruse the books of the Greek, Arabian, and Latin doctors once more, not omitting the Talmudists and Cabalists,[8] and by frequent dissections gain a perfect knowledge of that other world which is man. At some hours of the day also, begin to examine the Holy Scriptures. First the New Testament and the Epistles of the Apostles in Greek; and then the Old Testament, in Hebrew. In short, let me find you a veritable abyss of knowledge. For, later, when you have grown into a man, you will have to leave this quiet and repose of study, to learn chivalry and warfare, to defend my house, and to help our friends in every emergency against the attacks of evildoers.

---

[4]Cato the Elder (234–149 B.C.), a Roman statesman, was noted for his conservative morals and hostility to Greek influences in Roman society.
[5]Pausanias was a travel writer famous for his guides to the ancient monuments of Greece, and Athenaeus was a compiler of literary and philosophical writings. Both were Greeks of the second century A.D.
[6]Cosmographes are books on geography, geology, and astronomy.

[7]Lully alludes to Ramon Lull (c. 1236–1315), a Franciscan friar, a mystic, and a philosopher, who was falsely reputed to have authored various books on magic and alchemy.
[8]Talmudists are students of the collection of writings on Jewish civil and religious laws, and Cabalists refers to students of a medieval Jewish occult tradition based on a mystical interpretation of the Hebrew Scriptures.

# William Shakespeare
# HUMAN NATURE AND THE
# HUMAN CONDITION

By dealing with classical themes and figures, setting his plays in Renaissance Italy and ancient Greece, and probing the full range of people's motives, actions, and feelings, William Shakespeare (1564–1616), widely regarded as the world's finest playwright, gave expression to the Renaissance spirit. The following passages illustrate Shakespeare's brilliant insights into human nature and the human condition.

## THE NOBILITY OF THE HUMAN BEING
*Hamlet,* Act II, Scene ii. lines 310–313

What a piece of work is a man! How noble in reason! How infinite in faculties! in form and moving how express and admirable! in action how like an angel! in apprehension how like a god! the beauty of the world, the paragon of animals.

## THE DARK SIDE OF LIFE
*Henry the Eighth,* Act III, Scene ii. lines 414–428

Farewell! a long farewell, to all my greatness!
This is the state of man: to-day he puts forth
The tender leaves of hopes; to-morrow blossoms,
And bears his blushing honours thick upon him;
The third day come a frost, a killing frost,
And when he thinks, good easy man, full surely
His greatness is a-ripening, nips his root,
And then he falls, as I do. I have ventur'd,
Like little wanton boys that swim on bladders,
This many summers in a sea of glory,
But far beyond my depth: my high-blown pride
At length broke under me, and now has left me,
Weary and old with service, to the mercy
Of a rude stream, that must for ever hide me.
Vain pomp and glory of this world, I hate ye.

*Macbeth,* Act V, Scene v. lines 20–29

Tomorrow, and tomorrow, and tomorrow,
Creeps in this petty pace from day to day,

To the last syllable of recorded time;
And all our yesterdays have lighted fools
The way to dusty death. Out, out, brief candle!
Life's but a walking shadow, a poor player
That struts and frets his hour upon the stage,
And then is heard no more. It is a tale
Told by an idiot, full of sound and fury,
Signifying nothing.

*Measure for Measure,* Act III, Scene i. lines 130–144

Ay, but to die, and go we know not where,
To lie in cold obstruction and to rot,
This sensible warm motion to become
A kneaded clod; and the delighted spirit
To bathe in fiery floods, or to reside
In thrilling region of thick-ribbed ice,
To be imprison'd in the viewless winds,
And blown with restless violence round about
The pendent world; or to be worse than worst
Of those that lawless and incertain thought
Imagine howling: 'tis too horrible!
The weariest and most loathed worldly life
That age, ache, penury and imprisonment
Can lay on nature is a paradise
To what we fear of death.

## THE ROLES WE PLAY
*As You Like It,* Act II, Scene vii. lines 143–170

All the world's a stage,
And all the men and women merely players.
They have their exits and their entrances,
And one man in his time plays many parts,
His acts being seven ages. At first the infant,

---

311 faculties: powers
    express: well-modelled
312 apprehension: understanding

---

131 obstruction: stagnation (of the blood)
133 kneaded: i.e. like dough
135 thrilling: piercing with cold
136 viewless: invisible

Mewling and puking in the nurse's arms.
Then the whining schoolboy with his satchel
And shining morning face, creeping like snail
Unwillingly to school. And then the lover,
Sighing like furnace, with a woeful ballad
Made to his mistress' eyebrow. Then a soldier,
Full of strange oaths and bearded like the
     pard,
Jealous in honor, sudden and quick in quarrel,
Seeking the bubble Reputation
E'en in the cannon's mouth. And then the
     justice,
In fair round belly with good capon lin'd,
With eyes severe and beard of formal cut,
Full of wise saws and modern instances;
And so he plays his part. The sixt age shifts
Into the lean and slipper'd pantaloon,
With spectacles on nose and pouch on side;
His youthful hose well sav'd, a world too wide
For his shrunk shank, and his big manly voice,
Turning again toward childish treble, pipes
And whistles in his sound. Last scene of all,
That ends this strange eventful history,
Is second childishness and mere oblivion—
Sans teeth, sans eyes, sans taste, sans every-
     thing.

## LOVE AND LOVERS
*A Midsummer Night's Dream,* Act V,
Scene i. lines 4–11

Lovers and madmen have such seething brains,
Such shaping fantasies, that apprehend
More than cool reason ever comprehends.
The lunatic, the lover, and the poet,
Are of imagination all compact:
One sees more devils than vast hell can hold,

That is the madman; the lover, all as frantic,
Sees Helen's beauty in a brow of Egypt: . . .

*Troilus and Cressida,* Act III, Scene ii.
lines 144–146

     But you are wise,
Or else you love not; for to be wise and love
Exceeds man's might. That dwells with gods
     above.

*The Two Gentlemen of Verona,* Act III,
Scene i. lines 81–105

*Duke.* There is a lady of Verona here,
Whom I affect; but she is nice and coy
And nought esteems my aged eloquence.
Now therefore, would I have thee to my tutor,—
For long agone I have forgot to court;
Besides, the fashion of the time is chang'd—
How and which way I may bestow myself
To be regarded in her sun-bright eye.
     *Val{entine}.* Win her with gifts, if she
respect not words.
Dumb jewels often in their silent kind
More than quick words do move a woman's
     mind.
     *Duke.* But she did scorn a present that
I sent her.
     *Val.* A woman sometime scorns what best
contents her.
Send her another; never give her o'er,
For scorn at first makes after-love the more.
If she do frown, 'tis not in hate of you,
But rather to beget more love in you;
If she do chide, 'tis not to have you gone;
For why the fools are mad if left alone.
Take no repulse, whatever she doth say;
For 'get you gone,' she doth not mean 'away!'
Flatter and praise, commend, extol their graces;
Though ne'er so black, say they have angels'
     faces.

---

148 Mewling: crying, mewing like a cat
154 pard: leopard
155 Jealous in: suspiciously careful of
157 E'en: Even
160 saws: maxims
     modern instances: everyday illustrations
161 sixt: sixth
162 pantaloon: old dotard
169 mere: total
170 Sans: without

---

11 Helen: Helen of Troy
   brow of Egypt: gypsy's face
85 forgot: forgotten how
87 bestow: conduct
90 kind: nature
99 For why: because
103 black: dark-complexioned

That man that hath a tongue, I say, is no
   man,
If with his tongue he cannot win a
   woman.

*As You Like It,* Act III, Scene ii.
lines 359–364

   *Ros{alind}.* But are you so much in love
as your rhymes speak?

   *Orl{ando}.* Neither rhyme nor reason can
express how much.

   *Ros.* Love is merely a madness and, I tell
you, deserves as well a dark house and a whip
as madmen do. And the reason why they are
not so punish'd and cured is that the lunacy

is so ordinary that the whippers are in
love too.*

*Much Ado About Nothing,* Act II, Scene
iii. lines 60–68

Sigh no more, ladies, sigh no more,
   Men were deceivers ever;
One foot in sea, and one on shore,
   To one thing constant never.
     Then sigh not so,
     But let them go,
And be you blithe and bonny,
Converting all your sounds of woe
   Into Hey nonny, nonny.

––––––––

*The whip and the dark room represented the extent of
Elizabethan treatment of the insane.

## REVIEW QUESTIONS

1. In what ways did the curriculum recommended by Gargantua reflect the teachings
   of the Renaissance humanists?
2. How does the humanist educational program continue to influence the course of
   studies in modern universities?
3. How did Shakespeare express the Renaissance spirit?
4. Which lines do you consider the most insightful? Why?

# CHAPTER 10
# *The Reformation*

MARTIN LUTHER AND THE WITTENBERG REFORMERS (c. 1543), by Lucas Cranach, the Younger. With Luther (left) are Frederick of Saxony, Luther's protector, who dominates the painting, and the Swiss reformer Huldreich Zwingli (to the right of Frederick). *(The Toledo Museum of Art; Gift of Edward Drummond Libbey)*

The reformation of the church in the sixteenth century was rooted in demands for spiritual renewal and institutional change. These pressures began as early as the late fourteenth century and came from many sources.

The papacy and orthodox Catholic theology were challenged by English theologian John Wycliffe (c. 1320–1384) and Czech theologian John Huss (c. 1369–1415). Both attacked the bishops' involvement in temporal politics and urged a return to the simple practices of the early apostolic church; and both, claiming that the Bible alone—not the church hierarchy—was the highest authority for Christians, emphasized study of the Holy Scriptures by the laity and sermons in the common language of the people. Wycliffe, though not Huss, also undermined the clergy's authority by denying the priests' power to change the bread and wine into Christ's body and blood during the Mass. Despite severe persecution by church and state, followers of Wycliffe's and Huss's beliefs continued to exist and participated in the sixteenth-century Protestant movement.

Institutional reform from within was attempted through the Conciliar movement, which endeavored to restrict the pope's power through regular meetings of general councils of bishops. The Council of Constance (1414–1418) declared that a general council, not the papacy, was the supreme authority within the church and called for regular assemblies of bishops to consider the church's problems and initiate necessary reforms.

By the mid-fifteenth century, the Conciliar movement had collapsed, and the papacy, unreformed, freely exercised its supremacy. Fearful of losing its autonomy and power, the papacy resisted calling a new council from 1437 until 1512, when the Fifth Lateran Council met in Rome under close papal supervision. The council issued decrees aimed at improving education of the clergy, eliminating many abuses in church administration, and summoning a church council every five years. But the council's decrees were not implemented after the last session ended in 1517, the same year Martin Luther first challenged the papacy, thus starting the Protestant reform movement.

The principal source of the reform spirit was a widespread popular yearning for a more genuine spirituality. It took many forms: the rise of new pious practices; greater interest in mystical experiences and in the study of the Bible; the development of communal ways for lay people to live and work following the apostles' example; and a heightened search for ways within secular society to imitate more perfectly the life of Christ—called the New Devotion movement.

Several secular factors contributed to this heightening of spiritual feeling. The many wars, famines, and plagues of the late fourteenth and the fifteenth centuries had traumatized Europe. The increasing educational level of the urban middle class and skilled laborers and the invention of the printing press allowed the rapid and relatively inexpensive spread of new ideas. Finally, there was the influence of the humanist movement, particularly in northern Europe and Spain. Many humanists dedicated themselves to promoting higher levels of religious education. They stimulated public interest in biblical study by publishing new editions of the Holy Scriptures and the writings of the church fathers, along with new devotional literature. Nearly all the religious reformers of the sixteenth century were deeply influenced by the ideals and methods of the Christian humanist movement.

In Germany, a spirit of discontent with social and economic conditions coincided with the demand for reform of the church and religious life. For several decades before Luther's revolt against the papacy, the economic conditions of the knights, the peasants, and the lower-class urban workers had deteriorated. The knights' grievances included loss of their political power to the centralizing governments of the German princes and increasing restrictions on their customary feudal privileges. Peasants protested that lords had steadily withdrawn certain of their customary rights and had added burdens, increasing the lords' income and control over their estates. The knights and peasants were squeezed into an ever-worsening social and economic niche. In the cities, the lower-class artisans and laborers were similarly oppressed. Those in the urban upper classes, who controlled town governments, enhanced their own economic privileges at the expense of lower-class citizens. The church, which was a major landowner and active in commercial enterprises in the towns, played an important role in these conflicts. All these grievances formed the explosive background to Martin Luther's challenge to the authority of the church and the imperial government.

The success of the reformers, both Protestant and Catholic, depended on support from the ruling political forces in the various kingdoms, principalities, and city-states of Europe. Usually, the rulers' religious preference determined whether the church remained Catholic or became Lutheran, Calvinist, or some combination of all three, as in England. The rulers of large parts of Germany, especially the imperial city-states, and of the Scandinavian kingdoms adopted the Lutheran reform. The Austrian and Spanish Hapsburg emperors and the French kings remained Catholic, although Calvinism had many adherents in France. In eastern Europe, Protestantism was successful at first, but, under the influence of the Catholic reform movement, Catholicism later recovered its dominance. In Switzerland, allegiance was divided among Catholics and the followers of John Calvin, reformer of the church in Geneva, and of Ulrich Zwingli, reformer of the church in Zurich. Calvinism took root in Scotland, and its influence also grew in England where it inspired the Puritan movement.

These divisions in the Christian church marked a turning point in European history and culture, ending forever the coherent world-view of medieval Christendom. The Reformation split the peoples of Europe into two broad political, intellectual, and spiritual camps: Protestant and Catholic. With the moral, political, and ideological power of the church significantly diminished, post-Reformation society was open to increasing secularization on all fronts. By ending the religious unity of the Middle Ages and weakening the Catholic Church, the Reformation contributed significantly to the rise of modernity.

## 1   Late Medieval Attempts to Reform the Church

One of the most powerful forces for spiritual reform was the so-called New Devotion *(devotio moderna),* which had its roots in the preaching of Dutch priest Gerard Groote (1340–1384). Groote's disciples founded several reformed religious orders and inspired lay people to adopt his spiritual teaching in their daily lives. These followers were especially active in creating schools where children were taught religion from the Bible itself, often in translations from the Latin into vernacular languages. Groote's ideal of all Christians living in perfect imitation of Christ as depicted in the New Testament became the heart of the New Devotion, which spread throughout the Netherlands, Germany, and Spain in the fifteenth century. Desiderius Erasmus, Martin Luther, and Saint Ignatius Loyola were among the many religious reformers of the sixteenth century whose piety was shaped by this orthodox spiritual reform movement.

## Thomas à Kempis
## *THE IMITATION OF CHRIST*

The character of the New Devotion is best revealed in the following passages from *The Imitation of Christ* by Thomas à Kempis (1380–1471). An Augustinian priest, he was educated by the disciples of Gerard Groote. This work has never gone out of print and is considered one of the great works of practical Christian spirituality.

### BOOK 1, CHAPTER 1
*On the Imitation of Christ*

"He who follows Me shall not walk in darkness," says Our Lord.*

In these words Christ counsels us to follow His life and way if we desire true enlightenment and freedom from all blindness of heart. Let the life of Jesus Christ, then, be our first consideration.

The teaching of Jesus far transcends all the teachings of the Saints, and whosoever has His spirit will discover concealed in it heavenly manna.[1] But many people, although they often hear the Gospel, feel little desire to follow it, because they lack the spirit of Christ. Whoever desires to understand and take delight in the words of Christ must strive to conform his whole life to Him.

---

*John 8:12.

[1]Manna was the food provided by God for the Hebrews during their wanderings in the Sinai Desert.

Of what use is it to discourse learnedly on the Trinity [God the Father, Son, and Holy Spirit] if you lack humility and therefore displease the Trinity? Lofty words do not make a man just or holy; but a good life makes him dear to God. I would far rather feel contrition [remorse for one's sins] than be able to define it. If you knew the whole Bible by heart, and all the teachings of the philosophers, how would this help you without the grace and love of God?† "Vanity of vanities, and all is vanity," except to love God and serve Him alone. And this is supreme wisdom—to despise the world, and draw daily nearer the kingdom of heaven.

It is vanity to solicit honours, or to raise oneself to high station. It is vanity to be a slave to bodily desires and to crave for things which bring certain retribution. It is vanity to wish for long life, if you care little for a good life. It is vanity to give thought only to this present life, and to care nothing for the life to come. It is vanity to love things that so swiftly pass away, and not to hasten onwards to that place where everlasting joy abides.

Keep constantly in mind the saying, "The eye is not satisfied with seeing, nor the ear filled with hearing."‡ Strive to withdraw your heart from the love of visible things, and direct your affections to things invisible. For those who follow only their natural inclinations defile their conscience, and lose the grace of God.

## BOOK 1, CHAPTER 11
### On Peace and Spiritual Progress

If only we were completely dead to self, and free from inner conflict, we could savour spiritual things, and win experience of heavenly contemplation. But the greatest, and indeed the whole obstacle to our advance is that we are not free from passions and lusts, nor do we strive to follow the perfect way of the Saints. But when we encounter even a little trouble, we are quickly discouraged, and turn to human comfort.

If we strove to stand firm in the struggle like men of valour, we should not fail to experience the help of our Lord from heaven. For He is ever ready to help all who fight, trusting in His grace; He also affords us occasions to fight that we may conquer. If we rely only on the outward observances of religion, our devotion will rapidly wane. But let us lay the axe to the root—that, being cleansed from our passions, we may possess our souls in peace.

If each year we would root out one fault, we should soon become perfect. . . .

## BOOK 1, CHAPTER 23
### A Meditation on Death

Each morning remember that you may not live until evening; and in the evening, do not presume to promise yourself another day. Be ready at all times, and so live that death may never find you unprepared. Many die suddenly and unexpectedly; for at an hour that we do not know the Son of Man [Jesus Christ] will come. When your last hour strikes, you will begin to think very differently of your past life, and grieve deeply that you have been so careless and remiss.

Happy and wise is he who endeavours to be during his life as he wishes to be found at his death. For these things will afford us sure hope of a happy death; perfect contempt of the world; fervent desire to grow in holiness; love of discipline; the practice of penance; ready obedience; self-denial; the bearing of every trial for the love of Christ. While you enjoy health, you can do much good; but when sickness comes, little can be done. Few are made better by sickness, and those who make frequent pilgrimages seldom acquire holiness by so doing. . . .

## BOOK 4, CHAPTER 18
### How We Should Approach Christ's Sacrament Humbly, Submitting Reason to Holy Faith

. . . Beware of curious and unprofitable inquiry into the Mysteries of this most holy Sacrament

†Eccles. 1:2.
‡Eccles. 1:8.

[the Eucharist], if you would avoid being plunged into the depths of doubt; for those who attempt to search into the majesty of God will be overwhelmed with its glory. God can do more than man is able to comprehend; yet we may humbly and reverently search for truth, so long as the seeker is always willing to be taught, and to follow the sound teachings of the Fathers.

Blessed is that simplicity which rejects obscure inquiry and advances along the sure and open road of God's Commandments. Many have lost their devotion by attempting to pry into matters too high for them. It is faith and a holy life that are required of you, not a lofty intellect or knowledge of the profound mysteries of God. For if you cannot understand or grasp things that are beneath you, how will you comprehend those that are above you? Therefore submit yourself to God, and humble your reason to faith, and the light of knowledge shall be granted you in so far as it be profitable and necessary. . . .

Go forward, then, with simple, undoubting faith, and come to this Sacrament with humble reverence, confidently committing to almighty God whatever you are not able to understand. God never deceives; but man is deceived whenever he puts too much trust in himself. God walks with the simple, reveals Himself to the humble, gives understanding to little ones, discloses His secrets to pure minds and conceals His grace from the curious and conceited. . . .

## REVIEW QUESTIONS

1. What were the principal characteristics of the New Devotion?
2. According to Thomas à Kempis, what was the proper relationship between piety, learning, and intellectual curiosity?

## 2 A Catholic Critic of the Church

The greatest scholar and most popular humanist author of the early sixteenth century was the Dutch priest Desiderius Erasmus (1466–1536). Educated under the influence of the New Devotion and well trained in the new humanistic studies, Erasmus dedicated his life to purifying the Latin and Greek texts of the Bible and those of the early fathers of the church. He used his wit and humanistic learning in his preaching to advocate a simpler yet more intense Christian life modeled on Christ. Erasmus castigated those who pandered to the superstitions of people by encouraging magical beliefs about relics, the cults of the saints, indulgences (see the next section) and other abuses of pious practices. He also was hostile to the excessive influence of scholastic philosophers on the church's theology, believing that in their quibbling over obscure philosophical-theological issues, they mocked the Christian faith as revealed in the New Testament. An Augustinian monk who preferred to live outside the monastery, Erasmus severely criticized the lax practices of monks and clergy. He argued, too, that salvation was not based on ascetic and ceremonial acts, but on deeds of love.

Although Erasmus at first welcomed Martin Luther's call for reform, he quickly discerned that Luther was going far beyond what he, Erasmus, felt was wise or necessary. He urged, instead, reform within the church's framework. Although scandalized by a pope leading armies and engaging in international war against other Christians, Erasmus clung loyally to the hierarchical church. He urged peace and civility on all parties, condemned extremist positions, and tried to work for peaceful reconciliation and reform. In 1524, Erasmus wrote a reasoned defense of the role of free will in the process of salvation, taking a Catholic position on this difficult theological problem. Luther was furious with Erasmus for not supporting him, and Erasmus found himself abused by zealots from both camps. To the end, he remained a devout, loyal, but critical Catholic reformer. His preaching, piety, and literary scholarship exemplified the ideals of Christian humanism.

# Desiderius Erasmus
# *IN PRAISE OF FOLLY*

Erasmus's most famous work was *In Praise of Folly,* written in 1509, before Luther's first challenge to the church. In the following passages, speaking through the voice of Folly, Erasmus castigates monks, theologians, and other Christians for failing to discern the true purpose of the Christian life: the imitation of Christ. It was said of Erasmus that he laid the egg Luther hatched—a judgment Erasmus did not acknowledge.

As for the theologians, perhaps it would be better to pass them over in silence, *"not stirring up the hornets' nest"* and "not laying a finger on the stinkweed," since this race of men is incredibly arrogant and touchy. For they might rise up en masse and march in ranks against me with six hundred conclusions and force me to recant. And if I should refuse, they would immediately shout "heretic." For this is the thunderbolt they always keep ready at a moment's notice to terrify anyone to whom they are not very favorably inclined. . . .

. . . They are so blessed by their Selflove as to be fully persuaded that they themselves dwell in the third heaven, looking down from high above on all other mortals as if they were earth-creeping vermin almost worthy of their pity. They are so closely hedged in by rows of magistral definitions, conclusions, corollaries, explicit and implicit propositions, they have so many *"holes they can run to,"* that Vulcan [Roman god of fire] himself couldn't net them

tightly enough to keep them from escaping by means of distinctions, with which they cut all knots as cleanly as the fine-honed edge of "the headsman's axe"—so many new terms have they thought up and such monstrous jargon have they coined. . . .

In all of these there is so much erudition, so much difficulty, that I think the apostles themselves would need to be inspired by a different spirit if they were forced to match wits on such points with this new breed of theologians. Paul could provide a living example of faith, but when he said "Faith is the substance of things to be hoped for and the evidence of things not seen," his definition was not sufficiently magisterial. So too, he lived a life of perfect charity, but he neither distinguished it nor defined it with sufficient dialectical precision in the first epistle to the Corinthians, chapter 13. . . .

. . . But Christ, interrupting their boasts (which would otherwise never come to an end), will say, "Where did this new race of Jews [quibbling theologians] come from? The only law I recognize as truly mine is the only one I hear nothing about. Long ago, not speaking obliquely in parables but quite openly, I promised my Father's inheritance not to hoods [worn by monks], or trifling prayers, or fasts, but rather deeds of faith and charity. Nor do I acknowledge those who too readily acknowledge their own deeds: those who want to appear even holier than I am can go dwell in the heavens of the Abraxasians[1] if they like, or they can order that a new heaven be built for them by the men whose petty traditions they have placed before my precepts." When they hear this and see sailors and teamsters chosen in preference to them, how do you suppose their faces will look as they stare at each other? . . .

Almost as happy as the theologians are those men who are commonly called "religious" and "monks"—though both names are quite incorrect, since a good part of them are very far removed from religion and no one is encountered more frequently everywhere you go. I cannot imagine how anything could be more wretched than these men. . . . For even though everyone despises this breed of men so thoroughly that even a chance meeting with one of them is considered unlucky, still they maintain a splendid opinion of themselves. First of all, they consider it the very height of piety to have so little to do with literature as not even to be able to read. Moreover, when they roar out their psalms in church like braying asses (counting their prayers indeed, but understanding them not at all), then (of all things!) they imagine that the listening saints are soothed and caressed with manifold delight. Among them are some who make a great thing out of their squalor and beggary, who stand at the door bawling out their demands for bread—(indeed there is no inn or coach or ship where they do not make a disturbance), depriving other beggars of no small share of their income. And in

this manner these most agreeable fellows, with their filth, ignorance, coarseness, impudence, recreate for us, as they say, an image of the apostles. . . .

Closely related to such men are those who have adopted the very foolish (but nevertheless quite agreeable) belief that if they look at a painting or statue of that huge . . . Christopher, they will not die on that day; or, if they address a statue of Barbara with the prescribed words, they will return from battle unharmed, or, if they accost Erasmus on certain days, with certain wax tapers, and in certain little formulas of prayer, they will soon become rich.[2] Moreover, in George they have discovered a new Hercules. . . .[3] They all but worship George's horse, most religiously decked out in breastplates and bosses [ornaments], and from time to time oblige him with some little gift. To swear by his bronze helmet is thought to be an oath fit for a king.

Now what shall I [Folly] say about those who find great comfort in soothing self-delusions about fictitious pardons for their sins, measuring out the times in purgatory down to the droplets of a waterclock, parceling out centuries, years, months, days, hours, as if they were using mathematical tables. Or what about those who rely on certain little magical tokens and prayers thought up by some pious impostor for his own amusement or profit? They promise themselves anything and everything: wealth, honor, pleasure, an abundance of everything, perpetual health, a long life, flourishing old age, and finally a seat next to Christ among the saints, though this last they don't want for quite a while yet—that is, when

---

[1]A heretical sect that believed there were 365 "heavens."

[2]Christopher refers to Saint Christopher, a popular legendary giant and the patron saint of travelers. Barbara was a widely venerated but legendary early Christian martyr and saint. Erasmus, an Italian bishop and also a saint, was martyred in about A.D. 303.

[3]George, the patron saint of England and of the Crusaders, was believed to have been martyred in about A.D. 300. Saint George's battle with a dragon was a popular legend. Hercules, a Greek hero, performed twelve difficult tasks that won him immortality as a gift of the gods. He was himself worshiped as a god by later Greeks and Romans.

the pleasures of this life, to which they cling with all their might, have finally slipped through their fingers, then it will be soon enough to enter into the joys of the saints. Imagine here, if you please, some businessman or soldier or judge who thinks that if he throws into the collection basket one coin from all his plunder, the whole cesspool of his sinful life will be immediately wiped out. He thinks all his acts of perjury, lust, drunkenness, quarreling, murder, deception, dishonesty, betrayal are paid off like a mortgage, and paid off in such a way that he can start off once more on a whole new round of sinful pleasures.

Now who could be more foolish—rather, who could be happier—than those who assure themselves they will have the very ultimate felicity because they have recited daily those seven little verses from the holy psalms? A certain devil—certainly a merry one, but too loose-lipped to be very clever—is believed to have mentioned them to St. Bernard,[4] but the poor devil was cheated by a clever trick. Such absurdities are so foolish that even I am almost ashamed of them, but still they are approved not only by the common people but even by learned teachers of religion. . . .

But why have I embarked on this vast sea of superstitions?

Not if I had a hundred tongues, a hundred
    mouths,
A voice of iron, could I survey all kinds
Of fools, or run through all the forms of folly.[5]

So rife, so teeming with such delusions is the entire life of all Christians everywhere. And yet priests are not unwilling to allow and even foster such delusions because they are not unaware of how many emoluments accumulate from this source. In the midst of all this, if some odious wiseman should stand up and sing out the true state of affairs: "You will not die badly if you live well. You redeem your sins if to the coin you add a hatred of evil deeds, then tears, vigils, prayers, fasts, and if you change your whole way of life. This saint will help you if you imitate his life"—if that wiseman were to growl out such assertions and more like them, look how much happiness he would immediately take away from the minds of mortals, look at the confusion he would throw them into!

---

[4]Saint Bernard (1091–1153) was a leading theologian, Cistercian monk, and preacher.

[5]Virgil's *Aeneid* 6.625–627.

## REVIEW QUESTIONS

1. What criticisms did Desiderius Erasmus make of the institutional church?
2. What did he see as the solution to the ills afflicting the church?

---

# 3  The Lutheran Reformation

The reformation of the Western Christian church in the sixteenth century was precipitated by Martin Luther (1483–1546). A pious German Augustinian monk and theologian, Luther had no intention of founding a new church or overthrowing the political and ecclesiastical order of late medieval Europe. He was educated in the tradition of the New Devotion, and as a theology professor at the university in Wittenberg, Germany, he opposed rationalistic, scholastic theology. Sympathetic at first to the ideas of Christian humanists like Erasmus, Luther too sought a reform of morals and an end to abusive practices within the church. But a visit to the papal court in Rome in 1510 left him profoundly shocked at its worldliness and disillusioned with the papacy's role in the church's governance.

# Martin Luther
# ON PAPAL POWER, JUSTIFICATION BY FAITH, THE INTERPRETATION OF THE BIBLE, AND THE NATURE OF THE CLERGY

To finance the rebuilding of the church of St. Peter in Rome, the papacy in 1515 offered indulgences to those who gave alms for this pious work. An indulgence was a mitigation or remission of the penance imposed by a priest in absolving a penitent who confessed a sin and indicated remorse. Indulgences were granted by papal decrees for those who agreed to perform some act of charity, alms-giving, prayer, pilgrimage, or other pious work. Some preachers of this particular papal indulgence deceived people into believing that a "purchase" of this indulgence would win them, or even the dead, a secure place in heaven.

In 1517, Luther denounced the abuses connected with the preaching of papal indulgences. The quarrel led quickly to other and more profound theological issues. His opponents defended the use of indulgences on the basis of papal authority, shifting the debate to questions about the nature of papal power within the church. Luther responded with a vigorous attack on the whole system of papal governance. The principal points of his criticism were set out in his *Address to the Christian Nobility of the German Nation Concerning the Reform of the Christian Estate,* published in August 1520. In the first excerpt that follows, Luther argued that the papacy was blocking any reform of the church and appealed to the nobility of Germany to intervene by summoning a "free council" to reform the church.

A central point of contention between Luther and Catholic critics was his theological teaching on justification (salvation) by faith and on the role of good works in the scheme of salvation. Luther had suffered anguish about his unworthiness before God. Then, during a mystical experience, Luther suddenly perceived that his salvation came not because of his good works but as a free gift from God due to Luther's faith in Jesus Christ.

Thus, while never denying that a Christian was obliged to perform good works, Luther argued that such pious acts were not helpful in achieving salvation. His claim that salvation or justification was attained through faith in Jesus

Christ as Lord and Savior, and through that act of faith alone, became the rallying point of the Protestant reformers.

The Catholic position, not authoritatively clarified until the Council of Trent (1545–1563), argued that justification came not only through faith, but through hope and love as well, obeying God's commandments and doing good works. In *The Freedom of a Christian,* published in 1520, Luther outlined his teaching on justification by faith and on the inefficacy of good works; the second excerpt is from this work.

Another dispute between Luther and papal theologians was the question of interpretation of the Bible. In the medieval church, the final authority in any dispute over the meaning of Scriptural texts or church doctrine was ordinarily the pope alone, speaking as supreme head of the church or in concert with the bishops in an ecumenical council. The doctrine of papal infallibility (that the pope could not err in teaching matters of faith and morals) was already well known, but belief in this doctrine had not been formally required. Luther argued that the literal text of Scripture was alone the foundation of Christian truth, not the teaching of popes or councils. Moreover, Luther said that all believers were priests, and the clergy did not hold any power beyond that of the laity; therefore the special privileges of the clergy were unjustified. The third excerpt contains Luther's views on the interpretation of Scripture and the nature of priestly offices.

## ON PAPAL POWER

The Romanists [traditional Catholics loyal to the papacy] have very cleverly built three walls around themselves. Hitherto they have protected themselves by these walls in such a way that no one has been able to reform them. As a result, the whole of Christendom has fallen abominably.

In the first place, when pressed by the temporal power they have made decrees and declared that the temporal power had no jurisdiction over them, but that, on the contrary, the spiritual power is above the temporal. In the second place, when the attempt is made to reprove them with the Scriptures, they raise the objection that only the pope may interpret the Scriptures. In the third place, if threatened with a council, their story is that no one may summon a council but the pope.

In this way they have cunningly stolen our three rods from us, that they may go unpunished. They have [settled] themselves within the safe stronghold of these three walls so that they can practice all the knavery and wickedness which we see today. Even when they have been compelled to hold a council they have weakened its power in advance by putting the princes under oath to let them remain as they were. In addition, they have given the pope full authority over all decisions of a council, so that it is all the same whether there are many councils or no councils. They only deceive us with puppet shows and sham fights. They fear terribly for their skin in a really free council! They have so intimidated kings and princes with this technique that they believe it would be an offense against God not to be obedient to the Romanists in all their knavish and ghoulish deceits. . . .

The Romanists have no basis in Scripture for their claim that the pope alone has the right to call or confirm a council. This is just their own ruling, and it is only valid as long as it is not harmful to Christendom or contrary to the laws of God. Now when the pope deserves punishment, this ruling no longer obtains, for not to punish him by authority of a council is harmful to Christendom. . . .

Therefore, when necessity demands it, and the pope is an offense to Christendom, the first man who is able should, as a true member of the whole body, do what he can to bring about a truly free council. No one can do this so well as the temporal authorities, especially since they are also fellow-Christians, fellow-priests, fellow-members of the spiritual estate, fellow-lords over all things. Whenever it is necessary or profitable they ought to exercise the office and work which they have received from God over everyone.

## JUSTIFICATION BY FAITH

You may ask, "What then is the Word of God, and how shall it be used, since there are so many words of God?" I answer: The Apostle explains this in Romans 1. The Word is the gospel of God concerning his Son, who was made flesh, suffered, rose from the dead, and was glorified through the Spirit who sanctifies. To preach Christ means to feed the soul, make it righteous, set it free, and save it, provided it believes the preaching. Faith alone is the saving and efficacious use of the Word of God, according to Rom. 10(:9): "If you confess with your lips that Jesus is Lord and believe in your heart that God raised him from the dead, you will be saved." Furthermore, "Christ is the end of the law, that every one who has faith may be justified" (Rom. 10:4). Again, in Rom. 1 (:17), "He who through faith is righteous shall live." The Word of God cannot be received and cherished by any works whatever but only by faith. Therefore it is clear that, as the soul needs only the Word of God for its life and righteousness, so it is justified by faith alone and not any works; for if it could be justified by anything else, it would not need the Word, and consequently it would not need faith.

This faith cannot exist in connection with works—that is to say, if you at the same time claim to be justified by works, whatever their character—for that would be the same as "limping with two different opinions" (I Kings 18:21), as worshiping Baal and kissing one's own hand (Job 31:27–28), which, as Job says, is a very great iniquity. Therefore the moment you begin to have faith you learn that all things in you are altogether blameworthy, sinful, and damnable, as the Apostle says in Rom. 3(:23), "Since all have sinned and fall short of the glory of God," and, "None is righteous, no, not one: . . . all have turned aside, together they have gone wrong" (Rom.3:10–12). When you have learned this you will know that you need Christ, who suffered and rose again for you so that, if you believe in him, you may through this faith become a new man in so far as your sins are forgiven and you are justified by the merits of another, namely, of Christ alone.

Since, therefore, this faith can rule only in the inner man, as Rom. 10(:10) says, "For man believes with his heart and so is justified," and since faith alone justifies, it is clear that the inner man cannot be justified, freed, or saved by any outer work or action at all, and that these works, whatever their character, have nothing to do with this inner man. On the other hand, only ungodliness and unbelief of heart, and no outer work, make him guilty and a damnable servant of sin. Wherefore it ought to be the first concern of every Christian to lay aside all confidence in works and increasingly to strengthen faith alone and through faith to grow in the knowledge, not of works, but of Christ Jesus, who suffered and rose for him, as Peter teaches in the last chapter of his first Epistle (1 Pet. 5:10). No other work makes a Christian. . . .

Our faith in Christ does not free us from works but from false opinions concerning works, that is, from the foolish presumption that justification is acquired by works. Faith redeems, corrects, and preserves our consciences so that we know that righteousness does not consist in works, although works neither can nor ought to be wanting; just as we cannot be without food and drink and all the works of this mortal body, yet our right-eousness is not in them, but in faith; and yet those works of the body are not to be despised or neglected on that account. In this world we are bound by the needs of our bodily life, but we are not righteous because of them. "My kingship is not of this world" (John 18:36), says Christ. He does not, however, say, "My kingship is not here, that is, in this world." And Paul says, "Though we live in the world we are not carrying on a worldly war" (II Cor. 10:3), and in Gal. 2(:20), "The life I now live in the flesh I live by faith in the Son of God." Thus what we do, live, and are in works and ceremonies, we do because of the necessities of this life and of the effort to rule our body. Nevertheless we are right-eous, not in these, but in the faith of the Son of God.

## THE INTERPRETATION OF THE BIBLE AND THE NATURE OF THE CLERGY

They (the Roman Catholic Popes) want to be the only masters of Scriptures. . . . They assume sole authority for themselves and would persuade us with insolent juggling of words that the Pope, whether he be bad or good, cannot err in matters of faith. . . .

. . . They cannot produce a letter to prove that the interpretation of Scripture . . . belongs to the Pope alone. They themselves have usurped this power . . . and though they allege that this power was conferred on Peter when the keys were given to him, it is plain enough that the keys were not given to Peter alone but to the entire body of Christians (Matt. 16:19; 18:18). . . .

. . . Every baptized Christian is a priest already, not by appointment or ordination from the Pope or any other man, but because Christ Himself has begotten him as a priest . . . in baptism. . . .

The Pope has usurped the term "priest" for his anointed and tonsured hordes [clergy and monks]. By this means they have separated themselves from the ordinary Christians and have called themselves uniquely the "clergy of God," God's heritage and chosen people who must help other Christians by their sacrifice and worship. . . . Therefore the Pope argues that he alone has the right and power to ordain and do what he will. . . .

[But] the preaching office is no more than a public service which happens to be conferred on someone by the entire congregation all the members of which are priests. . . .

. . . The fact that a pope or bishop anoints, makes tonsures, ordains, consecrates [makes holy], and prescribes garb different from those of the laity . . . nevermore makes a Christian and a spiritual man. Accordingly, through baptism all of us are consecrated to the priest-hood, as St. Peter says . . . (I Peter 2:9).

To make it still clearer, if a small group of pious Christian laymen were taken captive and settled in a wilderness and had among them no priest consecrated by a bishop, if they were to agree to choose one from their midst, married or unmarried, and were to charge him with the office of baptizing, saying Mass, absolving [forgiving of sins], and preaching, such a man would be as truly a priest as he would if all bishops and popes had consecrated him.

## *REVIEW QUESTIONS*

1. Why did Martin Luther see the papacy as the crucial block to any meaningful reform of the Church?
2. How did Luther's teaching undermine the power of the clergy and traditional forms of piety?

# 4   The German Peasants' Revolt

After Luther was outlawed as a heretic by the Imperial Diet (parliament) at Worms in 1521, economic and political grievances among the knights, peasants, and lower-class urban workers fostered a series of rebellions. The uprisings were largely local affairs, mostly in southwestern Gemany. When the knights revolted against their lords in 1523, they were quickly crushed. A more widespread peasant revolt followed in 1525, accompanied in some places by sympathetic rebellions among the lower-class artisans and laborers of nearby towns. Driven to a frenzy by their grievances and religious enthusiasm, the German peasants seized lords' estates and pillaged churches and monasteries in a rebellion covering a third of the country. Lacking effective training and leaders, however, they were soon crushed by the lords' vengeful armies.

Although Luther was not primarily responsible for the peasants' revolt, his attacks on the abuses of the ruling nobles and the clergy coincided with the growing anger and resentment among knights, peasants, and lower-class townspeople. The peasants had hoped that Luther, who had denounced the lords' cruelty and oppression, would endorse if not lead their revolt. They were completely mistaken. Luther was preoccupied with the individual's relationship with God and with attaining salvation through faith. He did not intend to initiate social revolution and regarded rebellion against the constituted authority of the state as contrary to the Gospel's spirit. To Luther, subjects had the duty to obey state authority, since it was ordained by God.

## *THE TWELVE ARTICLES*

A manifesto was drawn up in 1524 by the leaders of the peasants of Swabia, a large duchy in southwestern Germany. The following passages from the Twelve Articles show the intermingling of Lutheran reform ideas with the peasants' demands for relief from their landlords' domination. In a pamphlet published just prior to the peasants' uprising, Martin Luther criticized the Twelve Articles, opposing what he feared was an egalitarian social revolution that threatened the hierarchical order of society and the legitimate property rights of the lords and clergy. He urged peaceful resolution of the crisis, pointing out the just grievances of the peasants.

*Peace to the Christian reader and the grace of God through Christ:*

There are many evil writings put forth of late which take occasion, on account of the assembling of the peasants, to cast scorn upon the Gospel, saying: "Is this the fruit of the new teaching, that no one should obey but all should everywhere rise in revolt, and rush together to reform, or perhaps destroy entirely, the authorities, both ecclesiastical and lay?" The articles below shall answer these godless and criminal fault-finders, and serve, in the first place, to remove the reproach from the word of God and, in the second place, to give a Christian excuse for the disobedience or even the revolt of the entire Peasantry. . . .

*The Second Article*  According as the just tithe [a tax paid in grain] is established by the Old Testament and fulfilled in the New, we are ready and willing to pay the fair tithe of grain. The word of God plainly provides that in giving . . . to God and distributing to his people the services of a pastor are required. We will that for the future our church provost [manager of a feudal estate], whomsoever the community may appoint, shall gather and receive this tithe. From this he shall give to the pastor, elected by the whole community, a decent and sufficient maintenance for him and his, as shall seem right to the whole community. . . . The small tithes,* whether ecclesiastical or lay, we will not pay at all, for the Lord God created cattle for the free use of man. We will not, therefore, pay farther an unseemly tithe which is of man's invention.

*The Third Article*  It has been the custom hitherto for men to hold us as their own property, which is pitiable enough, considering that Christ has delivered and redeemed us all, without exception, by the shedding of his precious blood, the lowly as well as the great. Accordingly it is consistent with Scripture that we should be free and should wish to be so. Not that we would wish to be absolutely free and under

---

*That is, tithes of other products than the staple crops—for example, tithes of pigs or lambs.

no authority. God does not teach us that we should lead a disorderly life in the lusts of the flesh, but that we should love the Lord our God and our neighbor. We would gladly observe all this as God has commanded us in the celebration of the communion. He has not commanded us not to obey the authorities, but rather that we should be humble, not only towards those in authority, but towards every one. We are thus ready to yield obedience according to God's law to our elected and regular authorities in all proper things becoming to a Christian. We therefore take it for granted that you will release us from serfdom as true Christians, unless it should be shown us from the gospel that we are serfs. . . .

*The Tenth Article*  In the tenth place, we are aggrieved by the appropriation by individuals of meadows and fields which at one time belonged to a community. These we will take again into our own hands. It may, however, happen that the land was rightfully purchased, but when the land has unfortunately been purchased in this way, some brotherly arrangement should be made according to circumstances.

*The Eleventh Article*  In the eleventh place, we will entirely abolish the due called [heriot, a death tax], and will no longer endure it, nor allow widows and orphans to be thus shamefully robbed against God's will. . . .

---

# Martin Luther
# AGAINST THE PEASANTS

When in the spring of 1525 the peasants finally took up arms against their manorial lords, they were joined by the lower-class artisans and workers in many towns. In a pamphlet entitled *Against the Thievish, Murderous Hordes of Peasants,* Luther reacted sternly, urging the princes to repress the rebels with every power at their command.

. . . They are starting a rebellion, and are violently robbing and plundering monasteries and castles which are not theirs; by this they

have doubly deserved death in body and soul as highwaymen and murderers. Furthermore, anyone who can be proved to be a seditious person is an outlaw before God and the emperor; and whoever is the first to put him to death does right and well. For if a man is in open rebellion, everyone is both his judge and his executioner; just as when a fire starts, the first man who can put it out is the best man to do the job. For rebellion is not just simple murder; it is like a great fire, which attacks and devastates a whole land. Thus rebellion brings with it a land filled with murder and bloodshed; it makes widows and orphans, and turns everything upside down, like the worst disaster. Therefore let everyone who can, smite, slay, and stab, secretly or openly, remembering that nothing can be more poisonous, hurtful, or devilish than a rebel. It is just as when one must kill a mad dog; if you do not strike him, he will strike you, and a whole land with you.

It does not help the peasants when they pretend that according to Genesis 1 and 2 all things were created free and common, and that all of us alike have been baptized. For under the New Testament, Moses does not count; for there stands our Master, Christ, and subjects us, along with our bodies and our property, to the emperor and the law of this world, when he says, "Render to Caesar the things that are Caesar's" (Luke 20:25). Paul, too, speaking in Romans 12 (13:1) to all baptized Christians, says, "Let every person be subject to the governing authorities." And Peter says, "Be subject to every ordinance of

man" (I Pet. 2:13). We are bound to live according to this teaching of Christ, as the Father commands from heaven, saying, "This is my beloved Son, listen to him" (Matt. 17:5).

For baptism does not make men free in body and property, but in soul; and the gospel does not make goods common, except in the case of those who, of their own free will, do what the apostles and disciples did in Acts 4 (:32–37). They did not demand, as do our insane peasants in their raging, that the goods of others—of Pilate and Herod—should be common, but only their own goods. Our peasants, however, want to make the goods of other men common, and keep their own for themselves. Fine Christians they are! I think there is not a devil left in hell; they have all gone into the peasants. Their raving has gone beyond all measure. . . .

. . . I will not oppose a ruler who, even though he does not tolerate the gospel, will smite and punish these peasants without first offering to submit the case to judgment. He is within his rights, since the peasants are not contending any longer for the gospel, but have become faithless, perjured, disobedient, rebellious murderers, robbers, and blasphemers, whom even a heathen ruler has the right and authority to punish. Indeed, it is his duty to punish such scoundrels, for this is why he bears the sword and is "the servant of God to execute his wrath on the wrongdoer," Romans 13 (:4).

## REVIEW QUESTIONS

1. Explain the revolutionary potential of the Scriptures as they were interpreted by the poor and oppressed German peasants.
2. How did Martin Luther use the Scriptures to respond to the peasants' claims?

## 5  Luther and the Jews

Initially, Luther hoped to attract Jews to his vision of reformed Christianity. In *That Jesus Was Born a Jew* (1523), the young Luther expressed sympathy for Jewish sufferings and denounced persecution as a barrier to conversion. He declared, "I hope that if one deals in a kindly way with the Jews and instructs them carefully from the Holy Scripture, many of them will become genuine

Christians. . . . We [Christians] are aliens and in-laws; they are blood relatives, cousins, and brothers of our Lord." When the Jews did not abandon their faith, however, Luther launched a diatribe against them.

# Martin Luther
## *ON THE JEWS AND THEIR LIES*

In *On the Jews and Their Lies* (1543), Martin Luther accepted at face value medieval prejudices against the Jews: that they engaged in sorcery and magic, poisoned the wells of Christians, desecrated the Eucharistic host, and ritually murdered Christian children. In the concluding section, excerpted here, Luther advises civil and clerical authorities to treat the Jews harshly. The authorities did not heed Luther's proposals to raze synagogues and homes—although some anti-Jewish measures were introduced—and for several centuries Lutheran theologians paid little mind to Luther's anti-Judaism. In the late nineteenth century, German nationalists revived Luther's treatise and the Nazis gleefully circulated his words as an authoritative endorsement of their anti-Semitic ideology.[1]

First, their synagogues or churches should be set on fire, and whatever does not burn up should be covered or spread over with dirt so that no one may ever be able to see a cinder or stone of it. And this ought to be done for the honour of God and of Christianity in order that God may see that we are Christians, and that we have not wittingly tolerated or approved of such public lying, cursing and blaspheming of His Son and His Christians. . . . Secondly, their homes should likewise be broken down and destroyed. For they perpetrate the same things there that they do in their synagogues. For this reason they ought to be put under one roof or in a stable, like gypsies, in order that they may realise that they are not masters in our land, as they boast, but miserable captives, as they complain of us incessantly before God

with bitter wailing. Thirdly, they should be deprived of their prayerbooks and Talmuds in which such idolatry, lies, cursing and blasphemy are taught. Fourthly, their rabbis must be forbidden under threat of death to teach any more. . . . Fifthly, passport and travelling privileges should be absolutely forbidden to the Jews. For they have no business in the rural districts since they are not nobles, nor officials, nor merchants, nor the like. Let them stay at home. Sixthly, they ought to be stopped from usury. All their cash and valuables of silver and gold ought to be taken from them and put aside for safekeeping. For this reason, as said before, everything that they possess they stole and robbed from us through their usury, for they have no other means of support. . . . Such evilly acquired money is cursed, unless, with God's blessing, it is put to some good and necessary use. . . . Seventhly, let the young and strong Jews and Jewesses be given the flail, the axe, the hoe, the spade, the distaff and spindle and let them earn their bread by the sweat of their noses as is enjoined upon Adam's children. For it is not proper that they should want us cursed *Goyyim* to work in the sweat of our brow and that they, pious crew, idle away their

---

[1]In 1994 the Church Council of the Evangelical Lutheran Church in America acknowledged "with pain . . . Luther's antiJudaic diatribes and violent recommendations . . . against Jews. . . . [W]e reject this violent invective, and yet more do we express our deep and abiding sorrow over its tragic effects on subsequent generations. In concert with the Lutheran World Federation, we particularly deplore the appropriation of Luther's words by modern anti-Semites for the teaching of hatred toward Judaism or toward Jewish people in our day."

days at the fireside in laziness, feasting and display. And in addition to this, they boast impiously that they have become masters of the Christians at our expense. We ought to drive the rascally lazy bones out of our system. If, however, we are afraid that they might harm us personally, or our wives, children, servants, cattle etc, when they serve us or work for us— since it is surely to be presumed that such noble lords of the world and poisonous bitter worms are not accustomed to any work and would very unwillingly humble themselves to such a degree among the cursed *Goyyim*—then let us apply the same cleverness (expulsion) as the other nations, such as France, Spain, Bohemia, etc. and settle with them for that which they have extorted usuriously from us, and after having divided it up fairly let us drive them out of the country for all time. For, as has been said, God's rage is so great against them that they only become worse and worse through mild mercy, and not much better through severe mercy. Therefore away with them. . . . To sum up, dear princes and nobles who have Jews in your domains, if this advice of mine does not suit you, then find a better one so that you and we may be free of this insufferable devilish burden—the Jews.

## REVIEW QUESTIONS

1. What factors seemed to motivate Martin Luther's attack against the Jews?
2. What steps did Luther advocate to reduce the role of the Jews in German society?

## 6   The Calvinist Reformation

In the first decade of the Lutheran movement, Protestant reform had not spread significantly outside Germany due to suppression by the royal governments in France, Spain, and England. But in 1534 a French clergyman, John Calvin (1509–1564), resigned his church offices and fled to Basel, a Swiss city that had accepted Protestant reforms. There he composed a summary of the new Protestant theology, *The Institutes of the Christian Religion,* which was to be revised four times before his death. Written in the elegant Latin style favored by humanists, the work was translated into French and soon became the principal theological text for French, Scottish, Dutch, and English Protestant reformers. Calvin himself settled in Geneva, Switzerland, where his influence dominated the civil and religious life of the townspeople. From Geneva, Calvin carried on an active mission, spreading his reformed faith throughout his native France and elsewhere.

In 1536, the newly Protestant-controlled government of Geneva asked Calvin to draw up a public confession of the reformed faith, a catechism, and rules for liturgical worship. But the Council of Geneva's demand that all citizens be forced to subscribe to the new confession resulted in a change of government at the elections in 1538. Calvin withdrew to Basel. By 1541, the political situation had changed again; Calvin was recalled, and his recommendations for a new government for the church were put into law. He remained the spiritual leader of Geneva and of many reformed Protestants elsewhere until his death. Calvinism was especially influential in England and Scotland, giving rise to the

Puritan movement in seventeenth-century England and the Presbyterian churches in Scotland and Ireland. Both of these religious traditions exercised great influence on the settlers of the English colonies in North America.

# John Calvin
## *THE INSTITUTES*
## ECCLESIASTICAL ORDINANCES, AND
## THE OBEDIENCE OWED RULERS

One doctrine that assumed greater and greater importance in the four separate revised editions of Calvin's *Institutes* was predestination: the belief that each person's salvation or damnation was already decided before birth. This doctrine raised a question about whether Christ offered salvation for all human beings or only for the elect—a chosen few who were predestined to be saved by God's sovereign will. Some argued that the latter interpretation, one strongly articulated by Saint Augustine, implied that God was a tyrant who created human beings to be damned and that they were not free to acquire salvation by faith. In effect, salvation and damnation were foreordained. To many Christians, this doctrine diminished the justice and mercy of God, made meaningless the idea of freedom of choice in the process of salvation, and stripped good works of any role in gaining salvation. In the first excerpt (from *The Institutes of the Christian Religion*), Calvin offered his definition of predestination and cited Saint Augustine as an authority.

Calvin's ecclesiastical ordinances became a model for Calvinist churches throughout Europe and America. Each local church was governed by four types of officers: ministers, teachers, elders, and deacons. The ministers preached the Word of God and administered the two sacraments: baptism and the Eucharist. The teachers taught children and candidate members. The elders closely supervised the morals of the congregation. The deacons cared for the poor and the sick. An especially important innovation was the consistory, composed of the ministers and elders who met weekly to hear accusations against and to discipline individuals whose conduct was contrary to the church's moral teachings. Persistent offenders were turned over to the city authorities for punishment.

Like Luther, Calvin had a horror of disobedience of the civil authorities. Although he tended to be skeptical about any good coming from kings, Calvin believed that all authority comes from God and that bad kings or tyrants were to be accepted as an expression of God's wrath and as just punishment for the people's sins.

Yet by 1561 Calvin was forced by circumstance (the severe persecution of his followers in France and elsewhere) to moderate his position. In his *Commentaries on the Book of the Prophet Daniel*, Calvin justified disobeying rulers who deny the rights of God (as understood by the Protestant reformers); an excerpt from this work concludes this selection of Calvin's writings. This teaching would lay the groundwork for Calvinists of France, the Netherlands, England, and Scotland to resist the legitimate Catholic and Anglican kings of those realms to the point of resorting to revolution.

# THE INSTITUTES
## *Predestination*

Predestination, by which God adopts some to the hope of life, and adjudges others to eternal death, no one, desirous of the credit of piety, dares absolutely to deny. But it is involved in many [disputes], especially by those who make foreknowledge the cause of [predestination]. We maintain, that both belong to God; but it is preposterous to represent one as dependent on the other. When we attribute foreknowledge to God, we mean that all things have ever been, and perpetually remain, before his eyes, so that to his knowledge nothing is future or past, but all things are present; and present in such a manner, that he does not merely conceive of them from ideas formed in his mind, as things remembered by us appear present to our minds, but really beholds and sees them as if actually placed before him. And this foreknowledge extends to the whole world, and to all the creatures. Predestination we call the eternal decree of God, by which he has determined in himself, what he would have to become of every individual of mankind. For they are not all created with a similar destiny; but eternal life is foreordained for some, and eternal damnation for others. Every man, therefore, being created for one or the other of these ends, we say, he is predestinated either to life or to death.[1] This God has not only testified [to this destiny] in particular persons, but has given a specimen of it in the whole posterity of Abraham, which should evidently show the future condition of every nation to depend upon his decision. "When the Most High divided the nations, when he separated the sons of Adam, the Lord's portion was his people; Jacob was the lot of his inheritance" [Deut. 32:8–9]. The separation is before the eyes of all: in the person of Abraham, as in the dry trunk of a tree, one people is peculiarly chosen to the rejection of others: no reason for this appears, except that Moses, to deprive their posterity of all occasion of glorying, teaches them that their exaltation is wholly from God's gratuitous love. . . .

This doctrine [predestination] is maliciously and impudently calumniated by others, as subversive of all exhortations to piety of life. This formerly brought great odium upon Augustine, which he removed by his Treatise on Correction and Grace. . . . A slight acquaintance with [Saint] Paul will enable any one to understand, without tedious arguments, how easily he reconciles things which they pretend to be repugnant to each other. Christ commands men to believe in him. Yet his limitation is neither false nor contrary to his command, when he says, "No man can come unto me, except it were given unto him of my Father" [John 6:65]. Let preaching therefore have its course to bring men to faith, and by a continual progress to promote their perseverance. Nor let the knowledge of predestination be prevented, that the obedient may not be proud as of any thing of their own, but may glory in the Lord. Christ had some particular meaning in saying, "Who hath ears to hear, let him hear" [Matt. 13:9]. . . . "But why (says Augustine) should some have ears, and others not? 'Who hath known the mind of the Lord?' [Rom. 11:34] Must that which is evident be denied, because that which is concealed cannot be comprehended?" These observations I have faithfully borrowed from Augustine; but as his words will perhaps have more authority than mine, I will proceed to

---

[1]The phrase "predestinated . . . death" means predestined to be saved (life) or to be damned (death).

an exact quotation of them. "If, on hearing this, some persons become torpid and slothful, and exchanging labour for lawless desire, pursue the various objects of concupiscence [lust], must what is declared concerning the foreknowledge of God be therefore accounted false? If God foreknew that they would be good, will they not be so, in whatever wickedness they now live? and if he foreknew that they would be wicked, will they not be so, in whatever goodness they now appear? Are these, then, sufficient causes why the truths which are declared concerning the foreknowledge of God should be either denied or passed over in silence? especially when the consequence of silence respecting these would be the adoption of other errors. The reason of concealing the truth (he says) is one thing, and the necessity of declaring it is another."

---

The Genevan ecclesiastical ordinances illuminate the character of the Calvinist system of public regulation of morals through community pressure and state power.

---

## ECCLESIASTICAL ORDINANCES
### *The Duties of Elders, or Presbyters*

The office of the elders is to watch over the conduct of every individual, to admonish lovingly those whom they see doing wrong or leading an irregular life. When there is need, they should lay the matter before the body deputed to inflict paternal discipline (i.e. the consistory), of which they are members. . . .

*The Consistory, or Session*   The elders, who have been described, shall assemble once a week with the ministers, namely Thursday morning, to see if there be any disorders in the Church and discuss together such remedies as shall be necessary. . . . If any one shall in contempt refuse to appear before them, it shall be their duty to inform the [town] council, so that it may supply a remedy. . . .

## EXTRACTS FROM CALVIN'S REGULATIONS FOR THE VILLAGES ABOUT GENEVA

The whole household shall attend the sermons on Sunday, except when some one shall be left at home to tend the children or cattle.

If there is preaching on week days, all who can must come,—unless there be some good excuse,—so that at least one from each household shall be present. Those who have menservants or maid-servants shall bring them when it is possible, so that they shall not live like beasts without instruction. . . . Should any one come after the sermon has begun, let him be warned. If he does not amend, let him pay a fine of three sous [coins]. Let the churches be closed except during service, so that no one may enter them at other hours from superstitious motives. If any one be discovered engaged in some superstition within or near the church, let him be admonished. If he will not give up his superstition, let him be punished.

*Persecution of Catholics*   Those who are found to have rosaries or idols to adore, let them be sent before the consistory, and in addition to the reproof they receive there, let them be sent before the council. Let the same be done with those who go on a pilgrimage. Those who observe feasts or papistical fasts shall only be admonished. Those who go to mass shall, besides being admonished, be sent before the council, and it shall consider the propriety of punishing the offenders by imprisonment or special fines, as it judges best.

He who blasphemes, swearing by the body or blood of our Lord, or in like manner, shall kiss the earth for the first offense, pay five sous for the second and ten for the third. He who contradicts the word of God shall be sent before the consistory for reproof, or before the council for punishment, as the case may require. If any one sings indecent, licentious songs, or dances . . . he shall be kept in prison three days and then sent to the council.*

---

*There are similar provisions for drunkenness, gambling, quarreling, taking more than five per cent interest, etc.

Commenting on the story of the Hebrew prophet Daniel (who clearly refused to obey the Persian king's order that he not worship the god of Israel) and denying that Daniel had committed any offense against the king, Calvin explains this apparent contradiction. He affirms the traditional Christian view that obedience to divine law takes precedence over obligations to obey the laws of earthly rulers. This view is the Christian basis for civil disobedience and even revolutionary action against a ruler perceived to be an enemy of God. The following passage starts with a biblical quote in which Daniel addresses the Persian king.

## OBEDIENCE TO SECULAR RULERS

*. . . And even before thee, O king, I have committed nothing wrong.* It is clear that the Prophet had violated the king's edict. Why, then, does he not ingenuously confess this? Nay, why does he contend that he has not transgressed against the king? Because he conducted himself with fidelity in all his duties, he could free himself from every [false charge] by which he knew himself oppressed, as if he had despised the king's sovereignty. But Daniel was not so bound to the king of the Persians when [the king] claimed for himself as a god what ought not to be offered to him. We know how earthly empires are constituted by God, only on the condition that [God] deprives himself of noth-

ing, but shines forth alone, and all magistrates must be set in regular order, and every authority in existence must be subject to his glory. Since, therefore, Daniel could not obey the king's edict without denying God, as we have previously seen, he did not transgress against the king by constantly persevering in that exercise of piety to which he had been accustomed, and by calling on his God three times a-day. To make this the more evident, we must remember that passage of [the Apostle] Peter, "Fear God, honour the king" (1 Pet. 2:17). The two commands are connected together, and cannot be separated from one another. The fear of God ought to precede, that kings may obtain their authority. For if any one begins his reverence of an earthly prince by rejecting that of God, he will act preposterously, since this is a complete perversion of the order of nature. Then let God be feared in the first place, and earthly princes will obtain their authority, if only God shines forth, as I have already said. Daniel, therefore, here defends himself with justice, since *he had not committed any crime against the king;* for he was compelled to obey the command of God, and he neglected what the king had ordered in opposition to it. For earthly princes lay aside all their power when they rise up against God, and are unworthy of being reckoned in the number of mankind. We ought rather utterly to defy than to obey them whenever they are so restive and wish to spoil God of his rights, and, as it were, to seize upon his throne and draw him down from heaven.

## REVIEW QUESTIONS

1. Why was the doctrine of predestination so troublesome to many Christian theologians?
2. Explain John Calvin's views on the proper relationship between Christians and the state.
3. The close policing of the morals of individuals is characteristic of Calvinist teachings and practice. What role has Calvinism (or Puritanism, as it was called in England and America) played historically in regulating morals in American society?

## 7   The Catholic Response to Protestantism

The criticisms of Catholic beliefs and practices by Luther, Calvin, and other Protestant reformers generated a host of theological defenses of traditional Catholicism. However, there was a general admission that grave abuses in Catholic clerical morals and discipline had been allowed to go uncorrected. Almost everyone agreed that a new general council of the church was necessary to clarify and affirm Catholic doctrine and institute reforms in clerical discipline and practices. Despite many promises to summon such a council, the popes delayed. Political conditions never seemed right, and the papacy, remembering the challenge to its power attempted by councils in the fifteenth century, feared that prematurely summoning a council could be a disaster for papal authority.

The council was finally convoked in 1545 at the Alpine city of Trent, on the borders between the German lands and Italy. The papacy was firmly in control and no Protestant theologians participated in the conciliar sessions. The council was suspended several times, the longest hiatus lasting for ten years (1552–1562), and concluded its work in 1563.

The council fathers confessed their responsibility for the evils that had grown up in the church and committed themselves to institutional reforms that would raise the standards of morality and learning among future bishops and clergy. The most significant pastoral reforms included creating an official catechism outlining the orthodox beliefs of the Roman church, establishing seminaries to direct the education of future clergy, and reforming the bishop's office by increasing his responsibilities for the pastoral life of his diocese.

# CANONS AND DECREES OF THE COUNCIL OF TRENT

On doctrinal matters, the council gave an authoritative Catholic response to Protestant teachings on a host of issues. In the following excerpt from the decrees of the Council of Trent (1545–1563), the council condemned the Protestant view that faith alone was necessary for salvation and insisted on the integration of both faith and good works in the process of salvation. This position allowed the council to defend such traditional Catholic practices as monasticism, indulgences, masses for the dead, alms giving, pilgrimages, veneration of saints, and other pious works.

### THE NECESSITY OF PREPARATION FOR JUSTIFICATION [SALVATION] IN ADULTS, AND WHENCE IT PROCEEDS

It is furthermore declared that in adults the beginning of that justification must proceed from the predisposing grace of God through Jesus Christ, that is, from His vocation, whereby, without any merits on their part, they are called; that they who by sin had been cut off from God, may be disposed through His quickening and helping grace to convert themselves to their own justification by freely assenting to and cooperating with that grace; so that, while God touches the heart of man through the illumination of the Holy Ghost, man himself neither does absolutely nothing while receiving that inspiration, since he can also reject it, nor yet is he able by his own free will and without the grace of God to move himself to justice in His sight. Hence, when it is said in the sacred writings: *Turn ye to me, and I will turn to you* [Zach. 1:3], we are reminded of our liberty; and when we reply: *Convert us, O Lord, to thee, and we shall be converted* [Lam. 5:21], we confess that we need the grace of God. . . .

## HOW THE GRATUITOUS JUSTIFICATION OF THE SINNER BY FAITH IS TO BE UNDERSTOOD

But when the Apostle [Paul] says that man is justified by faith and freely, these words are to be understood in that sense in which the uninterrupted unanimity of the Catholic Church has held and expressed them, namely, that we are therefore said to be justified by faith, because faith is the beginning of human salvation, the foundation and root of all justification, *without which it is impossible to please God* [Heb. 11:6] and to come to the fellowship of His sons; and we are therefore said to be justified gratuitously [unearned, as a freely given gift], because none of those things that precede justification, whether faith or works, merit the grace of justification. For, *if by grace, it is not now by works, otherwise,* as the Apostle says, *grace is no more grace* [Rom. 11:6]. . . .

## IN WHAT THE JUSTIFICATION OF THE SINNER CONSISTS, AND WHAT ARE ITS CAUSES

. . . For though no one can be just except he to whom the merits of the passion of our Lord Jesus Christ are communicated, yet this takes place in that justification of the sinner, when by the merit of the most holy passion, *the char-*

*ity of God is poured forth by the Holy Ghost in the hearts* [Rom. 5:5] of those who are justified and inheres in them; whence man through Jesus Christ, [with] whom he is [now one], receives in that justification, together with the remission of sins, all these infused at the same time, namely, faith, hope and charity. For faith, unless hope and charity be added to it, neither unites man perfectly with Christ nor makes him a living member of His body. For which reason it is most truly said that *faith without works is dead* [James 2:17, 20] and of no profit, and *in Christ Jesus neither circumcision availeth anything nor uncircumcision, but faith that worketh by charity* [Gal. 5:6, 6:15]. This faith, conformably to Apostolic tradition, catechumens [candidates for baptism] ask of the Church before the sacrament of baptism, when they ask for the faith that gives eternal life, which without hope and charity faith cannot give. Whence also they hear immediately the word of Christ: *If thou wilt enter into life, keep the commandments* [Matt. 19:17]. . . .

---

The council also condemned individual interpretation of the Bible and set up controls over the publication and sale of unauthorized religious books. It approved the cult of the saints and the use of images, practices condemned by Calvin and the Anabaptists.

---

Furthermore, to check unbridled spirits, it [the council] decrees that no one relying on his own judgment shall, in matters of faith and morals pertaining to the edification of Christian doctrine, distorting the Holy Scriptures in accordance with his own conceptions, presume to interpret them contrary to that sense which holy mother Church, to whom it belongs to judge of their true sense and interpretation, has held and holds, or even contrary to the unanimous teaching of the [church] Fathers, even though such interpretations should never at any time be published. Those who act contrary to this shall be made known by the ordinaries [bishops] and punished in accordance with the penalties prescribed by the law.

And wishing, as is proper, to impose a restraint in this matter on printers also, who, now without restraint, thinking what pleases them is permitted them, print without the permission of ecclesiastical superiors the books of the Holy Scriptures and the notes and commentaries thereon of all persons indiscriminately, often with the name of the press omitted, often also under a fictitious press-name, and what is worse, without the name of the author, and also indiscreetly have for sale such books printed elsewhere, (this council) decrees and ordains that in the future the Holy Scriptures, especially the old Vulgate [Latin] Edition, be printed in the most correct manner possible, and that it shall not be lawful for anyone to print or to have printed any books whatsoever dealing with sacred doctrinal matters without the name of the author, or in the future to sell them, or even to have them in possession, unless they have first been examined and approved by the ordinary [the local bishop], under penalty of anathema [condemnation and excommunication] and fine. . . .

## ON THE INVOCATION, VENERATION, AND RELICS OF SAINTS, AND ON SACRED IMAGES

The holy council commands all bishops and others who hold the office of teaching and have charge of the *cura animarum* [care of souls], that in accordance with the usage of the Catholic and Apostolic Church, received from the primitive times of the Christian religion, and with the unanimous teaching of the holy Fathers and the decrees of sacred councils, they above all instruct the faithful diligently in matters relating to intercession and invocation of the saints, the veneration of relics, and the legitimate use of images, teaching them that the saints who reign together with Christ offer up their prayers to God for men, that it is good and beneficial suppliantly

to invoke them and to have recourse to their prayers, assistance and support in order to obtain favors from God through His Son, Jesus Christ our Lord, who alone is our redeemer and savior. . . . Also, that the holy bodies of the holy martyrs and of others living with Christ, which were the living members of Christ and the temple of the Holy Ghost, to be awakened by Him to eternal life and to be glorified, are to be venerated by the faithful, through which many benefits are bestowed by God on men. . . . Moreover, that the images of Christ, of the Virgin Mother of God, and of the other saints are to be placed and retained especially in the churches, and that due honor and veneration is to be given them. . . .

---

The Council of Trent condemned the Protestant view that clergy were no different than lay people and reaffirmed the Catholic belief that the clergy, for their administration of the church's sacraments, are specially ordained intermediaries between God and human beings. Whereas Luther admitted only three sacraments—baptism, the Eucharist, and penance or confession— and Calvin only two—baptism and the Eucharist—the Council of Trent decreed that there were seven sacraments in the Catholic Church, including ordination of the clergy.

---

## CANONS ON THE SACRAMENTS IN GENERAL

Canon 1. If anyone says that the sacraments of the New Law were not all instituted by our Lord Jesus Christ, or that there are more or less than seven, namely, baptism, confirmation, Eucharist, penance, extreme unction, order and matrimony, or that any one of these seven is not truly and intrinsically a sacrament, let him be anathema [cursed]. . . .

Can. 10. If anyone says that all Christians have the power to administer the word and all the sacraments, let him be anathema. . . .

## CANONS ON THE SACRAMENT OF ORDER

Canon 1. If anyone says that there is not in the New Testament a visible and external priesthood, or that there is no power of consecrating and offering the true body and blood of the Lord and of forgiving . . . sins, but only the office and bare ministry of preaching the Gospel; or that those who do not preach are not priests at all, let him be anathema. . . .

Can. 4. If anyone says that by sacred ordination the Holy [Spirit] is not imparted and that therefore the bishops say in vain: *Receive ye the Holy* [*Spirit*], or that by it a character is not imprinted, or that he who has once been a priest can again become a layman, let him be anathema.

Can. 5. If anyone says that the holy unction which the Church uses in ordination is not only not required but is detestable and pernicious, as also are the other ceremonies of order, let him be anathema.

Can. 6. If anyone says that in the Catholic Church there is not instituted a hierarchy by divine ordinance, which consists of bishops, priests and ministers, let him be anathema.

Can. 7. If anyone says that bishops are not superior to priests, or that they have not the power to confirm and ordain, or that the power which they have is common to them and to priests, or that orders conferred by them without the consent or call of the people or of the secular power are invalid, or that those who have been neither rightly ordained nor sent by ecclesiastical and canonical authority, but come from elsewhere, are lawful ministers of the word and of the sacraments, let him be anathema.

# Saint Ignatius Loyola
# *THE SPIRITUAL EXERCISES*

Even before the Council of Trent had been called to respond to the challenge of Protestant teachings, the Basque nobleman Saint Ignatius Loyola (1491–1556) founded a new religious order, the Society of Jesus, popularly called the Jesuits. A former soldier, Ignatius underwent a spiritual conversion in 1521–1522 and, after seeking guidance about his vocation, decided to become a priest. Later, while studying at the University of Paris, Ignatius and several companions decided to found their order and received papal recognition in 1540.

The new Jesuit order was characterized by three unusual features. First, the members took a special oath of obedience to the pope, which bound them to support the papacy and its programs with special devotion. Second, they rejected the traditional monastic ideal of a life of contemplation and instead espoused a life of active service in the world. Third, they were especially committed to the Christian education of youth and to missionary work among pagans and heretics.

The Jesuits soon became the vanguard of the Roman Catholic Church's effort to resist what it believed to be Protestant errors and to hasten the restoration of Catholicism in those lands where it no longer was the dominant religion. Ignatius himself thought it vital for his followers, and for the Catholic laity as well, to "think with the mind of the Church." To help Catholics achieve a higher spiritual life, Ignatius composed a book during 1521–1535 called *The Spiritual Exercises*. It became a guide for Jesuit confessors or counselors in leading penitents to a greater spiritual maturity. It was a summary of practical ways to order one's life through the imitation of Christ.

In the last section of *The Spiritual Exercises,* written during the early 1530s, Ignatius gives final instructions to his followers: a set of rules for "thinking with the Church." These guidelines reflect the response of reformed Catholicism to the great theological issues raised by Luther, Calvin, and other Protestants.

## RULES FOR THINKING WITH THE CHURCH

In order to have the proper attitude of mind in the Church Militant [all active, living Christians] we should observe the following rules:

1. Putting aside all private judgment, we should keep our minds prepared and ready to obey promptly and in all things the true spouse of Christ our Lord, our Holy Mother, the hierarchical Church.

2. To praise sacramental confession and the reception of the Most Holy Sacrament [the Eucharist] once a year, and much better once a month, and better still every week, with the requisite and proper dispositions.

3. To praise the frequent hearing of Mass, singing of hymns and psalms, and the recitation of long prayers, both in and out of church; also the hours arranged for fixed times for the whole Divine Office, for prayers of all kinds and for the canonical hours.

4. To praise highly religious life, virginity, and continence; and also matrimony, but not as highly, as any of the foregoing.

5. To praise the vows of religion, obedience, poverty, chastity, and other works of perfection and supererogation.[1] It must be remembered that a vow is made in matters that lead to evangelical perfection. It is therefore improper to make a vow in matters that depart from this perfection; as, for example, to enter business, to get married, and so forth.

6. To praise the relics of the saints by venerating them and by praying to these saints. Also to praise the stations, pilgrimages, indulgences, jubilees,[2] Crusade indulgences, and the lighting of candles in the churches.

7. To praise the precepts concerning fasts and abstinences, such as those of Lent, Ember Days,[3] Vigils, Fridays, and Saturdays; likewise to praise acts of penance, both interior and exterior.

8. To praise the adornments and buildings of churches as well as sacred images, and to venerate them according to what they represent.

9. Finally, to praise all the precepts of the church, holding ourselves ready at all times to find reasons for their defense, and never offending against them.

10. We should be more inclined to approve and praise the directions and recommendations of our superiors as well as their personal behavior. Although sometimes these may not be or may not have been praiseworthy, to speak against them when preaching in public or in conversation with people would give rise to murmuring and scandal rather than to edification. As a result, the people would be angry with their superiors, whether temporal or spiritual. Still, while it does harm to our superiors in their absence to speak ill of them in the presence of the people, it might be useful to speak of their bad conduct to those who can apply a remedy.

---

[1]The performance of good works beyond what God requires.

[2]*Stations* refers to a set of prayers recited while meditating on certain moments in the passion and death of Christ. Jubilees were certain years set aside by the papacy during which special indulgences were offered to pilgrims attending certain shrines, particularly that of Saint Peter in Rome.

[3]Three Ember Days were set aside by the church each season for special prayers and fasting.

11. To praise both positive and scholastic theology, for as it is more characteristic of the [early church] doctors, such as St. Augustine, St. Jerome, St. Gregory, and others, to encourage the affections to greater love and service of God our Lord in all things, so it also is more characteristic of the [medieval] scholastic doctors, such as St. Thomas, St. Bonaventure, and the Master of the Sentences,[4] etc., to define and explain for our times the things necessary for eternal salvation, and to refute and expose all errors and fallacies. Also, the scholastic doctors, being of more recent date, not only have a clearer understanding of the Holy Scripture and of the teachings of the [early church] doctors, but also, being enlightened and inspired by the Divine Power, they are helped by the Councils, Canons, and Constitutions of our Holy Mother Church. . . .

13. If we wish to be sure that we are right in all things, we should always be ready to accept this principle: I will believe that the white that I see is black, if the hierarchical Church so defines it. For, I believe that between the Bridegroom, Christ our Lord, and the Bride, His Church, there is but one spirit, which governs and directs us for the salvation of our souls, for the same Spirit and Lord, who gave us the Ten Commandments, guides and governs our Holy Mother Church.

14. Although it be true that no one can be saved unless it be predestined and unless he have faith and grace, still we must be very careful of our manner of discussing and speaking of these matters. [See Calvin's *Institutes*, page 324.]

15. We should not make predestination an habitual subject of conversation. If it is sometimes mentioned we must speak in such a way that no person will fall into error, as happens on occasion when one will say, "It has already been determined whether I will be saved or lost, and in spite of all the good or evil that I do, this will not be changed." As a result, they become apathetic and neglect the works that are conducive to their salvation and to the spiritual growth of their souls.

16. In like manner, we must be careful lest by speaking too much and with too great emphasis on faith, without any distinction or explanation, we give occasion to the people to become indolent and lazy in the performance of good works, whether it be before or after their faith is founded in charity.

17. Also in our discourse we ought not to emphasize the doctrine that would destroy free will. We may therefore speak of faith and grace to the extent that God enables us to do so, for the greater praise of His Divine Majesty. But, in these dangerous times of ours, it must not be done in such a way that good works or free will suffer any detriment or be considered worthless.

---

[4]*Master of the Sentences* is a reference to Peter Lombard (c. 1100–c. 1160), an Italian theologian whose book *Sentences* was the most widely used theology textbook in the medieval universities.

## REVIEW QUESTIONS

1. What was the Catholic doctrine on justification by faith defined by the Council of Trent and how did it differ from the views of Luther and Calvin?
2. How did the Council of Trent approach the problem of authoritative interpretation of the Scriptures and of church doctrines?
3. How did Saint Ignatius' "rules for thinking with the church" respond to Protestant beliefs and practices?
4. The Jesuits became major patrons of the visual and fine arts during the Catholic reformation after the Council of Trent. What aspect of Ignatius' teachings might have drawn them to this role?

# CHAPTER 11
# *Early Modern Society and Politics*

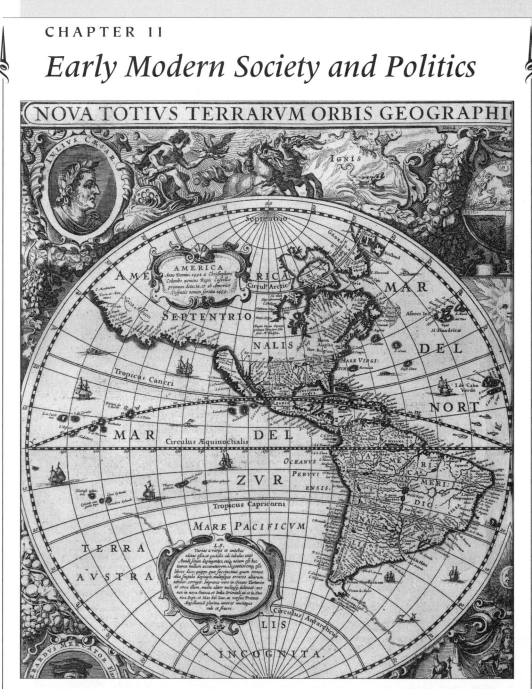

WESTERN HEMISPHERE, detail of Mercator's world map, 1636. Voyages of exploration throughout the sixteenth and seventeenth centuries opened up vast new trade opportunities for the Western Europeans. (*Mercator Hondius Janssonius,* Atlas or a Geographicke Description of the World *[Amsterdam, 1636].* Vol. I [Facsimile by Theatrum Orbis Terrarum B.V., 2 vols., 1967.] Courtesy of the Harvard Map Collection.)

The period from the Renaissance through the Scientific Revolution saw the breakdown of distinctively medieval cultural, political, and economic forms. The Renaissance produced a more secular attitude and expressed confidence in human capacities. Shortly afterward, the Protestant Reformation ended the religious unity of medieval Latin Christendom and weakened the political power of the church. At the same time the discovery of new trade routes to East Asia and of new lands across the Atlantic widened the imagination and ambitions of Christian Europeans and precipitated a commercial revolution. This great expansion of economic activity furthered capitalism and initiated a global economy—two developments associated with the modern world.

In the late fifteenth century, many Europeans encountered peoples whose cultures markedly differed from their own. The Portuguese, trying to break the Muslim monopoly over trade between Europe and eastern Asia, explored along the Atlantic coast of Africa, establishing their first links with the peoples and kingdoms of the sub-Saharan regions of modern Guinea, Ghana, Dahomey, and the Congo. Setting up fortified trading posts along the way, they eventually sailed around the Cape of Good Hope at the tip of Africa and reached India in 1498. By 1516, Portuguese merchants had reached the port of Canton in southern China. The Portuguese established fortified trading posts in India and Southeast Asia, some of which (Goa, Timor, Macao) they continued to hold into the late twentieth century.

In India, China, and Japan, the Portuguese found highly advanced civilizations that were able to resist European political and cultural domination fairly effectively. In contrast, the Spanish, with the discovery of the Caribbean islands by Christopher Columbus in 1492, encountered a local population living in a Stone Age culture. There were no cities, no state structures, no significant architecture or art; technology was primitive, and contacts with other peoples limited. However, after 1518 when the Spanish landed on the American mainland, they found in Mexico, Yucatán, and Peru advanced civilizations with great cities, well-developed governments, monumental architecture, and extensive commercial networks. The vast regions and diverse peoples of the Americas were gradually linked to Europe's Christian culture and expanding economy during the sixteenth and seventeenth centuries.

Exploration and commercial expansion created the foundations of a global economy in which the European economy was tied to Asian spices, African slaves, and American silver. A wide variety of goods circulated all over the globe. From the West Indies and East Asia, sugar, rice, tea, cacao, and tobacco flowed into Europe. From the Americas, potatoes, corn, sweet potatoes, and manioc (from which tapioca is made) spread to the rest of the world. Europeans paid for Asian silks and spices with American silver.

The increasing demand for goods and a rise in prices produced more opportunities for the accumulation and investment of capital by private individuals, which is the essence of capitalism. State policies designed to increase national wealth and power also stimulated the growth of capitalism. Governments subsidized new industries, chartered joint-stock companies to engage in overseas trade, and struck at internal tariffs and guild regulations that hampered domestic economic growth. Improvements in banking, shipbuilding, mining, and manufacturing further stimulated economic growth.

In the sixteenth and seventeenth centuries the old medieval political order dissolved, and the modern state began to emerge. The modern state has a strong central government that issues laws that apply throughout the land and a permanent army of professional soldiers paid by the state. Trained bureaucrats, responsible to the central government, collect taxes, enforce laws, and administer justice. The modern state has a secular character; promotion of religion is not the state's concern, and churches do not determine state policy. These features of the modern state were generally not prevalent in the Middle Ages, when the nobles, church, and towns possessed powers and privileges that impeded central authority, and kings were expected to rule in accordance with Christian principles. In the sixteenth and seventeenth centuries, monarchs were exercising central authority with ever-greater effectiveness at the expense of nobles and clergy. The secularization of the state became firmly established after the Thirty Years' War (1618–1648); with their states worn out by Catholic-Protestant conflicts, kings came to act less for religious motives than for reasons of national security and power.

Historically, the modern state has been characterized by a devotion to the nation and by feelings of national pride. There is a national language that is used throughout the land, and the people have a sense of sharing a common culture and history, of being distinct from other peoples. There were some signs of growing national feeling during the sixteenth and seventeenth centuries, but this feature of the modern state did not become a major part of European political life until the nineteenth century. During the early modern period, loyalty was largely given to a town, to a province, to a noble, or to the person of the king rather than to the nation, the people as a whole.

# 1 The Age of Exploration and Conquest

In 1498, a Portuguese explorer, Vasco da Gama (c. 1460–1524) sailed a fleet of four ships around Africa into the Indian Ocean and landed at the Indian port of Calicut. His voyage marked the first step in the creation of a Portuguese commercial empire in East Asia. For centuries afterward, Europeans competed by fair means and foul for access to and control of the Asian trade. The Dutch, English, and French eventually established trading posts and colonies along the same routes pioneered by the Portuguese. Meanwhile, the Spaniards, following the initial discovery of the Caribbean islands by Columbus in 1492, proceeded to explore, conquer, and settle the mainland of Central, South, and North America.

# Bernal Díaz del Castillo
# THE DISCOVERY AND CONQUEST
# OF MEXICO

In 1518, Spanish ships explored the mainland coast along the Gulf of Mexico near the Yucatán Peninsula. The following year an expedition under the leadership of Hernando Cortés (1485–1547) landed at the site of modern Veracruz to explore the newly discovered country. There the Spaniards were unexpectedly confronted with ambassadors from Montezuma (c. 1502–1520), the ruler of an extensive Aztec empire; the Aztecs presented Cortés with gifts made of jade, gold, and silver and with rich textiles, and urged that the Spaniards depart—Montezuma feared Cortés was the Aztec god Quetzalcoatl who had come to reclaim his kingdom. Having 555 troops together with 16 horses and some cannons, Cortés refused and announced that he was sent by his king to speak directly with Montezuma. Sinking his ships to prevent his troops from deserting, Cortés marched inland to the Aztec capital, Tenochtitlán, the site of today's Mexico City; the Spaniards found a civilization with a high level of social and political organization and advanced techniques of engineering, architecture, writing, astronomy, painting, and ceramics. Located on islands in the midst of a lake, Tenochtitlán was approached by three stone causeways that converged in a great central square, dominated by a high pyramidal temple. Other magnificent stone temples and palaces, paved marketplaces, canals with boats carrying products needed by the busy inhabitants, and cultivated gardens with aviaries presented impressive urban scenes. Thousands of priests, soldiers, civil servants, artisans, and laborers filled the streets and houses.

The following excerpts are from *The Discovery and Conquest of Mexico,* the personal memoir of Bernal Díaz del Castillo (c. 1492–1581). Díaz accompanied Cortés and wrote an eyewitness account of this first confrontation between Christian and Aztec civilizations. In the following passage Díaz described Montezuma and his courtiers. Although generally favorable in his account of Montezuma, Díaz reported a rumor that the Aztec emperor ate human flesh for dinner. Whether the Aztecs were cannibals is still disputed among scholars.

The Great Montezuma was about forty years old, of good height and well proportioned, slender and spare of flesh, not very swarthy, but of the natural colour and shade of an Indian. He did not wear his hair long, but so as just to cover his ears, his scanty black beard was well shaped and thin. His face was somewhat long, but cheerful, and he had good eyes and showed in his appearance and manner both tenderness and, when necessary, gravity. He was very neat and clean and bathed once every day in the afternoon. He had many women as mistresses, daughters of Chieftains, and he had two great Cacicas [noblewomen] as his legitimate wives. He was free from unnatural offences. The clothes that he wore one day, he did not put on again until four days later. He had over two hundred Chieftains in his guard, in other rooms close to his own, not that all were meant to converse with him, but only one or another, and when they went to speak to him they were obliged to take off their rich mantles [cloaks] and put on others of little worth, but they had to be clean, and they had to enter barefoot with their eyes lowered to the ground, and not to look up in his face. And they made him three obeisances [bows], and said: "Lord, my Lord, my Great Lord," before they came up to him, and then they made their report and with few words he dismissed them, and on taking leave they did not turn their backs, but kept their faces towards him with their eyes to the ground, and they did not turn their backs until they left the room. I noticed another thing, that when other great chiefs came from distant lands about disputes or business, when they reached the apartments of the Great Montezuma, they had to come barefoot and with poor mantles, and they might not enter directly into the Palace, but had to loiter about a little on one side of the Palace door, for to enter hurriedly was considered to be disrespectful. . . .

I have heard it said that they were wont to cook for him the flesh of young boys, but as he had such a variety of dishes, made of so many things, we could not succeed in seeing if they were of human flesh or of other things, for they daily cooked fowls, turkeys, pheasants, native partridges, quail, tame and wild ducks, venison, wild boar, reed birds, pigeons, hares and rabbits, and many sorts of birds and other things which are bred in this country, and they are so numerous that I cannot finish naming them in a hurry; so we had no insight into it;

but I know for certain that after our Captain [Cortés] censured the sacrifice of human beings, and the eating of their flesh, he ordered that such food should not be prepared for him thenceforth. . . .

. . . While Montezuma was at table eating, as I have described, there were waiting on him two other graceful women to bring him tortillas, kneaded with eggs and other sustaining ingredients, and these tortillas were very white, and they were brought on plates covered with clean napkins, and they also brought him another kind of bread, like long balls kneaded with other kinds of sustaining food, and *pan pachol,* for so they call it in this country, which is a sort of wafer. There were also placed on the table three tubes much painted and gilded, which held *liquidambar* [a sort of sweet gum] mixed with certain herbs which they call *tabaco,* and when he had finished eating, after they had danced before him and sung and the table was removed, he inhaled the smoke from one of those tubes, but he took very little of it and with that he fell asleep. . . .

Let us leave this and go on to another great house, where they keep many Idols, and they say that they are their fierce gods, and with them many kinds of carnivorous beasts of prey, tigers and two kinds of lions, and animals something like wolves and foxes, and other smaller carnivorous animals, and all these carnivores they feed with flesh, and the greater number of them breed in the house. They give them as food deer and fowls, dogs and other things which they are used to hunt, and I have heard it said that they feed them on the bodies of the Indians who have been sacrificed. It is in this way; you have already heard me say that when they sacrifice a wretched Indian they saw open the chest with stone knives and hasten to tear out the palpitating heart and blood, and offer it to their Idols, in whose name the sacrifice is made. Then they cut off the thighs, arms and head and eat the former at feasts and banquets, and the head they hang up on some beams, and the body of the man sacrificed is not eaten but given to these fierce animals. They also have in that cursed house many vipers and poisonous snakes which carry on their tails things that sound like bells. These are the worst vipers of all, and they keep them in jars and great pottery vessels with many feathers, and there they lay their eggs and rear their young, and they give them to eat the bodies of the Indians who have been sacrificed, and the flesh of dogs which they are in the habit of breeding.

Let me speak now of the infernal noise when the lions and tigers roared and the jackals and foxes howled and the serpents hissed, it was horrible to listen to and it seemed like a hell. Let us go on and speak of the skilled workmen Montezuma employed in every craft that was practised among them. We will begin with lapidaries [gem cutters] and workers in gold and silver and all the hollow work, which even the great goldsmiths in Spain were forced to admire. . . . Let us go on to the great craftsmen in feather work, and painters and sculptors who were most refined; then to the Indian women who did the weaving and the washing, who made such an immense quantity of fine fabrics with wonderful featherwork designs; the greater part of it was brought daily from some towns of the province on the north coast near Vera Cruz called Cotaxtla.

---

Díaz records with amazement the great central marketplace with its merchants and myriad products.

---

. . . When we arrived at the great market place, called Tlaltelolco, we were astounded at the number of people and the quantity of merchandise that it contained, and at the good order and control that was maintained, for we had never seen such a thing before. The chieftains who accompanied us acted as guides. Each kind of merchandise was kept by itself and had its fixed place marked out. Let us begin with the dealers in gold, silver, and precious stones, feathers, mantles, and embroi-

dered goods. Then there were other wares consisting of Indian slaves both men and women; and I say that they bring as many of them to that great market for sale as the Portuguese bring negroes from Guinea; and they brought them along tied to long poles, with collars round their necks so that they could not escape, and others they left free. Next there were other traders who sold great pieces of cloth and cotton, and articles of twisted thread, and there were *cacahuateros* who sold cacao. In this way one could see every sort of merchandise that is to be found in the whole of New Spain [Spain's name for Mexico]. . . .

. . . And we saw the fresh water that comes from Chapultepec [a wooded area near Tenochtitlán] which supplies the city, and we saw the bridges on the three causeways which were built at certain distances apart through which the water of the lake flowed in and out from one side to the other, and we beheld on that great lake a great multitude of canoes, some coming with supplies of food and others returning loaded with cargoes of merchandise; and we saw that from every house of that great city and of all the other cities that were built in the water it was impossible to pass from house to house, except by drawbridges which were made of wood or in canoes; and we saw in those cities Cues [pyramidal temples] and oratories like towers and fortresses and all gleaming white, and it was a wonderful thing to behold; then the houses with flat roofs, and on the causeways other small towers and oratories which were like fortresses.

After having examined and considered all that we had seen we turned to look at the great market place and the crowds of people that were in it, some buying and others selling, so that the murmur and hum of their voices and words that they used could be heard more than a league off. Some of the soldiers among us who had been in many parts of the world, in Constantinople, and all over Italy, and in Rome, said that so large a market place and so full of people, and so well regulated and arranged, they had never beheld before. . . .

---

When Cortés mocks the Aztec ruler's religious devotion to his gods and proposes setting up the Christian cross and image of the Virgin Mary, Montezuma reproaches him.

---

. . . Our Captain said to Montezuma through our interpreter, half laughing: "Señor Montezuma, I do not understand how such a great Prince and wise man as you are has not come to the conclusion, in your mind, that these idols of yours are not gods, but evil things that are called devils, and so that you may know it and all your priests may see it clearly, do me the favour to approve of my placing a cross here on the top of this tower, and that in one part of these oratories where your Huichilobos and Tezcatepuca [Aztec gods] stand we may divide off a space where we can set up an image of Our Lady (an image which Montezuma had already seen) and you will see by the fear in which these Idols hold it that they are deceiving you."

Montezuma replied half angrily (and the two priests who were with him showed great annoyance), and said: "Señor Malinche [Aztec name for Cortés], if I had known that you would have said such defamatory things I would not have shown you my gods, we consider them to be very good, for they give us health and rains and good seed times and seasons and as many victories as we desire, and we are obliged to worship them and make sacrifices, and I pray you not to say another word to their dishonour." . . .

---

The Spaniards decide to build a Christian chapel within the walls of the huge Aztec palace in which they are quartered, hoping to convert the Aztecs by the example of their own Christian religious devotions. By chance, they discover a secret door to a room filled with treasure.

---

. . . Now as there was a rumour and we had heard the story that Montezuma kept the treasure of his father Axayaca in that building, it was suspected that it might be in this chamber which had been closed up and cemented only a few days before. Yañes spoke about it to Juan Valásquez de Leon and Francisco de Lugo, and those Captains told the story to Cortés, and the door was secretly opened. When it was opened Cortés and some of his Captains went in first, and they saw such a number of jewels and slabs and plates of gold and chalchihuites [figures of goddesses] and other great riches, that they were quite carried away and did not know what to say about such wealth. The news soon spread among all the other Captains and soldiers, and very secretly we went in to see it. When I saw it I marvelled, and as at that time I was a youth and had never seen such riches as those in my life before, I took it for certain that there could not be another such store of wealth in the whole world. It was decided by all our captains and soldiers, that we should not dream of touching a particle of it, but that the stones should immediately be put back in the doorway and it should be sealed up and cemented just as we found it, and that it should not be spoken about, lest it should reach Montezuma's ears, until times should alter.

## REVIEW QUESTIONS

1. What evidence did Bernal Díaz del Castillo offer to show that the Aztecs were a highly civilized people?
2. What moral and religious practices of the Aztecs did the Spaniards find strange and contrary to Christian beliefs?

## 2   Toward the Modern Economy: The Example of Holland

The Spanish and Portuguese monopoly of trade was challenged in the late sixteenth century, first by English privateers who preyed on the Spanish fleets crossing the Atlantic and then by the Dutch who were in revolt against their sovereign, the Spanish king Philip II (1556–1598). Earlier, the Dutch had traded with both Spanish and Portuguese ports, but were not allowed to seek markets directly with the Americas or the East Indies. When Philip II, who was also king of Portugal from 1580, excluded the rebellious Dutch from trading in his ports—a policy that was renewed by his son, Philip III (1598–1621)—Dutch merchants decided to break the Portuguese monopoly over trade with the East Indies. In doing so, they launched the first of many commercial wars designed to win control over world trade markets.

To encourage trade with the East Indies, the Dutch government established a private limited stockholding company, the East India Company, and granted it a monopoly over trade and colonization anywhere east of the Cape of Good Hope or beyond the Straits of Magellan at the southern tip of South America. The company was granted the right to build fortresses, to raise armies, to establish laws and courts in territories it captured from the Spanish or the Portuguese, and to enter into diplomatic alliances with other princes. The East India Company was the foundation on which the Dutch built their colonial empire. Other European states established similar corporations to further trade and colonization.

## John Keymer
## DUTCH TRADE AND COMMERCE AS A MODEL

The rapid growth of Holland's wealth and the general prosperity of the Dutch people in the early seventeenth century drew the attention of many Europeans to what seemed an economic wonder. Despite the absence of notable natural resources, such as forests, minerals, or climate favorable for growing grain, the Dutch had become the dominant economic power in northern Europe.

In the early seventeenth century, an Englishman named John Keymer published a series of tracts urging major reforms in English economic policies to permit more rapid development of English industry and commerce. Like many other economists of the period, he looked at the Dutch economy as a model to be adopted by other nations. Although Keymer shared the prevalent view that national wealth was measured by stores of precious metals in bullion or coin, his description of the Dutch economy revealed a more complicated reality. In his tract *Observations Touching Trade and Commerce with the Hollanders, and Other Nations*—falsely attributed to Sir Walter Raleigh (c. 1552–1618), who was noted for his interest in promoting English overseas trade and colonization—Keymer described the unusual character of the Dutch economy and the factors leading to its great success.

*May it please your most Excellent Majesty,*

I have diligently, in my travels, observed how the countries herein mentioned [mainly Holland] do grow potent with abundance of all things to serve themselves and other nations, where nothing groweth; and that their never dryed fountains of wealth, by which they raise their estate to such an admirable height, [so] that they are . . . [now] a wonder to the world, [come] from your Majesty's seas and lands.

I thus moved, began to dive into the depth of their policies and circumventing practices, whereby they drain, and still covet to exhaust, the wealth and coin of this kingdom, and so with our own commodities to weaken us, and finally beat us quite out of trading in other countries. I found that they more fully obtained these their purposes by their convenient privileges, and settled constitutions, than *England* with all the laws, and superabundance of home-bred commodities which God hath [bestowed on] your sea and land. . . .

To bring this to pass they have many advantages of us; the one is, by their fashioned ships called boyers, hoy-barks, hoys, and others that are made to hold great bulk of merchandise, and to sail with a few men for profit. For example, . . . [Dutch ships] do serve the merchant better cheap by one hundred pounds [English money] in his freight than we can, by reason he hath but nine or ten mariners, and we near thirty; thus he saveth twenty men's meat and wages in a voyage; and so in all other their ships according to their burden, by which means they are freighted wheresoever they come, to great profit, whilst our ships lie still and decay. . . .

Of this their smallness of custom [duty] inwards and outwards, we have daily experience; for if two *English* ships, or two of any other nations be at *Bourdeaux* [a French port, exporting mainly wine], both laden with wine of three hundred tons apiece, the one bound for *Holland,* or any other petty [small] states, the other for *England,* the merchant shall pay about nine hundred pounds custom here, and other duties, when the other in *Holland,* or any other petty states, shall be cleared for less than fifty pounds, and so in all other wares and merchandizes accordingly, which draws all nations to traffick with them; and although it seems but small duties which they receive, yet the multitudes of all kind of commodities and coin that is brought in by themselves and others, and carried out by themselves and others, is so great, that they receive more custom and duties to the state, by the greatness of their commerce in one year, than *England* doth in two years. . . .

And if it happen that a trade be stopped by any foreign nation, which they heretofore usually had, or hear of any good trading which they never had, they will hinder others, and seek either by favour, money, or force, to open the gap of traffick for advancement of trade amongst themselves, and employment of their people.

And when there is a new course or trade erected, they give free custom inwards and outwards, for the better maintenance of navigation, and encouragement of the people to that business.

Thus they and others glean the wealth and strength from us to themselves; and these reasons following procure them this advantage of us.

1. The merchant[s] . . . which maketh all things in abundance, by reason of their store-houses continually replenished with all kind of commodities.
2. The liberty of free traffick for strangers to buy and sell in *Holland,* and other countries and states, as if they were free-born, maketh great intercourse.
3. The small duties levied upon merchants, draws all nations to trade with them.
4. Their fashioned ships continually freighted before ours, by reason of their few mariners and great bulk, serving the merchant cheap.
5. Their forwardness to further all manner of trading.
6. Their wonderful employment of their busses [herring boats] for fishing, and the great returns they make.
7. Their giving free custom inwards and outwards, for any new-erected trade, by means whereof they have gotten already almost the sole trade into their hands. . . .

The merchandises of *France, Portugal, Spain, Italy, Turkey, East* and *West-Indies,* are transported most by the *Hollanders,* and other petty states, into the east and northeast kingdoms of [Europe] . . . and the merchandises brought from the last-mentioned. . ., being wonderful many, are likewise by the *Hollanders* and other petty states most transported into the southern and western dominions, and yet the situation of *England* lieth far better for a storehouse to serve the south-east and north-east regions than theirs doth, and hath far better means to do it, if we will bend our course for it.

No sooner a dearth of fish, wine, or corn here, and other merchandise, but forthwith the *Emdeners, Hamburghers* [from the German ports of Emden and Hamburg], and *Hollanders,* out of their store-houses, [load] fifty or one hundred ships, or more, dispersing themselves round about this kingdom, and carry away great store of coin and wealth for little commodity, in those times of dearth; by which means they suck our commonwealth of

her riches, cut down our merchants, and decay our navigation; not with their natural commodities, which grow in their own countries, but the merchandises of other countries and kingdoms.

Therefore it is far more easy to serve ourselves, hold up our merchants, and increase our ships and mariners, and strengthen the kingdom; and not only keep our money in our own realm, which other nations still rob us of, but bring in theirs who carry ours away, and make the bank or coin a store-house to serve other nations as well, and far better cheap than they. . . .

The abundance of corn groweth in the east kingdoms [of Europe], but the great store-houses for grain to serve Christendom, and heathen countries in the time of dearth, is in the *Low-Countries* [Holland and modern-day Belgium], wherewith, upon every occasion of scarcity and dearth they do inrich themselves seven years after, employ their people, and get great freights for their ships in other countries, and we not one in that course.

The mighty vineyards and store of salt is in *France* and *Spain;* but the great vintage and staple of salt is in the *Low-Countries,* and they send near one thousand sail of ships with salt and wine only into the east kingdoms yearly, besides other places, and we not one in that course.

The exceeding groves of wood are in the east kingdoms, but the huge piles of [lumber] . . . and timber, is in the *Low-Countries,* where none grow, wherewith they serve themselves and other parts, and this kingdom with those commodities; they have five or six hundred great long ships continually using that trade, and we none in that course.

The wool, cloth, lead, tin, and divers other commodities, are in *England;* but by means of our wool and cloth going out rough, undress'd, and undy'd, there is an exceeding manufactory and drapery in the *Low-Countries,* wherewith they serve themselves and other nations, and advance greatly the employment of their people at home, and traffick abroad, and put down ours in foreign parts, where our merchants trade unto, with our own commodities. . . .

The *Low-Countries* send into the east kingdoms yearly, about three thousand ships, trading into every city and port-town, taking the advantage, and vending their commodities to exceeding profit, and buying and lading their ships with plenty of those commodities, which they have from every of those towns 20 *per cent.* cheaper than we, by reason of the difference of the coin, and their fish yields ready money, which greatly advanceth their traffick, and decayeth ours.

# William Carr
# CAPITALISM IN AMSTERDAM

In 1693, William Carr, the English consul at Amsterdam, wrote a travelers' guide to the leading cities of Holland, Flanders, northern Germany, and Scandinavia. Of these, the largest and wealthiest was Amsterdam in Holland. In less than a century, this once-small medieval city had grown to become the most important commercial port in the West and the center of European financial capitalism. In the following selections, Carr describes the products and items of trade that flowed through the hands of the Amsterdam merchants; the excerpts have been adapted, using modern language and spelling.

I now come to speak of Amsterdam, my home for several years, which I shall describe in more detail than I do other places. It is considered by intelligent men to be the second city in the world in the matters of trade and not inferior in wealth to any city. Certainly, Amsterdam is one of the most beautiful cities in the world; its buildings are large, and its streets for the most part are pleasantly planted with trees and neatly paved. And although, as I have already said, Amsterdam may justly be taken for the second or third city in the world after London and Paris, it has neither court nor university as they have.

Amsterdam, for the wise statesmen it has produced, is said to be a second Athens; others regard it as the storehouse of Europe, for it has such great stores of grain that it is able to supply many other nations. And second, it is known for the great stores of spices that are distributed all over Europe and the Indies by the East India Company. Third, it has an inconceivably great supply of war provisions, so that England and other countries purchase military supplies in Amsterdam. There are several shopkeepers in Amsterdam who can deliver arms for four thousand or five thousand men at a cheaper rate than can be obtained anywhere else; they can do this because of their great industry in controlling the market of products from iron works on the Rhine and other rivers that run into Holland. Fourth, Amsterdam has more stores of lumber for shipbuilding than can be found in any nation in the world; this is the reason why its neighboring town Sardam can build ships 20 per cent more cheaply than can be done in England or France. For this reason both France and Spain buy ships in Holland. . . . Fifth, Amsterdam . . . supplies Europe and many places in the Indies with vermillion [a bright red dye]. . . . Sixth, Amsterdam is the market from which the king of France [Louis XIV] bought marble for Versailles, the Louvre, and other palaces in France. There are such vast storehouses of marble in Amsterdam that one would think that there were marble quarries near the city gates. Seventh, Amsterdam has the most active bank in the world. . . . There are many other points I could list to demonstrate the great riches and trade of Amsterdam, including the vast quantities of wines and brandy-wines that its merchants sell in northern Europe, from which they import hemp, pitch, and tar to sell to France, Italy, and Spain. They also control much of the marketing of Sweden's copper and iron.

---

Carr then describes the commercial trading system of the famous Dutch East India Company, which established trading posts in South Africa, the Persian Gulf area, India, Ceylon, Bangladesh, Indonesia, China, and Japan. (Although not mentioned by Carr, the Dutch West India Company conducted similar operations in the Caribbean and North America. The Dutch trading post of New Amsterdam at the mouth of the Hudson River would become the city of New York, the world center of finance capitalism in the twentieth century.)

---

. . . The East India Company of the Netherlands is said to be a commonwealth within a commonwealth, and this is true when you consider the sovereign power and privileges the company has been granted by the States General [the ruling council of the Dutch Republic] and also consider its riches and vast number of subjects, and the many territories and colonies it possesses in the East Indies. The company is said to have 30,000 men in its constant employ and more than 200 capital ships, in addition to its sloops, ketches, and yachts. The company possesses many colonies formerly belonging to Spain, Portugal, and various Indian princes, and as good Christians company members have spread the Gospel of Christ in these lands, printing the Bible, prayer books, and catechisms in Indian languages and maintaining ministers and teachers to instruct those that are converted to the faith. Having said that this company is so extensive—as it were a commonwealth apart—I will demonstrate that

it is a commonwealth first by its power, riches, and strength in the East Indies, and second, by its position in Europe. . . . But I will begin at the Cape of Good Hope [Africa] where the company has built a fort where it maintains a garrison to defend its ships when they stop there for fresh water. From there let us view the company on the island of Java, where it has built a fair city called Batavia and fortified it with bastions like those in Amsterdam. This city is the residence of the company's grand minister of state, called the General of the Indies. He has six privy counsellors (ordinary) and two extraordinary; they oversee the concerns of the company throughout the Indies, including matters of war and peace. . . . The General of the Indies has horse and foot soldiers, officers, and servants—as if he were a sovereign prince—all paid for by the company. . . . So formidable is the company in the East Indies that it looks as though it aims to rule the South Seas. It also has a great trade with China and Japan. . . . With Persia also it has great commerce and is so confident that it wages war with the Persian monarch if he wrongs it in trade. It also has several colonies on the coast of Malabar and Coromandel [west coast of India] and in the country of the Great Mogul. . . . But especially let us examine the company on the rich island of Ceylon [Sri Lanka] where it controls the plains, so the king of the island is forced to live in the mountains while the company possesses the city of Colombo. . . . I will say no more of the company's power in the Indies, but let us examine its position in Europe. To begin with, in Amsterdam the company has two large stately palaces, one being in the old part of the city, and the other in the new; in the old part it keeps its court—where the Resident Committee of the company sits—and sells the company's goods.

---

The most important institutional support for the growth of capitalism in Amsterdam was the merchants' exchange bank. Founded in 1609 under municipal supervision, it provided a safe, convenient depository for the coined money and bullion of its several thousand depositors, who included both foreign and Dutch merchants, kings, princely nobles, and governments. The bank allowed merchants to pay debts and receive payments from debtors by a system of bills of exchange or paper notes; for a fee, it provided customers with a daily statement of their accounts. Carr's description of the bank follows.

. . . [T]he Merchants' Bank . . . is governed by divers commissioners, clerks and bookkeepers, and an assay-master who judges [the quality and value of] the gold and silver that at any time is brought into the bank uncoined. The security given for the bank's preservation are the States [the Dutch parliament] and Magistrates of Amsterdam. Now, if you have a mind to put money into the bank, perhaps 1,000 pounds sterling, more or less, you must go to the clerks and ask for a folio for your name, and then pay in your money at 3 or 4 percent [discount for the payee], according to whether the rate of the bank money is high or low. Or you may buy it of those called cashiers or brokers; then get the clerks to set down in the folio what you bring in. Having done so, you may draw this sum or sell it in what parcels you please, but then if you let your money lie seven years in the bank, you receive no interest for it. If you should ask me where the advantage is for the merchant? I would answer: first, you have your money ready at all times for answering bills of exchange and making other payments; you have no charge for bags [storage for

coins] or portage [the cost of shipping coins or bullion], no loss by false tale or bad money [counterfeit or badly clipped], no danger from thieves or unfaithful servants or fire; and above all, you have the accounts of your cash most punctually and justly kept without any trouble and without running the risk of goldsmith or cashiers [going broke] in your debt. For such is [the commissioners'] care that twice a year, or sometimes oftener, they shut up the bank for fourteen days and all that have concerns there must bring in their accounts to the clerks, who a few days after, having viewed their books, acquaint any who have brought in wrong accounts about their mistakes, requesting them to return to their books and to rectify their errors. . . . Besides the clerks' care in keeping and stating the accounts, the bank is obliged for five pounds a year to send to every merchant who desires it, their accounts every morning before Exchange-time, of the moneys written by them in the bank the day before upon any merchant's account, and what sums are written by others upon their accounts, so that the merchants may compare the bank's notes with their books and so save much of the charges of bookkeeping. . . .

[Also], . . . the Magistrates of the city take out of the Merchants' Bank a sufficient amount of money to supply the Lumbert, a bank that lends out money and is governed by four commissioners . . . [who have] officers who lend money [secured by any kind of collateral], from a pair of shoes to the richest jewel. This is a great convenience for poor people, yes, for merchants also, . . . and prevents the extraordinary extortion used by pawnbrokers in England, France, and other countries.

## REVIEW QUESTIONS

1. What fiscal and organizational policies of the Dutch government contributed to Holland's economic success?
2. What factors made Amsterdam the first successful center of modern capitalism?

## 3   The Atlantic Slave Trade

As the first Portuguese merchants began to penetrate southward along the coast of western Africa, they found that the local African societies engaged in an extensive trade in slave laborers. Like slaves in the Mediterranean region, African slaves were prisoners of war, criminals, or victims of violence and kidnapping. The Portuguese ships began carrying slaves from one local market to another along the African coast. Some slaves were taken back to Europe, but after 1500 the trade shifted largely to the Portuguese colony in Brazil and the Spanish colonies in the West Indies. In addition, Arabs and Portuguese competed in conveying slaves from East Africa to the markets of the Middle East. The widespread use of African slaves marked a new stage in the history of slavery. In the western world slavery became identified with race; the myth emerged that blacks were slaves by nature.

In the seventeenth century, the Dutch and English entered the West African slave trade, ousting the Portuguese as the principal slave traders to the West Indies and North America. The supply of laborers from Africa was essential to the New World's successful economic development. The Africans proved themselves to be skilled farmers and artisans who could endure the heavy labor of plantation life without the high rate of sickness and death that afflicted the local Indian populations. The Atlantic slave trade continued for more than three hundred years until finally suppressed by European governments in the nineteenth century. During that period, it is estimated that between 9.5 and 12 million African men, women, and children were shipped to the New World as slaves.

## Seventeenth-Century Slave Traders
# BUYING AND TRANSPORTING AFRICANS

Dealing in slaves was a profitable business that attracted numerous entrepreneurs. Following are two accounts written by slave traders in the seventeenth century.

As the slaves come down to Fida from the inland country, they are put into a booth, or prison, built for that purpose, near the beach, all of them together; and when the Europeans are to receive them, they are brought out into a large plain, where the surgeons examine every part of every one of them, to the smallest member, men and women being all stark naked. Such as are allowed good and sound, are set on the one side, and the others by themselves; which slaves so rejected are there called Mackrons, being above thirty five years of age, or defective in their limbs, eyes or teeth; or grown grey, or that have the venereal disease, or any other imperfection.

These being so set aside, each of the others, which have passed as good, is marked on the breast, with a red-hot iron, imprinting the mark of the French, English, or Dutch companies, that so each nation may distinguish their own, and to prevent their being chang'd by the natives for worse, as they are apt enough to do. In this particular, care is taken that the women, as tenderest, be not burnt too hard.

The branded slaves, after this, are returned to their former booth, where the factor [buyer] is to subsist them at his own charge, which amounts to about two-pence a day for each of them, with bread and water, which is all their allowance. There they continue sometimes ten or fifteen days, till the sea is still enough to send them aboard; for very often it continues too boisterous for so long a time, unless in January, February and March, which is commonly the calmest season: and when it is so, the slaves are carried off by parcels, in bar-canoes, and put aboard the ships in the road. Before they enter the canoes, or come out of the booth, their former Black masters strip them of every rag they have, without distinction of men or women; to supply which, in orderly ships, each of them as they come aboard is allowed a piece of canvas, to wrap around their waist, which is very acceptable to those poor wretches. . . . in the aforesaid months of January, February and March, which are the good season, ships are for the most part soon dispatched, if there be a good number of slaves at hand; so that they need not stay above four weeks for their cargo, and sometimes it is done in a fortnight.

The Blacks of Fida are so expeditious at this trade of slaves that they can deliver a thousand every month. . . . If there happens to be no stock of slaves at Fida, the factor must trust the Blacks with his goods, to the value of a hundred and fifty, or two hundred slaves; which goods they carry up into the inland, to buy slaves, at all the markets, for above two hundred leagues up the country, where they are kept like cattle [are kept] in Europe; the slaves sold there being generally prisoners

of war, taken from their enemies, like other booty, and perhaps some few sold by their own countrymen, in extreme want, or upon a famine; as also some as a punishment of heinous crimes: tho' many Europeans believe that parents sell their own children, men their wives and relations, which, if it ever happens, is so seldom, that it cannot justly be charged upon a whole nation, as a custom and common practice. . . .

---

A second slaver describes the loading and transporting of the newly acquired slaves.

---

When our slaves were come to the seaside, our canoes were ready to carry them off to the longboat, if the sea permitted, and she convey'd them aboard ship, where the men were all put in irons, two and two shackled together, to prevent their mutiny, or swimming ashore.

The negroes are so wilful and loth to leave their own country, that they have often leap'd out of the canoes, boat and ship, into the sea, and kept under water till they were drowned, to avoid being taken up and saved by our boats, which pursued them; they having a more dreadful apprehension of Barbadoes than we can have of hell, tho' in reality they live much better there than in their own country; but home is home, etc: we have likewise seen divers of them eaten by the sharks, of which a prodigious number kept about the ships in this place, and I have been told will follow her hence to Barbadoes, for the dead negroes that are thrown over-board in the passage. I am certain in our voyage there we did not want the sight of some every day, but that they were the same I can't affirm.

We had about 12 negroes did wilfully drown themselves, and others starv'd themselves to death; for 'tis their belief that when they die they return home to their own country and friends again.

I have been inform'd that some commanders have cut off the legs and arms of the most wilful, to terrify the rest, for they believe if they lose a member, they cannot return home again: I was advis'd by some of my officers to do the same, but I could not be perswaded to entertain the least thought of it, much less put in practice such barbarity and cruelty to poor creatures, who, excepting their want of christianity and true religion (their misfortune more than fault) are as much the works of God's hands, and no doubt as dear to him as ourselves; nor can I imagine why they should be despis'd for their colour, being what they cannot help, and the effect of the climate it has pleas'd God to appoint them. I can't think there is any intrinsick value in one colour more than another, nor that white is better than black, only we think so because we are so, and are prone to judge favourably in our own case, as well as the blacks, who in odium of the colour, say, the devil is white, and so paint him. . . .

When our slaves are aboard we shackle the men two and two, while we lie in port, and in sight of their own country, for 'tis then they attempt to make their escape, and mutiny; to prevent which we always keep centinels upon the hatchways, and have a chest full of small arms, ready loaden and prim'd, constantly lying at hand upon the quarter-deck, together with some granada shells; and two of our quarter-deck guns, pointing on the deck thence, and two more out of the steerage, the door of which is always kept shut, and well barr'd; they are fed twice a day, at 10 in the morning, and 4 in the evening, which is the time they are aptest to mutiny, being all upon deck; therefore all that time, what of our men are not employ'd in distributing their victuals to them, and settling them, stand to their arms; and some with lighted matches at the great guns that yaun upon them, loaden with partridge, till they have done and gone down to their kennels between decks. . . .

When we come to sea we let them all out of irons, they never attempting then to rebel, considering that should they kill or master us, they could not tell how to manage the ship, or must trust us, who would carry them where we pleas'd; therefore the only danger is while we are in sight of their own country, which they are loth to part with; but once out of sight out of mind: I never heard that they mutiny'd in any ships of consequence, that had a good number of men, and the least care; but in small tools [vessels] where they had but few men, and those negligent or drunk, then they surpriz'd and butcher'd them, cut the cables, and let the vessel drive ashore, and every one shift for himself. However, we have some 30 or 40 gold coast[1] negroes, which we buy, and are procur'd us there by our factors, to make guardians and overseers of the Whidaw negroes, and sleep among them to keep them from quarrelling; and in order, as well as to give us notice, if they can discover any caballing or plotting among them, which trust they will discharge with great diligence: they also take care to make the negroes scrape the decks where they lodge every morning very clean, to eschew any distempers that may engender from filth and nastiness; when we constitute a guardian, we give him a cat of nine tails [whip] as a badge of his office, which he is not a little proud of, and will exercise with great authority. We often at sea in the evenings would let the slaves come up into the sun to air themselves, and make them jump and dance for an hour or two to our bagpipes, harp, and fiddle, by which exercise to preserve them in health; but notwithstanding all our endeavour, 'twas my hard fortune to have great sickness and mortality among them.

Having bought my compliment of 700 slaves, *viz.* 480 men and 220 women, and finish'd all my business at Whidaw, I took my leave of the old king . . . and parted, with many affectionate expressions on both sides, being forced to promise him that I would return again the next year, with several things he desired me to bring him from England. . . .

---

[1]The Gold Coast was a section of coastal western Africa along the Gulf of Guinea, known for its trade in gold.

# Olaudah Equiano
# MEMOIRS OF A FORMER SLAVE

One eighteenth-century African, Olaudah Equiano, an Ibo from what is now Nigeria, wrote about his kidnapping and enslavement in Africa, his subsequent sale to English slave merchants, and his voyage to and first impressions of the West Indian port of Bridgetown, Barbados. Equiano's subsequent life diverged from the pattern of most slaves. He educated himself, engaged in petty trade, purchased his freedom, and traveled to England, Nicaragua, Syria, and New England. In 1786, he was involved in planning the first free black colony, at Freetown, Sierra Leone, in Africa and took an active part in the antislavery movement in England. In the following excerpts from his memoir, *The Interesting Narrative of Olaudah Equiano or Gustavus Vasa the African,* published in two volumes in London in 1789, he records his reactions at the age of eleven when he was placed aboard an English slave ship for the voyage to the West Indies.

The first object which saluted my eyes when I arrived on the coast was the sea, and a slaveship, which was then riding at anchor, and waiting for its cargo. These filled me with astonishment, which was soon converted into terror, which I am yet at a loss to describe, nor the then feelings of my mind. When I was carried on board I was immediately handled, and tossed up, to see if I were sound, by some of the crew; and I was now persuaded that I had got into a world of bad spirits, and that they were going to kill me. Their complexions too differing so much from ours, their long hair, and the language they spoke, which was very different from any I had ever heard, united to confirm me in this belief. Indeed, such were the horrors of my views and fears at the moment, that, if ten thousand worlds had been my own, I would have freely parted with them all to have exchanged my condition with that of the meanest slave in my own country. When I looked round the ship too, and saw a large furnace or copper [pot] boiling, and a multitude of black people of every description chained together, every one of their countenances expressing dejection and sorrow, I no longer doubted of my fate; and, quite overpowered with horror and anguish, I fell motionless on the deck and fainted. When I recovered a little, I found some black people about me, who I believed were some of those who brought me on board, and had been receiving their pay; they talked to me in order to cheer me, but all in vain. I asked them if we were not to be eaten by those white men with horrible looks, red faces, and long hair. They told me I was not. . . .

. . . Soon after this, the blacks who brought me on board went off, and left me abandoned to despair. I now saw myself deprived of all chance of returning to my native country, or even the least glimpse of hope of gaining the shore, which I now considered as friendly; and I even wished for my former slavery, in preference to my present situation, which was filled with horror of every kind, still heightened by my ignorance of what I was to undergo. I was not long suffered to indulge my grief; I was soon put down under the decks, and there I received such a salutation in my nostrils as I had never experienced in my life; so that, with the loathsomeness of the stench, and crying together, I became so sick and low that I was not able to eat, nor had I the least desire to taste any thing. I now wished for the last friend, death, to relieve me; but soon, to my grief, two of the white men offered me eatables; and, on my refusing to eat, one of them held me fast by the hands, and laid me across, I think, the windlass, and tied my feet while the other flogged me severely. I had never experienced any thing of this kind before; and, although not being used to the water, I naturally feared that element the first time I saw it; yet, nevertheless, could I have got over the nettings, I would have jumped over the side; but I could not; and, besides, the crew used to watch us very closely who were not chained down to the decks, lest we should leap into the water: and I have seen some of these poor African prisoners most severely cut for attempting to do so, and hourly whipped for not eating. This indeed was often the case with myself. . . .

. . . At last, when the ship we were in had got in all her cargo . . . we were all put under deck. . . . The closeness of the place, and the heat of the climate, added to the number in the ship, which was so crowded that each had scarcely room to turn himself, almost suffocated us. This produced copious perspirations, so that the air soon became unfit for respiration, from a variety of loathsome smells, and brought on a sickness amongst the slaves, of which many died, thus falling victims to the improvident avarice, as I may call it, of their purchasers. This wretched situation was again aggravated by the galling of the chains, now become insupportable; and filth of the necessary tubs, into which the children often fell, and were almost suffocated. The shrieks of the women, and the groans of the dying, rendered the whole a scene of horror almost inconceivable. Happily perhaps for myself I was soon reduced so low here that it was thought necessary to keep me almost always on deck; and from my extreme youth I was not put in fetters. In this situation I expected every hour to share the fate of my companions, some of whom were almost daily brought upon deck at the point of death, which I began to hope would soon put an end to my miseries. Often did I think many of the inhabitants of the deep much more happy than myself; I envied them the freedom they en-

joyed, and as often wished I could change my condition for theirs. Every circumstance I met with served only to render my state more painful, and heighten my apprehensions and my opinion of the cruelty of the whites. . . .

. . . In a little time after, amongst the poor chained men, I found some of my own nation, which in a small degree gave ease to my mind. I inquired of them what was to be done with us? They gave me to understand we were to be carried to these white people's country to work for them. I then was a little revived, and thought, if it were no worse than working, my situation was not so desperate: but still I feared I should be put to death, the white people looked and acted, as I thought, in so savage a manner; for I had never seen among any people such instances of brutal cruelty; and this not only shown towards us blacks, but also to some of the whites themselves. One white man in particular I saw, when we were permitted to be on deck, flogged so unmercifully with a large rope near the foremast, that he died in consequence of it; and they tossed him over the side as they would have done a brute. This made me fear these people the more; and I expected nothing less than to be treated in the same manner. I could not help expressing my fears and apprehensions to some of my countrymen.

---

The voyage from the African coast to the West Indies covered some 5,500 miles and normally took more than two months. (The mortality rate among the slaves sailing from the Niger Delta in the late eighteenth century averaged 9.7 percent.) Equiano's ship finally reaches Bridgetown, Barbados, where the slaves are to be sold.

---

. . . The white people got some old slaves from the land to pacify us. They told us we were not to be eaten, but to work, and were soon to go on land where we should see many of our country people. This report eased us much; and sure enough, soon after we landed, there came to us Africans of all languages. We were conducted immediately to the merchant's yard, where we were all pent up together like so many sheep in a fold, without regard to sex or age. As every object was new to me, everything I saw filled me with surprise. What struck me first was, that the houses were built with bricks, in stories, and in every other respect different from those I have seen in Africa: but I was still more astonished on seeing people on horseback. I did not know what this could mean; and indeed I thought these people were full of nothing but magical arts. While I was in this astonishment, one of my fellow prisoners spoke to a countryman of his about the horses, who said they were the same kind they had in their country. . . . We were not many days in the merchant's custody, before we were sold after their usual manner, which is this: on a signal given (as the beat of a drum), the buyers rush at once into the yard where the slaves are confined, and make choice of that parcel they like best. The noise and clamour with which this is attended, and the eagerness visible in the countenances of the buyers, serve not a little to increase the apprehension of the terrified Africans, who may well be supposed to consider them as the ministers of that destruction to which they think them-

selves devoted. In this manner, without scruple, are relations and friends separated, most of them never to see each other again. I remember in the vessel in which I was brought over, in the men's apartment, there were several brothers who, in the sale, were sold in different lots; and it was very moving on this occasion to see and hear their cries at parting. O, ye nominal Christians! might not an African ask you, learned you this from your God? who says unto you, Do unto all men as you would men should do unto you. Is it not enough that we are torn from our country and friends to toil for your luxury and lust of gain? Must every tender feeling be likewise sacrificed to your avarice? Are the dearest friends and relations, now rendered more dear by their separation from their kindred, still to be parted from each other, and thus preventing from cheering the gloom of slavery with the small comfort of being together, and mingling their sufferings and sorrows? Why are parents to love their children, brothers their sisters, or husbands their wives? Surely this is a new refinement in cruelty, which, while it has no advantage to atone for it, thus aggravates distress, and adds fresh horrors even to the wretchedness of slavery.

## REVIEW QUESTIONS

1. When were the African slaves most likely to try to escape? How did the slave traders try to prevent this?
2. Did either of the two slave traders express any humane feelings towards the captive Africans?
3. Compare the reaction of Olaudah Equiano on first encountering Europeans with that of the Spaniards encountering Aztecs (Section 1).
4. What did Equiano believe to be the worst evil of the slave system?

## 4 The Witch Craze

In both ancient and medieval times, it was widely believed that certain persons, called sorcerers or witches, had supernatural powers over both nature and human beings and that these powers enabled witches to harm people through magical practices. Those suspected of sorcery were greatly feared and were subject to execution. In the late Middle Ages, Europeans began to view suspected witches as having entered into a pact with the devil. The church began to treat them as devil worshippers, heretics, rebels against the church, and threats to society.

During the sixteenth and seventeenth centuries, both Roman Catholics and Protestants intensified the struggle to destroy alleged witches; thousands were questioned under torture, and if convicted of witchcraft, were put to death, a sentence justified by both the Old Testament and Roman law. Belief in witches was not limited to superstitious peasants and fanatics. Prominent intellectuals, theologians, philosophers, and scientists either supported the prosecution of witches or remained silent. Few doubted the existence of witches, and forced confessions were accepted as proof of sorcery; the idea of witchcraft offered credible explanations for otherwise inexplicable human experiences. Although the number of females accused of witchcraft outnumbered the males, during these times persons of all ages, social classes, education, and occupations could find themselves facing the charge of witchcraft. The regular use of torture during interrogation of suspects probably accounted for most confessions, and the alleged bizarre and sometimes lurid practices of suspects seem to have been the products of mental disorders and popular beliefs in occult powers.

# Jakob Sprenger and Heinrich Krämer
## *THE HAMMER OF WITCHES*

Written in 1486 by Jakob Sprenger and Heinrich Krämer, both Dominican inquisitors in Germany, *The Hammer of Witches* became a standard reference work for the beliefs and practices of witches. The work, excerpted below, tells us much about the mindset of early modern Europeans committed to a belief in witches who served the devil.

And this class [of witches] is made up of those who, against every instinct of human or animal nature, are in the habit of eating and devouring the children of their own species. And this is the most powerful class of witches, who practise innumerable other harms also. For they raise hailstorms and hurtful tempests and lightnings; cause sterility in men and animals; offer to devils, or otherwise kill, the children whom they do not devour. But these are only the children who have not been re-born by baptism at the font, for they cannot devour those who have been baptized, nor any without God's permission. They can also, before the eyes of their parents, and when no one is in sight, throw into the water children walking by the water side; they make horses go mad under their riders; they can transport themselves from place to place through the air, either in body or in imagination; they can affect Judges and Magistrates so that they cannot hurt them; they can cause themselves and others to keep silence under torture; they can bring about a great trembling in the hands and horror in the minds of those who would arrest them. . . . [T]hey can at times strike whom they will with lightning, and even kill some men and animals; they can make of no effect the generative desires, and even the power of copulation, cause abortion, kill infants in the mother's womb by a mere exterior touch; they can at times bewitch men and animals with a mere look, without touching them, and cause death; they dedicate their own children to devils; and in short, as has been said, they can cause all the plagues. . . . [I]t is common to all of them to practise carnal copulation with devils. . . .

[T]here are now [such witches], some in the country of Lombardy [in northern Italy], in the domains of the Duke of Austria, where the Inquisitor of Como, as we told in the former Part, caused forty-one witches to be burned in one year; and he was fifty-five years old, and still continues to labour in the Inquisition.

Now the method of profession is twofold. One is a solemn ceremony, like a solemn vow. The other is private, and can be made to the devil at any hour alone. The first method is when witches meet together in conclave on a set day, and the devil appears to them in the assumed body of a man, and urges them to keep faith with him, promising them worldly prosperity and length of life; and they recommend a novice to his acceptance. And the devil asks whether she will abjure the Faith, and forsake the holy Christian religion and the worship of the Anomalous Woman (for so they call the Most Blessed Virgin Mary), and never venerate the Sacraments; and if he finds the novice or disciple willing, then the devil stretches out his hand, and so does the novice, and she swears with upraised hand to keep that covenant. And when this is done, the devil at once adds that this is not enough; and when the disciple asks what more must be done, the devil demands the following oath of homage to himself: that she give herself to him, body and soul, for ever, and do her utmost to bring others of both sexes into his power. He adds, finally, that she is to make certain unguents [ointments] from the bones and limbs of children, especially those who have been baptized; by all which means she will be able to fulfil all her wishes with his help.

We Inquisitors had credible experience of this method in the town of Breisach in the diocese of Basel [in Switzerland] receiving full information from a young girl witch who had been converted, whose aunt also had been

burned in the diocese of Strasburg [in Germany]. And she added that she had become a witch by the method in which her aunt had first tried to seduce her. . . .

She said also that the greatest injuries were inflicted by midwives, because they were under an obligation to kill or offer to devils as many children as possible; and that she had been severely beaten by her aunt because she had opened a secret pot and found the heads of a great many children. And much more she told us, having first, as was proper, taken an oath to speak the truth.

And her account of the method of professing the devil's faith undoubtedly agrees with what has been written by that most eminent Doctor, John Nider, who even in our times has written very illuminatingly; and it may be especially remarked that he tells us the following, which he had from an Inquisitor of the diocese of Edua, who held many inquisitions on witches in that diocese, and caused many to be burned.

For he says that this Inquisitor told him that in the Duchy of Lausanne [in Switzerland] certain witches had cooked and eaten their own children, and that the following was the method in which they became initiated into such practices. The witches met together and, by their art, summoned a devil in the form of a man, to whom the novice was compelled to swear to deny the Christian religion, never to adore the Eucharist, and to tread the Cross underfoot whenever she could do so secretly.

Here is another example from the same source. There was lately a general report, brought to the notice of Peter the Judge in Boltingen, that thirteen infants had been devoured in the State of Berne [in Switzerland]; and public justice exacted full vengeance on the murderers. And when Peter asked one of the captive witches in what manner they ate children, she replied: "This is the manner of it. We set our snares chiefly for unbaptized children, and even for those that have been baptized, especially when they have not been protected by the sign of the Cross and prayers" (reader, notice that, at the devil's command, they take the unbaptized chiefly, in order that they may not be baptized), "and with our spells we kill them in their cradles or even when they are sleeping by their parents' side, in such a way that they afterwards are thought to have been overlain or to have died some other natural death. Then we secretly take them from their graves, and cook them in a cauldron, until the whole flesh comes away from the bones to make a soup which may easily be drunk. Of the more solid matter we make an unguent which is of virtue to help us in our arts and pleasures and our transportations; and with the liquid we fill a flask or skin, whoever drinks from which, with the addition of a few other ceremonies, immediately acquires much knowledge and becomes a leader in our sect."

---

# Johannes Junius
# *A CONFESSION OF WITCHCRAFT EXPLAINED*

In 1628 Johannes Junius, lord mayor of Bamberg, a city in Bavaria, Germany, was accused of practicing witchcraft. Junius denied the charge and he was tortured. He then confessed to having become a witch and was burned at the stake. The reasons for his confession are revealed in a letter he secretly sent to his daughter.

Many hundred thousand good-nights, dearly beloved daughter Veronica. Innocent have I come into prison, innocent have I been tortured, innocent must I die. For whoever comes into the witch prison must become a witch or be tortured until he invents something out of his head and—God pity him—bethinks him of something. I will tell you how it has gone with me. When I was the first time put to the torture, Dr. Braun, Dr. Kötzendörffer, and two strange doctors were there. Then Dr. Braun asks me, "Kinsman, how come you here?" I answer, "Through falsehood, through misfortune." "Hear, you," he says, "you are a witch; will you confess it voluntarily? If not, we'll bring in witnesses and the executioner for you." I said "I am no witch, I have a pure conscience in the matter; if there are a thousand witnesses, I am not anxious, but I'll gladly hear the witnesses." Now the chancellor's son was set before me . . . and afterward Hoppfen Elss. She had seen me dance on Haupts-moor. . . . I answered: "I have never renounced God, and will never do it—God graciously keep me from it. I'll rather bear whatever I must." And then came also—God in highest Heaven have mercy—the executioner, and put the thumbscrews on me, both hands bound together, so that the blood ran out at the nails and everywhere, so that for four weeks I could not use my hands, as you can see from the writing. . . . Thereafter they first stripped me, bound my hands behind me, and drew me up in the torture. Then I thought heaven and earth were at an end; eight times did they draw me up and let me fall again, so that I suffered terrible agony. . . .*

. . . When at last the executioner led me back into the prison, he said to me: "Sir, I beg

---

*This torture of the strappado, which was that in most common use by the courts, consisted of a rope, attached to the hands of the prisoner (bound behind his back) and carried over a pulley at the ceiling. By this he was drawn up and left hanging. To increase the pain, weights were attached to his feet or he was suddenly jerked up and let drop.

you, for God's sake confess something, whether it be true or not. Invent something, for you cannot endure the torture which you will be put to; and, even if you bear it all, yet you will not escape, not even if you were an earl [high nobleman], but one torture will follow after another until you say you are a witch. Not before that," he said, "will they let you go, as you may see by all their trials, for one is just like another."...

And so I begged, since I was in wretched plight, to be given one day for thought and a priest. The priest was refused me, but the time for thought was given. Now, my dear child, see in what hazard I stood and still stand. I must say that I am a witch, though I am not,—must now renounce God, though I have never done it before. Day and night I was deeply troubled, but at last there came to me a new idea. I would not be anxious, but, since I had been given no priest with whom I could take counsel, I would myself think of something and say it. It were surely better that I just say it with mouth and words, even though I had not really done it; and afterwards I would confess it to the priest, and let those answer for it who compel me to do it.... And so I made my confession, ... but it was all a lie.

Now follows, dear child, what I confessed in order to escape that great anguish and bitter torture, which it was impossible for me longer to bear. [He then describes his confession] ...

Now, dear child, here you have all my confession, for which I must die. And they are sheer lies and made-up things, so help me God. For all this I was forced to say through fear of the torture which was threatened beyond what I had already endured. For they never leave off with the torture till one confesses something be he ever so good, he must be a witch. Nobody escapes, though he were an earl. . . .

Dear child, keep this letter secret so that people do not find it, else I shall be tortured most piteously and the jailers will be beheaded. So strictly is it forbidden. . . . Dear child, pay this man a dollar. . . . I have taken several days to write this: my hands are both lame. I am in a sad plight. . . .

Good night, for your father Johannes Junius will never see you more. July 24, 1628.

[And on the margin of the letter he adds:]

Dear child, six have confessed against me at once: the Chancellor, his son, Neudecker, Zaner, Hoffmaisters Ursel, and Hoppfen Elss—all false, through compulsion, as they have all told me, and begged my forgiveness in God's name before they were executed. . . . They know nothing but good of me. They were forced to say it, just as I myself was. . . .

# Nicholas Malebranche
# *SEARCH AFTER TRUTH*

Greatly influenced by Descartes (see page 394), the French thinker Nicholas Malebranche (1638–1715) supplemented his training in philosophy and theology with the study of mathematics and natural science. His most important work, *Search After Truth,* which appeared in two volumes in 1674 and 1675, treated many technical, philosophical, and theological issues. In this work, from which an excerpt follows, he also analyzed the belief in witchcraft, attributing it to the unchecked power of people's imagination. Malebranche attempted a rational explanation of the witch craze and wanted the courts to dismiss charges of witchcraft. Nevertheless, he still believed that although "true witches are very rare," they do exist.

The strangest effect of the power of imagination is the disorderly fear of the apparition of spirits, of enchantments, of symbols, of the charms of Lycanthropes or Werewolves, and generally of everything which is supposed to depend upon the demon's power.

Nothing is more terrible or more frightening to the mind, or produces deeper vestiges on the brain, than the idea of an invisible power which thinks only about harming us and which is irresistible. Speeches which reveal this idea are always heard with fear and curiosity. Holding on to everything extraordinary, men take bizarre pleasure in recounting these surprising and prodigious stories about the power and malice of Witches, in order to frighten both others and themselves. So it is not astonishing if Witches are so common in some countries, where belief in the Sabbat [a secret meeting of witches where they engage in orgiastic rites] is too deeply rooted; where the most absurd stories about spells are listened to as authentic; and where madmen and seers whose imagination has become disordered. . . . from telling these stories . . . are burned as real Witches.

I well know that some people will take exception to my attributing most witchcraft to the power of imagination, because I know that men want to be made afraid, that they become angry with those who want to demystify them. . . .

Superstitions are not easily destroyed, and they cannot be attacked without finding a large number of defenders. It is easy enough to prove that the inclination to believe blindly all the dreams of Demonographers [those who study demons] is produced and maintained by the same cause which makes superstitious men stubborn. Nevertheless, that will not prevent me from describing in a few words how, I believe, such opinions get established.

A shepherd in his fold after dinner tells his wife and children about the adventures of the Sabbat. As his imagination is moderately inspired by vapours from wine, and since he believes that he has attended that imaginary assembly several times, he does not fail to speak about it in a strong and lively manner. His natural eloquence, together with the disposition of his entire family to hear such a new and terrible subject discussed, should doubtlessly produce strange traces in weak imaginations. It is naturally impossible that a woman and her children not remain completely frightened, full, and convinced of what they have heard said. This is a husband, a father, who is speaking about what he has seen and done; he is loved and respected; why should he not be believed? This Shepherd repeats it on different days. Little by little the mother's and children's imagination receives deeper traces from it. They grow used to it, the fears pass, and the conviction remains. . . .

Several times Witches of good faith have been found, who generally tell everybody that they have gone to the Sabbat, and who are so convinced of it, that although several persons watched them and assured them that they had not left their beds, they could not agree with their testimony. . . . So we should not be astonished if a man who thinks he has been to the Sabbat, and consequently talks about it in a firm voice and with an assured countenance, easily persuades some people who listen to him respectfully about all the circumstances which he describes, and thus transmits in their imagination traces similar to those which deceive him.

When men talk to us, they engrave in our brain traces similar to those which they possess. When they have deep traces, they talk to us in a manner which engraves deep ones in us; for they cannot speak without making us in some way similar to them. Children at their mother's breast only see what their mother sees. Even when they have become worldly-wise, they imagine few things of which their parents are not the cause, since even the wisest men conduct themselves more by the imagination of others, *i.e.,* by opinion and custom, then by the rules of reason. Thus in places where Witches are burned, a great number of them are found. Because in places where they are condemned to fire, men truly believe that they commit witchcraft, and this belief is fortified by the speeches which are made about it. If one were to stop punishing them and were to treat them like madmen, then it would be seen in time that there would no longer be any Witches, because those who do it only in imagination (who are surely the greater number) would then abandon their errors.

It is indubitable that real Witches deserve death. . . . But by punishing all [those who believe themselves or are believed by others to be witches] common opinion is strengthened, imaginary Witches are multiplied, and so an infinity of people are lost and damned. It is thus right that many Parlements [French courts] no longer punish Witches. There are many fewer of them in the lands of their jurisdictions; and the envy, hatred, or malice of evil men cannot use this pretext to destroy the innocent. . . .

It is ordinary enough for some people to have fairly lively dreams at night and to be able to remember them exactly when awake, although the subject of their dream is not in itself very terrible. Thus it is not difficult for people to persuade themselves that they have been at the Sabbat, for that merely requires that their brain preserves the traces made there during sleep.

The chief reason which prevents us from taking our dreams for realities is that we cannot link our dreams with the things we have done during our wakefulness. By that we recognize that they were only dreams. But Witches cannot recognize in this way that their imaginary Sabbat is a dream. . . .

I am persuaded that true Witches are very rare, that the Sabbat is only a dream, and that the Parlements who dismiss accusations of witchcraft are the most equitable. However, I do not doubt that Witches, charms, enchantments, etc., could exist, and that the demon sometimes exercises his malice upon men by special permission of a superior power.

## REVIEW QUESTIONS

1. According to *The Hammer of Witches,* what anti-Christian practices did witches engage in?
2. According to Johannes Junius, how were apparently innocent people successfully prosecuted for practicing witchcraft?
3. To what did Malebranche attribute a belief in witchcraft?

# 5 Justification of Absolute Monarchy by Divine Right

Effectively blocking royal absolutism in the Middle Ages were the dispersion of power between kings and feudal lords, the vigorous sense of personal freedom and urban autonomy of the townspeople, and the limitations on royal power imposed by the church. However, by the late sixteenth century, monarchs were asserting their authority over competing groups with ever-greater effectiveness. In this new balance of political forces, European kings implemented their claim to absolute power as monarchs chosen by and responsible to God alone. This theory, called the divine right of kings, became the dominant political ideology of seventeenth- and eighteenth-century Europe.

# James I
# *TRUE LAW OF FREE MONARCHIES* AND A SPEECH TO PARLIAMENT

One of the most articulate defenders of the divine right of monarchy was James VI, who was king of Scotland (1567–1625) and as James I (1603–1625) also was king of England. A scholar as well as a king, James in 1598 anonymously published a widely read book called the *True Law of Free Monarchies.* He claimed that the king alone was the true legislator. James's notions of the royal prerogative and of the role of Parliament are detailed in the following passages from the *True Law* and a speech to Parliament.

## TRUE LAW
### *Prerogative and Parliament*

According to these fundamental laws already alleged, we daily see that in the parliament (which is nothing else but the head court of the king and his vassals) the laws are but craved by his subjects, and only made by him at their [proposal] and with their advice: for albeit the king make daily statutes and ordinances, [imposing] such pains thereto as he thinks [fit], without any advice of parliament or estates, yet it lies in the power of no parliament to make any kind of law or statute, without his sceptre [that is, authority] be to it, for giving it the force of a law. . . . And as ye see it manifest that the king is over-lord of the whole land, so is he master over every person that inhabiteth the same, having power over the life and death of every one of them: for although a just prince will not take the life of any of his subjects without a clear law, yet the same laws whereby he taketh them are made by himself or his predecessors; and so the power flows always from himself. . . . Where he sees the law doubtsome or rigorous, he may interpret or mitigate the same, lest otherwise *summum jus* be *summa injuria* [the greatest right be the greatest wrong]: and therefore general laws made publicly in parliament may upon . . . [the king's] authority be mitigated and suspended upon causes only known to him.

As likewise, although I have said a good king will frame all his actions to be according to the law, yet is he not bound thereto but of his good will, and for good example-giving to his subjects. . . . So as I have already said, a good king, though he be above the law, will subject and frame his actions thereto, for example's sake to his subjects, and of his own free will, but not as subject or bound thereto. . . .

---

In a speech before the English Parliament in March 1610, James elaborated on his exalted theory of the monarch's absolute power.

---

## A SPEECH TO PARLIAMENT

. . . The state of monarchy is the supremest thing upon earth: for kings are not only God's lieutenants upon earth and sit upon God's throne, but even by God himself they are called gods. There be three principal [comparisons] that illustrate the state of monarchy: one taken out of the word of God, and the two other out of the grounds of policy and philosophy. In the Scriptures kings are called gods, and so their power after a certain relation compared to the Divine power. Kings are also compared to fathers of families: for a king is truly *parens patriae* [parent of the country], the politic father of his people. And lastly, kings are compared to the head of this microcosm of the body of man. . . .

I conclude then this point touching the power of kings with this axiom of divinity, That as to dispute what God may do is blasphemy, . . . so is it sedition in subjects to dispute what a king may do in the height of his power. But just kings will ever be willing to declare what they will do, if they will not incur the curse of God. I will not be content that my power be disputed upon; but I shall ever be willing to make the reason appear of all my doings, and rule my actions according to my laws. . . .

Now the second general ground whereof I am to speak concerns the matter of grievances. . . . First then, I am not to find fault that you inform yourselves of the particular just grievances of the people; nay I must tell you, ye can neither be just nor faithful to me or to your countries that trust and employ you, if you do it not. . . . But I would wish you to be careful to avoid [these] things in the matter of grievances.

First, that you do not meddle with the main points of government: that is my craft . . . to meddle with that, were to lessen me. I am now an old king . . .;

I must not be taught my office.

Secondly, I would not have you meddle with such ancient rights of mine as I have received from my predecessors, possessing them *more majorum* [as ancestral customs]: such things I would be sorry should be accounted for grievances. All novelties are dangerous as well in a politic as in a natural body: and therefore I would be loath to be quarrelled in my ancient rights and possessions: for that were to judge me unworthy of that which my predecessors had and left me.

## REVIEW QUESTIONS

1. What was the theory of kingship by divine authority embraced by King James I of England?
2. What was the proper role of Parliament for James I?

## 6  The Court of Louis XIV

During his seventy-two-year reign, Louis XIV (1643–1715) gave France greater unity and central authority than it had ever known. To prevent the great nobles from challenging royal authority, Louis XIV chose many of his ministers and provincial administrators from the middle class. The great nobles, "princes of the blood," enjoyed considerable social prestige but exercised no real power in the government. The king encouraged these "people of quality" to live at court where they contended with each other for his favor.

As the symbol of France and the greatest ruler of Europe, Louis insisted that the social life at Versailles provide an appropriate setting for his exalted person. During his long reign, France set the style for the whole of Europe. The splendor of Versailles was the talk of Europe, and other monarchs sought to imitate the fashions and manners of the Sun King's court.

# Duc de Saint-Simon
# AN ASSESSMENT OF LOUIS XIV

Louis de Rouvroi, duc de Saint-Simon (1675–1755), was an astute observer of Louis XIV and his court. The following description of Louis XIV comes from Saint-Simon's extensive *Memoirs*.

Louis XIV was made for a brilliant Court. In the midst of other men, his figure, his courage, his grace, his beauty, his grand mien, even the tone of his voice and the majestic and natural charm of all his person, distinguished him till his death. . . . The superior ability of his early ministers and his early generals soon wearied him. He liked nobody to be in any way superior to him. Thus he chose his ministers, not for their knowledge, but for their ignorance; not for their capacity, but for their want of it. He liked to form them, as he said; liked to teach them even the most trifling things. It was the same with his generals. He took credit to himself for instructing them; wished it to be thought that from his cabinet he commanded and directed all his armies. Naturally fond of trifles, he unceasingly occupied himself with the most petty details of his troops, his household, his mansions. This vanity, this unmeasured and unreasonable love of admiration, was his ruin. His ministers, his generals, his mistresses, his courtiers, soon perceived his weakness. They praised him with emulation and spoiled him. Those whom he liked owed his affection for them, to their untiring flatteries. This is what gave his ministers so much authority, and the opportunities they had for adulating him, of attributing everything to him, and of pretending to learn everything from him. Suppleness, meanness, an admiring, dependent, cringing manner—above all, an air of nothingness—were the sole means of pleasing him.

Though his intellect, as I have said, was beneath mediocrity, it was capable of being formed. He loved glory, was fond of order and regularity; was by disposition prudent, moderate, discreet, master of his movements and his tongue. Will it be believed? He was also by disposition good and just! God had sufficiently gifted him to enable him to be a good King; perhaps even *a tolerably great King!* All the evil came to him from elsewhere. His early education was . . . neglected. He was scarcely taught how to read or write, and remained so ignorant, that the most familiar historical and other facts were utterly unknown to him! He fell, accordingly, and sometimes even in public, into the grossest absurdities.

He was exceedingly jealous of the attention paid him. Not only did he notice the presence of the most distinguished courtiers, but those of inferior degree also. He looked to the right and to the left, not only upon rising but upon going to bed, at his meals, in passing through his apartments, or his gardens of Versailles, where alone the courtiers were allowed to follow him; he saw and noticed everybody; not one escaped him, not even those who hoped to remain unnoticed. He marked well all absentees from the court, found out the reason of their absence, and never lost an opportunity of acting towards them as the occasion might seem to justify. With some of the courtiers (the most distinguished), it was a demerit not to make the court their ordinary abode; with others 'twas a fault to come but rarely; for those who never or scarcely ever came it was certain disgrace. When their names were in any way mentioned, 'I do not know them,' the King would reply haughtily. Those who presented themselves but seldom were thus characterised: 'They are people I never see'; these decrees were irrevocable. He could not bear people who liked Paris [better than Versailles].

Louis XIV took great pains to be well informed of all that passed everywhere; in the public places, in the private houses, in society and familiar intercourse. His spies and telltales were infinite. He had them of all species; many who were ignorant that their information reached him; others who knew it; others who wrote to him direct, sending their letters through channels he indicated; and all these letters were seen by him alone, and always before everything else; others who sometimes spoke to him secretly in his cabinet, entering by the back stairs. These unknown means ruined an infinite number of people of all classes, who never could discover the cause; often ruined them very unjustly; for the King, once prejudiced, never altered his opinion, or so rarely, that nothing was more rare. He had, too, another fault, very dangerous for others and often for himself, since it deprived him of good subjects. He had an excellent memory; in this way, that if he saw a man who, twenty years before, perhaps, had in some manner offended him, he did not forget the man, though he might forget the offence. This was enough, however, to exclude the person from all favour. The representations of a minister, of a general, of his confessor even, could not move the King. He would not yield.

The most cruel means by which the King was informed of what was passing—for many years before anybody knew it—was that of opening letters. The promptitude and dexterity with which they were opened passes understanding. He saw extracts from all the letters in which there were passages that the chiefs of the post-office, and then the minister who governed it, thought ought to go before him; entire letters, too, were sent to him, when their contents seemed to justify the sending. Thus the chiefs of the post, nay, the principal clerks were in a position to suppose what they pleased and against whom they pleased. A word of contempt against the King or the government, a joke, a detached phrase, was enough. It is incredible how many people, justly or unjustly, were more or less ruined, always without resource, without trial, and without knowing why. . . .

Never was man so naturally polite, or of a politeness so measured, so graduated, so adapted to person, time, and place. Towards women his politeness was without parallel. Never did he pass the humblest petticoat without raising his hat; even to chambermaids, that he knew to be such, as often happened at Marly. For ladies he took his hat off completely. . . . He took it off for the princes of the blood, as for the ladies. If he accosted ladies he did not cover himself until he had quitted them. All this was out of doors, for in the house he was never covered. . . .

The King loved air and exercise very much, as long as he could make use of them. He had excelled in dancing, and at tennis and mall. On horseback he was admirable, even at a late age. He liked to see everything done with grace and address. To acquit yourself well or ill before him was a merit or a fault. . . . He was very fond of shooting, and there was not a better or more graceful shot than he. He had always in his cabi-

net seven or eight pointer bitches, and was fond of feeding them, to make himself known to them. He was very fond, too, of stag hunting. . . .

He liked splendour, magnificence, and profusion in everything: you pleased him if you shone through the brilliancy of your houses, your clothes, your table, your equipages.

As for the King himself, nobody ever approached his magnificence. His buildings, who could number them? At the same time, who was there who did not deplore the pride, the caprice, the bad taste seen in them? St. Germains, a lovely spot, with a marvellous view, rich forest, terraces, gardens, and water he abandoned for Versailles; the dullest and most ungrateful of all places, without prospect, without wood, without water, without soil; for the ground is all shifting sand or swamp, the air accordingly bad. . . .

Let me now speak of the amours of the King which were even more fatal to the state than his building mania.

Louis XIV in his youth more made for love than any of his subjects—being tired of gathering passing sweets, fixed himself at last upon La Vallière.[1] The progress and the result of his love are well known. . . .

When the King travelled his coach was always full of women; his mistresses, afterwards his bastards, his daughters-in-law, sometimes *Madame,* and other ladies when there was room. In the coach, during his journeys, there were always all sorts of things to eat, as meat, pastry, fruit. A quarter of a league was not passed over before the King asked if somebody would not eat. He never ate anything between meals himself, not even fruit; but he amused himself by seeing others do so, aye, and to bursting. You were obliged to be hungry, merry, and to eat with appetite, otherwise he was displeased and even showed it. And yet after this, if you supped with him at table the same day, you were compelled to eat with as good a countenance as though you had tasted

---

[1]Françoise-Louise de La Vallière was Louis XIV's mistress from 1661 to 1667; she held great influence over him and was the mother of four of his children. After being discarded as his mistress she retired to a convent in 1674.

nothing since the previous night. He was as inconsiderate in other and more delicate matters; and ladies, in his long drives and stations, had often occasion to curse him. The Duchesse de Chevreuse once rode all the way from Versailles to Fontainbleau in such extremity, that several times she was well-nigh losing consciousness. . . .

At ten o'clock his supper was served. The captain of the guard announced this to him. A quarter of an hour after the King came to supper, and from the ante-chamber of Madame de Maintenon[2] to the table again, any one spoke to him who wished. This supper was always on a grand scale, the royal household (that is, the sons and daughters of France), at table, and a large number of courtiers and ladies present, sitting or standing. . . .

During all his life, the King failed only once in his attendance at mass. It was with the army, during a forced march; he missed no fast day, unless really indisposed. Some days before Lent, he publicly declared that he should be very much displeased if any one ate meat or gave it to others, under any pretext.

---

[2]Françoise d'Aubigné (Madame de Maintenon) was the widow of a celebrated poet when she became governess to two of the king's children in 1669. He provided her with an estate and later married her secretly.

---

# Liselotte von der Pfalz (Elizabeth Charlotte d'Orleans) A SKETCH OF COURT LIFE

Deprived of power and usefulness, many great nobles lived a frivolous, if not debauched, existence at Versailles. The letters of Elizabeth Charlotte, Duchesse d'Orleans (1652–1722)—her German name was Liselotte von der Pfalz—describe this lifestyle. A native of Germany, the duchess was married to Louis XIV's only brother and spent fifty years at the king's court. During this period she wrote extensive letters, some of which are reproduced below, to her German relatives.

*Versailles, 13 February 1695*

Where in the world does one find a husband who loves only his spouse and does not have someone, be it mistresses or boys, on the side? If for this reason wives were to go in for the same behavior one could never be sure, as Godfather so rightly says, that the children of the house are the rightful heirs. Does the young duchess* not know that a woman's honor consists of having commerce with no one but her husband, and that for a man it is not shameful to have mistresses but shameful indeed to be a cuckold? . . . .

Your Grace would not believe how coarse and unmannerly French men have become in the last twelve or thirteen years. One would be hard put to find two young men of quality who know how to behave properly either in what they say or in what they do. There are two very different causes for this: namely, all the piety at court and the debauchery among men. Because of the first, men and women are not allowed to speak to each other in public, which used to be a way to give young gentlemen polish. And secondly, because they love the boys, they no longer want to please anyone but one another, and the most popular among them is the one who knows best how to be debauched, coarse, and insolent. This habit has become so ingrained that no one knows how to live properly any longer, and they are worse than peasants behind the plough. . . .

---

*Electress Sophie's daughter-in-law, who was caught in a scandalous adultery with Count Christoph von Koenigsmarck.

It is a great honor to sit next to the King during the sermon, but I would be happy to cede this honor to someone else, for His Majesty will not permit me to sleep. As soon as I go to sleep, the King nudges me with his elbow and wakes me up; thus I can never really go to sleep nor really stay awake. And that gives one a headache.

---

*Paris, 14 May 1695*

At every gathering here in France people do nothing but play *lansquenet*. This game is all the rage now. . . . The stakes are horrendously high here, and the people act like madmen when they are playing. One bawls, another hits the table with his fist so hard that the whole room shakes, and a third one blasphemes to make one's hair stand on end; in short, they show such despair that one is frightened even to look at them.

---

*Saint Cloud, 15 September 1695*

The story of Saint Cyr is worse than it is written in the book,† and funnier, too. The young maids there fell in love with each other and were caught in committing indecencies together. They say that Madame de Maintenon wept bitter tears about this and had all the relics exposed in order to drive out the demon of lewdness. Also, a preacher was dispatched to preach against lewdness. But he himself said such filthy things that the good and modest girls could not stand it and walked out of the church, while the others, the guilty ones, were so taken by the giggles that they could not hold them in.

---

*Versailles, 7 March 1696*

I will tell . . . how everything is here, and I will begin with Monsieur. All he has in his head are his young fellows, with whom he wants to gorge and guzzle all night long, and he gives them huge sums of money; nothing is too much or too costly for these boys. Meanwhile, his children and I barely have what we need. Whenever I need shirts or sheets it means no end of begging, yet at the same time he gives 10,000 *talers* to La Carte‡ so that he can buy his linens in Flanders. And since he knows that I am bound to find out where all the money goes, he is wary of me, afraid that I might speak about it to the King, who might chase the boys away. Whatever I may do or say to show that I do not object to his life, he still does not trust me and makes trouble for me with the King every day; even says that I hate the King. If there is any bad gossip, Monsieur tells the King that I have started it and even adds a few stout lies of his own, and sometimes he himself tells me about the terrible things he has said about me. Thereby he so turns the King against me that I can never be in his good graces. Monsieur also continually stirs up my children against me; since he does not want my son to realize how little is being done for his future, he always indulges him in his debaucheries and encourages them. Then if I suggest to my son that he should try to please the King more and abstain from vice, Monsieur and my son laugh in my face, and in Paris both of them lead an absolutely shameful life. My son's inclinations are good, and he could make something of himself if he were not corrupted by Monsieur. My daughter, thank God, he does not drag into debauchery, and to tell the truth, the girl does not have the slightest propensity for *galanterie* [flirtations and love affairs]. But Monsieur does not let me have control over her, always takes her places where I am not, and surrounds her with such rabble that it is a miracle that she has not been corrupted. Moreover, he is inculcating her with such hatred of the Germans that she can barely stand to be with me because I am German, and that makes me feel that she will end up like my son. . . . It is true that in public Monsieur is

---

† A book that had been sent to Madame by her aunt: among other things, it contained negative accounts of the convent school of Saint-Cyr, which had been founded by Madame de Maintenon.

‡ One of Monsieur's favorites, a particularly greedy character.

polite to me, but in fact he cannot stand me. As soon as he sees that any of my servants, be they male or female, become attached to me, he conceives an utter dislike for them and does them harm whenever he can; those who despise me, on the other hand, have all his favor. Monsieur is doing everything he can to make me hated, not only by the King, but also by Monsieur Le Dauphin, and everyone else too. . . . Indeed, the King is so well aware that Monsieur likes me to be treated with contempt that whenever there is trouble between them, the reconciliation always amounts to extra favors for Monsieur's beloved boys and bad treatment for me. All the silverware that came from the Palatinate Monsieur has melted down and sold, and all the proceeds were given to the boys; every day new ones show up, and all of his jewelry is being sold, pawned, pledged, and given to the young men so that if—God forbid—Monsieur should die today, tomorrow I would be thrown upon the King's mercy and not know where to find my daily bread. Monsieur says quite loudly and does not conceal from his daughter and from me that since he is getting old now, he feels that there is no time to lose and that he means to spare no expense to have a merry time until his end: he also says that those who will live longer than he will just have to see how they can get along and that he loves himself more than he loves me and his children. And indeed he practices what he preaches. If I were to tell Your Grace all the details, I would have to write a whole book. Everything here [at court] is pure self-interest and deviousness, and that makes life most unpleasant. If one does not want to get involved in intrigues and *galanteries,* one must live by oneself, which is also quite boring. In order to clear my head of these dismal reflections, I go hunting as often as possible, but this will come to an end as soon as my poor horses can no longer walk, for Monsieur has never bought me any new ones and is not likely to do so now. In the past the King used to give them to me, but now times are bad. . . . The young people are so brutal that he has to be afraid of them and does not feel like having anything to do with

them: the old ones are full of politics and only seek one's company after they see that one has the King's good graces.

————

*Versailles, 2 February 1698*

I firmly believe that the wild life that my son leads, carousing all night long and not going to bed until eight in the morning, will do him in before long. He often looks as if he had been pulled out of the grave: this is sure to kill him, but his father never wants to reprimand him. But since nothing I could say would do any good I will be quiet, although I do want to add that it is truly a shame that my son is being dragged into this profligate life, for if he had been accustomed to better and more honorable ways, he would have become a better person. He is not lacking in wit, nor is he ignorant, and from his youth he had every inclination for that which is good, commendable and befitting his rank; but ever since he has become his own master, a lot of contemptible wretches have attached themselves to him, making him keep company with, begging your leave, the vilest kinds of common whores, and he has changed so much that one does not recognize either his face or his temperament, and since he leads this life he no longer takes pleasure in anything; his pleasure in music, which used to be a passion, is gone too. In short, he has become quite insufferable, and I fear that in the end he will lose his very life over it.

————

*Versailles, 16 March 1698*

Monsieur is keener than ever on the boys and now takes lackeys out of the antechambers; every last penny he has is squandered in this way, and some day his children will be complete beggars, but he does not care about anything but providing for these pleasures of his. He opposes me in everything and avoids me at all times; he lets himself be ruled completely by these rakes and everything in his and my house is being sold for the benefit of these fellows. It is shameful what goes on here. My son has been completely captivated by Monsieur's favorites; since he loves women, they act as his pimps, sponge off him, gorge and guzzle with him, and drag him so deeply into debauchery that he cannot seem to get out of it; and since he knows that I do not approve of his ways, he avoids me and does not like me at all. Monsieur is glad that my son likes his favorites and not me and therefore puts up with everything from him. My son's wife does not love her husband; just as long as he is away from her, she is content, and in this respect they are well matched; all she cares about is her brothers' and sisters' grandeur. That is how things are here; so Your Grace can imagine what a pleasant life it is for me.

---

*Versailles, 8 March 1699*

Yesterday at table we talked about the Duchesse de Lesdiguières, who certainly has a strange temperament. All day long she does nothing but drink coffee or tea; she never reads or writes, nor does she do needlework or play cards. When she takes coffee, her chambermaids and herself must be dressed in the Turkish manner; when she takes tea, the servants who bring it must be dressed in the Indian manner. The chambermaids often weep bitter tears that they must change their clothes two or three times a day. If anyone comes to call on the lady, her antechamber is full of pages, lackeys, and noblemen; then one comes to a locked door, and when one knocks, a great big moor wearing a silver turban and a big sabre comes to open up and lets the lady or gentleman, whoever it may be, enter, but all alone. He leads the caller to a second door, which is also locked, and it is opened by another Moor who bolts it after the people have gone through, just as the first one had done. The same thing happens in the third room. In the fourth one there are two valets who lead the caller to the fifth room, where one finds the Duchess all by herself. All the portraits in her room are of her coach horses, which she had painted. These she has led one by one into the courtyard every morning and watches them from the window wearing spectacles, for she does not see well. In her room she also has a painting of the conclave, done in an unusual manner: the Pope and all the cardinals are depicted as Moors, and she also has a piece of yellow silk embroidered with a whole lot of Moors. In her garden, which is very beautiful, there is a marble column with an epitaph to one of her deceased cats which she had loved very much. If her son wants to see her, he must ask for an audience, and so must his wife: after they have inquired six or seven times whether they might be permitted to see her, she receives them, but with the same ceremonies as if they were strangers.

## REVIEW QUESTIONS

1. According to Saint-Simon, what were Louis XIV's likes and dislikes?
2. What were the Duchesse d'Orleans' major complaints about her life at court?

---

## 7 Constitutional Resistance to Royal Absolutism

Despite severe persecution of suspected Protestants by the French royal authorities, Calvinism in the sixteenth century had won a sizable minority of followers among all social ranks. In 1559, a Protestant national synod met in Paris to organize a national federation of congregations modeled on Calvin's church in Geneva. Within two years, more than two thousand congregations were gathered into a national church, governed by representative assemblies (called synods) organized on district, provincial, and national levels.

The French monarchy faltered when Henry II (1547–1559) and his son Francis II (1559–1560) died within a year and a half of each other. The country was left under the rule of a ten-year-old child, Charles IX (1560–1574), whose mother, Queen Catherine de Médici, supervised the government. The Calvinists (or Huguenots, as they were called) began openly to attack Roman Catholic churches, and a plot was uncovered to kidnap the child-king and legalize the Protestant religious reform. By spring 1562, France was engulfed in a civil war between Huguenots and Catholics that lasted on and off for some thirty years. When Henry IV (1589–1610), a Protestant, inherited the French throne, the Catholic majority resisted him until he decided to become a Catholic. In 1598, he issued the Edict of Nantes, granting limited religious toleration to the Huguenots.

# Philippe du Plessis-Mornay
# *DEFENSE OF LIBERTY AGAINST TYRANTS*

The Huguenots felt obliged to justify their rebellion against their rulers. Calvin had emphasized the obligation of Christians to obey the civil authorities even if persecuted, but this view became increasingly difficult to maintain in the circumstances the Huguenots faced. Out of this crisis, a number of Huguenot political writers sought to make a case for rebellion against or opposition to a king perceived to be their enemy.

*Vindiciae contra tyrannos (The Defense of Liberty Against Tyrants)* was published in 1579 anonymously by Philippe du Plessis-Mornay, a Huguenot noble and councilor to Henry of Navarre, later King Henry IV. The arguments of Mornay and other Huguenot political propagandists permanently affected the development of political thought and would provide a moral basis for the English Puritans in their struggle against English kings. Mornay began his work—excerpts from which follow—by asking a question crucial in his religious age: Are subjects bound to obey princes if their orders contradict the laws of God?

. . . The question here is whether it is permissible to resist a prince who is a violator of God's Law and is trying either to destroy His church or to obstruct its propagation. Holy Scripture, if only we accept its verdict, will provide us with an answer. For if, as may readily be shown, the Jewish people taken as a whole were not only so permitted but enjoined, none, I believe, will deny that the same must surely apply to the whole people of a Christian kingdom.

The prime consideration here is that God, in choosing the Jews from all the other nations as His chosen people, made a covenant with them that they would be God's people, which is documented throughout the Book of Deuteronomy. . . . Hence, we see that the whole people was obligated to maintain God's Law, to defend His Church, and thus to drive the idols of the gentiles [non-Jews] from the Land of Canaan, which stipulation cannot apply to individuals, but only to the people as a whole. And it is significant, in this respect, that all the tribes encamped around the Ark of the Lord,[1] so that what was entrusted to the care of all all were obliged to protect. . . .

---

Mornay saw the relationship between ruler and ruled as based on a kind of social contract, or as he called it, a compact or covenant.

---

. . . We have already shown that it is God who makes kings, gives kingdoms, and selects rulers. And now we say that it is the people that establishes kings, gives them kingdoms, and approves their selection by its vote. For God willed that every bit of authority held by kings should come from the people, after Him, so that kings would concentrate all their care, energy, and thought upon the people's interests. And kings are not to think that they are of a higher nature than the rest of men and rule as men rule over cattle. Born the same as all the rest of men, they are always to remember that they were raised up from below to their estates, upon all others' shoulders, as it were, so that thereafter the burdens of the commonwealth should fall, for the most part, upon theirs. . . .

Thus, at the beginning all kings were elected. And even those who seem today to come to the throne by succession must first be inaugurated by the people. Furthermore, even if a people has customarily chosen its kings from a particular family because of its outstanding merits, that decision is not so unconditional that if the established line degenerates, the people may not select another. Indeed, even the nearest kin of the selected family are not born kings but are made such. At their birth

they are considered not kings but rather candidates for kingship. . . .

## THE PEOPLE IS GREATER THAN THE KING

Since kings, then, are created by the people, it seems to follow that the people as a whole is greater than the king. This is an implication of the term itself, since one who is created by another is considered his inferior. . . . And the people sets up a king as a kind of minister to the commonwealth. . . .

Let kings obey the law, then, and acknowledge law to be their queen. "I command as I will. Reason is anything I wish" is how Juvenal[2] describes not the strength, but the weakness of a woman, and it should be taken as a form of madness. And let kings not feel that subjection to the law diminishes their dignity as rulers. Law is like an instrument, divinely given, through which human societies are ordered for the best and directed to a blessed end. A king who finds obedience to the law demeaning is therefore as ridiculous as a surveyor who considers the rule and compass and other instruments of skilled geometers to be disgraceful and absurd. . . .

. . . In all properly constituted kingdoms, the king receives laws from the people, which laws he is obligated to protect and observe. If he violates or evades them, he is judged unjust.

We have already said that the creation of a king involved a double compact. The first, between God, the king, and the people. . . . The second, between the king and the people, we shall now take up.

When Saul is made king, he accepts a *lex regia*[3] as the condition of his rule. David[4] at

---

[1]The laws of God, given to Moses on Mount Sinai and engraved on stone tablets, were preserved in a sacred ark, or chest, also called the Ark of the Covenant.

[2]Juvenal was a Roman satiric poet of the late first to early second century A.D.
[3]Saul, the first Hebrew king, reigned in the last part of the eleventh century B.C. *Lex regia* means the fundamental law of a kingdom.
[4]David (c. 1012–c. 972 B.C.) was the second Hebrew king. He was considered a religious model for kingship in medieval society.

Hebron, in the presence of God—with God, that is, as witness—enters into a covenant with all the elders of Israel, who represented the people as a whole. . . . And Josiah[5] also promises that he will observe the precepts, testimonies, and commandments included in the Book of the Covenant, and he is thus referring to the precepts of religion and justice.

In all the relevant passages, the compact is said to be made with the whole people, or the entire multitude, or all the elders, or all the men of Judah—so that we may understand, even if it were not expressly stated, that not only did the chiefs of the tribes attend, but also the lesser military chiefs and lower magistrates acting in the name of the towns, each of which covenanted of its own right with the king.

This compact created the king. For the people made the king, not the king the people. Therefore, there is no doubt that the people was the stipulator and the king the promiser. And the position of the stipulator is considered stronger under civil law. The people asked, by way of stipulation, whether the king would rule justly and according to the law. He then promised to do so. And the people, finally, replied that they would faithfully obey, as long as his commands were just. Hence, the promise of the king was absolute, that of the people was conditional; and if he does not perform, the people, by the same principle of civil law, are released from any obligation.

By the first covenant, or compact, religious piety becomes an obligation; by the second, justice. In the first the king promises to obey God religiously, in the second, to rule the people justly; in the former, to maintain God's glory, in the latter, to preserve the people's welfare. The condition in the first is: "If you will observe My Law"; the condition in the second is: "If you will render each his own." If the king does not perform the conditions of

the first, God is properly the avenger, while the whole people may lawfully punish nonperformance of the second.

In all legitimate governments a compact is always to be found. . . .

---

But what if the compact between the ruler and ruled is violated by the ruler? He thus becomes a tyrant, said Mornay, a criminal who forfeits his right to the obedience of his subjects, who may now exercise their right to rebel and form a new compact.

---

Tyranny is like a raging fever. At the beginning it is easy to cure but difficult to detect; afterwards, it is easy to recognize but very difficult to cure. The leading men, therefore, will oppose its beginnings and overlook nothing, no matter how trivial it seems. But if the prince persists, pays no heed to repeated remonstrations, and seems only to be aiming at a situation in which he can do anything he pleases with impunity, then the fact of tyranny is proven, and anything that may be done against a tyrant may now be done to him. . . .

We have shown, moreover, that kings receive their royal status from the people; that the whole people is greater than the king and is above him; that the king in his kingdom, the emperor in his empire, are supreme only as ministers and agents, while the people is the true proprietor. It follows, therefore, that a tyrant commits felony against the people who is, as it were, the owner of his fief; that he commits *lèse majesté* [treason] against the kingdom or the empire; and that he is no better than any other rebel since he violates the same laws, although as king he merits even graver punishments. And so, says Bartolus,[6] he may be either deposed by his superior or punished under the

---

[5]Josiah was a Hebrew king of Judah during the seventh century B.C. He reformed the Hebrew religion by basing his rule on the laws set down in the book of Deuteronomy.

[6]Bartolus of Saxoferrato (1314–1357) was a leading Italian jurist. He helped revolutionize the study of Roman law and contributed to the Italian city-states' efforts to legally defend their liberties against the Holy Roman Emperors' claims of sovereignty.

*lex Julia*[7] for acts against the public majesty. But the superior here is the whole people or those who represent it. . . . And if things have gone so far that the tyrant cannot be expelled without resort to force, they may call the people to arms, recruit an army, and use force, strategy, and all the engines of war against him who is the declared enemy of the country and the commonwealth. . . .

The obligation between prince and people is ever reciprocal and mutual. He promises to be

a just prince; they, to obey him if he is one. The people, therefore, is obligated to the prince conditionally, he to the people absolutely. If the condition is not fulfilled, the people are released, the compact voided, and the obligation nullified. The king is perjured if he rules unjustly; the people, if they fail to obey him when his rule is just. The people, however, is absolved from any charge of perjury if it publicly renounces a ruler who would rule unjustly or if it attempts, by force of arms, to evict a ruler who seeks to retain possession of the kingdom in contravention of the law.

---

[7]*Lex Julia* was the basic Roman law on treason.

## REVIEW QUESTIONS

1. Compare the views of Philippe du Plessis-Mornay with those of John of Salisbury (see page 260) on tyranny and the character of a true prince.
2. What were Mornay's views on the origin, status, and obligations of kings?
3. Compare Mornay's views with those of James I. What are the implications when these two theories confront each other in the field of practical politics?

---

## 8  A Secular Defense of Absolutism

Thomas Hobbes (1588–1679), a British philosopher and political theorist, witnessed the agonies of the English civil war, including the execution of Charles I in 1649. These developments fortified Hobbes's conviction that absolutism was the most desirable and logical form of government. Only the unlimited power of a sovereign, said Hobbes, could contain human passions that disrupt the social order and threaten civilized life; only absolute rule could provide an environment secure enough for people to pursue their individual interests.

*Leviathan* (1651), Hobbes's principal work of political thought, broke with medieval political theory. Medieval thinkers assigned each group of people— clergy, lords, serfs, guildsmen—a place in a fixed social order; an individual's social duties were set by ancient traditions believed to have been ordained by God. During early modern times, the great expansion of commerce and capitalism spurred the new individualism already pronounced in Renaissance culture; group ties were shattered by competition and accelerating social mobility. Hobbes gave expression to a society where people confronted each other as competing individuals.

# Thomas Hobbes
# *LEVIATHAN*

Hobbes was influenced by the new scientific thought that saw mathematical knowledge as the avenue to truth. Using geometry as a model, Hobbes began with what he believed were self-evident axioms regarding human nature, from which he deduced other truths. He aimed at constructing political philosophy on a scientific foundation and rejected the authority of tradition and religion as inconsistent with a science of politics. Thus, although Hobbes supported absolutism, he dismissed the idea advanced by other theorists of absolutism that the monarch's power derived from God. He also rejected the idea that the state should not be obeyed when it violated God's law. *Leviathan* is a rational and secular political statement. In this modern approach, rather than in Hobbes's justification of absolutism, lies the work's significance.

Hobbes had a pessimistic view of human nature. Believing that people are innately selfish and grasping, he maintained that competition and dissension, rather than cooperation, characterize human relations. Even when reason teaches that cooperation is more advantageous than competition, Hobbes observed that people are reluctant to alter their ways, because passion, not reason, governs their behavior. In the following passages from *Leviathan,* Hobbes described the causes of human conflicts.

Nature hath made men so equall, in the faculties of body, and mind; as that though there bee found one man sometimes manifestly stronger in body, or of quicker mind than another; yet when all is reckoned together, the difference between man, and man, is not so considerable, as that one man can thereupon claim to himselfe any benefit, to which another may not pretend, as well as he. For as to the strength of body, the weakest has strength enough to kill the strongest, either by secret machination, or by confederacy with others, that are in the same danger with himselfe. . . .

And as to the faculties of the mind . . . men are . . . [more] equall than unequall. . . .

From this equality of ability, ariseth equality of hope in the attaining of our Ends. And therefore if any two men desire the same thing, which neverthelesse they cannot both enjoy, they become enemies; and in the way to their End, . . . endeavour to destroy, or subdue one another. . . . If one plant, sow, build, or possesse a convenient Seat, others may probably be expected to come prepared with forces united, to dispossesse, and deprive him, not only of the fruit of his labour, but also of his life, or liberty. . . .

So that in the nature of man, we find three principall causes of quarrell. First, Competition; Secondly, Diffidence; Thirdly, Glory.

The first, maketh men invade for Gain; the second, for Safety; and the third, for Reputation. The first use Violence, to make themselves Masters of other men's persons, wives, children, and cattell; the second, to defend them; the third, for trifles, as a word, a smile, a different opinion, and any other signe of undervalue, either direct in their Persons, or by reflexion in their Kindred, their Friends, their Nation, their Profession, or their Name.

Hereby it is manifest, that during the time men live without a common Power to keep them all in awe, they are in that condition which is called Warre; and such a warre, as is of every man, against every man. . . .

Hobbes then described a state of nature—the hypothetical condition of humanity prior to the formation of the state—as a war of all against all. For Hobbes, the state of nature is a logical abstraction, a device employed to make his point. Only a strong ruling entity—the state—will end the perpetual strife and provide security. For Hobbes, the state is merely a useful arrangement that permits individuals to exchange goods and services in a secure environment. The ruling authority in the state, the sovereign, must have supreme power, or society will collapse and the anarchy of the state of nature will return.

---

Whatsoever therefore is consequent to a time of Warre, where every man is Enemy to every man; the same is consequent to the time, wherein men live without other security, than what their own strength, and their own invention shall furnish them withall. In such condition, there is no place for Industry; because the fruit thereof is uncertain: and consequently no Culture of the Earth; no Navigation, nor use of the commodities that may be imported by Sea; no commodious Building; no Instruments of moving, and removing such things as require much force; no Knowledge of the face of the Earth; no account of Time; no Arts; no Letters; no Society; and which is worst of all, continuall feare, and danger of violent death; And the life of man, solitary, poore, nasty, brutish, and short. . . .

The Passions that encline men to Peace, are Feare of Death; Desire of such things as are necessary to commodious living; and a Hope by their Industry to obtain them. And Reason suggesteth convenient Articles of Peace, upon which men may be drawn to agreement. . . .

And because the condition of Man, (as hath been declared in the precedent Chapter) is a condition of Warre of every one against every one; in which case every one is governed by his own Reason; and there is nothing he can make use of, that may not be a help unto him, in preserving his life against his enemyes; It followeth, that in such a condition, every man has a Right to every thing; even to one another's body. And therefore, as long as this naturall Right of every man to every thing endureth, there can be no security to any man, (how strong or wise soever he be,) of living out the time, which Nature ordinarily alloweth men to live. . . .

. . . If there be no Power erected, or not great enough for our security; every man will and may lawfully rely on his own strength and art, for caution against all other men. . . .

The only way to erect . . . a Common Power, as may be able to defend them from the invasion of [foreigners] and the injuries of one another, and thereby to secure them in such sort, as that by their owne industrie, and by the fruites of the Earth, they may nourish themselves and live contentedly; is, to conferre all their power and strength upon one Man, or upon one Assembly of men, that may reduce all their Wills, by plurality of voices, unto one Will . . . and therein to submit their Wills, every one to his Will, and their Judgements, to his Judgment. This is more than Consent, or Concord; it is a reall Unitie of them all, in one and the same Person, made by Covenant of every man with every man, in such manner, as if every man should say to every man, *I Authorise and give up my Right of Governing my selfe, to this Man, or to this Assembly of men, on this condition, that thou give up thy Right to him, and Authorise all his Actions in like manner.* This done, the Multitude so united in one Person, is called a COMMON-WEALTH. . . . For by this Authorite, given him by every particular man in the Common-wealth, he hath the use of so much Power and Strength . . . conferred on him, that by terror thereof, he is inabled to forme the wills of them all, to Peace at home, and mutuall [aid] against their enemies abroad. And in him consisteth the Essence of the Common-wealth; which (to define it,) is *One Person, of whose Acts a great Multitude, by mutuall Covenants one with another, have made themselves every one the Author, to the end he may use the strength and means of them all, as he shall think expedient, for their Peace and Common Defence.*

And he that carryeth this Person, is called SOVERAIGNE, and said to have *Soveraigne Power;* and every one besides, his SUBJECT. . . .

. . . They that have already Instituted a Common-wealth, being thereby bound by Covenant . . . cannot lawfully make a new Covenant, amongst themselves, to be obedient to any other, in any thing whatsoever, without his permission. And therefore, they that are subjects to a Monarch, cannot without his leave cast off Monarchy, and return to the confusion of a disunited Multitude; nor transferre their Person from him that beareth it, to another Man, or other Assembly of men: for they . . . are bound, every man to every man, to [acknowledge] . . . that he that already is their Soveraigne, shall do, and judge fit to be done; so that [those who do not obey] break their Covenant made to that man, which is injustice: and they have also

every man given the Soveraignty to him that beareth their Person; and therefore if they depose him, they take from him that which is his own, and so again it is injustice. . . . And whereas some men have pretended for their disobedience to their Soveraign, a new Covenant, made, not with men, but with God; this also is unjust: for there is no Covenant with God, but by mediation of some body that representeth God's Person; which none doth but God's Lieutenant, who hath the Soveraignty under God. But this pretence of Covenant with God, is so evident a [lie], even in the pretenders own consciences, that it is not onely an act of an unjust, but also of a vile, and unmanly disposition. . . .

. . . Consequently none of [the sovereign's] Subjects, by any pretence of forfeiture, can be freed from his Subjection.

## REVIEW QUESTIONS

1. What was Thomas Hobbes's view of human nature and what conclusions did he draw from it about the best form of government?
2. How did Hobbes deal with the arguments of political thinkers like Philippe du Plessis-Mornay?
3. What has been the political legacy of Hobbes's notion of the state?

---

# 9 The Triumph of Constitutional Monarchy in England: The Glorious Revolution

The struggle against absolute monarchy in England during the early seventeenth century reached a climax during the reign of Charles I (1625–1649). Parliament raised its own army as civil war broke out between its supporters and those of the king. Captured by the Scottish Presbyterian rebels in 1646 and turned over to the English parliamentary army in 1647, Charles was held prisoner for two years until the Puritan parliamentary general Oliver Cromwell (1599–1658) decided to put him on trial for treason. The king was found guilty and executed in 1649.

The revolutionary parliamentary regime evolved into a military dictatorship headed by Cromwell. After Cromwell's death, Parliament in 1660 restored the monarchy and invited the late king's heir to end his exile and take the throne. Charles II (1660–1685), by discretion and skillful statesmanship, managed to evade many difficulties caused by the hostility of those who opposed his policies. He attempted to ease religious discrimination by ending the laws that penalized dissenters who rejected the official Church of England. But the religious prejudices of Parliament forced the king to desist, and the laws penalizing both Protestant dissenters and Roman Catholics remained in force. The king's motives for establishing religious toleration were suspect, since he himself was married to a French Catholic and his brother and heir James, Duke of York, was also a staunch Catholic.

When James II (1685–1688) succeeded to the throne, he tried unsuccessfully to get Parliament to repeal the Test Act, a law that forbade anyone to hold a civil or military office or to enter a university unless he was a member in good standing of the Church of England. This law effectively barred both Catholics and Protestant dissenters from serving in the king's government. When Parliament refused to act, James got the legal Court of the King's Bench to approve his decree suspending the Test Act. The court affirmed that the king, based on his sovereign authority, had absolute power to suspend any law at his sole discretion. The prerogatives claimed by the king were seen by many as an attempt to impose absolute monarchy on the English people.

King James further roused enemies by appointing many Catholics to high government posts and by issuing his Declaration of Indulgence for Liberty of Conscience on April 4, 1687. This declaration established complete freedom of worship for all Englishmen, ending all civil penalties and discriminations based on religious dissent. Instead of hailing the declaration as a step forward in solving the religious quarrels within the kingdom, many persons viewed this suspension of the laws as a further act of absolutism because James acted unilaterally without consulting Parliament. This act united the king's enemies and alienated his former supporters.

When the king's wife gave birth to a son, making the heir to the throne another Catholic, almost all factions (except the Catholics) abandoned James II and invited the Dutch Protestant Prince William of Orange and his wife Mary, James II's Protestant daughter, to come to England. James and his Catholic family and friends fled to France. Parliament declared the throne vacant and offered it to William and Mary as joint sovereigns. As a result of the "Glorious Revolution," the English monarchy became clearly limited by the will of Parliament.

# THE ENGLISH DECLARATION OF RIGHTS

In depriving James II of the throne, Parliament had destroyed forever in Britain the theory of divine right as an operating principle of government and had firmly established a limited constitutional monarchy. The appointment of William and Mary was accompanied by a declaration of rights (later enacted as the Bill of Rights), which enumerated and declared illegal James II's arbitrary acts. The Declaration of Rights, excerpted below, compelled William and Mary and future monarchs to recognize the right of the people's representatives to dispose of the royal office and to set limits on its powers. These rights were subsequently formulated into laws passed by Parliament. Prior to the American Revolution, colonists protested that British actions in the American colonies violated certain rights guaranteed in the English Bill of Rights. Several of these rights were later included in the Constitution of the United States.

And whereas the said late king James the Second having abdicated the government and the throne being thereby vacant, His Highness the prince of Orange (whom it hath pleased Almighty God to make the glorious instrument of delivering this kingdom from popery and arbitrary power) did (by the advice of the lords spiritual and temporal and divers principal persons of the commons)[1] cause letters to be written to the lords spiritual and temporal, being Protestants; and other letters to the several counties, cities, universities, boroughs and Cinque ports[2] for the choosing of such persons to represent them, as were of right to be sent to parliament, to meet and sit at Westminster upon the two and twentieth day of January in this year one thousand six hundred eighty and eight,[3] in order to [guarantee] . . . that their religion, laws and liberties might not again be in danger of being subverted; upon which letters elections having been accordingly made.

And thereupon the said lords spiritual and temporal and commons pursuant to their respective letters and elections being now assembled in a full and free representative of this nation, taking into their most serious consideration the best means for attaining the ends aforesaid, do in the first place (as their ances-

tors in like case have usually done) for the vindicating and asserting their ancient rights and liberties, declare:

That the pretended power of suspending of laws or the execution of laws by regal authority without consent of parliament is illegal.

That the pretended power of dispensing with laws or the execution of laws by regal authority as it hath been assumed and exercised of late is illegal.

That the commission for erecting the late court of commissioners for ecclesiastical causes and all other commissions and courts of like nature are illegal and pernicious.

That the levying money for or to the use of the crown by pretence of prerogative without grant of parliament for a longer time or in other manner than the same is or shall be granted is illegal.

That it is the right of the subjects to petition the king and all commitments and prosecutions for such petitioning are illegal.

That the raising or keeping a standing army within the kingdom in time of peace unless it be with consent of parliament is against law.

That the subjects which are Protestants may have arms for their defence suitable to their conditions and as allowed by law.

That election of members of parliament ought to be free.

That the freedom of speech and debates or proceedings in parliament ought not to be impeached or questioned in any court or place out of parliament.

That excessive bail ought not to be required nor excessive fines imposed nor cruel and unusual punishments inflicted.

That jurors ought to be duly impanelled and returned and jurors which pass upon men in trials for high treason ought to be freeholders.

---

[1]The lords spiritual refers to the bishops of the Church of England who sat in the House of Lords, and the lords temporal refers to the nobility entitled to sit in the House of Lords. The commons refers to the elected representatives in the House of Commons.

[2]The Cinque ports along England's southeastern coast (originally five in number) enjoyed special privileges because of their military duties in providing for coastal defense.

[3]The year was in fact 1689 because until 1752, the English used March 25 as the beginning of the new year.

That all grants and promises of fines and forfeitures of particular persons before conviction are illegal and void.

And that for redress of all grievances and for the amending, strengthening and preserving of the laws parliaments ought to be held frequently.

And they do claim, demand and insist upon all and singular the premises as their undoubted rights and liberties and that no declarations, judgments, doings or proceedings to the prejudice of the people in any of the said premises ought in any wise to be drawn hereafter into consequence or example.

## REVIEW QUESTIONS

1. How did the Declaration of Rights limit royal authority? With what result?
2. In what ways did the Glorious Revolution impact upon the American rebellion in the 1770s?

# CHAPTER 12

# *The Scientific Revolution*

JOHANNES KEPLER'S vision of the "House of Astronomy" from his book *Tabulae Rudolphinae*, 1627. Each pillar bears the name of such important contributors to the new science as Ptolemy, Copernicus, and Tycho Brahe. Astronomical instruments of the time hang from the pillars. *(Fotomas Index)*

The Scientific Revolution of the sixteenth and seventeenth centuries replaced the medieval view of the universe with a new cosmology and produced a new way of investigating nature. It overthrew the medieval conception of nature as a hierarchical order ascending toward a realm of perfection. Rejecting reliance on authority, the thinkers of the Scientific Revolution affirmed the individual's ability to know the natural world through the method of mathematical reasoning, the direct observation of nature, and carefully controlled experiments.

The medieval view of the universe had blended the theories of Aristotle and Ptolemy, two ancient Greek thinkers, with Christian teachings. In that view, a stationary earth stood in the center of the universe just above hell. Revolving around the earth were seven planets: the moon, Mercury, Venus, the sun, Mars, Jupiter, and Saturn. Because people believed that earth did not move, it was not considered a planet. Each planet was attached to a transparent sphere that turned around the earth. Encompassing the universe was a sphere of fixed stars; beyond the stars lay three heavenly spheres, the outermost of which was the abode of God. An earth-centered universe accorded with the Christian idea that God had created the universe for men and women and that salvation was the aim of life.

Also agreeable to the medieval Christian view was Aristotle's division of the universe into a lower, earthly realm and a higher realm beyond the moon. Two sets of laws operated in the universe, one on earth and the other in the celestial realm. Earthly objects were composed of four elements: earth, water, fire, and air; celestial objects were composed of the divine ether—a substance too pure, too clear, too fine, too spiritual to be found on earth. Celestial objects naturally moved in perfectly circular orbits around the earth; earthly objects, composed mainly of the heavy elements of earth and water, naturally fell downward, whereas objects made of the lighter elements of air and fire naturally flew upward toward the sky.

The destruction of the medieval world picture began with the publication in 1543 of *On the Revolutions of the Heavenly Spheres*, by Nicolaus Copernicus, a Polish mathematician, astronomer, and clergyman. In Copernicus's system, the sun was in the center of the universe, and the earth was another planet that moved around the sun. Most thinkers of the time, committed to the Aristotelian-Ptolemaic system and to the biblical statements that seemed to support it, rejected Copernicus's conclusions.

The work of Galileo Galilei, an Italian mathematician, astronomer, and physicist, was decisive in the shattering of the medieval cosmos and the shaping of the modern scientific outlook. Galileo advanced the modern view that knowledge of nature derives from direct observation and from mathematics. For Galileo, the universe was a "grand book which . . . is written in the language of mathematics, and its characters are triangles, circles, and other geometric figures without which it is humanly impossible to understand a single word of it." Galileo also pioneered experimental physics, advanced the modern idea that nature is uniform throughout the universe, and attacked reliance on scholastic authority rather than on experimentation in resolving scientific controversies.

Johannes Kepler (1571–1630), a contemporary of Galileo, discovered three laws of planetary motion that greatly advanced astronomical knowledge. Kepler showed that the path of a planet was an ellipse, not a circle as Ptolemy (and Copernicus) had believed, and that planets do not move at uniform speed but accelerate as they near the sun. He devised formulas to calculate accurately both a planet's speed at each point in its orbit around the sun and a planet's location at a particular time. Kepler's laws provided further evidence that Copernicus had been right, for they made sense only in a sun-centered universe, but Kepler could not explain why planets stayed in their orbits rather than flying off into space or crashing into the sun. The resolution of that question was left to Sir Isaac Newton.

Newton's great achievement was integrating the findings of Copernicus, Galileo, and Kepler into a single theoretical system. In *Principia Mathematica* (1687), he formulated the mechanical laws of motion and attraction that govern celestial and terrestrial objects.

The creation of a new model of the universe was one great achievement of the Scientific Revolution; another accomplishment was the formulation of the scientific method. The scientific method encompasses two approaches to knowledge, which usually complement each other: the empirical (inductive) and the rational (deductive). Although all sciences use both approaches, the inductive method is generally more applicable in such descriptive sciences as biology, anatomy, and geology, which rely on the accumulation of data. In the inductive approach, general principles are derived from analyzing external experiences—observations and the results of experiments. In the deductive approach, used in mathematics and theoretical physics, truths are derived in successive steps from indubitable axioms. Whereas the inductive method builds its concepts from an analysis of sense experience, the deductive approach constructs its ideas from self-evident principles that are conceived by the mind itself without external experience. The deductive and inductive approaches to knowledge, and their interplay, have been a constantly recurring feature in Western intellectual history since the rationalism of Plato and the empiricism of Aristotle. The success of the scientific method in modern times arose from the skillful synchronization of induction and deduction by such giants as Leonardo, Copernicus, Kepler, Galileo, and Newton.

The Scientific Revolution was instrumental in shaping the modern outlook. It destroyed the medieval conception of the universe and established the scientific method as the means for investigating nature and acquiring knowledge, even in areas having little to do with the study of the physical world. By demonstrating the powers of the human mind, the Scientific Revolution gave thinkers great confidence in reason and led eventually to a rejection of traditional beliefs in magic, astrology, and witches. In the eighteenth century, this growing skepticism led thinkers to question miracles and other Christian beliefs that seemed contrary to reason.

# 1   The Copernican Revolution

In proclaiming that the earth was not stationary but revolved around the sun, Nicolaus Copernicus (1473–1543) revolutionized the science of astronomy. Fearing controversy and scorn, Copernicus long refused to publish his great work, *On the Revolutions of the Heavenly Spheres*. However, persuaded by friends, he finally relented and permitted publication; a copy of his book reached him on his deathbed. As Copernicus anticipated, his ideas aroused the ire of many thinkers.

Both Catholic and Protestant philosophers and theologians, including Martin Luther, attacked Copernicus for contradicting the Bible and Aristotle and Ptolemy, and they raised several specific objections. First, certain passages in the Bible imply a stationary earth and a sun that moves (for example, Psalm 93 says, "Yea, the world is established; it shall never be moved"; and in attacking Copernicus, Luther pointed out that "sacred Scripture tells us that Joshua commanded the sun to stand still, and not the earth"). Second, a body as heavy as the earth cannot move through space at such speed as Copernicus suggested. Third, if the earth spins on its axis, why does a stone dropped from a height land directly below instead of at a point behind where it was dropped? Fourth, if the earth moved, objects would fly off it. And finally, the moon cannot orbit both the earth and the sun at the same time.

# Nicolaus Copernicus
# *ON THE REVOLUTIONS OF THE HEAVENLY SPHERES*

*On the Revolutions of the Heavenly Spheres* was dedicated to Pope Paul III, whom Copernicus asked to protect him from vilification. In the dedication, Copernicus explains his reason for delaying publication of *Revolutions*.

*To His Holiness, Pope Paul III, Nicholas Copernicus' Preface to His Books on the Revolutions*

I can readily imagine, Holy Father, that as soon as some people hear that in this volume, which I have written about the revolutions of the spheres of the universe, I ascribe certain motions to the terrestrial globe, they will shout that I must be immediately repudiated together with this belief. For I am not so enamored of my own opinions that I disregard what others may think of them. I am aware that a philosopher's ideas are not subject to the judgement of ordinary persons, because it is his endeavor to seek the truth in all things, to the extent permitted to human reason by God. Yet I hold that completely erroneous views should be shunned. Those who know that the consensus of many centuries has sanctioned the conception that the earth remains at rest in the middle of the heaven as its center would, I reflected, regard it as an insane pronouncement if I made the opposite assertion that the earth moves. Therefore I debated with myself for a long time whether to publish the volume which I wrote to prove the earth's motion or rather to follow the example of the Pythagoreans[1] and certain others, who used to transmit philosophy's secrets only to kinsmen and friends, not in writing but by word of mouth. . . . And they did so, it seems to me, not, as some suppose, because they were in some way jealous about their teachings, which would be spread around; on the contrary, they wanted the very beautiful thoughts attained by great men of deep devotion not to be ridiculed by those who are reluctant to exert themselves vigorously in any literary pursuit unless it is lucrative; or if they are stimulated to the nonacquisitive study of philosophy by the exhortation and example of others, yet because of their dullness of mind they play the same part among philosophers as drones among bees. When I weighed these considerations, the scorn which I had reason to fear on account of the novelty and unconventionality of my opinion almost induced me to abandon completely the work which I had undertaken.

But while I hesitated for a long time and even resisted, my friends [encouraged me]. . . .

Foremost among them was the cardinal of Capua [a city in southern Italy], Nicholas Schönberg, renowned in every field of learning. Next to him was a man who loves me dearly, Tiedemann Giese, bishop of Chelmno [a city in northern Poland], a close student of sacred letters as well as of all good literature. For he repeatedly encouraged me and, sometimes adding reproaches, urgently requested me to publish this volume and finally permit it to appear after being buried among my papers and lying concealed not merely until the ninth year[2] but by now the fourth period of nine years. The same conduct was recommended to me by not a few other very eminent scholars. They exhorted me no longer to refuse, on account of the fear which I felt, to make my work available for the general use of students of astronomy. The crazier my doctrine of the earth's motion now appeared to most people, the argument ran, so much the more admiration and thanks would it gain after they saw the publication of my writings dispel the fog of absurdity by most luminous proofs. Influenced therefore by these persuasive men and by this hope, in the end I allowed my friends to bring out an edition of the volume, as they had long besought me to do. . . .

But you [your Holiness] are rather waiting to hear from me how it occurred to me to venture to conceive any motion of the earth, against the traditional opinion of astronomers and almost against common sense. . . . [Copernicus then describes some of the problems connected with the Ptolemaic system.]

For a long time, then, I reflected on this confusion in the astronomical traditions concerning the derivation of the motions of the universe's spheres. I began to be annoyed that the movements of the world machine, created for our sake by the best and most systematic

---

[1]Pythagoreans were followers of Pythagoras, a Greek mathematician and philosopher of the sixth century B.C.; they were particularly interested in cosmology.

[2]The Roman poet Horace, who lived in the first century B.C., suggested in *Ars Poetica* that writers should keep a new manuscript in a cupboard "until the ninth year" before publishing it. Only then, he argued, would they have enough objectivity to judge its value. Copernicus is referring to this famous piece of advice.

Artisan of all [God], were not understood with greater certainty by the philosophers, who otherwise examined so precisely the most insignificant trifles of this world. For this reason I undertook the task of rereading the works of all the philosophers which I could obtain to learn whether anyone had ever proposed other motions of the universe's spheres than those expounded by the teachers of astronomy in the schools. And in fact first I found in Cicero that Hicetas supposed the earth to move. Later I also discovered in Plutarch[3] that certain others were of this opinion. . . .

Therefore, having obtained the opportunity from these sources, I too began to consider the mobility of the earth. . . . I thought that I too would be readily permitted to ascertain whether explanations sounder than those of my predecessors could be found for the revolution of the celestial spheres on the assumption of some motion of the earth.

Having thus assumed the motions which I ascribe to the earth later on in the volume, by long and intense study I finally found that if the motions of the other planets are correlated with the orbiting of the earth, and are computed for the revolution of each planet, not only do their phenomena follow therefrom but also the order and size of all the planets and spheres, and heaven itself is so linked together that in no portion of it can anything be shifted without disrupting the remaining parts and the universe as a whole. Accordingly in the arrangement of the volume too I have adopted the following order. In the first book I set forth the entire distribution of the spheres together with the motions which I attribute to the earth, so that this book contains, as it were, the general structure of the universe. Then in the remaining books I correlate the motions of the other planets and of all the spheres with the movement of the earth so that I may thereby determine to what extent the motions and appearances of the other planets and spheres can be saved if they are correlated with the earth's motions. I have no doubt that acute and learned astronomers will agree with me if, as this discipline especially requires, they are willing to examine and consider, not superficially but thoroughly, what I adduce in this volume in proof of these matters. However, in order that the educated and uneducated alike may see that I do not run away from the judgement of anybody at all, I have preferred dedicating my studies to Your Holiness rather than to anyone else. For even in this very remote corner of the earth where I live you are considered the highest authority by virtue of the loftiness of your office and your love for all literature and astronomy too. Hence by your prestige and judgement you can easily suppress calumnious attacks although, as the proverb has it, there is no remedy for a backbite.

Perhaps there will be babblers who claim to be judges of astronomy although completely ignorant of the subject and, badly distorting some passage of Scripture to their purpose, will dare to find fault with my undertaking and censure it. I disregard them even to the extent of despising their criticism as unfounded. For it is not unknown that Lactantius,[4] otherwise an illustrious writer but hardly an astronomer, speaks quite childishly about the earth's shape, when he mocks those who declared that the earth has the form of a globe. Hence scholars need not be surprised if any such persons will likewise ridicule me. Astronomy is written for astronomers. To them my work too will seem, unless I am mistaken, to make some contribution.

---

[3]Hicetas, a Pythagorean philosopher of the fourth century B.C., taught that the earth rotated on its axis while the other heavenly bodies were at rest. Cicero was a Roman statesman of the first century B.C. Plutarch (A.D. c. 50–c. 120) was a Greek moral philosopher and biographer whose works were especially popular among Renaissance humanists.

[4]Renaissance humanists admired Lactantius (c. 240–c. 320), a Latin rhetorician and Christian apologist, for his classical, Ciceronian literary style.

# Cardinal Bellarmine
# ATTACK ON THE COPERNICAN THEORY

In 1615, Cardinal Bellarmine, who in the name of the Inquisition warned Galileo (see Sections 2 and 3) not to defend the Copernican theory, expressed his displeasure with heliocentrism in a letter to Paolo Antonio Foscarini. Foscarini, head of the Carmelites, an order of mendicant friars, in Calabria and professor of theology, had tried to show that the earth's motion was not incompatible with biblical statements.

*Cardinal Bellarmine to Foscarini (12 April 1615)*

My Very Reverend Father,

I have read with interest the letter in Italian and the essay in Latin which Your [Reverence] sent me; I thank you for the one and for the other and confess that they are full of intelligence and erudition. You ask for my opinion, and so I shall give it to you, but very briefly, since now you have little time for reading and I for writing.

First, . . . to want to affirm that in reality the sun is at the center of the world and only turns on itself without moving from east to west, and the earth . . . revolves with great speed around the sun . . . is a very dangerous thing, likely not only to irritate all scholastic philosophers and theologians, but also to harm the Holy Faith by rendering Holy Scripture false. For your [Reverence] has well shown many ways of interpreting Holy Scripture, but has not applied them to particular cases; without a doubt you would have encountered very great difficulties if you had wanted to interpret all those passages you yourself cited.

Second, I say that, as you know, the Council [of Trent] prohibits interpreting Scripture against the common consensus of the Holy Fathers; and if Your [Reverence] wants to read not only the Holy Fathers, but also the modern commentaries on Genesis, the Psalms, Ecclesiastes, and Joshua, you will find all agreeing in the literal interpretation that the sun is in heaven and turns around the earth with great speed, and that the earth is very far from heaven and sits motionless at the center of the world. Consider now, with your sense of prudence, whether the Church can tolerate giving Scripture a meaning contrary to the Holy Fathers and to all the Greek and Latin commentators. Nor can one answer that this is not a matter of faith, since if it is not a matter of faith "as regards the topic," it is a matter of faith "as regards the speaker"; and so it would be heretical to say that Abraham did not have two children and Jacob twelve, as well as to say that Christ was not born of a virgin, because both are said by the Holy Spirit through the mouth of the prophets and the apostles.

Third, I say that if there were a true demonstration that the sun is at the center of the world and the earth in the third heaven, and that the sun does not circle the earth but the earth circles the sun, then one would have to proceed with great care in explaining the Scriptures that appear contrary, and say rather that we do not understand them than that what is demonstrated is false. But I will not believe that there is such a demonstration, until it is shown to me. . . . and in case of doubt one must not abandon the Holy Scripture as interpreted by the Holy Fathers. I add that the one who wrote, "The sun also ariseth, and the sun goeth down, and hasteth to his place where he arose," was Solomon [King of ancient Israel], who not only spoke inspired by God, but was a man above all others wise and learned in the human sciences and in the knowledge of created things; he received all this wisdom from God; therefore it is not likely that he was affirming something that was contrary to truth already demonstrated or capable of being demonstrated.

*REVIEW QUESTIONS*

1. What led Nicolaus Copernicus to investigate the motions of the universe's spheres?
2. Why did he fear to publish his theory about the earth's motion?
3. On what grounds did Cardinal Bellarmine reject the Copernican theory?

---

## 2  Expanding the New Astronomy

The brilliant Italian scientist Galileo Galilei (1564–1642) rejected the medieval division of the universe into higher and lower realms and proclaimed the modern idea of nature's uniformity. Learning that a telescope had been invented in Holland, Galileo built one for himself and used it to investigate the heavens. Through his telescope, Galileo saw craters and mountains on the moon; he concluded that celestial bodies were not pure, perfect, and immutable, as had been believed. There was no difference in quality between heavenly and earthly bodies; nature was the same throughout.

## Galileo Galilei
## *THE STARRY MESSENGER*

In the following reading from *The Starry Messenger* (1610), Galileo reported the findings observed through his telescope, which led him to proclaim the uniformity of nature, a key principle of modern science.

About ten months ago a report reached my ears that a certain Fleming [a native of Flanders]* had constructed a spyglass by means of which visible objects, though very distant from the eye of the observer, were distinctly seen as if nearby. Of this truly remarkable effect several experiences were related, to which some persons gave credence while others denied them. A few days later the report was confirmed to me in a letter from a noble Frenchman at Paris, Jacques Badovere,† which caused me to apply myself wholeheartedly to inquire into the means by which I might arrive at the invention of a similar instrument. This I did shortly afterwards, my basis being the theory of refraction. First I prepared a tube of lead, at the ends of which I fitted two glass lenses, both plane on one side while on the other side one was spherically convex and the other concave. Then placing my eye near the concave lens I perceived objects satisfactorily large and near, for they appeared three times closer and nine times larger than when seen with the naked eye alone. Next I constructed another one, more accurate, which represented objects as enlarged more than sixty times. Finally, sparing neither labor nor expense, I succeeded in constructing for myself so excellent an instrument that objects seen by means of it appeared nearly one thousand times larger and over thirty times closer than when regarded with our natural vision.

---

*Credit for the original invention is generally assigned to Hans Lipperhey, a lens grinder in Holland who chanced upon this property of combined lenses and applied for a patent on it in 1608.

†Badovere studied in Italy toward the close of the sixteenth century and is said to have been a pupil of Galileo's in about 1598. When he wrote concerning the new instrument in 1609, he was in the French diplomatic service at Paris, where he died in 1620.

It would be superfluous to enumerate the number and importance of the advantages of such an instrument at sea as well as on land. But forsaking terrestrial observations, I turned to celestial ones, and first I saw the moon from as near at hand as if it were scarcely two terrestrial radii [a measure of distance, obscure today] away. After that I observed often with wondering delight both the planets and the fixed stars, and since I saw these latter to be very crowded, I began to seek (and eventually found) a method by which I might measure their distances apart. . . .

Now let us review the observations made during the past two months, once more inviting the attention of all who are eager for true philosophy to the first steps of such important contemplations. Let us speak first of that surface of the moon which faces us. For greater clarity I distinguish two parts of this surface, a lighter and a darker; the lighter part seems to surround and to pervade the whole hemisphere, while the darker part discolors the moon's surface like a kind of cloud, and makes it appear covered with spots. Now those spots which are fairly dark and rather large are plain to everyone and have been seen throughout the ages; these I shall call the "large" or "ancient" spots, distinguishing them from others that are smaller in size but so numerous as to occur all over the lunar surface, and especially the lighter part. The latter spots had never been seen by anyone before me. From observations of these spots repeated many times I have been led to the opinion and conviction that the surface of the moon is not smooth, uniform, and precisely spherical as a great number of philosophers believe it (and the other heavenly bodies) to be, but is uneven, rough, and full of cavities and prominences, being not unlike the face of the earth, relieved by chains of mountains and deep valleys. . . .

---

With his telescope, Galileo discovered four moons orbiting Jupiter, an observation that overcame a principal objection to the Copernican system. Galileo showed that a celestial body could indeed move around a center other than the earth; that earth was not the common center for all celestial bodies; that a celestial body (earth's moon or Jupiter's moons) could orbit a planet at the same time that the planet revolved around another body (namely, the sun).

---

On the seventh day of January in this present year 1610, at the first hour of night, when I was viewing the heavenly bodies with a telescope, Jupiter presented itself to me; and because I had prepared a very excellent instrument for myself, I perceived (as I had not before, on account of the weakness of my previous instrument) that beside the planet there were three starlets, small indeed, but very bright. Though I believed them to be among the host of fixed stars, they aroused my curiosity somewhat by appearing to lie in an exact straight line parallel to the ecliptic, and by their being more splendid than others of their size. Their arrangement with respect to Jupiter and each other was the following:

*East*　　✳　　✳　　**O**　　✳　　　*West*

that is, there were two stars on the eastern side and one to the west. The most easterly star and the western one appeared larger than the other. I paid no attention to the distances between them and Jupiter, for at the outset I thought them to be fixed stars, as I have said.‡ But returning to the same investigation on January eighth—led by what, I do not know—I found a very different arrangement. The three starlets

---

‡The reader should remember that the telescope was nightly revealing to Galileo hundreds of fixed stars never previously observed. His unusual gifts for astronomical observation are illustrated by his having noticed and remembered these three merely by reason of their alignment, and recalling them so well that when by chance he happened to see them the following night he was certain that they had changed their positions.

were now all to the west of Jupiter, closer together, and at equal intervals from one another
as shown in the following sketch:

*East*    O    *    *    *    *West*

On the tenth of January, however, the stars
appeared in this position with respect to
Jupiter:

*East*    *    *    O    *West*

that is, there were but two of them, both easterly, the third (as I supposed) being hidden behind Jupiter. . . . There was no way in which
such alterations could be attributed to Jupiter's motion, yet being certain that these were
still the same stars I had observed . . . my per-
plexity was now transformed into amazement.
I was sure that the apparent changes belonged
not to Jupiter but to the observed stars, and I
resolved to pursue this investigation with
greater care and attention. . . .

I had now decided beyond all question that
there existed in the heavens three stars wandering about Jupiter as do Venus and Mercury
about the sun, and this became plainer than
daylight from observations on similar occasions which followed. Nor were there just
three such stars; four wanderers complete their
revolutions about Jupiter. . . .

Here we have a fine and elegant argument for
quieting the doubts of those who, while accepting with tranquil mind the revolutions of the
planets about the sun in the Copernican system,
are mightily disturbed to have the moon alone
revolve about the earth and accompany it in an
annual rotation about the sun. Some have believed that this structure of the universe should
be rejected as impossible. But now we have not
just one planet rotating about another while
both run through a great orbit around the sun;
our own eyes show us four stars which wander
around Jupiter as does the moon around the
earth, while all together trace out a grand revolution about the sun in the space of twelve years.

## REVIEW QUESTIONS

1. What methods did Galileo Galilei use in his scientific investigations?
2. What was the implication for modern astronomy of Galileo's observation of the
   surface of the moon? Of the moons of Jupiter?

---

## 3 Critique of Authority

Galileo appealed to the Roman Catholic authorities asking them to halt their actions against the theories of Copernicus, but was unsuccessful. His support of
Copernicus aroused the ire of both clergy and scholastic philosophers. In 1616,
the church placed Copernicus's book on the index of forbidden books, and
Galileo was ordered to cease his defense of the Copernican theory. In 1632,
Galileo published *Dialogue Concerning the Two Chief World Systems* in which
he upheld the Copernican view. Widely distributed and acclaimed, the book
antagonized Galileo's enemies, who succeeded in halting further printing.
Summoned to Rome, the aging and infirm scientist was put on trial by the Inquisition and ordered to renounce the Copernican theory. Galileo bowed to the
Inquisition, which condemned the *Dialogue* and sentenced him to life imprisonment—largely house arrest at his own villa near Florence, where he was
treated humanely.

# Galileo Galilei
# LETTER TO THE GRAND DUCHESS CHRISTINA AND *DIALOGUE CONCERNING THE TWO CHIEF WORLD SYSTEMS— PTOLEMAIC AND COPERNICAN*

The first reading illustrates Galileo's active involvement in a struggle for freedom of inquiry many years before the *Dialogue* was published. In 1615, in a letter addressed to Grand Duchess Christina of Tuscany, Galileo argued that passages from the Bible had no authority in scientific disputes.

The second reading (from the *Dialogue*) reveals Galileo's views on Aristotle. Medieval scholastics regarded Aristotle as the supreme authority on questions concerning nature, an attitude that was perpetuated by early modern scholastics. Galileo insisted that such reliance on authority was a hindrance to scientific investigation, that it is through observation, experiment, and reason that one arrives at physical truth.

## BIBLICAL AUTHORITY

Some years ago, as Your Serene Highness well knows, I discovered in the heavens many things that had not been seen before our own age. The novelty of these things, as well as some consequences which followed from them in contradiction to the physical notions commonly held among academic philosophers, stirred up against me no small number of professors—as if I had placed these things in the sky with my own hands in order to upset nature and overturn the sciences. They seemed to forget that the increase of known truths stimulates the investigation, establishment, and growth of the arts; not their diminution or destruction.

Showing a greater fondness for their own opinions than for truth, they sought to deny and disprove the new things which, if they had cared to look for themselves, their own senses would have demonstrated to them. To this end they hurled various charges and published numerous writings filled with vain arguments, and they made the grave mistake of sprinkling these with passages taken from places in the Bible which they had failed to understand properly, and which were ill suited to their purposes. . . .

. . . Men who were well grounded in astronomical and physical science were persuaded as soon as they received my first message. There were others who denied them or remained in doubt only because of their novel and unexpected character, and because they had not yet had the opportunity to see for themselves. These men have by degrees come to be satisfied. But some, besides allegiance to their original error, possess I know not what fanciful interest in remaining hostile not so much toward the things in question as toward their discoverer. No longer being able to deny them, these men now take refuge in obstinate silence, but being more than ever exasperated by that which has pacified and quieted other men, they divert their thoughts to other fancies and seek new ways to damage me. . . .

. . . Possibly because they are disturbed by the known truth of other propositions of mine which differ from those commonly held, and therefore mistrusting their defense so long as they confine themselves to the field of philosophy, these men have resolved to fabricate a shield for their fallacies out of the mantle of pretended religion and the authority of the Bible. These they apply, with little judgment, to the refutation of arguments that they do not understand and have not even listened to.

First they have endeavored to spread the opinion that such propositions in general are contrary to the Bible and are consequently damnable and heretical. . . . Hence they have had no trouble in finding men who would preach the damnability and heresy of the new doctrine from their very pulpits with unwonted confidence, thus doing impious and inconsiderate injury not only to that doctrine and its followers but to all mathematics and mathematicians in general. . . .

. . . They go about invoking the Bible, which they would have minister to their deceitful purposes. Contrary to the sense of the Bible and the intention of the holy [Church] Fathers, if I am not mistaken, they would extend such authorities until even in purely physical matters—where faith is not involved—they would have us altogether abandon reason and the evidence of our senses in favor of some biblical passage, though under the surface meaning of its words this passage may contain a different sense.

I hope to show that I proceed with much greater piety than they do, when I argue not against condemning [Copernicus'] book, but against condemning it in the way they suggest—that is, without understanding it, weighing it, or so much as reading it. For Copernicus never discusses matters of religion or faith, nor does he use arguments that depend in any way upon the authority of sacred writings which he might have interpreted erroneously. He stands always upon physical conclusions pertaining to the celestial motions, and deals with them by astronomical and geometrical demonstrations, founded primarily upon sense experiences and very exact observations. He did not ignore the

Bible, but he knew very well that if his doctrine were proved, then it could not contradict the Scriptures when they were rightly understood. . . .

The reason produced for condemning the opinion that the earth moves and the sun stands still is that in many places in the Bible one may read that the sun moves and the earth stands still. Since the Bible cannot err, it follows as a necessary consequence that anyone takes an erroneous and heretical position who maintains that the sun is inherently motionless and the earth movable.

With regard to this argument, I think in the first place that it is very pious to say and prudent to affirm that the holy Bible can never speak untruth—whenever its true meaning is understood. But I believe nobody will deny that it is often very abstruse, and may say things which are quite different from what its bare words signify. Hence in expounding the Bible if one were always to confine oneself to the unadorned grammatical meaning, one might fall into error. . . .

. . . Now the Bible, merely to condescend to popular capacity, has not hesitated to obscure some very important pronouncements, attributing to God himself some qualities extremely remote from (and even contrary to) His essence. Who, then, would positively declare that this principle has been set aside, and the Bible has confined itself rigorously to the bare and restricted sense of its words, when speaking but casually of the earth, of water, of the sun, or of any other created thing? Especially in view of the fact that these things in no way concern the primary purpose of the sacred writings, which is the service of God and the salvation of souls—matters infinitely beyond the comprehension of the common people.

This being granted, I think that in discussions of physical problems we ought to begin not from the authority of scriptural passages, but from sense-experiences and necessary demonstrations. . . . Nothing physical which sense-experience sets before our eyes, or which necessary demonstrations prove to us, ought to be called in question (much less condemned) upon the testimony of biblical passages which may have some different meaning beneath their words. . . .

. . . I do not feel obliged to believe that that same God who has endowed us with senses, reason, and intellect has intended to forgo their use and by some other means to give us knowledge which we can attain by them. He would not require us to deny sense and reason in physical matters which are set before our eyes and minds by direct experience or necessary demonstrations. . . .

It is obvious that such [anti-Copernican] authors, not having penetrated the true senses of Scripture, would impose upon others an obligation to subscribe to conclusions that are repugnant to manifest reason and sense, if they had any authority to do so. God forbid that this sort of abuse should gain countenance and authority, for then in a short time it would be necessary to proscribe all the contemplative sciences. People who are unable to understand perfectly both the Bible and the sciences far outnumber those who do understand. The former, glancing superficially through the Bible, would arrogate to themselves the authority to decree upon every question of physics on the strength of some word which they have misunderstood, and which was employed by the sacred authors for some different purpose. And the smaller number of understanding men could not dam up the furious torrent of such people, who would gain the majority of followers simply because it is much more pleasant to gain a reputation for wisdom without effort or study than to consume oneself tirelessly in the most laborious disciplines.

---

Galileo attacked the unquestioning acceptance of Aristotle's teachings in his *Dialogue Concerning the Two Chief World Systems—Ptolemaic and Copernican*. In the *Dialogue*, Simplicio is an Aristotelian and Salviati is a spokesman for Galileo; Sagredo, a third participant, introduces the problem of relying on the authority of Aristotle.

---

## ARISTOTELIAN AUTHORITY

SAGREDO One day I was at the home of a very famous doctor in Venice, where many persons came on account of their studies, and others occasionally came out of curiosity to see some anatomical dissection performed by a man who was truly no less learned than he was a careful and expert anatomist. It happened on this day that he was investigating the source and origin of the nerves, about which there exists a notorious controversy between the Galenist and Peripatetic doctors.[1] The anatomist showed that the great trunk of nerves, leaving the brain and passing through the nape, extended on down the spine and then branched out through the whole body, and that only a single strand as fine as a thread arrived at the heart. Turning to a gentleman whom we knew to be a Peripatetic philosopher, and on whose account he had been exhibiting and demonstrating everything with unusual care, he asked this man whether he was at last satisfied and convinced that the nerves originated in the brain and not in the heart. The philosopher, after considering for awhile, answered: "You have made me see this matter so plainly and palpably that if Aristotle's text were not contrary to it, stating clearly that the nerves originate in the heart, I should be forced to admit it to be true." . . .

SIMPLICIO But if Aristotle is to be abandoned, whom shall we have for a guide in philosophy? Suppose you name some author.

SALVIATI We need guides in forests and in unknown lands, but on plains and in open places only the blind need guides. It is better for such people to stay at home, but anyone with eyes in his head and his wits about him could serve as a guide for them. In saying this, I do not mean that a person should not listen to Aristotle; indeed, I applaud the reading

---

[1]Galenist doctors followed the medical theories of Galen (A.D. 129–c. 199), a Greek anatomist and physician whose writings had great authority among medieval and early modern physicians. Peripatetic doctors followed Aristotle's teachings.

and careful study of his works, and I reproach only those who give themselves up as slaves to him in such a way as to subscribe blindly to everything he says and take it as an inviolable decree without looking for any other reasons. This abuse carries with it another profound disorder, that other people do not try harder to comprehend the strength of his demonstrations. And what is more revolting in a public dispute, when someone is dealing with demonstrable conclusions, than to hear him interrupted by a text (often written to some quite different purpose) thrown into his teeth by an opponent? If, indeed, you wish to continue in this method of studying, then put aside the name of philosophers and call yourselves historians, or memory experts; for it is not proper that those who never philosophize should usurp the honorable title of philosopher.

## REVIEW QUESTIONS

1. What was Galileo Galilei's objection to using the Bible as a source of knowledge of physical things? According to him, how did one acquire knowledge of nature?
2. What point was Galileo making in telling the story of the anatomical dissection?
3. What was Galileo's view on the use of Aristotle's works as a basis for scientific endeavors?

## 4 Prophet of Modern Science

Sir Francis Bacon (1561–1626), an English statesman and philosopher, vigorously supported the advancement of science and the scientific method. He believed that increased comprehension and mastery of nature would improve living conditions for people and therefore wanted science to encompass systematic research; he urged the state to fund scientific institutions. Bacon denounced universities for merely repeating Aristotelian concepts and discussing problems—Is matter formless? Are all natural substances composed of matter?—that did not increase understanding of nature or contribute to human betterment. The webs spun by these scholastics, he said, were ingenious but valueless. Bacon wanted an educational program that stressed direct contact with nature and fostered new discoveries.

Bacon was among the first to appreciate the new science's value and to explain its method clearly. Like Leonardo da Vinci, Bacon gave supreme value to the direct observation of nature; for this reason he is one of the founders of the empirical tradition in modern philosophy. Bacon upheld the inductive approach—careful investigation of nature, accumulation of data, and experimentation—as the way to truth and useful knowledge. Because he wanted science to serve a practical function, Bacon praised artisans and technicians who improved technology.

# Francis Bacon
# ATTACK ON AUTHORITY
# AND ADVOCACY OF
# EXPERIMENTAL SCIENCE

Bacon was not himself a scientist; he made no discoveries and had no laboratory. Nevertheless, for his advocacy of the scientific method, Bacon is deservedly regarded as a prophet of modern science. In the first passage from *Redargutio Philosophiarum (The Refutation of Philosophies)*, a treatise on the "idols of the theater"—fallacious ways of thinking based on given systems of philosophy—Bacon attacks the slavish reliance on Aristotle.

But even though Aristotle were the man he is thought to be I should still warn you against receiving as oracles the thoughts and opinions of one man. What justification can there be for this self-imposed servitude [that] . . . you are content to repeat Aristotle's after two thousand [years]? . . . But if you will be guided by me you will deny, not only to this man but to any mortal now living or who shall live hereafter, the right to dictate your opinions. . . . You will never be sorry for trusting your own strength, if you but once make trial of it. You may be inferior to Aristotle on the whole, but not in everything. Finally, and this is the head and front of the whole matter, there is at least one thing in which you are far ahead of him—in precedents, in experience, in the lessons of time. Aristotle, it is said, wrote a book in which he gathered together the laws and institutions of two hundred and fifty-five cities; yet I have no doubt that the customs of Rome are worth more than all of them combined so far as military and political science are concerned. The position is the same in natural philosophy. Are you of a mind to cast aside not only your own endowments but the gifts of time? Assert yourselves before it is too late. Apply yourselves to the study of things themselves. Be not for ever the property of one man.

With these scattered excerpts from *The New Organon* (new system of logic), in 1620

Bacon criticized contemporary methods used to inquire into nature. He expressed his ideas in the form of aphorisms—concise statements of principles or general truths.

I. Man, being the servant and interpreter of Nature, can do and understand so much and so much only as he has observed in fact or in thought of the course of nature: beyond this he neither knows anything nor can do anything.

VIII. . . . The sciences we now possess are merely systems for the nice ordering and setting forth of things already invented; not methods of invention or directions for new works.

XII. The logic now in use serves rather to fix and give stability to the errors which have their foundation in commonly received notions than to help the search after truth. So it does more harm than good.

XIX. There are and can be only two ways of searching into and discovering truth. The one flies from the senses and particulars to the most general axioms, and from these principles, the truth of which it takes for settled and immoveable, proceeds to judgment and to the discovery of middle axioms. And this way is now in fashion. The other derives axioms from the senses and particulars, rising by a gradual and unbroken ascent, so that it arrives at the most general axioms last of all. This is the true way, but as yet untried.

XXIII. There is a great difference between . . . certain empty dogmas, and the true signatures and marks set upon the works of creation as they are found in nature.

XXIV. It cannot be that axioms established by argumentation should avail for the discovery of new works; since the subtlety of nature is greater many times over than the subtlety of argument. But axioms duly and orderly formed from particulars easily discover the way to new particulars, and thus render sciences active.

XXXI. It is idle to expect any great advancement in science from the superinducing [adding] and engrafting of new things upon old. We must begin anew from the very foundations, unless we would revolve for ever in a circle with mean and contemptible progress.

CIX. There is therefore much ground for hoping that there are still laid up in the womb of nature many secrets of excellent use, having no affinity or parallelism with any thing that is now known, but lying entirely out of the beat of the imagination, which have not yet been found out. They too no doubt will some time or other, in the course and revolution of many ages, come to light of themselves, just as the others did; only by the method of which we are now treating they can be speedily and suddenly and simultaneously presented and anticipated.

---

Bacon describes those "idols" or false notions that hamper human understanding.

---

XXXVIII. The idols and false notions which are now in possession of the human understanding, and have taken deep root therein, not only so beset men's minds that truth can hardly find entrance, but even after entrance obtained, they will again in the very instauration [renewal] of the sciences meet and trouble us, unless men being forewarned of the danger fortify themselves as far as may be against their assaults.

XXXIX. There are four classes of Idols which beset men's minds. To these for distinc-

tion's sake I have assigned names,—calling the first class *Idols of the Tribe;* the second, *Idols of the Cave;* the third, *Idols of the Market-place;* the fourth, *Idols of the Theatre.*

XLI. The Idols of the Tribe have their foundation in human nature itself, and in the tribe or race of men. For it is a false assertion that the sense of man is the measure of things. On the contrary, all perceptions as well of the sense as of the mind are according to the measure of the universe. And the human understanding is like a false mirror, which, receiving rays irregularly, distorts and discolours the nature of things by mingling its own nature with it.

XLII. The Idols of the Cave are the idols of the individual man. For every one (besides the errors common to human nature in general) has a cave or den of his own, which refracts and discolours the light of nature; owing either to his own proper and peculiar nature; or to his education and conversation with others; or to the reading of books, and the authority of those whom he esteems and admires; or to the differences of impressions, accordingly as they take place in a mind preoccupied and predisposed or in a mind indifferent and settled; or the like. . . .

XLIII. There are also Idols formed by the intercourse and association of men with each other, which I call Idols of the Market-place, on account of the commerce and consort of men there. For it is by discourse that men associate; and words are imposed according to the apprehension of the vulgar. And therefore the ill and unfit choice of words wonderfully obstructs the understanding. Nor do the definitions or explanations wherewith in some things learned men are wont to guard and defend themselves, by any means set the matter right. But words plainly force and overrule the understanding, and throw all into confusion, and lead men away into numberless empty controversies and idle fancies.

XLIV. Lastly, there are Idols which have immigrated into men's minds from the various dogmas of philosophies, and also from wrong laws of demonstration. These I call Idols of the Theatre; because in my judgment all the received systems are but so many stage-plays, representing worlds of their own creation after an unreal and scenic fashion. Nor is it only of the systems now in vogue, or only of the ancient sects and philosophies, that I speak; for many more plays of the same kind may yet be composed and in like artificial manner set forth; seeing that errors the most widely differ-ent have nevertheless causes for the most part alike. Neither again do I mean this only of entire systems, but also of many principles and axioms in science, which by tradition, credulity, and negligence have come to be received.

But of these several kinds of Idols I must speak more largely and exactly, that the understanding may be duly cautioned.

## REVIEW QUESTIONS

1. What intellectual attitude did Francis Bacon believe obstructed new scientific discoveries in his time?
2. What method of scientific inquiry did Bacon advocate?
3. Explain how each one of Bacon's idols hampers human understanding.

---

## 5   The Circulation of the Blood

William Harvey (1578–1657), a British physician, showed that blood circulates in the body because of the pumping action of the heart muscle. Previous belief derived from Galen's theories. Galen (c. 138–c. 201), a Greco-Roman physician, claimed that there were two centers of blood, with the liver being the source of blood in the veins, and the heart being the source of arterial blood. In contrast, Harvey demonstrated that all blood passes through a single central organ, the heart, flowing away from the heart through the arteries and back to it through the veins, and that this constant, rotating circulation is caused by the rhythmic contractions of the heart muscle acting as a pump.

This discovery of the circulation of blood marked a break with medieval medical ideas (inherited from the ancient world) and signified the emergence of modern physiology. Harvey employed the inductive method championed by Sir Francis Bacon; he drew conclusions after carefully observing and experimenting with living animals.

## William Harvey
## *THE MOTION OF THE HEART AND BLOOD IN ANIMALS*

In *The Motion of the Heart and Blood in Animals* (1628), Harvey described the heart as a mechanical pump, a description that corresponded to Newton's view that the universe was a mechanical system. In this reading, Harvey discussed his reasons for writing the book and provided insights into his method.

When I first gave my mind to vivisections [cutting live animals open for experimentation], as a means of discovering the motions and uses of the heart, and sought to discover these from actual inspection, and not from the writings of others, I found the task so truly arduous, so full of difficulties, that I was almost tempted to think . . . that the motion of the heart was only to be comprehended by God. For I could neither rightly perceive at first when the systole and when the diastole took place, nor when and where dilatation and contraction occurred,[1] by reason of the rapidity of the motion, which in many animals is accomplished in the twinkling of an eye, coming and going like a flash of lightning; so that the systole presented itself to me now from this point, now from that; the diastole the same; and then everything was reversed, the motions occurring, as it seemed, variously and confusedly together. My mind was therefore greatly unsettled, nor did I know what I should myself conclude, nor what believe from others. . . .

At length, and by using greater and daily diligence, having frequent recourse to vivisections, employing a variety of animals for the purpose, and collating numerous observations, I thought that I had attained to the truth, that I should extricate myself and escape from this labyrinth [a maze, a confused state], and that I had discovered what I so much desired, both the motion and the use of the heart and arteries; since which time I have not hesitated to expose my views upon these subjects, not only in private to my friends, but also in public, in my anatomical lectures, after the manner of the Academy[2] of old.

These views, as usual, pleased some more, others less; some chid and calumniated me, and laid it to me as a crime that I had dared to depart from the precepts and opinion of all anatomists; others desired further explanations of the novelties, which they said were both worthy of consideration, and might perchance be found of signal use. At length, yielding to the requests of my friends, that all might be made participators in my labours, and partly moved by the envy of others, who, receiving my views with uncandid minds and understanding them indifferently, have essayed to traduce me publicly, I have been moved to commit these things to the press, in order that all may be enabled to form an opinion both of me and my labours. . . .

But lest any one should say that we give them words only, and make mere specious assertions without any foundation, and desire to innovate without sufficient cause, three points present themselves for confirmation, which being stated, I conceive that the truth I contend for will follow necessarily, and appear as a thing obvious to all. First,—the blood is incessantly transmitted by the action of the heart from the vena cava to the arteries in such quantity, that it cannot be supplied from the ingesta,[3] and in such wise that the whole mass must very quickly pass through the organ; Second,—the blood under the influence of the arterial pulse enters and is impelled in a continuous, equable, and incessant stream through every part and member of the body, in much larger quantity than were sufficient for nutrition, or than the whole mass of fluids could supply; Third,—the veins in like manner return this blood incessantly to the heart from all parts and members of the body. These points proved, I conceive it will be manifest that the blood circulates, revolves, propelled and then returning, from the heart to the extremities, from the extremities to the heart, and thus that it performs a kind of circular motion.

Let us assume either arbitrarily or from experiment, the quantity of blood which the left

---

[1] In dilatation, the heart muscle is relaxed, creating the diastole, or expansion of the heart's chambers, during which they fill with blood. The heart's contraction, or systole, forces blood out of the chambers in a pumping action.

[2] *The Academy* refers to the Athens school founded by Plato at which public lectures were given.

[3] The vena cava is the major vein that carries blood returning from the body into the heart. Ingesta refers to solid or liquid nutrients taken into the body.

ventricle[4] of the heart will contain when distended to be, say two ounces, three ounces, one ounce and a half—in the dead body I have found it to hold upwards of two ounces. Let us assume further, how much less the heart will hold in the contracted than in the dilated state; and how much blood it will project into the aorta[5] upon each contraction;—and all the world allows that with the systole something is always projected, a necessary consequence demonstrated in the third chapter, and obvious from the structure of the valves; and let us suppose as approaching the truth that the fourth, or fifth, or sixth, or even but the eighth part of its charge is thrown into the artery at each contraction; this would give either half an ounce, or three drachms, or one drachm [dram: ⅛ ounce] of blood as propelled by the heart at each pulse into the aorta; which quantity, by reason of the valves at the root of the vessel, can by no means return into the ventricle. Now in the course of half an hour, the heart will have made more than one thousand beats, in some as many as two, three, and even four

thousand. Multiplying the number of drachms propelled by the number of pulses, we shall have either one thousand half ounces, or one thousand times three drachms, or a like proportional quantity of blood, according to the amount which we assume as propelled with each stroke of the heart, sent from this organ into the artery; a larger quantity in every case than is contained in the whole body! In the same way, in the sheep or dog, say that but a single scruple [⅓ dram, ¼ ounce] of blood passes with each stroke of the heart, in one half hour we should have one thousand scruples, or about three pounds and a half of blood injected into the aorta; but the body of neither animal contains above four pounds of blood, a fact which I have myself ascertained in the case of the sheep.

Upon this supposition, therefore, assumed merely as a ground for reasoning, we see the whole mass of blood passing through the heart, from the veins to the arteries, and in like manner through the lungs.

But let it be said that this does not take place in half an hour, but in an hour, or even in a day; any way it is still manifest that more blood passes through the heart in consequence of its action, than can either be supplied by the whole of the ingesta, or than can be contained in the veins at the same moment.

[4]The heart consists of four chambers: a left and right ventricle (the lower chambers) and a left and right atrium (the upper chambers).

[5]The aorta is the major artery that carries blood out of the heart to the body.

## REVIEW QUESTIONS

1. What evidence led William Harvey to conclude that blood constantly circulates through the heart?
2. What method did he use to reach his conclusions?
3. Why did some of Harvey's colleagues refuse to believe his conclusions?
4. Why did Harvey publish his book?

## 6  The Autonomy of the Mind

**René Descartes (1596–1650), a French mathematician and philosopher, united the new currents of thought initiated during the Renaissance and the Scientific Revolution. Descartes said that the universe was a mechanical system whose inner laws could be discovered through mathematical thinking and formulated in mathematical terms. With Descartes' assertions on the power of thought,**

human beings became fully aware of their capacity to comprehend the world through their mental powers. For this reason he is regarded as the founder of modern philosophy.

The deductive approach stressed by Descartes presumes that inherent in the mind are mathematical principles, logical relationships, the principle of cause and effect, concepts of size and motion, and so on—ideas that exist independently of human experience with the external world. Descartes, for example, would say that the properties of a right-angle triangle ($a^2 + b^2 = c^2$) are implicit in human consciousness prior to any experience one might have with a triangle. These innate ideas, said Descartes, permit the mind to give order and coherence to the physical world. Descartes held that the mind arrives at truth when it "intuits" or comprehends the logical necessity of its own ideas and expresses these ideas with clarity, certainty, and precision.

# René Descartes
# *DISCOURSE ON METHOD*

In the *Discourse on Method* (1637), Descartes proclaimed the mind's autonomy and importance, and its ability and right to comprehend truth. In this work he offered a method whereby one could achieve certainty and thereby produce a comprehensive understanding of nature and human culture. In the following passage from the *Discourse on Method,* he explained the purpose of his inquiry. How he did so is almost as revolutionary as the ideas he wished to express. He spoke in the first person, autobiographically, as an individual employing his own reason, and he addressed himself to other individuals, inviting them to use their reason. He brought to his narrative an unprecedented confidence in the power of his own judgment and a deep disenchantment with the learning of his times.

## PART ONE

From my childhood I lived in a world of books, and since I was taught that by their help I could gain a clear and assured knowledge of everything useful in life, I was eager to learn from them. But as soon as I had finished the course of studies which usually admits one to the ranks of the learned, I changed my opinion completely. For I found myself saddled with so many doubts and errors that I seemed to have gained nothing in trying to educate myself unless it was to discover more and more fully how ignorant I was.

Nevertheless I had been in one of the most celebrated schools in Europe, where I thought there should be wise men if wise men existed anywhere on earth. I had learned there everything that others learned, and, not satisfied with merely the knowledge that was taught, I had perused as many books as I could find which contained more unusual and recondite knowledge. . . . And finally, it did not seem to me that our times were less flourishing and fertile than were any of the earlier periods. All this led me to conclude that I could judge others by myself, and to decide that there was no such wisdom in the world as I had previously hoped to find. . . .

I revered our theology, and hoped as much as anyone else to get to heaven, but having learned on great authority that the road was just as open to the most ignorant as to the most learned, and that the truths of revelation which lead thereto are beyond our understanding, I would not have dared to submit them to the weakness of my reasonings. I thought that to succeed in their examination it would be necessary to have some extraordinary assistance from heaven, and to be more than a man.

I will say nothing of philosophy except that it has been studied for many centuries by the most outstanding minds without having produced anything which is not in dispute and consequently doubtful. I did not have enough presumption to hope to succeed better than the others; and when I noticed how many different opinions learned men may hold on the same subject, despite the fact that no more than one of them can ever be right, I resolved to consider almost as false any opinion which was merely plausible. . . .

This is why I gave up my studies entirely as soon as I reached the age when I was no longer under the control of my teachers. I resolved to seek no other knowledge than that which I might find within myself, or perhaps in the great book of nature. I spent a few years of my adolescence traveling, seeing courts and armies, living with people of diverse types and stations of life, acquiring varied experience, testing myself in the episodes which fortune sent me, and, above all, thinking about the things around me so that I could derive some profit from them. For it seemed to me that I might find much more of the truth in the cogitations [reflections] which each man made on things which were important to him, and where he would be the loser if he judged badly, than in the cogitations of a man of letters in his study, concerned with speculations which produce no effect, and which have no consequences to him. . . .

. . . After spending several years in thus studying the book of nature and acquiring experience, I eventually reached the decision to study my own self, and to employ all my abilities to try to choose the right path. This produced much better results in my case, I think, than would have been produced if I had never left my books and my country. . . .

## PART TWO

. . . As far as the opinions which I had been receiving since my birth were concerned, I could not do better than to reject them completely for once in my lifetime, and to resume them afterwards, or perhaps accept better ones in their place, when I had determined how they fitted into a rational scheme. And I firmly believed that by this means I would succeed in conducting my life much better than if I built only upon the old foundations and gave credence to the principles which I had acquired in my childhood without ever having examined them to see whether they were true or not. . . .

. . . Never has my intention been more than to try to reform my own ideas, and rebuild them on foundations that would be wholly mine. . . . The decision to abandon all one's preconceived notions is not an example for all to follow. . . .

As for myself, I should no doubt have . . . [never attempted it] if I had had but a single teacher or if I had not known the differences which have always existed among the most learned. I had discovered in college that one cannot imagine anything so strange and unbelievable but that it has been upheld by some philosopher; and in my travels I had found that those who held opinions contrary to ours were neither barbarians nor savages, but that many of them were at least as reasonable as ourselves. I had considered how the same man, with the same capacity for reason, becomes different as a result of being brought up among Frenchmen or Germans than he would be if he had been brought up among Chinese or cannibals; and how, in our fashions, the thing which pleased us ten years ago and perhaps will please us again ten years in the future, now seems extravagant and ridiculous; and I felt that in all these ways we are much more greatly influenced by custom and example than by any certain knowledge. Faced with this divergence of opinion, I could not accept the testimony of the majority, for I thought it worthless as a proof of anything somewhat difficult to discover, since it is much more likely that a single man will have discovered it than a whole people. Nor, on the other hand, could I select anyone whose opinions seemed to me to be preferable to those of others, and I was thus constrained to embark on the investigation for myself.

Nevertheless, like a man who walks alone in the darkness, I resolved to go so slowly and circumspectly that if I did not get ahead very rapidly I was at least safe from falling. Also, I did not want to reject all the opinions which had slipped irrationally into my consciousness since birth, until I had first spent enough time planning how to accomplish the task which I was then undertaking, and seeking the true method of obtaining knowledge of everything which my mind was capable of understanding. . . .

---

Descartes' method consists of four principles that place the capacity to arrive at truth entirely within the province of the human mind. First one finds a self-evident principle, such as a geometric axiom. From this general principle, other truths are deduced through logical reasoning. This is accomplished by breaking a problem down into its elementary components and then, step by step, moving toward more complex knowledge.

---

. . . I thought that some other method [beside that of logic, algebra, and geometry] must be found to combine the advantages of these three and to escape their faults. Finally, just as the multitude of laws frequently furnishes an excuse for vice, and a state is much better governed with a few laws which are strictly adhered to, so I thought that instead of the great number of precepts of which logic is composed, I would have enough with the four following ones, provided that I made a firm and unalterable resolution not to violate them even in a single instance.

The first rule was never to accept anything as true unless I recognized it to be evidently such: that is, carefully to avoid precipitation and prejudgment, and to include nothing in my conclusions unless it presented itself so clearly and distinctly to my mind that there was no occasion to doubt it.

The second was to divide each of the difficulties which I encountered into as many parts as possible, and as might be required for an easier solution.

The third was to think in an orderly fashion, beginning with the things which were simplest and easiest to understand, and gradually and by degrees reaching toward more complex knowledge, even treating as though ordered materials which were not necessarily so.

The last was always to make enumerations so complete, and reviews so general, that I would be certain that nothing was omitted. . . .

What pleased me most about this method was that it enabled me to reason in all things, if not perfectly, at least as well as was in my power. In addition, I felt that in practicing it my mind was gradually becoming accustomed to conceive its objects more clearly and distinctly. . . .

---

Descartes was searching for an incontrovertible truth that could serve as the first principle of philosophy. His arrival at the famous dictum "I think, therefore I am" marks the beginning of modern philosophy.

---

## PART FOUR

. . . As I desired to devote myself wholly to the search for truth, I thought that I should . . . reject as absolutely false anything of which I could have the least doubt, in order to see whether anything would be left after this procedure which could be called wholly certain. Thus, as our senses deceive us at times, I was ready to suppose that nothing was at all the way our senses represented them to be. As there are men who make mistakes in reasoning even on the simplest topics in geometry, I judged that I was as liable to error as any other, and rejected as false all the reasoning which I had previously accepted as valid demonstration. Finally, as the same precepts which we have when awake may come to us when asleep without their being true, I decided to suppose that nothing that had ever entered my mind was more real than the illusions of my dreams. But I soon noticed that while I thus wished to think everything false, it was necessarily true that I who thought so was something. Since this truth, *I think, therefore I am,* was so firm and assured that all the most extravagant suppo-sitions of the sceptics[1] were unable to shake it, I judged that I could safely accept it as the first principle of the philosophy I was seeking.

---

[1]The skeptics belonged to the ancient Greek philosophic school that held true knowledge to be beyond human grasp and treated all knowledge as uncertain.

## REVIEW QUESTIONS

1. Why was René Descartes critical of the learning of his day?
2. What are the implications of Descartes' famous words: "I think, therefore I am"?
3. Compare Descartes' method with the approach advocated by Francis Bacon.

---

## 7   The Mechanical Universe

By demonstrating that all bodies in the universe—earthly objects as well as moons, planets, and stars—obey the same laws of motion and gravitation, Sir Isaac Newton (1646–1723) completed the destruction of the medieval view of the universe. The idea that the same laws governed the movement of earthly and heavenly bodies was completely foreign to medieval thinkers, who drew a sharp division between a higher celestial world and a lower terrestrial one. In the *Principia Mathematica* (1687), Newton showed that the same forces that hold celestial bodies in their orbits around the sun make apples fall to the ground. For Newton, the universe was like a giant clock, all of whose parts obeyed strict mechanical principles and worked together in perfect precision. To Newton's contemporaries, it seemed as if mystery had been banished from the universe.

## Isaac Newton
## *PRINCIPIA MATHEMATICA*

In the first of the following passages from *Principia Mathematica,* Newton stated the principle of universal law and lauded the experimental method as the means of acquiring knowledge.

### RULES OF REASONING IN PHILOSOPHY

*Rule I. We are to admit no more causes of natural things than such as are both true and sufficient to explain their appearances.*

To this purpose the philosophers say that Nature does nothing in vain, and more is in vain when less will serve; for Nature is pleased with simplicity, and affects not the pomp of superfluous causes.

*Rule II. Therefore to the same natural effects we must, as far as possible, assign the same causes.*

As to respiration in a man and in a beast; the descent of stones [meteorites] in *Europe* and in *America*; the light of our culinary fire and of the sun; the reflection of light in the earth, and in the planets.

*Rule III. The qualities of bodies, which admit neither [intensification] nor remission of degrees, and which are found to belong to all bodies within the reach of our experiments, are to be esteemed the universal qualities of all bodies whatsoever.*

For since the qualities of bodies are only known to us by experiments, we are to hold for universal all such as universally agree with experiments; and such as are not liable to diminution can never be quite taken away. We are certainly not to relinquish the evidence of experiments for the sake of dreams and vain fictions of our own devising; nor are we to recede from the analogy of Nature, which [is] . . . simple, and always consonant to itself. We no other way know the extension of bodies than by our senses, nor do these reach it in all bodies; but because we perceive extension in all that are sensible, therefore, we ascribe it universally to all others also. That abundance of bodies are hard, we learn by experience; and because the hardness of the whole arises from the hardness of the parts, we, therefore, justly infer the hardness of the undivided particles not only of the bodies we feel but of all others. That all bodies are impenetrable, we gather not from reason, but from sensation. The bodies which we handle we find impenetrable, and thence, conclude impenetrability to be an universal property of all bodies whatsoever. That all bodies are moveable, and endowed with certain powers (which we call . . . {*inertia*}) of persevering in their motion, or in their rest, we only infer from the like properties observed in the bodies which we have seen. The extension, hardness, impenetrability, mobility, . . . of the whole, result from the extension, hardness, impenetrability, mobility, . . . of the parts; and thence we conclude the least particles of all bodies to be also all extended, and hard and impenetrable, and

moveable, . . . And this is the foundation of all philosophy. . . .

Lastly, if it universally appears, by experiments and astronomical observations, that all bodies about the earth gravitate towards the earth, and that in proportion to the quantity of matter which they severally contain; that the moon likewise, according to the quantity of its matter, gravitates towards the earth; that, on the other hand, our sea gravitates towards the moon; and all the planets mutually one towards another; and the comets in like manner towards the sun; we must, in consequence of this rule, universally allow that all bodies whatsoever are endowed with a principle of mutual gravitation. . . .

*Rule IV. In experimental philosophy we are to look upon propositions collected by general induction from phenomena as accurately or very nearly true, notwithstanding any contrary hypotheses that may be imagined, till such time as other phenomena occur, by which they may either be made more accurate, or liable to exceptions.*

This rule we must follow, that the argument of induction may not be evaded by hypotheses.

---

Newton describes further his concepts of gravity and scientific methodology.

---

## GRAVITY

Hitherto, we have explained the phenomena of the heavens and of our sea by the power of gravity, but have not yet assigned the cause of this power. This is certain, that it must proceed from a cause that penetrates to the very centres of the sun and planets, without suffering the least diminution of its force; that operates not according to the quantity of the surfaces of the particles upon which it acts (as mechanical causes used to do) but according to the quantity of the solid matter which they contain, and propagates its virtue on all sides to immense distances, decreasing always in the duplicate portion of the distances. . . .

Hitherto I have not been able to discover the cause of those properties of gravity from the phenomena, and I frame no hypothesis; for whatever is not deduced from the phenomena is to be called an hypothesis; and hypotheses, whether metaphysical or physical, whether of occult qualities or mechanical, have no place in experimental philosophy. In this philosophy particular propositions are inferred from the phenomena, and afterward rendered general by induction. Thus it was the impenetrability, the mobility, and the impulsive forces of bodies, and the laws of motion and of gravitation were discovered. And to us it is enough that gravity does really exist, and acts according to the laws which we have explained, and abundantly serves to account for all the motions of the celestial bodies, and of our sea.

---

A devoted Anglican, Newton believed that God had created this superbly organized universe. The following selection is also from the *Principia*.

---

## GOD AND THE UNIVERSE

This most beautiful system of the sun, planets, and comets could only proceed from the counsel and dominion of an intelligent and powerful Being. And if the fixed stars are the centers of other like systems, these, being formed by the like wise counsel, must be all subject to the dominion of One, especially since the light of the fixed stars is of the same nature with the light of the sun and from every system light passes into all the other systems; and lest the systems of the fixed stars should, by their gravity, fall on each other mutually, he hath placed those systems at immense distances from one another.

This Being governs all things not as the soul of the world, but as Lord over all; and on account of his dominion he is wont to be called "Lord God" . . . or "Universal Ruler." . . . It is the dominion of a spiritual being which constitutes a God. . . . And from his true dominion it follows that the true God is a living, intelligent and powerful Being. . . . he governs all things, and knows all things that are or can be done. . . . He endures for ever, and is every where present; and by existing always and every where, he constitutes duration and space. . . . In him are all things contained and moved; yet neither affects the other: God suffers nothing from the motion of bodies; bodies find no resistance from the omnipresence of God. . . . As a blind man has no idea of colors so we have no idea of the manner by which the all-wise God preserves and understands all things. He is utterly void of all body and bodily figure, and can therefore neither be seen, nor heard, nor touched; nor ought to be worshipped under the representation of any corporeal thing. We have ideas of his attributes, but what the real substance of any thing is we know not. . . . Much less, then, have we any idea of the substance of God. We know him only by his most wise and excellent contrivances of things. . . . [W]e reverence and adore him as his servants; and a god without dominion, providence, and final causes, is nothing else but Fate and Nature. Blind metaphysical necessity, which is certainly the same always and everywhere, could produce no variety of things. All that diversity of natural things which we find suited to different times and places could arise from nothing but the ideas and will of a Being necessarily existing. . . . And thus much concerning God; to discourse of whom from the appearances of things does certainly belong to Natural Philosophy.

## REVIEW QUESTIONS

1. What did Isaac Newton mean by universal law? What examples of universal law did he provide?
2. What method for investigating nature did Newton advocate?
3. Summarize Newton's arguments for God's existence.
4. For Newton, what is God's relationship to the universe?

## CHAPTER 13

# The Enlightenment

THE GEOGRAPHY LESSON, Pietro Longhi, c. 1750. This scene depicting a bourgeois family's lesson in geography illustrates the widespread interest in intellectual pursuits that typified this age. *(Oil on canvas. Galleria Querini Stampalia, Venice. Scala/Art Resource, N.Y.)*

The Enlightenment of the eighteenth century culminated the movement toward modernity that started in the Renaissance era. The thinkers of the Enlightenment, called *philosophes,* attacked medieval otherworldliness, dethroned theology from its once-proud position as queen of the sciences, and based their understanding of nature and society on reason alone, unaided by revelation or priestly authority.

From the broad spectrum of Western history, several traditions flowed into the Enlightenment: the rational spirit born in classical Greece, the Stoic emphasis on natural law that applies to all human beings, and the Christian belief that all individuals are equal in God's eyes. A more immediate influence on the Enlightenment was Renaissance humanism, which focused on the individual and worldly human accomplishments and which criticized medieval theology-philosophy for its preoccupation with questions that seemed unrelated to the human condition. In many ways, the Enlightenment grew directly out of the Scientific Revolution. The philosophes praised both Newton's discovery of the mechanical laws that govern the universe and the scientific method that made this discovery possible. They wanted to transfer the scientific method—the reliance on experience and the critical use of the intellect—to the realm of society. They maintained that independent of clerical authority, human beings through reason could grasp the natural laws that govern the social world, just as Newton had uncovered the laws of nature that operate in the physical world. The philosophes said that those institutions and traditions that could not meet the test of reason, because they were based on authority, ignorance, or superstition, had to be reformed or dispensed with.

For medieval philosophers, reason had been subordinate to revelation; the Christian outlook determined the medieval concept of nature, morality, government, law, and life's purpose. During the Renaissance and Scientific Revolution, reason increasingly asserted its autonomy. For example, Machiavelli rejected the principle that politics should be based on Christian teachings; he recognized no higher world as the source of a higher truth. Galileo held that on questions regarding nature, one should trust to observation, experimentation, and mathematical reasoning and should not rely on Scripture. Descartes rejected reliance on past authority and maintained that through thought alone one could attain knowledge that has absolute certainty. Agreeing with Descartes that the mind is self-sufficient, the philosophes rejected the guidance of revelation and its priestly interpreters. They believed that through the use of reason, individuals could comprehend and reform society.

The Enlightenment philosophes articulated basic principles of the modern outlook: confidence in the self-sufficiency of the human mind, belief that individuals possess natural rights that governments should not violate, and the desire to reform society in accordance with rational principles. Their views influenced the reformers of the French Revolution and the Founding Fathers of the United States.

---

# 1  The Enlightenment Outlook

The critical use of the intellect was the central principle of the Enlightenment. The philosophes rejected beliefs and traditions that seemed to conflict with reason and attacked clerical and political authorities for interfering with the free use of the intellect.

## Immanuel Kant
## *WHAT IS ENLIGHTENMENT?*

The German philosopher Immanuel Kant (1724–1804) is a giant in the history of modern philosophy. Several twentieth-century philosophic movements have their origins in Kantian thought, and many issues raised by Kant still retain their importance. For example, in *Metaphysical Foundations of Morals* (1785), Kant set forth the categorical imperative that remains a crucial principle in moral philosophy. Kant asserted that when confronted with a moral choice, people should ask themselves: "Canst thou also will that thy maxim should be a universal law?" By this, Kant meant that people should ponder whether they would want the moral principle underlying their action to be elevated to a universal law that would govern others in similar circumstances. If they concluded that it should not, then the maxim should be rejected and the action avoided.

Kant valued the essential ideals of the Enlightenment and viewed the French Revolution, which put these ideals into law, as the triumph of liberty over despotism. In an essay entitled "What Is Enlightenment?" (1784), he contended that the Enlightenment marked a new way of thinking and eloquently affirmed the Enlightenment's confidence in and commitment to reason.

Enlightenment is man's leaving his self-caused immaturity. Immaturity is the incapacity to use one's intelligence without the guidance of another. Such immaturity is self-caused if it is not caused by lack of intelligence, but by lack of determination and courage to use one's intelligence without being guided by another. *Sapere Aude!* [Dare to know!] Have the courage to use your own intelligence! is therefore the motto of the enlightenment.

Through laziness and cowardice a large part of mankind, even after nature has freed them from alien guidance, gladly remain immature. It is because of laziness and cowardice that it is so easy for others to usurp the role of guardians. It is so comfortable to be a minor! If I have a book which provides meaning for me, a pastor who has conscience for me, a doctor who will judge my diet for me and so on, then I do not need to exert myself. I do not have any need to think; if I can pay, others will take over the tedious job for me. The guardians who have kindly undertaken the supervision will see to it that by far the largest part of mankind, including the entire "beautiful sex," should consider the step into maturity, not only as difficult but as very dangerous.

After having made their domestic animals dumb and having carefully prevented these quiet creatures from daring to take any step beyond the lead-strings to which they have fastened them, these guardians then show them the danger which threatens them, should they attempt to walk alone. Now this danger is not really so very great; for they would presumably learn to walk after some stumbling. However, an example of this kind intimidates and frightens people out of all further attempts.

It is difficult for the isolated individual to work himself out of the immaturity which has become almost natural for him. He has even become fond of it and for the time being is incapable of employing his own intelligence, because he has never been allowed to make the attempt. Statutes and formulas, these mechanical tools of a serviceable use, or rather misuse, of his natural faculties, are the ankle-chains of a continuous immaturity. Whoever threw it off would make an uncertain jump over the smallest trench because he is not accustomed to such free movement. Therefore there are only a few who have pursued a firm path and have succeeded in escaping from immaturity by their own cultivation of the mind.

But it is more nearly possible for a public to enlighten itself: this is even inescapable if only the public is given its freedom. For there will always be some people who think for themselves, even among the self-appointed guardians of the great mass who, after having thrown off the yoke of immaturity themselves, will spread about them the spirit of a reasonable estimate of their own value and of the need for every man to think for himself. . . . [A] public can only arrive at enlightenment slowly. Through revolution, the abandonment of personal despotism may be engendered and the end of profit-seeking and domineering oppression may occur, but never a true reform of the state of mind. Instead, new prejudices, just like the old ones, will serve as the guiding reins of the great, unthinking mass. . . .

All that is required for this enlightenment is *freedom*; and particularly the least harmful of all that may be called freedom, namely, the freedom for man to make *public use* of his reason in all matters. But I hear people clamor on all sides: Don't argue! The officer says: Don't argue, drill! The tax collector: Don't argue, pay! The pastor: Don't argue, believe! . . . Here we have restrictions on freedom everywhere. Which restriction is hampering enlightenment, and which does not, or even promotes it? I answer: The *public use* of a man's reason must be free at all times, and this alone can bring enlightenment among men. . . .

I mean by the public use of one's reason, the use which a scholar makes of it before the entire reading public. . . .

The question may now be put: Do we live at present in an enlightened age? The answer is: No, but in an age of enlightenment. Much still prevents men from being placed in a position . . . to use their own minds securely and well in matters of religion. But we do have very definite indications that this field of endeavor is being opened up for men to work freely and reduce gradually the hindrances preventing a general enlightenment and an escape from self-caused immaturity.

## REVIEW QUESTIONS

1. What did Immanuel Kant mean by the terms *enlightenment* and *freedom*?
2. In Kant's view, what factors delayed the progress of human enlightenment?
3. What are the political implications of Kant's views?

## 2  Political Liberty

John Locke (1632–1704), a British statesman, philosopher, and political theorist, was a principal source of the Enlightenment. Eighteenth-century thinkers were particularly influenced by Locke's advocacy of religious toleration, his reliance on experience as the source of knowledge, and his concern for liberty. In his first *Letter Concerning Toleration,* Locke declared that Christians who persecute others in the name of religion vitiate Christ's teachings. Locke's political philosophy as formulated in the *Two Treatises on Government* (1690) complements his theory of knowledge (see page 416); both were rational and secular attempts to understand and improve the human condition. The Lockean spirit pervades the American Declaration of Independence, the Constitution, and the Bill of Rights and is the basis of the liberal tradition that aims to protect individual liberty from despotic state authority.

Viewing human beings as brutish and selfish, Thomas Hobbes (see page 369) had prescribed a state with unlimited power; only in this way, he said, could people be protected from each other and civilized life preserved. Locke, regarding people as essentially good and humane, developed a conception of the state differing fundamentally from Hobbes's. Locke held that human beings are born with natural rights of life, liberty, and property; they establish the state to protect these rights. Consequently, neither executive nor legislature, neither king nor assembly has the authority to deprive individuals of their natural rights. Whereas Hobbes justified absolute monarchy, Locke explicitly endorsed constitutional government in which the power to govern derives from the consent of the governed and the state's authority is limited by agreement.

# John Locke
# *SECOND TREATISE ON GOVERNMENT*

Locke said that originally, in establishing a government, human beings had never agreed to surrender their natural rights to any state authority. The state's founders intended the new polity to preserve these natural rights and to implement the people's will. Therefore, as the following passage from Locke's *Second Treatise on Government* illustrates, the power exercised by magistrates cannot be absolute or arbitrary.

. . . *Political power* is that power, which every man having in the state of nature, has given up into the hands of the society, and therein to the governors, whom the society hath set over itself, with this express or tacit trust, that it shall be employed for their good, and

the preservation of their property: now this *power,* which every man has *in the state of nature,* and which he parts with to the society in all such cases where the society can secure him, is to use such means, for the preserving of his own property, as he thinks good, and nature allows him; and to punish the breach of the law of nature in others, so as (according to the best of his reason) may most conduce to the preservation of himself, and the rest of mankind. So that the *end and measure of this power,* when in every man's hands in the state of nature, being the preservation of all of his society, that is, all mankind in general, it can have no other *end or measure,* when in the hands of the magistrate, but to preserve the members of that society in their lives, liberties, and possessions; and so cannot be an absolute, arbitrary power over their lives and fortunes, which are as much as possible to be preserved; but a *power to make laws,* and annex such *penalties* to them, as may tend to the preservation of the whole, by cutting off those parts, and those only, which are so corrupt, that they threaten the sound and healthy, without which no severity is lawful. And this *power has its original only from compact,* and agreement, and the mutual consent of those who make up the community. . . .

These are the *bounds,* which the trust, that is put in them by the society, and the law of God and nature, have *set to the legislative* power of every common-wealth, in all forms of government.

First, They are to govern by *promulgated established laws,* not to be varied in particular cases, but to have one rule for rich and poor, for the favourite at court, and the country man at plough.

Secondly, These *laws* also ought to be designed *for* no other end ultimately, but *the good of the people.*

Thirdly, They must *not raise taxes* on the *property of the people, without the consent of the people,* given by themselves, or their deputies. And this properly concerns only such governments, where the *legislative* is always in being, or at least where the people have not reserved any part of the legislative to deputies, to be from time to time chosen by themselves.

Fourthly, The *legislative* neither must *nor can transfer the power of making laws* to any body else, or place it any where, but where the people have. . . .

> If government fails to fulfill the end for which it was established—the preservation of the individual's right to life, liberty, and property—the people have a right to dissolve that government.

. . . The *legislative acts against the trust* reposed in them, when they endeavour to invade the property of the subject, and to make themselves, or any part of the community, masters, or arbitrary disposers of the lives, liberties, or fortunes of the people.

The reason why men enter into society, is the preservation of their property; and the end why they chuse and authorize a legislative, is, that there may be laws made, and rules set, as guards and fences to the properties of all the members of the society, to limit the power, and moderate the dominion of every part and member of the society: for since it can never be supposed to be the will of the society, that the legislative should have a power to destroy that which every one designs to secure, by entering into society, and for which the people submitted themselves to legislators of their own making; whenever the *legislators endeavour to take away, and destroy the property of the people,* or to reduce them to slavery under arbitrary power, they put themselves into a state of war with the people, who are thereupon absolved from any farther obedience, and are left to the common refuge, which God hath provided for all men, against force and violence. Whensoever therefore the *legislative* shall transgress this fundamental rule of society; and either by ambition, fear, folly or corruption, *endeavour to grasp* themselves, *or put into the hands of any other, an absolute power* over the lives, liberties, and estates of the people; by this breach of trust they *forfeit the power* the people had put into their hands for quite contrary ends, and it devolves to the people, who have a right to resume their original liberty, and, by the establishment of a new legislative, (such as they shall think fit) provide for their own safety and security, which is the end for which they are in society. What I have said here, concerning the legislative in general, holds true also concerning the supreme executor, who having a double trust put in him, both to have a part in the legislative, and the supreme execution of the law, acts against both, when he goes about to set up his own arbitrary will as the law of the society. He *acts* also *contrary to his trust,* when he either employs the force, treasure, and offices of the society, to corrupt the *representatives,* and gain them to his purposes; or openly pre-engages the *electors,* and prescribes to their choice, such, whom he has, by sollicitations, threats, promises, or otherwise, won to his designs; and employs them to bring in such, who have promised beforehand what to vote, and what to enact. . . .

---

Locke responds to the charge that his theory will produce "frequent rebellion." Indeed, says Locke, the true rebels are the magistrates who, acting contrary to the trust granted them, violate the people's rights.

---

. . . Such *revolutions happen* not upon every little mismanagement in public affairs. *Great mistakes* in the ruling part, many wrong and inconvenient laws, and all the *slips* of human frailty, will be *borne by the people* without mutiny or murmur. But if a long train of abuses, prevarications and artifices, all tending the same way, make the design visible to the people, and they cannot but feel what they lie under, and see whither they are going; it is not to be wondered at, that they should then rouze themselves, and endeavour to put the rule into such hands which may secure to them the ends for which government was at first erected. . . .

. . . I answer, that *this doctrine* of a power in the people of providing for their safety a-new, by a new legislative, when their legislators have acted contrary to their trust, by invading their property, is *the best defence against rebellion,* and the probablest means to hinder it: for *rebellion* being an opposition, not to persons, but authority, which is founded only in the constitutions and laws of the government; those, whoever they be, who by force break through, and by force justify their violation of them, are truly and properly *rebels*: for when men, by entering into society and civil government, have excluded force, and introduced laws for the preservation of property, peace, and unity amongst themselves, those who set up force again in opposition to the laws, do [rebel], that is, bring back again the state of war, and are properly rebels: which they who are in power, (by the pretence they have to authority, the temptation of force they have in their hands, and the flattery of those about them) being likeliest to do; the properest way to prevent the evil, is to shew them the danger and injustice of it, who are under the greatest temptation to run into it.

The end of government is the good of mankind; and which is *best for mankind,* that the people should always be exposed to the boundless will of tyranny, or that the rulers should be sometimes liable to be opposed, when they grow exorbitant in the use of their power, and employ it for the destruction, and not the preservation of the properties of their people?

---

# Thomas Jefferson
# DECLARATION OF INDEPENDENCE

**Written by Thomas Jefferson (1743–1826) to justify the American colonists' break with Britain, the Declaration of Independence enumerated principles that were quite familiar to English statesmen and intellectuals. The preamble to the Declaration, excerpted below, articulated clearly Locke's philosophy of natural rights. Locke had viewed life, liberty, and property as the individual's essential natural rights; Jefferson substituted the "pursuit of happiness" for property.**

## A DECLARATION BY THE REPRESENTATIVES OF THE UNITED STATES OF AMERICA, IN GENERAL CONGRESS ASSEMBLED.

When in the Course of human Events, it becomes necessary for one People to dissolve the Political Bands which have connected them with another, and to assume among the Powers of the Earth, the separate and equal Station to which the Laws of Nature and of Nature's God entitle them, a decent Respect to the Opinions of Mankind requires that they should declare the causes which impel them to the Separation.

We hold these Truths to be self-evident, that all Men are created equal, that they are endowed by their Creator with certain unalienable Rights, that among these are Life, Liberty, and the Pursuit of Happiness—That to secure these Rights, Governments are instituted among Men, deriving their just Powers from the Consent of the Governed, That whenever any Form of Government becomes destructive of these Ends, it is the Right of the People to alter or to abolish it, and to institute new Government, laying its Foundation on such Principles, and organizing its Powers in such Form, as to them shall seem most likely to effect their Safety and Happiness. Prudence, indeed, will dictate that Governments long established should not be changed for light and transient Causes; and accordingly all Experience hath shewn, that Mankind are more disposed to suffer, while Evils are sufferable, than to right themselves by abolishing the Forms to which they are accustomed. But when a long Train of Abuses and Usurpations, pursuing invariably the same Object, evinces a Design to reduce them under absolute Despotism, it is their right, it is their duty, to throw off such Government, and to provide new Guards for their future Security. Such has been the patient Sufferance of these Colonies; and such is now the Necessity which constrains them to alter their former Systems of Government. The History of the present King of Great-Britain is a History of repeated Injuries and Usurpations, all having in direct Object the Establishment of an absolute Tyranny over these States. . . .

### REVIEW QUESTIONS

1. Compare the views of John Locke with those of Thomas Hobbes (see page 369) regarding the character of human nature, political authority, and the right to rebellion.
2. Compare Locke's theory of natural rights with the principles stated in the American Declaration of Independence.

---

## 3   Attack on the Old Regime

François Marie Arouet (1694–1778), known to the world as Voltaire, was the recognized leader of the French Enlightenment. Few of the philosophes had a better mind, and none had a sharper wit. A relentless critic of the Old Regime (the social structure in prerevolutionary France), Voltaire attacked superstition, religious fanaticism and persecution, censorship, and other abuses of eighteenth-century French society. Spending more than two years in Great Britain, Voltaire acquired a great admiration for English liberty, toleration, commerce, and science. In *Letters Concerning the English Nation* (1733), he drew unfavorable comparisons between a progressive Britain and a reactionary France.

Voltaire's angriest words were directed against established Christianity, to which he attributed many of the ills of modern society. Voltaire regarded Christianity as "the Christ-worshiping superstition" that someday would be destroyed "by the weapons of reason." He rejected revelation and the church hierarchy and was repulsed by Christian intolerance, but he accepted Christian morality and believed in God as the prime mover who set the universe in motion.

# Voltaire
# A PLEA FOR TOLERANCE AND REASON

The following passages compiled from Voltaire's works—grouped according to topic—provide insight into the outlook of the philosophes. The excerpts come from sources that include his *Candide* (1759), *Treatise on Tolerance* (1763), *The Philosophical Dictionary* (1764), and *Commentary on the Book of Crime and Punishments* (1766).

## TOLERANCE

It does not require any great art or studied elocution to prove that Christians ought to tolerate one another. I will go even further and say that we ought to look upon all men as our brothers. What! call a Turk, a Jew, and a Siamese, my brother? Yes, of course; for are we not all children of the same father, and the creatures of the same God?

———

What is tolerance? . . . We are all full of weakness and errors; let us mutually pardon our follies. This is the last law of nature. . . .

It is clear that every private individual who persecutes a man, his brother, because he is not of the same opinion, is a monster. . . .

Of all religions, the Christian ought doubtless to inspire the most tolerance, although hitherto the Christians have been the most intolerant of all men.

———

. . . Tolerance has never brought civil war; intolerance has covered the earth with carnage . . . .

What! Is each citizen to be permitted to believe and to think that which his reason rightly or wrongly dictates? He should indeed, provided that he does not disturb the public order; for it is not contingent on man to believe or not to believe; but it is contingent on him to respect the usages of his country; and if you say that it is a crime not to believe in the dominant religion, you accuse then yourself the first Christians, your ancestors, and you justify those whom you accuse of having martyred them.

You reply that there is a great difference, that all religions are the work of men, and that the Apostolic Roman Catholic Church is alone the work of God. But in good faith, ought our religion because it is divine reign through hate, violence, exiles, usurpation of property, prisons, tortures, murders, and thanksgivings to God for these murders? The more the Christian religion is divine, the less it pertains to man to require it; if God made it, God will sustain it without you. You know that intolerance produces only hypocrites or rebels; what distressing alternatives! In short, do you want to sustain through executioners the religion of a God whom executioners have put to death and who taught only gentleness and patience?

———

I shall never cease, my dear sir, to preach tolerance from the housetops, despite the complaints of your priests and the outcries of ours, until persecution is no more. The progress of reason is slow, the roots of prejudice lie deep. Doubtless, I shall never see the fruits of my efforts, but they are seeds which may one day germinate.

## DOGMA

. . . Is Jesus the Word? If He be the Word, did He emanate from God in time or before time? If He emanated from God, is He co-eternal and consubstantial with Him, or is He of a similar substance? Is He distinct from Him, or is He not? Is He made or begotten? Can He beget in His turn? Has He paternity? or productive virtue without paternity? Is the Holy Ghost made? or begotten? or produced? or proceeding from the Father? or proceeding from the Son? or proceeding from both? Can He beget? can He produce? is His hypostasis consubstantial with the hypostasis of the Father and the Son? and how is it that, having the same nature—the same essence as the Father and the Son, He cannot do the same things done by these persons who are Himself?

Assuredly, I understand nothing of this; no one has ever understood any of it, and that is why we have slaughtered one another.

The Christians tricked, cavilled, hated, and excommunicated one another, for some of these dogmas inaccessible to human intellect.

## FANATICISM

Fanaticism is to superstition what delirium is to fever, what rage is to anger. He who has ecstasies and visions, who takes dreams for realities, and his own imaginations for prophecies is an enthusiast; he who reinforces his madness by murder is a fanatic. . . .

The most detestable example of fanaticism is that exhibited on the night of St. Bartholomew,[1] when the people of Paris rushed from

---

[1]St. Bartholomew refers to the day of August 24, 1572, when the populace of Paris, instigated by King Charles IX at his mother's urging, began a week-long slaughter of Protestants.

house to house to stab, slaughter, throw out of the window, and tear in pieces their fellow citizens who did not go to mass.

There are some cold-blooded fanatics; such as those judges who sentence men to death for no other crime than that of thinking differently from themselves. . . .

Once fanaticism has infected a brain, the disease is almost incurable. I have seen convulsionaries who, while speaking of the miracles of Saint Paris [a fourth-century Italian bishop], gradually grew heated in spite of themselves. Their eyes became inflamed, their limbs shook, fury disfigured their face, and they would have killed anyone who contradicted them.

There is no other remedy for this epidemic malady than that philosophical spirit which, extending itself from one to another, at length softens the manners of men and prevents the access of the disease. For when the disorder has made any progress, we should, without loss of time, flee from it, and wait till the air has become purified.

## PERSECUTION

What is a persecutor? He whose wounded pride and furious fanaticism arouse princes and magistrates against innocent men, whose only crime is that of being of a different opinion. "Impudent man! you have worshipped God; you have preached and practiced virtue; you have served man; you have protected the orphan, have helped the poor; you have changed deserts, in which slaves dragged on a miserable existence, into fertile lands peopled by happy families; but I have discovered that you despise me, and have never read my controversial work. You know that I am a rogue; that I have forged G[od]'s signature, that I have stolen. You might tell these things; I must anticipate you. I will, therefore, go to the confessor [spiritual counselor] of the prime minister, or the magistrate; I will show them, with outstretched neck and twisted mouth, that you hold an erroneous opinion in relation to the cells in which the Septuagint was studied; that you have even spoken disrespectfully ten years ago of Tobit's dog,[2] which you asserted to have been a spaniel, while I proved that it was a greyhound. I will denounce you as the enemy of God and man!" Such is the language of the persecutor; and if precisely these words do not issue from his lips, they are engraven on his heart with the pointed steel of fanaticism steeped in the bitterness of envy. . . .

O God of mercy! If any man can resemble that evil being who is described as ceaselessly employed in the destruction of your works, is it not the persecutor?

## SUPERSTITION

In 1749 a woman was burned in the Bishopric of Würzburg [a city in central Germany], convicted of being a witch. This is an extraordinary phenomenon in the age in which we live. Is it possible that people who boast of their reformation and of trampling superstition under foot, who indeed supposed that they had reached the perfection of reason, could nevertheless believe in witchcraft, and this more than a hundred years after the so-called reformation of their reason?

In 1652 a peasant woman named Michelle Chaudron, living in the little territory of Geneva [a major city in Switzerland], met the devil going out of the city. The devil gave her a kiss, received her homage, and imprinted on her upper lip and right breast the mark that he customarily bestows on all whom he recognizes as his favorites. This seal of the devil is a little mark which makes the skin insensitive, as all the demonographical jurists of those times affirm.

The devil ordered Michelle Chaudron to bewitch two girls. She obeyed her master punctually. The girls' parents accused her of witchcraft before the law. The girls were questioned and confronted with the accused. They declared that they felt a continual pricking in certain parts of their bodies and that they were possessed. Doctors were called, or at least, those who passed for doctors at that time. They examined the girls. They looked for the devil's seal on Michelle's body—what the statement of the case called *satanic marks.* Into them they drove a long needle, already a painful torture. Blood flowed out, and Michelle made it known, by her cries, that satanic marks certainly do not make one insensitive. The judges, seeing no definite proof that Michelle Chaudron was a witch, proceeded to torture her, a method that infallibly produces the necessary proofs: this wretched woman, yielding to the violence of torture, at last confessed every thing they desired.

The doctors again looked for the satanic mark. They found a little black spot on one of her thighs. They drove in the needle. The torment of the torture had been so horrible that the poor creature hardly felt the needle; thus the crime was established. But as customs were becoming somewhat mild at that time, she was burned only after being hanged and strangled.

In those days every tribunal of Christian Europe resounded with similar arrests. The [twigs] were lit everywhere for witches, as for heretics. People reproached the Turks most for having neither witches nor demons among them. This absence of demons was considered an infallible proof of the falseness of a religion.

A zealous friend of public welfare, of humanity, of true religion, has stated in one of his writings on behalf of innocence, that Christian tribunals have condemned to death over a hundred thousand accused witches. If to these judicial murders are added the infinitely superior number of massacred heretics, that part of the world will seem to be nothing but a vast scaffold covered with torturers and victims, surrounded by judges, guards and spectators.

---

[2]The Septuagint, the version of the Hebrew Scriptures used by Saint Paul and other early Christians, was a Greek translation done by Hellenized Jews in Alexandria sometime in the late third or the second century B.C. *Tobit's dog* appears in the Book of Tobit, a Hebrew book contained in the Catholic version of the Bible.

The following passage is from *Candide,* Voltaire's most famous work of fiction. The king of the Bulgarians goes to war with the king of the Abares, and Candide is caught in the middle of the conflict.

## WAR

Nothing could be smarter, more splendid, more brilliant, better drawn up than the two armies. Trumpets, fifes, hautboys [oboes], drums, cannons, formed a harmony such as has never been heard even in hell. The cannons first of all laid flat about six thousand men on each side; then the musketry removed from the best of worlds some nine or ten thousand blackguards who infested its surface. The bayonet also was the sufficient reason for the death of some thousands of men. The whole might amount to thirty thousand souls. Candide, who trembled like a philosopher, hid himself as well as he could during this heroic butchery. At last, while the two Kings each commanded a Te Deum[3] in his camp, Candide decided to go elsewhere to reason about effects and causes. He clambered over heaps of dead and dying men and reached a neighboring village, which was in ashes; it was an Abare village which the Bulgarians had burned in accordance with international law. Here, old men dazed with blows watched the dying agonies of their murdered wives who clutched their children to their bleeding breasts; there, disemboweled girls who had been made to satisfy the natural appetites of heroes gasped their last sighs; others, half-burned, begged to be put to death. Brains were scattered on the ground among dismembered arms and legs. Candide fled to another village as fast as he could; it belonged to the Bulgarians, and Abarian heroes had treated it in the same way. Candide, stumbling over quivering limbs or across ruins, at last escaped from the theater of war. . . .

---

[3]A Te Deum is a special liturgical hymn praising and thanking God for granting some special favor, like a military victory or the end of a war.

## REVIEW QUESTIONS

1. What arguments did Voltaire offer in favor of religious toleration?
2. Why did Voltaire ridicule Christian theological disputation?
3. What did Voltaire mean by the term *fanaticism*? What examples of fanaticism did he provide? How was it to be cured?
4. What did Voltaire imply about the rationality and morality of war?

# 4  Attack on Religion

Christianity came under severe attack during the eighteenth century. The philosophes rejected Christian doctrines that seemed contrary to reason. Deism, the dominant religious outlook of the philosophes, taught that religion should accord with reason and natural law. To deists, it seemed reasonable to believe in God, for this superbly constructed universe required a creator in the same manner that a watch required a watchmaker. But, said the deists, after God had constructed the universe, he did not interfere in its operations; the universe was governed by mechanical laws. Deists denied that the Bible was God's work, rejected clerical authority, and dismissed miracles—like Jesus walking on water—as incompatible with natural law. To them, Jesus was not divine but an inspired teacher of morality. Many deists still considered themselves Christians; the clergy, however, viewed the deists' religious views with horror.

# Thomas Paine
## *THE AGE OF REASON*

Exemplifying the deist outlook was Thomas Paine (1737–1809), an Englishman who moved to America in 1774. Paine's *Common Sense* (1776) was an eloquent appeal for American independence. Paine is also famous for *The Rights of Man* (1791–1792), in which he defended the French Revolution. In *The Age of Reason* (1794–1795), he denounced Christian mysteries, miracles, and prophecies as superstition and called for a natural religion that accorded with reason and science.

I believe in one God, and no more; and I hope for happiness beyond this life.

I believe in the equality of man; and I believe that religious duties consist in doing justice, loving mercy, and endeavoring to make our fellow-creatures happy.

But, lest it should be supposed that I believe many other things in addition to these, I shall, in the progress of this work, declare the things I do not believe, and my reasons for not believing them.

I do not believe in the creed professed by the Jewish church, by the Roman church, by the Greek church, by the Turkish church, by the Protestant church, nor by any church that I know of. My own mind is my own church. . . .

When Moses told the children of Israel that he received the two tables of the [Ten] commandments from the hands of God, they were not obliged to believe him, because they had no other authority for it than his telling them so; and I have no other authority for it than some historian telling me so. The commandments carry no internal evidence of divinity with them; they contain some good moral precepts, such as any man qualified to be a lawgiver, or a legislator, could produce himself, without having recourse to supernatural intervention. . . .

When also I am told that a woman called the Virgin Mary, said, or gave out, that she was with child without any cohabitation with a man, and that her betrothed husband, Joseph, said that an angel told him so, I have a right to believe them or not; such a circumstance required a much stronger evidence than their bare word for it; but we have not even this— for neither Joseph nor Mary wrote any such matter themselves; it is only reported by others that *they said so*—it is hearsay upon hearsay, and I do not choose to rest my belief upon such evidence.

It is, however, not difficult to account for the credit that was given to the story of Jesus Christ being the son of God. He was born when the heathen mythology had still some fashion and repute in the world, and that mythology had prepared the people for the belief of such a story. Almost all the extraordinary men that lived under the heathen mythology were reputed to be the sons of some of their gods. It was not a new thing, at that time, to believe a man to have been celestially begotten; the intercourse of gods with women was then a matter of familiar opinion. Their Jupiter [chief Roman god], according to their accounts, had cohabited with hundreds: the story, therefore, had nothing in it either new, wonderful, or obscene; it was conformable to the opinions that then prevailed among the people called Gentiles, or Mythologists, and it was those people only that believed it. The Jews who had kept strictly to the belief of one God, and no more, and who had always rejected the heathen mythology, never credited the story. . . .

Nothing that is here said can apply, even with the most distant disrespect, to the real character of Jesus Christ. He was a virtuous and an amiable man. The morality that he preached and practised was of the most benevolent kind; and though similar systems of morality had been preached by Confucius [Chinese philosopher], and by some of the Greek philosophers, many years before; by the Quakers [members of the Society of Friends] since; and by many good men in all ages, it has not been exceeded by any. . . .

. . . The resurrection and ascension [of Jesus Christ], supposing them to have taken place, admitted of public and ocular demonstration, like that of the ascension of a balloon, or the sun at noon-day, to all Jerusalem at least. A thing which everybody is required to believe, requires that the proof and evidence of it should be equal to all, and universal; and as the public visibility of this last related act was the only evidence that could give sanction to the former part, the whole of it falls to the ground, because that evidence never was given. Instead of this, a small number of persons, not more than eight or nine, are introduced as proxies for the whole world, to say they saw it, and all the rest of the world are called upon to believe it. But it appears that Thomas [one of Jesus' disciples] did not believe the resurrection, and, as they say, would not believe without having ocular and manual demonstration himself. *So neither will I,* and the reason is equally as good for me, and for every other person, as for Thomas.

It is in vain to attempt to palliate or disguise this matter. The story, so far as relates to the supernatural part, has every mark of fraud and imposition stamped upon the face of it. Who were the authors of it is as impossible for us now to know, as it is for us to be assured that the books in which the account is related were written by the persons whose names they bear; the best surviving evidence we now have respecting this affair is the Jews. They are regularly descended from the people who lived in the times this resurrection and ascension is said to have happened, and they say, *it is not true.*

---

# Baron d'Holbach
# *GOOD SENSE*

More extreme than the deists were the atheists, who denied God's existence altogether. The foremost exponent of atheism was Paul-Henri Thiry, Baron d'Holbach (1723–1789), a prominent contributor to the *Encyclopedia* (see Section 6). Holbach hosted many leading intellectuals, including Diderot, Rousseau, and Condorcet (all represented later in this chapter), at his country estate outside of Paris. He regarded the idea of God as a product of ignorance, fear, and superstition and said that terrified by natural phenomena—storms, fire, floods—humanity's primitive ancestors attributed these occurrences to unseen spirits, whom they tried to appease through rituals. In denouncing religion, Holbach was also affirming core Enlightenment ideals—reason and freedom—as the following passage from *Good Sense* reveals.

In a word, whoever will deign to consult common sense upon religious opinions, and will bestow on this inquiry the attention that is commonly given to any objects we presume interesting, will easily perceive that those opinions have no foundation; that Religion is a mere castle in the air. Theology is but the ignorance of natural causes reduced to a system; a long tissue of fallacies and contradictions. In every country, it presents us with romances void of probability. . . .

Savage and furious nations, perpetually at war, adore, under divers names, some God, conformable to their ideas, that is to say, cruel, carnivorous, selfish, bloodthirsty. We find, in all the religions of the earth, "a God of armies," a "jealous God," an "avenging God," a "destroying God," a "God," who is pleased with carnage, and whom his worshippers consider it as a duty to serve to his taste. Lambs, bulls, children, men, heretics, infidels, kings, whole nations, are sacrificed to him. Do not the zealous servants of this barbarous God think themselves obliged even to offer up themselves as a sacrifice to him? Madmen may every where be seen who, after meditating upon their terrible God, imagine that to please him they must do themselves all possible injury, and inflict on themselves, for this honour, the most exquisite torments. The gloomy ideas more usefully formed of the Deity, far from consoling them under the evils of life, have every where disquieted their minds, and produced follies destructive to their happiness.

How could the human mind make any considerable progress, while tormented with frightful phantoms, and guided by men, interested in perpetuating its ignorance and fears? Man has been forced to vegetate in his primitive stupidity: he has been taught nothing but stories about invisible powers upon whom his happiness was supposed to depend. Occupied solely by his fears, and by unintelligible reveries, he has always been at the mercy of his priests, who have reserved to themselves the right of thinking for him, and directing his actions.

Thus man has remained a child without experience, a slave without courage, fearing to reason, and unable to extricate himself from the labyrinth, in which he has so long been wandering. He believes himself forced to bend under the yoke of his gods, known to him only by the fabulous accounts given by his ministers, who, after binding each unhappy mortal in the chains of his prejudice, remain his masters, or else abandon him defenceless to the absolute power of tyrants, no less terrible than the gods, of whom they are the representatives upon earth.

Oppressed by the double yoke of spiritual and temporal power, it has been impossible for the people to know and pursue their happiness. As Religion, so Politics and Morality became sacred things, which the profane were not permitted to handle. Men have had no other Morality, than what their legislators and priests brought down from the unknown regions of heaven. The human mind, confused by its theological opinions ceased to know its own powers, mistrusted experience, feared truth and disdained reason, in order to follow authority. Man has been a mere machine in the hands of tyrants and priests, who alone have had the right of directing his actions. Always treated as a slave, he has contracted the vices of a slave.

Such are the true causes of the corruption of morals, to which Religion opposes only ideal and ineffectual barriers. Ignorance and servitude are calculated to make men wicked and unhappy. Knowledge, Reason, and Liberty, can alone reform them, and make them happier. But every thing conspires to blind them and to confirm them in their errors. Priests cheat them, tyrants corrupt, the better to enslave them. Tyranny ever was, and ever will be, the true cause of man's depravity, and also of his habitual calamities. Almost always fascinated by religious fiction, poor mortals turn not their eyes to the natural and obvious causes of their misery; but attribute their vices to the imperfection of their natures, and their unhappiness to the anger of the gods. They offer up to heaven vows, sacrifices, and presents, to obtain the end of their sufferings, which in reality, are attributable only to the negligence, ignorance, and perversity of their guides, to the folly of their customs, to the unreasonableness of their laws, and above all, to the general want of knowledge. Let men's minds be filled with true ideas; let their reason be cultivated; let justice govern them; and there will be no need of opposing to the passions, such a feeble barrier, as the fear of the gods. Men will be good, when they are well instructed, well governed, and when they are punished or despised for the evil, and justly rewarded for the good, which they do to their fellow citizens.

To discover the true principles of Morality, men have no need of theology, of revelation, or of gods: They have need only of common sense. They have only to commune with themselves, to reflect upon their own nature, to consult their visible interests, to consider the objects of society, and of the individuals who compose it; and they will easily perceive, that virtue is advantageous, and vice disadvantageous to such beings as themselves. Let us persuade men to be just, beneficent, moderate, sociable; not because such conduct is demanded by the gods, but, because it is pleasure to men. Let us advise them to abstain from vice and crime; not because they will be punished in the other world, but because they will suffer for it in this.—*There are,* says a great man [Montesquieu], *means to prevent crimes, and these means are punishments; there are means to reform manners, and these means are good examples.* . . .

. . . Men are unhappy, only because they are ignorant; they are ignorant, only because every thing conspires to prevent their being enlightened; they are wicked, only because their reason is not sufficiently developed.

## REVIEW QUESTIONS

1. What Christian beliefs did Thomas Paine reject? Why?
2. How did Baron d'Holbach's critique of religion affirm basic Enlightenment ideals?

---

## 5  Epistemology and Education

The philosophes sought a naturalistic understanding of the human condition, one that examined human nature and society without reference to God's will. Toward this end, they sought to explain how the mind acquires knowledge; and as reformers, they stressed the importance of education in shaping a better person and a better society.

# John Locke
## *ESSAY CONCERNING HUMAN UNDERSTANDING*

In his *Essay Concerning Human Understanding* (1689–1693), a work of immense significance in the history of philosophy, John Locke argued that human beings are not born with innate ideas (the idea of God and principles of good and evil, for example) divinely implanted in their minds. Rather, said Locke, the human mind at birth is a blank slate upon which are imprinted sensations derived from contact with the world. These sensations, combined with the mind's reflections on them, are the source of ideas. In effect, knowledge is derived from experience. In the tradition of Francis Bacon, Locke's epistemology (theory of knowledge) implied that people should not dwell on insoluble questions, particularly sterile theological issues, but should seek practical knowledge that promotes human happiness and enlightens human beings and gives them control over their environment.

Locke's empiricism, which aspired to useful knowledge and stimulated an interest in political and ethical questions that focused on human concerns, helped to mold the utilitarian and reformist spirit of the Enlightenment. If there are no innate ideas, said the philosophes, then human beings are not born with original sin, contrary to what Christians believed. All that individuals are derives from their particular experiences. If people are provided with a proper environment and education, they will become intelligent and productive citizens. This was how the reform-minded philosophes interpreted Locke. They preferred to believe that evil stemmed from faulty institutions and poor education, both of which could be remedied, rather than from a defective human nature. Excerpts from *Essay Concerning Human Understanding* follow.

Let us then suppose the mind to be, as we say, white paper, void of all characters, without any ideas:—How comes it to be furnished? Whence comes it by that vast store which the busy and boundless fancy of man has painted on it with an almost endless variety? Whence has it all the *materials* of reason and knowledge? To this I answer, in one word, from EXPERIENCE. In that all our knowledge is founded; and from that it ultimately derives itself. Our observation employed either, about external sensible objects or about the internal operations of our minds perceived and reflected on by ourselves, is that which supplies our understandings with all the *materials* of thinking. These two are the fountains of knowledge, from whence all the ideas we have, or can naturally have, do spring.

First, our Senses, conversant about particular sensible objects, do convey into the mind several distinct perceptions of things, according to those various ways wherein those objects do affect them. And thus we come by those *ideas* we have of *yellow, white, heat, cold, soft, hard, bitter, sweet,* and all those which we call sensible qualities; which when I say the senses convey into the mind, I mean, they from external objects convey into the mind what produces there those perceptions. This great source of most of the ideas we have, depending wholly upon our senses, and derived by them to the understanding, I call SENSATION.

Secondly, the other fountain from which experience furnisheth the understanding with ideas is,—the perception of the operations of our own mind within us, as it is employed about the ideas it has got. . . .

And such are *perception, thinking, doubting, believing, reasoning, knowing, willing,* and all the different actings of our own minds;—which we being conscious of, and observing in ourselves, do from these receive into our understandings as distinct ideas as we do from bodies affecting our senses. This source of ideas every man has wholly in himself; and though it be not sense, as having nothing to do with external objects, yet it is very like it, and might properly enough be called *internal sense.* But as I call the other Sensation, so I call this REFLECTION, the ideas it affords being such only as the mind gets by reflecting on its own operations within itself. By reflection then, in the following part of this discourse, I would be understood to mean, that notice which the mind takes of its own operations, and the manner of them, by reason whereof there come to be ideas of these operations in the understanding. These two, I say, viz. external material things, as the objects of SENSATION, and the operations of our own minds within, as the objects of REFLECTION, are to me the only originals from whence all our ideas take their beginnings. . . .

The understanding seems to me not to have the least glimmering of any ideas which it doth not receive from one of these two. *External objects* furnish the mind with the ideas of sensible qualities, which are all those different perceptions they produce in us; and *the mind* furnishes the understanding with ideas of its own operations.

These, when we have taken a full survey of them, and their several modes, (combinations, and relations,) we shall find to contain all our whole stock of ideas; and that we have nothing in our minds which did not come in one of these two ways. Let any one examine his own thoughts, and thoroughly search into his understanding; and then let him tell me, whether all the original ideas he has there, are any other than of the objects of his senses, or of the operations of his mind, considered as objects of his reflection. And how great a mass of knowledge soever he imagines to be lodged there, he will, upon taking a strict view, see that he has not any idea in his mind but what one of these two have imprinted;—though perhaps, with infinite variety compounded and enlarged by the understanding, as we shall see hereafter.

He that attentively considers the state of a child, at his first coming into the world, will have little reason to think him stored with plenty of ideas, that are to be the matter of his future knowledge. It is *by degrees* he comes to be furnished with them.

---

# John Locke
# *SOME THOUGHTS CONCERNING EDUCATION*

In *Some Thoughts Concerning Education* (1693), excerpted below, Locke expressed a warm concern for children. Deploring rote learning and physical punishment, he maintained that parents and teachers should be mild but firm, teach sound habits by example, and utilize the child's natural disposition for play to good educational advantage.

I think I may say, that of all the Men we meet with, Nine Parts of Ten are what they are, Good or Evil, useful or not, by their Education. 'Tis that which makes the great Difference in Mankind: The little, and almost insensible Impressions on our tender Infancies, have very important and lasting Consequences: And there 'tis, as in the Fountains of some Rivers, where a gentle Application of the Hand turns the flexible Waters into Chanels, that make them take quite contrary Courses, and by this little Direction given them at first in the Source, they receive different Tendencies, and arrive at last, at very remote and distant Places. . . .

If what I have said in the beginning of this Discourse be true, as I do not doubt but it is, *viz.* That the difference to be found in the Manners and Abilities of Men, is owing more to their *Education* than to any thing else; we have reason to conclude, that great care is to be had of the forming Children's *Minds,* and giving them that seasoning early, which shall influence their Lives always after. . . .

The great Mistake I have observed in People's [rearing] their Children has been, that . . . the Mind has not been made obedient to Discipline, and pliant to Reason, when at first it was most tender, most easy to be bowed. . . .

The Difference lies not in the having or not having Appetites, but in the Power to govern, and deny our selves in them. He that is not used to submit his Will to the Reason of others, *when* he is *young,* will scarce hearken or submit to his own Reason, when he is of an Age to make use of it. And what a kind of a Man such an one is like to prove, is easie to foresee. . . .

I am very apt to think that *great Severity of* Punishment does but very little Good; nay, great Harm in Education: And I believe it will be found, that, *Cæteris paribus* [all other things being equal], those Children, who have been most *chastised,* seldom make the best Men. All that I have hitherto contended for, is, That whatsoever *Rigour* is necessary, it is more to be used the younger Children are; and having, by a due Application, wrought its Effect, it is to be relaxed, and changed into a milder Sort of Government. . . .

[I]f the *Mind* be curbed, and *humbled* too much in Children; if their *Spirits* be abased and *broken* much, by too strict an hand over them, they lose all their Vigor and Industry, and are in a worse State than the former. For extravagant young Fellows, that have Liveliness and Spirit, come sometimes to be set right, and so make Able and Great Men: But *dejected Minds,* timorous, and tame, and *low Spirits,* are hardly ever to be raised, and very seldom attain to any thing. To avoid the danger, that is on either hand, is the great Art; and he that has found a way, how to keep a Child's Spirit, easy, active and free; and yet, at the same time, to restrain him from many things he has a Mind to, and to draw him to things that are uneasy to him; he, I say, that knows how to reconcile these seeming Contradictions, has, in my Opinion, got the true Secret of Education. . . .

Beating then, and all other Sorts of slavish and corporal Punishments, are not the Discipline fit to be used in the Education of those we would have wise, good, and ingenuous Men; and therefore very rarely to be applied, and that only in great Occasions, and Cases of Extremity. On the other side, to flatter Children by *Rewards* of things, that are pleasant to them, is as carefully to be avoided.

But, if you take away the Rod on one hand, and these little Encouragements, which they are taken with, on the other, How then (will you say) shall Children be govern'd? Remove Hope and Fear, and there is an end of all Discipline. I grant, that Good and Evil, *Reward* and *Punishment,* are the only Motives to a rational Creature; these are the Spur and Reins, whereby all Mankind are set on work, and guided, and therefore they are to be made use of to Children too. For I advise their Parents and Governors always to carry this in their Minds, that Children are to be treated as rational Creatures. . . .

*Rewards,* I grant, and *Punishments* must be proposed to Children, if we intend to work upon them. The Mistake, I imagine, is, that those that are generally made use of, are *ill chosen.* The Pains and Pleasures of the Body are, I think, of ill consequence, when made the Rewards and Punishments, whereby Men would prevail on their Children. . . .

The *Rewards* and *Punishments* then, whereby we should keep Children in order, *are* quite of another kind, and of that force, that when we can get them once to work, the business, I think, is done, and the difficulty is over. *Esteem* and *Disgrace* are, of all others, the most powerful incentives to the Mind, when once it is brought to relish them. If you can once get into Children a love of Credit, and an apprehension of Shame and Disgrace, you have put into them the true Principle, which will constantly work, and incline them to the right. . . .

But to return to the Businesses of Rewards and Punishments. All the Actions of Childishness, and unfashionable Carriage . . . being . . . exempt from the Discipline of the Rod, there will not be so much need of beating Children, as is generally made use of. To which if we add

Learning to Read, Write, Dance, Foreign Languages, &c. as under the same Privilege, there will be but very rarely any Occasion for Blows or Force in an ingenuous Education. The right Way to teach them those Things is, to give them a Liking and Inclination to what you propose to them to be learn'd; and that will engage their Industry and Application. This I think no hard Matter to do, if Children be handled as they should be, and the Rewards and Punishments above-mentioned be carefully applied, and with them these few Rules observed in the Method of Instructing them. . . .

It will perhaps be wondered that I mention *Reasoning* with Children: And yet I cannot but think that the true Way of Dealing with them. They understand it as early as they do Language; and, if I misobserve not, they love to be treated as Rational Creatures sooner than is imagined. 'Tis a Pride should be cherished in them, and, as much as can be, made the great Instrument to turn them by.

But when I talk of *Reasoning,* I do not intend any other, but such as is suited to the Child's Capacity and Apprehension. No Body can think a Boy of Three, or Seven Years old, should be argued with, as a grown Man. Long Discourses, and Philosophical Reasonings, at best, amaze and confound, but do not instruct Children. When I say therefore, that they must be *treated as Rational Creatures,* I mean, that you should make them sensible by the Mildness of your Carriage, and the Composure even in your Correction of them, that what you do is reasonable in you, and useful and necessary for them: And that it is not out of *Caprichio,* Passion, or Fancy, that you command or forbid them any Thing. This they are capable of understanding; and there is no Vertue they should be excited to, nor Fault they should be kept from, which I do not think they may be convinced of; but it must be by such *Reasons* as their Age and Understanding are capable of, and those proposed always *in* very *few and plain Words.* . . .

But of all the Ways whereby Children are to be instructed, and their Manners formed, the plainest, easiest and most efficacious, is to set before their Eyes the *Examples* of those Things you would have them do, or avoid. Which, when they are pointed out to them, in the Practice of Persons within their Knowledge, with some Reflection on their Beauty or Unbecomingness, are of more force to draw or deterr their Imitation, than any Discourses which can be made to them.

# Claude Helvétius
# *ESSAYS ON THE MIND AND A TREATISE ON MAN*

Even more than did Locke, Claude-Adrien Helvétius (1715–1777) emphasized the importance of the environment in shaping the human mind. Disparities in intelligence and talent, said Helvétius, are due entirely to environmental conditions and not to inborn qualities. Since human beings are malleable and perfectible, their moral and intellectual growth depends on proper conditioning. For this reason he called for political reforms, particularly the implementation of a program of enlightened public education.

In 1758 Helvétius published *Essays on the Mind,* which treated ethics in a purely naturalistic way. Shocked by his separation of morality from God's commands and from fear of divine punishment, and his attacks on the clergy, the authorities suppressed the book. His second major work, *A Treatise on Man,* was published posthumously in 1777. Apparently Helvétius wanted to avoid another controversy. The following passages from both works illustrate Helvétius' belief that "education makes us what we are."

## ESSAYS ON THE MIND

The general conclusion of this discourse is, that genius is common, and the circumstances, proper to unfold it, very extraordinary. If we may compare what is profane to what is sacred, we may say in this respect, Many are called, but few are chosen.

The inequality observable among men, therefore, depends on the government under which they lie; on the greater or less happiness of the age in which they are born; on the education; on their desire of improvement, and on the importance of the ideas that are the subject of their contemplations.

The man of genius is then only produced by the circumstances in which he is placed.* Thus all the art of education consists in placing young men in such a concurrence of circumstances as are proper to unfold the buds of genius and virtue. [I am led to this conclusion by] the desire of promoting the happiness of mankind. I am convinced that a good education would diffuse light, virtue, and consequently, happiness in society; and that the

opinion, that geniuses and virtue are merely gifts of nature, is a great obstacle to the making any farther progress in the science of education, and in this respect is the great favourer of idleness and negligence. With this view, examining the effects which nature and education may have upon us, I have perceived that education makes us what we are; in consequence of which I have thought that it was the duty of a citizen to make known a truth proper to awaken the attention, with respect to the means of carrying this education to perfection.

## A TREATISE ON MAN

Some maintain that, *The understanding is the effect of a certain sort of interior temperament and organization.*

Locke and I say: *The inequality in minds or understandings, is the effect of a known cause, and this cause is the difference of education. . . .*

Among the great number of questions treated of in this work, one of the most important was to determine whether genius, virtue, and talents, to which nations owe their grandeur and felicity, were the effect of the difference of. . . . the organs of the five senses [that is, differences due to birth] . . . or if the same genius, the same virtues, and the same talents were the effect of education, over which the laws and the form of government are all powerful.

If I have proved the truth of the latter assertion, it must be allowed that the happiness of nations is in their own hands, and that it entirely depends on the greater or less interest they take in improving the science of education.

---

*The opinion I advance must appear very pleasing to the vanity of the greatest part of mankind, and therefore, ought to meet with a favourable reception. According to my principles, they ought not to attribute the inferiority of their abilities to the humbling cause of a less perfect organization, but to the education they have received, as well as to the circumstances in which they have been placed. Every man of moderate abilities, in conformity with my principles, has a right to think, that if he had been more favoured by fortune, if he had been born in a certain age or country, he had himself been like the great men whose genius he is forced to admire.

# Jean Jacques Rousseau
# *ÉMILE*

In *The Social Contract* (see Section 7), Jean Jacques Rousseau (1712–1778), who had only contempt for absolute monarchy, sought to provide a theoretical foundation for political liberty. In *Émile* (1762), he suggested another cure for the ills of modern society: educational reforms that would instill in children self-confidence, self-reliance, and emotional security. Rousseau understood that children should not be treated like little adults. He railed against chaining young children to desks and filling their heads with rote learning. Instead, he urged that children experience direct contact with the world to develop their ingenuity, resourcefulness, and imagination so that they might become productive and responsible citizens. Excerpts from Rousseau's influential treatise on education follow.

When I thus get rid of children's lessons, I get rid of the chief cause of their sorrows, namely their books. Reading is the curse of childhood, yet it is almost the only occupation you can find for children. Emile, at twelve years old, will hardly know what a book is. "But," you say, "he must, at least, know how to read." When reading is of use to him, I admit he must learn to read, but till then he will only find it a nuisance.

If children are not to be required to do anything as a matter of obedience, it follows that they will only learn what they perceive to be of real and present value, either for use or enjoyment; what other motive could they have for learning? . . .

People make a great fuss about discovering the best way to teach children to read. They invent "bureaux"* and cards, they turn the nursery into a printer's shop. Locke would have them taught to read by means of dice. What a fine idea! And the pity of it! There is a better way than any of those, and one which is generally overlooked—it consists in the desire to

learn. Arouse this desire in your scholar and have done with your "bureaux" and your dice—any method will serve.

Present interest, that is the motive power, the only motive power that takes us far and safely. Sometimes Emile receives notes of invitation from his father or mother, his relations or friends; he is invited to a dinner, a walk, a boating expedition, to see some public entertainment. These notes are short, clear, plain, and well written. Some one must read them to him, and he cannot always find anybody when wanted; no more consideration is shown to him than he himself showed to you yesterday. Time passes, the chance is lost. The note is read to him at last, but it is too late. Oh! if only he had known how to read! He receives other notes, so short, so interesting, he would like to try to read them. Sometimes he gets help, sometimes none. He does his best, and at last he makes out half the note; it is something about going to-morrow to drink cream—Where? With whom? He cannot tell—how hard he tries to make out the rest! I do not think Emile will need a "bureau." Shall I proceed to the teaching of writing? No, I am ashamed to toy with these trifles in a treatise on education. . . .

If, in accordance with the plan I have sketched, you follow rules which are just the

---

*Translator's note*—The "bureau" was a sort of case containing letters to be put together to form words. It was a favourite device for the teaching of reading and gave its name to a special method, called the bureau-method, of learning to read.

opposite of the established practice, if instead of taking your scholar far afield, instead of wandering with him in distant places, in far-off lands, in remote centuries, in the ends of the earth, and in the very heavens themselves, you try to keep him to himself, to his own concerns, you will then find him able to perceive, to remember, and even to reason; this is nature's order. . . . Give his body constant exercise, make it strong and healthy, in order to make him good and wise; let him work, let him do things, let him run and shout, let him be always on the go; make a man of him in strength, and he will soon be a man in reason.

Of course by this method you will make him stupid if you are always giving him directions, always saying come here, go there, stop, do this, don't do that. If your head always guides his hands, his own mind will become useless. . . .

It is a lamentable mistake to imagine that bodily activity hinders the working of the mind, as if these two kinds of activity ought not to advance hand in hand, and as if the one were not intended to act as guide to the other. . . .

. . . Your scholar is subject to a power which is continually giving him instruction; he acts only at the word of command; he dare not eat when he is hungry, nor laugh when he is merry, nor weep when he is sad, nor offer one hand rather than the other, nor stir a foot unless he is told to do it; before long he will not venture to breathe without orders. What would you have him think about, when you do all the thinking for him? . . .

As for my pupil, or rather Nature's pupil, he has been trained from the outset to be as self-reliant as possible, he has not formed the habit of constantly seeking help from others, still less of displaying his stores of learning. On the other hand, he exercises discrimination and forethought, he reasons about everything that concerns himself. He does not chatter, he acts. Not a word does he know of what is going on in the world at large, but he knows very thoroughly what affects himself. As he is always stirring he is compelled to notice many things, to recognise many effects; he soon acquires a good deal of experience. Nature, not man, is his schoolmaster, and he learns all the quicker because he is not aware that he has any lesson to learn. So mind and body work together. He is always carrying out his own ideas, not those of other people, and thus he unites thought and action; as he grows in health and strength he grows in wisdom and discernment.

## REVIEW QUESTIONS

1. According to John Locke, knowledge originates in experience and has two sources—the senses and reflection. What does this mean, and what makes this view of knowledge so revolutionary?
2. How does Locke's view of the origin of knowledge compare to that of René Descartes (see page 394)? Which view do you favor, or can you suggest another alternative?
3. How would you characterize Locke's general theory of education? Is it compatible with his theory of knowledge?
4. What implications do Locke's theory of knowledge and educational theory have for his conception of human nature?
5. In what way may Claude Helvétius be regarded as a disciple of John Locke, and how did he expand the significance of Locke's ideas?
6. What was Rousseau's basic approach to educating a child?
7. Compare Rousseau's theory of education with Locke's. How similar or different are their views, and what implications do they have for their respective conceptions of human nature?

## 6  Compendium of Knowledge

A 38-volume *Encyclopedia,* whose 150 or more contributors included leading Enlightenment thinkers, was undertaken in Paris during the 1740s as a monumental effort to bring together all human knowledge and to propagate Enlightenment ideas. The *Encyclopedia*'s numerous articles on science and technology and its limited coverage of theological questions attest to the new interests of eighteenth-century intellectuals. Serving as principal editor, Denis Diderot (1713–1784) steered the project through difficult periods, including the suspension of publication by French authorities. After the first two volumes were published, the authorities denounced the work for containing "maxims that would tend to destroy royal authority, foment a spirit of independence and revolt, . . . and lay the foundations for the corruption of morals and religion." In 1759, Pope Clement XIII condemned the *Encyclopedia* for having "scandalous doctrines [and] inducing scorn for religion." It required careful diplomacy and clever ruses to finish the project and still incorporate ideas considered dangerous by religious and governmental authorities. With the project's completion in 1772, Diderot and Enlightenment opinion triumphed over clerical censors and powerful elements at the French court.

## Denis Diderot
## *ENCYCLOPEDIA*

The *Encyclopedia* was a monument to the Enlightenment, as Diderot himself recognized. "This work will surely produce in time a revolution in the minds of man, and I hope that tyrants, oppressors, fanatics, and the intolerant will not gain thereby. We shall have served humanity." Some articles from the *Encyclopedia* follow.

*Encyclopedia* . . . In truth, the aim of an *encyclopedia* is to collect all the knowledge scattered over the face of the earth, to present its general outlines and structure to the men with whom we live, and to transmit this to those who will come after us, so that the work of past centuries may be useful to the following centuries, that our children, by becoming more educated, may at the same time become more virtuous and happier, and that we may not die without having deserved well of the human race. . . .

. . . We have seen that our *Encyclopedia* could only have been the endeavor of a philosophical century. . . .

I have said that it could only belong to a philosophical age to attempt an *encyclopedia*; and I have said this because such a work constantly demands more intellectual daring than is commonly found in [less courageous periods]. All things must be examined, debated, investigated without exception and without regard for anyone's feelings. . . . We must ride roughshod over all these ancient puerilities, overturn the barriers that reason never erected, give back to the arts and sciences the liberty that is so precious to them. . . . We have for quite some time needed a reasoning age when men would no longer seek the rules in classical authors but in nature. . . .

*Fanaticism* . . . is blind and passionate zeal born of superstitious opinions, causing people to commit ridiculous, unjust, and cruel actions, not only without any shame or remorse, but even with a kind of joy and comfort. *Fanaticism,* therefore, is only superstition put into practice. . . .

*Fanaticism* has done much more harm to the world than impiety. What do impious people claim? To free themselves of a yoke, while *fanatics* want to extend their chains over all the earth. Infernal zealomania! . . .

*Government* . . . The good of the people must be the great purpose of the *government.* The governors are appointed to fulfill it; and the civil constitution that invests them with this power is bound therein by the laws of nature and by the law of reason, which has determined that purpose in any form of *government* as the cause of its welfare. The greatest good of the people is its liberty. Liberty is to the body of the state what health is to each individual; without health man cannot enjoy pleasure; without liberty the state of welfare is excluded from nations. A patriotic governor will therefore see that the right to defend and to maintain liberty is the most sacred of his duties. . . .

If it happens that those who hold the reins of *government* find some resistance when they use their power for the destruction and not the conservation of things that rightfully belong to the people, they must blame themselves, because the public good and the advantage of society are the purposes of establishing a *government.* Hence it necessarily follows that power cannot be arbitrary and that it must be exercised according to the established laws so that the people may know its duty and be secure within the shelter of laws, and so that

governors at the same time should be held within just limits and not be tempted to employ the power they have in hand to do harmful things to the body politic. . . .

*History* . . . *On the usefullness of history.* The advantage consists of the comparison that a statesman or a citizen can make of foreign laws, morals, and customs with those of his country. This is what stimulates modern nations to surpass one another in the arts, in commerce, and in agriculture. The great mistakes of the past are useful in all areas. We cannot describe too often the crimes and misfortunes caused by absurd quarrels. It is certain that by refreshing our memory of these quarrels, we prevent a repetition of them. . . .

*Humanity* . . . is a benevolent feeling for all men, which hardly inflames anyone without a great and sensitive soul. This sublime and noble enthusiasm is troubled by the pains of other people and by the necessity to alleviate them. With these sentiments an individual would wish to cover the entire universe in order to abolish slavery, superstition, vice, and misfortune. . . .

*Intolerance* . . . Any method that would tend to stir up men, to arm nations, and to soak the earth with blood is impious.

It is impious to want to impose laws upon man's conscience: this is a universal rule of conduct. People must be enlightened and not constrained. . . .

What did Christ recommend to his disciples when he sent them among the Gentiles? Was it to kill or to die? Was it to persecute or to suffer? . . .

Which is the true voice of humanity, the persecutor who strikes or the persecuted who moans?

*Peace* . . . War is the fruit of man's depravity; it is a convulsive and violent sickness of the body politic. . . .

If reason governed men and had the influence over the heads of nations that it deserves, we would never see them inconsiderately surrender themselves to the fury of war; they would not show that ferocity that characterizes wild beasts. . . .

*Political Authority*  No man has received from nature the right to command others. Liberty is a gift from heaven, and each individual of the same species has the right to enjoy it as soon as he enjoys the use of reason. . . .

The prince owes to his very subjects the *authority* that he has over them; and this *authority* is limited by the laws of nature and the state. The laws of nature and the state are the conditions under which they have submitted or are supposed to have submitted to its government. . . .

Moreover the government, although hereditary in a family and placed in the hands of one person, is not private property, but public property that consequently can never be taken from the people, to whom it belongs exclusively, fundamentally, and as a freehold. Consequently it is always the people who make the lease or the agreement: they always intervene in the contract that adjudges its exercise. It is not the state that belongs to the prince, it is the prince who belongs to the state: but it does rest with the prince to govern in the state, because the state has chosen him for that purpose: he has bound himself to the people and the administration of affairs, and they in their turn are bound to obey him according to the laws. . . .

*The Press*  [*press* includes newspapers, magazines, books, and so forth] . . . People ask if freedom of the *press* is advantageous or prejudicial to a state. The answer is not difficult. It is of the greatest importance to conserve this practice in all states founded on liberty. I would even say that the disadvantages of this liberty are so inconsiderable compared to its advantages that this ought to be the common right of the universe, and it is certainly ad-

visable to authorize its practice in all governments. . . .

*The Slave Trade*  [This trade] is the buying of unfortunate Negroes by Europeans on the coast of Africa to use as slaves in their colonies. This buying of Negroes, to reduce them to slavery, is one business that violates religion, morality, natural laws, and all the rights of human nature.

Negroes, says a modern Englishman full of enlightenment and humanity, have not become slaves by the right of war; neither do they deliver themselves voluntarily into bondage, and consequently their children are not born slaves. Nobody is unaware that they are bought from their own princes, who claim to have the right to dispose of their liberty, and that traders have them transported in the same way as their other goods, either in their colonies or in America, where they are displayed for sale.

If commerce of this kind can be justified by a moral principle, there is no crime, however atrocious it may be, that cannot be made legitimate. Kings, princes, and magistrates are not the proprietors of their subjects: they do not, therefore, have the right to dispose of their liberty and to sell them as slaves.

On the other hand, no man has the right to buy them or to make himself their master. Men and their liberty are not objects of commerce; they can be neither sold nor bought nor paid for at any price. We must conclude from this that a man whose slave has run away should only blame himself, since he had acquired for money illicit goods whose acquisition is prohibited by all the laws of humanity and equity.

There is not, therefore, a single one of these unfortunate people regarded only as slaves who does not have the right to be declared free, since he has never lost his freedom, which he could not lose and which his prince, his father, and any person whatsoever in the world had not the power to dispose of. Consequently the sale that has been completed is invalid in itself. This Negro does not divest himself and can never divest himself of his natural right; he carries it everywhere with him, and he can demand everywhere that he be allowed to enjoy it. It is, therefore, patent inhumanity on the part of judges in free countries where he is transported, not to emancipate him immediately by declaring him free, since he is their fellow man, having a soul like them.

## REVIEW QUESTIONS

1. Why was the publication of the *Encyclopedia* a vital step in the philosophes' hopes for reform?
2. To what extent were John Locke's political ideals reflected in the *Encyclopedia*?
3. Why was freedom of the press of such significance to the enlightened philosophes?
4. Why did some philosophes condemn slavery?

---

## 7 Rousseau: Political Reform

To the philosophes, advances in the arts were hallmarks of progress. However, Jean Jacques Rousseau argued that the accumulation of knowledge improved human understanding but corrupted the morals of human beings. In *A Discourse on the Arts and Sciences* (1750) and *A Discourse on the Origin of Inequality* (1755), Rousseau diagnosed the illnesses of modern civilization. He said that human nature, which was originally good, had been corrupted by society. As a result, he stated at the beginning of *The Social Contract* (1762), "Man is born free; and everywhere he is in chains." How can humanity be made moral and free again? In *The Social Contract,* Rousseau suggested one cure: reforming the political system. He argued that in the existing civil society the rich and powerful who controlled the state oppressed the majority. Rousseau admired the small, ancient Greek city-state (polis), where citizens participated actively and directly in public affairs. A small state modeled after the ancient Greek polis, said Rousseau, would be best able to resolve the tensions between individual freedom and the requirements of the collective community.

## Jean Jacques Rousseau
## *THE SOCIAL CONTRACT*

In the opening chapters of *The Social Contract,* Rousseau rejected the principle that one person has a natural authority over others. All legitimate authority, he said, stemmed from human traditions, not from nature. Rousseau had only contempt for absolute monarchy and in *The Social Contract* sought to provide a theoretical foundation for political liberty.

[To rulers who argued that they provided security for their subjects, Rousseau responded as follows:]

It will be said that the despot assures his subjects civil tranquillity. Granted; but what do they gain, if the wars his ambition brings down upon them, his insatiable avidity, and the vexatious conduct of his ministers press harder on them than their own dissensions would have done? What do they gain, if the very tranquillity they enjoy is one of their miseries? Tranquillity is found also in dungeons; but is that enough to make them desirable places to live in? The Greeks imprisoned in the cave of the Cyclops lived there very tranquilly, while they were awaiting their turn to be devoured. . . .

Even if each man could alienate himself, he could not alienate his children: they are born men and free; their liberty belongs to them, and no one but they has the right to dispose of it. Before they come to years of discretion, the father can, in their name, lay down conditions for their preservation and well-being, but he cannot give them irrevocably and without conditions: such a gift is contrary to the ends of nature, and exceeds the rights of paternity. It would therefore be necessary, in order to legitimize an arbitrary government, that in every generation the people should be in a position to accept or reject it; but, were this so, the government would be no longer arbitrary.

To renounce liberty is to renounce being a man, to surrender the rights of humanity and even its duties. For him who renounces everything no indemnity is possible. Such a renunciation is incompatible with man's nature; to remove all liberty from his will is to remove all morality from his acts.

---

Like Hobbes and Locke, Rousseau refers to an original social contract that terminates the state of nature and establishes the civil state. The clash of particular interests in the state of nature necessitates the creation of civil authority.

---

I suppose men to have reached the point at which the obstacles in the way of their preservation in the state of nature show their power of resistance to be greater than the resources at the disposal of each individual for his maintenance in that state. That primitive condition can then subsist no longer; and the human race would perish unless it changed its manner of existence. . . .

This sum of forces can arise only where several persons come together: but, as the force and liberty of each man are the chief instruments of his self-preservation, how can he pledge them without harming his own interests, and neglecting the care he owes to himself? This difficulty, in its bearing on my present subject, may be stated in the following terms:

"The problem is to find a form of association which will defend and protect with the whole common force the person and goods of each associate, and in which each, while uniting himself with all, may still obey himself alone, and remain as free as before." This is the fundamental problem of which the *Social Contract* provides the solution.

---

In entering into the social contract, the individual surrenders his rights to the community as a whole, which governs in accordance with the general will—an underlying principle that expresses what is best for the community. The general will is a plainly visible truth that is easily discerned by reason and common sense purged of self-interest and unworthy motives. For Rousseau, the general will by definition is always right and always works to the community's advantage. True freedom consists of obedience to laws that coincide with the general will. Obedience to the general will transforms an individual motivated by self-interest, appetites, and passions into a higher type of person—a citizen committed to the general good. What happens, however, if a person's private will—that is, expressions of particular, selfish interests—clashes with the general will? As private interests could ruin the body politic, says Rousseau, "whoever refuses to obey the general will shall be compelled to do so by the whole body." Thus Rousseau rejects entirely the Lockean principle that citizens possess rights independently of and against the state. Because Rousseau grants the sovereign (the people constituted as a corporate body) virtually unlimited authority over the citizenry, some critics view him as a precursor of modern dictatorship.

---

The clauses of this contract. . . . properly understood, may be reduced to one—the total alienation of each associate, together with all his rights, to the whole community; for, in the first place, as each gives himself absolutely, the conditions are the same for all; and, this being so, no one has any interest in making them burdensome to others.

Moreover, the alienation being without reserve, the union is as perfect as it can be, and no associate has anything more to demand: for, if the individuals retained certain rights, as there would be no common superior to decide between them and the public, each, being on one point his own judge, would ask to be so on all; the state of nature would thus continue, and the association would necessarily become inoperative or tyrannical.

Finally, each man, in giving himself to all, gives himself to nobody; and as there is no associate over which he does not acquire the same right as he yields others over himself, he gains an equivalent for everything he loses, and an increase of force for the preservation of what he has.

If then we discard from the social compact what is not of its essence, we shall find that it reduces itself to the following terms:

*"Each of us puts his person and all his power in common under the supreme direction of the general will, and, in our corporate capacity, we receive each member as an indivisible part of the whole."*

At once, in place of the individual personality of each contracting party, this act of association creates a moral and collective body, composed of as many members as the assembly contains voters, and receiving from this act its unity, its common identity, its life, and its will. . . .

In order then that the social compact may not be an empty formula, it tacitly includes the undertaking, which alone can give force to the rest, that whoever refuses to obey the general will shall be compelled to do so by the whole body. This means nothing less than that he will be forced to be free; for this is the condition which, by giving each citizen to his country, secures him against all personal dependence. In this lies the key to the working of the political machine; this alone legitimizes civil undertakings, which, without it, would be absurd, tyrannical, and liable to the most frightful abuses.

The passage from the state of nature to the civil state produces a very remarkable change in man, by substituting justice for instinct in his conduct, and giving his actions the morality they had formerly lacked. Then only, when the voice of duty takes the place of physical impulses and right of appetite, does man, who so far had considered only himself, find that he is forced to act on different principles, and to consult his reason before listening to his inclinations. Although, in this state, he deprives himself of some advantages which he got from nature, he gains in return others so great, his faculties are so stimulated and developed, his ideas so extended, his feelings so ennobled, and his whole soul so uplifted, that, did not the abuses of this new condition often degrade him below that which he left, he would be bound to bless continually the happy moment which took him from it for ever, and, instead of a stupid and unimaginative animal, made him an intelligent being and a man.

Let us draw up the whole account in terms easily commensurable. What man loses by the social contract is his natural liberty and an unlimited right to everything he tries to get and succeeds in getting; what he gains is civil liberty and the proprietorship of all he possesses. If we are to avoid mistake in weighing one against the other, we must clearly distinguish natural liberty, which is bounded only by the strength of the individual, from civil liberty, which is limited by the general will; and possession, which is merely the effect of force or the right of the first occupier, from property, which can be founded only on a positive title.

We might, over and above all this, add, to what man acquires in the civil state, moral liberty, which alone makes him truly master of himself; for the mere impulse of appetite is slavery, while obedience to a law which we prescribe to ourselves is liberty. . . .

The first and most important deduction from the principles we have so far laid down is that the general will alone can direct the State according to the object for which it was instituted, i.e. the common good: for if the clashing of particular interests made the establishment of societies necessary, the agreement of these very interests made it possible. The common element in these different interests is what forms the social tie; and, were there no point of agreement between them all, no society could exist. It is solely on the basis of this common interest that every society should be governed. . . .

It follows from what has gone before that the general will is always right and tends to the public advantage; but it does not follow that the deliberations of the people are always equally correct. Our will is always for our own good, but we do not always see what that is; the people is never corrupted, but it is often deceived, and on such occasions only does it seem to will what is bad.

There is often a great deal of difference between the will of all and the general will; the latter considers only the common interest, while the former takes private interest into account, and is no more than a sum of particular wills: but take away from these same wills the pluses and minuses that cancel one another, and the general will remains as the sum of the differences.

If, when the people, being furnished with adequate information, held its deliberations, the citizens had no communication one with another, the grand total of the small differences would always give the general will, and the decision would always be good. But when factions arise, and partial associations are formed at the expense of the great association, the will of each of these associations becomes general in relation to its members, while it remains particular in relation to the State: it may then be said that there are no longer as many votes as there are men, but only as many as there are associations. The differences become less numerous and give a less general result. Lastly, when one of these associations is so great as to prevail over all the rest, the result is no longer a sum of small differences, but a single difference; in this case there is no longer a general will, and the opinion which prevails is purely particular.

It is therefore essential, if the general will is to be able to express itself, that there should be no partial society [factions] within the State, and that each citizen should think only his own thoughts. . . . But if there are partial societies, it is best to have as many as possible and to prevent them from being unequal. . . . These precautions are the only ones that can guarantee that the general will shall be always enlightened, and that the people shall in no way deceive itself.

## REVIEW QUESTIONS

1. What did Jean Jacques Rousseau mean by the "general will"? What function did it serve in his political theory?
2. Why do some thinkers view Rousseau as a champion of democracy, whereas others see him as a spiritual precursor of totalitarianism?

# 8  Judicial and Penal Reform

A humanitarian spirit pervaded the philosophes' outlook. Showing a warm concern for humanity, they attacked militarism, slavery, religious persecution, torture, and other violations of human dignity, as seen in passages from the *Encyclopedia* and Voltaire's works earlier in this chapter. Through reasoned arguments they sought to make humankind recognize and renounce its own barbarity. In the following selections, other eighteenth-century reformers denounce judicial torture and the abuse of prisoners.

## Caesare Beccaria
## *ON CRIME AND PUNISHMENTS*

In *On Crime and Punishments* (1764), Caesare Beccaria (1738–1794), an Italian economist and criminologist, condemned torture, commonly used to obtain confessions in many European countries, as irrational and inhuman.

The true relations between sovereigns and their subjects, and between nations, have been discovered. Commerce has been reanimated by the common knowledge of philosophical truths diffused by the art of printing, and there has sprung up among nations a tacit rivalry of industriousness that is most humane and truly worthy of rational beings. Such good things we owe to the productive enlightenment of this age. But very few persons have studied and fought against the cruelty of punishments and the irregularities of criminal procedures, a part of legislation that is as fundamental as it is widely neglected in almost all of Europe. Very few persons have undertaken to demolish the accumulated errors of centuries by rising to general principles, curbing, at least, with the sole force that acknowledged truths possess, the unbounded course of ill-directed power which has continually produced a long and authorized example of the most cold-blooded barbarity. And yet the groans of the weak, sacrificed to cruel ignorance and to opulent indolence; the barbarous torments, multiplied with lavish and useless severity, for crimes either not proved or wholly imaginary; the filth and hor-

rors of a prison, intensified by that cruellest tormentor of the miserable, uncertainty—all these ought to have roused that breed of magistrates who direct the opinions of men. . . .

But what are to be the proper punishments for such crimes?

Is the death-penalty really *useful* and *necessary* for the security and good order of society? Are torture and torments *just,* and do they attain the *end* for which laws are instituted? What is the best way to prevent crimes? Are the same punishments equally effective for all times? What influence have they on customary behavior? These problems deserve to be analyzed with that geometric precision which the mist of sophisms, seductive eloquence, and timorous doubt cannot withstand. If I could boast only of having been the first to present to Italy, with a little more clarity, what other nations have boldly written and are beginning to practice, I would account myself fortunate. But if, by defending the rights of man and of unconquerable truth, I should help to save from the spasm and agonies of death some wretched victim of tyranny or of no less fatal ignorance, the thanks and tears of one innocent mortal in his transports of joy would console me for the contempt of all mankind. . . .

A cruelty consecrated by the practice of most nations is torture of the accused during his trial, either to make him confess the crime or to clear up contradictory statements, or to discover accomplices, or to purge him of infamy in some metaphysical and incomprehensible way, or, finally, to discover other crimes of which he might be guilty but of which he is not accused.

No man can be called *guilty* before a judge has sentenced him, nor can society deprive him of public protection before it has been decided that he has in fact violated the conditions under which such protection was accorded him. What right is it, then, if not simply that of might, which empowers a judge to inflict punishment on a citizen while doubt still remains as to his guilt or innocence? Here is the dilemma, which is nothing new: the fact of the crime is either certain or uncertain; if certain, all that is due is the punishment established by the laws, and tortures are useless because the criminal's confession is useless; if uncertain, then one must not torture the innocent, for such, according to the laws, is a man whose crimes are not yet proved. . . .

. . . The impression of pain may become so great that, filling the entire sensory capacity of the tortured person, it leaves him free only to choose what for the moment is the shortest way of escape from pain. The response of the accused is then as inevitable as the impressions of fire and water. The sensitive innocent man will then confess himself guilty when he believes that, by so doing, he can put an end to his torment. Every difference between guilt and innocence disappears by virtue of the very means one pretends to be using to discover it. (Torture) is an infallible means indeed—for absolving robust scoundrels and for condemning innocent persons who happen to be weak. Such are the fatal defects of this so-called criterion of truth, a criterion fit for a cannibal. . . .

Of two men, equally innocent or equally guilty, the strong and courageous will be acquitted, the weak and timid condemned, by virtue of this rigorous rational argument: "I, the judge, was supposed to find you guilty of such and such a crime; you, the strong, have been able to resist the pain, and I therefore absolve you; you, the weak, have yielded, and I therefore condemn you. I am aware that a confession wrenched forth by torments ought to be of no weight whatsoever, but I'll torment you again if you don't confirm what you have confessed.". . .

A strange consequence that necessarily follows from the use of torture is that the innocent person is placed in a condition worse than that of the guilty, for if both are tortured, the circumstances are all against the former. Either he confesses the crime and is condemned, or he is declared innocent and has suffered a punishment he did not deserve. The guilty man, on the contrary, finds himself in a favorble situation; that is, if, as a consequence of having firmly resisted the torture, he is absolved as innocent, he will have escaped a greater punishment by enduring a lesser one. Thus the innocent cannot but lose, whereas the guilty may gain. . . .

It would be superfluous to [cite] . . . the innumerable examples of innocent persons who have confessed themselves criminals because of the agonies of torture; there is no nation, there is no age that does not have its own to cite.

# John Howard
# *PRISONS IN ENGLAND AND WALES*

**The efforts of John Howard (1726–1790), a British philanthropist, led Parliament in 1774 to enact prison reform. In 1777 Howard published *State of the Prisons in England and Wales,* excerpts from which follow.**

There are prisons, into which whoever looks will, at first sight of the people confined there, be convinced, that there is some great error in the management of them: the sallow meagre countenances declare, without words, that they are very miserable: many who went in healthy, are in a few months changed to emaciated dejected objects. Some are seen pining under diseases, *"sick and in prison;"* expiring on the floors, in loathsome cells, of pestilential fevers, and . . . small-pox: victims, I must not say to the cruelty, but I will say to the inattention, of sheriffs, and gentlemen in the commission of the peace.

The cause of this distress is, that many prisons are scantily supplied, and some almost totally unprovided with the necessaries of life.

There are several Bridewells [prisons for those convicted of lesser crimes such as vagrancy and disorderly conduct] (to begin with them) in which prisoners have no allowance of food at all. In some, the keeper farms what little is allowed them: and where he engages to supply each prisoner with one or two pennyworth of bread a day, I have known this shrunk to half, sometimes less than half the quantity, cut or broken from his own loaf.

It will perhaps be asked, does not their work maintain them? for every one knows that those offenders are committed to *hard labour.* The answer to that question, though true, will hardly be believed. There are very few Bridewells in which any work is done, or can be done. The prisoners have neither tools, nor materials of any kind; but spend their time in sloth, profaneness and debauchery, to a degree which, in some of those houses that I have seen, is extremely shocking. . . .

I have asked some keepers, since the late act for preserving the health of prisoners, why no care is taken of their sick: and have been answered, that the magistrates tell them *the act does not extend to Bridewells.*

In consequence of this, at the quarter sessions you see prisoners, covered (hardly covered) with rags; almost famished; and sick of diseases, which the discharged spread wherever they go, and with which those who are sent to the County-Gaols infect these prisons. . . .

Felons have in some Gaols two pennyworth of bread a day; in some three halfpennyworth; in some a pennyworth; in some a shilling a week. . . . I often weighed the bread in different prisons, and found the penny loaf 7½ to 8½ ounces, the other loaves in proportion. It is probable that when this allowance was fixed by its value, near double the quantity that the money will now purchase, might be bought for it: yet the allowance continues unaltered. . . .

This allowance being so far short of the cravings of nature, and in some prisons lessened by farming to the gaoler, many criminals are half starved: such of them as at their commitment were in health, come out almost famished, scarce able to move, and for weeks incapable of any labour.

Many prisons have NO WATER. This defect is frequent in Bridewells, and Town-Gaols. In the felons courts of some County-Gaols there is no water: in some places where there is water, prisoners are always locked up within doors, and have no more than the keeper or his servants think fit to bring them: in one place they are limited to three pints a day each—a scanty provision for drink and cleanliness! . . .

From hence any one may judge of the probability there is against the health and life of prisoners, crowded in close rooms, cells, and subterraneous dungeons, for fourteen or sixteen hours out of the four and twenty. In some of those caverns the floor is very damp: in others there is sometimes an inch or two of water; and the straw, or bedding is laid on such floors, seldom on barrack bedsteads. . . . Some Gaols have no sewers; and in those that have, if they be not properly attended to, they are, even to a visitant, offensive beyond expression: how noxious then to people constantly confined in those prisons!

In many Gaols, and in most Bridewells, there is no allowance of straw for prisoners to sleep on; and if by any means they get a little, it is not changed for months together, so that it is almost worn to dust. Some lie upon rags, others upon the bare floors. When I have complained of this to the keepers, their justification has been, "The county allows no straw; the prisoners have none but at my cost."

The evils mentioned hitherto affect the *health* and *life* of prisoners: I have now to complain of what is pernicious to their morals; and that is, the confining all sorts of prisoners together: debtors and felons; men and women; the young beginner and the old offender: and with all these, in some counties, such as are guilty of misdemeanors only. . . .

In some Gaols you see (and who can see it without pain?) boys of twelve or fourteen eagerly listening to the stories told by practised and experienced criminals, of their adventures, successes, stratagems, and escapes.

I must here add, that in some few Gaols are confined idiots and lunatics. . . . The insane, where they are not kept separate, disturb and terrify other prisoners. No care is taken of them, although it is probable that by medicines, and proper regimen, some of them might be restored to their senses, and to usefulness in life. . . .

A cruel custom obtains in most of our Gaols, which is that of the prisoners demanding of a new comer garnish, footing, or (as it is called in some London Gaols) chummage. "Pay or strip," are the fatal words. I say *fatal,* for they are so to some; who having no money, are obliged to give up part of their scanty apparel; and if they have no bedding or straw to sleep on, contract diseases, which I have known to prove mortal.

Loading prisoners with heavy irons, which make their walking, and even lying down to sleep, difficult and painful, is another custom which I cannot but condemn. In some County-Gaols the *women* do not escape this severity.

## REVIEW QUESTIONS

1. What were Caesare Beccaria's arguments against the use of torture in judicial proceedings?
2. What ideals of the Enlightenment philosophes are reflected in Beccaria's arguments?
3. List the abuses in British jails that John Howard disclosed.

---

## 9   On the Progress of Humanity

Marie Jean Antoine Nicolas Caritat, Marquis de Condorcet (1743–1794), was a French mathematician and historian of science. He contributed to the *Encyclopedia* and campaigned actively for religious toleration and the abolition of slavery. During the French Revolution, Condorcet attracted the enmity of the dominant Jacobin party and in 1793 was forced to go into hiding. Secluded in Paris, he wrote *Sketch for a Historical Picture of the Progress of the Human Mind.* Arrested in 1794, Condorcet died during his first night in prison from either exhaustion or self-inflicted poison.

## Marquis de Condorcet
# THE EVILS OF SLAVERY

Montesquieu, Voltaire, Hume, Benjamin Franklin, Thomas Paine, and several other philosophes condemned slavery and the slave trade. In Book 15 of *The*

*Spirit of the Laws,* Montesquieu scornfully refuted all justifications for slavery. Ultimately, he said, slavery, which violates the fundamental principle of justice underlying the universe, derived from base human desires to dominate and exploit other human beings. In 1780, Paine helped draft the act abolishing slavery in Pennsylvania. Five years earlier, he wrote:

> Our Traders in Men . . . must know the wickedness of that SLAVE-TRADE, if they attend to reasoning, or the dictates of their own hearts, and [those who] shun and stifle all these wilfully sacrifice Conscience, and the character of integrity to that Golden Idol. . . . Most shocking of all is alleging the sacred Scriptures to favour this wicked practice.

In 1788, Condorcet helped found The Society of the Friends of Blacks, which attacked slavery. Seven years earlier he had published a pamphlet denouncing slavery as a violation of human rights. Following are excerpts from this pamphlet.

### *"Dedicatory Epistle to the Negro Slaves"*

My Friends,

Although I am not the same color as you, I have always regarded you as my brothers. Nature formed you with the same spirit, the same reason, the same virtues as whites. . . . Your tyrants will reproach me with uttering only commonplaces and having nothing but chimerical [unrealistic] ideas: indeed, nothing is more common than the maxims of humanity and justice; nothing is more chimerical than to propose to men that they base their conduct on them.

Reducing a man to slavery, buying him, selling him, keeping him in servitude: these are truly crimes, and crimes worse than theft. In effect, they take from the slave, not only all forms of property but also the ability to acquire it, the control over his time, his strength, of everything that nature has given him to maintain his life and satisfy his needs. To this wrong they add that of taking from the slave the right to dispose of his own person. . . .

It follows from our principles that the inflexible justice to which kings and nations are subject like their citizens requires the destruction of slavery. We have shown that this destruction will harm neither commerce nor the wealth of a nation because it would not result in any decrease in cultivation. We have shown that the master had no right over his slave; that the act of keeping him in servitude is not

the enjoyment of a property right but a crime; that in freeing the slave the law does not attack property but rather ceases to tolerate an action which it should have punished with the death penalty. The sovereign therefore owes no compensation to the master of slaves just as he owes none to a thief whom a court judgment has deprived of the possession of a stolen good. The public tolerance of a crime may make punishment impossible but it cannot grant a real right to the profit from the crime.

---

Defenders of slavery, says Condorcet, will blame the philosophes for stirring up trouble in the same way opponents of reform attack the philosophes for supporting other progressive causes.

---

If writers protest against the slavery of Negroes, it is the *philosophes,* their opponents say, thinking they have won their case. . . . If some people have been saved by inoculation from the dangers of smallpox, it's by the advice of the *philosophes.* . . . If the custom of breaking the bones of the accused between boards to make them tell the truth has been recently suppressed, it's because the *philosophes* inveighed against the practice; and it is in spite of the *philosophes* that France has been lucky enough to save a remnant of the old laws and conserve the precious practice of applying torture to condemned criminals. . . . Who is it who dares to complain in France about the barbarism of the criminal laws, about the cruelty with which the French Protestants have been deprived of the rights of man and citizen, about the harshness and injustice of the laws against smuggling and on hunting? Who had the culpable boldness to pretend that it would be useful to the people and in accord with justice to insure liberty of commerce and industry? . . . We can see clearly that it was surely the *philosophes*.

---

# Marquis de Condorcet
# PROGRESS OF THE HUMAN MIND

Sharing the philosophes' confidence in human goodness and in reason, Condorcet was optimistic about humanity's future progress. Superstition, prejudice, intolerance, and tyranny—all barriers to progress in the past—would gradually be eliminated, and humanity would enter a golden age. The following excerpts are from Condorcet's *Sketch*.

. . . The aim of the work that I have undertaken, and its result will be to show by appeal to reason and fact that nature has set no term to the perfection of human faculties; that the perfectibility of man is truly indefinite; and that the progress of this perfectibility, from now onwards independent of any power that might wish to halt it, has no other limit than the duration of the globe upon which nature has cast us. This progress will doubtless vary in speed, but it will never be reversed as long as the earth occupies its present place in the system of the universe, and as long as the general laws of this system produce neither a general cataclysm nor such changes as will deprive the human race of its present faculties and its present resources. . . .

. . . It will be necessary to indicate by what stages what must appear to us today a fantastic hope ought in time to become possible, and even likely; to show why, in spite of the transitory successes of prejudice and the support that it receives from the corruption of governments or peoples, truth alone will obtain a lasting victory; we shall demonstrate how nature has joined together indissolubly the progress of knowledge and that of liberty, virtue and respect for the natural rights of man. . . .

After long periods of error, after being led astray by vague or incomplete theories, publicists have at last discovered the true rights of man and how they can all be deduced from the single truth, that *man is a sentient being, capable of reasoning and of acquiring moral ideas.* . . .

At last man could proclaim aloud his right, which for so long had been ignored, to submit all opinions to his own reason and to use in the search for truth the only instrument for its recognition that he has been given. Every man learnt with a sort of pride that nature had not forever condemned him to base his beliefs on the opinions of others; the superstitions of antiquity and the abasement of reason before the [rapture] of supernatural religion disappeared from society as from philosophy.

Thus an understanding of the natural rights of man, the belief that these rights are inalienable and [cannot be forfeited], a strongly expressed desire for liberty of thought and letters, of trade and industry, and for the alleviation of the people's suffering, for the [elimination] of all penal laws against religious dissenters and the abolition of torture and barbarous punishments, the desire for a milder system of criminal legislation and jurisprudence which should give complete security to the innocent, and for a simpler civil code, more in conformance with reason and nature, indifference in all matters of religion which now were relegated to the status of superstitions and political [deception], a hatred of hypocrisy and fanaticism, a contempt for prejudice, zeal for the propagation of enlightenment: all these principles, gradually filtering down from philosophical works to every class of society whose education went beyond the catechism and the alphabet, became the common faith . . . [of enlightened people]. In some countries these principles formed a public opinion sufficiently widespread for even the mass of the people to show a willingness to be guided by it and to obey it. . . .

Force or persuasion on the part of governments, priestly intolerance, and even national prejudices, had all lost their deadly power to smother the voice of truth, and nothing could now protect the enemies of reason or the oppressors of freedom from a sentence to which the whole of Europe would soon subscribe. . . .

Our hopes for the future condition of the human race can be subsumed under three important heads: the abolition of inequality between nations, the progress of equality within each nation, and the true perfection of mankind. Will all nations one day attain that state of civilization which the most enlightened, the freest and the least burdened by prejudices, such as the French and the Anglo-Americans [by virtue of their revolutions], have attained already? Will the vast gulf that separates these peoples from the slavery of nations under the rule of monarchs, from the barbarism of African tribes, from the ignorance of savages, little by little disappear? . . .

Is the human race to better itself, either by discoveries in the sciences and the arts, and so in the means to individual welfare and general prosperity; or by progress in the principles of conduct or practical morality; or by a true perfection of the intellectual, moral, or physical faculties of man, an improvement which may result from a perfection either of the instruments used to heighten the intensity of these faculties and to direct their use or of the natural constitution of man?

In answering these three questions we shall find in the experience of the past, in the observation of the progress that the sciences and civilization have already made, in the analysis of the progress of the human mind and of the development of its faculties, the strongest reasons for believing that nature has set no limit to the realization of our hopes. . . .

The time will therefore come when the sun will shine only on free men who know no other master but their reason; when tyrants and slaves, priests and their stupid or hypocritical instruments will exist only in works of history and on the stage; and when we shall think of them only to pity their victims and their dupes; to maintain ourselves in a state of vigilance by thinking on their excesses; and to learn how to recognize and so to destroy, by force of reason, the first seeds of tyranny and superstition, should they ever dare to reappear amongst us.

## REVIEW QUESTIONS

1. On what grounds did the Marquis de Condorcet attack slavery?
2. According to Condorcet, what economic, political, and cultural policies were sought by the philosophes?
3. Was the Enlightenment philosophy an alternative moral code to that of Christianity? Or was it an internal reformation of the traditional Christian moral order?
4. What image of human nature underlies Condorcet's theory of human progress?

**Chapter 1 cont.**
*Section 4* PP. 13, 14: Erman, Adolph, *The Ancient Egyptians.* Reprinted with permission of Methuen & Co. *Section 5* P. 15: From *Ancient Eastern Texts to the Old Testament,* 3/e with Supplement edited by James B. Pritchard, 1969, pp. 100, 101. Copyright © 1969 by Princeton University Press. *Section 6* PP. 17, 18: From Miriam Lichtheim, *Ancient Egyptian Literature: A Book of Readings, Vol. II,* pp. 182, 185, 183–184, 166–180. Copyright © 1973–1980 by the Regents of the University of California. Reprinted by permission of the University of California Press. *Section 7* P. 19: From R.F. Harper, *Assyrian and Babylonian Literature* (New York: D. Appleton, 1904), pp. 12–14. P. 20: From *Ancient Eastern Texts to the Old Testament,* 3/e with Supplement edited by James B. Pritchard, 1969, pp. 297–298. Copyright © 1969 by Princeton University Press. P. 20: *Inscription of Darius I* from Journal of the American Oriental Society, Vol. 51, No. 3. Used with permission. *Section 8* P. 23: "O Salt" and "Scorching Fire" from *The Intellectual Adventure of Ancient Man: An Essay on Speculative Thought in the Ancient Near East* by Henri Frankfort, H.A. Frankfort, John A. Wilson, Thorkild Jacobsen, and William A. Irwin. Copyright © 1946, 1977 by the University of Chicago. All rights reserved. Used by permission of The University of Chicago Press. P. 24: From *Ancient Eastern Texts to the Old Testament,* 3/e with Supplement edited by James B. Pritchard, 1969, pp. 297–298, 100, 101, 370. P. 25: Thorkild Jacobsen, *The Treasures of Darkness: A History of Mesopotamiam Religion.* Copyright © 1976 by Yale University Press. Used with permission.

**Chapter 2**
*Sections 1–5* PP. 29–42: Scripture quotations from the *Revised Standard Version of the Bible.* Copyright 1946, 1952, 1971 by the Division of Christian Education of the National Council of the Churches of Christ in the USA. Reprinted with permission.

**Chapter 3**
*Section 1* P. 47: From *The Iliad* by Homer, translated by E.V. Rieu. Copyright © 1950. Reprinted by permission of the Estate of E.V. Rieu. *Section 2* PP. 49–51: G.S. Kirk, J.E. Raven and M. Scholfield, *The Presocratic Philosophers.* Copyright © 1957, 2nd edition © 1984 by Cambridge University Press. Used with permission. *Section 3* P. 52: Reprinted by permission of the publishers and the Loeb Classical Library from Hippocrates: *Hippocrates,* Vol. II, translated by W.H.S. Jones, Cambridge, Mass.: Harvard University Press, 1923. P. 53: From *History of the Peloponnesian War* by Thucydides, translated by Rex Warner. Copyright © 1954. Reproduced by permission of Penguin Books Ltd., UK.

P. 54: Reprinted by permission of the publishers from *Ancilla To The Pre-Socratic Philosophers* by Kathleen Freeman, Cambridge, Mass.: Harvard University Press, 1948. *Section 4* P. 56: Poetry by Pindar, translated by H.D.F. Kitto in *The Greeks.* Revised Edition. Copyright © 1957. Reproduced by permission of Penguin Books, Ltd., UK. P. 56: *Antigone,* from *Three Theban Plays* by Sophocles, translated by Robert Fagles. Translation copyright © 1982 by Robert Fagles. Used by permission of Viking Penguin, a division of Penguin Books USA, Inc. *Section 5* P. 57: From Herodotus, *The Histories,* trans. by Aubrey de Selincourt, revised by A.R. Burn. (Penguin Classics, 1954.) *Section 6* P. 60: *Antigone,* from *Three Theban Plays* by Sophocles, translated by Robert Fagles. Translation copyright © 1982 by Robert Fagles. Used by permission of Viking Penguin, a division of Penguin Books USA, Inc. *Section 7* P. 66: Thucydides, *History of the Peloponnesian War,* translated by Rex Warner. Copyright © 1954 by Rex Warner. Reproduced by permission of Penguin Books Ltd. *Section 8* P. 68: Reprinted by permission of the publishers and The Loeb Classical Library from Xenophon: *Oeconomicus,* Vol. IV, translated by E.C. Marchant, Cambridge, Mass.: Harvard University Press, 1923. P. 69: Reprinted by permission from *Lysistrata,* copyright © 1991 by Ivan R. Dee, Inc., translation copyright © 1991 by Nicholas Rudall. All rights reserved. *Section 9* P. 74: Thucydides, *History of the Peloponnesian War,* translated by Rex Warner. Copyright © 1954 by Rex Warner. Reproduced by permission of Penguin Books Ltd. *Section 10* P. 79: From *The Trial and Death of Socrates,* trans. F.J. Church (London: Macmillan, 1880), pp. 37–41, 50–53, 56–57. *Section 11* P. 83: From *The Republic of Plato,* translated by F.M. Cornford, pp. 178–179, 181, 190–192, 228–231, 282–283, 286, 288–289. Copyright © 1941. Reprinted by permission of Oxford University Press. *Section 12* P. 90: From *The Oxford Translation of Aristotle,* edited by W.D. Ross. Copyright © 1925. Reprinted by permission of Oxford University Press. P. 90: Aristotle, *The Politics,* translated by T.A. Sinclair, revised by Trevor J. Saunders. Copyright © 1962 by the Estate of T.A. Sinclair, revised translation copyright © 1981 by Trevor J. Saunders. Reproduced by permission of Penguin Books Ltd. *Section 13* P. 95: From *Epicurus: The Extant Remains,* translated by Cyril Bailey, pp. 53, 83, 85, 89, 97, 101, 115, 117, 119. Copyright © 1926. Reprinted by permission of Oxford University Press. *Section 14* P. 97: Daniel, *First Maccabees, Second Maccabees,* (Wilmington: Michael Glazier, 1981; Collegeville: The Liturgical Press, 1990). Used with permission. P. 99: Reprinted by permission of the publishers and the Loeb Classical Library from Philo Judaeus, *The Special Laws, III,* 1–6, in *Philo,* Vol. VII, translated by F.H. Colson, Cambridge, Mass.: Harvard University Press, 1937. Copyright © 1937 by The Trustees of Harvard

University. P. 99: Reprinted by permission of the publishers and the Loeb Classical Library from Philo Judaeus, *Preliminary Studies in Philosophy,* Vol. IV, translated by F.H. Colson and G.H. Whitaker, Cambridge, Mass.: Harvard University Press, 1932. Copyright © 1932 by The Trustees of Harvard University. P. 100: Reprinted by permission of the publishers and the Loeb Classical Library from Philo Judaeus, *The Special Laws,* I, 32–40, in *Philo,* Vol. VII, translated by F.H. Colson, Cambridge, Mass.: Harvard University Press, 1937. Copyright © 1937 by The Trustees of Harvard University.

## Chapter 4

*Section 1* P. 103: From *The Rise of the Roman Empire,* translated by Ian Scott-Kilvert. Copyright © 1979 by Ian Scott-Kilvert. Reproduced by permission of Penguin Books Ltd., UK. *Section 2* P. 105: Livy, *The War With Hannibal,* translated by Audrey de Selincourt. Copyright © 1965 The Estate of Audrey de Selincourt. Reprinted by permission of Penguin Books Ltd., UK. P. 107: *The Roman History of Appian of Alexandria,* translated by Horace White (Macmillan, 1899), Vol. I, pp. 229– 232. *Section 3* P. 109: From *Selected Works* by Cicero, translated by Michael Grant. Copyright © 1971. Reproduced by permission of Penguin Books Ltd., UK. *Section 4* P. 112: Reprinted by permission of the publishers and The Loeb Classical Library from Diodorus of Sicily: *The Library of History,* Vol. III, translated by C.H. Oldfather, Cambridge, Mass.: Harvard University Press, 1939. Copyright © 1939 by The Trustees of Harvard University. *Section 5* P. 115: Reprinted by permission of the publishers and The Loeb Classical Library from Livy: *Ad Urbe Condita,* Vol. X, translated by Evan T. Sage, Cambridge, Mass.: Harvard University Press, 1935. Copyright © 1935 by The Trustees of Harvard University. P. 117: From *A Source Book of Roman History,* ed. Dana C. Munro (Boston: D.C. Heath, 1904), pp. 201–204. *Section 6* P. 119: Reprinted by permission of the publishers and The Loeb Classical Library from *Plutarch's Lives,* translated by Bernadotted Perrin, Cambridge, Mass.: Harvard University Press, 1921. Copyright © 1921 by The Trustees of Harvard University. *Section 7* P. 121: From *The Conspiracy of Catiline* by Sallust, translated by S.A. Handford. Copyright © 1963. Reproduced by permission of Penguin Books Ltd., UK. *Section 8* P. 124: Reprinted by permission of the publishers and The Loeb Classical Library from Cicero, *De Republica de Legibus,* translated by Clinton Walker Keyes in Cicero, Vol. XVI, Cambridge, Mass.: Harvard University Press, 1938. Copyright © 1938 by The Trustees of Harvard University. *Section 9* P. 126: From Cicero, *De Officiis* (Cambridge: Harvard University Press, 1913), p. 128. P. 127: Reprinted with permission of the publishers and The Loeb Classical Library from *Roman History,* Dio Cassius, translated by Ernest Cary, Cambridge, Mass., Harvard University Press, 1916.

## Chapter 5

*Section 1* P. 132: From "The Achievements of Divine Augustus" in *Res Gestae divi Augusti* by Augustus, edited by P.A. Brunt and J.M. Moore. Copyright © 1967. Reprinted by permission of Oxford University Press. P. 133: From Tacitus, *The Annals of Imperial Rome,* translated by Michael Grant. Copyright © 1971. Reproduced by permission of Penguin Books Ltd., UK. *Section 2* P. 135: From *The Aeneid* by Virgil, translated by Robert Fitzgerald. Translation copyright © 1980, 1982, 1983 by Robert Fitzgerald. Reprinted by permission of Random House, Inc. P. 135: Reprinted by permission of the publishers and The Loeb Classical Library from Quintilian: *The Instibutio Oratotia,* translated by H.E. Butler, Cambridge, Mass.: Harvard University Press, 1920. P. 138: Adapted from *The Satires of Juvenal,* translated by Hubert Creekmore (New York: The New American Library, 1963). Permission granted courtesy of Schaffner Agency, Inc. for the estate of Hubert Creekmore. *Section 3* P. 141: Reprinted by permission of the publishers and the Loeb Classical Library from *Moral Essays* by Seneca, Vol. I, (Cambridge, Mass.: Harvard University Press, 1963). All rights reserved. P. 143: From *Meditations* by Marcus Aurelius, translated by Maxwell Staniforth. Copyright © 1964. Reproduced by permission of Penguin Books Ltd., UK. *Section 4* P.146: S.P. Scott, translator, *Corpus Juris Civilis (The Civil Law),* 17 volumes. Copyright © 1932 by The Central Trust Company. Used with permission. *Section 5* P. 148: Reprinted by permission of the publishers and The Loeb Classical Library from Pliny: *Letters and Paneygyricus,* Vol. II, translated by Betty Radice, Cambridge, Mass.: Harvard University Press, 1923. Copyright © 1923 by The Trustees of Harvard University. *Section 6* P. 152: Moses Hadas, *The History of Rome.* Copyright © 1956 by Doubleday & Company, Inc. Used with permission. P. 154: From Tacitus, *On Britain and Germany,* translated by H. Mattingly. Copyright © 1948. Reproduced by permission of Penguin Books Ltd., UK. P. 155: From *The Jewish War* by Josephus, translated by G.A. Williamson (Penguin Classics 1959, revised edition 1970) Copyright © 1970. Reproduced by permission of Penguin Books Ltd., UK. *Section 7* P. 158: Reprinted by permission of the publishers and The Loeb Classical Library from Dio Cassius: *Roman History,* Vol. IX, translated by Earnest Cary, Cambridge, Mass.: Harvard University Press, 1927. Copyright © 1927 by The Trustees of Harvard University. P. 159: From *Roman Civilization,* ed. Naphtali Lewis and Meyer Reinhold (Harper & Row Torchbook edition, 1966), II, 454. Reprinted by permission of Columbia University Press. P. 160: Herodian, *History of the Roman Empire,* Edward C. Echols, translator. Copyright © 1961 by The University of California Press. Used with permission. *Section 8* P. 161: Salvian, *The Writings of Salvian. The Presbyter.* Copyright © 1962 by

The Catholic University of America Press. Used with permission. P. 163: From James Harvey Robinson, *Readings in European History* (Boston: Ginn, 1904), pp. 23–24. P. 164: From Gregory the Great, *Homiliarum in Exechielem* in *Gregory the Great,* trans. F. Homes Dudden (New York: Longmans, Green and Co., 1905), II, 18–20.

## Chapter 6

*Section 1* PP. 168–171: Reprinted by permission of the National Council of Churches in the USA. *Section 2* PP. 171–172: Reprinted by permission of The National Council of Churches in the USA. *Section 3* P. 174: From Athenagoras, "A Plea for Christians" in *The Writings of Justin Martyr and Athenagoras,* ed. Alexander Roberts and James Donaldson in *Ante-Nicene Christian Library* (Edinburgh: T. & T. Clark, 1867), Vol. 2, pp. 416–419. *Section 4* P. 176: From Eusebius, *Ecclesiastical History,* Book 5, Chap. 1, in *Translation and Reprints from the Original Sources of European History,* Vol. 4 (1897 series), ed. D. C. Munro and Edith Bramhall (Philadephia: University of Pennsylvania Press, 1898), pp. 11–19. *Section 5* P. 178: From *Early Latin Theology,* translated and edited by S.L. Greenslade (Volume V: The Library of Christian Classics). Published simultaneously in Great Britain and the USA by the SCM Press, Ltd., London, and the Westminster Press, Philadelphia. Used by permission of Westminster/John Knox Press, Louisville, KY. P. 179: From Clement of Alexandria, *Stromata (Miscellanies),* trans. William Wilson in A. Roberts and James Donaldson, Ante-Nicene Christian Library in *The Writings of Clement of Alexandria* (Edinburgh: T. & T. Clark, 1867–1872), Vol. 4, pp. 303–305, 307–310, 318. *Section 6* P. 181: From Oliver J. Thatcher, *Library of Original Sources* (Milwaukee, WI: University Research Extension Co., 1907), Vol. 4, pp. 130–133, 155, 144, 147–148, 153, 136–139. *Section 7* P. 185: St. Augustine, *The City of God.* Copyright © 1858 by Catholic University Press of America. Used with permission. P. 188: From Oliver J. Thatcher, *Library of Original Sources* (Milwaukee, WI: University Research Extension Co., 1907), Vol. 4, pp. 133–134. P. 189: Reprinted with permission of Simon & Schuster from *The Crisis of Church and State, 1050–1300* by Brian Tierney. Copyright © 1964 by Prentice-Hall, Inc., renewed 1992 by Brian Tierney.

## Chapter 7

*Section 1* P. 194: From *The Koran* by Muhammed, translated by N.J. Dalwood. Copyright © 1994. Reprinted by permission of Penguin Books Ltd., UK. *Section 2* P. 197: From Deno Geanakoplos (ed.), *Byzantium: Church, Society, and Civilization Seen through Contemporary Eyes,* pp. 396–397. Reprinted by permission of the publisher, The University of Chicago Press. Copyright © 1984 by the University of Chicago. P. 198: From Arthur J. Arberry, *Avicenna on Theology,*

pp. 9–13. Copyright © 1951. Reprinted by permission of John Murray (Publishers) Ltd. *Section 3* P. 201: From *A History of the English Church and People* by Bede, translated by Leo Sherley-Price. Reprinted by permission of Penguin Books Ltd., UK. P. 203: From *The Letters of St. Boniface,* translated with an introduction by Ephraim Emerton. Copyright © 1940. Columbia UniversityPress. Reprinted with permission of the publisher. P. 205: Einhard, *Life of Charlemagne,* tr. Samuel E. Turner. Copyright © 1960 by University of Michigan Press. Used with permission. *Section 4* P. 207: Cassiodorus Senator, *An Introduction to Divine and Human Readings,* translated by Leslie W. Jones. Copyright © 1946, renewed 1974 Columbia University Press. Used with permission. *Section 5* PP. 209–211: Einhard, *Life of Charlemagne,* tr. Samuel E. Turner. Copyright © 1960 by University of Michigan Press. Used with permission. *Section 6* PP. 212–213: From Galbert, "Commendation and Oath of Fealty" and Fulbert, "Obligations of Lords and Vassals" from *Translations and Reprints from the Original Sources of European History,* ed. E.P. Cheney (Philadelphia: University of Pennsylvania Press, 1895), Vol. 4, No. 3, pp. 18, 23–24. P. 213: Barbara Smythe, *Troubador Poet.* Copyright by Chatto & Windus Ltd. Used with permission. *Section 7* P. 215: From *The Ledgerbook of Vale Royal Abbey,* ed. John Brownbill (The Record Society for the Publication of Original Documents Relating to Lancashire and Cheshire, 1914), Vol. 68, pp. 117–120.

## Chapter 8

*Section 1* P. 221: Larson, *The King's Mirror.* Copyright © 1917 by The Scandinavian Foundation. Used with permission. P. 223: From P. Studor, *The Oak Book of Southampton* in Publications of the Southampton Record Society (Southampton: Cox & Sharland, 1910), Vol. I, no. 10, pp. 21, 25, 29, 37, 51, 53. *Section 2* P. 225: Ephraim Emerton, editor and translator, *The Correspondence of Pope Gregory VII.* Copyright 1932, renewed 1960 Columbia University Press. Used with permission. *Section 3* P. 229: From *Translations and Reprints from the Original Sources of European History,* ed. D. C. Munro (Philadelphia: University of Pennsylvania, 1897), pp. 5–8. *Section 4* P. 231: Bernard Gui, *Heresies of the High Middle Ages: Selected Sources,* translated by W.L. Wakefield and A.P. Evans. Copyright © 1969 by Columbia University Press. Used with permission. P. 233: James M. Powell, translator, *The Liber Augustalis or Constitution of Melfi.* Copyright © 1971 by Syracuse University Press. Used with permission. *Section 5* P. 235: David Ayerst and A.S.T. Fisher, editors, *Records of Christianity,* Vol. II. Copyright © 1977 by Basil Blackwell Publishers. Used with permission. P. 236: Anton Pegis, editor and translator, *The Basic Writings of St. Thomas Aquinas.* Copyright © 1945. Used with permission. P. 239: Anton C. Pegis, editor and translator, *Summa Contra Gentiles.* Copyright © 1955 by Doubleday, Dell Publishing Group, Inc. Used with permission. *Section 6* P. 240: From *The Metalogican of John of Salisbury* translated by Daniel D. McGarry. Copyright © 1982. P. 242: David Jones, translator, *The World of Medieval Learning.* Copyright © 1981 by Basil Blackwell Publisher. Used with permission. P. 242: From *The Canterbury Tales* by Geoffrey Chaucer, translated by Nevill Coghill. Penguin Classics, Revised Edition. Copyright ©1977. Reproduced by permission of Penguin Books Ltd., UK. P. 243: Charles Homer Haskins, *Studies in Medieval Culture.* Copyright © 1929 by Clarendon Press. Used with permission. P. 243: G.G. Coulton, *Life in the Middle Ages,* Vol 3. Copyright © 1928/29 by Cambridge University Press. Used with permission. *Section 7* P. 245: August C. Krey, editor, *The First Crusade.* Copyright © 1921 by Princeton University Press. Reprinted by permission of Princeton University Press. P. 246: From *A Source Book for Medieval History,* eds. Oliver J. Thatcher and Edgar H. McNeal (New York: Charles Scribner's Sons, 1905), pp. 212– 213. P. 246: From Joseph Jacobs, *The Jews of Angevin England* (London: David Nutt, 1893), p. 45. P. 247: From *The Teachings of Maimonides,* ed. A. Cohen (KTAV Publishing House, Inc., 1968), pp. 289–293, 236–237, 252–253, 262. *Section 8* P. 250: *Songs of the Troubadors* by Anthony Bonner. Copyright © 1972. Reprinted by permission of author. *Section 9* P. 252: J. Sprenger and H. Kramer in *Witchcraft in Europe 1100–1700,* eds. Alan C. Kors and Edward Peters (University of Pennsylvania Press, 1972), pp. 117, 120, 121, 123, 124, 127. Reprinted by permission. P. 254: Selection from *The Book of the City of Ladies* by Christine de Pisan, translated by Earl Jeffrey Richards. Copyright © 1982 by Persea Books, Inc. Reprinted by permission of Persea Books, Inc. P. 257: Excerpts from *A Medieval Home Companion* by Tania Bayard. Copyright © 1991 by Tania Bayard. Reprinted by permission of HarperCollins Publishers, Inc. *Section 10* P. 260: John of Salisbury from *The Statesman's Book of John of Salisbury,* trans. John Dickenson (New York: Russell and Russell, 1963), pp. 335–336. P. 260: From J.C. Holt (ed.), *Magna Carta.* Copyright © 1976. Reprinted by permission of Cambridge University Press. P. 262: Edward I, "Writs" from *A Sourcebook of English History,* ed. Elizabeth K. Kendall (London: Macmillan, 1900), pp. 89–91. *Section 11* P. 265: R.A. Newhall, editor, *The Chronicle of Jean de Venette,* translated by Jean Birdsall. Used with permission. *Section 12* P. 267: John Froissart, *The Chronicles of England, France, and Spain,* translated by Thomas Johnes. Copyright J.M. Dent & Everyman's Library. Reprinted by permission. *Section 13* P. 270: From *On the Misery of the Human Condition* by Lotharo dei Segni (Pope Innocent III) edited by Donald R. Howard, translated by Margaret Mary Dietz. Copyright © 1969. P. 272: Excerpts from *The Divine Comedy* by Dante Alighieri, translated by Howard R. Huse, reprinted by permission of Holt, Rinehart and Winston, Inc. All rights reserved.

## Chapter 9

*Section 1* P. 282: From J.H. Robinson and H.W. Rolfe, *Petrarch the First Modern Scholar and Man of Letters* (New York: G. P. Putnam's Sons, 1909), pp. 208, 210, 213. P. 283: "Love for Greek Literature" from Henry Osborn Taylor, *Thought and Expression in the Sixteenth Century,* 2nd rev. ed. (New York: Frederick Ungar, 1930, repub. 1959), Vol. 1, pp. 36–37, 291. "On Learning and Literature" from *Vittorino de Feltre and Other Humanist Educators,* ed. W. H. Woodward (Cambridge: Cambridge University Press, 1897), pp. 124, 127–129, 132–133. *Section 2* P. 286: *Oration on the Dignity of Man* by Pico della Mirandola, translated by Elizabeth L. Forbes from *The Renaissance Philosophy of Man,* edited by Ernst Cassirer, Paul Oskar Kristeller and John H. Randall, Jr., pp. 223–225. Reprinted by permission of the publisher, The University of Chicago Press. Copyright © 1948 by the University of Chicago. *Section 3* P. 288: From *The Prince* by Niccolo Machiavelli, translated by Luigi, revised by E.R.P. Vincent, pp. 92–93, 97, 98–99, 101–103. Copyright © 1935. Reprinted by permission of Oxford University Press. *Section 4* P. 292: From *The Greatness of Lorenzo de Medici* from *The History of Florence* by Francesco Guicciardini. Translated by Mario Domandi. Copyright © 1970 by Mario Domandi. Reprinted by permission of HarperCollins Publishers, Inc. P. 293: Reprinted by permission of the publishers from *Florentine Merchants in the Age of the Medici,* edited by Gertrude R.B. Richards, Cambridge, Mass.: Harvard University Press, 1932. *Section 5* P. 294: From *On Painting* by Leon Battista Alberti, translated by John Spencer. Copyright © 1966. Reprinted by permission of Yale Univeristy Press and Routledge & Kegan Paul. P. 296: Jonathan Cape for permission to quote from *The Notebooks of Leonardo da Vinci,* edited and translated by Edward MacCurdy. *Section 6* P. 299: From François Rabelais, *The Histories of Gargantua and Pantagruel,* translated by J.M. Cohen. Copyright © 1955. Reproduced by permission of Penguin Books Ltd., UK. P. 301: *The Yale Shakespeare,* ed. Wilbur L. Cross and Tucker Brooke. (New York: Barnes and Noble, 1993.)

## Chapter 10

*Section 1* P. 308: From *The Imitation of Christ* by Thomas à Kempis, translated by Leo Sherley-Price. Copyright © 1952. Reproduced by permission of Penguin Books Ltd., UK. *Section 2* P. 311: From *In Praise of Folly* by Desiderius Erasmus, translated by Clarence H. Miller. Copyright © 1979. Reprinted by permission of Yale University Press. *Section 3* P. 315: Reprinted from *Luther's Works,* Vol. 44, edited by James Atkinson, copyright © 1966 Fortress Press. Used by permission of Augsburg Fortress. P. 316: Reprinted from *Luther's Works,* Vol. 31, edited by H.J. Grimm, copyright © 1957 Fortress Press. Used with permission of Augsburg Fortress. P. 317: Luther, *What Luther Says:*

An Anthology, edited by Ewald Plass. Copyright © 1959 by Concordia Publishing House. Used with permission. *Section 4* P. 318: From *Translations and Reprints from the Original Sources of European History,* (1895 series) ed. D. C. Munro (Philadelphia: University of Pennsylvania, 1899), Vol. 2, pp. 25–30. P. 319: Reprinted from *Luther's Works,* Vol. 46, edited by Robert C. Schultz, copyright © 1967 Fortress Press. Used by permission of Augsburg Fortress. *Section 5* P. 321: Reprinted from *Luther's Works,* Vol. 47, edited by Franklin Sherman, copyright © 1971 Fortress Press. Used by permission of Augsburg Fortress. *Section 6* P. 324: From *Institutes of the Christian Religion* (Volume II), by John Calvin. Translated by John Allen, 1928. Used by permission of Westminster/John Knox Press. P. 325: From *Translations and Reprints from the Original Sources of European History* (Philadelphia: University of Pennsylvania Press, 1896), Vol. 3, No. 3, pp. 10–11. P. 326: From John Calvin, *Commentaries on the Book of the Prophet Daniel,* trans. Thomas Myers (Edinburgh: The Calvin Translation Society, 1852), Vol. 1, pp. 278–279, 281–282. *Section 7* P. 327: From H.J. Schroeder, tr., *Canons and Decrees of the Council of Trent.* Copyright © 1979 by TAN Books and Publications, Inc. P. 330: Anthony Mottola, translator, *The Spiritual Exercises of St. Ignatius.* Copyright © 1964 by Doubleday & Company, Inc. Used with permission.

## Chapter 11

*Section 1* P. 336: From *The Discovery and Conquest of Mexico* by Bernal Diaz del Castillo. Copyright © 1956. Published by Farrar, Straus & Giroux, Inc. Reprinted by permission of Farrar, Straus & Giroux, Inc. *Section 2* P. 340: Reprinted from John Keymer, *Observations Touching Trade and Commerce with the Hollanders, and Other Nations in A Select Collection of Scarce and Valuable Tracts on Commerce,* ed. John R. McCulloch (London: 1859; New York: Augustus M. Kelly Publisher, 1966), pp. 59, 13–14. P. 343: From William Carr, *Travels Through Holland, Germany, Sweden and Denmark by An English Gentleman* (London: Randall Taylor, 1693), pp. 14–18, 33–34, 60–64. *Section 3* P. 346: From *Documents Illustrative of the History of the Slave Trade to America,* Vol. I edited by Elizabeth Donnan. Copyright © 1935, published by Carnegie Institution. Reprinted by permission of Carnegie Institution of Washington. P. 349: From Philip D. Curtin, *Africa Remembered* (Madison, WI: University of Wisconsin Press, 1967), pp. 92–94, 95–96, 97–98. Reprinted by permission. *Section 4* P. 352: From *Witchcraft in Europe, 1100–1700: A Documentary History* edited by Alan C. Kors and Edward Peters. Copyright © 1972 by the University of Pennsylvania Press. Reprinted by permission of the publisher. P. 354: From *Translations and Reprints from the Original Sources of European History,* ed. George L. Burr (Philadelphia: University of Pennsyl-

vania, 1907), pp. 26–28. P 355: In Nicholas Malebranche, *Recherche de la vérité, Oeuvres complites,* published under the direction of Audré Robinet, Volume I, pp. 370–376, VRIN, Paris, 1962. Reprinted by permission. *Section 5* P. 358: From *Select Statutes and Other Constitutional Documents Illustrative of the Reigns of Elizabeth and James I,* 3rd ed., ed. G. W. Prothero (Oxford: Clarendon Press, 1906), pp. 293–294, 400–401. *Section 6* P. 359: From *Memoirs of the Duc de Saint-Simon* edited by W.H. Lewis. Copyright © 1964. P. 362: From Elborg Forster (trans.), *A Woman's Life in the Court of the Sun King: Letters of Liselotte von der Pfalz, 1652– 1722,* pp. 87, 88, 90, 91, 92, 106, 107, 111, 112, Copyright © 1984 by The Johns Hopkins University Press. Reprinted by permission of The Johns Hopkins University Press. *Section 7* P. 366: Reprinted with permission of Macmillan Publishing Company from *Constitutionalism and Resistance in the Sixteenth Century,* translated and edited by Julian H. Franklin. Copyright © 1969 by The Bobbs- Merrill Company. *Section 8* P. 370: From *The English Works of Thomas Hobbes of Malmesbury, Leviathan, or the Matter Form and Power of a Commonwealth Ecclesiastical and Civil,* collected and ed. Sir William Molesworth (London: John Bohn, 1839), Vol. 3, pp. 110–113, 116, 117, 154, 157–158, 160– 161. *Section 9* P. 373: From *Select Documents of English Constitutional History,* eds. George Burton Adams and H. Morse Stephens (New York: Macmillan Company, 1902), pp. 464–465.

## Chapter 12

*Section 1* P. 379: Copernicus, Nicolaus, *On the Revolutions,* translated by Edward Rosen, edited by Jerry Dbrzycki. Reprinted by permission of Macmillan Ltd. P. 382: Maurice A. Finocchiaro, ed., *Galileo Affair: A Documentary History,* pp. 67–68. Copyright © 1989 The Regents of the University of California. Reprinted by permission of the University of California Press. *Section 2* P. 383: From *Discoveries and Opinions of Galileo Galilei* by Galileo Galilei. Copyright © 1957 by Stillman Drake. Used by permission of Doubleday, a division of Bantam Doubleday Dell Publishing Group, Inc. *Section 3* P. 386: From *Dialogue Concerning the Two Chief World Systems by Galileo Galilei.* Translated by Stillman Drake, pp. 107–108, 112–113, 175–177, 179–184. Copyright © 1952, 1962, 1967 by The Regents of the University of California. Reprinted by permission of the University of California Press. *Section 4* P. 390: From *The Philosophy of Francis Bacon,* ed. and trans. Benjamin Farrington (Liverpool University Press, 1970), pp. 114–115. P. 391: From *The Works of Francis Bacon,* ed. Spedding, Ellis, and Heath (Boston: Taggard and Thompson, 1863), VIII, 67–69, 71–72, 74, 76–79, 142. *Section 5* P. 392: From *The Works of William Harvey,* ed. Robert & Willis (London: Sydenham Society, 1847), pp. 19–20, 40–49.

**Section 6** P. 395: From Descartes, *Philosophical Writings,* translated by Norman Kemp Smith. Reprinted by permission of Macmillan Press Ltd. **Section 7** P. 398: From Sir Isaac Newton, *The Mathematical Principles of Natural Philosophy, Book III,* trans. Andrew Motte (London: H.D. Symonds, 1803), II, 160–162, 310–314.

**Chapter 13**

**Section 1** P. 403: From *The Philosophy of Kant,* by Immanuel Kant, trans. by Carl J. Friedrich. Copyright © 1949 by Random House, Inc. **Section 2** P. 405: From John Locke, *Two Treatises on Civil Government* (London: 1688, 7th reprinting by J. Whiston et al., 1772), pp. 292, 315–316, 354–355, 358–359, 361–362. P. 408: First printing of the Declaration of Independence, July 4, 1776, Papers of the Continental Congress No. 1, Rough Journal of Congress, III. **Section 3** P. 409: From *Candide and Other Writings* by Voltaire, edited by Haskell M. Block. Copyright © 1956 and renewed 1984 by Random House, Inc. Reprinted by permission of Random House, Inc. **Section 4** P. 413: From Thomas Paine, *Age of Reason being an Investigation of True and Fabulous Theology* (New York: Peter Eckler, 1892), pp. 5–11. P. 414: From Paul Heinrich Dietrich Baron d'Holbach, *Good Sense or Natural Ideas opposed to Ideas that are Supernatural* (New York: G. Vale, 1856), pp. vii–xi. **Section 5** P. 418: From *Some Thoughts Concerning Education* by John Locke, pp. 83, 103, 105, 111, 112, 113–114, 115–116, 134, 142. Copyright © 1989. Reprinted by permission of Oxford University Press.

P. 420: Helvétius, *Essays on the Mind and Its Several Faculties,* trans. from the French (London: J.M. Richardson, 1809), pp. 361–363. P. 422: From Jean Jacques Rousseau, *Émile,* trans. Barbara Foxley, pp. 80–84. Everyman's Library Series, reprinted by permission of J.M. Dent and Everyman's Library as publishers. **Section 6** P. 424: From Denis Diderot, *The Encyclopedia Selections,* ed. and trans. Stephen J. Gendzier, pp. 92–93, 104, 124–125, 134, 136, 153, 183–187, 199, 229–230. Reprinted by permission of Stephen J. Gendzier. **Section 7** P. 427: From Jean Jacques Rousseau, *The Social Contract* in *The Social Contract and Discourses,* trans. G.D.H. Cole, pp. 8–9, 13–15, 18–19, 23 and 26–28. Reprinted by permission of J.M. Dent & Sons and Everyman's Library. **Section 8** P. 431: *On Crime and Punishments* by Cesare Beccaria, translated by Henry Paolucci. Copyright © 1963. Reprinted by permission of Prentice-Hall, Inc., Upper Saddle River, NJ. P. 432: John Howard, *The State of Prisons in England and Wales with Preliminary Observations, and an Account of Some Foreign Prisons.* (London: Warrington, 1777.) **Section 9** P. 434: From Lynn Hunt (ed. & trans.), *The French Revolution and Human Rights: A Brief Documentary History,* pp. 56–57. Copyright © 1996 by St. Martin's Press, Inc. Reprinted with permission of St. Martin's Press, Inc. P. 436: From *Sketch for a Historical Picture of the Progress of the Human Mind* by Antonie-Nicholas Condorcet, translated by June Barraclough, pp. 4–5, 9–10, 128, 136, 140–142, 173–175, 179. Reprinted by permission of the publisher, The Orion Publishing Group, Ltd.

# Index of Authors and Selections